About the Author

After thirty-three years as a member of the Columbia University Faculty of Political Science, Salo Wittmayer Baron became professor emeritus of Jewish history, literature, and institutions on the Miller Foundation in 1963. Since that time he has served as Philip L. Levin Visiting Professor at Rutgers University, Gottesman Visiting Professor at Brown University, and Alexander Marx Visiting Professor at the Jewish Theological Seminary of America. He is president of the American Academy for Jewish Research; a Fellow of the American Academy of Arts and Sciences; a corresponding member of the International Commission for a Scientific and Cultural History of Mankind; and has been editor of the quarterly *Jewish Social Studies* since its founding in 1939. In 1979 Columbia University honored him by establishing The Salo Wittmayer Baron Professorship in the Study of Jewish Society, Culture and Institutions. He has also been made Knight of the Order of Merit of the Republic of Italy.

Other books by Professor Baron include *The Jewish Community* (3 vols.), *Modern Nationalism and Religion, The Russian Jew Under Tsars and Soviets, History and Jewish Historians: Essays and Addresses, Ancient and Medieval Jewish History: Essays*, and *Steeled by Adversity: Essays and Addresses on American Jewish Life*. He is coeditor, with Joseph Blau, of *The Jews of the United States, 1790–1840: A Documentary History* (3 vols.).

A SOCIAL AND RELIGIOUS HISTORY OF THE JEWS

Late Middle Ages and Era of European Expansion 1200–1650

VOLUME XVII

BYZANTINES, MAMELUKES, AND MAGHRIBIANS

A SOCIAL AND RELIGIOUS HISTORY OF THE JEWS

By SALO WITTMAYER BARON

Second Edition, Revised and Enlarged

Late Middle Ages and Era of European Expansion
1200–1650

VOLUME XVII

BYZANTINES, MAMELUKES, AND MAGHRIBIANS

Columbia University Press
New York 1980

The Jewish Publication Society of America
Philadelphia 5740

COLUMBIA UNIVERSITY PRESS

NEW YORK AND GUILDFORD, SURREY

ISBN: 0-231-08854-X

LIBRARY OF CONGRESS CATALOG CARD NUMBER: 52-404

PRINTED IN THE UNITED STATES OF AMERICA

CONTENTS

A SOCIAL AND RELIGIOUS HISTORY OF THE JEWS

PUBLISHED VOLUMES

Ancient Times

I. TO THE BEGINNING OF THE CHRISTIAN ERA

I JEWISH SOCIETY AND RELIGION
II ISRAEL'S ORIGINS
III KINGS AND PROPHETS
IV CRUCIAL TEST
V RETHINKING FUNDAMENTALS
VI EXPANSION OF JUDAISM
VII PALESTINIAN CENTER
VIII SOCIAL TURMOIL

II. CHRISTIAN ERA: THE FIRST FIVE CENTURIES

IX NEW HORIZONS
X THE GREAT SCHISM
XI BREAKDOWN AND RECONSTRUCTION
XII CLOSING THE RANKS
XIII INCIPIENT MEDIEVALISM
XIV WORLD OF THE TALMUD
XV TALMUDIC LAW AND RELIGION

High Middle Ages

III. HEIRS OF ROME AND PERSIA

XVI THE PREISLAMIC WORLD
XVII MOHAMMED AND THE CALIPHATE
XVIII PROTECTED MINORITY
XIX EASTERN EUROPE

IV. MEETING OF EAST AND WEST

XX WESTERN CHRISTENDOM
XXI AGE OF CRUSADES
XXII ECONOMIC TRANSFORMATIONS

V. RELIGIOUS CONTROLS AND DISSENSIONS

XXIII COMMUNAL CONTROLS
XXIV SOCIORELIGIOUS CONTROVERSIES
XXV MESSIANISM AND SECTARIAN TRENDS
XXVI KARAITE SCHISM

VI. LAWS, HOMILIES, AND THE BIBLE

XXVII REIGN OF LAW
XXVIII HOMILIES AND HISTORIES
XXIX RESTUDY OF THE BIBLE

VII. HEBREW LANGUAGE AND LETTERS

XXX LINGUISTIC RENASCENCE
XXXI WORSHIP: UNITY AMIDST DIVERSITY
XXXII POETRY AND BELLES-LETTRES

VIII. PHILOSOPHY AND SCIENCE

XXXIII MAGIC AND MYSTICISM
XXXIV FAITH AND REASON
XXXV SCIENTIFIC EXPLORATION
XXXVI MEDICAL SCIENCE AND PRACTICE

INDEX TO VOLUMES I–VIII

Late Middle Ages and Era of European Expansion

BYZANTINES, MAMELUKES, AND MAGHRIBIANS

LXXI

BYZANTINE WORLD IN DECLINE

Leaving the territories of Poland and Lithuania, we must now turn back to the East-European areas under the sway of the Byzantine civilization. Despite its large number of Greek-Orthodox and Uniate subjects, the dual Polish-Lithuanian Commonwealth was essentially part of the Western group of nations. It shared the major developments of medieval western and central Europe under the spiritual control of the Papacy and, after a brief Humanist experience, it played an eminent role in the Reformation and Counter Reformation. In the Jewish question, too, the Commonwealth followed the patterns developed in the Holy Roman Empire and its dependencies to such an extent that, as we recall, the basic royal charters for the Jewries of both Poland and Lithuania originated as almost verbatim replicas of documents granting similar privileges to the Jews of Austria, Bohemia, and Hungary. These enactments themselves had had their roots in the legal evolution initiated by the rulers of the Carolingian Empire. East of the Polish-Lithuanian border, however, the old institutions developed in the Eastern Roman Empire since the time of Constantine the Great continued to prevail. We resume here the analysis of the socioreligious evolution of Jewish life after the Latin conquest of Constantinople in 1204. Despite this great crisis and the constant turmoil of the ever shifting power structure in the Balkans, Asia Minor, the East-Mediterranean islands, and the vast expanses of the growing Muscovite Empire, the Byzantine civilization revealed, in many ways, a remarkable continuity from the developments of the preceding centuries discussed in our earlier volumes.

Byzantium as such never recovered, to be sure, from the shock of 1204. Politically and economically it was but a shadow of its former self. Even after its gradual recuperation in the course of the thirteenth century and the recapture of Constantinople in 1261, it remained a fragmented country, of which a relatively small area continued under the control of the Greek emperors. The very title of "emperor and autocrat of the Romans" was now often assumed by other princes, including the Greek rulers of Epirus and the Serbian king Stephen Dushan. In what follows we shall have to deal mainly with three different groups of sovereignties—Greek, Latin, and Slavic—which shared the destinies of the Byzantine world until its partial reunification under Ottoman rule in the fourteenth to the sixteenth centuries. Though politically and socioeconomically greatly divided and frequently in armed combat with one another, the large majority of its inhabitants remained faithful to the Greek-Orthodox Church, headed by the Ecumenical Patriarchate of Constantinople. The spiritual underpinnings of the Byzantine civilization remained intact even after several Slavic nations achieved autonomous status under their so-called autocephalous metropolitanates and, ultimately, patriarchates in Bulgaria, Serbia, and Kiev-Moscow.

Understandably, the greatest degree of continuity existed in the areas under Greek rule. Beginning with the Empire of Nicaea in Asia Minor and, after the reconquest of Thessalonica in 1246 and Constantinople in 1261, having fairly defined (though still often fluctuating) borders in Europe and Asia, the Empire was controlled during the last two centuries of its existence by a single dynasty established by Michael VIII Palaeologus (1259–82). Its regime could pursue a relatively consistent policy, as did to some extent those of the "empire" and later despotate of Epirus in the west and the Empire of Trebizond on the Asian shore of the Black Sea. Much less uniform, however, were the areas under Western control. The Crusaders experienced great difficulty in holding on to their 1204 gains. As one example, Baldwin II, the last Latin "emperor" of Constantinople before its return to Greek rule, was in such financial straits that, in order to secure a loan from Venetian merchants, he had to pledge his only son and heir, Philip, as security.[1]

Some parts of the mainland now developed Western forms of life and almost resembled cities and villages in Italy, Spain, or France. This was particularly true of the Peloponnesus and some coastal areas on the Adriatic Sea. Of a different nature was the penetration of many important islands, including Rhodes, by the Western Order of the Hospitallers, or of St. John of Jerusalem, which later ruled over Malta. Equally important were the numerous islands (such as Crete, Euboea, and Corfu), as well as quite a few harbors both close to Constantinople and elsewhere, which had come under the enduring control of the Venetian Republic, the real initiator of the Latin conquest. But Venice soon found a powerful rival in the continually expanding Genoese empire. Stimulated by a treaty it concluded with Michael VIII in 1261, the Republic of Genoa established a number of colonies in the Aegean and Black Seas; it even exercised effective control over Galata, the harbor at the very doorstep of the Byzantine capital. However, all of these Latin powers pursued different policies in their diverse possessions, policies which often varied from one island to another in accordance with both deep-rooted local customs and temporary exigencies.

The third major area emerging from the old Byzantine Empire was inhabited by the now wholly independent Slavic peoples, notably in Bulgaria and Serbia. Each of these countries in turn found its boundaries expanding or shrinking as a result of the constantly changing power constellations and almost unceasing warfare. They sometimes acted in alliance with the remnants of the Greek Empire, the neighboring Walachians and Hungarians, or with each other, and sometimes as enemies in combat. To the north the Byzantine Church's influence extended to the semi-romanized areas of Walachia and Moldavia and also had an increasing impact on the quickly expanding Muscovite Empire. It was ultimately Moscow upon which the mantle of Byzantine leadership descended. The Muscovite Grand Duke Ivan III, married to Zoe-Sophia (a niece of the last Byzantine emperor, Constantine XI Palaeologus [1449–53]), assumed the formal title of "tsar," a variant of Caesar, and thereby laid the foundation for the ever more assertive doctrine of "Moscow, the third Rome." [2]

The destinies of the Jews in these three widely divergent groups of states differed greatly. During the Late Middle Ages, however, in the aggregate they constituted but a small minority of the Jewish people, and their impact on the cultural and religious life of world Jewry was relatively slight. They left behind few records of their socioeconomic life, with many basic aspects remaining obscure and controversial, before the new era which began for most of them after the successive Ottoman conquests. Thenceforth they shared the destinies of their coreligionists in the vast Ottoman Empire extending from Algiers, Cairo, and Baghdad to Budapest, Jassy, and the Crimea.

GREEK REVIVAL

After the Crusaders' conquest of Constantinople, the emergent small Greek states were further fragmented internally by the progress of feudalism. The feudal system of *pronoia,* which had been spreading in the Byzantine Empire even before 1204, now increasingly resembled the Western fief. Yet these states, and especially the resurgent Byzantine Empire, formed the nucleus for the reassertion of Greek civilization. Of course, the disturbances preceding the Crusaders' invasion and the catastrophic breakdown in 1203–1204 inflicted irreparable damage on Byzantine society. If under the regime of Manuel I Comnenus (1143–80) the Empire had retained some of its former glory, it quickly went downhill under Isaac II (1185–95) and Alexius IV (1195–1203). Its disorganization progressed so rapidly that its major backbone, the imperial bureaucracy, became more and more a purely mercenary force acting for the benefit of its own members rather than of society at large. According to the distinguished chronicler Nicetas Choniates, Isaac himself was selling offices "like vegetables on the market." The presence of some 60,000 Latins in the capital—many of them, like the Venetians, enjoying special privileges which helped them exploit the local economy rather than contribute to it—should also have been for keen observers an ominous portent of unavoidable ruin. Although generally living on fairly amicable terms with their Venetian and other Latin neighbors, the Jews of Constantinople readily became special objects of murder and pillage during the three-day conquest of the city (April 13–15, 1204) by the newly arriving Western legions, animated by both greed and a fanatical zeal to destroy infidels and heretics.[3]

Jews also probably suffered more than other citizens from the growing disarray during the preceding quarter century. No longer would travelers like Benjamin b. Jonah of Tudela and Petaḥiah b. Jacob of Ratisbon be impressed by the beauty, populousness, and wealth of both the capital and the provinces. We recall Petaḥiah's assertion that the Empire embraced "so many Jewish congregations that the Land of Israel could not contain them, were they settled therein." (This statement is reminiscent of the equally exaggerated account about Basil I's persecution of 873–74 which, according to Yehudah b. David, affected some 1,000 Jewish communities, of which only five were saved.) Even an outsider, like Elisha bar Shinaya, writing in the second quarter of the eleventh century, strongly emphasized the presence of a large Jewish population in the Empire. Yet within the great imperial population the Jews formed but a tiny minority even during the relatively flourishing time of Manuel I. Benjamin, who offers us the most comprehensive, if at times ambivalent, data on Jewish life in the area—for which he gathered the available evidence with a moderately critical eye—did not cover the entire territory. He also was often quite ambiguous as to whether the figures he cited were derived from autopsy, such as through observation of the number of worshipers at synagogue services, or from what he heard from local communal leaders. Nor are we certain when his figures refer to families, to adult males, or to all individuals. Hence modern scholars have cited them in partial support of their diverse estimates of the total Byzantine Jewish population of his time, estimates which range from 12,000 or 15,000 to 85,000 or 100,000 persons, representing 0.1–0.7 percent of the Empire's approximately 15,000,000 inhabitants. Moreover, during the four decades after Benjamin's visit in the mid-1160s and particularly during the fall of Constantinople in 1204, the Jewish ratio must have declined sharply because of the mass slaughter by the conquering hosts and the flight of countless refugees to neighboring lands. The Jewish community of the capital, for example, which may have numbered as many as 20,000 souls (if we accept Benjamin's figure of 2,000 Rabbanites and 500 Karaites as representing families settled in the main Jewish quarter in suburban Pera and add about 50 percent more for Jewish residents of other quarters), after 1204 became both small and inarticulate. In the first half of the thirteenth century many visitors actually commented on the relative paucity of residents seen on the city's streets. Certainly, Constantinople, which once may have accommodated as many as 1,000,000 persons and still may have numbered 400,000 to 500,000 inhabitants in the latter part of the twelfth century, was reduced now to a small fraction of that number. The Jewish decline doubtless was proportionately even greater.[4]

Initial steps to reconstruct the Empire were taken by the largest remnant of Greek rule, the Empire of Nicaea. Though for a time deprived of the main center in Constantinople, the Greek emperors of Nicaea Theodore I Lascaris (1204–1222) and John III Vatatzes (1222–54) took over most of the Byzantine possessions in Asia Minor and defended them not only against the Latin conquerors but also against their Seljuk neighbors in Anatolia. A part of Anatolia separated itself, however, and under the high-sounding name of the Empire of Trebizond continued an independent existence until it was conquered by the Turks in 1461, eight years after the fall of Constantinople. At the same time Nicaea also became the seat of the Greek-Orthodox Ecumenical Patriarchate, which retained the title of the Patriarchate of Constantinople and still claimed spiritual supremacy over the entire Greek-Orthodox world. Held first by the scholarly Michael Autoreianus, the office quickly overshadowed the Roman Catholic patriarchate established in Constantinople by the Latin conquerors and occupied by such alien priests as the Venetian Tomaso Morosini (1204–1211).

Carefully husbanding the resources of its Anatolian possessions, the new dynasty of Palaeologi gradually recaptured much of the former imperial territory on the European mainland. Its founder, Michael VIII, himself entered Constantinople in 1261 and transferred the seat of the Empire back to the ancient metropolis. The second largest city of the former Empire, Thessalonica (now Salonica), reconquered by a Nicaean army in 1246, served as a base for expansion into the other major segment of Greek rule, the despotate of Epirus. Finally the despotate was conquered by the Nicaeans in 1340. This expansion proved short lived. By 1348 the Serbian ruler Stephen III Dushan, who styled himself "emperor [*basileus*] and autocrat of Serbs and Romans," took over most of Epirus and Thessaly. But Serbia soon found an overpowering enemy in the Ottoman Turks, who crossed into Europe and defeated first Bulgaria in the Battle of Maritza in 1371 and then the Serbian army in the historic Battle of Kosovo Polye in 1389. Thenceforth Bulgaria became an integral part, and Serbia first a vassal state and later a province, of the rapidly expanding Ottoman Empire with its temporary capital in Adrianople. It was only the diversion of Ottoman energies to the defense of the Asian territories against the new, overwhelming power of the Mongolian hosts led by Timur (Tamerlane), who routed the Ottoman forces in the decisive battle of Ankara in 1402, that saved Constantinople from immediate capture by the Turks. It allowed Greek rule to continue there for half a century, while another small fragment of a Greek regime persisted for a while in the northern Morea.[5]

In all these areas under Greek domination, Jewish communities lived a shadowy existence. The old saying that a people is most happy when it has no history does not apply to the Jewries of the surviving parts of the Greek Empire. Occasional glimpses into the position of the Jews in the Nicaean Empire, recorded in a few early Greek and Jewish sources (often ambiguous and confused in their dates), reveal an increasingly antagonistic attitude of the regime toward its Jewish subjects. According to Jacob b. Elijah of Valencia (or Venice), when Theodore I Dukas Angelos reconquered Thessalonica in 1222–23, he confiscated much of their property in the city and generally refused to protect them against acts of injustice. More serious was another outburst of Byzantine intolerance aimed at suppressing the Jewish faith, such as had repeatedly occurred in previous centuries, although it seems to have had no more lasting effects than the earlier enactments. We learn that in 1253, toward the end of his reign, John III Vatatzes, though sometimes styled "the Merciful," was carried away by nationalist zeal. Although he and his contemporaries derived much comfort from comparing their own "temporary" exile to that of the ancient Israelites in Babylonia, he proclaimed a general outlawry of Judaism in his possessions. True, our information about the Jews in Nicaea and other Anatolian cities of the period is almost nil. But since the Crusaders had not occupied the Asian provinces of the Empire, they could not stage bloodbaths against heretics and infidels as they had in Constantinople. Hence the earlier presence of Jews—attested for Nicaea itself by the casual remark of a tenth-century writer that "Hebrews dwelt there for the sake of its trade and its other advantages"—doubtless continued into the thirteenth century. We may only deplore Benjamin of Tudela's decision not to visit Asia Minor. This restraint has deprived us of an eye-witness account of life in its Jewish communities. Presumably, Vatatzes' intolerant decree was not implemented, since he died the following year and was succeeded in 1258 by Michael VIII who, from the outset, took a much more liberal stance toward religious diversity. We note that the fourteenth-century Karaite scholar Aaron b. Elijah was called "of Nicomedia," a designation probably derived from his birthplace or former residence.[6]

Being limited to but a few references in later chronicles, we can only surmise the reasons for John Vatatzes' anti-Jewish attitude and Michael's more liberal one. From the beginning John had to appeal to the national and patriotic sentiments of the Greek population in order to resist the power of the Western knights. As in many other periods of Jewish history, a rising wave of nationalism engulfed Jewish communities in the ruler's quest for ethnoreligious uniformity of his subjects. Michael, on the other hand, especially after transferring his residence to Constantinople with its cosmopolitan population (including many Latins), took a much broader view. He realized that the greatly depleted old capital required a rapid increase in its population. Therefore he not only allowed the Jews to continue professing their inherited religion but also is said to have called together an assembly of Jewish leaders from all parts of his country and publicly announced to them his disapproval of Vatatzes' decree.[7]

Michael's immediate successors, Andronicus II (1282–1328) and Andronicus III (1328–41), continued his tolerant policies toward their multinational subjects. In fact, when Andronicus II's armies occupied parts of Epirus, the emperor confirmed in 1319 a municipal charter that had been granted to Iannina when his army commander, Syrgiannes Palaeologus Philanthropenus, conquered the city. This charter included such generally patriotic and liberal provisions as that the city would never be handed over to the Franks, that its citizens would enjoy freedom of trade throughout the Empire without the payment of commercial taxes, and that they would be free to elect their own judges. It also provided that the Jews of Iannina should enjoy freedom and not be molested. The entire tenor of that chrysobull, or formal decree, intimates that Jews were to enjoy a measure of equality with their non-Jewish neighbors. This insistence is the more noteworthy as it implied a desire to attract Jews to this locality which, a century and a half earlier, apparently had not merited a visit from Benjamin of Tudela. He stopped for a while in Arta or Leucas, but not in Iannina.[8]

Of course, the surviving Greek states basically continued to adhere to both the ecclesiastical ideology concerning the treatment of Jews, and the laws governing their legal status, as they had developed in the area since the early days of the Eastern Roman Empire. Notwithstanding occasional persecutions of Jews and even Vatatzes' attempt at outright suppression of Judaism, the Jewish inhabitants, when tolerated, lived along established legal and political patterns. Curiously, the Byzantines never adopted the Western doctrine of Jews as "serfs of the imperial Chamber." Nor did they look for such diverse ideological justifications as were advanced by the popes, the Holy Roman emperors, and the Western kings; these ideological divisions were largely obviated by the absence of a strict separation between state and Church in Byzantium. We only hear some echoes of Jewish subjection to Christian domination, as already formulated by certain Church Fathers and reflected in a few imperial enactments. For example, in the privilege granted in 1049 to the monastery of Nea Moné, on Chios, Constantine IX Monomachus wrote:

> God the great King, having rejected the Old Israel and chosen the new, preferred the latter to the former and named it the people of His own possession, the 'pleasant portion,' and His own lot. For this very reason He placed the Jewish race in subjection to the Christian and appointed the faithful and right-thinking people to rule over the faithless and ungrateful one.

Yet the emperors did not seem to derive therefrom the Western lesson that they were to collect a special Jewish tax. It appears that even the *aurum coronarium,* which in the fifth century had replaced the *fiscus judaicus* of ancient Rome, did not become a permanent institution that continued in all Byzantine regions. Whatever special taxes were occasionally recorded, like that imposed on the Jews of Chios for the monastery's benefit, had a local origin and impact. Even in that chrysobull of 1049, which was renewed by later emperors in 1062 and 1079 and recopied as late as the fifteenth century for the use of the monastery, the emperor balanced the new impost by freeing the Jews of Chios from all other taxes theretofore paid by them together with other inhabitants. On the other hand, such likely absence of any universal special Jewish tax in Byzantium, and its nominal yield wherever one may have been sporadically collected, made the presence of Jewish taxpayers of but minor importance to the imperial Treasury. This factor surely contributed to the relative ease which some emperors felt in outlawing Judaism and thus foregoing that income. At the same time, they tried to keep as many converted Jews as possible in the country, so as to minimize the damage to the economy.[9]

Nor is the following statement appearing in connection with the Byzantine-Venetian negotiations of 1319–20 any more enlightening. Discussing the location of the Venetian quarter near the *Judaica,* the writer asserts that "our Jews are an appropriate possession of the Empire. Thus a location was given them and assigned for their dwellings, where the inhabitants would exercise their crafts and pay the Empire what they were ordered to do." This high-sounding declaration, echoing the contemporary German pronouncements about Jews being "serfs of the [imperial] Chamber" and the recurrent Spanish references to Jews as a royal "treasure" and the like, probably meant only that Jews had to pay a regular rent for the land (and perhaps also for some buildings erected on it) assigned to them by the authorities. These rather ambivalent allusions may be compared with the far more explicit statement in the chrysobull of 1187, in which the weak emperor Isaac II had spoken of the Venetians, whose upsurging power was largely responsible for the Empire's downfall seventeen years later, as having been "not only at that juncture but also at other times and places serfs of the Romans [*Romeis servi erant*]." This servitude evidently went no further than that illustrated by the act of violence committed by the Byzantine authorities in 1171 when, in a single day, they arrested all Venetians in their country and confiscated their property, a fate which befell Jews in both East and West in connection with many decrees of expulsion or forced conversion.[10]

Also of interest in this connection is the 1333 gift of Andronicus III to a monk Jacob, which included both a church in Thebes and ten hyperpera from the Jews in the castle of Zichna (Macedonia). Although still recorded twelve years later under the Serbian King Stephen Dushan, this amount probably originated from an agreement about rent, rather than a tax. In general, concerning other than special payments, one needs but refer to the limited services usually rendered to the emperor by the Jews of Constantinople, as illustrated by the housing compact made by the Jews living in a section of the Venetian quarter and the factors of Emperor Andronicus II and the empress. The Jews, we are told, were leasing the requisite land and erecting dwellings on it. Although the buildings became wholly their own property, they had to pay an annual rental (*terraticum*) for the use of the land. We have little reason to doubt this information, later submitted by the Venetian bailo to his home authorities (1319–20), because such a transaction was perfectly legal under the existing Byzantine law. But a bilateral agreement of this sort certainly does not reflect any kind of master-serf relationship in the ordinary meaning of this term.[11]

Clearly one must not equate the status of Byzantine Jewry with the "Jewish serfdom" that developed in the West during the Late Middle Ages. Even Franz Dölger, the chief proponent of the existence of a special Jewish tax in Byzantium, calls it, in the case of the 1049 donation to the Chios monastery, a *Rekognitionssteuer*. This term is juridically very ambiguous, if not entirely meaningless. It certainly does not convey either the idea of Jews as "protected subjects" under Islam, or that of the Western "serfs of the Chamber." Even in thirteenth-century Germany, we recall, where the term *servi camerae* began to be used most frequently, it was long intended to convey a special fiscal allegiance of Jews to the imperial office, rather than any form of "bondage" and lack of freedoms; for instance, freedom to marry or to be judged by the person's own courts. To the end there was a fundamental difference between the "serfdom" of the Jews and that of the peasant "villeins," who, in fact, upon settling in a city also automatically secured freedom according to the old adage, *Stadtluft macht frei*. At the most the Byzantine concept of Jewish subjection to Christian masters, very sparingly used, carried a merely theological connotation similar to that given it in patristic and papal sources. It infringed upon the Jews' personal freedoms even less than did the bull *Sicut Judaeis* in Rome which, like most early imperial and royal laws in the West, was frequently reenacted for the *protection* of Jewish rights.[12]

Of a different nature seems to have been the status of the occasionally recorded Jewish "serfs" belonging to individual masters. Regrettably, the available documents are even less clear as to the extent of their servitude. In one case we learn that in 1321 three Jews, Laméris, David, and Samarias, and their sons "belonged" to the metropolitan of Iannina; the relationship appears to have been continued by the descendants of these "serfs" and the metropolitanate for some five centuries, deep into the period of Ottoman rule. However, all that appears to have been required of these "serfs" was that each render his master one day's service a week. There is neither an indication of what type of service was involved, nor of how this unusual relationship had originated. Possibly, it amounted to only that certain payments which the family had to make to the metropolitan see (whether as a result of an imperial donation as in Chios, or because of unpaid loans or other obligations) were converted into some form of service. Nor are we better informed about another family of Jewish "serfs," this time belonging to Jewish masters. We are told that one Moses ben R. Shabbetai Shem Ṭob Galimidi, who for some reason had to leave Thebes and settled in Negroponte, then under Venetian control, became dependent there on David Kalomiti, the powerful leader of the local Jewish community. Owing to David's good will, Moses had served as judge, scribe, and slaughterer of the Jewish community. Through circumstances that are unexplained in the single, rather equivocal source, Moses later became more dependent on his sponsor; he and his sons are described as David's "serfs" (*'abadim*), a status which was abused by the master's sons and was turned into a constant subjection of the Galimidi family. However, their "servile" status did not prevent four of Moses' six sons from leaving the island. One of them, even after his return there, proceeded to Rome and submitted a formal complaint against these abuses to the papal Curia. This unusual form of private Jewish servitude under a Jewish master is not recorded anywhere outside the Byzantine area. Pending further clarification by some new documents, it must be regarded as a singular exception. Such limited serfdom was, of course, entirely different from slavery, to which some Jews may have been condemned as a result of warlike disturbances or piracy. We learn, for example, that in 1430, when a Catalan adventurer was forced to relinquish his hold on the leading Euboean harbor of Clarentza, he carried away with him "all the Jews on his galleys," evidently in order to collect ransom for them. The chances are that, as in other cases, the ransom was speedily paid and the Jewish captives did not long remain in their unfree status.[13]

SOCIOPOLITICAL STATUS

On the whole, the legal codes issued by former emperors dating back to Theodosius the Great retained their validity, subject only to some specific modifications enacted in later imperial decrees. In addition to using the Theodosian Code and Justinian's *Corpus iuris civilis,* administrators and jurists usually acted in conformance with subsequent codes of law such as the *Eklogé, Procheiron, Epanagogé,* and particularly the most comprehensive of them, the *Basilika.* Considerable weight was also given to local customs observed in various regions. The difficulty of generalizing about the Jewish status in the Empire, which confronts every student of Byzantine history even in the periods of its greatest prosperity and power, is compounded in the late medieval period by the deep internal divisions and the fluidity of the frontiers under effective imperial control, as well as by the extreme paucity of relevant source material.[14]

It appears that basically the Jews, in so far as they were tolerated at all, enjoyed the same rights as their neighbors unless specific disabilities were imposed upon them by some general or local laws. The objectives of such restrictions reflected the traditional ecclesiastical demands that Jews be both segregated from and discriminated against in favor of Christians. The lengths to which the ecclesiastical organs were prepared to go in preventing close social relations between Jews and Christians are well illustrated by a series of "Questions and Answers" prepared by an official of the Ecumenical Patriarchate (*ca.* 1150). One question pertained to the penalties to be imposed upon Christians who, though forewarned, continued to have meals together with Armenians, Saracens, or Jews. The reply was unequivocal—the sinners ought to be placed under a ban and "all individuals associating with such persons shall be excommunicated until they abstain from these transgressions." Yet there were occasions when even high ecclesiastics had friendly relations with Jews. Such was the case, for instance, of Metropolitan Simeon of Thessalonica, whose demise in 1429 was greatly mourned by Jews as well as Christians, according to a contemporary chronicler. This friendship probably antedated the brief Venetian control over the city (1423–30).[15]

Of course, one must not generalize from such an episode and assume that the Thessalonican clergy or that of other places was generally friendly to Jews. A noteworthy incident in that city in 1337 sheds some light on the divided attitudes within the ecclesiastical establishment itself. We learn from a trial record that one Chionius, a royal official, took seriously his duty to defend Jews against outside attacks. On learning that some Jew-baiters had maltreated certain Jews and denigrated Jewish observances, he made an official complaint to the clerk of the metropolitanate, Deacon Strymbammon. Perhaps in an excess of zeal, he accused the assailants of anti-Christian behavior, because they had derided the law of Moses which, in the eyes of pious Christians, was appreciated as sacred Scripture. Chionius' opponents immediately attacked his own orthodoxy and even called him a Judaizer. Thereupon an ecclesiastical commission ordered his arrest. But when the matter was brought to the attention of the city council, the case was retried in the presence of the highest local dignitaries, the metropolitan, the prefect, the commander of the mercenary force, the president of the civil tribunal, and others. The testimonies were ultimately submitted to the Holy Synod, which acquitted all accused. In this connection the question arises whether and in what form Jews took their oath of fidelity to the emperor. First mentioned with respect to government officials only, this oath was later demanded of all subjects and is frequently referred to under the Palaeologi. Because of its constitutional importance, most likely the Jewish subjects would not have been exempted. And yet to recite it in its customary Christian wording must have been repugnant to conscientious Jews. At the same time, we do not hear of any special Jewish oath of fidelity, a sort of oath *more judaico,* though that legal procedure seems to have originated in Byzantium in connection with the formula of abjuration of new converts. Regrettably, no answer can be given to this intriguing problem on the basis of the meager documentation available.[16]

Effective segregation was greatly limited, moreover, by existing conditions. For instance, the separation of Jews from Christians in distinct quarters meant much less in the eastern countries, both Muslim and Byzantine, than in western and central Europe. In the first place, Jews were not the only religious minority in Byzantium. In many cities they lived side by side with Muslims, Armenians, and such Christian sectarians as the Paulicians and Bogomils, who usually were more sharply persecuted by the Orthodox rulers than the Muslim and Jewish "infidels." Secondly, it was customary in many Byzantine lands to maintain separate quarters for artisan guilds, even if all their members were Greek-Orthodox. That is why a typical reply by Archbishop Demetrios Chomatianos of Ochrida to Constantine Cabasilas, archbishop of Durazzo, merely asserted (*ca.* 1230–34) that

> people of alien tongues and alien beliefs, such as Jews, Armenians, Israelites [Karaites?], Hagarites [Ishmaelites, i.e., Muslims], and others such as these were permitted from of old to dwell in Christian countries and cities. For this reason quarters located either within or without the cities are set apart for each one of these groups that they may be restricted to these quarters and may not extend their residence beyond them.

Nevertheless we have good evidence that Jews resided in many parts of the major cities, especially Constantinople. There the majority may well have been concentrated in the suburb of Pera before 1204 and in the vicinity of the Venetian quarter after Michael VIII reoccupied the city. But synagogues also existed in other districts of Constantinople, undoubtedly because of the convenience for Jewish worshipers living nearby. A similar situation in Thessalonica after 1175 is reflected in an epistle by the local metropolitan, Eustathios. He was mainly concerned about the desecration of Christian icons. In his complaint to the ecumenical patriarch he wrote:

> During the incumbency of the saintly patriarchs who preceded my worthless self, the Hebrews were permitted to spread out. I know not whether this happened by oversight, or with their [the patriarchs'] knowledge, or because of an imperial rescript, for that cannot be

determined. Some of them occupied ruined Christian dwellings which they rebuilt, while others lived in houses occupied by Christians. Some of these houses had been decorated with religious pictures, before which hymns had been chanted, yet until the other day no one said a word about it.

Eustathios asked his superior how he was to proceed in order to stem potential further desecrations.[17]

The presence of special quarters in which various ethnic and occupational groups were concentrated in many Byzantine, as well as Muslim, cities in the Middle East is generally recognized. Such foreign colonists as the Venetians and Genoese actually benefited from this segregation because thus they could more fully enjoy their special privileges. Certainly, there was nothing derogatory about space being assigned to Jews for a quarter of their own. The only question is whether the quarter existing in Pera at the time of Benjamin's visit was based on the ethnic and religious segregation of Jews, or whether it was derived mainly from the location there of workshops belonging to members of the Jewish guilds of silk weavers and tanners.[18]

Eustathios' description of how the Jewish quarter of Thessalonica had "spread out" is probably typical of the organic growth of Jewish settlements in the Empire and its successor states when there was neither governmental support nor interference. The few references to "assignment" of quarters to Jews, Armenians, Venetians, Genoese, and so forth may indeed reflect some preceding negotiations between the parties and the authorities. At the same time, other quarters grew up by the simple concentration of individuals of the same ethnoreligious group who settled close to one another and then spread out as their numbers increased. This equivocal situation has led David Jacoby, an expert Byzantinist as well as Jewish historian, to present a simplified picture of three successive Jewish quarters in Constantinople. One, located within the city near the Golden Horn, began at an unknown date and lasted at least until 1061. A second quarter followed after the transfer of the Jewish habitat—the origins of which are likewise nowhere recorded—to Pera. This second quarter was burned by the Crusaders in 1203. Some eighty years later a third Jewish quarter existed in the district of Vlanga, where Jews lived from at least

1281 to 1453; it apparently did not long outlast the Turkish conquest. Its inhabitants seem to have been among the early victims of the Turkish assaults. Describing the events of May 29, 1453, the Venetian surgeon Niccolò Barbaro, who lived in Constantinople during the siege, states that the Turks "went on land there [on the side of the Dardanelles], part of them disembarking by the Giudecca, so as to have better opportunity of getting booty, there being great riches in the houses of the Jews, principally jewels." In addition, after 1324 there existed a special Jewish section within the Venetian quarter. It was inhabited largely by so-called White Venetians, that is, local and other non-Venetian Jews taken under Venetian protection (see below). Not surprisingly, the Jewish streets, headed by a *caput sinagogae* (presumably the ranking elder of the synagogue within the quarter), were the objects of an extended diplomatic controversy between the Venetian Republic and the Byzantine emperor, Andronicus III. The simultaneous existence of two Jewish quarters—and possibly other Jewish residences of single or multiple families—in the city makes it difficult to identify the one mentioned by such Muslim and Christian visitors as Muḥammad ibn al-Jazari, Abu 'Abd-Allah Muḥammad Ibn Baṭṭuṭa, or Stephan of Novgorod.[19]

More importantly, we have no texts of imperial decrees officially establishing such quarters or closing them down, nor do we hear of any formal relocations of Jews from one area to another, such as are recorded in Frankfort, Rome, and other cities. Even the phrase used by Archbishop Chomatianos about quarters being "set apart" for the respective groups so that they might not infect their Greek-Orthodox neighbors with their teachings and mores seems to be more a rationalization after the event than a reflection of an explicit aim of the government. In many cases quarters undoubtedly arose as a fact of life, rather than as the result of a predetermined legal order. Nor need we assume that, once a quarter was largely depopulated—whether because of a forced conversion, or as the result of an enemy attack like that of 1203, or simply from one of the recurrent fires or earthquakes—it remained totally abandoned by the particular group. We know from Western examples—which are generally much more familiar because of the richer source materials available and also because Jewish quarters there were of a more exceptional nature than in the Middle East—that many an area inhabited by Jews at one time often remained so, clandestinely or overtly, for many generations. It was no accident that the district beyond the river Tiber, which had accommodated most Jews in ancient Rome, later under the Italian name of Trastevere embraced a large proportion of Roman Jewry down to the Second World War. Similarly, it has been shown that the district apparently populated by Jews at the time when Paris was called Lutetia Parisiorum, in the ancient Roman province of Gaul, still had a rather important aggregation of Jews in the twentieth century. These examples can easily be multiplied. Under such circumstances we must not press the *argumentum ex silentio* too hard, particularly in an area with such a dearth of documentary evidence as is Jewish life in late medieval Byzantium. Rather, we may assume that in addition to the three successive quarters so meritoriously identified and documented by Jacoby, there simultaneously existed other localities with fewer Jewish inhabitants, some of which were able to maintain simple accommodations for worship.[20]

True, the extant sources are silent about Jewish residences outside the Jewish quarter or quarters. Probably there was no particular reason to mention them, especially in the few documents which have survived. However, we have intimations of such individual preferences in Manuel I Comnenus' decree of about 1166, which provided that the existing practice of Jews being judged exclusively by the *strategos* of the district of Stenon be replaced by their being allowed to appear before any tribunal. Evidently this provision was not intended to reduce the authority of that important official, but rather to enable residents of other quarters to appear before any court closer to them in so far as it was open to other citizens "in accordance with the law." [21]

Nor do we have enough information about the effects of fires or enemy attacks on Constantinople's Jewish quarters before the Turkish occupation. In the years between the devastation of one Jewish habitat by the Crusaders in 1203 and the pillage of another by the Turkish conquerors in 1453, the inhabitants, including Jews, seem to have suffered little from the vandalism of warring armies. The only conquest of the capital in the intervening period, the entry of Michael VIII in 1261, apparently took place without any bloodshed or major destruction. Large conflagrations likewise seem to have diminished in number and intensity during these two and a half centuries, probably because the greatly reduced population density in the city allowed for more open spaces and led to fewer accidental fires.[22]

RELIGIOUS AND ECONOMIC LIBERTIES

On the other hand, the presence of a synagogue in the capital did give rise to a complaint by Patriarch Athanasius I to Emperor Andronicus II Palaeologus sometime between 1304 and 1309, when the Jewish quarter in the Vlanga district still was very new. Complaining also about the presence in the capital of numerous Roman Catholics, Armenians, and Muslims, the patriarch laid particular stress on Jews:

> The pious King Hezekiah, in order to expiate for the blasphemies of a satrap of King Sennacherib, did not hesitate to cover himself with sackcloth; he had the merit of seeing 185,000 Assyrians exterminated in one blow. But the Byzantines simply tolerate that one should erect in public view of the Orthodox city a synagogue of the deicide people who ridicule that [city's] religion, its faith in Jesus Christ, its sacraments, and its worship of images. If a Christian dares to raise his voice [against them], he goes to prison. It is [George] Kôkalas to whom they owe their great power.

This alleged protector of Jews was indeed an important dignitary, whose daughter had married the emperor's nephew, and who is recorded as still holding a high office in 1326. Later Athanasius complained to Andronicus that many of society's shortcomings had been caused by the fact that "the masses have not only been allowed to live in ignorance, but have also been contaminated by the admission of Jews and Armenians." He added the warning that the ancient Jews "had perished only because of their disobedience [to God's laws] and their prevarications. Everybody knows it, and yet the iniquity is only getting worse." [23]

Remarkably, the patriarch did not refer in his complaints to the old canonical prohibition, enacted by the ancient Roman emperors, that Jews must not erect new synagogues without a special ecclesiastical or governmental authorization. This disability was clearly restated in the *Basilika,* under the severe sanction of a fine of 50 pounds of gold for each violation. Nonetheless it seems that, as in the earlier Middle Ages, the Jews continued to spread out into many new localities in the Empire—as well as into new districts in their older settlements—and that, as soon as they established a community, they also erected a house of worship. Similarly the Karaites, whose presence in the Empire is well attested from the eleventh century on, must often have felt the urge to erect synagogues where they could cultivate their own liturgy. Yet there is no record of either Rabbanites or Karaites applying for licenses to erect a synagogue or to enlarge an existing one. Nor do we hear of wanton destruction of synagogues by fanatical mobs similar to that of fifth-century Callinicum, which, as we recall, gave rise to the first major Church and state confrontation between the distinguished Church Father St. Ambrose, bishop of Milan, and Emperor Theodosius II. To be sure, an *argumentum ex silentio* is especially perilous in the Byzantine area, but if controversies on this score had arisen with any degree of frequency, they should have been alluded to in some Christian or Jewish source available today.[24]

Adherence of the Byzantine Jews to their respective rituals, and hence their need to worship in more than one synagogue, may be taken for granted, although we have few direct records of such separate institutions before the arrival of the masses of Iberian and other exiles in the Ottoman period. By the sixteenth century there were more than forty synagogues in Constantinople-Istanbul alone. Minor liturgical differences, derived from local customs rather than diverse theological doctrines, never assumed among Jews the importance they had in the Christian world, where the controversy about the inclusion of the word *filioque* in a crucial prayer reflected the Eastern conviction of the absolute equality of Father and Son in the Trinity and thus symbolized the major political, as well as theological, cleavage between the Eastern and the Western Churches. Yet it stands to reason that the Byzantine Jews, having had behind them an age-old tradition of ritualistic differences, were further stimulated to attach considerable significance to ritualistic minutiae. Regrettably, we have little evidence to this effect in the few extant Hebrew letters of the period, but there clearly was in this area, too, a line of continuity from the earlier Byzantine to the later Turkish period of Jewish history in the Balkans.[25]

In still another aspect the Byzantine Jewish community differed from its more autonomous Western counterparts. Whereas in Catholic countries the rabbis insisted that litigations among Jews be adjudicated exclusively in rabbinic courts, and often severely condemned a man suing a coreligionist before a general tribunal, in Byzantium litigations before general courts were the rule rather than exceptions. They were taken for granted even by the Italian rabbi Isaiah b. Mali of Trani, who visited the Balkans and maintained close relations with his confreres across the Adriatic Sea. He also was often approached by them for legal decisions in difficult cases. The general courts' judicial authority over Jews originated in the decree enacted by Theodosius I in 398, which for civil cases had converted Jewish courts into mere courts of arbitration to which the parties might willingly submit their disputes. Only through such a mutual agreement between the litigants did the sentences of these courts become binding upon them; they were also enforceable with the aid of the non-Jewish authorities. Of course, in religious and ritualistic matters the jurisdiction of rabbinical courts usually prevailed. This system was well defined by a sixth-century Byzantine jurist, Thalelaios, when he stated:

> Jews who live according to Roman and common law shall, in matters which by law and justice relate to their religion or to the market place, turn to the [regular] courts in a customary way; they shall be subject to all Roman laws and procedures. When, however, some of them, following the example of the "judge" among the Jews [of the Old Testament era], should by common agreement wish to litigate in civil matters [before arbiters of their choice], they shall not be hindered by public law from submitting themselves to such courts. The authorities shall accept the sentences of such courts as if they were decisions rendered by [governmental] officials.

Our evidence is regrettably much too limited for us to ascertain the extent to which Jewish parties made use of either alternative.[26]

It is amazing that even in the area of marital relations—often the most tenaciously conservative branch of civil law and custom—many Byzantine Jews almost obliterated the distinctions between the ceremonies at betrothals and weddings, and their respective legal consequences. This practice, unknown among the Jews under Islam or in Western lands, may have resulted from the imitation of non-Jewish ways in the Byzantine environment, or else both Jews and Gentiles may have adopted a procedure inherited from common Hellenistic predecessors. At any rate, this alien custom, too, was grudgingly approved by Isaiah b. Mali. Such acculturation to the Greek environment was particularly pronounced in regard to language. Speaking Greek for many generations (as we shall see in a later context, so-called Romaniot communities continued to do so in many Balkan areas even under the Ottoman domination), they used Greek loanwords even in some of their Hebrew halakhic writings. Such practices, carried over from the Hellenistic era, have recently been documented from works written after 1000 C.E. In fact, certain usages of Greek words found in the late medieval Hebrew writings shed interesting light on the evolution of medieval Greek in general.[27]

It may be assumed, however, that in the fourteenth century, when the corruption of judges became ever more flagrant—in 1337 Andronicus III had to remove, on this score, three of the four officiating general judges in Constantinople as part of his judicial reform, and in 1341–54 the increasing domestic dissension turned into a regular civil war—Jews preferred to use the services of their own rabbinic courts. This likelihood is increased by the fact that, as a tolerated minority, the Jews could not resort to self-help against corrupt bureaucrats; some organized Greek groups did so and in one case delivered an unnamed royal chamberlain (the fourteenth-ranking government official) to five fishwives for utterly humiliating treatment. Of course, briberies could also work in favor of a Jewish party unable to obtain redress against wrongs by ordinary legal methods.[28]

Most importantly, at this time Jews suffered little discrimination in the economic sphere. True, as before 1204 Jews were barred from holding public office. This prohibition was already in force in the ancient Christian Empire, which had deprived Jews of the *honos militiae et administrationis*. As feudalization of the country now proceeded at a faster pace, one could hardly expect Jews to serve as feudal lords controlling large numbers of Christian serfs. Hence we have no records of great Jewish landowners. But Jews seem to have freely acquired other, particularly urban, real estate. From the outset, some Jewish quarters were assigned to their early inhabitants by grants of land from the authorities, with the obligation for the new tenants to erect specified buildings. They were to pay rent to the government, usually for twenty-nine years, after which, by virtue of the old system of *emphyteusis,* they were to become full-fledged owners. They were also allowed to work in many branches of industry, often forming guilds of their own which, at times, played a very significant role in the local economy. It was, for example, the influential Jewish guild of tailors of silk and purple garments which had helped to make Thebes the greatest center of the silk industry in the Balkans and probably in all of Europe. Not surprisingly, it deeply impressed Benjamin of Tudela. Both the community and the industry survived the cataclysm of 1203–1204, and in 1218 they were glowingly described by another Spanish Jewish visitor, the poet Yehudah b. Solomon al-Ḥarizi. Sometimes, to be sure, Christian guilds tried to monopolize certain trades. We shall see that one such attempt, relating to the tanning of hides and the working of furs, affected both Jewish and non-Jewish Venetian subjects and gave rise to a long-lasting controversy between the Byzantine and Venetian administrations. On the whole, in the general make-up of Jewish communities artisans seem to have surpassed even merchants in importance. Although our information about Jewish commercial activities, too, is very limited, Jewish names sporadically appear in business records; for instance, nine Jews were entered into the Book of Accounts by the Venetian merchant Giacomo Badoer who spent the years 1436–39 in Constantinople. Some of these merchants are recorded with multiple transactions.[29]

As before 1204, we hear practically nothing about Jewish money-lenders in the Empire proper, though a number of them are recorded in Crete and other Italian colonies. Hardly any Jews are mentioned as traders in bullion or currency, although such business doubtless proved quite remunerative to expert money changers who could discern the ever declining ratios of gold or silver in the new coins. The period of monetary crisis in late medieval Byzantium, which had once gloried in the long-term stability of its coinage, must have offered many opportunities for agile capitalists to make quick gains. Similarly, the Treasury's frequent need to borrow from private bankers, especially in Venice, with substantial and often unusual collateral (like the aforementioned pledge of an emperor's son) were highly profitable for the lenders. Participation in that lucrative business must have been very tempting to wealthy Jews with cash on hand. Perhaps the existing legal restrictions of interest rates since the days of Justinian and the general insecurity for Jewish dependents in dealing with the government may have stymied some such desires. At the same time, the absence of Jewish "usurers" removed a major irritant from Judeo-Christian relations. In general, it probably was the more normal economic stratification of Byzantine Jewry which helped to reduce the tensions between the Jews and their urban neighbors and gave rise to fewer mass assaults on Jewish quarters than took place in the Western lands. Even the Black Death, which destroyed many lives in Byzantium before it reached central and western Europe, apparently passed without any untoward consequences for the status of Byzantine Jewry. Together with the rest of the population, Jews undoubtedly suffered from the high mortality occasioned by the plague. But they do not seem to have become victims of allegations, such as spread in the West, that they bore a special responsibility for that awesome contagion. In fact, our sources are almost totally silent about any Jewish aspects of that catastrophe in the entire Byzantine area.[30]

As may be seen from the above presentation, our information about the late medieval Jews in areas under direct control of the Byzantine emperors is extremely sketchy. It appears that neither the government, nor the chroniclers, nor even the Orthodox clergy took a particular interest in the presence of the small Jewish minority, scattered over many localities. Since many Jews bore typical Greek names, while many Orthodox Christians preferred to be called by Hebraic first names, we cannot use the usual onomatological criteria for identifying Jews, such as had been helpful in regard to ancient Babylonia or Hellenistic Egypt. We depend, therefore, on the few casual remarks in some literary writings and, more frequently, on incidental references in legal enactments, judicial decisions, and the like, to learn even about the mere existence of Jews in particular towns. At the same time the Jews seem to have been either too reticent or, for the most part, not sufficiently learned to leave behind historically relevant records. Those documents that might have proved helpful, had they survived, doubtless fell victim to the frequent fires and the destruction by conquering hosts under ever-changing masters.

A telling example of a community being enveloped in nearly total obscurity is that of Adrianople (later called Edirne in Turkish). As an important administrative and commercial center ever since it had been named after Emperor Hadrian, it was during the Middle Ages the third-largest city in the Balkans (after Constantinople and Thessalonica-Salonica). As such it surely attracted many Jews in various periods. After its occupation by the Turks it embraced a well-established Romaniot Jewish community, called *de los Griegos* (whose old synagogue was open to worshipers until destroyed by fire in 1905), and numerous Jewish tombstones which indicate that many Jews must have lived and died there before the Turkish occupation. However, even the general history of the city during the preceding period is so full of obscurities that the date of such a crucial event as the Turkish conquest, followed by the transfer of the Ottoman capital from Brusa to Adrianople (it remained there until the conquest of Constantinople in 1453), still is the subject of scholarly controversy.[31]

LATIN ROMANIA

Somewhat different were developments in the western parts of the Balkan Peninsula, including the Peloponnesus, the scene of much classical and modern Greek history. Conceivably it was the greater difference in faith (Catholic versus Orthodox), speech (Romance versus Greek), and culture between the Western conquerors and the local population that made people more keenly aware of the religious diversity of the Jews as well. Perhaps, too, coming from countries where the Jewish question was more frequently, often heatedly, debated in public, the Latin rulers—and indirectly the population under their rule—were prone to react to the Jews living among them, either positively or negatively. Be this as it may, extant records are far more helpful to modern investigators of the Jewish position in these lands, although they still lag far behind the much richer documentation available from the Italian colonies and from the merchant republic of Dubrovnik (Ragusa).

In the Late Middle Ages much of the area was best known as Morea; its northern parts were dominated by feudal lords and only on occasion, as the Byzantine Despotate of Morea, were controlled by the emperors residing in Constantinople; the southern section became the Latin or Frankish Morea. Even before the Crusaders' arrival the peninsula had lost its ancient glory and, especially as a result of the pestilence of 746 and the settlement of still backward Slavic tribes, was deeply impoverished culturally as well as economically. We may discount the exaggerations, bred by a feeling of Byzantine superiority, of the Constantinopolitan man of the world, John Cantacuzenus, who called the Latin Morea a region "more deserted than the land of the Scythians." His observation did not hinder this statesman-historian from retiring to the Peloponnesus for the last two years of his life. Yet it possessed more than a kernel of truth. The situation was further aggravated by the local society's broad acceptance of the contemporary Frankish feudal order and rather rigid class structure. "Here was established," observes George Ostrogorsky, "the French principality of Achaia or the Morea, the most remarkable of all the principalities which were set up in Byzantine territory, for it was entirely Western in its mode of life and at the same time reflected a clear-cut feudal differentiation of society. It was a part of France transplanted to Greek soil and it led its own way of life under William of Champlitte and later under the house of Villehardouin." In all respects it became a Latin "Romania" in the narrower sense of that term.[32]

Our information about the late medieval Jewries in this entire area, too, largely depends on incidental references to them in predominantly non-Jewish sources. After 1204 one of its most important Jewish communities lived in Patras, where Benjamin had found only some 50 Jewish inhabitants (or families). However, even this small number represented a respectable twelfth-century Jewish group in the Balkans and, under normal conditions, would have left behind some significant records, both Jewish and non-Jewish. However, apart from a brief reference to a 1279 visit to the city by the well-known Spanish mystic Abraham b. Samuel Abulafia (probably to escape persecution after his perilous journey to Rome to present his messianic message to the pope), we hear almost nothing about the Patras Jews from Jewish sources.[33]

Sporadic allusions to them in non-Jewish documents (particularly those pertaining to the periods of Venetian and Byzantine sovereignty, 1408–1430 and 1430–58, respectively) attest the presence of Jews in Patras among a population which, in addition to Easterners, embraced Frenchmen, Italians, Germans, and possibly Englishmen. The records mention individual Jewish moneylenders, a Jewish leaseholder of a farm in one of the city's suburbs, and another landowner who also owned urban property in the city. It appears that, although living under the rule of the archbishop, who often combined secular feudal with ecclesiastical powers, the Jews enjoyed many commercial liberties. But, like the rest of the population, they were adversely affected by the almost perpetual turmoil in the struggles for control over the city and its environs. In 1429, in particular, when the Byzantines laid siege to the city before they reoccupied it after an intermission of 225 years, the Jewish quarter, located near the "Jewish gate" outside the wall, suffered severely. Although Patras' Byzantine domination outlasted that of Constantinople by five years, it was too short to leave a permanent imprint on the destinies of the local Jews. Curiously, like many of their Christian compatriots, the Jews of Patras were frightened at the approach of the Turkish troops in 1458 and left the city for safer places. However, they were easily persuaded to return to it at the Sultan's invitation. Thenceforth, the Patras Jews shared the destiny of all Turkish Jewry, including the continued insecurity of travel on the Aegean and Mediterranean Seas, then infested by pirates. Apparently in 1533 an episode of piracy brought a number of Patras Jewish captives within the purview of the Jewish community of Candia in Crete. In consonance with the old rabbinic injunctions stressing the priority of ransoming captives over most other commandments, the Candiot elders sold some of the sacred objects belonging to their synagogue in order to free these victims. Similar incidental scraps of information may be gathered from other localities; they do not add up, however, to any comprehensive image of Jewish life over the last medieval centuries. Hopefully, future explorations may yield new relevant data.[34]

Remarkably, although they realized that piracy seriously interfered with their international trade, the Venetian authorities did not try to stop their own subjects who engaged in that widespread practice. Even special pledges to restrain them, such as were stipulated in treaties between Venice and the Ottoman Empire in 1502, were often broken. Sultan Bayezid II's complaints in 1504 on this score were to no avail. In 1532 Andrea Doria, the well-known Genoese warlord then in the service of Emperor Charles V, raided both Patras and Coron and carried off many local Jews and Turks in order to sell them as slaves or to collect ransom for them.[35]

Contemporary records throw no more light on the situation north and east of Patras, including the Duchy of Athens. On the whole, Jews suffered there more from the changing sovereignties and the arbitrary rule of local grandees than from the legislation of princes and would-be emperors. One need but quote the vicissitudes of the Jewry of Thebes, which in the days of Benjamin of Tudela appears to have been the second largest Jewish community in the Byzantine Empire. Apart from its relatively large Jewish population of some 2,000 persons and its significant contribution to the industrial output of the country, Thebes was an important center of Jewish learning. According to Benjamin, the rabbis of Thebes had "none equal to them in all of Greece except in Constantinople." This testimony is the more remarkable as we recall that in 1147, some twenty years earlier, Roger II, the Norman ruler of Sicily, had invaded the city and allegedly removed "all" Jews and many Christians to his home country. He thereby successfully started the important silk industry in Sicily. After that wholesale evacuation, the city's standing continually declined. In 1205 Thebes was occupied first by the Greek Leon Sguros and soon thereafter by Boniface de Montferrat and his associates, Albertino de Canossa and Guy de la Roche. More enduring was the reign of Bela de Saint-Omer (De la Roche's brother-in-law) and his family (*ca.* 1230). The district was next occupied by the enterprising princes of Navarre in 1365. Later it fell briefly under the rule of the rapacious Catalans, and finally of members of what originally was the business firm Acciajuoli, until it was incorporated into the Ottoman Empire soon after 1453. While the Jewish silk weavers did not suffer the fate of their ancestors who had been forcibly removed to Sicily, their industrial and commercial life must have been undermined by the instability generated by the constant wars and changing regimes. With their intellectual activity likewise muted, we hear little about their life during the successive Latin occupations.[36]

We know somewhat more about the communities, to the north and northwest of the Peloponnesus, which remained under the control of the despotate of Epirus. The first ruler, Michael I Angelos, seems to have maintained the status of the Jews with few local changes. However, his half-brother and successor Theodore I Dukas Angelos (1215–30), who after numerous victories and the conquest of Thessalonica assumed the imperial title in 1224, seems to have staged a major persecution of Jews. But in 1230 he died in Bulgarian captivity. Remarkably, on the island of Corfu, which seems to have had few Jews when taken over by Michael in 1214 (earlier, Benjamin had found there only one Jewish family), his efforts to attract population appear to have laid the foundations for a substantial Jewish community. As we shall see, it later played a significant role in Jewish history. Among the other communities under Greek rule, Corinth, where Benjamin had found about 300 Jews (or Jewish families), now became the capital of the despotate of Morea; Athens, which was for a time the capital of a separate duchy, and Sparta, then usually called Lakedemonia, deserve mention primarily because of their ancient connections with the Jewish people. We remember that already before the Maccabean Age a special relationship had been claimed between the Jewish people and the ancient Spartans. Jews had evidently survived the threatening advice of St. Nicon Metanoites that Lakedemonia should banish all Jews (*ca.* 985). In the Late Middle Ages these foci of ancient glory were overshadowed by Mistra which, as a fortress, played a strategic role far beyond its size. As early as 1261 it was regained for the Empire by Michael VIII Palaeologus and remained an essentially Greek city in a Latin-controlled region. The Jewish community, however, seems to have been quite small. Among the few surviving communal records is a request that the Jewish elders of Candia, Crete, induce the absentee husband of one of its female members to send her a writ of divorce.[37]

Yet it was in the smaller centers of Greek Morea, like Mistra, rather than in Constantinople or even Thessalonica that the basic trends in the development of Greek nationalism were shaped. Though somewhat dormant in the first centuries of Turkish rule, they finally erupted in the famous Greek War of Independence in 1821–29, which in many ways spelled the beginning of the end of the Ottoman Empire. In the fifteenth century, it was particularly the distinguished reformer Georgios Gemistos Plethon who appeared as "the great visionary of Greek nationalism." It is rightly assumed that the Anatolian residence of his early years, and particularly the influence of his Jewish teacher Elissaeus in Brusa (Bursa)—about whom nothing else is known—had greatly helped to shape his national ideology. Although he seems to have had no occasion to raise his voice in behalf of Jews, the tenor of his writings reflects a moderately tolerant stance nurtured on his Platonic prototypes. For instance, in the "Memorandum on the State of Affairs in the Peloponnesus" that he submitted to the emperor, he advocated a number of important reforms. Among the prerequisites of good citizenship he considered "good religious convictions," based upon three fundamental principles: (1) belief in the existence of the one and only God, (2) conviction that God takes care of man through justice according to His superior lights, and (3) certainty that He cannot be swayed from that course by offerings and mere exercise of religious ceremonies. Of course, normative Judaism had long accepted these principles as basic to its entire religious outlook. Even if Gemistos Plethon, while writing this memorandum in Mistra, may have paid no attention to the presence of Jews or Muslims in the area, he definitely could not exclude the Catholic Latins from whatever measures he wished to see adopted in the Byzantine state. Unfortunately, we often have to resort to inferences of this kind for the reconstruction of Jewish life in many medieval Balkans areas.[38]

Perhaps even less is known about the fate of Jewries in the southern Peloponnesus, which became the Frankish principality of Morea (except for the districts of Modon and Coron, which after 1204 were controlled by Venice). The feudal institutions of Western Europe were transplanted bodily into Frankish Morea and soon made life, in general as well as for the Jews, follow the French patterns. Yet, while animated by religious zeal and hatred of all infidels including Jews, the new regimes had to accommodate themselves to the Greek-Orthodox majority as well as some Jewish, Armenian, and Muslim inhabitants of the area. Even the Greek version of *The Chronicle of Morea* which, based on a French original, described the Latin conquest and subsequent rule in a generally anti-Greek vein, claimed that the Latin conquerors had declared at the outset: "From now on no Frank will force us [the Greeks] to change our faith for the faith of the Franks, nor our customs for the law of the Romans." In the Jewish case, moreover, some of the Frankish rulers may have remembered how speedily Philip II Augustus had to reverse himself and, in 1198, revoke his decree of 1182 expelling the Jews from royal France. Later on, to be sure, the house of Anjou, which maintained the interest of its Norman and Hohenstaufen predecessors in the areas east of the Adriatic Sea, could readily have been affected by the progressively more intolerant French regime of Louis IX and particularly by the anti-Jewish stance of the expanding Angevin domain in southern Italy, to impose more severe restrictions on the Jewries of the Balkans as well. Yet, even though Charles II banished the Jews, as well as the Lombards and Cahorsins, from his French possessions of Anjou and Maine and subsequently persecuted the Jews in Naples and Sicily, creating a large number of insincere converts (*neofiti*), the presence of a vast non-Catholic majority among his Balkan subjects seems to have tempered his and his successors' policies in that region. For example, in Corfu, over which the Angevins ruled for more than a century (1267–1386), they seem to have interfered little with the growth of the local Jewry into the sizable community it had become by the time the Venetians conquered the island in 1386. Regrettably, few details are known about this and other Balkan Jewries after they came under Angevin rule. But, since the rulers had considerable leeway to exploit the population economically and fiscally, it may be assumed that they were satisfied with treating their Jewish subjects as preferred targets of such exploitation.[39]

Jews faced an even more exacting regime when some of these areas were taken over by the Catalan freebooters. This corps of mercenaries, invited by Emperor Andronicus II in 1302–1304 to help him fight the Turks, called itself "the happy Frankish army located in Romania," but it was better known under the descriptive name of *Almugavares* (Catalan for soldiers of fortune). After its successes in Asia Minor, however, the Catalan Company became involved in power politics on a large scale. Its original backers, James II of Aragon and particularly Frederick III of Sicily, conceived the plan of using this corps to conquer the East-Mediterranean islands and thus to control Egypt's and Byzantium's usual commercial exchanges with the West. Ultimately they hoped, with the aid of the sympathetic Pope Benedict XI, to conquer both Egypt and the Byzantine capital and thus to carve out for themselves a large Middle-Eastern empire. This intrigue was nipped in its early stages by Genoa's warnings to Andronicus II and by its own preparations for war against the Catalan adventurers. However, after their Anatolian victories, the Catalonians started to use their military superiority to ravage various Byzantine possessions in Macedonia, Thessaly and, finally, in the duchy of Athens. After they defeated the flower of the Frankish nobility of Athens and its allies in 1311, they ruled for many years (nominally in behalf of either Charles of Valois or Frederick III) over the occupied territories with utter ruthlessness. Contemporary chroniclers and diplomats, who viewed these campaigns with mixed feelings of horror and fascination, paid little attention to their impact on the suffering masses of the population. Jews must have been preferred victims of the indiscriminate massacres and robberies. Those who did not join the large hosts of refugees from these barbarians had every reason to fear a treatment like that (recorded in 1430) by the aforementioned Catalan adventurer who took with him from Clarentza all the local Jews for sale into slavery or for ransom. It is small wonder that even today one of the most bloodthirsty curses to be heard in the area is: "May the Catalan vengeance overtake you." [40]

RHODES AND CYPRUS

Compared with these ever-changing constellations of power, the more enduring rule of the military Order of St. John of Jerusalem, or the Hospitallers (later also known as the Knights of Malta), offered a certain measure of security to Jewish persons and property. Outstanding among the Knights' possessions was the largest of the Dodecanese Islands, Rhodes, which they conquered in 1308. Despite Jewish connections with Rhodes, and especially its capital, that went back to the pre-Christian era, the Jews living there in the Byzantine period left few records. Yet, on his visit Benjamin found a sizable community of 400 Jews (or Jewish families). Along with the rest of the population, they must have suffered greatly during the stormy thirteenth century, when the island repeatedly changed masters: Crusaders, Nicaean Byzantines, Genoese, and Seljuk Turks from Anatolia (which was only 12 miles away).[41]

More information is forthcoming from the period of the Hospitallers, which lasted more than two centuries (1308–1522). If, under Grand Master Philibert de Naillac (1396–1421), for strategic rather than anti-Jewish reasons the boundaries of the Jewish quarter were pushed back, the original area was returned to the Jewish community by his successor, Antoine de Fluvià (1421–37). In general, the Hospitallers tried to defend their Jewish subjects against molestation by outsiders, such as the Genoese. On one recorded occasion (in 1442), the Order lodged a formal protest against the mistreatment of a Jewish passenger by a Genoese shipmaster. We learn most about the conditions of Rhodes' Jewry during the last half-century of Hospitaller rule, especially from travelers, Jewish and non-Jewish. For example, an anonymous pilgrim from Cologne recorded, in his travelogue of 1472, that "this city is inhabited by many Jews and particularly by beautiful Jewesses who produce many fine and costly silk girdles." In 1481, shortly after a severe Turkish attack, a Jewish traveler, Meshullam b. Menaḥem (Bonaventura di Manuello) da Volterra, visited the island and graphically described Rhodes' harbor and geographic location. He added:

The city is extremely beautiful and magnificent; all the cavalry is clad in splendid uniforms. I saw the Grand Master in person, a handsome man, straight like a rod; he stems from a French family, has a long beard, and is about fifty five years of age. I saw the Court and the reception room in the company of R. Abraham Rafa Ashkenazi who lives with another fine and honorable Jew. I saw the devastation wrought by the Turks, especially in the Jewish quarter where the main battle took place. They destroyed a number of houses including those of Messer Leon of Rhodes and R. Azariah the physician, as well as the wall close to the synagogue. According to the tale told me, more than 10,000 Turks ascended the wall, dislodging [the forces of] the Grand Master. But God confounded them and they fought one another, whereupon their hearts sank; and the Lord delivered the [local population]. Thereupon the city was rebuilt with new houses and fortifications, more beautiful than any I have seen. They also erected two churches close to the wall on two sides of the synagogue in the place where the miracle had occurred. The local Greeks besought the Grand Master to remove the synagogue, but he would not listen to them. For "He that keepeth Israel does neither slumber nor sleep" [Ps. 121:4].

Meshullam did not foresee, however, that soon the synagogue would suffer severely from the earthquakes of 1481–82, and that in 1488 the regime would turn it over to the church of Our Lady of Victory, erected in memory of the miraculous resistance. To lighten the impact of this move on the Jewish community, Grand Master Pierre D'Aubusson assigned another locale for a synagogue and even personally contributed 100 ducats toward the cost of the new building.[42]

In 1488–90, the Jews of Rhodes welcomed another distinguished visitor, Obadiah Yare b. Abraham di Bertinoro, a renowned commentator on the Mishnah, from whom we learn some further details. According to this visitor, many of the Jewish houses destroyed during the preceding disturbances had not been rebuilt, apparently because the Jewish population had been temporarily reduced to twenty-two families. Obadiah also recorded the difficulties of Rhodes' Jewry in securing ritually permissible meat and wine. Since the Rhodes Jews abstained from drinking wine touched by Christians, "as if it were pork," the ritually supervised beverage had to be imported from Crete. Obadiah added:

> I saw no one among the Rhodes Jews, small or big without exception, who did not belong to persons of intelligence and knowledge and did not converse in a fine language. They have good mores and fine manners and know how to get along with people. Even the leather workers among them, who are engaged in tanning, wear clean clothes, speak softly, and let their hairlocks grow so that they look like royal children. Such beautiful women as the Rhodians are nowhere to be found in the whole world; they perform all sorts of arts and crafts and maintain their husbands through their work for the governor and high officials deep into the night. The governing officials highly esteem the Jews, maintain social relations with them, and are daily found in their homes where they chat with the women performing their skilled work. Therefore the Jewish women of Rhodes have a bad reputation among Christians.

There was an undertone of criticism in the rabbi's last remark, but it could not be compared with the much sharper censure of the Christian women voiced by a Muslim visitor in 1522, as well as by an earlier French visitor of 1485, who claimed that many of the beautiful married ladies had poor morals and that some of them engaged in outright prostitution. The temptation to sexual laxity was undoubtedly heightened by the Rhodian love for luxurious attire, commented on by many travelers; for instance, the fifteenth-century German pilgrim from the Lower Rhine. Nor was it a mere coincidence that Canon Pietro Casola, who visited Rhodes in 1494, remarked: "I saw very beautiful women there of every nation. There are many and rich Jews, and they control the silk industry"—a rather curious juxtaposition.[43]

Before long, D'Aubusson and his councilors changed their tolerant attitude; on January 9, 1502, they decreed that, because Jews refused to recognize the Christian interpretation of the "miracle" of 1480, they must all leave the island within forty days or else be baptized. The same law was to apply to Cos and other islands. The reasons for D'Aubusson's sudden change of mind have never been satisfactorily explained. The interpretation offered, for example, by Abbé V. A. Vertot in his generally well-informed, but undocumented, presentation of the history of the Hospitallers, merely refers to long-existing conditions. After declaring that the decree of banishment from all possessions of the Order was issued with the approval of its Council, Vertot states: "that nation's [the Jews'] hereditary aversion to the adorable person of Jesus Christ, had made them hateful to the Grand Master. Besides, they ruined the Order's subjects by their enormous usuries, and they were accused of other pursuits even more shameful and infamous." He may be alluding here to possible widespread sexual relations between Jews and Christians on the island, but otherwise these allegations, unsupported by any further evidence, bear the earmarks of the anti-Jewish stereotypes often used to replace the true causes. Nor does the pathetic description of the sufferings and fortitude of the Jews imprisoned by the Rhodes authorities on this occasion, by the Jewish chronicler Elijah Capsali of Candia, go beyond the usual generalities. Possibly, the growth of Spanish influence on the Order ever since the 1421 election of Antoine de Fluvià as its grand master may have poisoned the attitude of its ruling circles toward the Jews, particularly after the Iberian expulsions in 1492–97. It appears that, since the exiles were not allowed by the authorities to proceed to the Ottoman Empire lest they increase the manpower and financial resources of that powerful enemy of Rhodes, many, perhaps the majority, went to Nice. After this expulsion, any Jews captured by the Hospitallers in their piratical expeditions were treated as slaves. Their number is said to have risen to 2,000 or 3,000 persons. Not surprisingly, these Jews viewed the later Turkish assailants on the island as liberators, while a small remnant of the older Jewish community, continuing to live in Rhodes as secret Judaizers, were fulfilling their citizens' duties in defending their country against the Ottoman attackers. The Turks proved victorious, however, and in 1522 occupied the island. They speedily granted the Jewish community the legal status enjoyed by its Turkish coreligionists who, as we shall see, were often treated better than the Christian subjects of the Porte.[44]

Different again, in many ways, was the situation in Cyprus under another branch of the Latin conquerors. In 1192 Richard Lion-Heart, angered by the lack of Byzantine cooperation in his crusade, conquered the island and handed it over to Guy de Lusignan, who five years before had lost the capital of his Latin Kingdom of Jerusalem to Saladin. The Lusignan family ruled over Cyprus for the following three centuries; their regime was but locally interrupted by the Genoese occupation of Famagusta from 1373 to 1464. In 1489 the control over the entire island was assumed by the Republic of Venice and held until 1571, when it was surrendered to the Porte despite the great Turkish defeat at Lepanto. During that half a millennium, Jews again played a role in Cypriot history. They thus resumed a checkered career which much earlier had included their uprising against Trajan in 115–17, followed by the Roman outlawry of Jewish settlement. They had returned, as we recall, in time to participate in 610 in the large Jewish expeditionary force dispatched from Cyprus, Damascus, and Palestine to help the Jews of Tyre in their uprising against Byzantine rule. When Benjamin of Tudela arrived in Cyprus in the 1160s, the Jewish population included Rabbanites and Karaites as well as a sectarian group of Mishawites (followers of Meswi) whom, according to Benjamin, the Jews had everywhere excommunicated, for "they profane the eve of the Sabbath, and observe the first night of the week." [45]

We do not have detailed information about the status of the Jews under the Lusignans, but it appears that they lived under the laws formulated in the *Assises de Jérusalem,* taken over from the Latin Kingdom of that city. Basically this code treated equitably the large majority of the Greek-Orthodox, Muslims, Christian sectarians, and others. For example, the testimony of a Jew (and Saracen), with an "oath taken according to his own law," was readily recognized. In another context the *Assises* specified that a Jew should swear on the Torah, while a Samaritan should use his own version of the five books of Moses. Otherwise they were all to appear along with Syrians, Saracens, Nestorians, and other sectarians before the same courts. However, from time to time we hear echoes of a Western type of discrimination. For example, the code restricted the rights of "idolaters," Jews, and Saracens in acquiring hereditary real estate without special permission of the authorities. There also were such ecclesiastical and secular pronouncements—fairly stereotyped in the West—as that adopted by the Church Synod of Limassol in 1298, demanding that Jews abstain from carnal intercourse with Christians. Other churchmen insisted that Jewish physicians not be allowed to treat Christian patients and that Jews wear yellow badges, particularly yellow turbans. In wishing to glorify Archbishop Jean del Conte of Cyprus, who had died in August 1332, the sixteenth-century Venetian chronicler Francesco Amadi stressed among the churchman's great achievements his "ordering the Jews and Jewesses to wear a yellow mark on their heads so that they be recognized." Despite such restrictions Jews became quite prosperous, as was attested by the "great harvest of money from the Jews of Nicosia, Famagusta and throughout the realm" collected by the usurper Raymond de Pins in 1310, and said to have yielded 100,000 bezants, or some 25,000 ducats. In 1373 Peter II's agreement with the Genoese to stop their heavy raids on the island included a promised indemnity to the Republic of 1,000,000 ducats, which the king tried to raise from his subjects. To that forced loan the Jews of Nicosia were to contribute 70,000, and those of Famagusta, 30,000 ducats; by comparison, the shares of the far more numerous Christian burghers of these two cities amounted to 100,000 and 200,000 ducats, respectively. Yet this heavy tribute did not completely stop the Genoese raids on Nicosia.

In time Genoa's extortions became so burdensome that in 1447 the Genoese consul in Limassol graphically described the animosity of the local population by informing his superiors that "in these parts I would rather be called a Jew than a Genoese." It is small wonder that in the course of the fifteenth century the conditions throughout the island speedily deteriorated and that by the middle of the sixteenth century the famous Famagusta was reduced to a population of only 8,000 persons.[46]

CHIAROSCURO SITUATION

Reviewing the preceding description of the Jewish situation during the last two and a half centuries of Byzantine history, one finds long patches of total obscurity occasionally interrupted by sudden rays of light. The sporadically recorded episodes stem from different localities and different periods; they hardly add up to a satisfactory total picture. Yet, historically the destinies of the Byzantine Empire, even in its decay, and of its Jewries cannot be glossed over lightly. After all, this empire was a link between the great Graeco-Roman civilization, the Empire's progenitor, and the highly important Ottoman Empire, its ultimate successor. For the Jews, too, the area of the Eastern Roman Empire, which became Byzantium, originally embraced the large majority of both the world Jewish communities and individuals and included all the important Jewish economic and cultural centers except that of Babylonia. Similarly, the Ottoman Empire embraced in its population the descendants of Middle-Eastern Jewry (often forming their own Romaniot congregations) and most of the exiles from Spain and Portugal, together with a number of Ashkenazic immigrants and their descendants. As such, Ottoman Jewry rivaled in importance that of Poland-Lithuania and exceeded those of Germany and Italy. Among them these four regions contributed most to the Jewish history of the early modern period. This intervening late Byzantine phase, which lasted only from 1204 to 1453, was so greatly fragmented and its Jewry lived under so many ever-changing dynasties and feudal lordships that the variety itself has frequently required explanation beyond the relative merits of the respective communities. Nevertheless, the "benign neglect" accorded to this entire area by most Jewish historians of the nineteenth century is no longer justified. Much has been done since Samuel Krauss's pioneering effort to detect and gather whatever scraps of information were available and to reconstruct from them an approximation of what actually happened to the Jewish segment of the heirs of the grandeur that was Rome's.

This paucity of our sources of information, however, is in itself a contribution to our knowledge. In view of the existence of a very large body of Greek and other writings on theology, law, philosophy, and history, as well as of the entire range of belles lettres, stemming from the late Byzantine period, the relative absence of references to Jews is doubly remarkable. Evidently the Byzantine government and people, even the Church, evinced little interest in the few Jews living in their country. In the West-European lands—where the Jewish question was subject to much open debate; where churchman after churchman wrote diatribes *adversus Judaeos;* where Christian preachers often fulminated against their Jewish compatriots, particularly during the Easter period; where princes and city councilors heaped ordinance upon ordinance regulating the ever-shrinking areas of Jewish activity; and where the populace at large believed in the demonic nature of its Jewish neighbors and hurled against them accusations of ritual murder, desecration of the host, and poisoning of wells, if it did not indeed resort to violence, even massacres—there the Jewish problem evidently was an important, sometimes a burning issue. None of this is recorded in the declining Byzantine Empire.

The old discriminatory and segregationist laws, summarized in the codes of the earlier Middle Ages to be sure, still retained their formal force, although we have little evidence of their practical application. Some Byzantine theologians still indulged in the game of assailing the teachings of Judaism, its historical record, or its daily rituals. But much of that fury has an artificial ring; it seems to be a stereotype which was useful to repeat, if only to fortify one's own followers against the heretical propaganda of Christian sectarian leaders. At the same time, there also were leading ecclesiastics like the fifteenth-century Salonican Metropolitan Simeon, who befriended the Jews, although this fact is mentioned but incidentally in connection with the participation of numerous Jews in his funeral procession (1429).

One must bear in mind, however, that much of the pertinent

late Byzantine literature is still unpublished. Yet, barring some startling discoveries, we must assume that to most Byzantine writers between 1204 and 1453 the Jewish issue, while of considerable historical interest for the understanding of the postulated *praeparatio evangelica* during the pre-Christian age, was of minor contemporary importance. Most of the chroniclers who began their historical narratives with the ancient Roman world allotted much space to the story of ancient Jewry but had little to say about Jews living after the fall of Jerusalem in 70 C.E. Even in his private correspondence, the fourteenth-century writer Demetrius Cydonius makes few references to contemporary Jews; they essentially reflect his theoretical or ritualistic concerns rather than practical considerations of a sociopolitical nature. Nor is the apologetical and polemical literature of the fourteenth and fifteenth centuries, in so far as it has been published, particularly enlightening with respect to the real position of Jews in Byzantine society. Going beyond the general neglect of Jewish history after Josephus, which is characteristic of the chroniclers, the prolific controversialist Theophanes III of Nicaea, a friend of John VI Cantacuzenus and Patriarch Philotheus, could actually deny that medieval Jewry had anything in common with the Jews of the Second Commonwealth. But even when a polemist presented an imaginary dialogue with a Jew, as did Cantacuzenus himself with his purported spokesman for Judaism, who bore the characteristic name Xenos (the alien)—the dialogue resulting in the traditionally hallowed defeat of the Jew and his conversion to Christianity—the anti-Jewish arguments are presented with considerable restraint. On the whole, the tenor of these writings lacks the heat and venom which often characterized the Western polemical literature in the Late Middle Ages. This relative moderation did not necessarily reflect a modicum of deliberate religious toleration. But in trying to prove the superiority of Christianity over its mother faith even the Byzantine Jew-baiters do not depict the contemporary Jew as the "demonic alien," as he often appears in the parallel Western letters of the period.[47]

Under these circumstances a good deal of Jewish assimilation must have taken place, without leaving traces in the extant records. Only occasionally do we learn of converts from Judaism. To be sure, allegations of Jewish descent, real or imaginary, could be used as a weapon to denigrate a person or family. This was the case, for example, when Cydonius accused Patriarch Philotheus of having had some Jewish ancestors. But such aspersions did not prevent Macabrius, a monk of Jewish descent, from serving as testamentary executor of Emperor Manuel II Palaeologus (d. 1425) and as an influential counselor to Manuel's successors. A case has even been made for the likelihood of intellectual cooperation between a high ecclesiastic and a convert from Judaism or even a professing Jew. When Archbishop Simeon Atamano of Thebes was preparing his famed *Biblia Triglotta* (Hebrew, Greek, and Latin; *ca.* 1380)—a century and a half before the appearance of the Complutensian Polyglot of Cardinal Ximénez de Cisneros—he seems to have been assisted in the Hebrew portions of this work by a professing or converted Jewish scholar. Moreover, most Byzantine Jews of that period bore Greek names and thus escaped the attention of contemporaries and later historians. They also predominantly spoke Greek, usually repaired to non-Jewish courts and, along with their Christian neighbors, shared the miseries of successive wars, plagues, and fires and thus were little differentiated from the non-Jewish majority. Shortly after the occupation of Modon by the Turks, the French traveler Jacques Le Saige of Douai observed that without their yellow hats the Jews were not identifiable as such (1518). This observation doubtless held true for many other Greek Jewish communities. Nor was there enough incentive for the Jews to write any literary works in Hebrew. It is, therefore, more surprising that the Jews survived as an identifiable group at all, and less so that many individuals probably disappeared from the Jewish scene.[48]

In short, Jewish life under late Byzantine rule in its various parts of the Balkans, Asia Minor, and the Aegean islands did not differ greatly from that of the other inhabitants (themselves divided into many diverse ethnic and religious groups) and hence did not appear worthy of being written about by outsiders. The Jews, too, seem to have lacked the vigor to write about their own values. This tale of spiritual woe did not quite apply, however, to the Jewries living under the newly emerging colonial and national regimes.

LXXII

ITALO-SLAVIC PENETRATION

BYZANTIUM'S DOWNFALL was owing to a large extent to the same forces which, a millennium before, had destroyed the Western Roman Empire. Because the barbarian migrations of the fourth and fifth centuries were large-scale transfers of population, they spelled the end of Western Rome much faster than their counterparts in the eastern Mediterranean. Here the penetration of the predominantly Slavic tribes from the north proceeded far more slowly. The Balkan area was not only gradually repopulated by what later became Bulgarians and Serbs but also by such non-Slavic groups as the Pechenegs, the Avars, the Vlachs (combined with the original Daco-Romans), the Albanians, and even the Magyars. These tribes were often at war with one another; some disappeared completely by mixing with both the native populations and the tribes which followed them. At the same time, various Turkic tribesmen from Central Asia continued to infiltrate Anatolia, gradually establishing marches and principalities of their own. From these Turkomans emerged the two leading dynasties of Seljuks and Osmanlis which ultimately overran and reunited the whole former Byzantine Empire under their regime.

An entirely new development took place with the invasions from the West. These were not backward peoples, largely seminomadic, who moved into established agricultural and urban areas, but Crusaders, volunteer armies of Frankish nobles, pursuing an ideal while at the same time acquiring rich spoils, who finally established the Latin Kingdom of Jerusalem and the short-lived Latin Empire of Byzantium, as well as the various feudal lordships described in the preceding chapter. Equally important were the Italian merchant-adventurers and naval conquerors who gradually established a number of independent colonies and secured special privileges for their autonomous quarters in many leading commercial centers throughout the eastern Mediterranean. This large-scale Italian colonization, particularly that emanating from Venice and Genoa, adumbrated in many ways the modern worldwide expansion of West-European civilization spreading from the Iberian kingdoms, the Netherlands, France, and England. Unlike the Slavic and Turkic tribes, the Italian city-states did not export a mass of manpower from their own native bases. They were satisfied with dispatching sufficient naval and land forces to occupy the new territories and a host of officials to administer them. While some of these colonials took root in their new environment, most officials returned home after completing their terms of duty.

As a result the vast majority of the colonial population continued to live its accustomed way of life, spoke its traditional language, particularly Greek, professed its inherited religion, and fulfilled its duties to the colonial regimes by paying taxes, frequently very burdensome, and performing certain physical labors, especially for the defense of the colonies against outside aggressors. These services often became extremely arduous and led to numerous uprisings, usually suppressed with great severity by the masters. In Crete alone there were fourteen such major, if unsuccessful, revolts in the first century and a half of Venetian rule (1207–1363).

On the whole, however, out of self-interest the colonial administrations established regimes of law and order in the territories under their control. They also pursued a general policy of increasing the agricultural and industrial productivity of the colonies and of intensifying their international commercial exchanges. While none of these procedures could be applied without some force, in the long run the colonies themselves began to flourish economically and to develop their own ruling classes, which became even more exploitative than the foreign masters. One of the greatest services performed by the Venetians and Genoese for the local population was to protect their shipping and coastal cities against international piracy, that perennial plague of the Mediterranean world in that period.

Within this new colonial system, Jews were able to carve out for themselves many new niches. Entering the growing international trade with considerable zest and some expertise, a number of them were able to accumulate substantial wealth and to invest part of their profits in the domestic production. They also were, for this very reason, objects of fiscal exploitation. Equally important to the colonial rulers was the availability of credit to finance new business or military ventures through loans, voluntary or enforced, from Jewish capitalists. This novel situation also opened up new opportunities for the development of a Jewish communal life and the cultivation of Jewish arts and sciences. Because of the greater articulateness of both masters and subjects and the fortunate preservation of extensive documentary material in the local and central archives, we know much more about the fate of these colonial Jews than about the destinies of their coreligionists in other places.

VENETIAN *STATO DEL MAR:* CRETE

Most important of these colonial possessions, generally as well as from the Jewish point of view, were the numerous Aegean and Ionian islands which came under Venetian domination. Ever since the treaty of 1082, the Republic of the Lagoons had played a vital role in the maritime trade of the Byzantine Empire. In 1204 it emerged as the main victor of the Fourth Crusade and, led by the energetic Doge Enrico Dandolo, it reserved for itself the major spoils. According to the treaty among the allies, Venice was to receive three-eighths of the area of both the capital and the other Byzantine territories. Not unjustly Dandolo called himself "lord of a quarter and of a half [of a quarter] of the Roman Empire." It has also been estimated that Venice received five-ninths of the large booty captured by the Crusaders, its share allegedly amounting to the enormous sum of 500,000 marks. In the city of Constantinople, to be sure, the sovereignty rested with the emperor, whether Latin or Greek, although Venice long claimed authority over the church of St. Sophia which, for a time, served as the cathedral of the Latin patriarchate. After 1261 the cathedral reverted to the Greek-Orthodox Ecumenical Patriarchate which returned from Nicaea to the old capital. But elsewhere the Venetian authorities exercised full sovereign powers over the territories assigned to them, except for those which they voluntarily relinquished. They correctly realized that the administration of these ethnically heterogeneous and turbulent areas would overtax the limited manpower of their Republic. Therefore, Venice gave up most of Peloponnesus, originally assigned to it by the treaty, in favor of the various feudal rulers, but it reserved for itself the districts of Modon and Coron, the harbors of which could be used to excellent advantage as maritime bases in both war and peace. In general, the Venetian expansion was bent much more on securing for the Republic a dominant role in the ever-expanding Levantine trade than on pure power politics. The aristocracy which ruled Venice over the centuries was also interested in providing both luxury goods and foodstuffs for the various classes of the population at home as a means of maintaining the Republic's much-praised internal stability. In addition, the Venetian Treasury often drew large revenues from the new subject populations in the shape of both taxes and loans. But the government evinced little interest in converting the local Greek population to Roman Catholicism and even less in encouraging Greeks, Slavs, Albanians, and other ethnic groups to become Venetians. Quite early it promised to respect the local customs and diverse ways of life, and it generally lived up to these pledges.[1]

In many respects most focal, and certainly most enduring, was the Venetian domination over the island of Crete. Firmly established in 1210, it lasted without a break until 1645. In the course of the following twenty-four years practically the entire island was occupied by the Turks, except for a few small coastal localities which remained Venetian until 1715. During these four and a half centuries the Venetian administration, closely supervised by the doge and Senate at home, respected many of the customs and institutions it found in the colony, but it synthesized them with various new practices and governmental forms imported from the Italian mainland.

Such a blending of old and new methods was even more pronounced in the case of the Jewish minority. Jews had age-old connections with the island, possibly reaching back to the Minoan civilization. The Philistine invaders of Palestine seem to have been part of those "people of the sea" (as the Egyptians called them) who suddenly appeared on the scene in the period following ancient Israel's conquest of parts of the country. Certainly, the Bible connects these perennial enemies of Israel with *Kaftor* and *Kretim*. Later on, Gortyna, the island's capital in the Graeco-Roman period, is mentioned among the cities to which, at Simon the Maccabean's suggestion, the Roman Senate had addressed its pro-Jewish circular (*ca.* 140 B.C.E.). Crete had also been the scene of the pseudo-messianic tragedy, led by one "Moses" in the early fifth century C.E., according to Sokrates Scholasticus. Yet there is little information about the Jews of the island under either the early Byzantine or the Arab domination (which had interrupted the Byzantine rule from 826 to 960). The Jewish community came to life again in the Late Middle Ages. To begin with, after the Venetian occupation there started a considerable wave of Jewish immigration from both central Europe and the Iberian Peninsula. The last three centuries of the Middle Ages, we recall, witnessed numerous expulsions of Jews from Western lands, culminating in their banishment from Spain in 1492 and their forced conversion in Portugal in 1496–97. Many Jewish refugees seeking shelter in the eastern Mediterranean found the Venetian regime more accommodating even at a time when the Republic still refused to tolerate Jews at home. In Crete, as in other islands, particularly Corfu, the Ashkenazic and Sephardic immigrants lived side by side with the older Greek Jewish groups. However, unlike in Corfu and ultimately also in Venice itself, these groups in Crete did not tend to form separate communities endowed with special privileges by public law and often at loggerheads with one another.[2]

Such a mixture of Byzantine and Western institutions came to the fore in many areas of political and economic life. As in the rest of the Byzantine Empire, the Cretan Jews did not insist upon their members repairing to Jewish courts of justice in litigations with other Jews. The local rabbis seem to have accepted the system prevailing on the Byzantine mainland, that all subjects should be tried before the same *curia prosoporum*. Evidently for this reason we find in Crete records of Jewish lawyers (1496, 1503) who probably were allowed to represent their clients before the general courts, a Jewish professional activity practically unknown in the West until the onset of Emancipation. It stands to reason, however, that here, too, the authorities did not object if the Jewish parties concerned chose to appear before a rabbinical tribunal as a "court of arbitration." Although we have no documentary evidence to this effect, the Venetians may also have respected the old Roman law that in such cases the sentences of the "arbiters" were to become binding and that their execution would be fully backed by government officials. Another specifically Byzantine institution, little known under either Western Christendom or Islam, was the Jewish executioner in all capital cases. In some instances the community had to use all sorts of inducements to locate an individual willing to serve in this capacity. On one occasion, we learn from the native Rabbi Elijah b. Elqana Capsali, all eligible Jewish men disappeared from Candia and hid in caves to avoid this service repugnant to them. Thereupon the authorities arrested the chief Jewish elder and tortured him until a young Jew agreed to do the job for the high fee of 50 florins. It required long negotiations before the Venetian rulers consented in 1465 to free the designated Jewish executioners from working on Sabbaths and Jewish holidays.[3]

Needless to say, Jews did not receive, nor did they apparently aspire to, appointment to any regular public office. Rarely held by any Jew in the old Byzantine administration, such functions were even more exclusively performed by Venetian citizens in the colonies. Occasionally, to be sure, the Venetian authorities in Crete and such other colonies as Negroponte (see below), as well as at home, may have found it useful to employ a Jew, especially in the commercial and fiscal areas where he could use his expert knowledge to the state's advantage. Such was the case of a Jewish elder, Sambati (Shabbetai), who is recorded as serving, in 1314, as a *messetus* in charge of collecting dues from each commercial transaction. His appointment aroused the ire of a visiting inquisitor, the Dominican friar Andrea Doto, whose reference to the canonical prohibition of entrusting an "infidel" with authority over Christians seems to have evoked a sympathetic response in the Cretan populace. But the central government in Venice, doubly irked by the inquisitor's intervention in purely secular affairs, secured favorable opinions from two leading jurists at home and kept Sambati in office for several years. We must bear in mind, however, that his "office" was not quite "public" because his remuneration came from his share in the revenue he gathered, rather than from a salary, and thus was in many ways a variant of tax farming, an activity long considered admissible in such Catholic countries as Spain, Germany, or Poland. Another semipublic position sometimes entrusted to Jews was that of state physicians, who often were needed to testify at trials of persons accused of assault and battery and other crimes. One such practitioner, Elias *fisicus,* whose appointment was confirmed by the duke and the Council, is recorded as having been summoned to court 140 times. On the other hand, the Venetians continued the old Byzantine practice—which had its counterpart in western Europe as well—of calling upon Jews to serve in the defense of the country through both the building of fortifications, especially in the sections assigned for their living quarters, and at times as actual combatants.[4]

On other occasions, too, the Republic of the Lagoons made use of the commercial and diplomatic skills of some Cretan Jews. An outstanding example was David b. Elijah Mavrogonato who, during the last decade of his life (1461–70), played a significant role in the Republic's domestic and foreign affairs. His first important service to Venice was an investigation and detection of the leaders of two "conspiracies" (1453–54 and 1460–62). These discoveries made David at first quite unpopular among the Cretans, Jewish as well as Christian. More widely admired were his four missions to Constantinople. The first in 1465 helped bring about the termination of the Turko-Venetian war which for two years had caused the loss of many lives and much treasure to both sides, but was more acutely felt by the ever cost-conscious Venetian patricians. In these endeavors Mavrogonato was aided by a coreligionist, Jacopo di Gaëta, who as early as 1457 had been described in a formal report to the Venetian Senate as the "physician of the Turkish monarch, who is held in great repute [by his master] and has great influence on him. He has always shown himself most favorably disposed toward all the concerns of our dominions and been helpful to our nobles, citizens, and merchants." But there is no evidence that either Jacopo or David was in any way involved in a scheme hatched several years later by Salomone of Piove di Sacco—who took care of Mavrogonato's affairs during his absence from Venice—to poison the formidable Sultan Meḥmed the Conqueror. More directly relevant to Cretan Jewry were Mavrogonato's frequently successful interventions with the Venetian authorities in behalf of his coreligionists in the struggle for residential rights, against the prohibition of work on Sundays and Christian holidays, and the like. On the other hand, some of his business interests clashed at times with those of the community.[5]

Jewish economic stratification in Crete was influenced by Western models. In general, Jews were free to engage in almost all occupations except in civil service or activities dependent on the ownership of land, since in Crete, too, such ownership was partially circumscribed by growing feudalism. However, the law seems not to have prevented Jewish lenders from taking over rural property of defaulting debtors. Loans extended by Jewish (and non-Jewish) moneylenders to noble landlords were quite frequent. When in 1416 the Venetian authorities appointed a commission to investigate the abuses which had crept into the banking system on the island, they could not find any local noble who was free of indebtedness and thus qualified to serve on the commission. They had to dispatch three officials from Venice to perform that task. Ultimately, Venice forbade feudal landlords to mortgage fiefs to Jews, a prohibition sharpened by a decree of September 26, 1423. It declared that, notwithstanding all earlier measures,

> many Jews inhabit our lands and localities, both on the land side and on that of the sea [in the *terra ferma* and in the *terra del mar*]. They not only engage in usury, but have also acquired and owned many houses, landed estates, and territories, and daily acquire more. This is done against the divine law and to the burden and shame of our dominion. What is worse, unless some provision is made for a healthy remedy, they will in a short time in most of our lands and localities possess more houses and real estate than the Christians.

Therefore, the Jews should not be allowed to acquire any landed estates throughout the Republic's possessions. Those they already owned, they were to dispose of within two years. Jews failing to do so were threatened with the loss of all such property, while any official promoting their evasion was to be fined up to 500 ducats. But it appears that, like numerous earlier enactments, this prohibition quickly went into oblivion. In fact, all along we find records of Jews living in such villages as Castelnuovo and Castelbonifacio, though we are not sure that their residence there was connected with personal agricultural pursuits. It is noteworthy that, after a massacre of Jews in Castelnuovo in 1364 and the ensuing departure of practically all Jews, a small Jewish community later began growing up again in that locality.[6]

In this connection Zvi Ankori has recently made a case for a significant Jewish contribution to Crete's agricultural production, the mainstay even today of the island's economy. While we have no evidence of actual Jewish tillers of the soil or even of the Jews' role as landowners—and, as in other phases of the region's Jewish history, an argument derived from the absence of recorded evidence is very precarious—Ankori has cogently argued for important Jewish contributions to the financing of agricultural enterprises and to the export of their yield, especially in viticulture. Perhaps it may yet be too early to speak of medieval Cretan Jewry as a whole (as Ankori does) as being of an "agro-urban" type, which may have anticipated the better-known later developments among Polish-Lithuanian Jews. But some such combination of functions may indeed help to explain many puzzling phenomena in the recorded aspects of Jewish economic life on the island.[7]

In all major cities, including the newly founded Canea (1252), there also were Jewish artisans. As usual the meat trade had ritualistic aspects which, at times, required special Jewish communal action. The community also intervened when, in 1324, it found that Jewish craftsmen employed many Gentile apprentices and servants, whose presence in Jewish households ran counter to the Venetian legislation and also had unwelcome internal consequences. Remarkably, the Jewish leather workers seem to have evoked no complaints about the odor of their hides or excessive refuse, such as were heard in Constantinople. But it appears that, compared with Thebes and other Byzantine mainland areas, silk production was not widespread on the island. Instead, like many of their Christian neighbors, numerous Jews were engaged in making and exporting wine, an activity to which they were encouraged by their religious law. Some Cretan rabbis actually objected to the participation of Christian workers in the production of wine in Jewish vineyards, particularly if some of that wine was to be used for Jewish consumption. The government also made considerable efforts to protect against unfair competition the high-quality Cretan wines, which in the export markets fetched, as a rule, 50 percent higher prices than those of the neighboring islands.[8]

On the other hand, there apparently were proportionately more Jewish moneylenders in Crete than anywhere else in the Byzantine world. Of course, we have no statistical data relating to their numbers, distribution over the island, or the size of loans usually negotiated by them. Nor was this occupation so greatly concentrated in Jewish hands as it was in parts of the West, where the pressure of the Papacy and Church councils made non-Jewish competition somewhat more arduous. The Greek-Orthodox Church seems to have objected much less to moneylending at interest, partly because it had read the pertinent passage in the Gospel of Luke (6:35) in the Greek original, *davidzete medena apelpidzontes* (lend without despairing of receiving back [the loan]), rather than in the more ambiguous phrasing of *mutuum date nihil inde sperantes* (lend, hoping for nothing again) in the Latin Vulgate. Nor were the Aristotelian economic doctrines, though more native to the Greek soil, as influential in eastern Mediterranean intellectual circles as they had become among the Catholic scholastics in the West. Even in the West, as we recall, accrual by interest was treated rather leniently by the Church during the first millennium, that is, before the Great Schism completed the basic cleavage between the Eastern and Western Churches. Thenceforth, the Byzantine Church shared but little in the intellectual evolution and legislation of the Papacy, scholastic theology, or universal councils, the ecumenicity of which after 787 the Patriarchate of Constantinople and other Eastern Church organs never recognized. Even those Byzantine emperors who flirted with the Papacy's desire to bring about a reunification of the Churches did so largely for political reasons and generally had very little following among their own people. Hence the strict interpretation of the Lukan passage referring to loans was never shared by the Eastern establishment, ecclesiastical or lay. For this reason there were numerous legitimate Christian moneylenders in Crete, some of them commanding much greater resources than the Jews to whom on occasion they lent money.[9]

The Venetian government was actually interested in preserving

Jewish moneylending as an important resource for its own borrowing. Such public loans, in part probably negotiated under pressure, are often recorded in the extant documents. For example, in 1410 the Venetian Senate authorized the local officials to borrow 2,000 ducats from the Cretan Jews for the formation of two companies of infantry to be sent to Negroponte. In 1413 it again allowed them to borrow funds from Jews for the repayment of debts they had previously contracted in Venice. In 1412 they were told to acquire additional grain at a low price for shipment to Venice and were given permission to borrow from Jews any funds needed in excess of the 30,000 hyperpera then available to the Crete Chamber. In 1421 they were ordered to pay 728 ducats for the dispatch of a galley to Gaeta and were again told that, if needed, they should borrow the required amount from Jews. Another loan in the substantial amount of 4,000 hyperpera was apparently obtained from Candiot Jews for the benefit of the Venetian castellan in Coron-Modon (1425). In most such cases Jewish lenders may have been reasonably confident that the loans would be repaid on time, since the Venetian economy was booming and the Signoria's credit was generally good. However, at times there were serious delays in repayment. For instance, on November 26, 1435, the Cretan authorities informed their home government that, because of "unbearable" expenses, they would be unable to deliver to the creditors the sum of 20,000 ducats, which the Jews had lent the government four years before. They would leave it to their superiors to decide when to start their reimbursements. The Jewish leaders probably preferred to be assured, as they were in connection with a new loan of 3,000 ducats contracted in January 1452, that they would be able to deduct this amount from their future taxes. But the government insisted that it would grant them no discount in this case. From time to time a total sum was divided among several Jewish communities. In 1431, the Senate ordered the rectors of the Levant to collect as speedily as possible 20,000 ducats from the Jews of Crete, 2,000 from those of Negroponte, 3,000 from Corfu, and 1,000 from Istria. In Crete a time limit for the collection was set at only two months.[10]

Since the time of Justinian, moreover, the money trade was officially regulated and maximum rates of interest were legally established. But rather than having the variables of 4–8 and, in especially risky cases, of up to 12 percent, as was provided by Justinian's legislation, or else following the monopolistic type of state banking with a regular interest rate of 16.66 percent as enacted by Nicephorus I (802–811), Cretan law usually provided for a uniform maximum rate of 12 percent for both Christian and Jewish lenders. In the frequent periods of crisis, however, and the ensuing shortages of funds, as well as during the growing monetary inflation which led to a considerable depreciation of the Byzantine hyperperon, the rates usually rose to between 20 and 30 percent. Of course, even these high rates did not compare with the extremely burdensome interest rates in many Western countries. In any case, even the local Jew-baiters like Ludovico Foscarini who, as we shall presently see, hurled all sorts of accusations at the Jews, did not make a major issue of Jewish "usury." They did speak occasionally of the general abuses in sales of merchandise on credit and the Jews' general rapacity which, to quote the rector of Rethimo's complaint of 1412, had made them "lords of the money and the men of this region." Western travelers, like Mariano da Siena, wrote of the large number "of very rich Jews" (1431), or like Felix Fabri complained of the "very great power" exercised by the Jews on the island (1480). Mariano and Fabri repeated here what they heard from local Christians, including some government officials. These assertions could be used to good advantage by the fiscal authorities in Venice, who were anxious to tighten the screws on Jewish taxpayers. In attempting to levy, in 1447, a new impost of 5,000 ducats in order to help defray the expenses of equipping seven galleys for better surveillance on Lake Garda, they argued that the Jews could afford such an extra payment because they were *multi et divites* (numerous and rich). The same phrase had been used in 1439 to justify a new impost of 4,000 ducats annually for three years as a contribution to finance the war. But such generalizations were leveled more at the large Jewish share in shopkeeping and other commercial undertakings than at Jewish moneylending. Fabri doubtless also echoed the resentment of a relatively small group of local Christian druggists when he illustrated the allegedly excessive Jewish power by referring to the Cretan Jewish apothecaries as owning "the best and richest pharmacies." [11]

Clearly such conflicts between law and life lent themselves to numerous abuses. In one drastic case, we are told, in 1358 a Venetian burgher living in Crete had borrowed from a Jew, Jeremiah, 70 hyperpera and had already repaid him 64 hyperpera. Yet, because the borrower had gone to Venice, Jeremiah's son, Salacagia, demanded the repayment of 180 hyperpera, which was to include interest. The Senate ordered the local authorities to investigate. In other cases, it arbitrarily reduced the amounts due or the rate of interest. For example, in 1428 the Senate by a vote of 92 to 14 and 15 abstentions, lowered by one quarter the debt of 2,914 hyperpera owed Jews by 36 impoverished archers and extended the due date so that the loan might be repaid in ten annual installments. In a *cause célèbre* of 1416, which extended over several years, a special Commission tried to mediate between Jewish claimants and their Christian debtors. It proposed to divide the debtors into three classes: (1) those most able to pay were to be granted an extension of two to five years, during which period they were to be charged only an annual interest of 5 percent; (2) a middle group of less well-to-do was to be given twelve years to repay and likewise charged at the rate of 5 percent (subsequently the rate was to go up to 12 percent); and (3) the least wealthy were to be allowed to repay over twenty years and to have their debts reduced or even canceled outright. This proposal satisfied none of the parties. Two years later only 138 of a total of 1,970 claims were accepted under these conditions. As late as 1421 most debtors still refused to pay. When in 1449 the feudalists complained once more about the excessive usuries charged them by their creditors, Venice again sent three investigators to the island at a cost of 1,800 ducats. The outcome was a decree that thenceforth Jews should be allowed to lend money only on pawns. There is no evidence that this ordinance was carried out for any length of time. Four years later a prominent Christian refugee from Constantinople complained to the Cretan authorities that, because he had lost almost all his possessions during the Turkish siege of the Byzantine capital, he was unable to pay his debts to the Cretan Jews. Thereupon the authorities in Candia rather arbitrarily decided that his debts mainly represented accruals of excessive interest arrears and reduced them to an amount computed at the legal rate of but 10 percent. Such examples can easily be multiplied. Yet, these measures were far less drastic than the wholesale cancellations of debts owed to Jews, as occasionally practiced in the West.[12]

Less need be said about the Jewish role in general commerce, whether international or domestic. In their mercantile endeavors Jews seem to have enjoyed, on the whole, a measure of equality of opportunity. Our sources, in so far as they have been examined by modern historians, refer to Jewish merchants and shopkeepers mainly when some legal questions were raised by competitors, suppliers, or customers. Even those are known to us, as a rule, only if they were brought to the attention of the Senate in Venice. Some burghers (in Rethimo, for instance) at times protested against Jews opening shops outside their own quarter. Other complainants objected to Jewish traders selling on credit, or evading the acceptance of payment on time so that they might charge 12 percent interest on the overdue balances. The authorities tried to stem these and other abuses by various means. They sometimes offered partial cancellations of debts, reductions of interest rates, or other compromise solutions, in order to avert the debtors' flight deep into the Cretan mountains or other countries. Such cases seem to have been quite frequent. None of these measures apparently had much success. Similarly unavailing was the 1433 prohibition for Jews to serve as commercial agents for Christian purchasers and for Christians to employ Jews as middlemen—an occupation widely pursued by Jews in other countries. However, the general legal status, numerical strength, and role in the island's business of Jewish commercial agents still are open questions. The one prohibition alluded to in the sources stems from an *ad hoc* regulation issued by two Cretan noblemen, who in 1433 applied for senatorial approval. They forbade Jews to serve as *Sansarii aut Missete alicuius mercati,* a juxtaposition which gives the impression of referring to semipublic officials. We recall that a *messetus* was an appointed collector of customs, although his income consisted of a share in his collections. This impression is reinforced by the applicants' statement, mentioned in the Senate ordinance, that it appeared preferable that "the said arrangement [*ordo*] should be honest, praiseworthy to God and the world, and useful to Christians." The resolution itself also refers to the laws of God, according to which "the faithless Jews should be deprived of any office and Christian benefice." Yet, all these difficulties did not prevent a large segment, perhaps a majority, of Cretan Jewry from earning a living through mercantile activities, which could at times be combined with a craft or Jewish communal employment.[13]

It should be noted, however, that, compared with viticulture and the wine trade, sales of other major commodities, particularly grain and salt, showed less active Jewish participation. There is no question about the importance of both these articles of commerce not only for the Cretan economy but also for Venice itself. The City of the Lagoons depended on the importation of grain for the sustenance of its people to such an extent that Emmanuel Piloti, a Venetian living in Crete, sharply reacted against the papal prohibition of trading with Alexandria, which was a major emporium for the export of foodstuffs. Piloti went so far as to advocate a Venetian conquest of Egypt. Incidentally, such papal embargoes, going back to 1340, generally played into the hands of Jewish traders. Since many Cretan and other Venetian colonials evaded them by secret trading with Muslim lands, Jews had the greater advantage of dealing with numerous coreligionists in Syria and Egypt. Salt, too, was an important commodity. Until the conquest of Corfu with its salt mines, Venice depended on the production, however small, of Cretan salines and on imports from other countries to provide an ever growing citizenry with this indispensable condiment and preservative. The scarcity of references to the Jewish role in these two branches of business in the Venetian possessions—contrasting with the active share of Jews in the production and distribution of both these commodities in Poland and Lithuania—was doubtless owing to this trade being a Venetian state monopoly run by Christian government officials, for the most part recruited from among the Venetian Catholics.[14]

A number of Crete's Jewish heads of families undoubtedly made a living through services to the Jewish community as rabbis, cantors, scribes, ritual slaughterers, sextons, and the like. Since these officials rarely had dealings with the Venetian authorities, we only learn about their existence through the relatively few extant Hebrew sources. More is known about communal elders, some of whom were also playing important roles in business and the professions. A scholar like Elijah Capsali simultaneously served as rabbi and physician. Moreover, Jewish doctors often transmitted their craft to their sons and grandsons. The prominent family Delmedigo contributed dedicated members to the medical profession over a period of two and a half centuries (1400–1650). Discussing social life in the Byzantine areas, R. J. H. Jenkins observed that "the best doctors in the East, as in the West, were the Jews." Similarly, in his survey of Byzantine science K. Vogel concluded that "medical teaching in Byzantium ended with John Actuarius and the practice of medicine passed to Jewish doctors." This shift had been noted explicitly by Joseph Briennius (fl. 1387–1405), who tried to clarify the reasons for this change. Perhaps the growing reliance of the non-Jewish doctors on tradition and their resulting practice of "defensive medicine" gave an edge to more innovative Jewish doctors who maintained good contacts with the old centers of Arab medicine and the newly upsurging medical science in the West. The presence of an increasing number of physicians made itself felt in various phases of Jewish communal life, too. While some doctors are recorded as having performed numerous self-sacrificing charitable acts far beyond the line of duty, especially during the recurrent plagues, others steadily invoked their privileged position as tax-exempt subjects of the Republic. Such immunity from tax payments by favored, often very wealthy, individuals, here as elsewhere, was detrimental to the Jewish community at large, which had to make up the loss in revenue by taxing the less well-to-do members at higher rates. This abuse was but partially restricted by the government's revocation of many such discriminatory privileges in 1441. We also recall the more unusual activities of Jewish lawyers in Crete (such as representing clients in court), some of which have become known to us only through their recorded wills.[15]

Regrettably, the economic data currently available are too meager to allow for a reconstruction of the occupational stratification of Crete's Jewish community. If the Jewish population outside Candia was indeed limited to some 300 souls, as is indicated in the census of 1627 (see below), divided over two larger towns (Rethimo and Canea) and some rural communities, one can hardly expect much diversity in their occupational structure. Even the Jewry of Candia, if limited to less than 200 families, could not be represented in too many occupations. The chances are that especially some wealthy Jews were involved in a variety of commercial and financial activities which, through mortgage loans on land or the promotion of viticulture, led them also into direct contacts with agricultural pursuits. They may have performed these tasks personally or through employees, Jewish as well as non-Jewish. All of this naturally would have a bearing on the Jewish economic structure as a whole, but the existing documentation supplies us too few data for even remote "guesstimates" about the percentages of Jews thus engaged.[16]

Not much more is known about the Jewish share in the island's taxation. Our information is derived from a few sporadic references in the sources, most of which have been reviewed by Joshua Starr and need not be repeated here in detail. On the whole, it appears that, while Jews paid taxes as a corporate body rather than as individuals—the actual distribution among members was left to the Jewish communal elders, as in many other places and periods—they generally paid more than their proportionate share within the population. Such excess taxation was occasionally justified by the authorities through reference to the Jews "being numerous and rich," or "powerful and rich," but this may have been owing to an optical illusion, if not to special pleading. The fact that there were many Jewish moneylenders, full-time or part-time, whereas the fortunes of Christian landlords and burghers were mostly invested in urban or rural real estate or stocks of merchandise, made it easier for tax collectors to impose large cash payments on the Jews. The methods of collection also were quite drastic. For example, in the aforementioned case of December 27, 1447, when the authorities in Candia were ordered speedily to raise 5,000 ducats from Jews as an extraordinary tax for the arming of seven galleys, the Jewish taxpayers were told to pay within a month; otherwise the levy would be raised by 25 percent. The income from this penalty was to be equally divided among the city, the Republic, and those who would perform the necessary monetary transactions, thus adding a further incentive to the local collectors. In addition, Jewish moneylenders were often approached for loans which were but partly voluntary, although the Venetian government was much more likely to repay its debts eventually than were the Western rulers. However, any repayment over many years caused the lenders loss of interest which, if paid at all, was greatly reduced (in one recorded case in 1370 to 4 percent instead of the going rate of 12 percent or more) and the loss from depreciation of the currency.[17]

A more regular impost was the annual Jewish tax of 980 hyperpera recorded during most of the thirteenth and fourteenth centuries. This amount was temporarily lowered to 840 hyperpera in 1310–20, but was restored thereafter and only slightly raised to 1,000 hyperpera in 1386. In 1389 the authorities tried to increase the annual payment to 3,500 hyperpera but, after negotiations with the Jewish elders, reduced it to 2,000 hyperpera. In 1395 they revised it again upward to 4,000 hyperpera. More burdensome were the special levies, as we have noted, for the most part connected with wars or internal uprisings. One of the largest assessments was that of 1363 when 30,000 hyperpera were required for the defenses of the Candia harbor, one half of which was to be levied from the feudal vassals and the other half from burghers and Jews. The apparent ratio was about one-quarter for the Jews alone. More explicit was the ordinance issued on April 13, 1431, ordering the Cretan authorities to equip two warlike galleys to be sent to Corfu. The expenses were to be equally divided between the feudalists, the clergy, and the Jews. Curiously, the numerically largest group of taxpayers, the burghers, was not to be taxed at all. On the other hand, in 1462, after the fall of Constantinople, the Turkish peril loomed very large, and it was decided to fortify the city of Candia by a new wall. On this occasion the Jews were told to contribute one-quarter of the total cost, the feudalists and the burghers jointly one-half, while the state Treasury was to disburse the remaining quarter. For some reason the clergy was totally exempted. Large Jewish quotas also reappear in connection with some other extraordinary levies.[18]

A complicating factor in all such assessments was the question of principle concerning the fiscal contributions of the clergy. On the whole, not only the Catholic priests but also the Greek-Orthodox churchmen were powerful enough to secure general tax exemptions. But, more than elsewhere, in emergencies, the churches were made to contribute a share. Apparently not designated as a *donum charitativum* as in some other countries, such payments from ecclesiastical sources, primarily Greek-Orthodox, must have somewhat alleviated the rest of the population's burdens which, in periods of economic stringency, could become ruinous. Another complication in trying to estimate the Jewish share in the total taxation arises from the fact that, among the few payments recorded, some are given in Byzantine hyperpera and others in Venetian ducats. Over the centuries of Venetian domination the respective values of these currencies changed, the ducat being the relatively more stable currency.[19]

At the same time Jews were frequently exempted from various physical services resembling corvées. As early as 1356 Samargia, a Jew of Rethimo, protested to the Senate (also in behalf of his coreligionists) against the imposition, by a former rector of the city, of an *angaria* upon Jews. This service was to be performed in addition to their contribution to the annual payment of 1,000 hyperpera by all Cretan Jewry. Samargia claimed that the Jews would thereby be converted into villeins of the Republic. The Venetian authorities conceded the justification of this complaint and freed the Jews from all corvée labor. Later, however, Jews seem to have been occasionally drafted for some forced labor. At least in his instructions of May 10, 1485 to Francisco Bragadeno (Bragadin), Doge Giovanni Mocenigo bluntly stated that "no Jew and Jewess shall be able to free themselves from some *angaria,* except through accepting baptism. And we herewith command you thus to observe [this regulation]." Nor were the Jews free from some special levies arbitrarily instituted by the authorities, such as the strange 10 percent tax on all dowries received by Jewish newlyweds. Even more burdensome undoubtedly was a 5 percent surtax on all merchandise shipped by Jews to or from Crete, recorded in 1290–1318, since they played a major role in Crete's international trade, particularly with the neighboring Muslim countries. Suffice it to mention that merchandise shipped to Alexandria ranged from 42 to 51 percent, and to Beirut from 22 to 32 percent, of all Cretan exports in the years 1400–1412 and 1443–56 as against a mere 22–26 percent which went to all of Romania. Hence the Cretan Jews must have found the 5 percent surtax an impediment to their competition with numerous gifted Greek, Venetian, and other local traders. Apart from taxes, moreover, Jews occasionally made voluntary contributions to the Treasury. One characteristic patriotic gift consisted of 1,000 hyperpera donated by the Jews of Candia to the Venetian government to aid the suppression of a revolt in Zara. This gift was acknowledged by the Senate with formal thanks to the Jewish community (January 10, 1346).[20]

Despite the frequent and often arbitrary imposts, Jews were less harassed in Crete than in most other countries. Along with the rest of the population, they suffered more from the all-too-frequent wars and domestic uprisings than from excessive taxation. It appears, therefore, that relatively few Jews felt the urge to leave Crete for other countries. Even the great pull exercised by the Ottoman Empire on the Jews of many lands did not cause any major exodus from Candia and the other Cretan communities. When Meḥmed the Conqueror demanded that Venice return to Turkey the Jews who had fled from Constantinople before and after its occupation by the Turkish troops in 1453, the Senate decided to comply (October 20, 1457). But it added the reservation that those Jews who would evince the desire to remain under Venetian protection should be allowed to do so. There is no evidence that many refugees or other Cretan Jews responded to Meḥmed's call. Later, however, the progressive decline of the Republic's power and of the Levant trade—largely as a result of the epochal Atlantic discoveries and the West-European expansion—unavoidably affected also the East-Mediterranean islands and their Jews. The resulting economic crisis might have caused the descendants of these refugees to move back to the Ottoman lands. But by the time most of Crete was occupied by the Turks in 1687, the Ottoman Empire was in a general state of decline, economically as well as politically, and the exchange of masters was of little benefit to them. Moreover, having lost much of its importance in international trade, the entire Venetian colonial empire including Crete was deteriorating militarily, politically, and economically, in a way which could not leave the Jews unscathed.[21]

JUDEO-CHRISTIAN SYMBIOSIS

While in comparison with the earlier, less tolerant Byzantine regimes, Venetian rule bestowed many benefits upon the Cretan

Jews, it also brought with it some major negative importations from the West. Occasionally we even hear of the age-old accusations of Jewish ritual murder and host desecration. The Blood Accusation, in particular, found attentive listeners among the Greek majority of the area (including the Greek inhabitants of Syria during the well-known Damascus Affair of 1840), whereas the host libel seems to have retained its clearly foreign origin and remained quite rare. Nonetheless, it could cause much grief not only to the accused persons but also to the communal leaders held responsible for such alleged misdeeds by members. In 1451–54, such an accusation by a single person (the wife of a local Greek priest) sufficed to bring about the arrest of nine Jewish elders and their transportation in chains for trial in Venice. Two of the prisoners died from the hardships of the journey and torture, whereas the remaining seven defendants were acquitted. This was not enough. Their enemies claimed that some of the judges had been bribed and secured a retrial. But ultimately the seven men were again acquitted and allowed to return home for the second time. Nor were desecrators of Jewish cemeteries absent from the scene. Two culprits were apprehended by Candiot Jews in the early 1450s; after being turned over to the governing duke, they received appropriate punishment. Sometimes graves of wealthy persons had to be guarded for several nights after burial, a custom recorded in 1492. Remarkably, even the Jews of Candia had to be warned not to profane their own cemetery. In 1521 the old prohibition against funeral corteges being conducted as if they were joyous occasions had to be renewed by the communal authorities.[22]

Candiot Jewry did not completely escape interference from ecclesiastical inquisitors, however. As early as 1314, we recall, Inquisitor Andrea Doto had unsuccessfully tried to prevent the Jewish elder, Sambati (Shabbetai), from serving in the semipublic office of *messetus*. In 1320–25, we learn from indirect sources about inquisitors (probably including Doto) in search of a number of relapsed converts from Judaism who had escaped to Crete. In an interesting *consilium* by the well-known jurist Oldrado da Ponte of Avignon (who otherwise was not unfriendly to Jews) we read:

Certain Jews, formerly baptized in various regions, settled on the island of Crete and lived there as Jews. While the Inquisitor was investigating them some Jews who knew them as former Christians annoyed them, so that they left the island. They could not therefore be arrested by the inquisitor and caused to revert to Christianity because they had been made to depart. They had received passage money and expenses from the local Jews whom, as is known, the inquisitor prosecuted and arrested, whereas the former Jews escaped to Saracen lands.

These refugees probably were of Italian origin and the inquisitor was undoubtedly sent to Crete by the Roman Holy Office with whom, especially in the period of the Popes' "Babylonian Exile," Avignonese canonists like Oldrado were in constant communication. It is possible that these relapsed converts had come from among the southern Italian *neofiti,* left behind by the anti-Jewish legislation of Charles II, as suggested by Joshua Starr. But they may also have been joined by originally professing Christians, some of whom are recorded to have then or later voluntarily joined Judaism. On the other hand, we have little information about any repercussions on Crete of the inquisitorial prosecutions of the Iberian Marranos, such as repeatedly took place in Venice. Nor do we hear of any governmental efforts to implement the decrees issued by the Venetian Signoria in 1497 and 1550, banishing all New Christians from the city and its possessions. That some such *conversos* reached Cretan shores and lived among the island's communities as professing Jews may be taken for granted. It is only their presence which could have induced the Candiot elders to publicize in their community two communications from abroad, including one signed by R. David Ibn abi Zimra, R. Joseph Karo, and their associates in Safed on July 11, 1568, demanding severe punishment for any Jew reminding a repentant *converso* of his former transgressions and calling him a "renegade." Such behavior had already been outlawed by R. Gershom the Light of the Exile in the tenth century. The Jewry of Candia followed suit and enacted an ordinance to this effect in its own name. Undoubtedly prompted by commercial considerations, which largely accounted for the great laxity in the execution of the 1497 and 1550 decrees in Venice itself, the colonial authorities seem to have done nothing to implement them in the former Byzantine lands. Needless to say, they were completely disregarded after the Turkish occupation of Crete in the seventeenth century.[23]

Some Venetian officials contributed to the spread of anti-Jewish propaganda, however. One of them, Ludovico Foscarini, played a particularly sinister role in what he called a "perpetual war" against the Jews. Referring to a widespread local prejudice that, before Passover, Jews were acquiring lambs in order to crucify them and thus publicly deride Christ's Passion, Foscarini expanded the libel to include crucifixion of human beings as well. He repeated a miracle tale he had heard from an unnamed pauper, that, because a certain cattle breeder had sold a lamb to a Jew for ritual purposes, wolves had devoured his sheep during that year, and, despite many costly precautions, also in the following year. In the third year the breeder himself and his family died of the plague. On Foscarini's denunciation, the Venetian Council of Forty ordered the Cretan officials to cause an announcement to be read at the Candiot synagogue. All persons familiar with any such misdeeds being perpetrated then or later were to be urged to inform the authorities. Mere failure to denounce the culprits was to be punishable by life imprisonment in a dungeon and confiscation of property. Such a harsh sentence was to be pronounced "in any locality of our Signoria, be it on the sea or on land." Any convicted transgressor, moreover, was to pay an enormous fine of 2,000 gold ducats, the community at large being responsible for its payment in full. Remarkably, a century later, another Foscarini (Giacomo, Proveditor General of the island in 1574–77), fulminated against the close social contacts between Jews and Christians:

> The association and social relations of the Jewish ladies with Christians was so public and open and their intimacy so great that the Jewesses frequented all the feasts which were held not only in private homes [of the upper-class Italians], in which it is not customary for the Greek ladies to appear, but in the other houses which unfortunately set a scandalous example (may I be pardoned): it is only with these and with no other women that feasts were held; such was the public entertainment, such the public pastime and in those places there developed at length the principal brothel and from them were born innumerable creatures of Christian seed.

Yet even he did not invoke in this connection the old canonical demands that carnal relations between Jews and Christians be punished by execution. Nor must we overlook cases of individual officials who went out of their way to favor Jews. For instance, a fourteenth-century officer, Johannes Galliando, paid dearly for his apparently illegal freeing of a Jew, Sachali, imprisoned for nonpayment of debts. For this action—perhaps not completely disinterested—Galliando was condemned to three hours in pillory and dismissal from office.[24]

Such rapprochement between Jews and Gentiles was surely stimulated by the impact of the Renaissance. We hear of such other manifestations of Jewish assimilation of Italian cultural patterns as the appearance of forty young Cretan Jews performing dances at the ducal palace in Venice. In general, Cretan Jewry produced not only distinguished rabbis but also philosophers, scientists, and historians who had acquired a general Renaissance education. We recall the great role played, upon his arrival in Florence, by Elijah del Medigo (*ca.* 1450–93), scion of the distinguished Cretan medical family. Elijah became part of the philosophic circle around Marsilio Ficino and also instructed Pico della Mirandola and others in Greek and Jewish philosophy, as well as in his own philosophic ideas. He had the unique distinction of writing philosophic works not only in Hebrew but also in Latin, a language generally shunned by Western Jews as being a vehicle for Christian ecclesiastical lore. Two centuries later another Delmedigo, Joseph Solomon, left Crete and became a world traveler. We encountered him in Muscovy, Vilna, Amsterdam, Frankfort, and other localities, where he was welcomed with open arms as a learned rabbi and author of scientific works. More surprisingly, Candiot Jewry, generally orthodox as it was, did not mind asking its members to follow the sounding of the bells in the Greek Church of St. Peter in timing their cessation of work on Fridays. In short, Crete was not only a point of attraction for many refugees from other lands, but it also made its intellectual mark on large segments of world Jewry.[25]

Remarkably, these close Judeo-Christian social relations were little hindered by the introduction into Crete of a compulsory type of Jewish ghetto. Originally, as in most East-Mediterranean countries, the majority of Jews themselves preferred to live in their own quarters in consonance with the general topographical segregation of various religious, ethnic, and occupational groups. This kind of voluntary separation undoubtedly existed also in Candia and even in such a newly founded city as Canea. Because Jews belonged to the older settlers of some of these cities, the location of their quarter usually was in what became later the center of town. Such developments, some of them going back to Graeco-Roman times, have been noted also in many Western cities, including Paris. However, originally Jews were not constrained to live in their chosen street or streets. As late as 1299 they were specifically allowed by the Venetian authorities in Candia to live wherever they wished. They were also permitted to own real estate outside their quarter, especially if they acquired it through the foreclosure of mortgages. As we recall, the law had specifically forbidden only mortgages on feudal fiefs (1416). Yet, in 1325 a Venetian decree provided that "it shall be in the discretion of the rectors of Canea and its city council to place the Jews in a particular area of the city [*burgis*]." Nine years later such a quarter in Candia was taken for granted. Here the document refers to "the definitive boundaries within which the Jews have to live and stay according to our order." Yet at the same time the Venetian Senate left it to the discretion of the local authorities whether they wished to approve a Christian landowner's petition to lease to a Jew his property located in the "immediate vicinity of the Jewish quarter." Jews did not seem to object to this type of segregation, which helped strengthen the self-government of their own *qahal*. This Hebrew term was used for both the community at large and the territory it occupied, corresponding to the Latin-Italian term *Judaica* or *Zudeca* (with many variants thereof), or the Greek *Hebraiké*.[26]

In trying to reconstruct the locale of the main Jewish quarters in the major Cretan cities, Zvi Ankori had to overcome the difficulties caused by the rebuilding of these areas in later generations. He rightly minimized the 1571 observation of a Venetian official, Lorenzo da Mula, that the Candia Jewish quarter was located "in the most elegant part of the city, close to the sea, with most beautiful houses and institutions." Obviously, behind the impressive facade of some ornate buildings occupied by wealthy families were many inferior structures inhabited by the majority of Jews. Even in Venice itself, at the height of its prosperity, the narrow streets behind the marble-fronted palaces along the major canals included many slum-like dwellings. Perhaps the Cretan Jewish quarters never developed a truly shabby and neglected appearance because each accommodated but a relatively small population. Certainly, in terms of light and sanitation the Cretan cities were better off than Venice, where many streets were hemmed in by the numerous canals and most of the city's growing population had to live in tall structures which allowed for little air and light on the lower floors.[27]

It is not surprising, therefore, that harassed Jews from many lands settling in Crete were grateful to the Venetian authorities for their modicum of toleration. They also enjoyed Crete's economic, as well as cultural, opportunities. Hence loyalty to the Venetian government was an outstanding characteristic of Cretan Jewry, especially in emergencies. This was, indeed, the traditional behavior of the Jews who, ever since Prophet Jeremiah's injunction (29:7), prayed regularly for the welfare of the country in which they happened to live, whereby they usually understood also the welfare of the rulers. Loyalty to the regime was also dictated by self-interest under the conditions then prevailing in the eastern Mediterranean, where only the power of the Venetian navy and occasional interventions by Venetian diplomats prevented the Cretan and other colonial traders from suffering even greater losses than they did from both pirates and hostile local authorities. Widespread piracy was not only a long-established and, hence, tolerated evil, but it often found theoretical defenders. For example, when in 1318 the duke and some landowners of Crete complained to the Venetian authorities about the constant depredations by the Turks and the Catalan freebooters, King Frederick III (II) of Sicily replied on September 9 to the pertinent Venetian protest that, since the particular ship captured by the Catalans was sailing under the flag of the Kingdom of Thessalonica, "which kingdom is under the dominion of the emperor of Constantinople, an enemy of the Roman Church and of all faithful Christians," the ship and its passengers were legitimate booty of the Catalans.[28]

Jewish loyalty to the government often antagonized the opposing forces in Crete, however. During the reiterated uprisings of the Cretan population against their Venetian masters (Pierre Antoine Daru counted no less than fourteen major revolts in the period of 1207–1365 alone, the most important being that of 1361–64), Jews were viewed by the rebels as allies of the oppressive regime. As usual, they suffered from the disturbances even more than did the Venetians, because of their ready accessibility to the insurgents and their own relative defenselessness. To be sure, Jewish men were not only often called upon to help in building fortifications, but also manned their section of the walls in Candia and other cities and defended them against foreign assailants. They probably would have been able and willing to put up a strong self-defense against anti-Jewish mobs. But they were frequently restrained by their elders. For example, during Suleiman the Magnificent's attack on the island in 1538, Jews who worked on building ramparts were accused by their enemies of spying for the Turks—an age-old accusation voiced by Jew-baiters at many such critical junctures. The population was urged to stage a riot against the Jewish quarter and to loot its shops and residences. Jews, though on that day handicapped by the observance of the fast-day of Tammuz 17, wanted to rush to the defense of their homes but were held back by the fear of becoming involved in a battle with the majority of their neighbors. The worst was avoided, however, by the strong intervention of the Venetian garrison. Thereupon the Jews proclaimed the eighteenth day of Tammuz as an annual commemorative day of their deliverance. This local Purim was thenceforth celebrated by the community of Candia down to the twentieth century.[29]

On the other hand, their ambiguous position between the oppressive Venetian regime and the suffering masses—a position shared by the Candiot Jews with their coreligionists in many lands—could benefit certain individuals. For example, shortly after the Turkish conquest of Constantinople in 1453, the rising tide of Greek nationalism added force to the Cretan revolutionary movement. In that period, as we recall, David Mavrogonato helped the Venetian authorities to suppress it. Because of these services, Mavrogonato was rewarded by the government with a cash payment of 3,000 hyperpera and an annual pension of 500 hyperpera. After his death in 1470, that pension continued to be paid to his children. It is small wonder that his activity caused much ill will among the Greeks and, in 1464, Mavrogonato had to be given permission to carry arms "for the security of his person." While the influence thus exerted with the ruling circles in Venice by

Mavrogonato and other pro-Venetian partisans brought some benefit to the entire Jewish community, it also increased the hatred of all Jews by segments of the native population.[30]

As a result of these crisscross currents, Crete's Jewish population did not grow in numbers the way one might have expected. To be sure, we have no reliable demographic data for the Jews on the island in the early period of Venetian sovereignty, just as we are not certain whether a substantial number of them had lived there before 1204. Our usual twelfth-century authority, Benjamin of Tudela, did not visit Crete and hence does not mention it in his *Itinerary*. But the few recorded figures relating to the fifteenth, sixteenth, and seventeenth centuries, though not in complete agreement with one another, show that the number of Jews on the whole island probably did not greatly exceed at any time the 1,160 souls in a total population of 192,725 counted in the official census of 1627. No other contemporary source agrees with R. Meshullam da Volterra who, on his visit in 1481, claimed to have found in Candia alone 600 Jewish householders, that is, some 2,500–3,000 persons. Certainly, if in 1481 the city's total population probably did not greatly exceed the 11,474 mentioned in the 1627 census, then such a high percentage of Jews appears very problematic. Even the figure of 800 Jews in Candia alone, as quoted in that census, showed that, although more than two-thirds of all Cretan Jews lived in that city, they numbered only 6 percent of its population. Closer to the truth seems to be the 1577 report by Giacomo Foscarini who, in discussing the various ethnic groups inhabiting Candia, mentioned specifically that "there are approximately 700 Jews" in a total population of 1,700 (exclusive of soldiers). While it stands to reason that in the 96 years since Meshullam's journey the Jewish population had diminished more rapidly than that of the city as a whole, it is not likely that even in 1481 it had greatly exceeded 1,000 persons.[31]

OTHER VENETIAN POSSESSIONS

The story of Cretan Jewry and its political and economic conditions under Venetian rule have been described here at somewhat greater length than seems indicated by the relatively small number and size of the Jewish communities on the island. Because much documentation has been preserved in the Venetian archives and a considerable number of competent modern historians have investigated almost every facet of life on the island, this story offers perhaps the best illustration of how Jewish life was affected by the incipient Western Expansion. Here we have one of the first colonial regimes, which lasted almost half a millennium and which exerted a powerful influence on a number of Jewish settlements, especially that of Candia. Despite numerous external and internal unheavals, Candiot Jewry did succeed in maintaining its unbroken historic continuity and individual identity.[32]

At the same time there were numerous variations within the Venetian *stato del mar*. Since the Venetians tried to preserve much of the ethnocultural and religious autonomy of the various groups in the population—whose composition and traditions often materially differed from locality to locality—while insisting on a strongly centralized administration, fiscal supremacy, and economic control by the ruling circles in the metropolis, these local variations offer an illuminating example of a successful blend of "unity within diversity."

Among the eastern Mediterranean islands held by Venice, classical Euboea (in the Late Middle Ages better known under the Italian name of its major city, Negroponte—the Greek Chalcis) played, along with Crete, an important role in Jewish history. At first, Venice consented in 1209 to the island being placed under the control of three Veronese knights. But gradually these "Lombards" felt more secure under Venetian tutelage, especially after the temporary reoccupation of Negroponte by the imperial troops in 1275. In time these fiefs were bought up by the Venetian Republic. The island remained under Venetian rule until 1470, when it was incorporated into the Ottoman Empire.

In general, the rule of Venice in Negroponte followed the patterns developed in Crete, Jews being considered by the authorities primarily as choice targets for fiscal exploitation. While sharing the general taxes with the rest of the population, they were charged a variety of additional fees for special services, discriminatory duties on imported merchandise, rents for the dwellings they occupied in the Jewish quarter which expanded with the growth of the Jewish population (for which we have no fairly reliable estimates since Benjamin of Tudela's mention of 200 Jews in the 1160s), and so forth. They were also forced to perform such personal services as helping to build walls around the enlarged Venetian quarter, and digging trenches before an expected enemy attack. Without warning, for example, in 1340 the annual tax paid by a group of Jews who had voluntarily transferred their allegiance from the feudal barons to Venice was doubled to 200 hyperpera. Although this impost was reduced ten years later at the pleading of Jewish spokesmen in Venice, it was speedily reinstated at the higher rate. Together with other Jews the new group now paid a regular annual tax of 500 hyperpera. In 1410 the Venetian officials demanded from the community an additional single payment of 1,000 hyperpera. Two documents dated 1425 and 1429 mention regular annual payments of 600 and 1,000 hyperpera, respectively. Yet the growing Jewish share in the island's international trade seems to have made this fiscal burden sustainable. On the other hand, in 1318, on the recommendation by the local authorities themselves, the Venetian government freed the Jews of Negroponte from the 5 percent export and import tax. Similarly when the Turkish menace to the city increased, and many Jews had left their exposed quarter and lived dispersed among Christians, the Venetian Senate ordered that some new safe location be assigned to them. Clearly, Venice as well as the local officials recognized (as was explicitly stated in a document of 1439) that the Jews were "beneficial to the said city [of Negroponte], for it is largely they who carry on trade and enhance our receipts." [33]

In connection with these fiscal negotiations we hear of a special plea by a Jewish representative which raises some basic questions. Protesting against a higher levy in 1414, the Jewish petitioner stated "that in consideration of their poverty, for in their majority they are serfs [*servi sive vilani*], we [the Senate] should graciously provide that they [the Jews] should not carry such burdens which they cannot sustain." Since almost all the Jewish inhabitants of the island lived in the major city, this designation raises the problem of an unparalleled urban type of serfdom. Although slightly supported by the aforementioned status of subjection of the family of Moses b. Shabbetai Shem Ṭob Galimidi to David Kalomiti and his descendants—the Hebrew document, undated and otherwise imprecise, uses here the even more ambiguous term *'abadim,* which may mean anything from servants to slaves—it appears that this special pleading before the Senate need not be taken literally. Whether the envoy had in mind the former subjection of some of his coreligionists to the feudal lords on the island, or else thought of something akin to the Western designation of Jews being "serfs of the Chamber," his intention clearly was to overstate the community's indigence and its inability to pay the higher tax. Even when the issue of borrowing funds from local Jewish bankers was raised in Venice by an envoy of the city of Negroponte in 1429, the Senate insisted that Jews must not be burdened "beyond what is appropriate and honest [*debitum et honestum*]," for the Republic did not wish to "impinge on the privileges and concessions granted by us to the Jews and the Jewish communities of our maritime possessions." This resolution was adopted by the Senate with an overwhelming majority of 82 to 6 votes and 10 abstentions. Needless to say, when in 1431 the Republic was in urgent need of money, it imposed upon the Negroponte Jewish community an enforced loan of 2,000 ducats. This amount compared, however, with 20,000 ducats demanded from its coreligionists in Crete, 3,000 from the Corfiote Jewry, and 1,000 from that of Istria. In short, the entire documentation pertaining to Negroponte gives us a picture of a fairly prosperous Jewish community which included merchants, moneylenders, and doubtless artisans of various kinds. It also enjoyed considerable educational and cultural amenities and extensive connections with other Jewries. This general image certainly is a far cry from that of a group of villeins.[34]

Except for their discriminatory taxation and their restriction to a more or less compulsory Jewish quarter in Negroponte—it was established in 1353, long before such legislation was enacted in Venice itself in 1516—Jews were generally treated like other non-Venetians. True, the government tried to prevent them from acquiring any land outside the Jewish quarter, even through the widely accepted mortgage and default route. In his report of May 30, 1402 to the Senate, the former bailo of Negroponte, Nicolaus Vallaresso, used rather harsh language to describe the situation on the island. He contended that, unless countermeasures were speedily adopted, "the immovable property and villeins of our island would for the most part fall into Jewish hands, a situation which certainly must appear abominable to all Christians. It would accrue to the detriment of the Commune [Republic], since it would also affect the feudal possessions." By a vote of 50 to 22 with 20 abstentions the Senate outlawed future acquisitions of land in Negroponte by Jews and ordered them to sell all such property already in their hands within one year. It also provided that the numerous gates leading into the Jewish quarter should be permanently closed, except for three gates through which Jews would enter and leave their street. Yet by 1440 the Senate admitted that from time immemorial Jews owned many houses contiguous to their quarter. With specified exceptions, it again forbade their acquiring or renting such property in the future under the severe sanction of banishment and a fine of 500 ducats for the Jewish buyer or tenant and of 100 ducats for the Christian seller or lessor. Nonetheless, the same resolution, adopted by a lopsided vote of 77 to 8, with 11 abstentions, admitted that the Jews "are useful to the said city." [35]

Jews did not object to segregation as such. In 1425 they actually took the initiative in securing permission to erect a wall around two streets in their quarter. Despite the restrictions on their ownership of real estate, they enjoyed many civil rights, particularly in the economic sphere. A small minority among them even acquired the formal status of Venetian citizens. Of course, in the Middle Ages this term did not connote the exercise of all "rights of citizenship," as envisaged by modern jurists. Used more or less loosely, in the case of Jews it was essentially tantamount to the conferral upon certain individuals or groups of mutually understood special privileges, commercial or fiscal. It certainly did not imply, for example, the free admission of Jews to public office. Perhaps to appease his conscience, Doge Cristoforo Mauro submitted to the distinguished Cardinal Johannes Bessarion a query as to the validity, from the Catholic viewpoint, of the Republic's agreements previously made with Jews. The cardinal's reply read:

> We allow Jews to live among Christians. . . . The pacts concluded by Jews with cities, burghers, and communities in your provinces, castles, and the aforementioned localities, or such as may be concluded in the

future, if confirmed by your authority, that of your predecessors or successors, shall be observed and freely applied. In this fashion the Jews may be permitted peacefully and quietly to dwell among, and to converse and do business with these [communities and individuals].

This policy, which was consonant with the long-accepted norms of canon law (more fully discussed in our earlier volumes), was also imposed by Bessarion upon the anti-Jewish clergy of Negroponte. It conformed with a previous ordinance of May 11, 1462 which ordered officials to extend equal justice to Jews, abrogated their obligation to provide executioners, and even ordered the rectors of the outlying localities of Oreos and Karystos to cease mistreating the Jews. Incidentally, this is the only mention of a Jewish presence in these towns during that period.[36]

This relatively liberal policy of the Venetian regime in the mid-fifteenth century was no doubt aimed at strengthening the loyalty of the small, but fairly influential, Jewish population in the face of the Turkish danger which was ever present in the minds of the Venetian administrators. The conquest of Constantinople by the Turks in 1453 and the subsequent efforts of the Ottoman authorities to attract settlers to the depopulated capital induced some Negropontine Jews to settle there. In 1458 the Venetians tried to persuade them to return to the island by abolishing the special "supplementary" Jewish tax of 750 ducats introduced in 1439, thus reversing their rejection of a pertinent request made by the Jews of Negroponte as late as 1452. A year later they also argued with the Turkish authorities that these new settlers were but refugees from a plague in Negroponte and hence should be allowed to return to their former residence. All this became immaterial, however, after the Turkish occupation of Negroponte in 1470. During the preceding siege of the city, the ghetto and its adjacent districts were destroyed by cannon fire, and the population suffered severely. At that time more Negropontine Jews left the island, settled in Constantinople-Istanbul, and quickly established there a new "Negropontine" congregation. Those remaining behind maintained close relations with their Constantinople coreligionists, despite the difficulties of travel to the Turkish capital which, as late as 1686, required a sea journey of eight days. Moreover, both communities were reinforced by new Jewish arrivals, particularly from the Iberian Peninsula, sharing in the subsequent three and a half centuries the benefits as well as the disadvantages of Turkish domination.[37]

Less far-reaching was the transition from the Lusignan to Venetian domination of Cyprus, which lasted from 1489 to 1571. On the whole, the Republic introduced few major changes in the prevailing conditions on the island, which had developed during the previous four centuries of Western rule. Recovering somewhat from the wounds inflicted by the recurrent Genoese attacks and nearly a century of Genoese occupation of Famagusta (1373–1464), the Cypriots regained a measure of prosperity. For a time the Jewish population of Famagusta, which was described by Meshullam da Volterra in 1481 as "the most beautiful of all" Cypriot cities, was supposed to have numbered 2,000 souls. But the subsequent disturbances caused the large majority to leave the country. By 1522 the visiting Moses b. Mordecai Bassola, a rabbi of Pesaro, found there only 12 Jewish families. He described the whole of Famagusta as being

> a city as large as Fano, surrounded by fortified walls, with two gates of great strength and grace. Within it are beautiful houses and the city street in front of the governor's court is lovely as is the palace, appropriate for a place of its size. Meat is inexpensive . . . a hundred lambs and fattened goats, with eggs and poultry in plenty, as are pomegranates, grapes, and vegetables of various kinds. Only bread was expensive because of the locust which had spread in that year, but it was very inexpensive on my return trip. . . . There, as well as in Corfu and Zante, no Jew must touch bread or any other victuals, unless he buys them, for the Greeks refuse to eat or drink anything touched by a Jew. The Jews are few and sinful, altogether some 12 households, constantly quarreling with one another, and drinking "wine of libation" [in contact with Gentiles]. The majority stem from Sicily. They have a nice and orderly synagogue, with a *sukkah* [for the Feast of Tabernacles] in front, where I ate and slept on the ground during all the half-holidays.

Forty years later (1563) another Jewish visitor, Elijah of Pesaro, found there 25 families.[38]

Remarkably, Famagusta's Jewish community was divided into three congregations of Sicilians, Sephardim, and Levantines, which were involved in unending disputes. Except for two physicians, allowed as in Venice to wear black hats with yellow stripes as opposed to the majority obliged to wear yellow hats (this badge had been introduced into the island in the 1320s), the local Jews derived their livelihood in the main from commerce and moneylending. The city's volatile population included some pro-Turkish elements which, according to rumor transmitted from Constantinople to Venice, were incited in 1568 by the Constantinople Jewish statesman, Don Joseph Nasi, to stage a rebellion against the Venetian rulers in anticipation of the Turko-Venetian war which was soon to follow. On May 26, 1568 the Venetian governor was ordered to arrest the Jewish and Christian culprits, including four Cypriots "who had turned Muslim and traveled up and down the island, rendering Joseph an account of their treasonable activities." The governor was also told to ascertain the number and occupations of the Jews of Famagusta. Curiously, in the important city of Limassol the Jews seemed to have constituted a majority of the population, according to a German visitor, Johann Helffrich, who also reported that they lived in slumlike houses but had a plentiful supply of food.[39]

During the sixteenth century Cyprus lost much of its commercial and military importance. Hemmed in between Turkish-occupied territories, it largely depended on its trade with Egypt, Syria, and Asia Minor, and was ever exposed to Turkish attacks. As a result, even after the victory of Venice and her allies at Lepanto, the Republic had to surrender the island to the Ottoman Empire. The war of 1570–73 must have added to the population's feeling of insecurity, and many inhabitants, including Jews, seem to have left for more promising regions. That is why almost immediately after the occupation of Cyprus the Ottoman regime undertook a large-scale colonization to repopulate its deserted cities, especially Famagusta. To accelerate that process, the Turkish authorities resorted to forcible transplantation of their own subjects from other provinces to the island. We do not know what role the Jewish statesman, Don Joseph Nasi, duke of Naxos—who is said to have been promised the royal throne of Cyprus under Ottoman suzereinty—played in this intensive effort. But we have the record of three decrees issued by the sultan in 1577–78, ordering a mass transfer of Jews from Palestine, especially Safed, to Cyprus. This relocation was to embrace no less than 2,000 Jewish families. Probably the Turkish rulers took a dim view of the prospects for developing Palestine and particularly Safed into a flourishing industrial or commercial center; they might have been further discouraged by the failure of Don Joseph's attempt to colonize some of his coreligionists in Tiberias and its vicinity. However, perhaps because of protests of the Turkish Jewish communal leaders, the deportation of their Palestinian coreligionists was suspended on May 23, 1578. Thenceforth there was practically no significant Jewish community in Cyprus until the nineteenth century.[40]

Closer to home, Venice used the small but strategically located harbors of Modon and Coron as naval and mercantile bases. Conversely, half a century after its incorporation into the Ottoman Empire in 1500, Modon was called the "Key to Turkey" by the French traveler, Pierre Belon. The two cities were briefly described by the Spanish traveler Pero Tafur, who in 1436 spent six days in them:

> There are 2,000 inhabitants [in Modon], and the sea encloses it on both sides. It is well walled and sufficiently strong, but flat. I saw there numerous gardens supplied with all kinds of fruit, and the soil is very productive, like that of Andalucia. . . . Six miles away is Coron. . . . It is a large town, and a powerful fortress. . . . The Venetians have these possessions in Morea because they are vital for their trade. The people are very wealthy, for these places are the ports of discharge for Greece and the Black Sea for all classes of merchandise.

We may assume that the local Jews had a share in that flourishing trade, although we have but little information about the impact of Venetian rule on them during the thirteenth and fourteenth centuries. In 1431 Mariano da Siena merely tells us that Modon embraced "a great number of Jews engaged in all crafts. They include extremely rich persons."[41]

Only in the 1480s and 1490s do we hear from successive non-Jewish and Jewish visitors about the location of the Jewish quarter in Modon and aspects of life in it. To be sure, Meshullam da Volterra's estimate of 300 Jewish households in 1481 may be exaggerated, though some fifteen years later the same figure is quoted by the Christian traveler Johann von Hassenstein, while in 1485 another Christian visitor, Georges Lengherand, merely mentioned "beaucoup de juifs" living in a quarter where one could find better food than anywhere else in town. In 1496 Arnold von Harff further commented on the city's first suburb, "in which is a very long street inhabited solely by Jews whose womenfolk do beautiful work in silk, making girdles, hoods, veils, and face coverings, some of which I bought." The manufacture of silk and silk products in Modon also played a great role in its commercial exchanges with Venice. On the other hand, a 1494 visitor, Canon Pietro Casola, who called Modon a "sparsely populated" city, referred to the Jewish part in the silk industry and added: "They are very dirty people in every way and full of very bad smells. Their society did not please me; I speak, however, of those outside the city." He evidently referred to Jewish tanners, who played a major role in Modon's extensive leather industry; he also may have confused them with neighboring gypsies and Albanians. Commercially, the Jews were quite influential. We remember the statement by another visitor, Felix Fabri of Ulm, who had visited the region in 1480, that Jews had almost monopolized the trade in Oriental drugs and cosmetics, with which they supplied almost all European pharmacies. Others emphasized Jewish trade in Turkish carpets, as well as moneylending. We also learn about local Jewish sheep breeders, though not about Jewish exporters of Balkan grain to Venice, on which the mother city greatly depended.[42]

Among the legal forms of discrimination was the obligation for the community to provide Jewish executioners for capital punishment, an obligation carried down from Byzantine times. More remarkably, apart from paying special taxes some Jews of both sexes had to perform certain distinct services for the government. Of interest also are the unusually strict laws concerning Sunday abstention from work. In 1414 the list of such obligatory rest days comprised twenty-one additional Christian holidays and the whole week following Christmas. According to an ordinance of 1450, the Jews were even forbidden to acquire victuals and firewood on Sundays, surely a great hardship for families who had abstained from such purchases since the sundown on Friday and found it difficult to prevent the putrefaction of food, especially on hot summer days. Relatively small as the Jewish population and its financial resources were, the Turkish attack on Modon in 1500 caused the Venetian authorities to demand from it the high contribution of 25,000 ducats for the war effort. We do not know how much of that sum was actually paid, but the demand itself added impetus for the Jews' flight from the city. But since Modon and Coron were speedily occupied by the Turks in that year, some Jews returned to their homes and tried to rebuild their communities under the Ottoman regime. They were overwhelmed, however, by a sudden attack of the famous buccaneer Andrea Doria in 1532. The pirate carried away hundreds of Jewish captives from the Coron and Patras areas. According to a circular letter issued on February 27, 1533 by David b. Joseph Ibn Yaḥya of Naples, urging several North-Italian communities to raise funds for their redemption, by that date 25 of these captives had been sold as slaves in Sicily, 96 in Calabria, and 145 in Apulia. After the Neapolitan community had strained its dwindling resources (it was facing the final banishment of Jews from southern Italy, which was to be fully carried out in 1540) to ransom a great number, 100 still remained in captivity awaiting liberation by their Italian coreligionists. In the end neither Coron nor Modon, nor their Jewish communities, ever regained the importance they had had in the late medieval period when they had helped guard the Venetian lifeline to the Middle East.[43]

In many respects the developments in Corfu were quite exceptional. Throughout the Venetian rule in 1386–1797 the Corfiote Jews received an unusually favorable treatment from the authorities. In fact, the island's very terms of surrender to Venice in 1386, containing the stipulation that the Republic must uphold all privileges previously granted to any segment of the population, were arranged by a six-man mission of local inhabitants, including a Jew, David Semo. The same procedure was followed in 1515, when another six-man delegation, one of them the Jew Joseph Maycha, came to the City of the Lagoons to ask for further concessions. On other occasions, the Jewish community sent its own delegates to negotiate with the doge or Senate. This influential position cannot be attributed to the Jews' numerical strength, since in 1481 and 1522, respectively, Meshullam da Volterra and Moses Bassola found in Corfu only 300 or 200 Jewish families, at a time when the city (with its environs) embraced close to 40,000 inhabitants, according to a computation dated 1537. (Because of the insecurity engendered by Venice's failure to modernize its fortifications, the city's population suffered severely from piratical attacks and is said to have declined to 19,000 by 1588.) Corfiote Jewry's favorable status attracted numerous Jewish refugees from other countries, including some from the Iberian Peninsula. Outstanding among the new arrivals was, in 1495, the eminent scholar-statesman Don Isaac Abravanel; together with his family, however, he returned to the Italian mainland after a brief sojourn during which he met the Lisbon preacher David Ibn Yaḥya, the physician Eliezer Tanusi, and others. Abravanel was generally disheartened by the materialistic and hedonistic way of life of most Corfiote Jews. A century later we find among the island's temporary residents Immanuel Aboab who, in 1607, engaged in a learned correspondence with the Venetian commander Horatio del Monte. According to a contemporary historian of Corfu, Andrea Marmora, there were in 1665 no fewer than 500 Jewish households on the island. But this may have been one of the fairly frequent exaggerations by Jew-baiting observers.[44]

Sometimes the older Jewish settlers were less friendly to newly arriving coreligionists than were the Venetian authorities. The Greek Jewish community, which had placidly accepted Italo-German newcomers and did not oppose their establishing a separate congregation of their own rite, feared that the mass immigration of Iberian settlers might endanger its own status. The Greeks particularly resented the demand of the new Ponentine-Portuguese congregation, presented "with its customary ardor," to be given all the privileges granted to their own long-established congregation. The Greek-speaking elders appealed, therefore, to the Venetian officials in 1611 to settle that intracommunal controversy. However, the Venetian rulers did not like to interfere in religious controversies and even tried to ward off such interventions from either the popes or the Greek ecumenical patriarchs. Though themselves conforming Catholics, the officials insisted "that the Greeks should have the liberty to preach and teach the holy word, provided only that they say nothing against the Republic or the Latin religion." To a large extent this principle was also applied to the Jews.[45]

Legally, the Corfiote Jews suffered from few restrictions, although they were forbidden to own Christian serfs or to acquire land valued at more than 4,000 ducats outside their own quarter. In justification Andrea Marmora was later to argue that even taking land away from Jews was perfectly legitimate since these Christ-killers, "deserving death, merit no landownership except for their graves." The 4,000 ducats maximum could easily be evaded by the use of Christian intermediaries, however. Professionally, too, Jews were allowed to practice law, at a time when the city of Venice expressly excluded them from that occupation. Nor was the fiscal system particularly oppressive, even when it included special Jewish contributions for the defense of the island; for instance, in 1431 the Venetian Senate "borrowed" 3,000 ducats from the Jewish communities for military purposes. We recall that, on this occasion, it was Cretan Jewry which, together with the feudalists and the clergy of their island, had to pay for two galleys for use at Corfu. If under Angevin rule Jews had not only been forced at times to equip galleys at their own expense, but also to serve on them in person—we recall how arduous and even deadly a prolonged service of this kind could become—this abuse was quickly discontinued, probably before the Venetian occupation of the island. But during the Turkish siege of 1537 Jews fought alongside their Christian compatriots. This was but another illustration of Corfiote Jewry's general loyalty to Venice and of its gratitude for being able to pursue its historic career without the usual impediments imposed by a hostile legislation and society. Even the storm unleashed by the Turko-Venetian war of 1570–73, which led to the decree of expulsion of Jews from Venice and thus endangered the survival of Corfiote Jewry as well, passed when, at the request of a Corfiote Jewish delegation, the community was specifically exempted from the ban on December 14, 1571, a year and a half before its total abrogation (July 14, 1573). Intellectually and commercially these islanders were in contact with Jewish scholars and traders in many communities in both East and West. In one particular respect, moreover, they played an interterritorial Jewish role—down to the twentieth century they supplied many Jewish communities in Europe and the Americas with citrons of their own cultivation for the observance of the Feast of Tabernacles.[46]

In passing we may also mention the island of Zante which, after its occupation by Venice in 1482, began to attract Jewish settlers. For a long time Venice paid an annual tribute of 500 ducats to Turkey for being left in peaceful possession of the island, until the Treaty of Karlowitz in 1699 assigned to it full sovereignty. The presence of a small Jewish population on the island, estimated by Meshullam da Volterra and Elijah of Pesaro at 30 and 20 Jewish families, respectively (1522 and 1563), was confirmed by a contemporary Venetian report, dated September 8, 1527. It indicated a total of 204 Jewish persons in a population of 17,255 and 47 Jewish houses among the 3,374 houses in Zante. The number of Jews may have increased considerably thereafter, though the figure of 2,000 Jews, mentioned in the eighteenth century, seems highly inflated. The patterns of life resembled those of the Jewish communities of other Venetian possessions, with a Jewish quarter, badge (introduced in 1518), and much self-government. But we do not know any of its rabbis by name until 1634, when we learn of the demise of its spiritual leader Jacob b. Israel ha-Levi, a native of Morea.[47]

Of a different order was the Venetian Republic's treatment of Jews in areas which remained under the control of the Byzantine Empire or other sovereign powers. From the beginning Venice was more interested in commercial than in political expansion. We have seen how the Republic voluntarily forfeited its treaty rights to most of the Balkan mainland (except Modon and Coron) and even assumed the administration of Euboea-Negroponte only after the passage of many decades and the largely voluntary surrender of sovereignty by the "Lombard" barons. In the long run this economic imperialism, if it may thus be designated, led Venice to demand from the Byzantine emperor (especially in the treaties of 1268 and 1277) and the Lusignan kings of Cyprus that Venetian citizens be granted special rights, including exemption from a variety of taxes and customs duties, as well as that the Venetian bailo be given the authority to protect their rights against interference by local officials. Before long such protection began to be granted also to selected groups of non-citizens whose activities were considered advantageous to Venice—a right reluctantly recognized by the local powers. These Venetian "protégés" came to be called "white Venetians," whether or not they resided in Venetian quarters, such as existed in Constantinople and Thessalonica.[48]

It is small wonder that many Jews found it to their advantage to secure such protection. Remarkably, they succeeded in obtaining it from the same Republic which in 932 had tried to persuade the Holy Roman Empire to force Jews to adopt Christianity, and in 992 had accepted without protest the Byzantine decree excluding Jews from the use of Venetian shipping to Byzantium, and which even in the fifteenth century did not allow Jews to settle in Venice itself but restricted their residence to suburban Mestre. In contrast, in the eastern Mediterranean Venice had been constantly admitting many non-Venetian Jewish merchants to residence in the Venetian quarter of Constantinople, located near the new Jewish quarter. More, it also extended its protective umbrella over numerous Jewish residents in other important emporia. Of course, Venice did not act indiscriminately; it probably took under its wing only those Jews (as well as Greeks and members of other ethnic groups) whose activities promised to be of advantage to Venetian trade or to the supply of needed raw materials for the metropolis. Special consideration was, understandably, given to the *gasmuli,* offspring of mixed marriages between Venetian fathers and Greek and other non-Venetian women who may have included converted Jewesses. Once accepted, the "white Venetians" were adamantly sheltered under the provisions of the respective treaties and even beyond them. Time and again the Venetian diplomacy without much ado rejected protests by the imperial authorities of Constantinople against such infringement of Byzantine sovereignty.[49]

Within the group of "white Venetians," to be sure, Jews were discriminated against by being subjected to specific payments, in cash or in kind, to the bailo on his installation in office and, subsequently, during certain stated periods of each year. It has been estimated that the prescribed annual delivery of seven barrels of wine alone cost the Jews some 7 hyperpera. In their external relations, however, Jews were treated on a basis of equality with other "white Venetians." For example, in 1319 the Byzantine emperor Adronicus II forbade Jews to pursue their traditional craft of tanning and leather work. Thereupon some "Venetian" Jews, who had previously agreed with the guild of Byzantine Jewish leather workers to restrict themselves to producing finished furs, tried to take over the tanning of hides as well. The Byzantine authorities reacted sharply and forbade all Venetians, Christian as well as Jewish, to engage in tanning. Some Jewish tanners were dispossessed from their workshops and suffered losses estimated by the bailo at 1,741.5 hyperpera. This affair became the subject of diplomatic negotiations between Venice and the Byzantine court. Although this was a period of détente between the two powers, their representatives presented a whole series of mutual grievances, which often related to conflicting interpretations of the existing treaties. The final outcome in the Jewish case is not recorded, but it seems that "white Venetians" could continue plying their leather trade without hindrance.[50]

This situation, unusual even under the rudimentary international law of the time, brought forth a number of other disputes between the respective regimes, but as a rule Venice, backed by its economic and naval supremacy, retained the upper hand. Of great importance also was the hereditary character of these protective relationships. According to a noteworthy document of 1423, some Constantinople Jews claimed that they and their ancestors had lived under Venetian protection for eighty years and successfully demanded its continuation. It may be observed that such protection was extended not only to artisans in crafts needed by Venetians, or to merchants who imported or exported goods favorable to Venice's international trade, but also to Jewish moneylenders. Probably Jewish capital was found very useful to the Republic as a source of both public loans, voluntary or semi-enforced, and the financing of trade or industrial production serving Venetian interests. On one occasion, in 1359, the Venetian authorities of Coron and Modon imposed a tax upon the Greek traders to reimburse a Jew for losses inflicted upon his business by the Turks. Upon the protest of the Byzantine ambassador the Senate instructed the castellani of Coron and Modon to limit the amounts thus collected to the 100 hyperpera lost by the Jew and return the surplus to the Greek merchants. These relationships continued down to the fall of Constantinople in 1453. Curiously, even after the renewal of the Venetian quarter in the new capital of the Ottoman Empire, and of certain privileges for it by the sultan, the Venetians were still willing to continue that relationship with their "white" Jewish protégés. At this time, however, many Jews lost interest in Venetian protection, because the civil rights and communal autonomy extended to them by the first sultans residing in Constantinople-Istanbul appeared to them equally favorable. Only two or three centuries later, under the changed conditions in the Ottoman Empire, did many of its Jewish subjects once again seek protection from one or another foreign power under the new system of "capitulations." [51]

Significantly, however, we have no evidence for similar Venetian interventions in behalf of non-citizens in the other great Byzantine harbor city of Thessalonica. Unless this silence is fortuitous—and with the paucity of documentation in the pre-Turkish period we must not draw any definite conclusions from the absence of specific data—it may have meant that the local Venetian representatives there were either less powerful or less accommodating to outsiders than the chiefs of the Venetian mission in the capital. It is also possible that, because no such arrangement had existed in the area when Thessalonica was an independent despotate or a part of the despotate of Epirus, or else because of its closeness to the shifting powers of Bulgaria and Serbia, the Venetians had fewer occasions and less incentive to interfere. In contrast, during the brief interval between the Ottoman conquest of Constantinople in 1453 and that of Negroponte seventeen years later, Venice did try to intervene with the Turkish authorities in behalf of the new Negropontine settlers in Constantinople.

GENOESE COLONIES

In extending their regime into the eastern Mediterranean, from the outset the Venetian patricians ran into stiff competition from equally enterprising Pisan, Florentine, and particularly Genoese merchants. The Genoese-Venetian rivalry often exploded into armed conflict, especially regarding the control over particular islands. After the Fourth Crusade this rivalry enabled the Byzantine emperors and their heirs in the various principalities to play off one republic against the other and thus helped to neutralize the overwhelming power of either, which might otherwise have been irresistible.

Obviously, the Genoese empire in the eastern Mediterranean never equaled in size and commercial importance that established by the Venetian Signoria. But in its own way it played a considerable role during the last centuries of the Middle Ages and early modern times until the colonial possessions of both republics came under Ottoman rule. In one area Genoa long proved even more successful than Venice: after concluding a treaty with Emperor Manuel I in 1169, the Ligurian city negotiated a more lasting alliance with Michael VIII Palaeologus in 1261–70, soon after the emperor recaptured Constantinople. It thereby secured imperial privileges enabling it to establish a semi-autonomous colony in Galata (the former Pera), a suburb of Constantinople which had long accommodated the Jewish quarter, until its destruction by the Crusaders in 1203–1204. Located at the strategic narrow entrance from the Straits into the Black Sea, Galata controlled much of the shipping through that important artery of commerce and thus Genoa was in a position to play a preeminent role in the Black Sea trade centered around its colony of Kaffa (ancient Theodosia, later Russian Feodosiya) until the latter fell to the Tatars in 1475. South of the Straits, too, Genoa's mercantile power was second only to that of Venice.[52]

At home the Genoese were even less tolerant toward Jews than the Venetians. Except for two brief periods, we recall, Jews were not allowed to live in the Ligurian republic at all, and even during the short intervals of admission and readmission their numbers were very slight. The tragic experience of the Spanish refugees who, in 1492, were forced by a storm to land on Genoese shores and were refused entry by the Republic, called forth a critical comment by its own Chancellor Bartolomeo Senarega. Even the eminent physician, Joseph b. Joshua ha-Kohen, whose family was allowed to live in Genoa for a while, was forced by the decree of expulsion of 1550 to leave the city for a small nearby town. Only a tiny Jewish community weathered the recurrent decrees of expulsion, and was ultimately forced after 1660 to live in a formal ghetto. On the other hand, realizing the importance of Jewish traders and capitalists for the commerce and industry of the eastern Mediterranean countries, the Genoese pursued a much more lenient policy in regard to Jewish subjects in their colonies. Not only did they treat the established Jewish population with considerable moderation, but they frequently also opened the gates to Jewish exiles from other lands and treated them on a par with the older Jewish settlers.[53]

Little is known about the Jews in Pera-Galata in the period of Genoese autonomy. In general the Ligurian republic welcomed the accretion of manpower by a number of Greeks and other local inhabitants even if they posed as Genoese citizens in order to secure exemption from Byzantine taxes or tolls. In many cases such claims were fortified by certificates from Genoese authorities confirming the citizenship of certain individuals. This practice elicited in 1317 a complaint from the Venetian bailo, Marco Minotto, to his doge that "in Romania we constantly diminish, while the Genoese increase in number." He suggested that the Venetian government leave it to his and the future bailos' discretion to admit outsiders to Venetian citizenship, as well as to secure from the Byzantine officials an ordinance that such attestations be accepted without demurrer. Yet while the Venetians drew the aforementioned rather sharp distinction between their "white" and regular citizens, the Genoese apparently treated them all as Genoese nationals without discrimination. That may be why it is so difficult to identify Jewish residents in Pera-Galata in the extant records, unless they are specifically called Jews. In 1391 one Leonidus Judeus is mentioned as having been fined. In 1343 the Venetian Senate protested to the Genoese podesta in Pera, as well as to the doge of Genoa and the empress of Byzantium, against the sequestration of the goods of a Venetian Jew who had been found on a Genoese ship. In 1407 the authorities of Pera seized twenty-three bottles of wine belonging to a Cretan Jew because a Genoese fugitive from a Cretan prison had sued the Cretan duke for 300 ducats in damages for his unlawful arrest. A few other Jewish names appear in the notarial records or travelogues. But the number of Jews probably was not large enough for them to establish in Pera-Galata a regular Jewish community, with a synagogue of its own.[54]

A better example of Genoese rule is offered by the island of Chios. Although even here our specific information is rather scanty, the Jewish community on this important island seems to have maintained a measure of continuity during the Byzantine rule. When Benjamin of Tudela visited the area in the 1160s, he reported finding in Chios about 400 Jews headed by two leaders, R. Elijah Heman and R. Shabta. He added, "Here grow the trees from which mastic is obtained." This product was so rare that it almost became a Chios monopoly and commanded very high prices. It also facilitated the symbiosis of Jewish traders with the new Genoese rulers. Apparently both weathered the thirteenth-century upheavals until the fabulously wealthy Genoese entrepreneur-conqueror Benedetto Zaccaria took over the island in 1304 as a fief of the Byzantine Empire and his family held it until 1329, when it was recaptured by the Byzantines. However, in 1346 a Genoese company of individual entrepreneurs, who assumed the designation Giustiniani (perhaps from their seat in a palace bearing that name), took over the rule of the island and held it until it was incorporated into the Ottoman Empire in 1566. That semiprivate association, also bearing the name of Mahona (or Maona, the etymology of which still is debatable), ruled the island under the suzereignty of the Ligurian republic along lines of the later Dutch and English East India and West India Companies. Theoretically, to be sure, the Genoese authorities at first extended that privilege to the Mahona for a period of only twenty years or until they indemnified the association for all its expenses in the conquest of the island. Since the Genoese Treasury never repaid that investment, the Mahonesi were able to maintain their control until the final Turkish occupation, although from the late fifteenth century onward Bayezid II forced them to pay a regular tribute to the Porte. In turn, the company was often indebted to Jewish moneylenders, so that it had to pledge them considerable quantities of mastic which, in order to secure partial repayment of these loans, Jewish merchants were allowed over the years to ship to various recipients.[55]

From the outset the Mahonesi treated the Jews rather well. Although they introduced the Genoese legislative system as the basic law of the colony, they discarded many anti-Jewish decrees enacted by the earlier Genoese rulers. To secure strong defenses for themselves they built a formidable castle in the capital and surrounded the adjoining district, renamed Kastro, with extensive fortifications. It embraced 200 houses from which the Greek inhabitants were evacuated and replaced by Genoese and Jews. The sixteenth-century historian Hieronimo Giustiniani quoted Martin Crusius, an informed German scholar-traveler, as saying that the Jewish street was located "in the most beautiful part of the city" and explained that "this place [*contrada*] was handed over to them [the Jews] by the masters for their security so that they should not be molested by the people which, by its very nature, is hostile to these infidels." In Chios this explanation rings truer than in many other cities where it often is but a later rationalization of the historic fact that the Jewish quarter was located near the center of town and the governor's castle merely because the Jews had belonged to the earliest settlers. Such a concentration of Jewish dwellings did not prevent individual Chios Jews, however, from acquiring houses and other landed property, including vineyards, in other parts of the city and countryside. But we cannot be certain whether any Jews actually resided outside their quarter, for the few pertinent notarial documents principally refer to transfers of property, rather than to the houses' occupancy.[56]

Another feature consisted of a Jewish distinguishing mark. Although originating from the Muslim environment in the Mid-Eastern countries, the Chios badge seems to have been imported from the West. We have no record of any decree issued to this effect, although from the outset the government may have expected that Jews would be outwardly recognizable as such. The relative absence of distinguishing marks is well illustrated by an incident reported by Giustiniani. We are told that, at one time, some young Jews attended a Christian religious festival—in itself a testimony of considerable social integration—and at first were not recognized as such. When their presence was finally detected, they were pelted with oranges by the aroused worshipers, but the attack was quickly suppressed by the guards. Such easy mingling of members of the two faiths was brought to the attention of Pope Martin V, who reacted by a letter addressed in 1423 to Bishop Leonardo of Chios which stated:

> You have lately taken care to notify us that the Jews living on the island of Chios and in your diocese, and those arriving there from

other parts, are obliged, both by law and by the accepted custom, to wear clothing distinct from the dress of Christians. Nevertheless, they do not scrupulously wear such, but go about in outer apparel similar to that of Christians, from whom they cannot be distinguished by any indication in their clothing. Because of this circumstance it frequently happens that these people [the Jews] intermingle with similar-looking Christians, to the grave scandal and danger to faithful souls. Wishing to provide against this practice, We order you, in regard to whom in this and other matters We place full assurance in God, to see to it that all Jews of either sex, both the permanent inhabitants of the said island and those coming from outside, should be distinguished from Christians by some sign on their clothing.

Jews refusing to obey this order should be "arrested, fined and incarcerated" under papal authority. Later travelers indeed observed Jews wearing special hats. Nicolas de Nicolay, who visited Chios in 1551, claimed that the Jews "in order to be distinguishable from others, are forced to wear as a mark a large cap in the shape of a cross-bow [*bonnet à arbaleste*] of yellow color." Remarkably, that type of cap happened to be worn extensively in Nicolay's native France at that time. It seems likely, therefore, that at least the shape was imported from France at an unspecified period, just as after the Turkish occupation of the island, Jews began wearing yellow turbans of their own kind.[57]

Within the Jewish quarter there existed a synagogue which bore the noteworthy name of *Ba'al ha-Ṭurim* (Author of the Pillars). This probably was but one of several houses of worship; according to the French traveler André Thévet, in his book published in 1575, shortly after the Ottoman occupation, there existed a number of synagogues in the city, or perhaps on the island. The basis of this attribution was a legend accepted by the Jews of Chios that R. Jacob b. Asher (1269–1343), author of the famous code of laws *Arba'ah Ṭurim* (Four Pillars), in company with several others had visited Chios on the way to the Holy Land, but together with his companions had died there from the plague. In the local cemetery there also was a tombstone supposedly placed on his grave. Evidently unhistorical, since R. Jacob is known to have been buried in his home community of Toledo, Castile, this legend has not yet been satisfactorily explained. In general, the Jews enjoyed considerable communal autonomy. They had their own rabbis, though in the Genoese period only one is definitely known by name: R. Abraham ibn Shoshan, recorded as officiating in 1541. He probably adjudicated many controversies among Jews, even if, as elsewhere in formerly Byzantine possessions, he may have merely functioned as one of the numerous "arbiters" on the island, mentioned in the sources. Many Jews, however, seem to have repaired to general, rather than to Jewish, courts.[58]

An interesting variant was found in Chios when, in 1555–56, on two different occasions, a Jewish plaintiff sued another Jew before the local ecclesiastical tribunal. One of the two cases is particularly significant, because it related to a controversy between two Jewish cantors who had arranged to conduct the synagogue services on alternate Sabbaths. For some reason this agreement was broken and the matter was submitted to the local bishop for adjudication. In itself this appeal to an outside forensic authority in a matter relating to synagogue services is not entirely surprising, since no less a personality than Emperor Justinian had, apparently on the prompting of a Jewish faction, interfered with the Jewish liturgy and educational system by forcing the Jews of Constantinople, and probably of the entire Empire, to recite their weekly lessons in the Greek translation of the Septuagint and by forbidding them to study the Oral Law (*deuterosis*). Yet, an intervention by an ecclesiastical court was quite unprecedented and the secular commissioners frowned on these proceedings. But the matter became entangled in local political struggles and the Genoese central authorities were reluctant to back up the commissioners against an aroused public. The affair took on such a dangerous turn that the bishop was able to threaten the Republic that it might lose the island. We do not know the ultimate outcome of this controversy, but the zealous inquisitor who had led the anti-Jewish faction was rewarded by a promotion to the bishopric of Naxos. In general, however, the Inquisition made little headway on the island. When in the course of the fifteenth century many Spanish Jews began arriving in Chios, they surely included a number of relapsed *conversos*. Perhaps for this reason, the Genoa Holy Office delegated Friar Antonio Giustiniani, probably a member of the ruling clan in Chios, to investigate cases of "heretical depravity" there. But the civil authorities, sensing that these activities would ultimately involve not only Judaizers but also schismatic Greeks, infidel Muslims, and others, speedily got rid of the inquisitor.[59]

Economically, Jews seem to have suffered from no special restrictions. We have a record not only of Jewish landowners and vintners but also of doctors and artisans, especially those who plied the traditional Balkan Jewish craft of dyeing. The money trade here, as on the other islands, was a two-way business. In the records of a single Christian notary covering five months of 1398 we find a notarial deed issued for the Jew Elias Sacerdote attesting the repayment by him of the substantial loan of 416 ducats he had owed to the Florentine Nani de Pacis (May 7), and the promissory note of the Jew Samaria Bonavita, also in his daughter Tova's name, pledging to pay up his debt of 12 denarii. A number of Chios Jews were involved in general merchandising, often in association with their coreligionists in Pera-Galata and elsewhere, as well as with Greeks. But they encountered stiff competition from the local merchants, who prided themselves on their business acumen. A popular proverb had it that "two Cephalonians [cannot cheat] one Jew, nor two Jews one Chian"—clearly a variant of the oft-repeated Balkan adage that "it takes two Jews to cheat a Greek and two Greeks to cheat an Armenian." A longer form of this proverb added the link that it takes two Greeks to cheat a Macedonian and two Macedonians to cheat one Armenian. As in Rhodes and Crete, many Jews were engaged in producing wine and exporting it to various countries. Chios wine seems to have been both plentiful and of high quality. In modern times the island is supposed to have produced as much as 500,000 pounds of grapes a year. But somehow the local Jewish ritualistic supervision did not quite satisfy some rigidly Orthodox Jews, and the rabbinate of Rhodes, after adopting in 1537 an *escama* instituting close controls over the wine trade, singled out Chios as one of the islands (along with Crete and Naxos) whose wines were not meeting the required ritualistic standards. Yet we do not learn of any diminution of Chios Jewish wine sales on this score. Except for their share in the island's nearly monopolistic export of mastic, the Chios Jews thus seem to resemble those of Crete in their socioeconomic stratification. If, as is likely, the wine trade depended in part on their financing of vintners, as well as their production of wine from their own vineyards, they must have maintained close contacts with the island's peasantry. In the absence, however, of any reference to Jewish settlers in the rural communities, comparable to the aforementioned Jewish residents of the two Cretan villages, it is difficult to postulate even the minimal "agro-urban" Jewish stratification suggested by Zvi Ankori for Crete.[60]

It may be mentioned in this connection that neither in Chios nor in any other Aegean or Ionian colony do Jews appear as slave traders. Even the long-held assumption that they played a leading role in this branch of business in the Black Sea area has been considerably weakened by newly available evidence. True, slave trade flourished along the northern shores of that Sea, because the Tatar raids into the neighboring Slavic countries yielded much human booty. But from the notarial and other records in commercial centers such as Kilia it appears that the Tatars themselves had enough businessmen to transport their Christian captives—primarily young girls in great demand for Turkish harems—and to sell them at a high price. There may have been some Jewish traders, too, who served as agents or even as direct purchasers and sellers of slaves, but very few Jewish names appear in the extant documentary records. On the contrary, we hear of Jewish prisoners taken from the Polish-Ukrainian areas, especially during the Cossack massacres of 1648–49, and sold as slaves in the Balkan markets. We also learn about certain Polish Jews traveling to the Middle East on errands of mercy to redeem some Christian as well as Jewish prisoners. But the supposedly large-scale Jewish slave trade of the fifteenth century may be as much a part of historical mythology as that of the Carolingian age.[61]

Although we do not have direct evidence of any statistical nature, it stands to reason that, as almost everywhere else, Jews were subject to discriminatory taxation. To be sure, it appears that the old obligation of Chios Jews to support the monastery of Nea Moné was not renewed. Despite the existence of a fifteenth-century transcript of the original privileges enacted by the Byzantine emperors in the eleventh century (possibly prepared by an ecclesiastical copyist to support some claims by the monastery), we do not hear of any Genoese enactment referring to that particular impost. Evidently, as Catholics, the Genoese were not interested in subsidizing a Greek-Orthodox establishment which owned one-fifth of Chios' land and had additional farms and rents elsewhere. Moreover, the Mahona certainly did not wish to uphold the other regulation in those privileges which, in return for the payment of that annual "head-tax" (*kephaleiton*) to the monastery, had freed the original fifteen Jewish families and their descendants from all other taxes and duties. Perhaps if the original eleventh-century Jewish contribution to the monastery consisted of a certain fixed sum of hyperpera, the monastery itself may have interveningly lost interest in that annual revenue, which had greatly depreciated during the following three centuries.[62]

Instead, the Jews not only were obligated to pay all the taxes imposed upon the Greeks and other ethnic groups, but they doubtless were forced to make additional contributions in the form of gifts or forced loans. One obligation was particularly noteworthy. On the eve of every Christmas the Jewish community had to provide the authorities with a new Chios flag adorned by the cross of St. George—surely an irksome duty for pious Jews—and to present it to them at a public procession, of which they formed the tail end. Similarly, the local etiquette required that Jews bring their Christmas greetings to the leading Mahonesi dignitaries at a banquet, the officials remaining in their seats as a sign of their deprecation of Jewish "infidelity." We know very little about the other imposts, except that Nicolas de Nicolay was undoubtedly right when he stated that Jews lived in Chios "in large numbers as tributaries to the *Seigneurie*," that is, to the Mahona. More questionable is a tax bearing the Latin name *caragium*, the equivalent of the Arabic-Turkish *kharaj*, which here referred to a land tax, payable in kind by all residents including the Latins. This meaning, though harking back to the *kharga* of the Sassanian-talmudic period, diverged from the frequent medieval identification of *kharaj* with the capitation tax paid in cash by the "protected" religious minorities in the Great Caliphate and its successor states. The document of 1484 referring to that impost does not indicate, however, whether the revenue was to be collected for the benefit of the local Genoese authorities or, more likely, that of the central Treasury of the Republic. Clearly, Genoa needed these funds, since the Turks were exacting a regular tribute from the island in return for a temporary respite from raids. But on November 23, 1567, one year after the incorporation of Chios into the Ottoman Empire, the Jewish statesman Don Joseph Nasi, duke of neighboring Naxos, came to the island as Sultan Selim II's representative and proclaimed an imperial ordinance imposing a land tax indiscriminately upon all landowners, "whether married or celibatarian." [63]

Among the Aegean Islands one may also mention small Cos (Kos, opposite the ancient Halicarnasus or modern Turkish Bodrum), which had Jewish connections dating back to the Maccabean Age, and Mytilene, the ancient Lesbos (Turkish Midilini), where Benjamin of Tudela found no less than ten synagogues in various localities. Both of these islands had been visited by King Herod, according to Josephus. Yet, despite the probable presence of a very sizable Jewish community in twelfth-century Mytilene, we hear very little about it until the Turkish occupation; even then our information is rather scant. The presence of Jews on the island may have been a factor in the sultan's appointment of the newly arrived Jewish businessman-statesman, Dom Alvaro Mendes (Solomon ibn Ya'ish), as duke of Mytilene. Like Joseph Nasi, Dom Alvaro, after a brilliant career in Western Europe, played a significant international role as adviser to the Porte. Regrettably, most of our information about the Jews on these islands and many others in the area (Lemnos, Kastellorizo, Patmos, and so on) dates from the Turkish period, at a time when most of their communities were declining.[64]

Unlike Venice, Genoa did not as a rule extend any of its wide-ranging privileges to a select category of half-citizens, corresponding to "white Venetians," among the local residents. This difference may, perhaps, be explained by the growing xenophobia in the Genoese homeland. While Venice became an increasingly cosmopolitan center of international trade, Genoa in the Late Middle Ages and early modern times endeavored to retain most of the commercial privileges for its citizens. Of course, it could not pursue the same exclusivist policy in the colonies, with their vast motley of races, faiths, and ethnic groups. Only occasionally, when it accrued to Genoese commercial advantage (as in the aforementioned instances in Pera-Galata), was the Republic apparently hospitable enough to take a number of foreigners under its special protection by claiming Genoese citizenship for them. Most oppressive was Genoa's administration in those areas which it did not expect to keep for any length of time. For instance, its occupation of Famagusta, Cyprus, in 1373 had begun only as a raid to capture as much booty as possible in a short time. Unexpectedly, the occupation lasted for more than ninety years (until 1464). During that time the Genoese soldiery indiscriminately plundered the possessions of the entire population and even staged raids on Nicosia and other cities. To secure some measure of peaceful coexistence the Lusignan king of Cyprus, Peter II, had agreed in 1373 to pay the Genoese a tremendous indemnity of 1 million ducats, toward which the Jews of Famagusta were to contribute 30,000, and those of Nicosia fully 100,000 ducats. Since, despite all his efforts to enforce these exorbitant demands, the king could not deliver the promised amount, the Genoese resumed their plundering expeditions.[65]

In their more permanent possessions, however, the Genoese enabled not only Jews but also Greeks, Turks, and other groups to enjoy a wide range of rights. Regrettably our information about the Jewish share in the commerce and other phases of life in the Black Sea colonies during the first two centuries of the Genoese domination is extremely limited. We only have a few references to Jews in the preserved Genoese notarial records from Kaffa (Feodosiya); for instance, in those of Lamberto di Sambuceto of 1289–90. Here the notary registered the statement by a Jew Iffuso, son of Minamini (perhaps a variant of Benjamin), that he owed two Christian merchants 3,700 aspers for the balance of his purchase of sheepskins from them—evidently a substantial transaction. This document also included a guarantee signed by one Milanus de Asti and a Jew Abramus. Certainly, the Genoese did not wish to interfere in any way with their highly profitable colonial trade. Suffice it to mention that the sums involved in 32 contracts certified by a single notary in Kilia during two months (March 8 to May 13, 1361) amounted to 7,770 gold hyperpera, or about a quarter of the total Byzantine imperial revenue from customs duties in 1348. Hence Genoa's merchants were rational enough not to allow their private prejudices to impinge on the ways of life of a subject population which was able to generate such financial benefits for their country. But at home they could afford, or believed that they were able, to keep the Jews permanently away from Genoa itself, where they might prosper at the expense of the native majority. Such differences between home country and colonies have not been unusual in modern colonial systems. With respect to Jews, a well-known example concerns England's administration of her North American colonies. In 1740 the English Parliament passed a Naturalization Act making specific allowances for Jews in order to facilitate their naturalization in the colonies. This law was passed "by both Houses without opposition." At the same time, no Jew could be naturalized under similar conditions in the English mother country. When this disparity became too obvious and Prime Minister Pelham in 1753 persuaded Parliament to pass a somewhat analogous law (his so-called Jew Bill), there was a sufficiently loud outcry in the country to cause Parliament, at the suggestion of the prime minister himself, to repeal that bill. Yet, with typical inconsistency, it simultaneously rejected a motion to revoke the Naturalization Act for the colonies, at least in so far as it concerned Jews. This rejection was by a substantial majority of 208 to 88 votes. In some respects Venice, but not Genoa, modified its Jewish policies at home to align them a little more closely with the legislation it enacted in its East-Mediterranean colonies, by extending broader privileges to the Levantine Jewish communities in the capital as contrasted with those governing the life of the German, Italian, and Ponentine (Iberian) Jews.[66]

SOUTHERN SLAVS AND RUMANIANS

Developments in the late medieval Byzantine Empire greatly affected Jewish life among the southern Slavic peoples and, because of the pervasive influence of the Greek-Orthodox Church, also the neighboring Albanians, Walachians, Moldavians, Ukrainians, and Muscovites. In its period of weakness after 1204, Byzantium not only lost control over the Bulgarians and Serbians, but at critical junctures often depended on their troops to help salvage Byzantine possessions from predatory outsiders. At times, however, these Slavs turned against their former Byzantine overlords and even came close to capturing the seat of the Empire in Constantinople. Bulgarian rulers now not only bore the high-sounding title of "tsar," but some monarchs also assumed the designation of "*basileus* and autocrat," previously reserved for the Byzantine imperial office alone. Rulers as far apart as Simeon (893–927) and Ivan Alexander (1331–71) even more specifically called themselves "emperor and autocrat of all Bulgarians and Greeks." Ivan Alexander's contemporary, the Serbian ruler Stephen Dushan (1331–55), proclaimed himself "emperor and autocrat of Serbia and Romania." Bulgarians and Serbs also made repeated drives toward Thessalonica, their best natural outlet to the Aegean and the Mediterranean Sea. However, these attempts at expanding their respective dominions were frustrated by their mutual hostility, with Bulgaria first achieving ascendancy but then being subdued by the Serbs. On their part, the Serbs also expanded their frontiers westward and northwestward and embraced many areas in Dalmatia, Slovenia, and Croatia that had come under the influence of Western Catholicism and thus were quite different in faith, script, and general culture from their Serbian fellow ethnics. Although thus partially removed from Byzantine influence, they nevertheless often shared the political, as well as the cultural, development among their Greek compatriots and neighbors.[67]

Jews had had manifold connections with all these areas since ancient times. In Macedonia, particularly, which often was the main battleground for the contending Byzantine, Bulgarian, and Serbian, as well as Western, armies, Jewish communities had existed even in the pre-Christian era. Some of them were mentioned in the famous epistle addressed by King Agrippa I (41–44), to his childhood friend Emperor Gaius Caligula (37–41) who, in his egomaniac attempt to force Jews to worship him as a deity, almost brought about a premature outbreak of the great Jewish revolt. To point out to the emperor the dangers of antagonizing the widespread Jewish diaspora, the Jewish king pleaded that Jerusalem was a "metropolis" of many dispersed Jewish communities which included

> Pamphylia, Cilicia, most of Asia as far as Bithynia and the remote corners of Pontus, and in the same way to Europe, to Thessaly, Boeotia. Macedonia, Aetolia, Attica, Argos, Corinth, and most of the best parts

of the Peloponnese. It is not only the continents that are full of Jewish colonies. So are the best known of the islands, Euboea, Cyprus, and Crete. I say nothing about the regions beyond the Euphrates.

Soon thereafter the Apostle to the Gentiles, Paul, made missionary journeys to these areas and it is known that he mainly visited communities inhabited by Jews, in whose synagogues he could preach his new gospel. We also recall that the small town of Stobi (near Monastir) has preserved an inscription dating from about 165 C.E., which recorded the gifts of a local Jewish citizen for the erection of a synagogue, the oldest epigraphically documented synagogue in that region. An inscribed Hebrew tombstone in Bulgaria and another in Gran, Pannonia, both of the third century, have also been found and carefully analyzed.[68]

Yet, despite its early antecedents, Jewish life in Bulgaria before and after the settlement there of the Slavic Bulgarians is still shrouded in obscurity. It is only assumed that in 811 when Krum, ruler of the First Bulgarian Empire, defeated a Byzantine army under Emperor Nicephorus I and captured many Byzantine prisoners, some Jewish captives from Thessalonica and other communities settled permanently in his country. Whether or not Jewish influence contributed to the downfall of Bulgarian paganism, the conversion of King Boris I Michael to Christianity under the emperor's sponsorship in 864 raised a number of old problems in Judeo-Christian relations. In his inquiry addressed to Pope Nicholas I in 866, Boris asked how he was to treat judaizing Christians, the extent to which he was obliged to observe the Sabbath and the ritual commandments of the Old Testament, and the like. In his reply the pope said, among other things, that the Jewish informant to whom the king had referred ought to be investigated as to whether he had been converted to Christianity. We also recall the Hebraic influences on the great missionaries to the Slavonic world, the brothers Cyril and Methodius, who were of Bulgarian descent. The influence of the Hebrew alphabet, especially, was perpetuated by them and their disciples in both the Glagolitic and Cyrillic scripts. However, in the reference to Bulgarians in his much-debated correspondence, Ḥisdai Ibn Shapruṭ may have had in mind the Volga Bulgars rather than those south of the Danube.[69]

Somewhat better known is the story of the Bulgarian Jewish

communities in the eleventh and twelfth centuries. A Jewish congregation, recorded in Sardica (present-day Sofia) since 967, continued with a membership predominantly bearing Greek family names down to 1888. There were also communities in Nicopolis, Silistra (ancient Durostorum), and elsewhere. Among the Jewish writers in the later Bulgarian-dominated areas was a novelist, Simeon Seti (*ca.* 1080), author of a Greek novel translated into Bulgarian under the title *Stefanit i Ihrilati,* as well as the most distinguished Balkan Jewish exegete and homilist in the Middle Ages, R. Ṭobiah b. Eliezer of Castoria, author of the work *Leqaḥ Ṭob* (written and revised in 1097–1108). From Castorian Jewry also emerged the convert Leo Mung, who reached the pinnacle of his ecclesiastical career as archbishop of Ochrida and primate of Bulgaria. It was only in the Second Bulgarian Empire, however, under the rule of the Assenides that numerous Jewish communities sprang up in the land. These powerful and ambitious rulers wished to increase the commerce and industry of their country by attracting settlers from other Balkan territories who would be able to compete with the merchants of Dubrovnik (Ragusa) and other Dalmatian and Aegean cities. The tolerant policies of the Assenides, understandably, did not meet with the approval of the Papacy. His confidence raised by the Latin domination of large parts of the Byzantine Empire, the generally aggressive Pope Gregory IX tried to persuade John Assen II (1218–41) to be less friendly to Jews and Christian sectarians. Unsuccessful in these efforts, the pope attempted to organize an anti-Bulgarian crusade in 1238. He first tried to convince King Bela IV of Hungary and later Baldwin II, the Latin emperor of Constantinople, to attack the uncooperative Bulgarian ruler. Both monarchs turned a deaf ear to these proposals.[70]

Among the leading Jewish communities during the Second Bulgarian Empire was that in its capital, Trnovo. An old cemetery, accidentally discovered at the beginning of this century near the city, included two tombstones bearing Jewish names. Other finds attested a measure of affluence in the neighboring Jewish quarter, which retained that name into the nineteenth century. The last mighty Bulgarian king, Ivan Alexander, actually married a Jewess, Sara, who assumed the name Theodora when she was converted to Greek Orthodoxy. Their daughter Tamar or Mara was later to marry the Ottoman Sultan Murad I (1362–89) and to give birth to Bayezid I (1389–1402), the conqueror of Bulgaria. Despite her change of faith, Theodora seems to have favored her former coreligionists, whose number in the country increased considerably both by immigration and by conversion of some natives to Judaism.[71]

There was an additional influx of refugees from Hungary and Bavaria after the expulsions from these countries in 1360 and 1376, although in 1352 a Bulgarian Church synod had tried to outlaw Judaism along with the Christian heresies. Despite this attempt, Jews generally benefited from the growing autonomy of the regional Churches, culminating in the establishment of Slavonic patriarchates, first in Bulgaria and then in Serbia. Among other effects, such independence made it easier for the Slavic rulers to treat their Jewish subjects according to their national interests, rather than to follow the dictates of the Patriarchate of Constantinople which, as a rule, was more religiously intolerant than the Slavic clergy. At the same time the heretical Bogomil sect was—through its dualistic faith, its Marcion-like rejection of the Old Testament, its opposition to marriage and procreation, as well as its strong Bulgarian nationalism—a greater menace to Jewish survival than was the established Church. From the period of the Second Bulgarian Empire we have records of Jewish communities in Sardica-Sofia, Trnovo, Vidin, Philippopolis, Castoria, and Ochrida. The differences between the new arrivals and the native Jews led to considerable friction, however, so that a special assembly in 1376 had to pass regulations regarding the jurisdiction of both Jewish and non-Jewish courts, suppression of polygamy, and the like. About that time R. Shalom of Neustadt established a regular rabbinical school in Vidin.[72]

Before these new Bulgarian-Jewish relations were able to reach full fruition the country was overrun by the Turks who, after conquering several major cities (Sofia was occupied in 1382), established their long-lasting rule over the entire country with the capture of Trnovo in 1393 and of Vidin in 1396. From then until the Bulgarian independence in 1878, Bulgarian Jewry shared the destinies of its coreligionists in the Ottoman Empire. If, upon their arrival, the Turks found a fairly large number of synagogues in the land, they had every reason to promote the growth of a population whose loyalty to them was assured.

During that period of constantly shifting power constellations and fluid frontiers, some of the communities here mentioned, such as Ochrida, were often occupied by the neighboring Serbs and formed part of the Serbian kingdom or empire. In Serbia, too, Jewish history goes back to the pre-Christian period. Under Byzantine rule Jews were recorded as settlers in what was for a time part of Bulgaria but later became southern Serbia. It was included in Pope Nicholas I's aforementioned reply to King Boris of 866, in which he insisted that the numerous proselytes to Judaism be induced to undergo baptism and to abstain from observing the Jewish Sabbath and the commandments relating to ritual food. Later on, Jews settled in a number of other southern communities including Skoplje (Ueskiib) and Bitolj (Monastir) and subsequently also in northern Serbia, especially Belgrade (Beograd). In 1337 there even existed a valley not far from Prilep which bore the characteristic name of Yudova, possibly because it originally was the scene of a predominantly Jewish settlement. From the pertinent document issued by Stephen Dushan, through which, in 1361, his son Stephen Uruš transferred to a monastery his claim to a Jewish tax, some scholars have deduced the presence of Jewish landowners in that area. Jews enjoyed considerable rights, especially in the north-central section, where Jewish tax farmers are recorded, for instance, in Priština in 1462 and Belgrade. Jews were also engaged in farming (a Jewish vintner is mentioned by Archbishop Demetrios Chomatianos in a village near Castoria), a variety of crafts, and particularly in commerce, some of their merchants doing business with more distant localities such as Constantinople, Thessalonica, and Vienna.[73]

Such a modicum of religious toleration was stimulated by the long oscillation of the Serbian dynasty between the Eastern and the Latin Churches. Stephen Nemanja (*ca.* 1167–96), in many ways the founder of the medieval Serbian kingdom, himself underwent a double baptism. His second son Stephen (1196–*ca.* 1228) received the crown from a papal legate and the approval of an autonomous Church from Byzantium. At the same time the elder son, St. Sava, who was to become medieval Serbia's greatest national hero, was consecrated as an Orthodox bishop. Only the conquest of formerly Byzantine territories, especially by Stephen Dushan (1331–55; tsar from 1345), greatly increased the influence of the Byzantine Church. His *Zakonik,* one of Serbia's outstanding codes of law, included regulations such as, "If anywhere a half-believer [probably referring to a Roman Catholic] takes a Christian [Orthodox] woman to wife" and refuses to be "baptized unto Christianity [Othodoxy]," he should be deprived of his family and be driven out. Also, "If any heretic [Bogomil] be found living among Christians, let him be branded on the face and driven forth, and whosoever shall harbor him, he too shall be branded." Even the mere utterance of heretical words was to be severely punished.[74]

It seems that none of these provisions applied to Jews, although they may have proved serious obstacles to the formation of regular congregations and the erection of synagogues, of which we have no traces in the extant records before the Ottoman conquest. Regrettably, like most Balkan Jews of the period, those in Serbia left behind little documentation about their life until the Turkish period. We cannot even tell to what, if any, extent Jews were involved in the preparation of the early Slavonic translations from the Hebrew Bible and the Apocrypha and Pseudoepigrapha. One must greet with satisfaction, therefore, even such belated data as are found in the description of the sufferings inflicted upon the surviving Jewish residents after the Austrians conquered Belgrade in 1688.[75]

Of a different character were the western provinces of the expanded Serbian empire, where Latin traditions persisted with considerable force. Serbia's subjects living along the Adriatic coast often came under direct Italian influence and ultimately even sovereignty; from the outset the Jews of Split (Spalato) and Dubrovnik (Ragusa) in Dalmatia, and Durazzo and Valona (Vlona or Vlora) in Albania were exchanging goods and ideas with their coreligionists across the Adriatic Sea. Among these communities Salona (now Solin) has the oldest extant records. A Jewish cemetery dating back to the third century was discovered in its vicinity; the tombstones bear traditional Jewish decorations of a palm tree, candelabrum, shofar, and the like. One such inscription reads:

"Aurelius Dionysius, Jew of Tiberias, aged 40 and father of three children." It appears that when the city was destroyed by the Avars in 641 most Jews moved to neighboring Split, which was later taken over by Venice. After a long hiatus during which we hear nothing about Jews, we suddenly learn of an interesting memorandum submitted to the Venetian Senate in 1577 by Daniel Rodrigues, apparently a new Iberian arrival. Called Michel Rodriguez by the later Doge Niccolò Contarini (died in office, 1631), he was characterized by the Venetian statesman as "a man of unmatched commercial acumen." Rodrigues proposed to the authorities the development of a new harbor and erection of the necessary subsidary buildings so as to make Split competitive with neighboring emporia. The Venetian administration accepted the proposal, and subsequently Rodrigues served not only as head of the Jewish community but also as a frequent consultant to the Venetian authorities on the Levantine trade. Another Sephardic Jew, Joseph Penso, later served in a similar double capacity as "consul" of the Jewish community and Split's diplomatic agent (about 1630). When the so-called *Uscocchi* (*uskoči*), Dalmatian pirates preying on Adriatic shipping, seized a number of Venetian vessels, the Signoria dispatched Rodrigues to negotiate the release of the captured women and children, a mission which he accomplished.[76]

Quite different again was the situation in Dubrovnik (Ragusa). This city was apparently founded by refugees from the turbulence of the seventh-century wars in the Balkans. For a long time thereafter it was hospitable to refugees of various ethnic groups, including Jews. Before long the city began to play a significant role in the Levant trade, particularly as the intermediate station between Venice and Byzantium and its successor states. Having conquered a part of the coastline, Dubrovnik remained essentially autonomous, although it came under the "protection" of Venice from 1204 to 1358, then under that of Hungary until the Hungarian defeat at the battle of Mohács of 1526. More direct was the subsequent overlordship of the Ottoman Empire until 1808, though the Turks, too, allowed Dubrovnik to enjoy a semisovereign status. The small republic reached the height of its affluence and cultural achievements between the fifteenth and seventeenth centuries; the disastrous earthquake of 1667 destroyed much of the city and at least 20 percent of its population. Being weakened by a variety of external and internal factors, it never fully recovered from that blow, as it had from the catastrophic Black Death of 1348, which is estimated to have destroyed 7,000–10,000 of its population of 30,000–40,000. Because of its extraordinary sociopolitical and cultural history, as well as of its preservation of very rich archival documentation, the story of Dubrovnik's Jewry illuminates, directly or indirectly, the destinies of the Jewish people in the entire region and deserves somewhat fuller treatment.[77]

Jews may have inhabited the area in Roman and early Byzantine times. But reliable information begins to flow only during the fourteenth century, for which the Dubrovnik municipal archives—though not those of the Jewish community—serve as valuable sources of information. To be sure, the extant documents do not provide us with the comprehensive data available for some Western communities, since they deal almost exclusively with the general legal status of the Jews, especially at certain dramatic moments, and with business transactions, in which Jews most often participated together with non-Jews. We learn little, however, about their internal, communal, and intellectual life. When such distinguished persons as Don Isaac Abravanel and his son Yehudah (Leone Ebreo) appear in the records, we are only told about a grain shipment in which these men were involved on the side, rather than about anything connected with the father's diplomatic and exegetical contributions or the son's philosophical studies. Even those Jews whose names are prominently mentioned in the archival records, such as Aron and David Koen, appear to us almost exclusively as traders, whereas their communal functions, or whatever type of rabbinical services Aron performed, are merely alluded to casually.[78]

It is nevertheless noteworthy that we hear of hardly any Jewish moneylenders. Seemingly, the Dubrovnik Jews were more often borrowers than lenders on credit, even in connection with sales of merchandise. An interesting case of Jewish indebtedness is recorded on September 15, 1488: One Jacob, son of Solomon of Trani, obligated himself to repay 48 "Venetian ducats of good gold and just weight" to two Christians who had redeemed him from captivity. His owner, a Turk, had acquired him from Turkish pirates who had seized him on a ship. Jacob now had to promise to repay that outlay and an additional 4 silver carlinos for interest and damages within ten days after his arrival in Franchauille (Francavilla or Francheville?). Many Jews also appear as partners of Christian merchants or as guarantors or witnesses for contracts concluded among their Christian neighbors. For example, in an agreement of 1402, a Candiot Jew Menohellius and a Christian citizen of Venice pledged themselves to pay 24 ducats to a Ragusan merchant. In another deed dated May 24, 1431, Bonaventura Leonis, a Jew of Trani residing in Dubrovnik, is named as a guarantor in a complicated transaction of 1422, whereby a Catalan Christian undertook to transport corals worth 374 hyperpera to Beirut, Damascus, and Alexandria, on behalf of another Catalan, and bring back with him some merchandise for sale. The profits were to be shared by the owner of the corals and the shipper in a ratio of 3:1, while the guarantor's remuneration is not mentioned. We do possess, however, a few interesting specimens of Jewish marriage contracts and testaments which give us glimpses of daily life in the Jewish community.[79]

Jews seem to have played a significant role in Dubrovnik's international trade. Although at times suspicious of Jewish traders, the local elders knew that they could not get along without Jewish assistance, especially in the period of Ottoman overlordship. In a characteristic instruction to a *supracarico* of 1587, they informed him: "Beware of the Jews and do not let them know our business, since acting as spies they can only do harm to us." Nevertheless, the Dubrovnik authorities did not hesitate to appoint Jewish consuls to represent them in some emporia. The men thus appointed were not necessarily Dubrovnik residents but were often selected from those living in a particular locality where the Dubrovnik merchants wished to be represented. Hence we are not surprised that, on March 11, 1577, in ordering another *supracarico* to ship a load of grain with the assistance of their consul in Valona, the elders wrote:

> The Jew who is our consul is more on the side of the Turks than on ours; therefore take care not to inform him of our secrets; nevertheless, should he give you spontaneously a good piece of advice, then you may

accept it if you deem it to be useful to us; and do not fail to treat him affectionately and feign friendship.

Most remarkably, the republic appointed quite a succession of Jewish consuls in Valona. At the beginning of the sixteenth century, Isaac Trinch (Trinque) served in that capacity. In 1540 another Jew, Samuel Angelo, occupied a similar post. Another Jew, Jacob Coduto, served as consul there for almost twenty years, beginning in 1557. He was followed a few decades later by Daniel Coduto and, beginning in 1637, by Angelo Coduto. In between, in 1627, the name of the Jewish consul was Zechariah Graciani (Gracijani). These officials, who were largely honorary (although they may have profited from particular mercantile transactions in which they assisted), were especially helpful to Dubrovnik's population in acquiring grain, which was not always easy to obtain. Certain other articles of commerce were also subject to restrictive policies by local authorities, as when the Turkish administration forbade the export of specified woolens from Salonica at the request of the local Jews, who claimed that they needed them for their own use. Some of the Jewish consuls also seem to have been instrumental in the redemption of Dubrovnik captives seized by either pirates or Turkish officials. On the other hand, we do not hear of any Jewish share in the flourishing slave trade, in which Dubrovnik often served as an intermediary station. We also learn very little about Dubrovnik's mercantile exchanges with the Jewish community of Kaffa, on the Black Sea.[80]

Not that all relations between the Jews and Christians were amicable. It seems that the arrival of Iberian New Christians led to a sharp anti-Jewish reaction. Similarly, involvement of leading Constantinople Jewish statesmen in international affairs often generated hostile repercussions not only in belligerent Christian countries but also in semineutral Dubrovnik. As a result, the small republic issued no less than three different decrees of expulsion of Jews from its territory, in 1514–15, 1545, and 1571. The resolution adopted on May 4, 1515 by a vote of 34 to 6 was quite explicit:

The said Marranos and Jews, collectively and individually, male and female, living and residing in the city, suburbs, islands, and other localities of our district, shall be obliged to depart, together with their families and offspring, from our said city and all our localities not later than at the end of the present month under the penalty of 100 ducats for any one acting to the contrary of this order. However, whether the fine is paid or not, they shall nevertheless be bound to depart. In the future, too, no Marrano nor Jew shall be allowed to visit our city and the said localities in the whole district in order to stay there with his family. The only exception would be those who will arrive with goods and merchandise [*grassis*] without families; they shall be able to stay here until they sell those goods and merchandise which they brought with them, but no longer, under the above penalty. Yet they shall be obliged to pay rent for the houses presently occupied by the Marranos and Jews only up to the day and hour of their departure.

This decision evidently was not carried out. Curiously, those designated as "Marranos" are distinguished from "New Christians" in three ordinances of 1498, probably because they were more or less overtly professing Judaism. The decree of June 16, 1571 anticipated by four months the famous battle of Lepanto (not far from Dubrovnik) and the ensuing similar ordinance issued in Venice on December 14, 1571 in reaction to the Turko-Venetian war which, despite the Turks' naval defeat, led to the Turkish conquest of Cyprus. We recall, however, that in 1573 it was the Jewish ambassador of the Sultan, Solomon Ashkenazi, who was one of the main promoters of the peace treaty concluded by the City of the Lagoons with the Porte. Although we do not have documentary evidence to this effect, it is quite possible that Dubrovnik then followed the example of Venice and revoked the decree of expulsion. In fact, because the war had made all shipping in the eastern Mediterranean extremely perilous, much of the international trade increasingly used the land routes across the Balkan Peninsula. As a result, the number of Jews and other traders using Dubrovnik grew considerably and the city was forced to allow Jews to reside in several streets outside the ghetto. At that time no less than 30 (out of a total of 50) commercial agents were Jews. On the other hand, the restoration of peace so diminished its role in international commerce that, in 1583, Daniel Rodrigues was able to force Dubrovnik to lower the customs duties on the goods he transshipped through it. When subsequently this concession was withdrawn, Rodrigues moved his operations to Split.[81]

Jews were not the only sufferers from the Dalmatian republic's religious intolerance, however. Predominantly Catholic, Dubrovnik was particularly suspicious of the neighboring Greek-Orthodox masses whom it considered a permanent menace to the survival of its own Latin traditions. After the great earthquake of 1667, when some 600 Orthodox families applied for admission to the city, the Dubrovnik fathers refused, though they were greatly concerned over the sudden loss of thousands of inhabitants in the city. At the same time, the government must have withstood pressures to establish a Holy Office to prosecute heretics, including Marranos, notwithstanding the availability of numerous local Dominican friars, who elsewhere frequently furnished the necessary manpower for the Inquisition. Internationally, moreover, Dubrovnik greatly depended on help from the Papacy which, as a result, exerted considerable influence on its domestic affairs, too. Nonetheless, its elders always jealously resisted encroachments on their self-determination in the religious sphere as well. As late as 1724, when Archbishop Galliani complained that the people in his archdiocese were beginning to read French books deriding Catholic customs, "he was told by the Senate that the [papal] *Index* [*librorum prohibitorum*] had not been officially sanctioned by the Ragusan government and was therefore not in effect." [82]

After 1526, the Ottoman Empire extended its protective shield over the Jews of Dubrovnik. It is quite likely that the decrees of expulsion of 1545 and 1571 were not carried into effect because of Turkish interventions. At any rate, so long as Jews were allowed to live in the republic they could prosper in business and some professions. True, they could not serve as lawyers, as they did in some other formerly Byzantine communities, because this profession was reserved for the noble class and the majority of Christian burghers were excluded as well. But quite a few Jews were active as physicians. In 1414 we hear of a Magister Samuel Ebreus being a *cirosicus* or *medicus chirurgus,* specializing in diseases of the eye. A surgeon was generally held in lower repute than a regular doctor, who was called *magister medicus physicus* and later *doctor artis medicinae.* At first the recompense was regulated by the state, which called for free services to residents by physicians in return for an annual salary of 400 ducats for doctors and 200 ducats for surgeons. Nonresidents were not protected, however, and we possess a number of contracts between patients and doctors—for instance, one dated 1313 in which the doctor promised, for a specified fee, to cure the other party's son within three months. It may be assumed if a physician of international renown happened to arrive, as did the Jewish doctor Amatus Lusitanus, who stayed briefly in Dubrovnik on his way to Turkey, he probably was not subjected to restrictions of this kind. The number of Jewish doctors increased from time to time. Among the 110 doctors known by name in Dubrovnik during the fourteenth, fifteenth, and sixteenth centuries there were no fewer than 14 Jews.[83]

Amatus Lusitanus' visit to Dubrovnik in 1558 lasted only a few months because the doctor was anxious to proceed to Salonica, where ten years later he died from the plague. It seems, however, that there was some local agitation against his presence, especially from ecclesiastical circles, which viewed with a jaundiced eye a New Christian officially professing Judaism. It is also possible that professional jealousy inspired some local Christian doctors to join that opposition. But neither set of opponents has left specific traces in the existing documentation. Other distinguished New Christians who had found their way to Dubrovnik included Didacus Pirus, Amatus' friend and fellow Marrano, who wrote and published a number of Latin poems during his stay in Dubrovnik, Gracia Mendes, and the family of Alvaro Mendes. These visitors, too, had the Ottoman Empire (in this case Constantinople, or rather Istanbul) as their goal.[84]

Jews were also given free rein in business. We learn not only of Jewish shippers of goods as so-called *mercatores,* but also as owners (*patrones*) or part-owners of ships. At least in the years 1744–59 members of various classes participated in owning shares (*karats*) in ships; among them were 78 nobles, 162 burghers, 97 captains, 20 priests, and 14 Jews. Contrary to the intent of the legislators, who prohibited any individual from acquiring more than 4 (of 24) shares, however, a number of recorded contracts reveal that some partners owned between 7 and 10 shares each; one priest held 17 shares, and the Jew Samuel Ambonetti was the possessor of 14 shares, and thus he and the priest had become majority shareholders in their respective deals. Although we do not have similar studies for the earlier periods, that system was doubtless established long before the earthquake of 1667. There also surely were some Jewish artisans, though the few extant lists naming various craftsmen do not include Jewish-sounding names. However, such onomastic criteria are unreliable since, for example, the prominent noble family Juda, frequently mentioned in the Dubrovnik records of 1205–1336, apparently had no Jewish antecedents. It is also possible that the artisan lists referred to members of Christian guilds, while Jews, as a rule, operated outside the guild system.[85]

Needless to say, Jews also suffered from certain specific disabilities and occasional manifestations of popular hostility. As in many other localities, the Jews of Dubrovnik lived in a quarter of their own—called in Venetian fashion *Judeca* in the fourteenth century and *ghetto* in early modern times—and were expected to wear distinguishing marks. But we cannot tell to what extent these regulations were enforced. Only occasionally were the relationships between the Jews and their neighbors marred by such incidents as the accusation of ritual murder against Isaac Yeshurun in 1622. Under the excitement created by this accusation, Aron Coen (Koen), a rabbi and leading businessman, and others were arrested. Since Yeshurun resisted all torture without confessing and the evidence against him was extremely tenuous, he was only condemned to a prison term of twenty years, in contrast to the Christian woman, his alleged fellow conspirator, who was executed. It appears that the authorities merely yielded to popular clamor and, when the excitement died down, they released Yeshurun after three years and allowed him to depart for Palestine. Remarkably, however, notwithstanding Dubrovnik's close ties with the West, the other folkloristic accusations of Jewish desecration of hosts or poisoning of wells rarely, if ever, became significant issues. To be sure, more than a century after the Black Death, the local writer N. Ragnina contended that in 1348–49 many people had believed that the great plague was caused by the Jews wilfully contaminating the town's waters. However, there is no confirmation of this libel—so widespread in the West—in contemporary sources. Nor is it alluded to in connection with the frequently recurring pestilences which subsequently ravaged the community. In short, Jewish life in Dubrovnik was relatively stable and moderately secure. Yet, with the general decline of the Levant trade and Dubrovnik's role therein, both the city and the Jewish community lost much of their importance after the middle of the seventeenth century.[86]

By contrast, very little is known about the history of the Jews in medieval Croatia and its capital city of Zagreb (Agram). Although the two Jews Saul and Joseph, included in the delegation of the king of "Gebalim" and mentioned in the letter by Ḥisdai Ibn Shapruṭ in the tenth century, seem to have come from that area, little reliable evidence has come down to us about the Jewish communities of this region until the eighteenth century. (Some of these meager data have been summarized here in an earlier volume.) The same may be said about medieval Slovenia which, for the most part, shared the circumstances of the other Austrian possessions, especially under the Habsburgs.[87]

Most profound was the Roman influence on Walachia and Moldavia, which ultimately formed the nuclei for the modern state of Rumania. Originally much of that area was occupied by the Romans and converted into the province of Dacia, the population of which included a number of Roman legionnaires, colonists, and merchants. Among them apparently were quite a few Jews, although we do not possess for them the kind of epigraphic evidence preserved from the neighboring Roman province of Pannonia (Hungary). It is possible that the Jewish settlement in the region antedated even the Roman annexation. In any case, today the Rumanians still speak a Romance language and feel strong kinship to the Western peoples, although their culture has absorbed a great many Yugoslav, Hungarian, Ukrainian, and Turkish ingredients.[88]

Recorded Jewish history in the area begins only in the Late Middle Ages, in so far as it can be reconstructed from a few hints in the scant and fragile source materials available. Some Walachians had moved deep into the Balkans and settled in Macedonia and Thrace, especially in mountainous regions. Even Benjamin of Tudela was struck by these tribesmen, whom he observed after his visit to the city of Sinon Potamo (with diverse readings in several manuscripts). He writes:

> The city is situated at the foot of the hills of Walachia. The nation called Walachians live in those mountains. They are as swift as hinds, and they sweep down from the mountains to despoil and ravage the

land of Greece. No man can go up and do battle against them and no king can rule over them. They do not hold fast to the faith of the Nazarenes, but give themselves Jewish names. Some people say that they are Jews, and, in fact, they call the Jews their brethren, and when they meet with them, though they rob them, they refrain from killing them as they kill the Greeks. They are altogether lawless.

We have little confirmation of these assertions from other sources. But there seems to be some connection between them and the tradition that, in the eighth century, Jewish armed detachments had come down from the north (Khazaria?) into both Moldavia and Walachia and mingled there with the local Jews. As a result, we are told, "for many years the Jewish religion reigned supreme in the land." Be this as it may, Jews seem indeed to have exerted considerable influence on the local population, especially in Moldavia. When Radu Negru came across the Carpathian Mountains in 1290 and established his rule over Moldavia, he is said to have brought with him a number of Jews. Similarly, the city of Roman, founded by Roman I in the 1390s, attracted many Jews whom he exempted from military service in return for the payment of 3 löwenthalers per person. Under Stephen Voda (1457–1504) a Jassy Jew, Isaac b. Benjamin Shor, achieved the high rank of *logofet* (*logothet,* chancellor) of the realm, a position he continued to hold under Stephen's successor, Bogdan (1504–1517). This title was borrowed from the ramified Byzantine bureaucracy, which included several *logothets,* however, as heads of departments. In contrast, a tyrannical ruler like Vlad IV of Walachia (1456–62, and 1476), known as Tepesh (the Impaler), maltreated the Jews perhaps even more than his other subjects. Nevertheless, both the Walachian and the Moldavian Jews were for the most part relatively prosperous under the varying regimes. Ultimately they too came under the control of the Ottoman Empire; particularly in Moldavia, however, the Ottomans found powerful rivals in the Habsburg empire, Poland-Lithuania, and Muscovy.[89]

For a moment it looked as if the three main branches of the Rumanian people could be united under one ruler. In his meteoric career Michael the Brave (1593–1601) succeeded, through some devious manipulations and sanguinary intrigues, in temporarily reigning over Walachia, Moldavia, and Transylvania. He made use of the long Austro-Turkish war (1593–1606) to throw off Ottoman sovereignty and declare his nation's independence. Because of this momentary act of unification, though it was achieved for selfish rather than patriotic reasons, Michael became a heroic figure in Rumania's popular imagination and was glorified as a great forerunner of Rumanian national unity. It augured ill for the future of Rumanian Jewry that Michael also engineered one of the earliest blood baths in the history of Walachian Jews. During the years he had spent in Constantinople, he had enjoyed the support of leading Turks and Jews, and his initial advances into Walachia were entirely financed by Turkish and Jewish money—he had borrowed some 400,000 ducats for presents to high officials of the Porte alone—but he turned sharply against his benefactors. According to a contemporary chronicler, early in his reign (November 13, 1594) he suddenly ordered the seizure and execution of 2,000 Janissaries who had allegedly settled in Walachia without permission. Michael "likewise put to death all Jews who, as was their habit, conducted themselves as traitors to the country." For many centuries similar accusations had served to justify attacks on Jews in various Christian lands. Here, too, the Jew-baiting rumormongers probably needed no further evidence than the generally known Jewish loyalty to the Ottoman regime, which for several generations past had proved most hospitable to the harassed Jewries of the Mediterranean world.[90]

MOSCOW, "THE THIRD ROME"

Byzantine influence was most enduring and, from the standpoint of world history, most decisive in Muscovy and later in Russia and the Soviet Union. Needless to say, important modifications occurred as the result of the particular antecedents of the northern Slavs, the great historic vicissitudes of the Russian people, the varying degrees of Western influence, and finally, the Communist Revolution. But certain significant patterns of thinking and living endured despite all storms of change. Although even after the conversion of the Kievan Grand Duke Vladimir the Rus tribes' pagan heritage still was strongly felt, the subjugation of Muscovy by the Tatar Golden Horde (lasting from 1242 to 1462 or even 1480) caused the Russian people to gather around its Church as the main bastion of Russian identity and culture. This feeling was reinforced by the sharp internal divisions of the time when the various feudal principalities bitterly fought one another, while the Orthodox Church and, on a less conscious level, the Rus language served as the main unifying forces. When ultimately the struggle for independence from the Teutonic Knights and later the Tatars—a struggle in part led by princes like "Saint" Alexander Nevskii, grand duke of Vladimir (*ca.* 1220–63), and Dimitri (Demetrius) Donskoi, grand duke of Vladimir and Moscow (1350–89), the first victor over the Tatars at Kulikovo (1380)—strengthened this intimate alliance of nationality and Church, it endured until the final liberation from the Golden Horde during the reign of Ivan III (1462–1505).

At the same time the declining powers of the Byzantine Empire shifted the center of gravity of the Orthodox world from the old metropolis of Constantinople to the newly rising imperial capital of Moscow. Emulating the tsars of the Second Bulgarian Empire, the Muscovite rulers now took over the old Byzantine claim to world leadership. This example was transmitted to them through the Bulgarian translation of the Greek chronicle of Manasses, which graphically described the fall of Western Rome and the rise of Byzantium, and by a number of Bulgarian refugees after the Turkish conquest of Trnovo in 1393. Outstanding among the new arrivals was Kiprian, who soon became the metropolitan of Moscow. Impressed by the fall of their Constantinopolitan center into the hands of the "infidel" Turks, some Russian thinkers and statesmen readily drew the lesson that Byzantium's decline implied God's wish to transfer the supremacy to Moscow. A Russian chronicler of 1512 wrote: "Constantine's city is fallen, but our Russian land through the help of the Mother of God and the saints grows and is young and exalted." Like his Bulgarian predecessors, Ivan III considered himself the heir of the Byzantine Crown and called himself *tsar.* This claim was doubly meaningful because of his marriage to the niece of the last Byzantine emperor, Constantine XI. The new concept was most clearly formulated in the first quarter of the sixteenth century by the monk Philotheus of the Pskov monastery, who wrote:

I wish to add a few words on the present Orthodox Empire of our ruler: he is on earth the sole Emperor (Tsar) of the Christians, the leader of the Apostolic Church which stands no longer in Rome or in Constantinople, but in the blessed city of Moscow. She alone shines in the whole world brighter than the sun. . . . Two Romes have fallen, but the third stands and a fourth there will not be.

The tsars' imperial title later was supported also by a reconstructed genealogy of Rurik, the founder of the Russian state, which supposedly showed that he was a descendant of the family of Augustus Caesar. Yet, characteristically, no one seems to have contended that the Russian tsars were the hereditary overlords of all the Jews of the dispersion. This claim, so often used by the Western Holy Roman emperors and their juridical advisers from the thirteenth century on, was not echoed in Moscow, perhaps because the tsars had not found it employed in Byzantium. Nor did they wish to assume the corresponding responsibility for protecting the Jewish "serfs of the [Imperial] Chamber." Nonetheless the Jews, too, accepted these Byzantine antecedents of Russia and began calling all Rus people *Yevanim* (Greeks, later Byzantines).[91]

Such a combination of orthodoxy and nationalism was a bad omen for the future of Jews in the Muscovite state. We recall that in Kievan Russia the relatively few Jews had played a disproportionate role in both the country's economy and its political evolution, a role which elicited occasional outbreaks of hostility against them. But their influence, in part emanating from the powerful empire of Khazaria (which was largely displaced by the Kievan Rus and Tatar peoples), continued to make itself felt in those Rus areas which were occupied by Lithuania. It is especially regrettable, therefore, that Benjamin of Tudela never visited that part of eastern Europe. On his return trip he did reach Prague, where he heard various tales about the Rus people. But apart from identifying the whole Slavic group of nations with descendants of Canaan, son of Ham and grandson of Noah, he only had the following curious observation:

These are the men of Russia, which is a great empire stretching from the gate of Prague to the gates of Kiev, the large city which is at the extremity of that empire. It is a land of mountains and forests, where there are to be found the animals called ermine, sable, and vair [a species of marten]. No one issues forth from his house in winter-time on account of the cold. People are to be found there who have lost the tips of their noses by reason of the frost. Thus far reaches the empire of Russia.

But despite his general curiosity about the life of his coreligionists, apparently the main stimulus to his journey, he had nothing to say about the Jews of that region, of whom we know practically nothing after the Mongolian invasion of 1242. To the extent that they survived the invaders' wholesale slaughter of the populations, they must have suffered greatly under the arbitrary domination of the Rus feudal lords and later under the increasingly centralized rule of the Muscovite princes, who in time became less and less tolerant of religious diversity.[92]

Under Ivan III, Muscovy's religious intolerance was somewhat moderated by international, as well as domestic, considerations. Novgorod, the prime commercial center of Russia and in many ways superior to Moscow in material and intellectual civilization, continued to be a member of the Hanseatic League and to develop its strong mercantile relations with the West. On his part, Ivan tried to maintain amicable contacts with the Crimean Tatars and for this purpose used some influential Jews living under the reign of the khans. The Crimea and other Black Sea areas already had a long Jewish history reaching back to various Hellenistic colonies; they left behind a number of significant inscriptions in different localities. Their assimilation to Greek culture had progressed to the extent that the Greek language and institutions penetrated the very synagogue precincts. Such Hellenistic influences are well illustrated, for instance, in the emancipation of slaves in the *proseuché* (at a synagogue assembly) according to the Graeco-Roman practice. Jews continued to live in these areas, and from time to time presumably grew in numbers by immigration from Khazaria, the Great Caliphate, and particularly from Byzantium after each of the expulsions and forced conversions from the seventh to the eleventh centuries. About 1260 some of the main harbors, especially Kaffa and Soldaia (Sudak), came under Genoese domination. As at Chios, the Genoese regime was quite tolerant of the various religious groups inhabiting the cities along the Black Sea whenever they proved useful to the Republic's commercial interests. In 1455, control over Kaffa was transferred to the old Bank of San

Giorgio in Genoa, further underscoring the city's preeminently commercial role. The Bank continued the tolerant policies of the republican regime until it lost Kaffa to the Ottoman Turks in 1475. The importance of the Jewish community, consisting of both Rabbanites and Karaites, is attested by a number of inscriptions; some of these, however, originally reproduced by Abraham Firkovich, are of dubious authenticity in whole or in part. Jews are also mentioned by such foreign visitors as the German Johannes Schiltberger who, in his extensive travels through parts of Europe, Asia, and Africa in the years 1396–1427, claims to have found in Kaffa and its suburbs a Jewish population inhabiting 4,000 houses—a decided exaggeration. Among the other ethnoreligious groups were Armenians (whose leaders at one time claimed that they embraced two-thirds of the population), Greeks, Tatars, and some 2,000–3,000 Italians, legally the most privileged group.[93]

Ivan III established contacts with some leaders of the Kaffa Jewish community in order to influence the khans' policies through them. Particularly Khoza Kokos' mediation was instrumental in bringing about an alliance between Ivan and the powerful Crimean Khan Mengli-Girai or Gherai (1466–74, 1475–76, 1478–1514). Remarkably, in one of his letters to Kokos, Ivan asked him not to use Hebrew but to use either the Russian or the Tatar language and script, since apparently the tsar found it difficult to locate a competent Hebrew interpreter in Moscow. In 1486 Ivan instructed the Russian ambassador to inform Kokos about the tsar's gratitude for his previous services and his promise to reward him "with palaces, amethysts, and fine pearls." Another influential person with whom Ivan entertained close relations was Zacharias de Guizolfi (Giexulfis), who actually ruled over the principality of Taman on the east coast of the Black Sea. Although a scion of an old Genoese Christian family, Guizolfi was suspected by some contemporaries of being a Judaizer. When threatened by the Ottoman invasion, he turned for assistance to the Bank of San Giorgio in Genoa, then in control of Kaffa, requesting a subsidy of 1,000 ducats for his Goth mercenaries to resist the Turkish advance. Unable to stop the Ottoman avalanche, however, Guizolfi seriously considered abandoning his land and settling in Moscow. In reply, Ivan wrote to the allegedly Judaizing prince:

You have written to Us through Gabriel Petrov, Our guest, that you desire to come to Us. It is Our wish that you do so. When you are with Us We will give you evidence of Our favorable disposition toward you. If you wish to serve Us, Our desire will be to confer distinction upon you; but should you not wish to remain with Us and prefer to return to your own country, you shall be free to go.

But nothing came out of these negotiations and, with the elimination of the Genoese colonies from the Black Sea, most Jews looked to the new Turkish capital of Istanbul-Constantinople for guidance in their commercial and communal relations.[94]

Internally, the Muscovite regime was troubled not only by the struggles of various groups of boyars against the centralizing tendencies of the tsar but also by great sectarian divisions in the Russian Church. Among these separatist groups, that of the *Judaizanti* or *Zhidovstvuiushchaia eres* (Judaizing Heresy) played a fateful role in subsequent Judeo-Russian relations. It was initiated in Novgorod by another Zechariah (Skharia), formerly of Kiev, who, his opponents asserted, had "studied astrology, necromancy, and a variety of magic arts." Perhaps identical with Zechariah b. Aaron ha-Kohen, a Kiev copyist of a Hebrew tract bearing on astronomy (1468), he was joined by several Jewish immigrants from Lithuania. The sect found a fertile ground in Novgorod, where Bogomilism, imported from the Balkans, had undermined the uniform adherence to the traditional Church among the Russian ruling classes. At first Ivan III, who conquered Novgorod in 1471, was not unsympathetic to the new movement, which had appealed to such influential persons as his daughter-in-law Helena and his chancellor Fedor Kuritsin (d. 1498). In fact, Ivan himself brought to Moscow two clerics inclined toward the new heresy. Among other teachings this "Judaizing" sect repudiated the Trinitarian dogma and the divinity of Christ, claiming that the Messiah was yet to come. It also deprecated the worship of icons, opposed monasticism, which was one of the strongest pillars of Moscow's ecclesiastical structure, and adopted a number of other "Jewish" doctrines and practices. It encountered, however, considerable resistance from the established Church. Under the leadership of Joseph Sanin, founder of the Volokolamsk monastery, and Archbishop Gennadius of Novgorod, the conservative forces sharply repressed the leadership of the new sect. After a series of church councils in 1488–1504 severely condemned the "Judaizing Heresy," Ivan sentenced some of its leaders in both Novgorod and Moscow (including Kuritsin's brother, Volk) to burning at the stake. Thenceforth the sect remained outlawed in the Muscovite state, although its underground persistence was felt in later generations in such sects as the *Molokani*. It partly resurfaced at the beginning of the nineteenth century under the name of *Subotniki* (Sabbath Observers).[95]

As a result of these conflicts, Jews remained eternally suspect. Under Ivan III's successors, Vasili III (1505–1533) and Ivan IV the Terrible (1533–84), hostility to Jews, even temporary visitors and traders, constantly increased. With his customary ruthlessness, Ivan IV tried to eliminate all vestiges of Judaism in his country. We recall his cruel treatment of Jews after his conquest of Polish-Lithuanian Polotsk in 1563. At that time he forced all the local Jews either to convert to the Russian Orthodox faith or else be drowned in the Dvina. This persecution ended only with the recapture of Polotsk by the Poles in 1579. In fact, Ivan the Terrible made his position very clear in his reply to Sigismund Augustus' proposal of 1550, that some Lithuanian Jews be admitted to Muscovy for mercantile purposes in accordance with the existing commercial treaty between the two countries. Ivan stated bluntly: "It is not convenient to allow Jews to come with their goods to Russia, since many evils result from them. For they import poisonous herbs into Our realm, and lead astray the Russians from Christianity. Therefore he, the [Polish] King, should no more write about these Jews." [96]

Such an exclusivist policy was maintained by Ivan's successors. In the "Time of Troubles" at the beginning of the seventeenth century, to be sure, a number of Jews seem to have entered the country, particularly with the powerful aid of Poland. With an overdose of zeal a contemporary chronicler, describing the appearance of pseudo-Dimitri (Demetrius), the first of three successive pretenders to the tsarist throne, declared that the kingdom was so overrun with foreign heretics, Poles, Lithuanians, and Jews that one could hardly find a Russian on the street (1605). When Wladislaw Vasa, son of Sigismund III and later king of Poland as Wladislaw IV, appeared as a candidate for the Muscovite throne in 1610, he had to sign an agreement with his partisans among the Muscovite nobles before they would promise to vote for him in the election. Among the twenty clauses of this pact, the fourth reads: "No churches or temples of the Latin or any other faith shall be allowed in Russia. No one shall be induced to adopt the Roman or any other religion, and the Jews shall not be allowed to enter the Muscovite Empire either on business or in connection with any other affairs." In the following years Michael I (1613–45, founder of the Romanov dynasty which was to rule Russia until the Revolution of 1917), though personally not a religious zealot, sensed the popular antagonism to Jews and resisted all efforts to legalize any Jewish settlements in the country. If in 1634 he ordered the governor of Perm to release all Lithuanian prisoners of war, including Jews, Germans, and Tatars, this humanitarian gesture did not alter his basic policy of barring unconverted Jews from entry into his country. Four years later Michael rejected Wladislaw IV's request that his Jewish agent, Aaron b. Mordecai Markowicz, be allowed to come to Moscow and be freed from customs duties on his merchandise. The tsar answered bluntly that he would "allow any Polish merchant to come, but not a Jew, since none such had lived in Russia and the Christians had no contacts with them." [97]

This policy was maintained by Michael's successor, Alexis Mikhailovich (1645–76). In his legal code of 1649 the tsar avoided mentioning the existing legal restrictions on Jews. But when the Muscovite armies invaded Lithuania soon thereafter, as a result of the Cossack uprising against the Polish regime, Jews were among the main victims of the ensuing massacres of civilians in occupied territories and of the sale of many survivors into slavery. At the same time the incorporation of certain East-Ukrainian provinces into the Muscovite state according to the armistice of Andruszów (Andrusovo) of 1667 automatically brought some Jewish communities under the rule of Russia, thereby opening a tentative new chapter in the history of the Jews. However, their uneasy sojourn under the rule of the tsars was repeatedly interrupted by outbreaks of Muscovite intolerance; this instability lasted until the partitions of Poland. Obviously, much of the popular as well as governmental antagonism to Jews received its inspiration from the Russian Church, whose sharply anti-Jewish attitude had long been encouraged by the ecclesiastical circles in Constantinople. According to the Muscovite merchant Basil Posniakov, who visited the Turkish capital in 1558, he informed the ecumenical patriarch that no Jews were tolerated in his native land. Thereupon the churchman, who had lived amicably side by side with Constantinople's flourishing Jewish community and whose office greatly depended on the good-will of the reigning "infidel" sultans, allegedly arose from his seat and, bowing to the ground, pronounced the prayer: "May God forgive [the sins] of the Lord Tsar and Grand Duke of all Russia, Ivan Vasilievich and his sons, Dukes Ivan and Fedor, for they have expelled the iniquitous Jews, like the wolves, from the Christian herd." [98]

A STUDY IN CONTRASTS

In reviewing the situation of East-European Jewry under the neighboring regimes of Poland and Russia in early modern times, one is struck by the sharp contrast between the Polish policy of toleration and opening the country to a mass immigration of Jews, and the Muscovite attempt, with few exceptions, to shut its borders tightly even to Jewish visitors. The results also were startlingly different. The Dual Commonwealth of Poland-Lithuania accommodated from the mid-fifteenth to the mid-eighteenth centuries the most important center of Jewish life and learning. Its great concentration of Jews became the main reservoir of Jewish manpower, physical and intellectual, not only for eastern Europe but also for the entire Western world. At the same time neighboring Muscovy, if it sporadically admitted Jews, kept them permanently off balance by the threat of instantaneous expulsion at the ruler's whim, thus preventing them from developing any kind of sustained Jewish communal life. This situation changed only, and rather abruptly, when the majority of Poles and almost all the Russians and Ukrainians were united under the tsarist scepter as a result of the three partitions of Poland in 1772–95 and the Napoleonic wars ending in 1815. Because of her unlimited expansionist appetites, Catherine II tried to absorb not only the lands inhabited by large numbers of Rus peoples, whether or not they recognized themselves as branches of the Great Russian nation, but also millions of Poles, Lithuanians, Latvians, Estonians, and Finns with their deep-rooted national cultures, totally at variance from the customary patterns of Russian life. In a quarter of a century Russia changed from a country with practically no Jews to that with the largest Jewish settlement in the world. But if she hoped to assimilate all these nationalities as she had many tribes inhabiting the regions east of the Dnieper and Volga, her hopes came to naught. Like the other northwestern nationalities, Russian Jewry defended its national and religious identity with increasing emphasis and vigor, even while remaining a minority surrounded almost everywhere by predominantly hostile majorities.

One cannot escape the impression that this divergence between the western and the eastern Slavs was largely attributable to the difference in religion. The Poles, the Czechs, and a segment of the southern Slavs had early come under the aegis of the Catholic Church and Latin culture. The Russians, despite all attempts at westernization, permanently remained the chief protagonists of the Orthodox Church and heirs of the Byzantine civilization. Quite obvious was the contrast between the Western separation of Church and state and the unbreakable tie between the two in the Orthodox East. Whether or not one cares to designate the Byzantine system "Caesaropapism"—the arguments against the use of that term as applied to the Byzantine world appear to be more semantic than substantive—there is no question that the emperor in Constantinople, and following him, the Muscovite tsar, was not only formally the head of the Church but also in fact dominated the ecclesiastical establishment in a way no Roman Catholic monarch was able to do. There certainly was no room in the Byzantine sphere of influence for a struggle between the *basileus* and the patriarch in any way resembling the centuries-long conflict between the Western Papacy and the Holy Roman Empire. Whatever pretensions to universal supremacy the Western emperors could advance for themselves had to be delimited by the similar, ideologically even superior, claims to universal leadership of the Holy See in Rome. In Byzantium and its successor states the concentration of the two sources of power in the supposedly universal empire of

Constantinople, the second Rome, or Moscow, the third Rome, encountered no such rivaling claims from the ecclesiastical establishment. True, the realities of life proved to be stronger: while Byzantium's political and military power crumbled and the country in its entirety was occupied by a Muslim power, the unity of the Orthodox world was continued only on the basis of its adherence to one faith. But within the confines of Russia the tsars could, with some justification, continue to cherish the old dream of achieving a universal empire.

Differences between the Western Churches and Orthodoxy in their basic attitudes to learning likewise colored their underlying views on Jews and Judaism. While in different periods mysticism played an enormous role in Western Catholicism (as well as in Judaism), it never so completely overshadowed the quest for *knowledge* of God as it did among the Orthodox theologians. Phrases like "Do not seek learning, seek humility" or "Learning is the coming of the Anti-Christ," as well as the general rejection of the idea that book learning could bring men closer to the understanding of God, were far more widely accepted among Eastern than Western churchmen. Emphasizing the ineffability of God's will, many Orthodox theologians condemned all efforts to "know" God as a sign of intellectual arrogance. The quest for learning, both sacred and profane, and in the religious sphere based to a large extent on the Hebrew Bible as well as on the Graeco-Latin New Testament, helped to build many bridges between Western religious thinkers and learned Jews. It thus generated a modicum of rapprochement to Judaism. Such individual Judeo-Christian scholarly exchanges were quite rare in the Byzantine world.

Combined with important demographic, economic, and political divergences, this contrast between East and West made it possible for Poland in her Golden Age to become religiously the most tolerant and, therefore, also one of the most highly creative and innovative countries in sixteenth-century Europe. Although this development was cut short by the onset of the Polish Counter Reformation at the end of that century, much religious diversity remained in the country in both theory and practice. This situation had no parallel in the East, at least not until the beginning of the Enlightenment, the impact of which turned out to be rather superficial and short-lived there. It was under Poland's regime of religious toleration, even if limited and at times curtailed under ecclesiastical influence, that the Jewish community could develop its autonomous forces of creativity and extensive self-determination. In Russia, on the contrary, even in the nineteenth century the modicum of toleration grudgingly granted to heretics and infidels was regarded by the ruling circles as but a temporary necessity. The regnant ideal still consisted in the expectation that, before long, there would be a total amalgamation of the population under the doctrine of "Orthodoxy, Autocracy, and Nationality," as summarized by Sergei S. Uvarov, Minister of Public Enlightenment under the autocratic Tsar Nicholas I.

In the final analysis the Muscovite national drive, though a little less conscious than that for religious conformity, was a powerful factor in shaping the destiny of the Russian people and, through it, also of the subjected minorities including Jews. In the period here under review, the nationalist forces developed gradually, first through the strengthening of the centralized powers of tsardom so as to overcome the centrifugal forces of the tribal principalities and, later, through the unrelenting drive toward the conquest of all Rus lands and their unification under the tsarist scepter. During that drive toward the western Rus lands, even if interrupted by occasional periods of weakness such as the "Time of Troubles" in the early seventeenth century, all peoples of diverse languages and cultures were felt to be foreign bodies which sooner or later were to be absorbed. There was indeed no room for Jews in this ethnoreligious structure erected by the Russian tsars who, notwithstanding their universalist claims, built their power entirely on the Russian nation.

Of course, there were various other rationales for the rejection of Jews. The most obvious explanation in the minds of the masses was the fact of Jewish "infidelity," the story of the Jews' part in the crucifixion of Jesus, and the danger of their undermining the unity of Russian Orthodoxy by helping to shape sectarian movements along judaizing forms. Still another reason was suggested by Dimitri Gerasimov, Tsar Vassili's envoy to Rome, who was seeking coordination of efforts of the Christian world to forestall the Turkish menace. In his discussion with the famous Italian publicist Paolo Giovio, Dimitri declared that Jews were not admitted to his country because they generally were a malevolent people, harmful to their environment, and responsible for instructing the Turks in the art of manufacturing gunpowder and cannons.[99]

All these were but weak rationalizations of a deep animosity toward Jews, nurtured by the depths of both national and religious feelings. This heritage has animated much of Russian policy not only under the tsars but also under the supposedly thoroughly atheistic Soviets.

LXXIII

LATE MEDIEVAL ISLAM

At the beginning of the thirteenth century, the world of Islam gave the appearance of somewhat greater stability than had existed in the previous generations. In the West the Almohades held sway over large parts of North Africa and Spain. In the Near and Middle East the decaying Faṭimid Empire gave way to more vigorous regimes established under the leadership of Turkic tribesmen in Egypt, Syria, and Asia Minor. Their efforts helped curb the earlier rejuvenation of the Byzantine Empire and the inroads made by the Latin Crusaders. In fact, Saladin's rapid successes in both Egypt and Syria and his further thrusts into the Arabian peninsula and Armenia made it possible for him to dream of reestablishing the Great Caliphate. In short, it appeared that Islam was on the move again.[1]

However, two independent developments checked the new Muslim expansion and caused partial retreats. In the West the Spanish *reconquista* converted the Iberian Peninsula into a wholly Christian domain except for the small kingdom of Granada. North Africa became a scene of great turbulence; one dynasty followed another in quick succession, while internecine wars and recurrent attacks by Berber tribes sapped much of the vitality from the areas that later became Morocco, Algeria, Tunisia, and Libya. The decisive blow was administered in the east, however, when the Mongols overran Persia and Iraq, putting an end to the Caliphate of Baghdad in 1258–60. To be sure, this Mongolian expansion was stemmed at the borders of Syria. And soon thereafter the Latin Kingdom of Jerusalem was destroyed by successive Muslim campaigns, which had begun with the conquests of Edessa in 1144 and Jerusalem in 1187, and concluded with the conquest of Acco (Acre) in 1291. Yet, the great power of the Italian merchant republics, though economically helpful to the Muslim Middle East by expanding its international trade with Europe, frequently menaced the coastal areas of North Africa, Syria, and Egypt, including raids into Damietta and Alexandria in Egypt, Smyrna in Asia Minor, and other localities. This situation did not change until after the penetration of Asia Minor by the Osmanli Turks and their gradual occupation of European territories in the fourteenth and fifteenth centuries, crowned by the conquest of Constantinople in 1453. Thenceforth the growing Ottoman Empire was not only able to revive the glory of the medieval Caliphate but also for the first time to occupy vast areas in the Balkans, deep into Hungary, the Danubian Principalities, and the Crimea. Twice (in 1529 and 1683) Ottoman troops besieged Vienna. During that period the "Turkish menace" constantly haunted the minds of popes and statesmen, religious reformers, and individual citizens throughout Christian Europe.

Not until this phenomenal Ottoman expansion (1357–1574) did the center of gravity of Mediterranean Jewry move back from the western countries to the Middle East. In the thirteenth and fourteenth centuries the Middle Eastern Jewries still were constantly losing ground numerically, economically, and culturally. The general decline of Muslim civilization during the late medieval period likewise affected Jewish life, including its cultural manifestations. After the death of Maimonides in 1204, Jewish intellectual creativity declined in most Muslim countries and increasingly became the domain of epigoni closely following the footsteps of their ancestors. This withering of the quality of Jewish letters lasted until the revival of creative élan brought about by the influx of Iberian Jews into North Africa and the Middle East after the massacres of 1391, the expulsion from Spain in 1492, and the forced conversion in Portugal in 1497. These Iberian exiles were joined by Ashkenazic immigrants from the constantly diminishing area of Jewish settlement in Europe north of the Pyrenees and Alps.[2]

AYYUBIDS

The replacement of the decaying Faṭimid Caliphate by the regime of the Ayyubid dynasty had mixed effects on Jews. On the one hand, the gradual reconquest of territories by Muslim generals opened many communities to Jewish settlement even before the great advances under Saladin (Ṣalaḥ ad-Din b. Ayyub; 1171–93). In 1144 Zangi of Mosul conquered Edessa and settled there 300 Jewish families. Twenty years later Benjamin of Tudela found some 5,000 Jews in Muslim Aleppo. Such restoration of Jews to the Syro-Palestinian communities was accelerated by Saladin's conquests. According to Yehudah al-Ḥarizi, who visited Palestine in 1218, the sultan had formally invited Jews to settle in Jerusalem in 1191, four years after his conquest of the Holy City. Although he found it necessary strategically to destroy Ascalon so as to remove it from the grasp of the Crusaders, he opened the gates of Jerusalem to Jewish and Muslim refugees from that city, thus giving rise to an "Ascalon" Jewish congregation there. At that time Jerusalem also embraced two other Jewish congregations of Maghribian (North-African) and Frankish (Ashkenazic) settlers. The Europeans had first come from the territories recaptured from the Latins by the Ayyubids. They were reinforced by fresh arrivals from Europe, including the 300 Western rabbis who came from France in 1211.[3]

On the other hand, the fact that Saladin and his successors professed Sunni rather than Shi'ite Islam removed a major incentive of their Faṭimid predecessors to appoint numerous Jewish and Christian officials to government posts. As Shi'ites the Faṭimid rulers often sensed the hostility of their predominantly Sunnite Muslim subjects and had good reasons to trust more fully the officials and doctors recruited from among their "protected" (*dhimmi*) subjects. In contrast, as an orthodox Sunnite Saladin renewed the old Islamic prohibition against employing "infidels" in any governing capacity which enabled them to control Muslim compatriots. Although the sultan's pertinent decree of 1172 was not fully carried into effect, it induced some Christian and Jewish officeholders to adopt Islam in order to save their jobs. In addition, it laid the foundation for the later increasing exclusion of *dhimmis* from government service. The sultan and his advisers also emphasized the other provisions of the Covenant of 'Umar, imposing upon the "infidels" the wearing of distinguishing attire, forbidding them to ride on horseback, and so forth. The Ayyubids went a step further and prohibited unbelievers from riding on mules as well, restricting them to camels and donkeys.[4]

Nonetheless, Saladin entrusted his and his family's health to Jewish and Christian doctors. Ibn abi 'Uṣaibi'a, the famed historian of Arabian medicine, mentions at least fifteen non-Muslim doctors in the sultan's entourage. Outstanding among them was Hibbat Allah (Nathaniel) ibn Jumay', considered by some contemporaries the outstanding Egyptian physician of his generation. If Maimonides appears not to have ministered to Saladin personally—though he was frequently consulted by the sultan's family—the reason probably is that, by the time he achieved his great medical reputation in Fusṭaṭ (where he had settled in 1165), Saladin was mostly away from Egypt, spending the last thirteen years of his life on campaigns in Syria. The Jewish doctor most likely was too engrossed in his literary and communal activities to volunteer his services by accompanying the monarch on his circuits through the various Syrian localities.[5]

Certainly, the rumors sometimes spread by Arab apologists that Saladin at one time wished to expel the Jews from Egypt are totally unfounded. Nevertheless the sultan's constant invocation of the supremacy of the Baghdadian caliph over the entire world (an argument he used effectively to justify his own military conquests) must have sounded threatening to all non-Muslims. At one point he transferred the Kurdistan province of Shahrazm to Baghdad's sovereignty, allegedly pacifying some of his councilors by explaining: "The caliph is the lord of mankind and the repository of the true faith; if he were to join us here I should give him all these lands—so what of Shahrazm!" Such repeated assertions, though primarily used to pressure recalcitrant Muslim princes into joining him in his anti-Frankish Crusade, doubtless sounded menacing to Christians and, to a lesser extent, to Jews. For example, when he addressed some petty princes of the Jezira, he declared:

> We appeal to all the true believers of the lands of Islam, to the holy war against its enemies and we shall unite them all for the exaltation of the Word of the faith. . . . Those who help Us . . . will enjoy abundant benefits from Us; those, however, who will fail to fulfill their duty and busy themselves only with the vanities of this world, will be removed forthwith.[6]

Saladin's religious orthodoxy undoubtedly raised in the minds of many thoughtful Jews the specter of ultimate intolerance. Some of them may have learned of the execution, late in 1191, of the Muslim Ṣufi Shihab ad-Din al-Suhrawardi who, like Hussain ibn Manṣur al-Ḥallaj and 'Ayn al-Qudat al-Hamadhani in their days (922 and 1131), suffered martyrdom because of his "mystic heresies." On occasion sharp religious reactions threatened many Jewish livelihoods. When Raynald of Châtillon, the unruly crusader, made frequent raids on Muslim territories in disobedience to his own superiors, and once even ventured an attack on the Red Sea aimed at Mecca itself, Saladin impulsively closed all navigation of that sea to non-Muslims (1183). He thereby blocked a great source of commercial enterprise to Egyptian Jews and Christians and almost choked off their participation in the lucrative India trade. It was only after the ruling circles in Egypt realized how much harm was done to Egyptian commerce by that sudden exclusion of valuable traders that the sultan changed his mind and reopened the Red Sea to interfaith commerce. Nevertheless, thenceforth the Muslim India traders, especially the so-called *Karimi* merchants, had the upper hand over their *dhimmi* competitors, some of whom now joined them after adopting Islam. Saladin's fiscal policies, too, lay heavily on the shoulders of unbelievers. We shall see that the traditional *dhimmi* poll tax was now exacted with greater vigor and ruthlessness than in late Faṭimid times. Always short of gold to finance his large conquests, Saladin resorted to the old scheme of debasing the coinage issued by his mint. At least some of the gold coins preserved from his period have a relatively low gold content.[7]

Fiscal considerations doubtless reinforced Saladin's protective attitude toward the *dhimmis*. Not long after the conquest of Aleppo (1183), his chief adviser, Al-Qadhi al-Fadhil, issued a sharp decree, probably with the sultan's consent if not on his direct order, "against a group of evildoers and lawbreakers who had directed their hands and tongues against the protected subjects and thus caused them damage in what the Covenant had liberally provided with respect to their livelihood and civil status." Although the edict's sharp tone may have stemmed from Al-Fadhil's personal friendliness to Jews (see below), the news about this favorable proclamation must have spread rapidly among the Middle-Eastern Jews. Hence, the image of Saladin loomed ever more glorious in the eyes of his *dhimmi* contemporaries, as it did among the Western nations. Jews, to be sure, had no occasion to extol his chivalry, his benevolent treatment of prisoners of war as in the much-heralded case of Richard Lion-Heart, or his promotion of Muslim learning through the establishment of new colleges. But like the Christians they were much impressed by his sense of justice. The chronicler Abraham bar Hillel doubtless voiced the prevailing Jewish opinion when he called Saladin "the righteous king, repairer of the breach, remover of fear, and enemy of bribery." [8]

Saladin's sense of justice was sufficient, indeed, to make him support Jewish religious autonomy in both Egypt and Syria. However, he could not, and probably did not even try, to prevent the serious manifestations of internal dissension within the Jewish communities. We recall the machinations of the adventurous and unscrupulous Zuṭa who, after the death of Samuel b. Ḥananiah (the *nagid* of Egyptian Jews), three times seized the reins as the chief administrator of Egyptian Jewry, over the protests of the other leaders including Maimonides. These conflicts greatly contributed to the temporary suspension of that office, which was not reestablished until Abraham b. Moses Maimonides assumed the title after the death of his illustrious father in 1204. Its wide range is well described by Jacob Mann, a pioneer in the history of medieval Egyptian Jewry, in stating that the *nagid*'s functions

> were to represent all the Jews, to serve them as legal authority and as judge in conformity with their laws, to watch over the contracting of marriages, the pronouncing of the ban, and the turning in prayer to the proper *Kiblah* [the direction of Jerusalem]. The Muhammedans looked to him for protection against Jews. The custom has been that the *Rais* [*al-Yahud,* the Arabic equivalent of *nagid*] should be of the Rabbanite community to the exclusion of the other communities, though he sat in judgment over all the three sections, Rabbanite, Karaite, and Samaritan. In short, the *Rais* of the Jews took the place of the Patriarch of the Christians.

This high office continued thereafter, with some interruptions, until the Turkish conquest of Egypt in 1517. As we recall, this example set by Egypt was emulated in Kairuwan, Yemen, and Spain.[9]

As orthodox Sunnites, however, the Ayyubid rulers occasionally lent a willing ear to conservative opponents of any "innovations" within the Jewish community. When appealed to, they did not hesitate on occasion to decide, in an antireformist vein, even a controversy relating to synagogue services. Abraham Maimuni (Maimonides) recognized this attitude when, as a confirmed pietist, he tried (sometime between 1205 and 1218) to introduce some minor liturgical reforms as well as to alter the existing seating arrangement in his synagogue so that all worshipers could look in the direction to Jerusalem. He had to explain to Sultan Al-'Adil I that these changes, intended to underscore the devotional character of the divine services, had not been imposed upon the Jewish communities at large. He had merely introduced them into his private synagogue as a matter of personal piety. The *nagid*'s explanation was supported by a written declaration by the synagogue's entire membership of some two hundred persons.[10]

On the whole, however, Abraham Maimonides enjoyed the full support of the Ayyubid administration under both Sultan Al-'Adil Sayf-ad-Din (Saladin's brother, known in the West as Saphadin, 1199–1218) and his son Al-Malik al-Kamil (1218–38). Although generally maintaining Saladin's policies, the brother and nephew often relaxed some of the rigidities of the Sunnite reaction during the regime of the dynasty's founder. Al-Kamil, especially, was far less interested in enforcing the discriminatory laws of the Covenant of 'Umar. He even reverted to the appointment of Christian, and probably also Jewish, officials whenever it suited his purposes.

However, Al-Kamil imposed some special fiscal contributions on his "protected subjects." While Saladin had generally endeavored to restore the basic canonical system of taxation as laid down in the early days of the Great Caliphate, Al-Kamil, who faced a dangerous Third Crusade (1219) at the beginning of his reign, forced the Melchites of Syria and the Copts of Egypt to contribute 3,000 dinars each to the war effort, or else see their members drafted into military service. Given the fanaticism aroused on both sides by the Crusades and holy wars, such service involved grave dangers for non-Muslim combatants not only from enemies but also from their Muslim fellow soldiers. Jews were probably included in most of these extraordinary imposts. At the same time

Al-Kamil, too, refrained from interfering in the internal squabbles within the Jewish community. For example, the newly revived Jewish settlement in Jerusalem embraced two Oriental communities following the Babylonian and Palestinian rites, as well as some new arrivals from western Europe. There also was, according to Al-Ḥarizi, a fierce ideological dispute connected with the anti-Maimonidean controversy. A French scholar, R. Joseph b. Gershom, complained, at the beginning of the 1230s, that the chief of Damascus Jewry "called all Frenchmen heretics and apostates because they lend to the Creator a body, image, and form; he maligned scholars after their death and excommunicated any Roman or Frenchman who would make use of his [the leader's] property." [11]

CRUSADER HERITAGE

The source of these arguments must be sought partly in the great sense of insecurity pervading the Jewish communities, especially in the Syro-Palestinian area. The community of Jerusalem, in particular, must have viewed itself as living on a permanent volcano. Located between the warring Muslim and Christian armies, it faced the threat of annihilation from both sides. Curiously, compared with the enormity of the wholesale slaughter of non-Christian civilians (in Jerusalem alone the number of victims was exaggeratingly given as 70,000), the sale into slavery of thousands of survivors, and the complete elimination of "infidels" from some localities, the initial psychological impact of the Crusades on the Middle-Eastern population was rather small. Some Jewish and Eastern Christian refugees into other lands surely felt like the Muslim qadhi or religious judge, who had escaped to Homs and there poetically asked: "Which misfortune has most painfully overcome me? / Is it the death of the heads of my family, the property lost? / Or is it the alienation from my native land, or the loss of my livelihood?" Others may have more matter-of-factly echoed the observation of the Egyptian Jewish pilgrim who, prevented from reaching Jerusalem, explained: "The Franks arrived and killed everybody in the city whether from *Ishmael* [Arabs] or from *Israel;* and the few who survived the slaughter were made prisoners. Some of these have been ransomed since, while others are still in captivity in all parts of the world." Moreover, even before 1099, many inhabitants of Syria and Palestine must have heard echoes of the propaganda for the Crusades, which had filled western and central Europe during the preceding several years, and of the atrocities committed by the Crusaders in their home countries and on their march to the Middle East. Yet, most of them seemed to have viewed the arrival of these armed hosts from distant lands as merely another episode in the centuries-old conflict between Christian Byzantium and Islam. Locally, too, the turbulent decades preceding the First Crusade, the occupation of Jerusalem by the Seljuk invaders in 1070, and the subsequent changes of masters which had led to reoccupation of the Holy City by the Faṭimid Egyptians in August 1098 (only a year before the arrival of the Western nobles), seem to have inured the residents to the ever-changing fortunes of war and the permanent menace of enemy occupation.[12]

At first the local Christians may have hoped for favorable treatment from their conquering coreligionists. Whether or not they had heard about Pope Urban II's address of November 27,1095 at the Council of Clermont, which proclaimed the Crusade as a means of helping the oppressed Christians in Muslim lands, they probably expected that removal of the Muslim "oppressors" would greatly improve their own way of living. They were severely disappointed when, from the outset, the new masters treated most of them as heretics rather than as full-fledged coreligionists. The Armenians, Jacobites, Copts, and others thus became objects of intensive missionizing. The Greek-Orthodox masses, on the other hand, were considered mere separatists who only required the replacement of their own hierarchy by priests of the Catholic Church in order to bring about their speedy amalgamation with the newcomers. In the first flush of victory the conquerors expelled the Armenians, Greeks, Copts, and Georgians from their monasteries, though they later reconsidered this move. Characteristic of their attitude was a letter addressed to the pope by the expedition's leaders even before the conquest of Jerusalem (September 11, 1098). "We conquered the Turks and pagans," they declared, "but we could not defeat the heretics, the Greeks and Armenians,

Syrians and Jacobites. We requested then and now repeat our request, our beloved father, that . . . you should come . . . and eradicate all the heresies whatever they might be, and destroy them by your authority and our valour." Needless to say, even if the pope had come to the Holy Land, his conversionist efforts would certainly have run into the stone wall of local, deep-rooted non-Catholic traditions and rituals. Perhaps he might have had some success among the Maronites, who always evinced certain sympathies for Roman Catholicism and many of whom had come down from their mountains to help the invading Crusaders (this rapprochment ultimately resulted in the Union of 1736). But they constituted a small minority of the Eastern Christians. The Greek-Orthodox clergy, in particular, must have viewed with dismay the removal of their patriarchs of Antioch and Jerusalem and the replacement of their bishops and many local churchmen by Roman Catholic priests. If, in protest, the Byzantine Church continued to maintain both patriarchates in Constantinople, the remote controls of that "ecclesiastical government in exile" over the destinies of its adherents in the occupied territories were very weak, indeed. Nonetheless, the conquerors hesitated to appoint a new Catholic patriarch or archbishop of Jerusalem and contented themselves with installing a lower-ranking bishop. Pious Eastern Christians were justified in viewing these proceedings as a severe religious persecution, contrasting with the considerable autonomy in religious matters granted to all *dhimmis* by the Muslim authorities.[13]

More remarkably, even the mass slaughter of Muslims and Jews in Jerusalem and other cities, which left behind a frightful memory for generations, did not immediately cause Muslim and Jewish leaders to reassess the extent and likely duration of the Crusaders' conquest. To be sure, as in other periods of great transformation, Jewish utopian dreamers saw in this upheaval a sign of the approaching steps of the Messiah. Some of them may have remembered views expressed by such former teachers as Saadiah and Hai (reacting to the recurrent crises of the Muslim Empire in their days) that the replacement of Ishmael's (Muslim) rule by that of Edom (Christians) over the Holy Land would be a clear harbinger of the Redeemer. But the realists, even among the Jewish pilgrims to Palestine, merely sought to adjust themselves to what they considered a temporary emergency. In an Arabic letter probably written in the spring of 1100—less than a year after the Crusaders' entry into Jerusalem on July 15, 1099—the Jewish writer stated:

> Now, all of us had anticipated that our [Egyptian] Sultan—may God bestow glory upon his victories—would set out against them [the Franks] with his troops and chase them away. But time after time our hope failed. Yet, to this very moment we do hope that God will give his [the Sultan's] enemies into his hands. For it is inevitable that the armies will join in battle this year; and, if God grants us victory through him [the Sultan] and he conquers Jerusalem—and so it may be, with God's will—I for one shall not be amongst those who will linger, but shall go there to behold the city.

In the meantime he and many other like-minded Jews had their hands full in trying to ransom the numerous Jewish captives taken by the Crusaders and in helping refugees who had escaped during the occupation of their cities. Redemptions were eased by the sharp drop in prices of slaves, owing to the sudden increase in supply. We recall Tancred's boast that (in obvious retaliation for Judas' betrayal of Jesus for 30 shekels) he had sold 30 Jewish prisoners for one dinar. This price contrasted with the prevailing rate of 33⅓ dinars per slave. On the other hand, most Jewish villagers seem to have been spared by the conquerors who realized that, without maintaining the agricultural production of the country on a fairly high level, they would have great difficulties in supplying their own armies with food and other materials.[14]

Different again was the position of the Muslim population. It suddenly found itself transformed from a ruling class into a suspected and oppressed religious group. Although that change in status helped to strengthen the unity of the Muslim *'umma* (community), the suddenness of this reversal was only somewhat mitigated by the suspension of the intercommunal strife which had divided the Syro-Egyptian Islamic world into conflicting sects of Sunnites and Shi'ites, while the adherence to one or another of the four schools of Muslim jurisprudence had caused less serious cleavages. Yet, the immediate reaction among the Muslim masses seems to have been fatalistic acquiescence to enemy domination. In time, however, quite a few Muslims chose voluntary expatriation to a Muslim country. For instance, many inhabitants of Palestinian Nablus left for Damascus. Others, like their Jewish counterparts, sought the greater security of more distant Egypt or Iraq.[15]

After the first decade, the conquerors' zeal and intolerance of religious diversity gradually diminished. From 1110 on, life in the Latin Kingdom of Jerusalem became more bearable for the subject population, including Jews. Below the small privileged class of Western nobles, the other segments of the population enjoyed a measure of equality of rights. For example, throughout the Latin Kingdom the wergeld for the murder of a Frank was set at 100 bezants to be paid to the lord and 100 to the family of the victim. The murder of any non-Catholic called for a fine of only half these amounts. While the government did not recognize the rabbinic courts (just as it did not give official sanction to Muslim tribunals), it did not prevent the "unbelievers" from voluntarily repairing to their own judges. Interfaith litigations, too, were adjudicated more equitably. The leading law code, *Livre des Assises de la Cour de Bourgeois,* explicitly provided that "if a Greek claims against a Jew and the latter denies—the law stipulates that the Greek should bring Jewish witnesses and these witnesses should take an oath according to their law that there is truth in the claim and that they saw the defendant perpetrate the transgression or heard him uttering the insult." Increasing toleration also found expression in the growth of communities outside Jerusalem. To be sure, Haifa, where Jewry had played a role in the city's defense against the onrushing Crusaders, suffered a long-lasting eclipse. But other communities resumed their prewar functions. That of Tyre, for example, which after the Seljuk devastation of Jerusalem in 1070 had accommodated the Jewish academy of the Holy City, continued to serve as a major socioeconomic and cultural center even after its occupation by the Franks in 1123. Characteristically, when Benjamin of Tudela arrived there about 1170 he found a prosperous community of 500 (according to another version, 400) Jews, headed by two newcomers, R. Ephraim, the "Egyptian," and R. Meir "of Carcassonne." Tyre soon found a rival in Acco, where Benjamin found 200 Jews. Because of its location within the territory of biblical Israel, Acco soon outstripped Tyre in Jewish leadership.[16]

Economic factors, too, played a considerable role. The Jews, plying their traditional crafts, continued to devote themselves in particular, to such specialties as dyeing and glassblowing, in which they had long excelled. Totally misunderstanding the situation, Jacques of Vitry, bishop of Acco, contrasted the situation in Europe, where Christian princes allowed Jews to enslave Christians by their "inhuman usury," with that in Muslim lands, where most Jews were earning a living through inferior manual labor. He saw therein the effects of Saracen hatred and contempt for the Jews, an observation which merely reflected his own upper-class bias against physical labor. He should have realized that his predecessor, William of Tyre, had actually blamed his fellow-Crusaders for frequently using Jewish doctors, and that King Amalric (Amaury, 1162–74) was willing to employ an Egyptian-Jewish expert like Maimonides as his court physician. It was the sage of Fusṭaṭ who refused the offer. Jacques also overlooked the presence in Tyre of Jewish shipowners and merchants of high standing. More importantly, one of the propelling forces for the Crusades was the drive of some Italian republics to gain direct access to the East-Mediterranean emporia and thus more profitably to participate in the lucrative commercial exchanges between Europe and the Far and Middle East. It has often been noted that the export of Oriental products to Europe far exceeded in value the recriprocal European exports of slaves and raw materials to the Middle East. The resulting deficits in Europe's balance of trade had to be made up by payments in gold and silver, creating a constant drain on the Western holdings of these precious metals. As a result, there arose in many cities of the Latin Kingdom of Jerusalem and in the other Crusader principalities special Pisan, Genoese, and Venetian quarters. Although the Italian competition had previously displaced the Jewish merchants who had played a leading role in the international trade of the Mediterranean world, these foreign merchants apparently found local Mid-Eastern Jews quite useful as intermediaries in establishing the necessary commercial contacts; they often accommodated such Jewish agents in their own residential and business districts.[17]

In time the Crusaders' expansive zeal became more subdued, and with the conquest of Tyre in 1123, their great crusading élan expended itself. True, there were a few additional European expeditions, some commanded by leading Western monarchs such as the Holy Roman Emperor, Frederick I Barbarossa (the Second Crusade, 1146–49), Philip IV of France and Richard Lion-Heart of England (the Third Crusade, 1189–92), Frederick II, the last of the Hohenstaufen (the Sixth Crusade, 1228–29), and Louis IX of France, later known as St. Louis (the Seventh Crusade, 1248–54). Thereafter several more futile efforts were made until Pope Pius II's death in Ancona, his projected port of embarkation (1464). The local Latin princes likewise made independent forays into the neighboring Muslim-dominated territories. Amalric of Jerusalem alone staged five raids into Egypt, conquering the city of Damietta, as Louis IX did later. But these were relatively minor episodes; in each case the Christian monarch was forced to retreat. On his march from Damietta to Cairo, St. Louis was defeated and taken prisoner together with his brother and other nobles. He was freed only after payment of the huge ransom of 400,000 pounds *tournois* or 800,000 bezants. More significantly, the local Christian princes constantly quarreled with one another, preventing any sustained unified action. At the siege of Damascus in 1148, writes an anonymous Syriac chronicler, "the inhabitants, in their distress, wanted to surrender, but the wicked jealousy of the Franks, who cannot bear another's success, was their undoing." Similarly Ascalon would have fallen into the Crusaders' hands long before 1153 were it not for the disunity among the Christian commanders. Perhaps most fatal was the fact that many Crusaders considered their mission accomplished after a few years in the field and returned to Europe. An increasing number of those who took the Cross in the twelfth century and still more of those in the thirteenth century preferred to secure an ecclesiastical release from their vows in return for payment of a prescribed fee—which thus became an important source of revenue for the Church. As a result, the Crusader ruling class in the Latin Kingdom remained a tiny minority of the population and their control over the multitude of non-Catholics could be maintained only by force. It increasingly bore the marks of colonial exploitation.[18]

A turning point in the destiny of the Latin Kingdom came with the conquest of Edessa by Zangi in 1144. After evacuating the

Christians, especially the Armenians, for security reasons, Zangi tried to replace them by new Muslim and Jewish settlers. Three hundred Jewish families were formally established in that important city. Zangi's offensive was followed by the conquests of Nur ad-Din and Saladin. It was in the last decades of the twelfth century that the Muslims responded to the Christian holy war by a strong emphasis upon their own *jihad*. The obligation to sacrifice one's life for Islam, long cherished by the leaders of that faith, was now elevated to the rank of Islam's sixth fundamental commandment, next to (1) the profession of the monotheistic faith, (2) five daily prayers, (3) charity, (4) fasts, especially during the Ramadan period, and (5) pilgrimage to Mecca. In ideological justification of the war there also was a new Muslim emphasis on the "sanctity of Jerusalem." Initiated by the 'Umayyad caliphs of Damascus in the seventh century in order to counteract the influence of the Meccan leadership, the high appreciation of Jerusalem as the third holiest city of Islam had been muted in the following generations. But it was now revived by the Seljuk propaganda and served Zangi, Nur ad-Din, and Saladin in very good stead. As usual, sayings attributed to Mohammed buttressed such glorification. One such statement allegedly advised pious Muslims that "there was no nobler purpose than a visit to three mosques, the Mosque of Mecca, his own Mosque [in Medina], and the Mosque of Beit al-Maqdus." This officially sponsored glorification of the city now found expressions in numerous tracts and poems, principally written by Syrian and other West-Asian Muslims.[19]

In contrast to this widespread rhetoric, the Muslim rulers paid more attention to their imperial and strategic interests. At first they turned a deaf ear to Innocent III's appeal to them in 1216 that they voluntarily return Jerusalem to Christian rule. However, when the hosts of the Fifth Crusade arrived in the Middle East (1219), the Muslim public must have been shocked to learn that their ruler Mu'aẓẓam Sharaf ad-din 'Isa (1218–27) was so frightened at the prospect of another Latin invasion that he threatened to level the city, following Saladin's procedure in Ascalon a quarter of a century earlier. Although we do not have any direct testimony to that effect, we may assume that many Jews joined the majority of their Muslim compatriots in fleeing the Holy City before the Latin attack materialized. Those who remained in, or returned to, Jerusalem had only a short respite. After the arrival of Emperor Frederick II in 1228 as a leader of the Sixth Crusade, Sultan Al-Kamil reached an amicable settlement with him by peacefully allowing the emperor to take over Jerusalem with the exception of its Muslim sanctuaries. This last emperor of the Hohenstaufen dynasty was a man of great intelligence, whose wide erudition had earned him the nickname *stupor mundi;* he also spoke Arabic and thus greatly impressed the sultan. Unlike most ardent Crusaders, to be sure, he was living under a papal excommunication and therefore had to place the crown of Jerusalem on his own head. Later (in 1239) he was publicly accused by his archenemy Pope Gregory IX of having written the blasphemous tract, *De tribus impostoribus,* referring to Moses, Jesus, and Mohammed as the three greatest prevaricators in world history. Yet even the emperor did not dare to defy the long-established Frankish policy of discouraging non-Christians from living in the Holy City. Hence in 1229 Jews once again had to leave Jerusalem, not to return until after its "liberation" by the Muslim Khwarizmians in 1244, a liberation which was combined with widespread looting and wanton destruction. However, only a few Jews seem to have resettled immediately. This restraint proved beneficial because, in 1260, the Mongolian hosts under Hulagu reached Palestine and occupied most of the country. News of the wholesale massacres staged by the new invaders throughout western Asia must have struck terror in the hearts of all inhabitants. Not surprisingly, therefore, in 1267 the newly arrived Naḥmanides found only one Jew, a dyer, in the city—a sharp contrast, indeed, with the three Jewish congregations functioning in Jerusalem during Al-Ḥarizi's visit half a century before. Needless to say, Jews not only suffered from the military campaigns but, together with the other inhabitants, were also victims of such recurrent elemental catastrophes as the plague, which on several occasions ravaged the Latin Kingdom, and the Syrian earthquake of 1202.[20]

Jewish reactions to the titanic struggle between Islam and Christendom took many forms. All Jews understandably mourned the deaths of the Jewish martyrs massacred by the Crusaders in

Europe and in the Holy Land. On the ideological level this world-historical struggle must have inspired poets and thinkers like Yehudah Halevi to elevate the Jewish people's powerlessness, on a par with personal martyrdom, into a hallowed religious trait, conferring a distinction upon the suffering people. On the popular level there arose a number of messianic movements which saw in this great conflict between the two daughter religions omens of the final redemption. This was, indeed, one of "the messianically most excited periods in Jewish history." On the other hand, some of the Western Jewish jurists, confronted with the practical problems arising from the establishment of the Latin Kingdom of Jerusalem and the constant wars in the Middle East, had to make decisions affecting Jewish behavior. For example, the old talmudic provision that a wife had to follow her husband if he chose to settle in the Holy Land or else accept a divorce without the contractual marriage settlement pledged in her *ketubah,* could not justifiably be enforced during that emergency period. Hence a leading Tosafist, R. Ḥayyim b. Ḥananel ha-Kohen of Paris, a pupil of R. Jacob Tam, rendered a decision that this talmudic provision "no longer applies today because the roads have become too risky to travel." R. Ḥayyim went further and declared: "In our days we are no longer obliged to live in the Holy Land. A great many commandments are connected with residence in Palestine and their neglect is subject to severe penalties. But we are no longer able scrupulously to observe them." Such neglect of a traditional talmudic provision was illustrated by no less a rabbinic authority than Maimonides when he left Acco for Egypt, despite the oft-quoted assertion of the tannaitic midrash, Sifre, that the commandment of living in the Holy Land outweighed all other commandments of the Torah, and Maimonides' own declaration that leaving Palestine for another country was strictly prohibited.[21]

After the conquest of Jerusalem by Saladin, however, Jewish public opinion, particularly in the Western countries, reverted to the old glorification of Jerusalem. Not only did the number of pious Jewish pilgrims reaching the Holy Land increase significantly, but there was even an attempt at group migration to the Holy Land. In 1211, we are told by the later chronicler Shem Ṭob Sonzolo, 300 rabbis from France and England, led by the distinguished scholar Simson b. Abraham of Sens, left their native lands and proceeded to Palestine. Simson, probably discouraged by the internal quarrels among the three Jewish congregations in Jerusalem after Saladin's purported invitation for Jews to settle in the Holy City, established his academy in Tyre. Another distinguished French rabbi, Yeḥiel b. Joseph of Paris, followed suit and opened his own school of higher Jewish learning in Acco (1253). Before long the "sages of Acco" achieved an international reputation and were reverently cited even by Solomon ibn Adret, the leading halakhic authority in contemporary Spain. The most renowned scholar to reach Jerusalem in the thirteenth century was Naḥmanides (Moses b. Naḥman). We recall that, after his eloquent defense of Judaism at the famous disputation in Barcelona in 1263, his enemies made his life in Aragon unbearable and he considered it the better part of wisdom to proceed to Palestine. In many passages in his *Commentary* on the Pentateuch, which he completed in the Holy Land, he expatiated on the duty of every Jew to try to live in his ancestral country. In one characteristic exegetical excursus, the rabbi even developed a remarkable nationalistic theory. He interpreted the biblical prediction, "And I will bring the land into desolation; and your enemies that dwell therein shall be astonished at it" (Lev. 26:32), as a prediction of the general instability of any non-Jewish rule in the Holy Land, as illustrated by its ever-changing foreign regimes. He explained the enemies' confusion as

> a message of glad tidings to all the communities of the Exile that our land does not accept our enemies. It also is a great proof and reassurance for us that the land, so fertile and rich in ancient times, had become utterly desolate today. All that because, since we [Jews] departed from it, it has not accepted any single people; they all tried to settle in it but did not succeed.

Similarly, in his *Commentary* on Maimonides' *Book of Commandments* Naḥmanides objected to the more casual Maimonidean treatment of the precept to settle in Palestine: "We were ordered to inherit the land promised by God to our forefathers, Abraham, Isaac, and Jacob, and we ought never to abandon it to any nation, neither leave it in desolation." When these words were written, sometime before the author's death in 1275, the Jewish community in Palestine was very small. Together with its non-Jewish neighbors it had undergone the harrowing experience of the Mongolian invasion, which had brought about the ruin of many Palestinian settlements, Jewish and non-Jewish alike.[22]

MONGOL DELUGE

At the beginning of the thirteenth century the Syro-Egyptian Jewish communities were overshadowed in cultural and economic importance by those of Babylonia (Iraq), especially Baghdad. We recall the enthusiastic reports of the twelfth-century visitors, Benjamin of Tudela and Petaḥiah of Ratisbon, about what they saw of the Jews in the old imperial capital. True, the dissolution of the Great Caliphate had left only a small segment of the empire under the caliph's control. Internally, too, his authority was circumscribed by his purported advisers, the Buwayhids, and later the Seljuks who bore the title of sultans. On the whole, both the cities and the countryside still were in a flourishing state, notwithstanding the numerous manifestations of spreading internal moral and economic decay. However, the center of gravity had gradually been moving to neighboring Persia, whose cultural upsurge was well exemplified by three contemporaries: the vizier and political scientist Nizam al-Mulk, the poet Omar Khayyam, and Hassan Sabbah, the founder of the notorious nihilist sect of "Assassins" (they died in 1092, 1123, and 1124, respectively).[23]

Within the Jewish community, too, remnants of the old glory mingled with many forms of disintegration. It was this semichaotic state in numerous communities and the general insecurity of life under the ever-changing regimes which generated such movements as that of the pseudomessiah, David Alroy. Not surprisingly, the exilarchic authority, which, based on the widely accepted claim to its unbroken continuity from the captive king Jehoiachim during the Babylonian Exile, had been the longest-lived dynasty in human history and, as such, the pride of Eastern Jewry, shrank from generation to generation. Finally, beginning in the first half of the eleventh century some members of the exilarchic family left Baghdad and established independent provincial centers in Mosul, Yemen, and other places. The most enduring dynasty was that of Mosul, where in the 1160s Benjamin of Tudela found a flourishing

Jewish community embracing 7,000 members. Its authority apparently ended only because of some drastic action during the reign of Timur (Tamerlane) about 1400 C.E. Although a branch of the exilarchic house had remained in Baghdad, it allowed the mantle of leadership to rest exclusively upon the shoulders of the geonim. Under the vigorous leadership of Samuel b. 'Ali (1164–94), the gaonate reasserted itself far beyond the boundaries of the caliphal state and tried to reach out to Jerusalem and Cairo-Fusṭaṭ. The gaon also replaced the exilarch as the main representative of the Jewish communities before the caliph, ultimately receiving from the rulers an official decree of appointment, along the lines of the original certificate handed to each newly elected prince of captivity.[24]

Among Samuel b. 'Ali's most worthy successors was Abu'l Fatḥ Isḥāq ibn al-Shuwaikh (1218–47). He was highly praised by his contemporaries, such as the poet Eleazar b. Jacob ha-Bavli and the more distant Egyptian *nagid,* Abraham Maimonides. An Arab chronicler, referring to his demise in 1247, called him a "man of virtue and erudition, with a beautiful handwriting, author of excellent poems, and a remarkably well-informed student of astronomy." Even Yehudah al-Ḥarizi, biting critic though he was at times, described R. Isaac as "the man of a precious soul and righteous ways of living." This poet-visitor was far less kindly, however, to the Baghdad community at large. He wrote:

> The keeners shall weep over the Jews of Baghdad, and all eyes shall shed tears . . . over the community which was the most beautiful of all the communities; its ancients had been scholars, its elders peers of heavenly angels, while its young people overflowed with the milk of human kindness. Today these fine attributes turned into bad traits, praise into blame, glory into shame, and the blessings into lamentations. Hence instead of a [liberal] distribution of funds there is miserliness; in lieu of wisdom, stupidity; and every gross ignoramus considers himself the Aristotle of his time.

We need not take these generalizations too seriously, for Al-Ḥarizi often judged communities and individuals by the amount of patronage he personally received. He was also conscious of his power to denigrate people as a means of extorting from them sizable "gifts." Nevertheless, we may believe him that the general level of education and philanthropy had declined from the heights once achieved by Baghdad Jewry. Certainly, it is rather unlikely that the community still filled two large Jewish quarters and possessed more than thirty synagogues and ten Jewish academies of learning, as it had in the 1160s, although according to an Arab chronicler's exaggerating report, before its destruction in 1258, it embraced 36,000 Jewish taxpayers. Nor were the caliphs of the thirteenth century nearly as friendly to the Jews as their predecessors had been during the visits of the two famous Jewish travelers half a century before. According to Benjamin, doubtless referring to the caliph Al-Mustanjid (1160–70), "[he] is kind unto Israel, and many belonging to the people of Israel are his attendants. He knows all languages and is well versed in the law of Israel. He reads and writes the holy language [Hebrew]." These are obvious exaggerations, on a par with Petaḥiah b. Jacob's assertion that 2,000 pupils attended Samuel b. 'Ali's academy.[25]

A contrary, equally exaggerated, picture emerges from the scathing comments of a Muslim official, Abu 'Abdallah Muḥammad ibn Yaḥya abu Fadhlan, in his letter of 1228. After complaining that the Jews did not pay a sufficiently high poll tax—he insisted that some Jewish officials of the Diwan charged the government more for expenses of one day than the amount they paid for their poll tax in a year—he censured the Jewish community for not living up to the Covenant of 'Umar and its manifold restrictions. According to him, Jewish doctors, though ill-prepared for their calling through their insufficient study of medical literature, nevertheless enjoyed a vogue among Muslim patients, accumulated riches, and appeared in public in luxurious and showy attire. He also blamed the Jewish artisans and petty merchants for cheating on weights and measures and for debasing the gold and silver objects they were selling, at the expense of their Muslim customers. Whether or not there was any truth in these accusations, we recall the studied humiliations to which individual Jewish (and Christian) taxpayers were exposed in the early thirteenth century, whenever they personally had to deliver the required poll taxes.[26]

These misfortunes were far overshadowed by the catastrophe which befell Mid-Eastern Jewry and its neighbors during the Mongol "deluge"—a term used by the invaders themselves. From the beginning Jenghiz, or Genghis, Khan (*ca.* 1167–1227) and his successors throughout the thirteenth century had a sense of mission to conquer the world. They preferred to use the title of world conqueror or world emperor rather than any other and did not hesitate to devastate entire countries in their march toward a universal empire. Even when they welcomed cooperation from Christian Europe in combating the Muslim world, they expected Christendom's ultimate surrender rather than partnership.

Typical of their attitude was the insolent letter addressed by Great Khan Göyük to Pope Innocent IV in November 1246. It included the following characteristic passage: "Jenghiz Khan and the Great Khan [Ogotai] have both transmitted to me God's order [that all the world should be subordinated to the Mongols]. . . . You personally, at the head of the [Christian] kings, shall come, one and all, to pay homage to me, and to serve me; then we shall take your submission. If, however, you do not accept God's wish and act against Our order, we shall know that you are Our enemies." What is most remarkable is that, unlike the other medieval drives for world domination, this one had a purely secular character. Although invoking God's commandments, the Mongols did not profess a religion with a well-formulated set of beliefs and rituals and were on the whole rather tolerant of religious diversity. As Gregory Barhebraeus, the well-informed Syriac historian of the thirteenth century, observed, "with the Mongols there is neither slave nor free man, neither believer nor pagan, neither Christian nor Jew; but they regard all men as belonging to one and the same stock." All they insisted on was quick surrender to their armies, whereupon the conquered population was to be spared. Resistance was punishable by total extermination, with the occasional enslaving of women and children. One country after another, deep into European Russia, felt the terror of the Mongol flood. We remember that in 1241 even Germany averted the Tatar attack with great difficulty and, in fact, mainly because the Mongol drive was weakened by serious troubles at home.[27]

The great crisis for Babylonian Jewry and its neighbors came in 1257–60, when Hulagu invaded the western provinces of the residual caliphate. Although, years earlier, his father Ogotai had been stopped after the occupation of several Babylonian cities including Mosul, Hulagu's troops quickly overcame all resistance and took Baghdad by storm on February 10, 1258. The Mongol hosts are said to have massacred 800,000 of its inhabitants (even more exaggeratingly, Al-Maqrizi contended that 2,000,000 persons were slaughtered), a disaster from which that imperial city never fully recovered. During that year Hulagu also conquered Aleppo and, without serious resistance, Damascus, penetrating into the Nablus and Gaza regions. While quietly surrendering cities along with their inhabitants were usually spared, theoretically all persons and properties were taken over by the conquerors. Ultimately, it was only Hulagu's departure with most of his armies, because of renewed troubles at home, which made it possible for the Egyptian army to stop the remaining Mongol force, not exceeding 10,000 men, in the battle of 'Ayn Jalut (Spring of Goliath) of September 3, 1260. This Muslim victory was celebrated for centuries thereafter as having saved Egypt and the rest of North Africa from the Mongol scourge. This relatively small encounter indeed marked a turning point in the history of the Middle East, just as the battle of Tours and Poitiers of 732, despite its equally small dimensions, had saved France and its neighboring countries from the Moorish occupation.[28]

Although the Mongols were much more hostile to the ruling Muslims than to the "protected subjects," Jews suffered severely from the often indiscriminate massacres. Only the Christians were occasionally spared because of the influence exerted upon Hulagu by his Nestorian wife and her Christian relatives. Also the possible alliance with the Western Christian powers against their common Muslim enemy may well have tempered the vengeance of the Mongols on that segment of the population which, in any case, appears to have less staunchly resisted their drive toward a Mongol world domination. Regrettably, we are not well informed about the attitude of the regime toward the Jews during these military campaigns. But it seems that at least after the restoration of peace the old restrictive policies of the Muslim authorities toward the *dhimmis* were largely discontinued. Jews could now take a much more active part in the administration of the country, some of them, like Sa'd ad-Daula, reaching the highest echelons of officialdom in the administration of the state and its provinces. According to an Arab report, it was a Jewish counselor who persuaded Hulagu not to dismiss his learned courtiers and astrologers, as had been suggested by his Mongol advisers.[29]

Jews also participated actively in the religious disputation staged at Hulagu's court. There was indeed some cause for Christian apprehensions that Jews might convert leading Mongols to Judaism, as their predecessors had successfully proselytized among the Khazars. Such fears were expressed, for instance, by Raymond Lull who, in presenting his missionary program to Pope Celestine V and the Roman cardinals, wrote:

> It is also an appropriate thing that the Church should do all in its power to conquer the Tatars by disputations. Such a conquest should be quite easy, because they do not have any religion of their own and because they allow the preachment of the faith of Christ in their land. Also because anyone wishing to do so may become a Christian without fear of the regime. Such a mission is highly imperative, for if the Tatars adopt a religion of their own, as Mohammed did, or if the Saracens or Jews succeed in converting them to their faith, all of Christendom will be in great danger.

According to the well-informed chronicler, Juvaini, Jenghiz Khan himself believed in a sole ominipotent Deity and allowed some of his sons to embrace Christianity and others to adopt Judaism. Not surprisingly, as in other periods of great stress, some Jews viewed these world-shaking events as ushering in the messianic age, especially since they involved the defeat of the Muslim, as well as the Crusader, rulers of the Holy Land. The poet Meshullam b. Solomon Dapiera predicted: "In our days the kingdom will be restored to our forlorn people and dispersed communities." A letter writer from Catania, Sicily, was more specific. Perhaps hearing rumors of Ogotai's (Ögedey's) arrogant letter to Innocent IV, he claimed that the "mysterious king" sent letters to the kings of Spain and Germany, asking them to assist his messengers in gathering the Jews of their countries and enabling them to proceed to the Holy Land.[30]

At the same time, however, in the areas under Mongol domination certain laws taken over from Jenghiz Khan's legislation must have proved quite awkward for the Jewish subjects. For example, the prohibition against slaughtering animals for food in any manner other than by slitting their breasts, rather than their throats—as prescribed by the Mongols under the sanction of a death penalty—if strictly enforced, might have played havoc with the Jewish *sheḥiṭah.* But it seems that many of these laws were not carried into effect toward non-Mongols. Similarly, the erection of a memorial statue for Jenghiz Khan and the practice of offering sacrifices to that "idol" could not be imposed upon Christians and Jews without violating their fundamental religious laws. Yet we do not hear of any Jews being specifically excused from such a performance; one or another may have suffered martyrdom on this score, as did the Christian Grand Duke Michael of Chernigov and his adviser who encouraged him to plead that his conscience would not allow him to commit that kind of idolatry. The considerable laxity of the Mongolian rulers in the sexual domain might also have been disruptive to the traditional life of the Jewish community. Quite apart from the excesses of a victorious army in conquered territories, which often led to the indiscriminate rape of women, the law provided that even in peacetime the khan could select any girl or married woman of the subject population and make her his concubine. However, we rarely hear of such forcible interference with Jewish, Christian, or even the more polygamous Muslim family life.[31]

In general, the "barbarian" Mongols were religiously far more tolerant than most of the regimes they replaced. Some observers might actually have called the establishment of the vast Mongolian Empire a blessing to the subject populations. It certainly ended much of the continuous tribal warfare which was the dominant way of life in most sections of Asia. Sanguine interpreters might even draw a comparison between this sort of *pax Mongolica* and the nineteenth-century *pax Britannica.* Such comparison would be quite fallacious, of course, since the Mongol yoke weighed much more heavily upon the subject peoples and internal peace was by no means safeguarded. Moreover, there are numerous scholars, particularly among the descendants of the peoples most victimized by the Mongols, who continue the old lamentations about the utter destructiveness of the Mongolian conquests and buttress them with much newly available evidence from archaeological digs. For example, the Soviet historian A. M. Sakharov finds in the remains of mass graves and of innumerable destroyed buildings mute testimony to the extent of the catastrophe which had befallen the populations of medieval Russia. The aftereffects of the Mongolian flood upon Jewish life and creativity were equally tragic and enduring.[32]

Nonetheless, a certain *modus vivendi* was rather speedily established, and in the following decades many Jewish communities reorganized themselves, albeit on a lower level, and resumed their more or less normal daily life. However, as a result of the ensuing political transformation Babylonia and its adjoining provinces came under the sway of Persia and its Mongolian "Il-Khan" dynasty, which in the days of Ghazzan adopted Islam (1295). Thenceforth the Jewry of that whole area shared the destinies of its Persian coreligionists down into the sixteenth century, when it came under the rule of the Ottoman Empire. Its history from the end of the thirteenth century will therefore be treated here in connection with the history of the Jews of Persia and the Ottoman Empire, in the forthcoming chapters.

MAMELUKE EMPIRE

After stemming the great Mongol invasion in the battle of ʻAyn Jalut, the Mameluke dynasty established itself firmly. For the first time only a succession of former slaves could occupy the royal throne, as well as the governorships of the various provinces and other high offices in the army. The term Mameluke, apparently appearing first as a synonym for "slave soldier" in a document of 687 C.E., was also the common name of dynasties of various descent which ruled over Egypt and Syria from 1250 until 1517, when the area was incorporated into the Ottoman Empire. Already ʻAbd ar-Raḥman Ibn Khaldun (1332–1406) recognized that these men from the steppes had saved Egypt and Syria from the Mongol occupation, a feat which he attributed to the working of divine Providence. While the majority of the new rulers originated from Turkestan and other "Turkic" areas, some had been acquired as slaves from the Golden Horde while it dominated the Kipchak steppes, now part of the European Soviet Union. How little discrimination was practiced at first in the selection of the new sultans may be seen in the coronation of Lachin or Lajin who, according to some rumors, had been a Christian Crusader born in either Western Europe or Byzantium. Taken prisoner, he had ultimately become the slave of Sultan Qala'un, who set him free. After serving as governor of Syria, he himself became the sultan in 1296, living as a pious Muslim, abstaining from wine and forbidden games, and every year fasting for three months. His election may have been facilitated by his marriage to the daughter of Baybars (1260–77), one of the heroes of 'Ayn Jalut. However, no Jew, professing or converted, is recorded among the leading Mamelukes. Even the poet Nur ad-Din 'Ali (d. 1468) and Azbek Ash-Sharifi (d. 1511), who appear to have been of Jewish descent, hardly had any contacts with their Jewish contemporaries. Perhaps the speedy ransoming of most Jewish captives by their coreligionists left only a small residuum of unfree young Jews able and willing to pursue a military career after undergoing conversion to Islam.[33]

Although chronologically the fourth ruler, Baybars was the true founder of the Mameluke regime. In the short span of seventeen years, he not only successfully combated the Crusaders—in 1265–66 he conquered Caesarea, Haifa, Safed, and other Crusader strongholds—but quickly expanded his dominion in both the north and south by penetrating Asia Minor and for the first time annexing Nubia, an achievement which had eluded his Faṭimid predecessors. He also reorganized the internal administration and laid the foundations for a constitutional structure which, though extremely oppressive and often arbitrary, effectively served the militaristic ambitions of the new sovereigns. With respect to the *dhimmis*, an unfortunate early episode threatened to undermine their continued toleration. According to contemporary Arab historians, some Christians, violently reacting to Baybars' conquests in the Latin Kingdom, set fire to many buildings in Cairo. This conflagration devastated a large part of the city and left a permanent mark on the memory of its inhabitants. Upon his return to the capital, we are told, Baybars ordered the burning of all the Christians and Jews he could seize (a large number had fled the city). At the last moment, however, he was persuaded by a high official to commute the penalty to a fine of 500,000 dinars (according to Al-Maqrizi, only 50,000 dinars). Despite the evidence for arson allegedly marshaled by the authorities, it is possible that, from the outset, the sultan's ruthless threat to the "protected subjects" was merely a means of extorting the high ransom from them. Certainly, Jews had played no role in starting the fires, and yet they were included in Baybars' drastic order. This affair was an evil augury for the future relations between the new regime and the religious minorities. Basic hostility from the top, politically and fiscally rather than religiously inspired, was also demonstrated by other incidents such as the governmental toleration of an anti-*dhimmi* outbreak in Damascus led by a Ṣufi protégé of Baybars, whose elevation to the sultanate the mystic had supposedly predicted. This attack led to the seizure of the largest synagogue in the Syrian capital and its conversion into a mosque (1271). It took the Jews eight years to secure the return of their sanctuary, a success doubtless facilitated by the intervening disgrace of the Ṣufi agitator, his arrest, and death in prison in 1277.[34]

In general, the new rulers consciously kept themselves apart from the majority of the population. To the end, they and their associates in army and government continued speaking Turkic dialects, rather than Arabic. One reason they were tolerated by the Arab majority—despite occasional popular uprisings—was gratitude for their maintaining a modicum of law and order throughout the realm. Even more importantly, the population appreciated their safeguarding the security of the borderlands, not only against foreign enemies but also against Bedouin raiders, and took pride in their country's victories during the period of Mameluke expansion as far north as Armenia and Asia Minor. Militarily, the Mamelukes were able to withstand the later Mongol incursions of 1299 and 1303 and even staved off the second highly threatening invasion by Timur (Tamerlane) in 1400–1404, reminiscent of that by Hulagu in 1257–60. The deliberate separatism did not cease until the small Mameluke minority was finally absorbed by the Egyptian Arab majority in the eighteenth and nineteenth centuries. This succession of foreign rulers inspired an eighteenth-century Turkish poet to comment bitterly: "Why do they call Egypt a 'mother of the world'? She is only a prostitute who has given herself up each century to all the nations." [35]

Needless to say, the term "Arab" population does not imply a monolithic ethnic majority opposing the alien Mamelukes. Cities like Cairo and Damascus were quite cosmopolitan in composition, despite the predominance of the Arabic language in most groups other than the ruling circles. The linguistic assimilation which had progressed very speedily in the earlier centuries put a veneer of relative uniformity on the diverse elements of the population. However, as A. S. Tritton stated, "it is astonishing how soon the Arabs fade out of Muslim history, Arabia itself excepted." Only the preeminent role of religion in all public affairs and the fact that the new Turkic rulers shared the majority's profession of Sunni Islam made it appear as if Egypt and Syria were parts of an all-embracing Arab world.[36]

The basic estrangement of the ruling minority from the subject population frequently had contradictory effects on their approach to the *dhimmis*. On the one hand, in order to get widespread backing among the Muslim masses, most rulers were, or pretended to be, extremely pious and punctiliously observant of every commandment of Muslim law. This attitude often led them to enforce the discriminatory provision against the "infidels" demanded by many leading Arab theologians and jurists. Themselves possessing little education, since their lifelong training consisted primarily in fighting wars, they were hardly able to argue with such experts about the meaning or range of certain regulations. This deficiency often came to the fore despite the undeniable native abilities for domestic government and international relations which characterized the more distinguished sultans, especially in the first, so-called Baḥri, era (1250–1382). At the same time the sultans found Coptic and other Christian, as well as Jewish, advisers indispensable in administering their large and variegated empire, collecting its taxes, and running its growing bureaucracy. They also had to take into account the international situation. While Christians were frequently suspected of siding with foreign enemies and, during the Mongol invasions, of cherishing the idea of an alliance between the Mongols and the European powers which might spell an end to Muslim rule, the Mameluke sultans also realized the indispensable function of the Italian, French, and other Western merchants for their country's welfare. Any direct anti-Christian move, moreover, often provoked the intervention of the Aragonese kings, Byzantine emperors, or other Christian rulers. The Jews, whose loyalty appeared less suspect, on the other hand, had no such foreign protectors. Nevertheless, formally Jews and Christians belonged to the same class of *dhimmis*, to whom the pertinent laws applied indiscriminately. It was only in the execution of these laws and in daily practice that the treatment of the religious minorities differed according to the exigencies of the moment or the individual temperaments of the sultans or governors.[37]

Another source of weakness for all "protected subjects" was the prevailing governmental instability. Already among the eleven Faṭimid caliphs who had occupied the Egypto-Syrian throne during the tenth and eleventh centuries, three had ascended the throne as children and four as adolescents. This meant that the actual power was exercised by viziers and other officials whose tenure of office depended entirely on the rulers' whims. But at least there was dynastic continuity. Under the Mamelukes, by contrast, there were very frequent changes resulting from palace revolts and conspiracies among powerful emirs. Among the Baḥri Mamelukes (1250–1382), only five—Baybars (1260–77), Qala'un (1279–90), Naṣir Muḥammad (1293–94, 1298–1308, 1309–1340), Naṣir Ḥasan (1347–51, 1354–61), and Ashraf Sha'ban (1363–76)—had reasonably long periods of reign, totaling, with interruptions, some 94 years. Twenty others occupied the throne for very brief periods, often only for a few months, to a total of 38 years. Somewhat better off were the Burji sultans (1382–1517), of whom Barquq (1382–98), Naṣir Faraj (1398–1405, 1406–1412), Mu'ayyad Shaykh (1412–21), Barsbay (1422–38), Jaqmaq (1438–53), Ashraf Inal (1453–60), Khushqadam (1461–67), Qa'it-Bey (1468–95), and Ashraf Qanṣuh-Ghuri (1500–1516) held sway for a fair number of years, while each of the fourteen others had a short reign. The proportion here was 125 years of moderately long-lasting to 70 years of speedily changing sultans. In many cases the term "short-lived" rulers applied in the literal sense, since their power ended by assasination. Moreover, the rulers of the fourteenth and fifteenth centuries were partly recruited from different families and often were of different foreign stocks.[38]

Consequently, the monarchical power often was greatly diffused; its range depended on the personality of the individual monarch, as well as on outward circumstances. Constitutionally, too, the sultan was merely a *primus inter pares* who depended on the cooperation of the emirs, who often functioned as great landowners, powerful governors, and/or army commanders. They in turn could be deposed by a powerful sultan without notice and banished from their seats of power, if allowed to survive at all. In addition, the Abbasid caliphs, after their removal in 1258 from Baghdad to Cairo, had some influence, although most of them lived a shadowy existence, in the capital or nearby, and were largely used by the sultans to lend the prestige of their office to some more daring enactments. In any case, neither the caliph, even in the period of his greatest power and prestige, nor the sultan was a monarch "by grace divine" in European terms; only the Shi'ites attributed to the *imam* some sort of supernatural endowment. Under these circumstances, Jews enjoyed only as much protection from the individual ruler as he was able and willing to extend to them. To be sure, the reign of justice had been preached by jurists and theologians as a supreme virtue for generations. A much-quoted old tradition had stated that "one day of a great *imam* stands higher than the [ordinary] man's religious observance in 60 years," and another attributed to Mohammed the saying that "on the day of Resurrection the just *imam* will be nearest to me." Yet, Mameluke rule was generally characterized by much arbitrariness in both legislation and administration, a situation aggravated by numerous acts of violence and distortion of the law by subordinates down to the lowly Mameluke soldiers. For example, women on the streets were often molested by Mamelukes of all ranks.[39]

The presence of other governmental institutions, in part counterbalancing Mameluke rule, did not fully benefit the non-Muslim population. The legal profession, particularly the qadhis, was the principal agent of continuity and, by upholding the supremacy of Muslim law, served as a unifying force in the otherwise greatly fragmented population. True, even Muslim law was not uniform, since in almost all major urban centers it was represented by the four schools of jurisprudence. In adjudicating major conflicts, particularly those affecting Jews and Christians, the sultans often summoned the four chief judges and listened to their opinions before reaching a decision. Being Sunni Muslims themselves, the Mameluke sultans had to pay less attention to Shi'ite and other sectarian views, although these sects were generally tolerated. Even more important were the tribal divisions within the Muslim majority. They frequently resulted in the formation of *futuwwas,* corporate groups which regulated the internal life of their members. Many achieved autonomous status. They thus brought about a semblance of municipal self-government.[40]

On the whole, these variegated components of the major cities were more antagonistic to the Jews than was the central government. However, these and other local authorities enjoyed far less autonomy than their opposite numbers in Christian Europe. For example, the police was not controlled by local elders, but by the central organs of the state. As a rule the qadhis enforced their sentences mainly through spiritual censures. Although neither as powerful nor as intolerant as some of the European burghers and their guilds, the Muslim populace and its leaders often staged local riots against its Jewish and Christian neighbors. Such disturbances were suppressed by the government officials, particularly if they included Christian or Jewish members in sufficiently influential positions to enforce the legally prescribed protective measures toward their own coreligionists. At the same time, the mere presence of such "unbelieving" high officials evoked many a violent reaction among the hostile majority.[41]

POPULATION MOVEMENTS

Certainly, such conditions were not conducive to a normal development of the Jewish communities. It appears that, despite fluctuations, the Jewish population was generally declining, both numerically and culturally, throughout the Mameluke period. Regrettably, our information concerning such basic facts as the size of the Jewish population in various parts of the empire is extremely limited. True, the accuracy of the earlier figures mentioned by Benjamin of Tudela in the 1160s may be subject to considerable doubt; they also cover only a minority of the Syro-Egyptian communities because the famous traveler usually described only settlements he had personally visited. Yet, his data give us at least an inkling of the dimensions of those communities, from which some conclusions may also be drawn about the other areas. No such detailed enumerations are available for the subsequent three centuries. At times a Jewish or Christian traveler or pilgrim on his way to, and from, the Holy Land may mention some figures related to the Jewish population. But such references are too sporadic and too unrelated to one another to allow for more extensive computations. Only toward the very end of the fifteenth century do we hear a little more about demographic facts from the Italian Jewish visitors Meshullam b. Menaḥem da Volterra and Obadiah di Bertinoro. Almost as an act of desperation, Shelomo Dov Goitein resorted to lists of charities collected in an Egyptian community for the ransom of captives, in order to deduce the number of donors and indirectly the size of the community at large. From these and other data he succeeded in producing estimates somewhat more worthwhile than those based upon other sources.[42]

One may perceive more clearly the conditions conducive to a demographic decline. Apart from the instability created by constant governmental changes and arbitrary acts, there were the usual negative demographic factors at play. The almost constant state of war and the frequent incursions of hostile troops into Syria and, to a lesser extent, into Egypt, were combined with the extremely cruel treatment of conquered populations not only by the Mongols but also by the Mamelukes and Crusaders. They caused a constant drain on both the belligerent and civilian manpower. In general, the Mameluke armies were not very large. Some major battles, it is estimated, were fought by 16,000 to 20,000 Mamelukes, aided by auxiliary contingents recruited from subject or friendly tribesmen. Yet the losses among the Mamelukes were staggering.

> Fighting [states William Muir] was their principal interest in life, even with each other, or with the people of the country, in order to keep them down. . . . Very few of this soldiery died at home in their own bed; nearly ninety, or perhaps more, per cent used to die a violent death, and most of them were under thirty or thirty-five years of age. At death . . . everything went to their master, to their murderer, or to the State, whichever was the strongest.

However, the annual importation of some 2,000 slaves and of a few volunteers, who gladly submitted themselves to such a rewarding form of slavery, sufficed to replenish the ranks. Only rarely did the force drop to as few as the 4,000 Mameluke soldiers said to have been at Barquq's disposal.[43]

Losses among civilians were even more staggering. It may not be quite true that the Mongols slaughtered 800,000 persons in Baghdad alone. But the massacre of the population of Bilbays by the Crusaders is another example of what frequently happened to cities which failed to surrender and were taken in battle. Pestilences, such as that which raged in Egypt in 1202–1203, likewise victimized great multitudes. Before Europe was stricken by the Black Plague in 1348, that deadly disease first devastated the Far-Eastern and then the Middle-Eastern populations; according to some contemporary historians, Cairo alone lost 800,000 souls in two months. During the last hundred years of the Burji regime, no fewer than fourteen major epidemics struck the ill-fated Egyptian masses (1416, 1419, 1426, 1430, 1438, 1444, 1449, 1460, 1469, 1477, 1492, 1498, 1505, 1513), in addition to lesser contagions recurring every spring. In Syria, where as early as 1434 a traveler found entire districts practically emptied of inhabitants, several major plagues (in 1437, 1460, 1468, 1476, 1491, 1497, and 1513–14) continued to decimate the surviving settlements. Some of them doubtless were as costly in human lives as was that of 1392–93, during which 1,000 victims were said to have died every day in Aleppo. Muḥammad ibn Ṣaṣra was later informed by a local scribe:

> I wanted to report accurately how many died in Aleppo and its province; I worked it out and found that from the beginning of the epidemic to its end three hundred and sixty thousand persons died: men, women, children, Jews, and Christians—mostly children. One hundred and fifty thousand died within the city; the remainder from outside the city and its vicinity.

Even if the scribe included in his count the entire region of Aleppo, which in M. Gaudefroy-Demombyne's survey included parts of Armenia and Mesopotamia, a loss of 360,000 inhabitants was a serious demographic blow. Regrettably, we do not possess contemporary Hebrew sources describing the sufferings of the Jews during those emergency periods. The frequent fires which destroyed large sections of Jewish, as well as non-Jewish, quarters must have added to the staggering number of victims. These elemental catastrophes were further aggravated by famines, partly generated by the oppressive fiscal system and mismanaged governmental monopolies. Not surprisingly, the widespread sufferings of the masses also resulted in a large number of suicides.[44]

Estimates of the Jewish population in Egypt and Syria in the Late Middle Ages are, therefore, even more tenuous than those for other countries of the period. Research in this field is made doubly difficult by the nearly complete absence of reliable data on the size of the total population of the individual cities or provinces, or of the area as a whole—despite the information given to Meshullam da Volterra that his protector, the dragoman Taghri Birdi, received every evening a complete report about all births and deaths in Cairo during the preceding day. The main sources, moreover, for gauging the size of Jewish communities in the West—tax lists of medieval communities or regions—have rarely been preserved in the Middle-Eastern archives; only a few are occasionally alluded to by the Arab historians. Nonetheless, for reasons elaborated in our earlier volumes, we must make efforts to gather whatever demographic data may be available and extend them by reasonable hypotheses so as to reach at least a minimal understanding of that vital historical factor.[45]

The scholar who has done most of the work in this field, Eli Ashtor (Strauss), originally estimated the Jewish populations of Egypt and Syria in the Mameluke period at about 40,000 each. Subsequently, he lowered the estimate for Egypt to a maximum of 12,000 to 15,000, allotting to Fusṭaṭ–Cairo no more than 1,500 souls. This seems to be much too low a figure even for the Rabbanite Jews, without the Karaites and Samaritans, although the government often treated all three groups as a unit headed by a single chief (*ra'is* or, in Hebrew, *nagid*). Even in 1481, in the period of their decline, Meshullam da Volterra claimed to have found 800 Rabbanite, 150 Karaite, and 50 Samaritan families, or over 5,000 persons, in the metropolis. Nor is it likely that a community of 1,500 persons should have played the significant role it did in a city that probably still numbered well over half a million inhabitants. Even in the early fifteenth century the Italian visitor Bertrando de Mignanelli admiringly wrote about "the wonderful city of Cairo, which has a population beyond estimating." That many of the Jews moved from Fusṭaṭ to Cairo—with their usual conservatism, even later the rabbis designated Cairo as "located near Fusṭaṭ" in such official documents as marriage contracts and divorce writs—need not be questioned. Yet, the depopulated Fusṭaṭ community still maintained its old synagogues intact. S. D. Goitein's estimate of 3,300 Jews in Fusṭaṭ–Cairo, derived from the aforementioned list of charitable donors and the assumption that the ratio between donors and recipients was four to one, seems to overlook the undoubtedly significant number of communal members who were above the poverty level and yet unable to contribute their share to charities, however urgent. Hence, the original figure of 7,000 Fusṭaṭ Jews mentioned by Benjamin of Tudela may have approximated the fifteenth-century reality somewhat more closely.[46]

Similar differences of opinion are reflected in the reports of visitors to Jerusalem in the 1480s. While Meshullam estimated the size of the Jewish population at 250 families in 1481, that is, at over 1,200 souls, the Christian pilgrims Felix Fabri and Bernard von Breydenbach mentioned in 1483 only about 500 (in one of Breydenbach's texts: 400) persons. In 1487 Obadiah di Bertinoro spoke of only 70 families, while explaining that earlier "there had been nearly 300 families in the city. But they gradually left one by one because of the heavy burden of taxes imposed upon them by the elders." And Jerusalem was the cynosure of the eyes of all four men, who certainly were deeply concerned about all facets of life in the Holy City.[47]

Nor was the flow of Jewish immigrants into the Syro-Egyptian area large enough—at least till the mass immigration from the Iberian Peninsula after 1492—to make up for this gradual decline. True, from time to time individual Jews from foreign lands arrived in the Mameluke possessions. The original East to West migration, which during the Faṭimid era had caused the rise of many Iraqi (Babylonian) Jewish congregations in both Syria and Egypt and even brought many Persian Jews, both Rabbanite and Karaite, to the Nile Valley, was perceptibly slowed by the Mongol destruction of many communities in the former Sassanian areas. However, a trickle continued from that direction. More numerous were the arrivals from Europe. We recall the immigration to Palestine of 300 French rabbis in 1211. The Holy Land had a special attraction to Jewish and Christian travelers and settlers, but some Palestinian immigrants later moved on to other parts of the Faṭimid or the Mameluke Empire. The most notable example is Moses Maimonides who, despite his own admission that any Jewish departure from Palestine to Egypt was prohibited, found it necessary to leave Acco and settle in Fusṭaṭ. Earlier in the twelfth century, two of the three judges functioning in the Cairo community came from Palestine, the other from Andalusia. Alexandria's Jewish judge at that time stemmed from Morocco.[48]

The mobility of Mediterranean Jews was not seriously impeded by fears of the local communities that new arrivals, through their competition, might undermine the livelihood of the established residents or, if impecunious, would become a burden on the communal charities. In some cases communal leadership welcomed newcomers as future taxpayers. Because of that ambivalence the Mid-Eastern communities seem not to have adopted the protectionist system of a *ḥerem ha-yishub* along European models. On the other hand, it appears that quite a few of these new arrivals, uprooted from their homelands, adopted Islam.[49]

Apart from the economic difficulties generated by the relative stagnation of the Mameluke civilization, Jewish immigrants from some Christian countries occasionally faced special legal prohibitions against travel to the Muslim Middle East. We have the record of the Aragonese Treasury collecting fines from various Jews who had defied that prohibition in 1341–44. In 1428, Venice ordained that no Venetian vessel should transport any Jew to the Middle East, thereby renewing an older prohibition which had gone into oblivion. Jewish travelers had to use other ships (Da Volterra traveled on a Genoese vessel) to reach their destination. More permanently, the flow of Jewish migrants and visitors was hindered by the spread of piracy, which, beyond the natural hazards of storms, made all sea travel extremely dangerous. At the same time, in the Middle East there were no mass expulsions of Jews, like those which were occurring in one European country and city after another. Occasionally we hear of proposals, and even hesitant enactments, aimed at forcing the Jews out of Cairo or Damascus, but they seem never to have been implemented. This is doubly remarkable, for we do know of actual expulsions of

Persians and Indians from Cairo in 1418 and 1436, respectively. Evidently, the toleration of Jews dating back to the early period of Islam had been accepted as a permanent religious accommodation, and it was adhered to even by some unfriendly Mameluke rulers.[50]

LEGAL STATUS

Despite the abundance of modern debates on various legal aspects of Jewish life under Islam and the considerable number of enactments issued by Mameluke rulers and provincial governors, our knowledge of the actual legislation and its implementation in practice is rather limited. To begin with, the governmental archives of the period probably never were in a satisfactory state and their preservation through the ages has been extremely haphazard. Modern scholars have often been stymied in their quest for originals of decrees attributed to certain sultans. Early in this century Richard J. H. Gottheil complained of that inability especially in regard to Egypt, although he was able to publish certain documents which he located in the Karaite communal archives of Cairo. A much larger collection of decrees, judgments, and other legal materials was assembled in the famous St. Catherine Monastery in Sinai. But documents preserved exclusively by recipients, rather than the issuing authorities, leave many questions open. Apart from the likelihood that recipients might keep in their collections favorable records, but set aside unfavorable ones, many of those extant today consist of secondary or tertiary copies prepared generations after the original enactments. Such copies were, of course, open to interpolations or deletions, and even to outright forgeries. We are familiar with such procedures all over medieval Europe, and there is no reason for assuming that Mid-Eastern copyists were more faithful to their originals, particularly if they wrote under orders from interested parties. Hence, we have to rely largely on the historians of the period, who habitually quoted verbatim many excerpts from contemporary enactments. However, the reliability varied from one writer to another and also depended on how much time had passed from the enactment to its reproduction by the chronicler. Nevertheless, because of the availability of a large body of historical literature, often multi-volumed, modern historians have been able to reconstruct much of the legal history of the Mameluke Empire with greater success than in many other countries.[51]

An even more staggering difficulty consists in the very nature of Muslim jurisprudence. From the beginning Islam, like Judaism and many Eastern Churches, heavily relied on oral traditions, which were first selectively incorporated in the *Ḥadith*. Largely consisting of sayings attributed to Mohammed, these traditions proliferated in the first three centuries of Islam in an unprecedented fashion. We recall that Aḥmad ibn Ḥanbal (d. 855) was already able to compile some 30,000 traditions ascribed to 700 of Mohammed's "companions," which he reproduced in a manuscript of 2,885 closely written pages. Al-Bukhari (d. 870) left behind an even more famous compilation of some 7,500 traditions, reputedly selected from a total of 6,000,000 which he had at his disposal. The progress of Muslim jurisprudence in subsequent generations vastly increased the literature available to every judge and lawyer in Cairo, Damascus, or Aleppo. Moreover, as observed by the widely traveled Ibn al-'Arabi (1165–1240): "The acceptance of one opinion as prevailing over another, does not entail the total exclusion of the latter. On the contrary, one ought to preserve it on account of its dignity." Joseph Schacht, a leading expert in Islamic law, had listed many such contradictory opinions and quoted an old adage that there "exists a blessing in the divergence among the *imams*." These divergences enabled later jurists to make their own choices out of some personal bias, or in order to meet changing contingencies. Like the Jewish judges, who faced somewhat similar, if less numerous, choices, many Muslim jurists felt more immune to pietist criticism if they selected stricter alternatives. They and their Jewish confreres were also aided by the assumption that maxims adopted by scholars of an earlier age were to be treated with greater reverence than decisions rendered by courts or juridical authors in more recent times.[52]

Unlike Jewish jurisprudence, however, Arab juridical lore was confronted by the frequent ambiguity of basic terminology. Two scholars recently assembled four hundred heteronyms in the juridical field alone. For example, the term *'abbana* could mean blame or praise of a deceased person; *mawla* could denote both a slave and his master. Somewhat less equivocal is the important term *jahbadh.* Of Persian origin, this word may refer to a moneychanger, a moneylender, or a tax collector. Even *dhimma,* so frequently used in connection with the *ahl ad-dhimma* ("the protected people" or, more literally, "the people of the Covenant"), juridically may mean either the legal capacity of a person or the debtor's obligation. Principally because of such ambiguities As-Suyuti (1445–1505) claimed that two-thirds of all juridical cases had been subjected to reasonings based on doubt. More fundamentally, both Muslim law and theology often include paradoxes even in such fundamentals as whether God occasionally approved of evil deeds. The orthodox Sunnites insisted upon God's omnipotence (and omniscience) and hence assumed that even sinful actions must be performed with God's approval. In contrast, the Mu'tazila school argued that God's omnipotence is limited by His self-imposed sense of justice and that, hence, He cannot possibly condone evil. One is reminded in this connection of the somewhat related rabbinic doctrine of a *miṣvah ha-ba'ah ba-'averah* (fulfillment of a commandment through a sinful act) utilized by mystics, like Abraham Cardozo of the Shabbetian variety, to justify serious violations of the Jewish law and faith. Notwithstanding these major difficulties in interpreting detailed decisions, particularly on certain aspects of civil law, the regulations concerning the "protected subjects" seem on the whole to be fairly unequivocal. At least in their basic principles, they were accepted by a general consensus, *ijma',* which in itself plays a decisive role in Muslim law. However, manifold details were often subject to diverse interpretations not only stemming from the varying approaches adopted by the four schools of jurisprudence but also from differing opinions of individual spokesmen. Such differences of opinion came to the fore especially at the assemblies of jurists and theologians often convoked by the Mameluke rulers to deal with the *dhimmi* question.[53]

On the whole, it appears that in more peaceful times the protection extended to Jewish life, limb, and property was reasonably adequate. The wergeld (*diya*) for the slaying of an unbeliever was set on a par for *dhimmis* and Muslims only by Abu Ḥanifa and his followers, whereas the other three schools of jurisprudence tried to reduce it to one-half for Jews and Christians, and to one-fifteenth for the Parsees. Moreover, arbitrary acts with respect to property and violent treatment of individuals were not uncommon. Although some Muslim apologists extolled the judicial administration of Muslim courts, miscarriage of justice was not infrequent. Ibn Taimiya's claim that some Christians preferred to apply to Muslim courts rather than their own was purely ideological; it was based on the assumption that, because the New Testament emphasizes forgiveness and goodness, Christian judges were less prone than their Muslim counterparts to protect the property rights of coreligionists. There also was the proven remedy, frequently practiced, especially by minorities, throughout the Middle East, of combating a judge's prejudice by douceurs. In extreme cases we often hear that due punishment was inflicted even upon high dignitaries for crimes committed against the "protected subjects." An incident of 1271, described by the chroniclers Ibn al-Furat and An-Nuwairi, illustrates the occasional redress in such cases by higher authority. When Sheikh Ḥidr ibn Abi Bak attacked the largest synagogue in Damascus and celebrated this brutal act with an exuberant festival led by female singers, he was haled before the government. Simultaneously accused of illegal entry into the Holy Sepulchre in Jerusalem and killing a priest there, he was kept in prison until his death nine years later. However, such occurrences were rarely recorded. Certainly, the slaughter of Jews or Christians by a Muslim mob aroused by rumors that fires were laid by *dhimmi* arsonists, or that they sided with the enemy in wartime, usually went unpunished. Yet, compared with the contemporary massacres in Christian Europe, anti-Jewish riots were both less frequent and less bloody. As a rule they were limited to certain localities and did not assume the epidemic proportions of the assaults by Crusaders or by the frenzied European mobs of 1348–49 or 1391.[54]

Nonetheless, Jews had no particular reason to be appreciative of their government. Many doubtless shared the antigovernment prejudices of enlightened Arabs who, although not necessarily concurring with the Western Christians' scholastic view of the state as born from sin, considered government offices very unattractive. Army service, once a proud privilege of the Arab conquerors, was now in the hands of foreign "barbarians," for the most part imported slaves. Even administrative offices were so permeated with venality and unreasoning submissiveness to superiors that the observation of these conditions in Morocco and Egypt led Ibn Khaldun to the bitter conclusions that "a country conquered by the Arabs is speedily ruined," and that "of all the peoples the Arabs are the most incapable to govern." No wonder that

> religious people shunned government service and regarded government in general as the very substance of the forces which opposed God's rule on earth. A pious man would not accept an invitation to dine from a government official. The food offered there could not be regarded as *halal* (religiously permissible), in the moral sense of the word, since most of government's revenue was thought to emanate from extortions, law-breaking, and oppression of the weak.

This observation of Shelomo Dov Goitein, a leading expert on medieval Islam, applied with even greater force to devout Jews. They must have remembered the old aggadic saying that "no one is named leader of the community unless he carries a bag of impure reptiles on his back," that is, he is prepared to cast aside all ethical compunctions. It was in this vein that Maimonides advised his coreligionists to avoid living in a locality with reprehensible morals and evil rulers. He added:

> If all the cities a man knows, or has heard of, follow a bad course as in our day, or if he is prevented through the insecurity of the roads, or through illness, from emigrating to a city where good customs prevail, he ought to live a lonely life. . . . But if evildoers and sinners made it impossible for him to stay in the city without mixing with them and adopting their wicked customs, he ought to withdraw into a cave, an abandoned field, or a desert.

Should such escapism be impossible, the Jew was to submit to the powers that were and follow the old rabbinic adage that the law of the kingdom is law. Evidently Mid-Eastern Jewry, long under the heel of tyrannical regimes, was more than usually submissive.[55]

Moreover Jews not only were irked by being forced to submit to foreign domination but also particularly resented Muslim rule since they recognized the Arabs' claim of being descendants of Ishmael, Abraham's son from a slave girl. The dispute over the superiority of Ishmael as Abraham's elder son or Isaac, his younger son from a lawful wife, played a considerable role in the religious polemics between the two faiths at the time. In fact, like Christian leaders, some spokesmen of Islam pointed up the Jews' political inferiority, loss of sovereignty, and submission to foreign rule as signs of the wrath divine over the recalcitrant Jewish people. Lower officials deputized by the rulers were doubly suspect. No less a thinker than Niẓam al-Mulk, himself a vizier of a Persian Seljuk sultan, warned monarchs not to put any trust in their servants but rather place spies in their offices and hold public hearings so that all people could freely voice their grievances. Needless to say, these were minority opinions as far as one's personal conduct was concerned. Few Jews or Christians refused employment in high offices when it was offered or when they could achieve it through talent, hard work, or effective intrigue. Yet, they sometimes had to defend themselves before their brethren's public opinion. One of them, we recall, argued that he was serving in public office not to "require assistance from Jews" but in order to accumulate enough wealth to be enabled "to bestow upon Israel some of the bounty given me by the Lord." They also might have argued, with some degree of plausibility, that their presence at court and influence on the ruling circles could effectively stave off some threatening anti-Jewish legislation or administrative measures.[56]

As in previous periods, however, the favorable impression made by the good offices rendered by high Jewish officials was counterbalanced by the anger their presence aroused among the Muslim subjects. We recall the situation in Faṭimid Egypt and the Arab poet's satirical exclamation that "the very sky has become Jewish." The high offices held by Jews or Christians constituted an ever-recurrent grievance voiced not only by potential competitors but also by the Muslim masses at large. To be sure, like their Faṭimid predecessors the Mameluke rulers often found that certain individuals from the "unbelieving" communities were far more talented and well trained for the services needed than were their own coreligionists. Because the rulers professed Sunni Islam, they could expect more loyalty from their Muslim officials, but these, too, were essentially foreigners who, through a stroke of good fortune, had found their way from lowly serfdom to the throne. For this reason the Baḥri Mamelukes were often forced to employ *dhimmis* unless they were compelled by public opinion, incited by theologians and jurists, to dismiss their "infidel" councilors. Muslim controversialists furnished a variety of arguments why *dhimmi* officials should be discharged. Gazi ibn al-Wasiti, for example, emphasized their general unreliability, since Christians were likely to conspire with European powers against their own country, while Jews, who unscrupulously extorted money from Muslims by their usury and shady commercial dealings, could not be expected to be more honest in public office. In contrast, he asserted, Muslim officials excelled through four attributes: modesty toward women; love for justice; mercy toward coreligionists; and giving honest advice to fellow Muslims. The sultans often found that calling together assemblies of learned Muslim spokesmen and having them pass resolutions requiring the dismissal of "unbelieving" administrators, sufficed, for a time, to pacify an aroused citizenry. After partially implementing such resolutions, however, some rulers became dissatisfied with their new Muslim appointees and restored their *dhimmi* advisers. To be sure, only few Jews attained the eminence of some outstanding predecessors. Certainly, there was no Ibn Killis, Samuel ha-Nagid, or a family like the sons of Neṭira among them. But in the second and third echelons of officials, Jews seem to have played a significant part, although it was in the nature of contemporary Arab historiography (from which most of our information is derived) not to discuss such lower officials in the largely biographical treatments of the dignitaries. It appears that after 1382, under the Burji Mamelukes, the question was less heatedly debated, whether because by that time more qualified Muslim officials were available, or because government service had lost much of its glamour. Yet, the issue was never allowed to lie completely dormant, and the existing sources reflect almost constant ups and downs in this area. A decade of relative silence, like that between 1453 and 1463, was rather exceptional. In short, as in the earlier periods, the Jewish communities paid a relatively high price for the elevation of some of their members to high administrative offices.[57]

Evidently, other factors were also at play to cause the dismissal of public officials. We recall that even powerful emirs were uncertain of their tenure; many were dismissed at the pleasure of the sultan, some with dire consequences to themselves. In the case of *dhimmis*, sultans or governors had the additional incentives of (1) pressure of public opinion; (2) the quest to bring about the conversion to Islam of some influential advisers wishing to retain their positions, although some extremist Muslim jurists tried to shut out converts, too, from public service; (3) the use of discharges as a simple device to squeeze out of the threatened officials, or of the community trying to protect them, some additional fiscal payments. A drastic illustration of that procedure was offered by Sultan Mu'ayyad. In 1412, he called the leaders of Egyptian Jews and Copts to a hearing in the presence of several qadhis, theologians, and emirs. After listening to polemical addresses by Muslim jurists, he imposed upon the two communities an additional tax which yielded 10,000 dinars in 1412, and 11,400 in 1413. Not yet satisfied, he demanded further payments of an annual total of 20,000 dinars, arbitrarily dividing this amount by allotting 2,000 dinars to the diminishing number of Jews and 18,000 to the Coptic group. These pressures continued in the following years.[58]

High office did not include military command, however; that was reserved, as a rule, to Mamelukes. Even ordinary Muslims were not admitted to this elite corps of soldiers, though they did serve in various auxiliary detachments, particularly recruited from allied tribesmen. We do not have any information about what had happened to such a warlike Jewish population as that of Palmyra which, in the days of Benjamin of Tudela, embraced some 2,000 Jews (or Jewish families). According to the famed traveler, these Jews "are valiant in war and fight with the Christians and with the Arabs, which latter are under the dominion of Nur ad-Din the King, and they help their neighbors, the Ishmaelites." Perhaps they did not survive the Mongolian "deluge." In any case, the legal exclusion of Jews and Christians from military service had already been quoted by the eleventh-century Ḥanafite jurist, Muḥammad b. Aḥmad al-Sarakhsi, as one of the three justifications —next to chastisement for their "infidelity," and opening the opportunity for them to learn something about the beauties of Islam and thus become ripe for conversion—for their toleration and their capitation tax. Nor was Al-Sarakhsi the only Muslim scholar whose conscience was troubled by the nexus between the tax and the principle of toleration. In historic reality, too, we hear rarely of Jews or Christians being called upon to participate actively in local defense. Such an incident is recorded in Muḥammad Ibn Ṣaṣra's *Chronicle of Damascus* during the long-lasting civil war between Mintash, a former slave who had been acquired by Barquq for 3,000 dinars and then freed, and Barquq himself, who had risen from slavery to the throne as the first Burji sultan. During the battle for Damascus in June 1391, we are told, the local qadhis advised Yalbuga an-Naṣiri, the commander of the sultan's forces, to issue a call to arms to the entire population of the city and its environs, so that "neither great nor small should remain behind, but should go forth to risk his life for the victory of Sultan al-Malik al-Zahir Barqūq." Resisters were threatened with forfeiture of life and property.

> Even the Christians and Jews went out and were compelled to fight. They assembled, each sect by sect, each market by market, each quarter by quarter, with bow and arrow, supplies and weapons—everyone who had any strength, according to his ability; and many people gathered outside the city.

However, such emergency measures merely confirmed the old Islamic practice of enlisting only Muslims (including the recently acquired and deeply indoctrinated Mamelukes) in the Empire's regular armed forces.[59]

A special category of high officials, the court physicians, required exceptional handling. In the early centuries of Islam, as we recall, the Jews had not played a very significant role in medical science or practice and, in the ninth century, Al-Jaḥiẓ could generalize that Jews were incapable of abstract thinking. In contrast, from the tenth century on, with their growing integration into the Islamic Renaissance society, the Jewish communities included a considerable number of distinguished physicians. A medical career often became the chosen route to both wealth and political influence. According to S. D. Goitein, "almost every distinguished doctor served in the entourage of a caliph, a sultan, a vizier, a general, or a governor. He shared the glory of the great of his world without being involved in their crimes and their hateful ways of oppression." As mentioned above, Saladin's family, despite its profession of strict orthodoxy, used the daily medical visits by Moses Maimonides to good advantage. A characteristic letter found in the Cairo Genizah clearly illustrates how even the admission to the medical profession in Egypt, at least in Faṭimid days, to a large extent had depended on the good will of such Jewish (or Christian) court physicians and their subordinates. An applicant, seeking an appointment to a hospital in his native Alexandria, was counseled by his cousin:

I advise you to obtain letters of recommendation to the wālī (chief of police), to the qadhi, to "the Successful" [most probably the famous Ibn Jumay'], to Ben Tammām and Ben Ṣadaqa [two well-known physicians, the first Jewish, the second a Samaritan]. This would not be bad, for Ben Tammām is today the superintendent. . . . Do not worry about anything except that certificate. If you get it, you have everything you need.

On occasion, a highly placed Jewish physician was actually able to choose his patients, especially if they lived in a distant locality. An eminent Jewish doctor of Tripoli, Libya, is said to have been invited to the court of the ailing sultan of Gabès with the promise of an honorarium of 1,000 dinars (until the recent dollar devaluations, the equivalent of $4,000 in gold, but worth very much more in purchasing power). The doctor was reluctant to accept the call and even tried to bribe his way out by offering 50 dinars to the local Bedouin chieftains if he was left alone. However, the Bedouins insisted and even imprisoned the local Jewish leaders until the physician promised to depart.[60]

Frequently the medical profession was pursued by members of the same family, such as that of Maimonides, for several generations. The attacks of Muslim theologians against entrenched *dhimmi* court physicians, which grew more intense during the Mameluke age, often proved unavailing. However, with the increasing religious reaction in the fourteenth and fifteenth centuries, we frequently hear of the dismissal of Jewish court physicians. The argument that "unbelieving" doctors would badly serve their Muslim patients, perhaps even poison them, was reinforced by the imputation that a physician might use his great influence on an ailing patient for religiously disturbing his soul. (The reciprocal segregationist drive among Jews had caused the ancient rabbis to advise Jewish doctors not to minister to heathen patients, an advice expressed as a prohibition by Maimonides himself in his legal code. This theoretical prohibition was clearly not applied to monotheistic Muslim or Christian patients, as was evidenced by the fact that the sage of Fusṭaṭ himself made his living from curing high-placed Muslims.) Perhaps, by a curious inversion, this prohibition echoing an old rabbinic ruling gave rise to the malicious rumor that Maimonides held his Jewish fellow physicians in very low esteem. Ultimately, the anti-*dhimmi* propaganda proved successful and in 1476(?) a formal decree forbade Jewish doctors to treat Muslim patients. At that time there were a sufficient number of Muslim practitioners available in most Syro-Egyptian areas to make the prohibition fairly effective. However, there is little documentation available which would prove the decline of Jewish medical practice; if it occurred at all, it was brought about more by the general economic and cultural stagnation of the late medieval Mid-Eastern society, including its Jewish community, than by the growing deterioration in interfaith relations.[61]

Most important was the continued Mameluke acceptance of the principle of religious toleration of Jews and Christians. In reality, too, Jewish religious practices were, on the whole, little interfered with by the powers that were. True, from the outset, Muslim rulers had insisted that all Jewish ceremonies be performed without offense to Muslim believers. For example, the blowing of the *shofar* (horn) at synagogue services was not to disturb neighboring Muslims, just as Christians were not to display their crosses in public or to ring their church bells. But complete adherence to Jewish rituals was greatly facilitated by the long-established custom that members of different denominational, ethnic, or professional groups voluntarily settled in their own quarters. At times Jews lived in suburbs for local historical reasons. Long after the foundation of Cairo in 982, for example, the majority of Jews continued to inhabit neighboring Fusṭaṭ. It was only toward the end of the medieval period that the focus of the Jewish community moved to the capital itself. Islamization of "Old Miṣr" continued in modern times, until in 1947 Fusṭaṭ embraced a Muslim majority of 92 percent and in 1960, after the Arab-Israeli war of 1956, one of 94 percent. Nonetheless, Jewish scribes, as we recall, continued to describe Cairo as "located near Fusṭaṭ." In San'a, the capital of Yemen, such separation originated in an expulsion of the Jews from the capital. Upon their return soon thereafter, they found their synagogue replaced by a mosque and their houses occupied by Muslims, including some of great local influence, who refused to restore that property to the original owners. Most Jewish returnees settled, therefore, in a neighboring suburb. Such segregation, without carrying the later stigma of a European ghetto, contributed greatly to the Jews' communal autonomy and enhanced the effectiveness of their synagogues, schools, and social welfare institutions.[62]

The existence in many cities of separate sectarian and ethnic quarters in no way curtailed the freedom of movement of the non-Muslim inhabitants. Fusṭaṭ Jews could move into Cairo without any interference. It was only their own preference and general inertia that made the majority stay on in Fusṭaṭ for generations. While, for example, Maimonides continued living in Fusṭaṭ and endured the arduous daily journey to the royal court in Cairo, his contemporary Mevorakh spent most of his time in Cairo and occupied his house in Fusṭaṭ only during the Jewish holidays. By 1400, however, the majority of Jews had moved to Cairo, though their old synagogues and other religious institutions continued to function in Fusṭaṭ. Nor was the character of the Jewish quarters entirely pure. We have records of five houses jointly owned by Jewish and Christian partners and three other houses in the joint possession of Jews and Muslims. Absence of strict segregation in dwellings is also reflected in a remarkable story retold by the fourteenth-century chronicler Ibn Ṣaṣra, about the early Caliph 'Abd al-Malik (705–715), who had a very close friend living in the Jewish quarter. Explaining to the caliph why he had failed to pay his usual visit to the court on the preceding day, this friend reported that, through his window facing the synagogue, he had overheard the Jewish preacher declaring at length why after death Jews and Christians were being admitted to Paradise, whereas the much larger multitude of Muslims had to stay out "in the sun." The caliph, though amused by the report (perhaps with reference to Qur'an 2:105), is said to have summoned the preacher and obliged him to supply tents for the Muslim crowds waiting in the sun. This punishment was converted into an annual fine of 5,000 dinars, a tribute soon discontinued by 'Umar II (717–20).[63]

In the purely religious sphere, however, the segregation was intended to be rather strict. Jews and Christians were not supposed to enter mosques, while Muslim visits to synagogues and churches were discouraged by the religious leaders of all three faiths. At the same time, conversions of Christians to Judaism and vice versa were considered a sufficient ground for withdrawal of the *dhimmi* "protection" from the individual renegades. Moreover, the state tried to safeguard the orthodoxy of the minority faiths as well. According to Ibn Taimiya,

> One may find among the *dhimmi* people a heretic who in his inner conviction denies the Creator, the Prophets, the revealed Scripture, divine laws, and the Hereafter, but who, externally, makes it appear that he professes the faith of the "people of the Book." Such a person ought to be killed without any doubt, just as one ought to put to death a "protected subject" who apostasizes from his faith in order to adhere to the doctrine of the negation of divine attributes.

The final sentence expressed the writer's private opinion, but it shows the extent to which a leading theologian could postulate the denial of protection to a member of the minority faiths for deviating from his or her own normative religion. It also places into sharper relief the background of the anti-Maimonidean controversy, which, as we shall see in a later volume, was largely based upon Maimonides' repudiation of the corporeality of God and, to some extent, also on his doctrine of negative attributes.[64]

Only on extraordinary occasions did the ruling classes allow ceremonies to be conducted jointly by the leaders of the three faiths. During the great emergency created by the Black Death, for example, the horror-stricken population gladly listened to prayers jointly recited by Muslims, Jews, and Christians to appease the divine wrath. Similarly, on the arrival of a new sovereign in the capital, bishops and rabbis with their respective lay elders were permitted to join the dignitaries of the Mosque in extending a festive welcome to their new ruler. On such occasions Jews appeared with their scrolls of law and recited their Hebrew benedictions.[65]

SOCIOCULTURAL VARIATIONS

This well-established *modus vivendi* between the three monotheistic faiths under Islam did not meet with complete approval from the more zealous spokesmen of the dominant religion. Their attacks on the fundamentals, as well as specific provisions, of the Jewish and Christian traditions multiplied under the intolerant climate of Mameluke rule. It was in the Mameluke period that much of the Arabic polemical literature was written, some of it by leading theologians of the day. Following the examples set by such distinguished Muslim apologists as Al-Jaḥiẓ (d. 869) and Ibn Ḥazm (d. 1064), writers like Aḥmad al-Qarafi (d. 1285), Ibn Taimiya (d. 1328), and Ibn an-Naqqash (d. 1361) attacked with particular vigor the Jews' supposed falsification of the Old Testament texts and insisted that Mohammed had already been predicted in the Hebrew Scripture. They defended the Qur'an against attacks by unbelievers who pointed out its inconsistencies and particularly its frequent inaccuracies in quotations from the Bible. They could not attack Judaism, as they did Christianity, for its trinitarian doctrine and image worship, but instead aimed their shafts at the corporeality attributed to God in the Hebrew Scripture. They also echoed the biblical reproach of Jewish stiffneckedness. At the same time, they strained their ingenuity in defending the extensive materialistic rewards in the Hereafter promised by the Qur'an for good behavior in one's lifetime.[66]

In addition many accusations against the Jews and Christians were of a sociopolitical nature. These often culminated in the assertion, also widespread in the Christian world, that the Jews' loss of national independence was a clear sign of God's wrath against His formerly chosen people because of its stubbornness and sinfulness. Yet these controversies were far overshadowed in the eyes of both authors and readers by those relating to dogmatic and theological fundamentals, which will be reviewed in a later volume. They did not materially differ from those analyzed in our earlier volumes, however.

Because of the deep concern of Muslim controversialists with the authenticity and meaning of numerous biblical passages, ordinary Muslims were discouraged from studying the Old and New Testaments. The excuse usually given was, in the form circulated in the Muslim world, that they were partially falsified by Jewish and Christian scribes. They were also allegedly superseded by the Qur'an. This did not hinder some Arab students from making considerable use of homiletical and hermeneutic elements in aggadic and patristic literatures, probably largely transmitted to them by some Jewish or Christian friends, particularly converts. For example, they quoted the passage, "In the same way you would like people to treat you, you treat them," but they attributed to Moses the famous saying of Hillel emphasizing the negative "golden mean," rather than the positive biblical commandment of loving one's neighbor like oneself. This type of material, consisting mainly of stories, carried the special designation of *Israiliyyat.* The study of Jewish and Christian traditions relating to tenets and observances also was forbidden, because they supposedly had been abrogated after the rise of Islam.[67]

Some Muslim apologists were particularly proud of what they considered their own golden mean between Christian and Jewish extremes. For example, Al-Qarafi pointed out that biblical unrestricted polygamy was one-sided in favoring the man, while Christian monogamy favored the woman, a condition which was particularly irksome if one had an unsuitable wife. In contrast, Islam by allowing marriage to four wives adopted the plausible middle road. Nowhere did the Muslim polemists take cognizance, however, of the widely prevalent contemporary Jewish practice for a husband to write into the marriage contract that he would not marry another woman in his bride's lifetime, at least not without her consent. Similarly, they contended, in its cultic regulations Islam held the middle ground between Jewish rigidity and Christian laxity. The Islamic veneration for Mohammed also was, in their opinion, a reasonable compromise between the deification of Christ and the hostility of the ancient Israelites toward their prophets, whom they sometimes killed. With a characteristic argumentation Al-Qarafi pointed out that Christians were most bellicose and murderous while professing a religion of brotherly love and forgiveness even to enemies. As an example he cited the practice in Barcelona, Florence, and Marseilles, which set aside three days every year during which severe persecutions of Jews, including bloodshed, were permitted. At the same time he glorified the hero cult in Islam and the exaltation of soldiers who fell in battle for Islam's quest to extend its reign over the whole world. These examples can easily be multiplied.[68]

Curiously, it was in the very midst of that cacophony of apologetics for, and mutual polemics among, the three faiths that a moderating appeal was sounded in 1284 by the Jewish thinker Sa'id ibn Manṣur Ibn Kammuna. We recall his blunt assertion that he had not seen anybody "who would adopt Islam without being impelled to it by fear, the striving for a respected social position, the threat of a high tax or imprisonment, the love for a Muslim woman, or some other motives like those." Needless to say, such voices were not heeded by the Muslim intelligentsia (with a few notable exceptions) and ultimately Ibn Kammuna himself paid dearly for his outspokenness. In that era of holy wars, the aging philosopher's public utterance of such tolerant sentiments was sufficient reason for the Baghdad mob to stage a riot which was stemmed only by the police chief's promise that the "culprit" would be burned on the following morning. Doubtless with the chief's connivance, Ibn Kammuna was smuggled out in a chest during the night to Hilla. He soon died there, probably as a result of that harrowing experience.[69]

Polemics such as Al-Qarafi's were intended mainly to strengthen the faith of professing Muslims, but they also were often used to missionize among "unbelievers." Through the ages Islam has proved its mettle as a first-rate missionizing religion. Even in modern times its proselytizing efforts, without support from organized missionary societies, often proved more successful in Asia and Africa than the Western missions. Its spokesmen in the Late Middle Ages were no less bent upon expanding their faith than had been their predecessors in the classical period. True, forced conversion, especially of individuals, was forbidden by law, but indirect pressures were often applied. Certainly, the numerous courtiers and officials facing dismissal after an outbreak of intolerance were often given the choice of adopting Islam and keeping their posts. Jews and Christians, accused of committing serious crimes, usually could secure total amnesty by lip-service to the dominant faith. Mass conversions, too, were sometimes practiced, particularly by such sectarian movements as those of the Almohades in North Africa and Spain or the Shi'ite Persians in Meshed.

Forced converts were often unreliable, however. An interesting poem by Moses b. Samuel, a Jewish *katib* (secretary) in Damascus around 1290, describes how he had been induced to adopt Islam by Qala'un's prohibition against employing *dhimmi*s in public office. Subsequently, he was even forced by his employer to join him on the pilgrimage to Mecca, where as a Jew he certainly could not have set foot. But later he repented and returned to Judaism. This poem has the characteristic title: "I Moses b. R. Samuel Who Returned With Full Repentance by One Who Chose the Law of Moses and Israel." The Muslim leaders were doubtless cognizant of the presence of numerous such insincere converts. We hear of occasional trials, and even executions, of Muslim mystics and other dissenters as well as of *dhimmi*s accused of "blasphemy" against Mohammed and the like. In 1351 a group of Jews was seized for allegedly chanting anti-Muslim prayers, and most of them saved their lives by adopting Islam. But there were no regular inquisitorial tribunals established for the prosecution of heretics, similar to those existing in the West. Even under the extreme Almohade intolerance, the semi-inquisitorial investigations of religious nonconformity were rather superficial and ineffective. That is why the Almohades continued to insist that even converts bear distinguishing marks. Without resorting to this radical measure, in the Mameluke Empire some rulers treated converts with much suspicion.[70]

Nonetheless, the fostering of a Jew's voluntary conversion to Islam was considered a meritorious act, though his conversion to Christianity—or a Christian's conversion to Judaism—was forbidden by Muslim law. Quite different was the response to conversion from one sect to another within the same faith, which was permitted ever since Al-Ma'mun's decree of 825 C.E. On one occasion (in 1465), the Muslim authorities would not allow the Rabbanite elders in Cairo to prevent a recent arrival from Toledo (probably a relapsed *converso*) from joining the Karaite community. The representatives of the four schools of Muslim jurisprudence agreed that (to quote the opinion rendered by the

Shafi'ite qadhi) "there can be no objection raised either way because the Jews form one community as regards the principles of faith." (Despite occasional outbreaks of mutual intolerance, these four schools generally recognized one another's right to adhere to its own tradition; their representatives often acted in unison when summoned by the rulers to express an opinion on a controversial legal issue.) Moreover, after every major riot or sweeping anti-*dhimmi* decree there remained a residuum of Jews and Christians who saved their lives by accepting conversion. A characteristic description of such effects is preserved in the seventeenth-century Hebrew chronicle by Joseph Sambari. Referring to outbreaks connected with the renewal of the Covenant of 'Umar in 1301, the chronicler writes:

> The people assaulted Jews and Christians and the law was issued in Cairo to attack Christians and Jews with Ishmael's sword [*be-ḥereb Yishmael*]. . . . They looted through the city, took all of their [the *dhimmis*'] possessions. Because of the great suffering and oppression, thousands and tens of thousands of Jews and Christians apostasized; especially in the city of Bulbais, adults and minors. Until today [seventeenth century] one can see an inscription written in square Hebrew characters in one of the mosques and it is said that it had been a synagogue.

These conversions, whether by individuals or en masse, greatly contributed to the decline of the Jewish population in the Mameluke Empire. However, the core of the Jewish communities valiantly carried on and survived to see better days under the Ottoman regime.[71]

Remarkably, in Islamic as well as Christian countries an inheritance left by the parent of a Jewish convert to their faith was treated legally as still belonging to his Jewish heirs or to the Jewish community at large. We recall that voices opposing this rule had been heard in the Christian world since ancient times. But under Islam even Ibn Taimiya merely tried to draw a distinction between property the deceased convert personally had held before his conversion—which, the theologian conceded, should remain in Jewish hands—and that acquired by him as a Muslim, which should go to his Muslim heirs. Behind all these theories loomed the legal fiction, taken over by both Christianity and Islam from

Judaism, that the act of conversion to their respective faiths was equivalent to the convert's total rebirth and that he was to be treated, therefore, as a propertyless, newly born child. This principle was but occasionally compromised by leaders who realized that its application to inheritances in civil law might seriously impede their conversionist efforts.[72]

Other provisions of the Covenant of 'Umar were in some respects more difficult for the government to enforce because of the great variety of detail appearing in the different versions of that fundamental law. Clearly, many texts included varying accretions taken from enactments by later caliphs or sultans, or from interpretations by leading jurists. Sultan Al-Malik aṣ-Ṣaliḥ, Qala'un's grandson, whose decree of 1354 was largely reproduced by Al-Qalqashandi, climaxed his anti-*dhimmi* legislation by purportedly quoting a text attributed to 'Umar Ibn al-Khaṭṭab. Yet, in conclusion he wrote: "all these statements are based upon the rulings adopted by experts in the exalted law." Moreover, individual teachers sometimes went to extremes in explaining the discretion left to the ruler in enforcing the Covenant's provisions. According to a more extreme interpreter, Ibn Taimiya, the compact made with the "protected subjects" was to serve only so long as it was useful to the Muslim peoples. The moment a country no longer needed to tolerate "infidels," its *imam* could readily abrogate the entire agreement. Similarly, an individual *dhimmi* who violated certain fundamental laws automatically lost the protection extended to him by the Covenant and became a rightless individual. But the majority opinion and the corresponding practice were far more lenient. In addition the edict of 1354 included such relatively novel provisions as "that they [the *dhimmis*] shall not harbor any spies or plot against Muslims; . . . nor shall they prevent any relatives from adopting Islam," and so forth. In fact, this text even included diverse regulations concerning *dhimmi* males and females at public baths. The men were merely ordered to wear distinguishing signs around their necks when entering the baths, whereas *dhimmi* women were supposed to have separate bathhouses set aside for them. Nonetheless, the very complexity of the various enactments and of their different origins from disparate underlying traditions or circumstances made it easier for many "protected subjects" to circumvent them in whole or in part with the aid of corrupt officials.[73]

The enforcement of the discriminatory laws could actually be turned into a source of fiscal revenue, as when the *dhimmis* voluntarily, or under pressure, offered major financial contributions to the Treasury in return for the modification of some restrictions. Since by closing technically illegal synagogues or churches, the ruler gained much approval from the Muslim public, a mere threat of closing, or granting a permit to reopen, a house of prayer caused the parties concerned to offer a substantial sum to the Treasury.

In general, like their predecessors, the Mamelukes evinced great interest in public buildings. True, none of them could afford to be a reckless spender like Caliph Mutawakkil (847–61), who built nineteen palaces and is said to have spent on them no less than 247,000,000 dirhems and 100,000,000 dinars. (Yet the same monarch did not hesitate to destroy synagogues and churches, even some which antedated Islam.) But many Mameluke rulers, too, spent more public funds on large edifices of various kinds than was prudent under the prevailing fiscal stringency. The sight of the numerous monumental structures left behind by the Crusaders in the Latin Kingdom of Jerusalem must also have served as an incentive for vast monetary outlays which could be obtained only by tightening the fiscal screws on all taxpayers, but particularly the *dhimmis*. On the other hand, the love for new buildings, intended to be showplaces illustrating the power and glory of the reigning sultan, did not extend to any appreciation and preservation of ancient monuments. Even the famous pyramids of Egypt did not completely escape the hands of vandals. An old legend, referring to the biblical story of the Egyptian pharaohs, contended that the generation before Noah, having received advance warnings about the forthcoming Deluge, hid many valuables in these imposing receptacles. That story stimulated much popular treasure hunting. The Sphinx seems to have escaped damage only because of a widespread folkloristic belief that it was the statue of a god watching over the entire district. Some Mameluke subjects in the Nile Valley, it appears, did appreciate the ancient Egyptian antecedents of their people. A debater with a Jewish convert to Islam once declared that he thought more highly of the biblical pharaoh than of Moses, to whom the "sincerely converted" Jew replied: "For me I keep Moses; you go to your pharaoh." This spokesman probably was not alone in his esteem for ancient Egyptian paganism.[74]

The issue of new buildings and those requiring major repairs, likewise complicated Jewish communal life thoughout the two and a half centuries of Mameluke rule. The old laws, dating back to the ancient Roman Empire, provided that Jews were not to build new synagogues but they might keep old synagogues in repair, under the condition that any alterations would not increase their size or make them more beautiful. The rationale for this limited permissiveness was its alleged inclusion in the original treaty between 'Umar I and the surrendering Christians of Jerusalem in 636, but its extent lent itself to a variety of interpretations. Some anti-*dhimmi* jurists argued that a similar treaty of submission had to be proved in every locality, and that particularly Jews, who had not been partners to the original compact of Jerusalem, had no claim to its application. More obviously, some of the largest cities founded after the rise of Islam, including Cairo, could not have had churches or synagogues before Mohammed, and, hence, all such structures must have been "new" at the time of their erection. In reply the more liberal jurists contended that even these new cities had been built on land originally belonging to small villages, the Christian or Jewish inhabitants of which may have had houses of worship of their own. These ambiguities were conducive to fabrication of evidence, as in the Aleppo and Fusṭaṭ inscriptions which allegedly proved the existence of synagogues there before the *hejira*. There also were a host of new arguments, pro and con, presented by the two sides. In the relatively few recorded cases when a "new" synagogue was razed to the ground on order of the authorities, this symbolic act caused general rejoicing in the Muslim community. The destruction of the Karaite synagogue in Damascus on a Jewish Sabbath (August 15, 1321) even inspired a Muslim eye-witness to compose a poem which included the following dithyrambic verses:

All sects, except the Muslims, live in humility, calamity, perdition, and ruin
Through God's judgment the Hebrew became tearful [a pun on *'ibri,* Hebrew, and *'ibar,* tear], there is no greater downfall than his.

You will see the Isaacs crushed, and to the Ezras punishment has come from Him,
Their synagogue is destroyed. Oh, they are humbled forever, there is no altering the power of God.

How seriously the authorities sometimes regarded any infringement of the Covenant's prescriptions may also be noted from an incident in Cairo in connection with some relatively minor repairs at a church, which went beyond the concession granted to its head. We are told that the Christian leader was "beaten severely and painfully, and in a state of nudity, as a reprimand to himself and to those who were like him, he was carried around the streets as a criminal, and clapped into the Dailan prison in al-Ḳahirah for some days." [75]

It is not surprising, therefore, that with respect to specific details the chief qadhis of the four schools of jurisprudence often held divergent opinions; on occasion, they presented them to the sultan at the assemblies convoked to decide the fate of a particular house of prayer. Even minor repairs were often subjected to close scrutiny. Muslim architects were sometimes sent into the Jewish quarter to measure in advance the exact dimensions of every part requiring replacement; each deviation, however small, called forth a new debate. In one case Muslim public opinion was so aroused that the Mameluke official in charge secretly removed the objectionable segment, in order to forestall an attack on the Jewish quarter. However, beyond these legalistic quibbles loomed the great historic transformation of the population since the beginnings of Islam. The conquering Muslim minority of the early period, which had been surrounded by a sea of Christians, Zoroastrians, and Jews, had by the end of the Middle Ages become the overwhelming majority of inhabitants in Egypt and Syria. Only the concentrated settlements of Copts in Egypt and Maronites in Lebanon constituted substantial reminders of the former dominant Christian populations. The Jewish communities played too insignificant a demographic role to offer a serious challenge to the Muslim majority. They were sufficiently influential, however, to become frequent objects of controversy among judges, administrative officials, and writers.[76]

At times the administration felt that it ought to enlist the cooperation of the "protected subjects" in securing compliance with the provisions of the Covenant. In 1442, on Sultan Jaqmaq's invitation, there appeared at court Yuhannis, the Jacobite patriarch; Philoteus, the chief of the Melkite Church; 'Abd al-Laṭif, Faraj Allah, and Abraham, heads of the Rabbanite Jews, the Karaites, and the Samaritans, respectively. They were met by the leading Muslim theologians and jurists. After some negotiations they were persuaded to submit a memorandum in the form of a petition, reading in part:

We ask your protection for ourselves, our posterity, our possessions, and our coreligionists. We covenant to you as regards our own persons, that we will not build in our city nor in its neighborhood any convent, church, cell, or hut for a monk, nor will we rebuild them should they fall into ruin. We will not replace that which has been demolished in the quarters where Muḥammadans live. We will not prevent any Muḥammadans from entering our places of prayer or our convents by night or by day. We will open our doors for those that pass by and for the traveler. If a Muḥammadan traveler should take refuge in them we will feed him as a guest for three nights. We will not teach our children the Koran. We will not openly vaunt our religion, nor try to convert any one to it. We will not seek to prevent any of our relatives from accepting Islām, if he should wish. We will show respect for Muḥammadans. We will rise up from our seats when one of their prominent men wishes to sit down. We will not copy them in their manner of riding and addressing—not even in their head-gear, their sandals, or in their way of parting the hair. We will not use their peculiar expressions of speech nor their surnames. We will not ride upon saddles, nor gird our swords, neither possess nor carry any weapons. We will not engrave in Arabic upon our seals. We will not further the sale of wine. We will shave the front part of our heads. Wherever we may be we will put a restraint upon ourselves. . . . Should any one of us be wronged, it is the duty of the Muḥammadans to repel such wrong and to punish the evil-doers. Should any one of us violate this pact, he shall forfeit protection and the pact; and you are permitted to treat him as enemies and rebels are treated.

In reply to this petition the government spokesman, the Shafi'ite head, Shihab ad-Din al-'Asqalani did not discuss the Covenant's detailed provisions, but stated succinctly: "I confirm you in the right to dwell in any country of Islam except the Ḥijaz, and to journey through it except holy Mecca, in accordance with these conditions, if you pay the capitulation tax according to established custom."[77]

Various other provisions of the Covenant were equally ambiguous, or else appeared in some, but not in other, versions. The field was thus left wide open for a variety of restrictive laws and court decisions to be superimposed upon, even inserted into, the basic texts. While we have no record of any imitation of Al-Ḥakim's ridiculous distinguishing marks, numerous other ordinances provided for special badges, permissible sizes and colors of headgear, and included, for example, such humiliations as forcing *dhimmi* women to wear shoes of nonmatching colors. The prohibition against Jews riding on horseback was generally upheld, although on arduous overland journeys in caravans, Jewish travelers like Meshullam da Volterra could freely use horses on a par with the other passengers; they merely had to conceal their Jewishness when facing highwaymen. At times *dhimmi*s were forbidden to mount camels or donkeys. In a few decrees they were told not to speak to a Muslim unless they were spoken to first. In general the Middle-Eastern mind laid great stress on appearances and tried to save "face" under all circumstances. The main objective of all that legislation was to express contempt for "unbelievers" and to establish the undisputed superiority of Muslims over *dhimmi*s. In consequence, many local riots started at the sight of a Christian or Jew riding on horseback, particularly if the rider was followed by a retinue of slaves or, serving as a high official, was surrounded by Muslims begging him for favors. We recall that such an incident in 1301 deeply shocked the visiting Moroccan vizier and gave rise to a major public disturbance and ultimately led to the sharp renewal of the restrictive laws. Nor must we overlook the preference of many pious Jews to be distinguished in their attire from their Gentile neighbors. Many of them doubtless remembered the injunction included in the revered Maimonidean Code, telling the Jews: "One must not follow the Gentile ways of life nor try to resemble them in clothing or hair-do. . . . A Jew ought to be differentiated from them [the Gentiles] and be recognizable as such through his attire and in other behavioral patterns, just as he is differentiated in his outlook and opinions." Maimonides had only exempted a Jew "serving in the entourage of a king who has to appear before the ruler, when his appearance at variance with that of the other courtiers would be reprehensible. Such a Jew is allowed to wear similar attire and even to shave the way the others are doing." [78]

It would lead us too far astray to try to do justice to the kaleidoscopic variety of the pertinent regulations and the even greater differences prevailing in their implementation. Suffice it to mention two aspects which greatly contributed to the differentiation between the religious minorities and the Muslim majority. A frequent source of contention between them was the sale of wines and other fermented drinks to Muslims, who were forbidden by their law to imbibe alcoholic beverages. (As in other areas of civil law, sales among the "protected subjects" were valid, if they conformed with their own laws, although Jews and Christians were often accused of selling inferior wines even to their coreligionists.) At times the authorities tried to enlist the cooperation of *dhimmi* leaders in enforcing these Muslim prohibitions. For example, in the aforementioned assembly Patriarch Yuhannis was forced to promise "that he would not give wine to Muslims either by selling it or in any other fashion whatsoever, nor would he cause a Muslim to drink it." However, since Islamic law permitted the consumption of grapes and unfermented grape juice, vineyards were often cultivated by Muslim landowners. On one occasion a Homs Muslim, who had received a vineyard through a bequest but was unable to sell the produce, was allowed by the government to convert it into wine for sale.[79]

Needless to say, given human frailty, it appears that many Muslims of the Late Middle Ages defied that prohibition and enjoyed repasts with alcoholic beverages. This practice was sufficiently frequent for R. David b. Solomon Ibn abi Zimra to warn his coreligionists that "it is best for an Israelite to keep away from a group of drinking non-Jews, for the Israelite might learn their ways and thus be drawn into transgressions of the law," and again that "it is not fitting that a Jew should drink together with a non-Jew even such liquors which are permitted to a Jew, for Israel is a holy people." It is also noteworthy that, unlike in the early period of Islam, Jews are rarely mentioned as tavern keepers in the Mameluke

Empire. We recall that the reason previously given for the rabbinic discouragement of serving drinks to non-Jews was likewise derived from the attempt at social separation, rather than from the Jewish fear of drinking "wine of libation" or from the governmental prohibition against serving alcoholic drinks to Muslims. The argument at that time was that some of the guests were in the habit of "ogling" the tavern keepers' wives, which the rabbis wished to prevent.[80]

Of great interest also is the particular form of the oath *more judaico*. While we do not have much evidence that such oaths were regularly imposed upon Jewish parties or witnesses appearing before Muslim courts (usually in litigations with Muslim parties), the few records of such formulas are sufficiently curious to be illustrated here by a lengthy quotation. The following excerpt from a rather extraordinary text seems to have been formulated by a Jewish convert to Islam who was familiar with the New Testament. It is cited here from an Arabic manuscript translated into Hebrew by L. A. Mayer:

(I swear) by God . . . who sent Moses with the true message and strengthened his arms and loins through his brother Aaron, (I swear) by the revered Torah through what it contains, by the Ten Commandments which had been given to Moses on tables of sapphire and by what was found in the Tent of Meeting. If I should not tell the truth, I should become a slave of Pharaoh and Haman and cut off from Israel; I should convert to the Christian faith, recognize the truth of the Annunciation to Mary, and justify Joseph the carpenter; I should deny the words (spoken by God to the children of Israel). If I should [have done the following:] approach Mt. Sinai in a state of impurity; call the Rock [in the Temple of Jerusalem, an assumed parallel to the Meccan Ka'ba] impure; be Nebuchadnezzar's partner in the destruction of the Temple and in the slaying of the children of Israel; stand next to the harlots on the Day of John [Judgment]; say that the flame which had consumed the burning bush was a deception; been with those who have shut the way to Midian to Moses and maligned the daughters of Jethro; consorted with the sorcerers against Moses and separated from those who believed in him; belonged to those who have incited [Pharaoh] to pursue the refugees [during the Exodus] and who advised to leave Joseph's casket behind in Egypt; greeted like a friend the Samaritan [who persuaded the Children of Israel to bow down to the Golden Calf] and settled in Jericho, the city of the giants; agreed with the deeds of the Sodomites and not observed the commandments of the Torah; declared the Sabbath to be profane and broke its commandments; pronounced the Festival of Tabernacles to be an error and Hanukkah senseless; insisted that God does not care about the commandments and that, in my opinion, it is permitted to break the laws; declared that Jesus son of Mary is the Messiah foretold by Moses son of Amram, and exchanged Judaism for another faith; considered a camel's flesh, fat, intestines, and all that is mixed in the bone, permissible nourishment; interpreted the law to mean that he who makes use of the price paid for forbidden things is not equal to one who makes use of the forbidden things themselves; agreed with what the Babylonians have said about Abraham—If I shall not tell the truth I shall be subject to the excommunication which will be imposed upon me by the group of rabbis and for the sake of which they will turn over the matting in the synagogue; that they will conduct me into the desert without manna or quails being given me; that they will separate me from all the tribes of Israel to be placed among those who, despite their good health, evaded participation in the war against the giants [of Canaan].

This long formula had little relationship to the other formulas used under Islam or, for that matter, to those current in the Byzantine and Catholic worlds. But in whatever form, such discriminatory treatment of Jews in taking oaths was particularly important, since for a long time Muslim courts relied on oral testimony much more than on documentary evidence. To be sure, just as ancient Jewish law had long before begun attributing increasing significance to documents—and hence Jews in their internal dealings, too, placed ever greater weight on evidence derived from letters, ledgers, and other writings—the attitude of Muslim jurists was gradually changing on this score. Yet, the use of oaths still played a vital role in the court procedures of both legal systems.[81]

On the whole, Jews and Christians learned to live with such offensive treatment. It appears that some European pilgrims were correct in stating that Jews were more severely mishandled by the authorities than were the Christians. However, an observer trying to penetrate beyond the hue and cry of the contemporary writers, who usually recorded exceptional occurrences rather than daily undramatic happenings, must realize that in ordinary times the various groups in the population often entertained pleasant, even amicable, personal relations. They all were much more concerned with the difficulties of earning a living and were even helping one another rather than listening to the extremist voices sowing discord among them.

Certainly, there was much interdenominational cooperation in the recurrent emergencies. Even intolerant Ibn Taimiya agreed that Jewish or Christian prisoners of war ought to be ransomed by Muslim governments and individual Muslims. He even claimed that on one such occasion, acting in his official capacity, he had personally redeemed a Jewish prisoner. On his visit to the Middle East, Obadiah di Bertinoro was amazed to observe that "among the Muslims Jews do not live in exile at all. I have traveled through the length and breadth of that whole territory, and nobody objected. They actually take pity on any stranger, particularly one who is unfamiliar with their language, and when they see a group of Jews congregating together they do not resent them at all." In another context, to be sure, the same traveler noted that, because the Muslims believed that the Jews ought to be poor, his coreligionists were generally concealing their well-being. "It is necessary for a Jew to appear under the Muslims bowed down and meek and he must humble himself and not brag about being wealthy, for they might concoct some accusation against him in order to despoil him of his money." In short, Bertinoro was not altogether wrong when he claimed that, compared with the conditions in Europe, the Middle-Eastern Jews lived a more peaceful and secure life. And we must remember that he had come from Renaissance Italy, where the Jews' legal status and daily relationships with their neighbors were far more favorable than in almost any other Christian country! [82]

SLOW DETERIORATION

Documentation for the economic conditions in the Mameluke Empire is in some respects even harder to come by than that concerning legal and political developments. Compared with the preservation of archives (including municipal, family, and business holdings) in the Western countries, the relatively meager finds extant from the late medieval Middle East leave much to be desired, although far more is available than has as yet been thoroughly investigated. Despite the herculean efforts of Adolf Grohmann and others, the papyrological evidence for the first centuries of Islam has not yet been fully utilized. Vienna alone is supposed to harbor some 28,000 such papyri, which have but partially been explored. In view of the enormous variety of occupations, individual and collective transactions, and the constantly changing conditions in different localities and periods, such scanty and disparate records are hardly sufficient for any reliable statistical computation or broader generalization—a situation especially frustrating for the quantitative school of economic historians. Epigraphic evidence is extremely limited for the older periods because of the relative paucity of surviving inscriptions. At the same time the more numerous juridical references to economic phenomena in the available legal literature suffer from the perennial dichotomy between the *Sollen* and the *Sein,* the legal theory and the economic reality. To be sure, one should not underestimate the realistic value of even abstruse juridical lucubrations. As Abraham Udovitch pointed out, a careful comparison of the practices reflected in the Genizah texts with the postulates and decisions recorded in the medieval Hebrew juridical literature has shown such a close correspondence that "we can assert that many of the latter were indeed transformed into actual economic institutions." This is doubly true in the case of responsa in which the questioners usually summarized, however briefly, some actual events, while the replies consisted of judgments rendered out of an existing practice and in response to specific social needs.[83]

Additional information can also be gathered from such auxiliary materials as coins. True, it is hard to distinguish coins put into circulation, or handled, by Jews from those used by their neighbors of other faiths. However, at least in regard to Jews working in mints, we can establish, or hypothesize, some particular connection between the producer and his ethnoreligious origin. On the whole it appears, although it cannot be fully proved from the meager extant documentary and numismatic evidence, that Jews, who had once played a considerable role in the Faṭimid mints, had little share in producing the ever-deteriorating coins of the Mameluke Empire.[84]

Nevertheless, there has been a fair consensus among scholars, medieval as well as modern, concerning the general economic decline of the Mid-Eastern countries during the last three centuries of the Middle Ages. In the most tangible monetary area, we note the considerable deterioration in the quality of the coins in circulation and the resulting financial instability which necessarily affected all business relations.

Originally the gold dinar had a theoretical value of 13½ *nuqra* (pure) silver dirhems, or, in practice, some 40 dirhems of lower quality. The growing scarcity of gold, especially after the gradual exhaustion of the Nubian mines, created an increasing disparity between the two sets of coins. In the fourteenth century the prevailing ratio of 20–25 *nuqra* dirhems to 1 dinar was maintained for the most part. But during the severe economic crisis of 1384–1404, which coincided with the rise of the new Burji dynasty, the value of gold increased so rapidly that by 1407 a dinar fetched 140, and in 1412, 240 dirhems. Later the balance between the two metals became somewhat more stable, except that in the meantime the gold dinars had been largely replaced by European coins, particularly the Venetian ducats and zecchini, the Florentine florins, and the imperial augustales. In most local transactions neither gold nor even silver was generally used. Payments for retail purchases, daily wages, and the like were now, as a rule, made with copper coins, which were often traded by weight. There also was a good deal of barter, particularly in the provinces.[85]

This situation was further aggravated by the relatively constant economic progress of the European civilization. Rather than having a favorable balance of trade and payments, as it did in the early Middle Ages, the Middle East now had deficits in both. To begin with, the very structure of the Mameluke Empire required the importation of some 2,000 high-priced Mamelukes each year, causing an annual drain of some 200,000 dinars on the country's cash resources. In addition, Mameluke society imported many other male and female slaves who, even if costing an average of about 33⅓ dinars, had to be paid for by cash or exported merchandise. The general exchange of goods, too, leaned ever more heavily in favor of the European businessmen. In the Late Middle Ages the European exports to the Middle East, especially of textiles, became quite substantial. Piracy, too, that perennial plague of Mediterranean shipping, whether governmentally sponsored or conducted as a private enterprise, was less damaging to the European traders, often protected by powerful navies, than to their ever-weakening Middle-Eastern counterparts. Even more decisive was the increasing feudalization of the Syro-Egyptian areas. From the outset the Mamelukes had arranged for the redistribution of land, the mainstay of their economy, and as a result the share of the governmental estates and those held by emirs exceeded the total owned by civilian landlords. Subsequent redistributions of confiscated landholdings from condemned culprits and heirless estates further increased the area held by the large feudal landlords. Their possessions often extended over one to ten entire villages and some portions of villages scattered through various parts of the country. Under the existing system, the emirs theoretically controlled the land given to them only so long as they continued in office. Hereditary rights could be secured only indirectly by such evasions as the proprietors transferring their lands to a charitable or educational foundation (a *waqf*) which, while no longer owned, was nevertheless effectively administered by their families. Because of the uncertainty of tenure, the landowners had little interest in investing money for improving their often widely scattered properties but rather were bent on squeezing out of them as much revenue as possible in a short time. Moreover, the emirs, usually recruited from among former slaves, frequently were absentee landlords preoccupied with their own military and administrative tasks and rarely had any previous experience in managing agricultural estates. On their part the peasants, increasingly converted into estate-bound serfs, had little share in either the profits or the decision-making. They surely were not a most efficient agricultural labor force. On the other hand, land transferred to a perpetual *waqf* turned into a regular mortmain and as such was a drag on the economy of the country. Carl H. Becker was not exaggerating when he observed that "the *waqf* system was one of the major causes for the economic decline of the East." In short, for these and other reasons, the level of agricultural production and the internal, as well as external, exchange of goods were in a sad state.[86]

Such a concatenation of adverse circumstances could not fail to affect the Jewish population as well. Most obvious was the constant decline in the share of land owned and cultivated by Jews. We recall that already at the beginning of Islam the discriminatory land tax imposed upon "unbelievers," which often amounted to one-fifth or more of the entire harvest, had caused a mass flight of *dhimmi* farmers to the cities. This process continued throughout the Middle Ages, but now also embraced a growing number of Muslim peasants. As a result of neglect, much of Egypt's immemorial irrigation system was allowed to deteriorate badly, converting many previously flourishing farms into wastelands. And Jews, even more than Christians, avoided partaking of the growing dependence of the peasant class, which not only ran counter to their general aspirations of freedom of movement and guiding their own destinies but also seriously interfered with their observance of Jewish law. In addition, like most urbanites regardless of faith and ethnic identity, they undoubtedly viewed with contempt the oppressed fellahin. A Jerusalem Jew, using what sounded like a superlative description of his mistreatment by the recipient of his letter, wrote: "I feel myself in relation to you like a fellah honored by a most illustrious lord." The Jewish majority, living in the capital and other major cities, even looked down upon the inhabitants of the provincial towns (the *rif*), who did not enjoy the metropolitan amenities, as uncivilized boors. These additional difficulties confronting Jewish farmers became more pressing as their number diminished. Unlike their Coptic, Maronite, and other Christian compatriots, Jewish tillers of the soil did not live in close settlements and certainly did not occupy entire villages. To live as families scattered among hostile Muslim neighbors was for them doubly difficult, since they could not easily enjoy the religious and educational amenities offered by urban or suburban Jewish communities. The attitude of many Muslim neighbors was well characterized by the remark of some Muslim guards (overheard by the fifteenth-century German visitor Arnold von Harff), calling Christians and Jews "more filthy than dogs." [87]

In Egypt, Jews may also have been deterred from acquiring land by the country's exceptional dependence on the annual flood of the Nile, which seems to have varied in seven-year cycles, and by the uncertainties surrounding the inheritance of property left behind by an heirless *dhimmi* owner. The traditional practice was to hand over such property to the religious community to which the deceased had belonged. But some would-be landowners must have known that leading jurists of the Ḥanafite and Hanbalite schools had long argued that all heirless property of the "unbelievers" should devolve to the Treasury. Even the Malekite school, which opposed such indiscriminate confiscation, merely demanded that only in voluntarily surrendered areas should *dhimmi* property be used for the benefit of the deceased persons' community. While this controversy related to all heirless property, movable objects could much more readily be transferred to one's community by the *morituri* than could landed possessions. However, Maimonides sweepingly denied the existence of truly heirless Jewish property; he claimed that somewhere an heir must be in existence and would eventually be discovered. Perhaps this assertion was aimed at encouraging Jewish communal leaders to resist the demands of the intolerant teachers of Muslim law and of greedy Treasury officials.[88]

In general, Jews were not forbidden to own land. Yet, most often they appear to have acquired agricultural property mainly in order to sell it and its produce with profit. This situation is well illustrated by passages in the responsa of Moses Maimonides, such as the following: "Some people give money to Gentiles in order to purchase, and to take care of, sheep and goats, or else entrust Gentiles with cattle already in their possession and these are sent out to the steppes where they give birth to offspring. . . . These Gentiles retain only the wool and milk. . . . Similarly some Jews hand over vineyards, fields, or orchards to Gentiles for cultivation against a share in the produce." The inquirers did not object to this practice as such, but they were concerned about possible violations of the Sabbath and holiday commandments through sales on those days of rest. This alienation from direct agricultural work progressed in the following three centuries to such an extent that R. David Ibn abi Zimra generalized: "In this country Jews are not accustomed to own fields or vineyards and for many reasons refrain from pursuing that occupation. This fact has become so widely known among the Gentiles that it gave rise to the foolish rumor that if a Jew sows seed it never sprouts." In another context Ibn abi Zimra conceded that some Jews still owned farm lands. But undoubtedly in many, perhaps most, cases the actual tilling of the soil was performed by non-Jewish laborers. This self-imposed alienation from agriculture was stimulated by the uncertainties about the ultimate prices of farm produce which depended on the unpredictable future supply and demand, as well as on arbitrary decisions by frequently unfriendly local bureaucrats. This situation did not prevent a certain number of Jews from cultivating orchards and vineyards near their urban habitations. Because of the difficulties of transportation, even cattle used to be raised close to the urban centers that wished to be supplied with milk, dairy products, and meats on a daily basis. Jews encountered even less difficulty in acquiring urban real estate. We know of numerous instances of Jews owning houses as neighbors of both Muslims and Christians. There also were many cases of adjacent dwellings being rented by members of different faiths, although most ethnoreligious groups seem to have preferred to live in their respective quarters.[89]

In regard to the local demand for agricultural produce, it is noteworthy that rice, for example, played a relatively minor role in the diet of the average Middle Easterner, partly because it usually was at least 50 percent more expensive than wheat or barley. Oil, which—because of its extensive uses in Mid-Eastern cuisine, lighting, cosmetics, and medicines—played a vital role in the economy of the area, was still being produced in Egypt mainly from sesame plants. Jews, who in antiquity had introduced the olive tree into Babylonia and thus helped to replace much of the sesame oil there, apparently did not perform the same pioneering service, although they did develop viticulture, in Egypt. Despite their prohibition against drinking wine, we recall, the Muslims owned and cultivated vineyards for the grapes, which they were allowed to eat or drink as grape juice. Jews and Christians, of course, were able to utilize the crop of their vineyards (which throughout the country theoretically belonged to the Mameluke sultans) principally to produce wine for domestic use, for sale to non-Muslims, or for export. The wine presses of the time were quite primitive and apparently were employed in a great many households as well as by professional wine pressers.[90]

INDUSTRY

In contrast to their small share in agriculture, the Jews played a considerable role in most branches of industry. Here, too, the government controls exercised by an inefficient and corrupt bureaucracy, as well as the earthquakes, famines, plagues, and particularly the wars, greatly hindered the artisans' orderly pursuit of their calling. Syria and its neighboring areas, though not Egypt, suffered severely from Timur's invasions (1400–1404) which, notwithstanding the ultimately successful Mameluke resistance, played havoc with the local industrial production. Apart from leaving behind cities burned to the ground and cruelly slaughtering thousands upon thousands of men, women, and children, the ruthless conqueror forcibly removed a great many skilled craftsmen from the West-Asian cities to his capital, Samarkand, before himself retiring to the heartland of his vast empire. The void thus created could not easily have been filled even if the Mameluke regime had still possessed the dynamism of its early years. Given the Empire's declining economy in the fifteenth century, the damage proved well-nigh irreparable.[91]

In general, few Syro-Egyptian enterprises lent themselves to large-scale production, since most work had to be done by hand. Transportation of merchandise, too, was rather costly and hazardous in view of the almost ubiquitous piracy at sea and highway robbery on land. As a rule, larger industrial enterprises were conducted by partnerships, whether formed *ad hoc* or operating for many years. Sometimes partners divided the labors by assigning to some the task of production and to others the responsibility for transportation and merchandising. Outstanding among the larger industries were sugar refining and textile manufacturing. Family names related to sugar production do not necessarily mean, to be sure, that the particular individuals concentrated on this area for generations or even throughout their own lifetimes. Yet such long-term continuity cannot be ruled out, in view of sugar's great role in food, medicine, and other needs, which made its production and sale very remunerative. For this reason it also whetted the appetites of certain emirs who wished to acquire complete control over its manufacture in their administrative districts; ultimately sugar became one of the governmental monopolies under the Burji dynasty. Perhaps because of bureaucratic inefficiency and the producers' passive resistance, these efforts often failed. Under Barsbay alone this monopoly was proclaimed in October 1423 and revoked three months later; in June 1425 it was reintroduced, but was again speedily abolished; reinstated in 1429, it did not even last a month, since many sugar refiners and merchants simply closed their shops and fled. As a result the sultan had to promise that he would no longer force merchants to acquire certain quantities of sugar at an arbitrarily high price. Such a pledge was actually inscribed on a column in the 'Umayyad mosque in Damascus, and it apparently was adhered to in the following years. But these "on again–off again" policies inevitably disrupted established businesses and aggravated the other factors impeding orderly and profitable production. In the case of textiles, on the other hand, it was more the growing competition from European exporters which reduced the local output, the quality of which, too, constantly deteriorated. Through this vicious circle the textile industry likewise found itself in a chaotic state.[92]

Most manufactured goods, however, were produced by an enormous variety of craftsmen, usually working with members of their own families. Slavery hardly played a role in these productive efforts; it was largely limited to domestic service. In view of the relatively high prices paid for ordinary slaves, which usually ranged from 33⅓ dinars upwards (equivalent to the cost of a small house), it simply did not pay to invest capital in slaves for industrial labor. This was particularly true of the religious minorities, since Jewish or Christian masters had to take into account the possibility that their slaves might escape and, by adopting Islam, secure freedom. This difficulty may have been partly responsible for the rather small number of Jews engaged in slave trading. For the most part we hear of slaves, if at all, as serving in Jewish homes but of practically none employed in any industrial or agricultural capacity. It should be noted that diversification in Jewish crafts went very far, indeed. Shelomo Dov Goitein identified no less than 450 special occupations of Jews mentioned in the Genizah, each of which bore a different Arabic designation. Of course, a man named as a craftsman in a very narrow field may have simultaneously produced goods of a similar kind technically belonging to another category. In many cases he may not have limited himself to the production of goods in his field but, by trying to sell the finished product to the public, may have become a merchant as well.[93]

Nevertheless, craftsmanship was probably the major occupation of a large segment of Syro-Egyptian Jewry. Unfortunately, we possess few occupational statistics of Jewish artisans in the Mameluke Empire. Eli Ashtor was able closely to examine only three documents, published by Joseph Braslavsky, R. J. H. Gottheil and W. H. Worrell, and himself, which happened to show a considerable variation in the ratio of artisans to merchants. One document reflected a proportion of 52.1 percent craftsmen as against 17.3 percent merchants and moneylenders. In the second document the disparity was reduced to 43.7 as against 37.5 percent. The third document revealed a ratio of 38.4 to 32.6 percent. Regrettably, these records embraced only 23, 18, and 54 persons, respectively (including persons of other occupations), certainly too small a sample to yield any significant statistical conclusions. Moreover, all three documents are undated; at least the first two may antedate the Mameluke regime. The only conclusion they seem to justify, therefore, is that the percentage of Jewish artisans was very large.[94]

Of great importance to the Jewish craftsmen was the fact that they were not seriously hampered by guild restrictions similar to those in contemporary Europe. True, the Middle East, too, had some professional associations. But the long-held view that these organizations had some of the monopolistic and authoritarian traits of the European guilds has been effectively refuted by recent investigators. Moreover, one must bear in mind that the powerful European guilds could develop only under the strong autonomy enjoyed by the Western cities. Even where the artisans failed to achieve control over the municipal administrations, they were strongly backed, as a rule, by the municipal authorities in their exercise of rigid controls over the training of apprentices and journeymen, the admission of new master artisans, the enforcement of their internal regulations, and their other economic and social functions. The Muslim guilds, on the contrary, closely supervised by state officials, were by their very structure sufficiently latitudinarian sometimes even to admit Jews or Christians to membership; this despite the general religious coloring of each such association. On the entrepreneurial side, too, we find occasional references to Jewish and Muslim partners running joint industrial enterprises. Nor, seemingly, were any major obstacles placed in the way of Jewish or Christian itinerant artisans visiting Muslim villages. We have the record of *dhimmi* shoemakers, for example, spending some time in one village in order to provide the local population with shoes or shoe repairs, and then moving on to another village. They often did not return home for weeks or months. According to a contemporary Hebrew source, they were generally well treated by the Muslim villagers, supplied with food and lodging, and paid fair wages. Clearly, theirs was nevertheless a more or less perilous way of life facing all solitary travelers.[95]

Jews frequently excelled in certain branches of industry. From time immemorial they played a special role in the production of textiles and their conversion into clothing, in dyeing, and in metal work of all kinds. While much sewing was done at home by the women in the family, the production of certain more costly textiles required great professional skills and many years of specialization. The medieval Muslim and *dhimmi* home usually required many more textiles for its furnishing than do modern homes. Much of the furniture consisted of carpets, drapes, coverings of all kinds; some of these objects were so durable and costly that they were inherited and used for several generations, or else, after prolonged possession, disposed of in the public market at prices not much lower than for new manufactures. At times valuable pieces of embroidery, carpets, and other objects made of precious fibers or silk served as means of exchange, particularly in barter trade. Of course, quality and prices of various textiles differed greatly. On the basis of extant records, which include a number of Judeo-Arabic marriage contracts, Eli Ashtor has shown that, during the fourteenth century, linen produced in Alexandria cost 35 dinars a piece, while the same article embroidered with gold thread commanded double that price. Later in the century the basic prices went up by about 50 percent. Cotton goods showed a similar increase after 1396. During the crisis of the fifteenth century, however, there was a considerable decline in the number of looms. Al-Jazari's estimate of 12,000 looms functioning in Alexandria before 1296 is questionable, but we may perhaps accept his assertion that, after the following famine and plague, their number had diminished to 1,000. Equally exaggerated seem to be the reports of other Arab historians, that the number of looms in

Cairo was reduced from 14,000 in 1395 to a mere 800 by 1434. Whatever one's doubts concerning the accuracy of these figures, there is no question that production had sharply diminished.[96]

With respect to dyes needed for coloring the textiles—they ranged over many more shades of color than appears practical today—we must bear in mind the high prices paid for them by the dyers, which, of course, they passed on to their customers. Indigo, for example, which in 1347 in Alexandria cost 28–32 dinars for 1.1 qinṭars (approximately 110 pounds), fetched 25 dinars in 1396, and 45 dinars in 1414. Curiously, while dyeing was a very skilled profession, its remuneration was not always high. In one document we read of a consignment of cloth valued at 500 dinars being given to a dyer, who was to provide the necessary coloring for a price of only 20 dinars. Similarly, weaving was very inexpensive. Possibly for this reason it was an occupation looked down upon by society at large, although we sometimes hear of important scholars deriving a livelihood from this lowly craft. However, interlacing damask with gold or silver threads could result in much-sought-after, high-priced products. As in ancient times and in medieval Europe, the glass industry also provided a livelihood for many Jews in the Mameluke Empire. So did gold- and silversmithing and various crafts connected with copper and brass production. We even hear of occasional Jewish ironsmiths. In addition to these major areas of occupation, we find records of Jewish craftsmen in almost all other branches of industry.[97]

Understandably, the mass of Jewish craftsmen was concentrated in the lower echelons of industrial workers. To be sure, Muqaddasi's (or Maqdisi's) aforementioned statement that "for the most part, the assayers of corn, dyers, bankers, and tanners, are Jews; while it is usual for the physicians and the scribes to be Christians" was not fully justified even in the tenth century. It was less and less true as time went on, although in the thirteenth century Gregory Abu'l Faraj Barhebraeus, the catholicos of the Syrian Jacobite Church, still contended that "from the time the Arab people spread in the world to the present day no Jew achieved a high position. You will find among them only tanners, dyers, and tailors, the most honored and wealthiest among them become physicians or officials, but only in places where others find these occupations beneath their dignity." Shelomo Dov Goitein is far more correct in asserting that the Genizah documents, mainly antedating 1250, show Jewish participation in almost all industrial occupations. Most remarkably, tanning, which because of the odors emanating from the hides was in general disrepute and often forced the municipal authorities to relocate such workshops outside the cities, seems to have greatly declined as a Jewish occupation. We certainly do not hear much about controversies raging between the Jewish tanners and their non-Jewish neighbors, such as were recorded in Byzantium. As Goitein has pointed out, tanners appear only sporadically in the lists of taxpayers, donors, or recipients of alms, so amply preserved in the Genizah.[98]

On the other hand, Jews seem frequently to have shunned serving as laborers for other entrepreneurs. We need not take too seriously the complaint of a displaced merchant who had lost all his possessions in a shipwreck and was forced to take any job available. He wrote: "I eat bread in the service of others; every minute of the day I gulp the cup of death because of my degradation and that of my children." In fact, from what we know about the labor market and the general xenophobia prevailing even in the Jewish communities, which since ancient times had strenuously tried to protect the "acquired rights" of the local inhabitants, he should have been happy to have found employment at all. Moses Maimonides' rhetorical exclamation in the lengthy epistle to his pupil Joseph b. Yehudah Ibn 'Aqnin, that "even one dirhem earned by an employee from tailoring, carpentry, or weaving appears to me preferable to the revenue [from public funds] received by the prince of captivity," did not necessarily convey the idea that such employment was easily obtainable for a new, untrained arrival in a community. In fact, Joseph was advised in the same context to devote his time to business and a medical career, while also setting aside time for the study of the Torah. In fact, many crafts required skills which could only be learned in years of training. Unless a young man or woman could acquire such skills at home, he or she had to serve as a helper of an established craftsman before becoming a master artisan. Without the sharp guild controls existing in medieval Europe and with the absence of strict regulations concerning the required years of, and gradations in, training, quite a few artisans must have been ill prepared for their tasks. Yet the occasional grumblings by employers and customers mentioned in the Genizah and other documents were muted by the prevailing scarcity of competent labor. This was at least the case during the Faṭimid age, whereas in the declining economy of the Mameluke period, workers, though probably less well trained, may have been more readily available. They must also have worked with inferior materials, as is attested by the surviving specimens displayed in the world's museums. However, in the absence of reliable and detailed documentation all these assumptions must remain conjectural.[99]

In any case, the remuneration of most workers even in the earlier period was not very high, often ranging between 2 and 5 dirhems a day; in some cases this was supplemented by a midday dinner valued at 3/4 to 1 1/4 dirhems. These amounts were subject to change, especially in the inflationary period of the fifteenth century, under the Burji sultans. Nonetheless, it appears that the workers' wages generally kept pace with both the debasement of the currency and the price inflation. Remarkably, the "real" wages actually went up, if measured by their purchasing power with respect to some major commodities. According to Eli Ashtor, the average wage which could secure between 405 and 476 pounds of bread during the twelfth through the fourteenth centuries, could purchase 666 pounds in the fifteenth century. A salary which in the eleventh century could purchase 43 kilograms of oil, in the thirteenth century could acquire 80 kilograms, and in the fifteenth century, 90 kilograms. Similarly, a twelfth-century wage equal in value to 33 kilograms of cheese rose in the fourteenth century to the equivalent of 75 kilograms and in the fifteenth century to 80 kilograms. Less consistent was the progress in relation to meat. Earnings equivalent in value to 26.6 kilograms of meat in the eleventh century were equal to 45.4 kilograms two centuries later, but dropped back to 25 kilograms in the fourteenth century. They regained the purchasing power of some 47 kilograms in the following century. In contrast, the amount of sugar purchasable by the same wages dropped from 19 kilograms in the eleventh century to 15 in the fourteenth century, and to 9 kilograms in the fifteenth. This sharp decline was the result of short-sighted monopolistic practices by government and emirs during the last two centuries of the Mameluke regime.[100]

Despite the gains in certain forms of purchasing power, the general impoverishment of the population in the Burji period forced many Jews, including women, to seek employment as laborers for entrepreneurs, Jewish or non-Jewish. A pathetic inquiry addressed to R. David Ibn abi Zimra raised the issue as to "the custom in Egypt for women to perform work in Gentile houses, staying in them for three or four days and nights at a time. Occasionally, they include the wives of *kohanim* [descendants of priestly lineage who were subject to more rigid religious controls]." The rabbi's answer was as expected:

These proceedings represent an unmitigated licentiousness. They have already been the object of ordinances issued against them by the *negidim* [the leaders of Egyptian Jewry]. Some [women workers] have, indeed, abstained from that practice, but a number of others have been unable to [give up these jobs] for they are poverty stricken and their husbands are unable to provide them and their children with clothing or covers against the cold. They must, therefore, seek a livelihood and they go there [to the Gentile houses] with their husbands' permission. All that we could achieve, therefore, was to persuade them while weaving not to sit at the same tables [with men].

Yet, this was an extreme case. The overwhelming majority of Jewish workers undoubtedly found some employment in Jewish shops, primarily in workshops run by their own relatives.[101]

COMMERCE AND BANKING

Many factors operated toward a reduction, and subsequently almost the elimination, of the Jewish preeminence in the international trade of the Middle-Eastern countries. Jewish influence had been declining, we recall, since the tenth century when the Italian merchant republics, buttressed by their naval power, began seizing control over an increasing share of Europe's trade with the Middle East and indirectly also with that of India and the Far East. The Mameluke Empire's new sociopolitical orientation and its growing need to import Mamelukes for its army and the highest echelons of its administration created a situation which found eloquent expression in a decree issued by Baybars. The sultan tried to encourage the importation of slaves from both East and West, promising full protection to the slave traders, and offering them important tax concessions. He declared:

> Importers of Mamelukes and young slave girls are able to sell their wares at prices higher than they anticipate. Like other importers from neighboring or distant lands, they are free to set their prices at their own discretion. We desire only that our armed forces be increased. . . . In fact, Islam owes these troops its power to unfurl its flag. The Mamelukes, whom we have acquired in this way, have emerged from darkness into light, the shame of their infidelity having given way to the high praise now being lavished on their new faith. They now fight for the victory of the Islamic commonwealth and the people.

In this area, too, the Jewish international traders could hardly compete with their major rivals, local or foreign. Since most of the Mamelukes were recruited from Eastern Europe or Central Asia, the small Jewish populations in those areas could offer little assistance to would-be Jewish slave traders. Even in the early Middle Ages, we have noted, the share of Jews in the disposal of that human cargo was much smaller than has often been assumed. But now that the highest prices were paid for gifted soldier material, as well as for beautiful or artistically talented young women, Muslim traders easily replaced the few Jews wishing to pursue that occupation.[102]

Jewish, as well as Christian, competition with Muslim big business was further curtailed by the *dhimmis*' limited access to the Red Sea, the major artery of communication between the Mediterranean and the Indian Ocean. Ever since Raynald of Châtillon's foolhardy attempt to establish a Crusader stronghold on that sea had provoked Saladin to forbid Jews and Christians to settle anywhere along its shores, their contacts with Aden, called "the gate to China," were greatly hampered. Although the Jewish communities of Aden and Yemen continued to flourish for centuries thereafter, they lost their once vital role in the exchanges between India and Egypt. Their capital resources certainly could not compare with the great financial power of the Karimi consortium. By offering valuable gifts and advancing substantial loans to rulers all along the various routes, the Karimis were able to dominate most of the international commerce of the area. One of them, Naṣir ad-Din Muḥammad ibn Musallam (d. 1374) was characterized by Ibn Ḥajar al-'Asqalani as a merchant who "was, as far as his fortune was concerned, the marvel of his time. It was said that no one could estimate its size." True, a somewhat similar comment had earlier been made about two Jewish brothers, Abu Sa'id at-Tustari and Abu Naṣr Harun, of eleventh-century Cairo. But certainly no such assets could be accumulated in the fourteenth century by any Jewish banker, even if he held a high office at the Mameluke court. The long-lasting cohesion among Karimi members further magnified the financial power and political influence of the syndicate. To be sure, on their way to the Nile Valley, Jews still frequently traveled from Aden to Aydhab (Old Suakin), the main harbor at the midpoint of the Red Sea. They seem to have enjoyed a rather high standing there. However, their stay in other localities along the route was rather circumscribed. And, of course, entry into Mecca was barred to non-Muslims under the sanction of capital punishment. This prohibition also had direct commercial implications, since Mecca had long been a major emporium for international trade. The annual arrival of thousands of pilgrims from all Muslim countries converted Islam's holiest city into the seat of a great international fair during which merchants from various lands exchanged goods, wrote contracts for later deliveries, and established contacts with their compeers residing hundreds, even thousands, of miles away. No *dhimmi* dared to set foot in that area except after formal conversion to Islam.[103]

Tense relations between the West-European and the East-Mediterranean countries during the period of the Crusades likewise impeded Jewish trade with India, as well as Europe. To be sure, the holy wars mutually proclaimed by Islam and Western Christendom did not completely halt visits by Christians to Muslim countries and by Muslims to Christian lands. A twelfth-century Muslim observer, Muḥammad b. Aḥmed ibn Jubair, remarked: "One of the strangest things in the world is to see Muslim caravans entering into Frankish possessions, as well as Frankish commerce penetrating Muslim lands." Yet the frequent military and naval clashes made such journeys more perilous. In particular, after the fall of the last Crusaders' citadel in Acco in 1291, the papal prohibition against shipment of any war materiel in the broadest sense (including, for instance, lumber), and later extended to any trade with Muslim lands, for a while seriously interfered with large-scale exchanges of goods between the two areas. However, these prohibitions were frequently violated and, later, formally circumvented by special licenses granted by the popes themselves to Venetian, Genoese, and other Christian traders. Ultimately, Martin V extended a general license to Venice for a period of twenty-five years. Since licenses were renewable, they largely nullified the entire boycott movement. Yet, during the century or more that this system lasted, it often was evaded with impunity only by merchants enjoying the protection of powerful Christian monarchs or republics, and it certainly made breaches by Jewish traders much more risky. In 1428 Venice went so far as to forbid Venetian shipmasters to accommodate Jewish passengers on their journeys to the Middle East. As late as 1504 it required much effort to prevent the Venetian authorities from confiscating some Eastern goods brought to the Republic by Jews, who at that time had no right to settle or trade in the City of the Lagoons. Under these circumstances we rarely hear of Jewish merchants traveling from Christian Europe through the Middle East to India or China and vice versa. Of course, if a Jew underwent conversion to either Christianity or Islam, his difficulties could be much more readily overcome. Even in Asia, only a convert (or son of a convert) from Aleppo, 'Abd al-Aziz ibn Manṣur, was able to amass a fortune estimated at 1,000,000 dinars through making five journeys to China and bringing back large quantities of Chinese merchandise (including slaves), which was greatly in demand in his own country.[104]

One route, however, still was relatively open to Jews. We remember that in the ninth century the Jewish traders whom Ibn Khurdadhbah called Radhanites had often used the northern route via eastern Europe and the Caucasian area to reach the Persian Gulf and beyond. Although this route was no longer quite so accessible after the Mongol invasion and the overriding control by the Golden Horde, the possibility of exporting slaves and other goods through the Black Sea harbors or on land through northern Armenia to Persia was still partially open. It was developed particularly by the merchants of the small empire of Trebizond and the Genoese and Venetian colonists established along the shores of the Black Sea. With the cooperation of these Italian republics, we remember, some Jews settled in the Crimea, in Genoese Kaffa, and other localities. From there they could export goods to the Byzantine Empire for transshipment to Egypt, Syria, and other Muslim lands. Some wares were also transported through Armenian Cilicia to the Iranian Plateau. It probably was in the main for the purpose of interrupting this traffic that, following the example set by Baybars in 1267 and 1275, Mameluke rulers repeatedly attacked Armenia in 1355, 1369 and finally conquered Cilicia in 1375, taking its king, Leo VI, prisoner. In the Black Sea area a few Jews are recorded as slave traders also in the fifteenth century. Nevertheless, the number of Jewish merchant-travelers must have greatly diminished. This was particularly true during the fifteen century, when the upsurge of the Muscovite Empire caused the downfall of the Golden Horde and thereby removed the relative calm which, under the *pax Mongolica,* had facilitated some overland exchanges with the Middle East and India. At that time R. David Ibn abi Zimra answered an inquiry concerning Cochin Jewry, on the west coast of India:

> They have not been known to us until about twenty years ago after the Portuguese had conquered India. I remember that some letters came from that community asking us to send them books which they did not possess, such as the Mishnah, the Talmud, and the law codes.

To that extent had Egyptian Jewry, thus represented by one of its outstanding leaders, become oblivious of the formerly intensive business relations which had led many of its ancestors from Fusṭaṭ and Alexandria to Aden and the Indian subcontinent.[105]

Apart from these external pressures, there were more fundamental forces which brought about the sharp decline in Egypt's international trade and caused the Jewish share therein to become ever smaller. We recall the constant slowdown in the growth of the Jewish population which, at best, was able to hold its own in the course of the last three centuries of pre-Ottoman rule. Egypt's general population decline seems to have been more severe. As a result of the recurrent plagues—between the Black Death (1348) and 1517 no less than eighteen major, and many smaller, epidemics had ravaged the Middle East—the occasional famines, and the decline of agricultural production, the working population was reduced from generation to generation. The migration from the village to the city, accelerated by the mismanagement of the Mameluke landlords, may have further contributed to a somewhat reduced birth rate, as happened in many other areas. The importation of slaves, as evidenced by the figures reconstructed by David Ayalon from the existing records, had also sharply declined, despite the desire of the ruling circles to maintain the military manpower at its full strength. The scarcity of civilian slaves contributed greatly to the sharp increase in wages of craftsmen and laborers which, with its stagnating economy, the country could ill afford. Most slaves, moreover, including the soldiers, were not channeled into any productive occupation but merely added to the consuming public which became a burden on the declining industrial and agricultural sector. Even the once famous textile industry, as we recall, barely kept pace with the needs of the country itself; it had small surpluses, if any, for export. Together with the deterioration of the currency, the growing exhaustion of the Nubian gold mines, and the generally chaotic monetary system, Egypt's position in international commerce would have become almost untenable were it not for the revival of the spice trade in the fifteenth century. This commercial activity owed its growth far more to the unquenchable thirst of the European aristocracy and bourgeoisie for these goods than to the vigor of the Egyptian exporters.[106]

Because of the new power constellation the European traders, defying the papal pronunciamentos, began playing an ever more assertive role and were also able to secure a greater measure of protection from the local potentates. Because of the treaties between the Western countries and the Mameluke rulers, the Italian, French, and Spanish merchants not only often attained a sort of self-government which exceeded that of the *dhimmis*, but also anticipated the future development of the exclusive consular jurisdiction over their respective nationals under the modern capitulation system. The Jewish position, on the other hand, had seriously deteriorated in Europe in the period of the great expulsions after 1290. Even earlier, as we recall, Jewish international traders were losing ground in their competition with the Italian merchants who increasingly controlled Mediterranean shipping. At times, some cities, such as Venice or Marseilles, forbade their nationals to transport more than a few, if any, Jewish passengers on their ships. That is why, as A. O. Citarella observed, the Genizah contains many records of Eastern Jews dealing with European Christian merchants but not with their own coreligionists.[107]

Nevertheless, in one form or another, commerce, both international and local, still furnished a livelihood to many Jewish traders. Despite the growth of feudalism and the deprecation of the local bourgeoisie by some leading Mamelukes, as a calling commerce was still highly appreciated. The fact that since pre-Islamic days Mecca itself was a center of Arabian trade and that the Messenger had been a businessman by profession prevented any kind of a stigma being attached to the merchant class as such. Nor were the writings of Muḥammad ash-Shaybani (d. 804) or Al-Jaḥiẓ (d. 869) altogether forgotten. In his classic work, *A Praise of Merchants and Condemnation of Officials,* Al-Jaḥiẓ had argued that by earning a living through trade one fulfilled a superior religious duty as well. Hence many Mameluke grandees pursued part-time mercantile activity on the side. In the fourteenth and fifteenth centuries it became quite customary for emirs to dominate the trade in their respective districts. They sometimes went to the extreme of forcing Muslim, as well as *dhimmi,* merchants to purchase some goods from them at arbitrarily fixed high prices and to absorb the losses engendered through their resale below cost.[108]

From time immemorial Jews had emphasized the obligation of every individual to provide for himself and his family by whatever work he could obtain. "Skin carcasses in the market [the lowest occupation] and earn your wages," rather than depend on public support, was an old talmudic injunction. Having for major historical reasons become an intensively mercantile population, Jews understandably considered business activities perfectly legitimate and honorable. However, because of the increasing difficulties and dangers accompanying even short-distance travel, most of them preferred to pursue their respective trades in a sedentary fashion. These different attitudes had already come to the fore in the eleventh century, when ships and caravans traversing long distances were readily available and the perils of travel could be minimized. S. D. Goitein contrasts two eleventh-century Cairo Jewish magnates, Joseph ibn 'Awkal, who did his business mostly by delegating chores to traveling agents, and Nahrai b. Nissim, who spent much of his time on the road. Understandably, long absences from home, sometimes extending over several years, greatly complicated family life and doubtless also interfered with the education of children as well as with the pursuit of studies by the merchants themselves. On the other hand, there were many itinerant scholars, Jewish as well as Muslim, who traversed great distances in order to visit different seats of learning and to collect diverse local traditions.[109]

Surely a much greater number of Jewish traders made a living from domestic commerce. The documentation in this area is much less comprehensive, because most transactions were informally completed between seller and buyer by the delivery of goods against cash payments or barter. S. D. Goitein's observation that the Genizah papers reveal a very large number of credit sales, in both the retail and the wholesale business, may only be the result of the sellers' habit of recording credit transactions as an aid for subsequent collections. Informal payments, on the other hand, may at best have been entered in some ledgers of larger firms, but were hardly ever consistently written down by small shopkeepers or peddlers. It is noteworthy that Jewish retail traders often were assigned space in Muslim bazaars, although at least one source mentions a Jewish bazaar in Cairo. But there is no way of telling whether some special streets devoted to a single trade, like the Tanners' or Soapmakers' Streets in Aleppo, which probably included merchants as well as craftsmen, also accommodated Jews. The objects displayed for sale even by petty traders were of an infinite variety. Although a particular firm may have been named after some specialty such as that of perfumer, leather merchant, or jeweler, the chances are that it offered for sale merchandise of a much greater variety. The same holds true even for wholesale firms. If, according to a list computed by S. D. Goitein, the India trade showed exports from India of 77 categories (of which 36 consisted of spices and related objects) while imports consisted of 103 items (36 in textiles), these objects doubtless joined many others available for sale in Cairo's domestic markets. The prices, of course, varied from object to object and from period to period. By way of generalization one may assert that in the thirteenth and fourteenth centuries prices were fairly stable and subject mainly to seasonal variations or such extraordinary events as wars, famines, or elementary catastrophes. In the fifteenth century, however, there was a rather constant inflationary push, occasioned by both the arbitrarily exercised government monopolies and the growing depreciation of the currency.[110]

Understandably, the merchants often needed assistance. Only occasionally do we hear of slaves functioning as business employees. Much collaboration was achieved by partnerships, in which some partners contributed all or most of the capital while the others devoted themselves to merchandising. However, there also was a fairly large class of agents and brokers, including women brokers, who mediated between sellers and buyers. Sometimes functions of this type were performed by a member of another denomination. This was particularly the case with the *waqil al-tujjar* (in Hebrew, *peqid ha-soḥrim*) or representative of the merchants (usually selected from the distinguished leaders of the community), who by his contacts with the authorities, as well as his personal resources, was able to serve his clients in more ways than as a mere mediator. One such official, Yehudah b. Moses ibn Sighmar, a native of Kairuwan whose name frequently appears in the Genizah during the years 1055–98, was highly praised in a letter from Jerusalem:

In His grace God has brought abū Zikrī [Ibn Sighmar's byname], the member of the academy, from the West, so that he should be in Miṣr [Old Cairo] a support for everyone coming from anywhere: from Iraq, Syria and Palestine, the West, or the countries of the Rum [Europe], being kind to them, spending on them his fortune, and using his high social position [*jāh*] for their best. May God preserve the wealth He has given him and increase it, and let him witness the joy [i.e., the wedding] of his son.

A similar position was held in Aden by four generations of the family of Maḍmun b. Japheth (d. 1172), whose name occurs even more frequently in the Genizah documents. He and his son Ḥalfon were each addressed by the exilarch as "prince of the land of Yemen." No Jewish representatives of such high standing are recorded under the Mameluke regime, although this silence may be due more to the relative paucity of extant documentation than to the unfavorable status of the Jewish subjects. But there is little doubt that the new instrumentalities of business, such as the *suftaja* (draft, prototype of our check), particularly useful in international business relations, which had been developed by earlier generations of Muslims in cooperation with Jews and Christians remained in widespread use to the end of the Middle Ages and beyond.[111]

Such instruments were particularly important in various phases of the money trade, which played a great role in the economy of the Mameluke Empire. While, as we have seen, the Jews' share in the Muslim mints had greatly declined and in the last medieval centuries played a very minor role, receipt of deposits against a fee seems to have been of some importance. We have less evidence from the Mameluke period than from the Great Caliphate that deposits with bankers were used as a means of concealing one's cash resources from rapacious officials and tax farmers. But cases like that of the Ḥanbalite chief judge under Baybars who failed to pay the required taxes on deposits he had held from merchants in Baghdad, Ḥarran, and Damascus and, when caught, lost his post, must often have gone undetected. In general, deposits played an important role in the circulation of money. As in modern times, they were frequently used by merchants to secure from their bankers drafts on their correspondents in distant localities for payment for goods purchased there. (These *suftaja*s thus functioned in a way similar to our letters of credit.) Even long-term deposits were far from infrequent. Jewish bankers of note and recognized honesty could well serve as depositaries despite the ever-present suspicion that such transactions may have served to camouflage some hidden forms of usury. True, Jews could hardly offer the depositors security equal to that supplied by the Templars (until their suppression by Philip IV of France in 1312), who usually kept such treasures in their heavily fortified castles. Nor could the Jewish bankers compete on an equal footing with the branch offices established by Italian and other Frankish merchants in various Mid-Eastern cities. But they certainly could attract substantial deposits from their own coreligionists. Depositaries were usually allowed to use funds deposited with them and only return an equivalent sum of money to the depositors, while some Muslim jurists insisted on the bankers' duty to return the identical coins to their owners. The profit derived from such investment by the depositary in return for his responsibility for funds held by him in trust was not considered usurious by the rabbis. This is, indeed, the tenor of Maimonides' discussions of the money trade in his legal, as well as philosophical, works.[112]

More important was the function of the money changer. Under the existing conditions throughout the Muslim world, where coins minted in Muslim lands from India to Spain and many others brought in by European merchants freely circulated, their intrinsic value greatly differed. As Maimonides stated, "the banker alone knows the coin, its deficiencies, and its monetary value." Such expertise was needed in the case of gold and silver coins whose mutual relationships often varied according to their places of origin and the dates of their production. Quite a few coins lost in value simply because they were worn down by extensive use over a long period of time. Equally knowledgeable was the dealer in copper coins, which generally were assessed only by weight. The procedure of having such coins (at times including more precious currency) collected in purses, the weight of which was attested by a reputable firm, did not prevent suspicious recipients from having them weighed by experts. Of course, many small localities had no such experts in their midst, nor even possessed the necessary fine scales. From the existing literature we learn that villagers often had to travel great distances before ascertaining the monetary value of purses or individual coins. In the cities, on the other hand, until the twentieth century, one could readily find money changers on numerous street corners prepared to use their judgment in assessing the value of coins and exchanging them into the local currency. Jews seemed to have had their share among these "experts" and quite a few made a living from that occupation.[113]

Moneylending as such seems to have played a smaller role in the Jewish economy. Jewish, as well as Muslim and Christian, laws forbade charging "usury." While there were considerable differences in the definition of that term, the three faiths agreed that money should be lent merely as a matter of charity and should yield no profit. However, they were much more indulgent in regard to loans extended to members of other faiths. Being, as a rule, a small minority in the population, the Jews were in the privileged position of being able to extend profitable loans to a majority of their neighbors. Moreover, jurists of all three faiths found numerous loopholes to evade the strict prohibitions, despite the attempts of legislators and juristic interpreters to hedge them by detailed safeguards. The reality that most large-scale business transactions and even many retail purchases depended on credit made one or another form of evasion, or *hilal,* an absolute necessity. Hence Jewish bankers, though proportionately far less numerous than in the Western countries, were able to lend money on interest with little difficulty, although for the most part they seem to have done so as a part of their broader business interests. Yet, because of the legal difficulties, the rate of interest was hardly ever spelled out. It can be deduced, if at all, only from the difference between the amounts lent and those repaid in cash or in kind. Remarkably, despite the risks involved and the frequently long periods elapsing before full repayment, the rates seem to have been rather moderate. If from early Syriac records, Eduard Sachau was able to compute that Jewish bankers charged, as a rule, 30 percent, while Christians lent money to fellow Christians at the rate of only 20 percent, this situation may even then have been quite exceptional. From the numerous documents relating to loans in the Genizah archives, S. D. Goitein was able to reconstruct only a few data revealing the rates charged. They seemed to range around only 11 percent. Practically no information on this subject seems to be available from the Mameluke period.[114]

At times the Jews, like their Muslim and Christian compatriots, were expected, however unwillingly, to extend loans to the sultans themselves. They had learned from experience that princes, in both East and West, were poor credit risks. Time and again, moreover, rapacious Mameluke rulers used one or another subterfuge to extort large outright payments from wealthy subjects or entire communities. An extreme case of this kind occurred in 1511, when a Jewish banker named Samuel and his wife were arrested under some trumped-up accusation. Even after paying the huge ransom of 500,000 dinars, both were kept in prison and soon died there. That in the unstable economy of the declining Mameluke Empire the Jewish bankers lived under a cloud of suspicion is attested, for example, by the German travelers Arnold von Harff and Sebald Rieter, Jr. After spending three weeks in prison in Gezerah (Gaza), Palestine, Harff advised every pilgrim and merchant traveling there "not to refuse to pay duty, if so advised, by Christians, Jews and Heathens, since one must pay courtesy or duty at every town or village; further to beware of associating with heathen women, also with Jews who live in those parts and know our tongue well, who deceive, betray and ruin us." Rieter, who visited Palestine in 1479, uncritically repeated the widespread rumor that many Jews were engaged in coin clipping. There is no evidence to support that insinuation, particularly since the frequent depreciation of the currencies in circulation was largely the effect of deliberate governmental policies to alleviate the pressures on the ever-penurious Treasury. By that time the number of very wealthy Jews had greatly diminished. In the fifteenth century the vast majority of Syro-Egyptian Jewry consisted of poverty-stricken masses with a mere sprinkling of well-to-do persons at the top of the social ladder. Some of these did lend money on interest, according to contemporary Jewish travelers of 1495 and 1522 and R. David Ibn abi Zimra. But the interest rate of 24 percent, usually charged by these lenders, often hardly sufficed to compensate them for the losses sustained through the decline in the value of the currency. Therefore, the wealthiest members of the Jewish community usually made a living by combining a variety of occupations, of which moneylending and currency exchange were only a minor phase. Merchandising, as such, often was much more lucrative and less risky. It also was less subject to censure by Jewish pietists within their own community and by Jew-baiters from the outside.[115]

The question of Jewish professionals need not greatly concern us here. Compared with modern times when the legal profession has embraced a great many Jewish practitioners, law then was part of the professional training of theologians and it was administered to Jews by their own judges trained in the Jewish *halakhah*. The preachers, cantors, beadles, and other synagogue officials were part of the Jewish communal bureaucracy. Scribes, whether devoting their energies to copying books, preparing scrolls of law, or composing the necessary deeds for commercial transactions or family relations, even if engaged in free-lance work, were closely supervised by Jewish communal organs. Although their documents were, for the most part, recognized by Muslim courts and civil authorities, Jewish scribes were considered members of the Jewish communal officialdom, trained by Jewish experts and working for an exclusively Jewish clientele. They will be dealt with at some length in connection with our analysis of Jewish communal life in a later volume.[116]

Only the Jewish medical profession played a considerable role beyond the confines of its own community. Not only Jewish court physicians and those serving in some other semigovernmental capacity, but also ordinary practitioners were often subjected to hostile attacks from rivals and religious fanatics. The most frequent accusation, that they were sworn enemies of all Gentiles, persisted in the face of their repeated denials supported by their effective ministrations to non-Jewish patients. A contemporary Muslim poet declaimed: "Cursed shall be the Jews and the Christians: / Through trickery they have succeeded in realizing their ambitions. / They have become physicians and comptrollers. / And thus manipulate both souls and fortunes." More dangerous was the denunciation, occasionally hurled against Jewish arrivals from other lands, that they had once professed Islam but subsequently relapsed to their ancestral faith. Such relapses were treated as mortal offenses under Muslim law. We recall that no less a personality than Moses Maimonides had been thus denounced by a young Arab doctor whom he had graciously received and showered with favors. Since Maimonides had come to Cairo after living for a number of years in Spain and Morocco under the intolerant Almohade regime, which had formally suppressed Judaism and Christianity throughout its realm, it could easily be construed that he must have been a relapsed convert. Only the intervention of highly placed friends saved him from a very severe penalty. Nevertheless, a considerable number of Jewish doctors continued to flourish in both Egypt and Syria to the end of the Mameluke regime. Connected with the medical profession was that of pharmacy, a semicommercial and semiprofessional occupation. In fact, many experts in medical drugs were also dealers in perfumes and other cosmetics. Some of them took part in the extensive international traffic of imports and exports of a variety of drugs stemming from different countries which were said to offer the most effective cures for specific ailments.[117]

FISCAL JUNGLE

In all these activities Jews enjoyed a modicum of equal opportunity. Whatever their occupation, however, Jews and Christians suffered from the yoke of taxation, whether it lay heavily on the general population or rested specifically on them. The simplistic tax system prevailing under early Islam had long since given way to a wide variety of taxes, some of which were from the outset more discriminatory against the *dhimmis*. According to Maqrizi's list, there existed 88 different taxes in the Faṭimid Empire that were considered noncanonical because they had no backing in early Islamic traditions. Upon seizing power, Saladin abolished them. However, because of the great fiscal needs of his expanding empire and his constant wars with the Crusaders or other neighbors, he and his successors had to reintroduce many of the discarded imposts. It was particularly Baybars who, even after the victory at 'Ayn Jalut, revived some old, and invented many new, methods of squeezing revenue out of impoverished subjects. True, in 1279 Qala'un revoked some of Baybars' fiscal decrees, but the great pressures, both international and domestic, forced him and his successors to reenact some of them and continually devise new fiscal methods to increase the revenues of the Treasury. Such backtracking was also repeated after the much-praised fiscal reform by An-Naṣir in 1315. That relatively long-lived sultan was constrained in the final years of his reign greatly to expand the fiscal exactions. The worst was still to come. Having disposed of much landed property by their semifeudal donations to their emirs (through the *iqta'* system), the sultans of the declining Baḥri period bequeathed to the Burji dynasty in 1382 a depleted Treasury and a fiscal structure in bad disarray. Hence Barsbay and his successors had to resort to the aforementioned ill-functioning government monopolies, which greatly interfered with the freedom of trade and ultimately contributed to the downfall of the Mameluke Empire. Under this system, the forced sales of monopolized goods at highly inflated prices to helpless merchants (including Jews and Christians) had all the earmarks of an artificial sales tax, which few traders were able entirely to pass on to the consumers.[118]

From the beginning of Muslim rule, however, there existed built-in discriminatory taxes whereby the *dhimmis* were supposed to be paying for their protection. Going back to the Qur'an and early Ḥadith, these taxes enjoyed canonical prestige and were collected in all medieval and early modern Muslim lands. While the original land tax (*kharaj*) became less and less significant to Jews, whose landholdings had been shrinking for both political and economic reasons, the main sufferers now were the Muslim peasants. Under the burgeoning feudal system the landed aristocracy holding the *iqta'* villages—though theoretically not owning them as private property—exploited the farming population through its excessive shares in crops, the peasants' corvée labor, and other services. But the capitation tax (*jizya,* in Egypt long known as *jaliya*), collected only from the *dhimmis*, remained a permanent feature of the fiscal system.

Remarkably, the force of tradition was sufficiently strong to keep the size and character of the poll tax more or less intact. Basically, the law provided for numerous exemptions of women, children, the aged, the sick, and the demonstrably poor; while the taxpaying male population was divided into three groups paying 1, 2, or 4 dinars. This division continued to operate in the twelfth and thirteenth centuries, although here and there some fractions of a dinar were added. In the late twelfth century the tax ranged from 2¼ to 4⅛ dinars; in practice the Treasury's revenue from it usually yielded only an average of 2 dinars a person. Occasionally, a ruler like Al-Ḥakim defied tradition and doubled the capitation tax, or an emir like Sa'īf ad-Din al-Fakri of Damascus forced the *dhimmis* in 1341–42 to pay the tax for three years in advance. Similarly, the poor, who were originally freed from taxation, were now often forced to disburse varying, arbitrarily assessed, amounts because only after making his payment did an Egyptian Jew or Christian obtain a formal receipt. This certificate (*bara'a*) had to be produced on many occasions, especially on travels from one locality to another; failure to present one on an official's request made the *dhimmi* subject to instant arrest. In a typical letter dated *ca.* 1225 a schoolteacher in a small Egyptian town complained to a relative that his income from teaching and copying books did not even cover his expenses for the poll tax and clothing, not to speak of food for himself and his family. He had in vain waited for a year for the *nagid* to take care of his *jaliya* as promised. Another defaulting taxpayer wrote:

My present state is marked by illness, infirmity, want, and excessive fear, since I am sought by the comptroller of revenue, who is hard upon me and writes out warrants of arrest, sending "runners" to track me down. I am afraid they will find out my hiding place. If I fall into their hands, I shall die under their chastisement or will have to go to prison and die there. Now I take my refuge with God and with you.

In such cases, the community at large often had to pay the *jaliya* for impecunious members even if it had to borrow money for that purpose, as it did in a famine year. In 1409, during the great economic crisis, it was even forced to sell three lots of real estate belonging to its philanthropic fund (the *waqf*). Yet the Jews had long learned to live somehow with that special tax.[119]

More burdensome were the recurrent extraordinary imposts such as the war tax of 1 dinar a year, which was more or less regularly collected, especially from the *dhimmis*. On major occasions, such as preparations for a campaign, defensive or offensive, special contributions were exacted either from the religious communities as a whole or from their wealthy members. This system lent itself to much abuse. According to the contemporary annalist, Muḥammad b. Aḥmad Ibn Iyas, by May–June 1493 Sultan Qa'it-Bey had raised large amounts for the Treasury because of a threatening Ottoman attack. He had gathered

the revenue of a five-months' rent imposed upon all real estate [including that] belonging to *Waqf*s of mosques, colleges, and the hospital, and the sums extorted from the Jewish and Christian communities, the European and North-African merchants, the fishermen on Lake Borollos, the most conspicuous tradesmen, and the rich burghers.

Although the Ottoman attack had not materialized at that time, the sultan did not refund these imposts to the respective taxpayers. Instead he lavished some 400,000 dinars on his Mamelukes. Even without any war emergency, sultans or emirs managed time and again to collect major contributions from the *dhimmis* under various excuses. As discussed earlier, Baybars had threatened all Cairo Jews and Christians with extermination because some Christians had been accused of large-scale arson, in revenge for the Mameluke victories over the Crusaders. Only after lengthy negotiations did the sultan accept the large fine of 500,000 dinars (according to some versions 50,000 dinars) as a "voluntary" contribution by the two religious communities. Such "fines" were not infrequently collected thereafter. The death of a childless *dhimmi,* especially a foreigner, offered the opportunity for confiscating an entire estate, although this was contrary to the established law which provided that heirless estates of non-Muslims should be inherited by their respective religious communities. These and many other abuses made earning a living increasingly difficult for the *dhimmi*s. Even the bribing of officials to stave off bureaucratic interference—a widespread way of life in the Middle East—merely added another significant expense to the legitimate pursuit of almost any calling.[120]

Equally discriminatory could be the system of collecting license fees and customs duties. In practice, many government officials granting such licenses (for example, to shopkeepers or brokers) often collected more from "infidels" than from their own coreligionists. Such fees must have been particularly burdensome to Jews, since so large a percentage of their population made a living as artisans, agents, and petty traders in large cities, especially Fusṭaṭ-Cairo, Alexandria, and Damascus. If on one occasion the license fees for *dhimmi*s were reduced from a 10 percent internal toll to 5 percent, the respective charges were doubtless considerably increased by the usual bribes. At one time the import duties on merchandise, set at 2½ percent *ad valorem* for the Muslims, amounted to 5 percent for native *dhimmi*s and 10 percent for foreigners. Ships landing in Alexandria had to pay a duty of up to 30 percent of the value of their imported cargo. According to an ancient Middle-Eastern usage, moreover, a creditor could seize not only merchandise brought in by his defaulting debtor but also that belonging to the debtor's compatriots. This system had been adopted by the Jewish communities as well. They often held merchants hailing from the same city coresponsible for obligations entered into by any one of their compatriots. Nor were import duties limited to the first place of entry, since many provinces collected customs duties on their own account. Merchants traveling from Syria to Egypt had to pass the border station of Qaṭya in eastern Egypt, which maintained a major customs station of its own. According to Ibn Baṭṭuṭa, who visited Qaṭya in 1326–27, that station collected the very large sum of 1,000 gold dinars daily. In addition various authorities collected export duties.[121]

This often chaotic fiscal system was worsened by the unpredictably fitful legislation. We recall Qala'un's abolition of certain taxes in 1279 and the great tax reform of An-Naṣir in 1315, both enacted to alleviate the unsustainable burdens of the population, that gave way within a few years to the reenactment of the same or new imposts. The subsequent fiscal developments clearly demonstrated that Mameluke taxation was bent more on producing the largest possible revenue for the state and its rapacious officials than on promoting the welfare of the population. How wrong this approach was, even from the standpoint of their self-interest, the Mameluke sultans could have learned from the example set by their neighbor, the Rasulid ruler of Yemen, Mu'ayyad Dawud (1297–1321). In order to restore the prosperity of his state, Mu'ayyad in 1298 abolished all excessive customs duties and ordered his officials to treat merchants benevolently. As a result, he found that within twenty years his cash accumulation had grown to 300,000 dinars.[122]

On the other hand, the Mamelukes' almost unmanageable fiscal system opened up new opportunities to a small enterprising minority, the tax collectors. Since the state was in no position directly to raise all taxes due from the population, the authorities had to employ tax farmers (*dhamins*) to gather some revenue on a semicommercial basis. This occurred despite the warnings against such delegation of power already voiced under Harun ar-Rashid (786–809) by the then leading fiscal expert, Ya'qub b. Ibrahim Abu Yusuf. Nor did the presence in Cairo of a highly developed bureaucratic apparatus effectively prevent tax evasions. In the case of the poll tax, the central office was supposed to receive regular reports about all new settlers, newly born children, and males reaching maturity, as well as about departures or deaths of prospective taxpayers. In this way the government was able for a long time to collect the capitation tax through its own officials, just as the *kharaj* was raised directly by the beneficiaries of the *iqta'* system or by government agents. Most other taxes, however, were entrusted to tax farmers who, against a stipulated annual amount paid to the authorities, were to collect them under clearly spelled out conditions. Nevertheless, the tax farmers usually managed to amass larger amounts than had originally been estimated and thus were able to accumulate considerable surpluses.[123]

However, there also were cases of collections falling below expectations and the tax farmers being forced to borrow money from the government to meet their obligations. This was a risky procedure because, when unable to repay such loans or otherwise to meet their payments on time, these entrepreneurs were often arrested and subjected to severe torture. Moreover, contracts were usually written on an annual basis and their renewal depended on the whim of the contracting officials. On its part, the Jewish community tried to prevent overbidding by outsiders—which would merely have whetted the appetites of sultans or emirs—by threatening unfair Jewish competitors with excommunication. But it appears that, under the Burji regime, with the tightening of fiscal controls and the general economic and moral decline, such competition by "interlopers" increased also in the Jewish camp. There may, nevertheless, have remained in the minds of some Muslim and Jewish intellectuals a general suspicion of tax farming as such. In the classical Muslim jurisprudence, voices were heard equating gains from tax farming with usury (*riba* in its widest interpretation). Similarly, students of the talmudic literature and Christian students of the New Testament could not help harboring compunctions about the ethics of any *mokhes* (publican), so greatly deprecated by their forebears. However, the economic realities made the employment of tax farmers a necessity and rendered the potential profits, however risky, extremely alluring to the tax collectors. These considerations seem to have greatly lessened opposition to that occupation as such. Nor could the potential critics overlook the vast opportunities for employment thus offered to countless individuals, who otherwise would merely have swelled the ranks of the poor. Needless to say, the advantages accruing to Jewish tax farmers and their employees did not entirely balance the damage caused to the masses of the Jewish population by the increasingly burdensome yoke of taxation.[124]

"WHEN A SLAVE BECOMES KING"

On the whole, the two and a half centuries of Mameluke rule were a sad chapter in the history of Mid-Eastern Jewry. Although its vicissitudes during that period compared rather favorably with the tragic destinies of the West-European Jews, they presented a sorry interlude between the flourishing Jewish life under the Great and Faṭimid Caliphates on the one hand, and that under the Ottoman Empire on the other. True, there were no large-scale massacres or wholesale uprootings of Jewish communities through decrees of expulsion. The occasional anti-Jewish riots usually bore a local character; as a rule they were quite sporadic and had little connection with one another. On the whole, security for life and limb continued to be vouchsafed by law while the occasional losses sustained by individuals may not have proportionately exceeded those occasioned by the internecine struggles within the turbulent Muslim majority.

Simultaneously, there was no stability in the entire fabric of sociopolitical life. While the Mameluke armies succeeded for the most part in staving off foreign invasions and particularly served to stem the Mongolian "deluge" with its extreme destructiveness to the lives and possessions of all subjects, there was a great deal of economic disorder and fiscal pressure which made earning a living extremely arduous for the majority of the population, and doubly so for the "protected subjects." Even the few individual Jews who, by personal endowment or good luck, were able to break through the barriers erected by law and mass prejudice and become higher government officials, busy physicians, or successful businessmen, were never sure of their wealth and social position. Especially during the Burji period the rapacity of the sultans and their fiscal advisers was such that no one could plan ahead for more than a few weeks or months. In addition, the general economic policies, based upon increasingly rigid monopolies, became ruinous to the country at large and the *dhimmis* in particular. A. S. Tritton correctly asserts that in the late medieval Middle East "the position of the *dhimmis* did change for the worse. They were more liable to suffer from the violence of the crowd, and the popular fanaticism was accompanied by an increasing strictness among the educated. The spiritual isolation of Islam was accomplished." The obverse of this condition was a growing spiritual isolation of the religious minorities. No longer did Jewish intellectuals make significant contributions to Arabic letters and sciences. Nor were they, for that matter, very creative in the fields of Jewish learning.[125]

It may well have crossed the minds of many Syro-Egyptian Jews, viewing the meteoric rise of former slaves to the throne, that this regime fully exemplified the old talmudic adage about the harshness meted out to subject groups "when a slave becomes king." If throughout their earlier history many thoughtful Jews had resented the rule of Islam over their communities as the reign of the "son of a slave girl" (Ishmael, son of Hagar), they must now have felt that they were living in a double bondage.

LXXIV

NORTH AFRICA AND MUSLIM SPAIN

ALTHOUGH FOR A while they were united with the Syro-Egyptian heartland of medieval Islam under the rule of the Great Caliphate and, in part, again under the early Faṭimid Empire, the countries west of Egypt pursued a basically different historical career. To be sure, the great Christian-Muslim confrontation during the Crusades affected the entire Mediterranean basin, and, for several generations, Spain became the major theater of the wars between Western Europe and Western Islam, although the Spanish *reconquista* soon reunited practically all of Spain under Christian rule. Yet this great ideological conflict and the enthusiasm generated, particularly on the Christian side, by the idea of liberating the Holy Land with its holy sepulchre and other surviving monuments of early Christianity were far less intensive in the West. And only here and there did missionary dreamers like Raymond Lull and King Louis IX conceive of converting the North African Muslims as a great Christian ideal. On the whole, the armed clashes between the Iberian Christians and their North African Muslim neighbors from Morocco to Tunisia pursued more obvious sociopolitical designs than did the expeditions to the Middle East, where the basic economic drive of the Italian merchant republics was long submerged under the idealistic motivations of most Crusaders, led by the Papacy and the Western nobility.

On the Muslim side, in contrast, the reaction was more outspokenly religious. In the eleventh and twelfth centuries, it was largely in the name of religion that the Almoravides and then the Almohades succeeded in reuniting the forces of North African Islam and in adding large parts of Spain to their united empire. However, this religiously motivated drive quickly spent itself. It was followed by a gradual retreat into the North African possessions, which themselves fell apart into several regional entities under various dynasties competing with one another for control over kingdoms with ever-changing frontiers. The early expeditions of Moroccan kings to Spain clearly bore the stamp of strategic and imperial efforts rather than of a holy war in behalf of Islam. Even these efforts ceased after the thirteenth century. At that time Christian Iberia was gradually gaining the upper hand, and in the fourteenth through the sixteenth centuries it made successful incursions into North Africa, establishing a number of bridgeheads along the Mediterranean and Atlantic shores. This expansion was stemmed only by the upsurging power of the Ottoman Empire.

Internally, too, the assimilation of the conquered populations proceeded much more slowly in North Africa west of Egypt than it did in the Middle East. The West-Asian conglomerates of ethnic and sectarian groups (apart from the Persians and, of course, Jews and Christians) rather quickly adopted, along with Islam and the Arabic language, the sort of melting-pot ideology of the caliphal regime which speedily converted all these populations into a more unified Arab civilization. In contrast, the Berbers of North Africa, though likewise adopting Islam and to some extent the Arabic language, retained much of their identity throughout the medieval period. Constantly reinforced from the Berber tribes living around the fringes of the Sahara Desert, this element left an indelible mark on the entire evolution of North African culture and policy. The medieval Latin writers were fully justified in using the term "Moors," rather than the more generic "Saracens," for the North African conquerors of Spain and their compatriots in their home countries.[1]

All these trends, of necessity, affected the North African Jewish minority. However, its destinies were far more deeply influenced by the intolerant Almohade regime, which caused a definite break in the historic continuity of its North African and Spanish communities. In fact, it took several generations after the catastrophic Almohade wave had passed before Jewish communal life could be fully revived. In many ways the North African Jews had to start afresh and endeavor to rebuild their communal structures from the ashes of their formerly glorious civilization.

UNITARIAN EXTREMISM

At the beginning of the thirteenth century the vast West-Islamic area, extending from the frontiers of Egypt to the Atlantic Ocean and across Gibraltar into large parts of Spain, was united under the Almohade regime. That its unification was not as enduring as had seemed at its inception was owing, in part, to the very factors which at first favored the rapid Almohade expansion. Ibn Tumart's "unitarian" ideology, which gave the movement its name, was very appealing to the Moorish masses in North Africa and Spain and so helped sweep away all resistance. In the victorious march of 'Abd al-Mu'min (1130–63) from the desert into the flourishing areas of north-central and north-west Africa and, finally, into Spain, the preaching of "pure" monotheism received a resounding echo. Its effect was magnified by the disturbing domestic situation in the petty Moorish kingdoms (of *taifas*) after the dissolution of the Spanish Caliphate in the early eleventh century and the beginnings of the Christian reconquest on the Iberian Peninsula. In a short time, however, the extreme intolerance of that movement and its attempt to suppress not only Christianity and Judaism but also various divergent Muslim sects and schools of theology became the Achilles heel of the new regime and, within little more than half a century, the empire began breaking asunder.[2]

During the following decades the Spanish Christians succeeded in reducing the Muslim control to a small southeastern corner of the Iberian Peninsula: the principality of Granada, which managed to survive as an independent state until 1492. Simultaneously, the disruptive forces on the North African continent, nurtured by the ever turbulent Berber tribes in the Sahara Desert and its vicinity, broke up the provinces of the Almohade empire into different sovereignties, out of which ultimately emerged the modern states of Morocco, Algeria, Tunisia, and Tripolitania-Libya. Their dynasties included the Marinids of Morocco (1196–1470), the Ziyanids of Algeria (1235–1393), who were followed for a while by the expanding Marinids, and the Ḥafṣids of Tunisia (1228–1574). All of these countries, together with Libya but with the significant exception of Morocco, were incorporated into the

Ottoman Empire by the middle of the sixteenth century. The last three medieval centuries belong to the most tempestuous periods in North African history, the sharp internal divisions being aggravated by invasions of European powers, particularly Portugal, Spain, and France, in the first decades of the modern era. These powers occupied some important Atlantic and Mediterranean harbors until most of these colonies were taken over by enterprising corsairs. These buccaneers continued their operations even after most of the Maghrib (known in Europe as the Barbary States) came under Ottoman overlordship. Only in the nineteenth and early twentieth centuries were France, Spain, and Italy able to occupy and colonize some of these territories until their emergence as independent Arab states in recent decades.[3]

During the Late Middle Ages and early modern times, the Jewish chronology in North Africa and Muslim Spain may be divided into five periods: (1) the severe oppression under the declining Almohade regime in the first half of the thirteenth century; (2) the resurgence of Jewish life under the newly independent smaller principalities before 1391; (3) the large-scale Spanish Jewish immigration to North Africa following the Castilian and Aragonese massacres of 1391 and the emergence of the complicated *converso* problem on the Iberian Peninsula; (4) the acceleration of that migratory movement after the fall of Granada and the expulsion of the Jews from Spain in 1492 and the forced conversion of Portuguese Jewry in 1496–97, followed ten years later by a certain relaxation of the ban on Jewish emigration; and (5) the new situation created by the Ottoman occupation.

At the beginning of the thirteenth century the Almohade regime still adhered to the policy stated, as we recall, in 'Abd al-Mu'min's reputed address to the Jewish and Christian leaders which emphasized that, after the expiration of the 500-year term of the original Covenant and the evident failure of the Jewish Messiah to come and of Christ to reappear, "We must not allow you to persevere in your error; nor do we desire any of your tribute. You have only the choice of Islam or death." 'Abd Al-Mu'min formulated here merely the ultimate consequences of the teachings and practices advocated by the founder of the Almohade movement, Muḥammad b. 'Abdallah Ibn Tumart. After his early successes, the reformer had concluded that he was the Mahdi and leading imam of his generation (if he obviously lacked one of the essential qualifications—descent from Mohammed—his followers quickly supplied him with a spurious genealogy up to the Messenger's daughter Faṭima). He soon insisted that the charismatic imam of every generation was the inspired holder of divine truth and as such made the final determination of right and wrong. A chapter in one of his writings bears the characteristic heading:

> On the knowledge, that is, the indispensability for the entire community of the belief in the imamate. It is the pillar of religion and one of the mainstays of the Law. The maintenance of truth in the world is unthinkable without the indispensable belief that the imamate shall exist at all times without a break down to the [world's] final hour.

In his detailed elaboration of this basic belief, Ibn Tumart emphasized that, in fulfillment of this religious duty, "it is indispensable for the entire community to believe in him and to acknowledge the truth of his message. All must submit to him and accept his judgment." This doctrine had long antecedents in the earlier Islamic theology; it even deeply affected such an outsider as Saadiah Gaon. Two centuries before Ibn Tumart, the great gaon had sounded his rallying cry:

> God does not leave His people in any generation without a scholar whom he inspires and enlightens so that he in turn may instruct and teach the people and make it prosper through him. And the occasion thereto has been what I have personally experienced in what God, in His grace, has done for me and for the people.

But only the disciples of the North African Muslim leader were able to establish, in his name, a wide-ranging authoritarian regime, whose demands ultimately included complete religious conformity in the teachings of Islam according to Ibn Tumart's interpretation.[4]

The practical enforcement of this policy is well illustrated by a letter written early in 1148 by Shlomo Cohen to his father Yehudah Sijilmasi, while the Almohade conquest of North Africa was still in progress. According to reports heard from eye-witnesses, upon the voluntary surrender of the famous southern city of Sijilmassa, 'Abd al-Mu'min ordered the Jews and Christians there to accept Islam. "After debates extending over seven months, during which the Jewish community fasted and prayed, a [Muslim] commander ordered speedy conversion of all." One hundred and fifty Jewish resisters were slain, while the rest, led by their judge, Joseph b. Amram, adopted Islam. Elsewhere, particularly in cities taken by storm, wholesale conversion seems to have been ruthlessly enforced immediately after occupation. Some Jews followed the old advice given by a gaon—to use the earliest opportunity for leaving the country. Although the Almohade administration had become suspicious of would-be travelers and threatened them with the death penalty for unauthorized departure, many Jews, like the family of Maimonides or his pupil Joseph Ibn 'Aqnin, found ways to emigrate to safer regions. Others, observing that mere lip service to Islam often satisfied the authorities, remained behind while secretly continuing to observe Jewish customs and particularly the Sabbath rest commandment. Until the modern period, there were some families of genuinely professing Muslims who closed their shops on Saturday and wore white clothing on Friday night, without realizing that they thus unconsciously continued a deeply rooted family tradition from the days when their ancestors professed Judaism.[5]

Secret Jews of this type were sufficiently numerous to attract the rulers' attention. After more than half a century of Almohade domination the theologically well-trained Caliph Abu-Yusuf Ya'qub al-Manṣur (1184–99) was quoted as saying: "If I knew for certain that they became faithful Muslims, I would allow them to mix and intermarry with Muslims; if I knew for certain that they are infidels, I would kill the men, and hand their children and their property over to Muslims. However, neither fact is certain." As a result, the former Jews, as well as Christians, were treated as second-class citizens. They were not allowed to engage in trade or to marry Old Muslims, while their children were frequently placed with Old Muslim families for orthodox Islamic upbringing. This situation, as we recall, may have been inspired by traditions of the late Visigothic discrimination against the Jews five centuries earlier. The prohibition against former *dhimmis* engaging in commercial transactions not only went further than the Visigothic King Egica's restrictive legislation but also was more significant psychologically, inasmuch as the Muslim civilization held commerce in much higher esteem than did the then regnant Christian opinion.[6]

This generally accepted notion of the extreme severity of Almohade enactments has recently been controverted by a competent Israeli scholar of Moroccan ancestry, David Corcos-Abulafia. After submitting the pertinent Arabic historical sources, especially those by Al-Marrakushi and Adh-Dhahabi, to a devastating critique and interpreting away some intimations in the later Jewish chronicles, Corcos reached the conclusion that

> (a) There was a general atmosphere of terror in the Al-Murabat cities conquered by the Almohades. It was because of this fear that Jews embraced Islam and not because of any consistent or declared policy of forced conversion. . . . (b) A change for the worse took place only in 1165, when the leader of the Jewish community of Fez, R. Judah ha-Cohen ibn Sussan, was cruelly executed. This marked the beginning of a short period during which a policy of forced mass-conversions was in effect. It was at this time that the family of Maimonides fled to the east. (c) With the death of the persecuting ruler [Abu Ya'qub Yusuf I, 1163–84], the situation of the Jews began to improve. In 1232 professing Jews are found in Marrakesh, and some time later they gradually make their appearance in other cities of northern Africa.

Despite that author's meritorious research and his clarification of many important details, the weight of evidence still favors the generally accepted assumption that the Almohade regime went much further in its outlawry of religious dissent and that it also discriminated against the ever suspect descendants of the forced converts. Yet we must not overlook the fact that, even at the height of their power before 1200, the Almohade rulers' law-enforcement capabilities were hampered by the presence in their newly conquered areas of only a rather small minority of genuine Almohade devotees. Even in such a metropolitan area as Seville (next to Marrakesh perhaps the most important center of the Almohade empire), life seems to have proceeded largely along its previously established patterns for most inhabitants, doubtless including the nominal converts from Judaism and Christianity. It stands to reason that the farther away from the seats of Almohade power the New Muslims lived, the less effective was the governmentally inspired supervision of their daily life. In the long run, moreover, whatever differentiation may have been actually applied between earlier Muslims and descendants of Jews, for decades after their ancestors' original conversion, often merely served to stiffen the New Muslims' resistance. As a result, quite a few grandchildren and great-grandchildren of the original apostates found their way back to their ancestral faith with relative ease and, as soon as they were able to, began to reassert their Jewish identity more or less openly.[7]

Such reassertion was facilitated by a gradual relaxation in the enforcement of the original decree. Al-Manṣur himself broke some of these regulations when, in his Moroccan capital of Marrakesh, he employed a bodyguard largely recruited from Christian Spaniards. Later (on June 10, 1251) another caliph, 'Umar al-Murtadha (1248–66), actually wrote a letter to Pope Innocent IV asking him to send "a man of superior intelligence and good conduct who would take care of their [the guardsmen's] religious interests and see to it that they observe their customary laws"—a request with which the pope complied. Perhaps, observing what was happening at the Faṭimid and other courts which had gradually come under the control of their praetorian guards, these monarchs had greater confidence in "unbelieving" soldiers than in an all-Muslim guard whose commanders might conspire against the throne. Al-Manṣur is also recorded as having allowed some Christian churches to reopen. In 1232, while Caliph Abu l'Ala Idris Ma'mun (1229–32) was engaged in besieging Ceuta, the rebel chieftain Yaḥya ibn an-Naṣir had occupied Marrakesh. "His first concern was to destroy the Christian church, to massacre a great many Jews and Beni Fardhan [Christians] and to seize their goods." Although in general these late Almohade caliphs did not tolerate Christian or Jewish religious displays and in 1220 five Franciscan missionaries were mercilessly slain, the pertinent report indicates the presence of both a church and professing Jews in the capital.[8]

EAST-CENTRAL MAGHRIB

Seemingly the farther away a particular province was from the center of the western Muslim–Christian conflict on the Iberian Peninsula, the less rigid became the attitude of the late Almohade rulers toward religiously suspect subjects. Not only did they allow a mosque converted from a church in Tunis to be named the Mosque of Jesus—this concession could still be reconciled with the traditional Muslim recognition of Jesus as a genuine prophet—but they apparently looked the other way when a synagogue reemerged there. At least according to a later tradition, an old Tunisian synagogue remained in operation until it was gradually abandoned, probably in the fourteenth century, necessitating the erection of a new house of worship close to the newly established Jewish quarter (*hara*) in the vicinity of the royal palace and the Great Mosque. This particular moderation may have been secured, however, through the personal intervention of Sidi Mahrez, who was later revered by the Tunisians as their city's patron. He had been aided by Jews in Al-Mu'min's successful campaign to recapture Tunis from the Normans in 1159–60. Possibly as a reward for their patriotic help, the Jews retained possession of their house of worship. In general, however, the Jews lived under the shadow of the titanic struggle between Islam and Christendom, as exemplified by the two crusades of Louis IX. The second expedition, in particular, which ended with the king's landing in Tunisia and his tragic death in 1270 (possibly from the epidemic dysentery then raging in the country), must have demonstrated to Tunisian Jewry that the Christian missionary fervor, though aimed principally at the Holy Land, constituted a permanent menace to the Jewish survival in all Moorish midway points. The Tunisian Jews may also have heard by that time about the persecution of their French coreligionists under the regime of Saint Louis and his brother, Count Alphonse de Poitou.[9]

In any case, it appears that almost all other synagogues remained closed and that, even after the dissolution of the Almohade empire and the reestablishment of some religious liberties, the Jewish communities were deprived of their communal institutions and increasingly sank into a state of dismal ignorance of their Jewish heritage. Maimonides, who during his emigration to the Middle East in 1165 had briefly visited Tunisia, is said to have commented later on the low level of their culture. In a letter which he supposedly wrote to his son Abraham toward the end of his life, he singled out the Jewry of the island of Jerba, offering the following advice:

Beware of some people residing in the Maghrib on the island of Jerba who come from localities in the Berber areas, for they are of a dry and crude disposition. You should generally be on guard against persons living between Tunis and Alexandria of Egypt or residing in the Berber mountains because they are, in my opinion, more stupid than are other people. This despite their being strong in their belief. The Lord is my witness that they appear to me like the Karaites who deny the Oral Law. In their business transactions they have no concern at all for the Torah, Bible, or Talmud, nor do they properly preach on the basis of the Aggadah or Halakhah, even though some of them serve as judges.

The majority of Jewish inhabitants on the island, which was to play a role in North African Jewish history, were predominantly of Berber origin even in the twentieth century. They bore Berber family names, used a Hebrew dialect and pronunciation which must have offended the ears of Spanish Hebrew purists like the Maimuni family, and were indeed far removed from the mainstream of Jewish cultural life. As an example taken from daily life which showed their utter ignorance of Jewish law, that purportedly Maimonidean letter mentioned their extreme rigidity with respect to a menstruating woman, at whom they did not deign to look and with whom they did not talk; they even refused to step on places previously touched by her feet. In fact, under the first Ḥafṣids Jewish communal life in the entire eastern region of the former Almohade empire remained on a generally very low level. As far as we can tell, neither Tunisia nor Tripolitania-Libya had officiating rabbis during the thirteenth and fourteenth centuries. Even their litigations had to be adjudicated by lay elders who, because of their ignorance of Jewish law, served as arbiters rather than as judges. In some cases they blithely referred to Muslim law to back up their decisions.[10]

Serious weaknesses in Jewish life in the east-central Maghrib came to the fore long before the Almohade conquest. About 1045, the once flourishing Jewish cultural center of Kairuwan had been destroyed by the invasion of the Berber Hilal and Sulaym tribes, partially instigated by the Fatimids in revenge for the separation of Tunisia and Tripolitania from their empire. As on some other occasions, a truly vigorous Jewish community might have speedily revived after that sudden onslaught. As it happened, however, this destruction left an indelible imprint upon north-central African Jewries, most of which took centuries to recover. Under the Almohade regime, Kairuwan and Ḥammamet were declared holy Islamic cities. Even after the rise of the more tolerant Ḥafṣid dynasty, "infidel" visitors were forbidden to enter the two cities; their spending a night there was punishable by death. Of course, converted Jews could remain, or even settle anew, in both localities. For centuries thereafter, Ḥammamet included some streets mainly inhabited by descendants of Jews who had adopted Islam during the great persecution. We do not know the specific dates and causes for that segregation, but it undoubtedly helped to preserve a certain element of continuity among these settlers of Jewish origin. As late as the beginning of the twentieth century, some of these offshoots of Ḥammamet's Jewish community maintained certain distinctive Friday night observances which were at variance with those customary among their Old Muslim compatriots. Like their similarly conservative coreligionists in late medieval Spain, they were generally unaware that these practices had been derived from old Jewish forms of celebrating the Sabbath, but they merely followed family traditions reaching back to the Middle Ages. Thus the Kairuwan region, which had once been the major focus of Jewish learning and communal autonomy outside the Palestino-Babylonian center, now practically disappeared from the annals of Jewish history.[11]

Nonetheless, on general grounds we may assume that the relatively brief interlude of extreme Almohade intolerance did not completely eliminate the continuity of Jewish life in the east-central Maghrib. At the same time the influence of the Berber tribes, whether still residing in their ancient habitats along the Sahara Desert or strongly represented in the urban centers, was an ever present factor. In their constant exchanges with their Muslim neighbors, Jews consisting of descendants of ancient settlers and early Islamic immigrants from the Middle East, and of offshoots of Berber tribes converted to Judaism at an early time, naturally appeared strange to Jews arriving from Syro-Egyptian or Iberian environments. Even if the new arrivals listened to the many local legends which greatly embellished and often distorted the historic realities, they could not quite comprehend the significant antecedents of these developments which, going back to Roman-Byzantine times, had led to the flowering of these communities under the cultural leadership of the Kairuwan sages and the Al-Mahdiyya merchants, and later to their sharp decline in 1050–1250.[12]

Jewish newcomers in the Late Middle Ages and early modern times must have been most amazed by the presence of unfamiliar types of Jews in various parts of North Africa. The farther away from the Mediterranean shores they moved toward the great Sahara Desert, the stranger must have appeared the ways of life of the diverse groups of Berber-looking and -speaking persons professing Judaism. On his numerous visits before the First World War, Nahum Slouschz encountered

> in every part of the desert traces—and even survivals—of a primitive Judaism which at one time played an important role in the whole region of the Sahara from Senegal to the very borders of Somaliland, and which even in our day has been a help in the French occupation. The oral traditions which are everywhere found concerning the early Jewish history of this country [the border regions of the Sahara] are beginning to find confirmation in Arab writings and even in inscriptions of Jewish origin.

Such encounters, which over generations have intrigued diplomatic, business, and scientific travelers, as well as tourists, of many nations, have given rise to numerous more recent scholarly researches. A number of archeologists, linguists, anthropologists, and historians have opened new, more dependable, vistas on the long chain of Judeo-Berber and Judeo-Negro relations which over the ages had existed in those vast expanses across the African continent from the Atlantic to the Indian Ocean.[13]

Closer to the seats of ancient Roman and medieval Muslim civilization, Kairuwan's place was to some extent taken by neighboring Tunis. Regrettably, few Jewish records dating from the late medieval centuries have been preserved. The contemporary Arab chroniclers, too, have but little to say about the Jewish population in Tunisia and Tripolitania before the sixteenth century. Only casually does Abi-Dinar al-Kairuani, for instance, refer to the major persecutions suffered by Tunisian Jewry under Muḥammad I al-Mustanṣir (1249–77). We learn a little more about some aspects of Jewish life in the area from European archives, especially from negotiations, commercial as well as diplomatic, conducted by the Italian merchant republics with the Tunisian rulers. For example, the Pisan archives have preserved a Tunisian courtier's request in 1224 that Podesta Uvaldo Visconti assist a Tunisian Jewish merchant in the pursuit of a claim against a Pisan coreligionist and his son-in-law, a convert to Christianity. Thirteen years later the same podesta received a letter from two Tunisian Muslims asking for assistance for another Tunisian Jew. Similarly, the Catalan archives have revealed that in 1276, on Muḥammad I's recommendation, King Pedro III of Aragon rented a workshop at the entrance to the Valencian Jewish quarter to a Jew from Tunis. Nine years later Pedro paid out to another Tunisian Jew one-half of the revenue received from the Aragonese *funduq* in Tunis. More significantly, in 1293 James II of Aragon sent a Jew named Bondavi on a secret mission to Tlemcen and Tunis. Such stray bits of information testify to the revival of Jewish life in Tunisia but do not offer any real picture of the way the survivors of the Almohade flood had succeeded in rebuilding their shattered fortunes. We rarely hear of any religious movements within the Jewish settlements in the country, but adherence to the Jewish faith was strong enough for the emergence, in the 1220s, of a Jewish messianic movement echoed even in distant France.[14]

In state papers Jews were specifically mentioned for the first time as a collective entity in the peace treaty of 1360 between Pedro IV of Aragon and Sultan Abu Isḥaq Ibrahim II al-Mustanṣir (1350–69) of Tunisia. This treaty provided that the Tunisian authorities would protect the shops belonging to Aragonese subjects, both Christian and non-Christian, and that the Aragonese consuls in Tunisia would exercise exclusive jurisdiction in litigations between Christians and Jews from Aragon. Pedro promised not to allow Muslim or Jewish Tunisians to be taken captive in Aragonese possessions and that those already in captivity would be set free. Abu Isḥaq Ibrahim made the reciprocal pledge with respect to Aragonese captives and in addition promised to refund 2,000 gold dinars annually from customs duties collected on Aragonese goods imported to, or exported from, Tunisia.[15]

Much more information is furnished by some fifteenth-century

Jewish sources. The emigration of Spanish Jews to North Africa, after the massacres of 1391 and the hostile legislation enacted in both Castile and Aragon during the following quarter century, brought into the Maghrib a number of prominent rabbis who, among their other contributions, helped the North African Jewish leaders to resolve certain difficult questions in Jewish law. The responsa of R. Isaac b. Sheshet Perfet and R. Simon b. Ṣemaḥ Duran, who were followed by Duran's learned descendants, also opened up to modern scholarship a vital source of information about many internal and external aspects of Jewish life throughout the western and central Maghrib. We find among the questioners Jewish scholars like Ḥayyim Melilli, a merchant, and Samuel Ḥakim, who was serving as a judge (*dayyan*) in Tunis; their questions are formulated on the level of learned discussions among scholars. Melilli also showed some expertise in commercial affairs. We learn, for example, of occasional conflicts between Muslim and Jewish law or between the will of the ruler and the established practices in the Jewish community. In one such case, R. Simon b. Ṣemaḥ was asked what should be done about the king's assignment of living quarters in Tunis to one of his Jewish favorites, an assignment which infringed upon a communal agreement concerning that particular property. Some of the questions characteristically referred to a private Jewish *funduq* in which foreign Jewish visitors were accommodated with board and lodging, although in 1495 a pupil of Obadiah di Bertinoro complained that he could not find sleeping quarters except in a dilapidated house without a roof. Some interesting insights are also offered by European travelers. According to the Flemish nobleman Anselm Adorne, who visited Tunis in the early 1470s:

> Jews enjoy no freedoms. They all pay a heavy poll tax, wear special clothes different from the attire of the Muslims. Failure to do so subjects them to stoning. Hence they wear a yellow cloth on their heads or necks, while their women do not venture to wear shoes. They are greatly despised and hated, even more than the Latin Christians who are called Frangi.

This status was, of course, not exceptional in the Muslim world. But the Jews of Tunisia, like most of those residing in the Mameluke Empire, usually disregarded such chicaneries with a measure of equanimity.[16]

In this way the Tunisian and neighboring communities carried on until the end of the Middle Ages, when the new disturbances created by the Spanish, Portuguese, and French occupation of some major harbors, as well as the gradual recapture of these cities by the Barbary corsairs led by Khair adh-Dhin (called Barbarossa by the Europeans because of his red beard), created a new situation full of both perils and opportunities for the Jews. According to C. A. Julien, "Khair adh-Dhin authorized the permanent settlement of Jews in the Regency [of Algeria], though he placed a limit on the number of their places of business." Finally, the formal take-over by the Turks—Tunis was one of the last North African centers east of Morocco to be officially annexed by the Ottoman Empire, in 1574—brought North African Jewry fully within the orbit of the mass settlement of Jews under Ottoman rule. Even in the transition period before the Turkish occupation, the power struggle over the Mediterranean possessions deeply affected Tunisian and the rest of North African Jewry, as will become clearer in our treatment of Ottoman Jewry at large in the next volume.[17]

Tunisian rule often extended to neighboring Tripolitania and Libya, which, however, since the days of Saladin frequently gravitated toward Egypt. In general, the frontiers between these areas both east and west of Tunisia were quite fluid. The extent to which sovereignty was exercised by the Ḥafṣids over one or another neighboring territory often depended on the incursions of the Berber tribes from the South. Unfortunately, our information concerning the Jews in Tripolitania and Libya during the last three medieval centuries is extremely limited. The ancient Jewish center in Cyrenaica, which had produced many freedom fighters against Roman oppression and included a Jewish historian of the rank of Jason of Cyrene (whose work is regrettably lost), had continued its activities through the first centuries of Islam. The frequent references to it in the Genizah and other records, largely dating before 1250, indicate the presence of at least 12 Jewish communities in Tripolitania and 4 in Libya, as against 12 in Tunisia, 14 in Algeria, and 17 in Morocco. But despite the availability of good bibliographical compilations, our knowledge is limited to relatively few business transactions or to such incidents as the aforementioned refusal of a Jewish physician in Tripoli to accept the invitation of the sultan of Gabès despite the large sum offered for his services. He yielded only when, to accommodate their neighbor, the Tripolitanian Berber chiefs imprisoned the leading Jews of Tripoli and held them as hostages until the doctor departed. On another occasion the Jewish community of Tripoli sequestered the goods left behind by the agent of an Egyptian Jewish merchant who, en route to Sicily, died on board ship before it landed in Tripoli. The sequestration of these goods for the benefit of the agent's widow and orphans, and the community's demand that they should not be delivered to anyone without adequate proof of his or her claim in a lawsuit, resulted from the elders' apprehension that the merchandise might be confiscated by the local authorities. From Aragonese sources we also learn about individual Tripolitanian Jews who were given safe-conducts by James I to settle in Aragon (1278). A Jewish merchant-interpreter, Maymos b. Nono, proved helpful to Aragonese diplomats in their negotiations with local rulers. Commercial contracts with Majorca were also frequently recorded. However, even after 1391 and 1492 the refugees reaching these distant communities left relatively few traces.[18]

When the Spaniards conquered Tripoli in 1510, most Jews fled to neighboring locations. The few who remained behind were carried into captivity, like their coreligionists of Bougie, Algeria, occupied by the Spanish troops a year earlier. Many of them were sold into slavery in Naples. Yet, before long quite a few Jews returned to the city and, with the aid of R. Simeon b. Labi, reorganized their community in 1549. Simeon, a "Western" (Moroccan?) pilgrim to the Holy Land, gave up his journey when he noticed how ignorant the Tripolitan Jews were of the Torah and how incorrectly they even recited their prayers and blessings. He decided that remaining in the city and teaching the local Jews the proper understanding of the "Torah and the fear of God" ranked higher than a pilgrimage to Jerusalem. "And he almost succeeded in converting them" (Azulai). Outwardly, however, the condition of the local Jews did not improve when in 1559 Emperor Charles V handed the city over to the Knights of Malta. A full restoration of Jewish life in the area did not occur until after its incorporation into the Ottoman Empire.[19]

Little more can be said about late medieval Algerian Jewry. To be sure, being closer to the center of Almohade power in Morocco, the Jews of what was to become Algeria sustained the full measure of Almohade intolerance. As in Morocco and Spain, many Jews and Christians submitted to the will of the "unitarian" rulers and adopted Islam. Others merely paid lip service or embraced a variety of syncretistic observances such as attending the mosque assemblies and even loudly reciting the *sha'ada,* the main Muslim profession of faith: "There is no god but Allah; Mohammed is the Messenger of Allah." They either omitted the final phrase relating to the Messenger or made the mental reservation that God used many messengers.

Here too, therefore, we find that some third- or fourth-generation secret Jews publicly professed Judaism when the pressure was removed. It was with reference to these survivors of Almohade persecution that, in his oft-quoted letter to Pablo Christiani, Jacob de Lattes of Valencia or Venice, formerly of Carcassonne, gloated over the oppressors' downfall. After describing the haughty self-assertion of the original conquerors, which had led to the wholesale destruction of synagogues, the burning of Jewish books, and the violation of the Sabbath and holidays, he boasted that, despite these persecutions

> the Lord's people had not forgotten their Covenant with the Lord, the God of their forefathers, and had not given up their Torah, but each one in his own home prepared for himself a place for concealment. Thus they were able to break the orders of the evildoer while observing the Lord's commandments. Yet the children of Israel sighed from their bondage and the Lord heard their outcry. Our God did not linger in taking revenge on these evildoers and smote them, discomfiting them utterly. . . . And their large empire sank in miry clay and it became the lowest among the kingdoms. In fact, these oppressors and the kings of their dynasty completely vanished.

However, no meaningful restoration of Jewish life was achieved until more than a century later, with the arrival in Algeria of many refugees from the Spanish massacres of 1391.[20]

In the intervening period Tlemcen, rather than Algiers, served as the capital and major military center of the kingdom. Commercially, however, the value of Tlemcen's total annual trade with Majorca in 1327 was estimated at no more than 15,000 to 20,000 dinars. Other parts of Algeria, including their Jewish communities, participated more actively in large-scale exchanges of goods with Spain. But it was particularly the arrival of R. Isaac b. Sheshet Perfet (1326–1408) and R. Simon b. Ṣemaḥ Duran (1361–1444) which injected new life into the Jewish communities of the entire region. In 1464 ʻAbdalbasiṭ b. Ḥalil al-Ḥanafi (1440–1514), son of a high Mameluke dignitary, visited Tlemcen. Although engaged in business, he evinced great interest in the leading scientists of the community and was very much impressed by the Jewish physician Mushi b. Samuil b. Yahuda al-Isra'ili al-Malaqi al-Andalusi, also called Ibn al-Ashqar. ʻAbdalbasiṭ only wished that "the highest God would bring him [Mushi] over to Islam." He added:

> I have never seen nor heard of a *dhimmi* equally expert in that [medical] science nor so versed in the drawing up of magical squares and calendars, as well as in a certain ancient lore. Nevertheless he is very pious in his own religion. . . . He was born in Málaga before 820 (1417), had studied under his father and other teachers, and had become prominent in the art of medicine. He established himself in Tlemcen where a great many distinguished persons came to him to be instructed. I have attached myself to him over a period of time; I learned from him a great deal in both medicine and other subjects.

ʻAbdalbasiṭ later learned that Mushi had become chief of medicine of Tlemcen and was well received at the royal court. "But he has the intelligence and the will not to mix in any governmental affairs." This caution was doubly necessary in Tlemcen, which in that period was the focus of many conflicting interests and was often occupied by the Moroccan rulers.[21]

Less fortunate were the Jews of Oran (in Arabic, Wahran) which, because of its location on the Bay of Oran, played a significant role in Mediterranean shipping and commerce. Like other Algerian Jewish communities, that of Oran received an influx of Spanish refugees after 1391, and its fifteenth-century rabbi Amram b. Merwas Ephrati enjoyed a considerable reputation among his confreres. Other waves of immigrants reached the city in 1492 and 1502, although on one occasion the sudden arrival of a large shipload of Jewish immigrants met with a hostile reception. According to an Arab chronicler, the local inhabitants thought

> that enemies were descending upon them and killed a number. But afterward the Muslim prince took pity on them and, through the in-

tervention of an influential Jew of the country named Dodiham, permitted them to land. He had board cabins erected outside the city for them and the cattle they had brought with them.

The fears of a foreign invasion among the population were not unjustified, for only a few years later (1509) the troops of Ferdinand the Catholic succeeded in occupying the city and, with a relatively short interruption in 1708–1732, Spain ruled over Oran as a Spanish colony until 1792. Probably quite a few Jews fled on the arrival of their sworn enemies. Yet those who remained were allowed to carry on until 1679, when the entire community was uprooted by a decree of banishment.[22]

Obviously, even in the much larger Algerian areas which remained under Muslim domination not all Muslim intellectuals were of as tolerant a disposition as 'Abdalbasiṭ. Not long after that visitor's highly laudatory comment about the local Jewish scientist, another Tlemcen writer, the jurist Muḥammad b. 'Abd al-Karim al-Majili (d. between 1503 and 1505) composed a violently anti-Jewish diatribe, entitled *Aḥkam ahl adh-dhimma* (Against the Protected People). Perhaps reflecting the widespread hostility generated by the arrival of numerous Jewish refugees, Al-Majili contended that every believing Muslim ought to consider any Jew a devil incarnate, bent only on denying his (the Muslim) religion, making him consume meat which the Jews reject, such as carrion and fermented food, as well as involving him in usurious transactions. That is why, the jurist insisted, 'Umar Ibn al-Khaṭṭab had provided that the Jews should not be allowed to exercise the professions of money changers and butchers and that they ought to be excluded from all Muslim bazaars. He even suggested that, since the infringement of any provision of the Covenant of 'Umar made a *dhimmi* lose the legal "protection" guaranteed by that agreement, the Jews, who were violating it in many ways, should be declared outlaws. Al-Majili also made a number of specific proposals affecting the Jewish legal status and economic endeavors. It seems, however, that his sharp attack found no sympathetic echo among the authorities in Tlemcen. Undismayed, the anti-Jewish agitator proceeded to Tuat, in the more "backward" environment of which he hoped to find a more receptive audience. Now often called Al-Tuati, he went to the extreme of advocating the destruction of all synagogues and the killing of all Jews. He also combined his verbal attacks with a promise of a prize of 7 mithkals to any assassin of a Jew. Through correspondence he secured some support from several muftis and qadhis in Fez and Tlemcen. Subsequently he also traveled through the Sudan pursuing his anti-Jewish crusade. On learning of the death of his son in Tuat, he returned to that town to accuse Jews of murdering the son and to demand their total elimination. This time he succeeded in persuading the local ruler to imprison all local Jews. But he was evidently unable to prove his allegations of their guilt and had to witness with dismay their complete exoneration. He seems to have died soon thereafter, without leaving a permanent anti-Jewish heritage in any of these areas.[23]

MOROCCO

The boundaries between what were to become Algeria and Morocco were constantly changing. Both territories, moreover, were subject to frequent incursions from the southern Berber areas, and rarely could the central government exercise any effective control over the country as a whole. Nevertheless, Morocco developed into the most important center of the Maghrib. Fez, especially, founded in 808 by Idris II, became a focus of the entire political, economic, and cultural life of northwest Africa, and its influence extended both eastward to the Egyptian border and north into all that remained of Muslim Spain during and after the *reconquista.*

Nevertheless, even under the long-lasting Marinid dynasty Morocco revealed certain fundamental weaknesses in both its international policies and its domestic affairs. Commenting on the achievements of that dynasty's real founder, Abu-Yusuf Ya'qub (1258–86), Henri Terrasse observed that, despite the sultan's great military successes, his policy was "behind its time. He who on the military front was the victor over the last Almohades, spiritually remained their slave: all his life he dreamed of resuming their foreign policy without realizing that an Islamic and imperial policy was too large an undertaking for him and that it belonged to a period long past." Nor were Morocco's internal conditions more favorable.

While superficially the reigns of Abu-Yusuf and his son Abu-Ya'qub Yusuf (1286–1307) appeared sufficiently brilliant to deserve the high praise showered upon them by later Muslim historians, the underlying deficiencies quickly became manifest under their immediate successor, Abu-Thabit (1307–1308). To quote Terrasse again: "All the shortcomings of the Marinid dynasty [now] came to the fore: the inner dissensions within the central government revealed by the proliferation of pretenders; the Moroccan South's persistent hostility to the dynasty; and the Arab segment's incessant turbulence which caused much trouble and ruin." To be sure, a quarter century later, under the reign of Abu'l Ḥasan 'Ali (1331–48), it appeared that the Marinids were again on the move to reestablish the Almohade empire. The sultan's reconquest of Gibraltar in 1332 was followed by a number of successful campaigns in Africa, culminating in his occupation of Tlemcen in 1337 and his overlordship over Tunis in 1347. But these external successes were marred by internal discord affecting even Abu'l Ḥasan's large family—he is said to have fathered 1,862 children—and his empire began to crumble during the relatively short reign of his son, Abu-'Inan Faris (1348–59). It is not surprising that, looking back on the often anarchical developments during the fourteenth century, 'Abd ar-Raḥman Ibn Khaldun (1332–1406) arrived at the general conclusion that successful Berber dynasties lasted no longer than four (or exceptionally six) generations. Curiously, in support of this theory, the eminent historian, himself a native of Seville of Berber descent, cited the biblical passage of God's vengeance "unto the fourth generation." [24]

Such a state of instability and frequent turmoil did not augur well for Jewish life in the country. Yet, with remarkable tenacity the Moroccan Jews succeeded in reestablishing a modicum of communal and cultural life. Emerging from the Almohade persecution, largely as Jews who had secretly professed their religion in the face of all dangers—in 1220 there was not one synagogue in the entire Maghrib, according to 'Abd al-Wahid al-Idhari al-Marrakushi—they were from time to time reinforced by immigrants from the Iberian Peninsula, where both Christian and Muslim successor states, including Granada, tolerated Judaism. As in the early history of Muslim domination, the great Moroccan cities attracted increasing numbers of Jews and other uprooted persons from various parts of the Mediterranean world. For example, we are told by the chronicler Ibn abi Zar that soon after its foundation in 808 Fez had attracted a multitude of settlers because of "its excellent soil, very sweet water, and temperate climate." Among them were many Jews who "were allowed to establish themselves there in return for the payment of an annual capitation tax which Idris II [the founder] had fixed at 30,000 dinars." Similarly, after the dissolution of the Almohade empire the surviving underground Jewish remnant drew a growing number of coreligionists from less tolerant localities.[25]

The Marinids and their successors never tried to suppress the Jewish faith or indulged in a wholesale expulsion of Jews. Yet, because of the internal dissensions and the fanaticism generated by both the continued Crusading ventures on the Christian side and the extreme Islamic zeal fostered among the masses by preachers and writers, Jewish life was never completely secure. The Jewish communities throughout North Africa perpetually remembered the harrowing experiences during the Almohade regime, a memory strengthened by recurrent violent anti-Jewish episodes or clashes between hostile Muslim factions in which Jews became embroiled against their will.

In 1276 a Fez Jew was slain because of a rumor that he had molested a Muslim woman. Thereupon the populace started an anti-Jewish riot. The incipient massacre, with 14 Jewish fatalities already, was stopped only by the personal intervention of Sultan Abu-Yusuf Ya'qub. The spread of Ṣufi mysticism among the masses, as well as in the leading intellectual circles, greatly contributed to the undermining of law and order and strengthened the forces of xenophobia and religious fanaticism. In 1437 the alleged discovery in Fez of the grave of Idris II aroused the religious-nationalist emotions among the populace to such a pitch that it rioted against the Jews. A major additional factor in both promoting Jewish welfare and ruining it was the frequent presence of influential Jewish advisers at the Marinid courts. We recall 'Abdalbasiṭ's observation that the Tlemcen physician Mushi was wise enough to steer clear of politics. This was not the case with other North African Jewish dignitaries who, prompted by ambition and financial interest, often sought and achieved considerable power in the country's fiscal and administrative affairs. So long as their power lasted, it benefited many other Jews employed by them in various capacities, as well as the Jewish community as a whole. Like their Spanish compeers, some of these North African Jewish grandees must have viewed their good fortune as a part of God's design to help their people. They undoubtedly saw in the biblical figures of Joseph in Egypt and Mordecai in Susa splendid prototypes of Jewish courtiers selected by divine Providence for their services to Jewry. This nexus had frequently been emphasized by such Spanish scholars as the kabbalist Don Joseph ben Shushan, who wrote: "It is the duty of every Jew in a position of power . . . to consider himself as a divine messenger . . . whom God caused to find favor in the eye of the king so that his words are listened to and complied with when he stands in the breach for his Lord's holy people." On the other hand, their frequently speedy downfall under the ever fluid power constellations of the central or provincial administrations often entailed not only the death of these leaders and much loss of their and other Jewish property, but at times also endangered the survival of the entire community and brought about at least a temporary deterioration in the standing of Jewry at large.[26]

Nor were these Jewish courtiers themselves too secure. Abu-Ya'qub Yusuf, who was reputed to love wine (despite its prohibition in Muslim law) and women, had in his youth a Jewish playmate named Khalifa Ibn Waqqaṣa (or Ruqqaṣa). After ascending the throne in 1286, he appointed his Jewish friend as supervisor over the palace and, according to some sources, also as his chamberlain. To all intents and purposes Ibn Waqqaṣa served as chief adviser to the sultan for many years, but with the changes in fortune characteristic of Muslim courts during that period, in 1302 he and many members of his family were executed. However, it seems that some other relatives survived and continued playing an important political role in the country. At least according to an Aragonese document, James II in 1309 recommended his ambassador Castellnou to several Moroccan courtiers, including another Khalifa ibn Waqqaṣa. Even more dramatic was the rise and fall of Harun (Aaron b. Shemṭob), the Jewish courtier of the last Marinid ruler, 'Abd al-Ḥaqq (1428–65). The sultan, who had formally been raised to the throne at the age of one, remained very long under the tutelage of his Waṭṭasid viziers. Finally, with the aid of Harun he gradually removed the last vizier and started to rule by himself. Harun assumed most of the vizierial obligations (though not the title) because, as the chronicler ʿAbdalbasiṭ b. Ḥalil reports, the sultan felt safer with a Jew who, because of his faith, would not dare to overstep his bounds. Harun antagonized many Muslims, however, by raising taxes, including those paid by the *dhimmis,* and by adopting other unpopular measures. The result was that, when in 1465 the sultan and his Jewish adviser left the capital for the vicinity of Ceuta (the city itself had been held by the Portuguese since 1415), the Fez populace, inspired by a fanatical preacher, used the opportunity to proclaim a "holy war" against the Jews. To legitimize the upheaval, the rebels tried to obtain an appropriate *fatwa,* or responsum, from the leading local jurist. When the conscientious scholar refused, they forced his hand by declaring: "We, too, have authority and power; we have risen for God's cause and we are entirely devoted to it. Here is our demand for a consultation to which we ask you to answer through a *fatwa* conforming to the judgment of the Highest God; otherwise we shall take your life, for you would be a scholar whose actions do not conform with his knowledge." In other words, they knew better what his legal conscience should have dictated to him than he did himself. Thus threatened, the jurist could no longer resist and legalized their violent action. In consequence, Harun was assassinated and, when the monarch himself returned to Fez to restore order, he was seized by the mob and ritualistically butchered in the slaughterhouse. Thus ingloriously ended the Marinid dynasty, in all but name. At the same time, there were severe anti-Jewish riots in both the capital and the provinces.[27]

After the restoration of order, the Marinid dynasty gave way to that of the Banu Waṭṭas, who had long furnished the truly ruling viziers or regents. The Waṭṭasids were fortunate in having relatively long-reigning monarchs when compared with their opposite numbers in most other North African countries. Muḥammad Saʿid ash-Shaykh (1472–1505) was followed by his son, Muḥammad b. Saʿid (1505–1524), nicknamed "the Portuguese" because in his youth he had spent time in Portugal as a hostage, guaranteeing his father's treaty with that country. He in turn was succeeded by his son Aḥmad (1524–45, and again in 1547–49). Despite this relative dynastic stability, there was little peace in the country. The old clashes between the various tribal and regional units—several provincial emirs ruled over their provinces like independent monarchs—were aggravated by the spread of Ṣufism, which now greatly appealed even to trained theologians and jurists, and by the rise of numerous confraternities which clamored for and often obtained much autonomy. With this domestic unrest grew a deep hostility toward foreigners, which necessarily affected also the relations between the Muslim majority and the *dhimmi* minorities. The sultans often followed the adage, "If you cannot beat them, join them." When Muḥammad ash-Shaykh al-Mahdi (1549–57) was unable to suppress the independent emir of Debdu and was defeated in battle, he secured peace by giving two of his daughters in marriage to the emir's two sons. Among the independent acts of Debdu's true ruler was the admission of numerous Spanish Jewish refugees to his emirate. Nor did the Banu Waṭṭas' successors of the Sa'adian or first Sharifian dynasty, whose claim to renown was derived from their alleged descent from Mohammed's grandson Ḥasan (a descent which had long been a prerequisite for the office of caliph but not sultan), alter this governmental attitude. According to a rumor cited by Joseph ha-Kohen, it was a Jew, Mas'ud Maṣliaḥ, who foretold the rise of the Sa'adian dynasty. Upon his conquest of Fez in 1549, Muḥammad ash-Shaykh al-Mahdi promoted Jewish immigration from the Iberian Peninsula and generally treated the older and more recent Jewish settlers with much compassion. He was followed by 'Abdallah al-Ghalib (1557–74) and notably Aḥmad al-Manṣur (1578–1603). Subsequently, Al-Manṣur's sons, in constant rivalry for succession, ruled partially from Fez and partially from Marrakesh only. The Moroccan realm, which under Al-Manṣur extended from Senegal to Bornu (near Lake Chad), now fell apart; it was restored only later under another branch of the Sharifian family, the Filalis, especially under Mulay Ismail as-Samin (1672–1727). All along, in return for the generally favorable treatment they received from the early Sa'adian monarchs, some Jews played an active role in supporting them against their numerous enemies, who were at times abetted by Turkish troops stationed in Algeria.[28]

The deep internal divisions in Morocco's Muslim society were paralleled by similar cleavages within the Jewish community. During the sixteenth century and long after, there was not only the basic differentiation between the newcomers and the old settlers, but within each of these major groups between several subcultures, which militated against joint communal action and even against mutual understanding. As early as 1526, a major intracommunal conflict arose in Fez and lasted nine years. Thenceforth, according to David Corcos, five distinct groups left their traces in Moroccan Jewish life down to the nineteenth century and beyond. They consisted of: (1) Berber Jews who conversed in Berber dialects and dressed like Berbers; (2) Arabic-speaking Jews from the vicinity of the Sahara, who may have originally arrived from southern Arabia, particularly Khaibar; (3) Spanish exiles from Castile and Aragon, using their respective Spanish dialects; (4) similar exiles from Muslim Spain, whose speech consisted of a Morisco idiom intermingled with old Spanish, Arabic, and Hebrew; and (5) Jews from Portugal, increasingly recruited from New Christians whose mores considerably differed from those of their other Iberian coreligionists. Since many of the new arrivals spread into the southern mountainous regions, where they encountered descendants of the old Berber tribes, their amalgamation must have proceeded even more slowly there. The observations of William Lemprière, an English visitor of the late eighteenth century, must have held true during several previous generations:

> Besides the Brebes, many Jews reside in the valleys and possess separate habitations and villages. These people are employed in trifling mechanical occupations which the Brebes require. Indeed I believe there is no part of the world where the Jews are so completely diffused over the face of the country.[29]

Hatred of foreigners was intensified by the constant decline of Morocco's external power. This was the period of Portuguese and Spanish expansion, which led not only to the conquest of new worlds overseas but also to the occupation of a number of coastal cities in North Africa. The Portuguese conquests, which started in 1415 with the occupation of Ceuta, concentrated in the first seventy years on capturing town after town along the Straits of Gibraltar and farther east along the Mediterranean coast. In the subsequent half-century the Lisbon regime focused its attention on the Atlantic coast, where it occupied Safi (1508), Azammur or Azemmour (1513), Mazagan (1514), and other localities. Almost immediately it turned also to missionary efforts, even if it applied them with less force than did some Spaniards in their colonies in the center of the Mediterranean littoral. (Fortunately for the two Iberian monarchies, they had concluded, under papal sponsorship, the Treaties of Alcáçovas [1479] and Tordesillas [1494], which geographically delimited their spheres of interest so that in territorial respects they did not work at cross purposes.) The Portuguese speedily established three Catholic bishoprics in Ceuta, Tangier, and Safi, thus testifying to their religious zeal as heirs of the medieval Crusaders. Curiously, among the "dreamers" of a Portuguese conquest of Fez was the prominent humanist Diogo de Gouvea, probably a New Christian, who cherished the hope of some day serving as the bishop of Fez and of spreading the Christian gospel there under a Portuguese regime. However, the primary political and economic motivations of the Portuguese rulers consisted in their wish to safeguard their navigation along the Atlantic coast to the Cape of Good Hope, and their need for continued regular supplies of Moroccan grain, flax, and horses. They made Portuguese rule in the occupied cities religiously rather tolerant, at least until Portugal itself had a fully functioning Inquisition in 1547. By that time, however, the Portuguese had been ousted from most of their coastal positions by Muslims led by the famous Barbary corsairs, Arruj and his brother Khair adh-Dhin Barbarossa. Unable to challenge the great power of Spain with his own meager resources, Barbarossa submitted his domain to Turkish suzerainty and thus secured the support of the equally powerful Ottoman Empire. Sultan Selim I appointed him governor-general (*berglerbey*) of what soon became the permanent regencies of Algeria and Tunisia; ultimately, however, these were converted into regular Ottoman pashaliks.[30]

Needless to say, along with the Muslim majority Jews suffered severely during the frequent raids of Christian pirates on the North African coastal cities. For example, during Filippo Doria's attack on Tripoli in 1510, we are told by one of its participants, Batistino de Tonsis, that 5,000 of the 10,000 Muslim inhabitants of the city and "some Jews" were carried away into captivity.

Many others were slain, with the exception of "the few who saved themselves by jumping over the walls of the *Judería*" in the northern section. In 1541 the Jewish community of Algiers heaved a sigh of relief over Spain's failure to occupy the city and instituted an annual Purim festival which was observed for many generations. Similarly, in 1578 Tetuan, called by a modern historian the "little Jerusalem," was besieged but not captured by the Spaniards, and the local Jews began to celebrate an annual "Purim de los Cristianos." In the same year (on August 4) the defeat and death of the Portuguese King Sebastian in the famous "battle of the three kings" at Alcazarquivir (Al-Kasr al-Kabir) gave the community of Tangier a double reason to observe their own Purim annually on Ellul 1, because they had undoubtedly heard about Sebastian's missionary designs and about the anti-Jewish persecutions by his ally Muḥammad al-Mutawakkil al-Maslukh during his brief occupation of Marrakesh. Such expression of the relief from pent-up fears by Jewish communities was often practiced in various parts of the world.[31]

This stormy period in the history of the Mediterranean world was accompanied by the vast exodus of Jews and later Moriscos from the Iberian Peninsula. A very large number of refugees crossed over to the neighboring Maghrib, although some of them eventually proceeded farther east to Egypt, western Asia, or the Balkans. At first, we recall, the forcibly converted masses of Portuguese Jewry, which after 1492 also included the largest segment of Spanish exiles, were forbidden to leave their country. The government rightly feared that the emigration of tens of thousands of Jews to North Africa would greatly increase the manpower of Portugal's potential enemies and furnish them a number of talented individuals with commercial, industrial, and military know-how. Hence, because of their clandestine departures, many refugees became ready targets for fraud and deceit, as when a captain collected 6,000 doubloons as advance payment for their passage to Morocco and then vanished together with his ship. But the would-be exiles could not be too particular. They may have known that another captain, Gonçalo de Lulé, had been severely punished by the Portuguese for assisting some early Jewish refugees to cross the Straits. Even those hardy souls who succeeded in reaching a major French harbor, such as Marseilles, hoping to secure transportation to a North African country, still faced numerous legal and financial obstacles. Certainly, the Marseilles captains who charged 2 gold ducats a person for transporting Jewish passengers to neighboring Italy must have demanded much more from those who had to leave in a hurry because the local authorities refused to give them permission to linger for more than three days, if at all. Moreover, the population at large in Morocco and Algeria was often hostile to the new arrivals; it feared that a large influx of new settlers would create shortages of food and other commodities and otherwise interfere with its normal pursuits. Later on, Salé closed its gates even to the Moriscos who had left Spain after the expulsion of 1609–1614, because of their Spanish speech, dress, and manners, and purportedly also their lack of shame and dignity.[32]

Such hostility was greatly intensified in the case of Jews by both the xenophobia and religious fanaticism aroused by the Ṣufi propaganda. We hear of cases of the inhabitants of coastal cities rising up in arms against ships bringing in large groups of refugees. According to one of the exiles, "most of the Muslims did not allow them into their cities and many of them died in the fields from hunger, thirst, and lack of everything." Almost all other immigrants suffered untold hardships before they were able to establish themselves in a more tolerant environment. A dramatic illustration is offered by R. Yehudah Ḥayyat's introduction to a rabbinic work that he completed some years later in Mantua. Right after his arrival in an unnamed Moroccan locality, we are told, a former Muslim compatriot from Granada accused him of having collaborated with the Christian conquerors of that city and of participating in the celebration of the Spanish victory. Arrested by the authorities, he was finally ransomed by the Jews of Xauen, in French called Chechaouen. In gratitude he donated to the community 200 books he had succeeded in salvaging. Proceeding to the "great city of Fez," he had the ill luck of finding the metropolis in the throes of a severe famine,

> so that we ate the grass of the field. Every day I ground the grain in the house of an Arab, with both my arms, for a small and extremely thin slice of bread, not fit even for dogs. At night, my belly cleaved to

the ground because of the biting autumnal cold and lack of covering against it and no house to lodge in, we dug ditches in the town dung and put ourselves into them. Thus came true the biblical verse of "They that were brought up in scarlet, embrace dunghills" [Lam. 4:5].

Similar complaints were voiced by other refugees and were frequently echoed in the contemporary or near-contemporary Jewish historical literature.[33]

Remarkably, despite their general tendency to combine colonial expansion with the ideal of converting natives to Christianity, even the Spaniards often refrained from overt missionary activity outside the North African localities they conquered. This was true at least until the arrival of the more zealous Jesuit Order, inspired by the spirit of the Counter Reformation. That is why we hear little about friction between Christians and the relatively few Jews who remained after the initial sales into slavery and other persecutions in Iberia's colonial possessions as well as in the much larger Jewish communities in the Muslim-dominated territories. In fact, on his arrival in Fez in 1540, the fine Christian Hebraist, Nicolas Clénard (Cleynaerts) of Brabant, was amazed to notice that the local Jews (among whom he was to live for most of his fifteen-month sojourn in Morocco) "are even more astonished about the continued existence of Christians [in North Africa] than are we when we see that some Jews still exist. Why should we wonder? After all they know nothing about us except that we burn them with enthusiasm." [34]

Overcoming the initial difficulties, the Iberian exiles settled all over the Maghrib. As we shall see, they entered various occupations from little-esteemed manual labor and peddling to high-ranking business and government service. They included such influential diplomats as Jacob Rosales and Jacob Ruti (Rute). They settled in both northern and southern localities, including the harbor cities occupied by the Portuguese and even in Spanish-controlled Badis and Peñon de Vélez de la Gomera. The same Philip II who greatly intensified the persecution of New Christians at home and in the New World, in 1564 allowed professing Jews (doubtless including some former *conversos*) to settle in Peñon de Vélez under the condition that they not build a wall or carry arms. A number of exiles settled in many parts of the Atlas Mountains, where they joined some of the older Jewish residents who had lived among the Berbers since pre-Islamic times. A family named Perez established itself in the Dades district in the central Atlas region. It engaged in agricultural, as well as in industrial, pursuits and occupied two entire townships in the district. These two localities, with a center in a fortified castle named Kalaat Ait Pereṣ (now called Klaa), remained autonomous until the late seventeenth century, when Mulay Ismail imposed upon them a mild form of serfdom. There, to quote one of the Perez descendants living in Europe, "no stranger, not of their fathers' house and bearing their name, passed in their midst, and they would marry no woman of another family." We have the testimony of a modern Jewish historian, David Corcos-Abulafia, that the Perez family continued to live in the area well into the twentieth century, still adhering to their strict endogamy and thus retaining their wholly Jewish character through the centuries.[35]

The largest concentration of Spanish exiles was in Fez where, in the mid-sixteenth century, their number was estimated between 4,000 and 10,000 by such non-Jewish writers as Clénard, who in 1541 mentioned the lower figure twice, and the Spaniard Luis de Marmol Carvajal, who referred to 10,000 just six years later. After a year's residence in the Jewish quarter of Fez, Clénard probably was much better informed about the number of Jews in the city than Marmol, who was prone to exaggerate. While admitting that the Jews of Fez were assigned a very fine residential quarter—we know from other sources that, for greater security, the residences of foreign diplomats and other dignitaries were also located there—Marmol emphasized the anti-Jewish discrimination by the authorities. He sweepingly asserted:

This [Jewish] people is very much oppressed in Africa. They spit into their faces on the streets, they beat them, they do not allow them to wear shoes, except for the few individuals who usually visit the sultan and the dignitaries; the other Jews possess only shoes made of rubber[?]. When they appear before the ruler they must take off their shoes. They are also obliged to wear black turbans and on them or their hats, as well as on their clothing, they must wear a badge to distinguish them from the other inhabitants. If there is a wealthy Jew, the sultan confiscates his property and frequently takes his life as well. Yet the Jews know how to adjust themselves beautifully and they are very clever in their business dealings so that the king and the higher officials entrust them with the management of their affairs and their revenues. This is a task shunned by the regular Moors who do not understand these matters so that each dignitary has a Jewish administrator.

It is not surprising that, in the midst of the largely stagnating Moroccan society of the sixteenth through the nineteenth centuries, the differences in economic, cultural, and religious traditions originally existing between the newcomers and the older Jewish settlers long persisted. In Moroccan society at large, too, despite centuries of coexistence under Islamic rule, there never was a complete amalgamation of the native Berber tribes with the Arab settlers brought into the country in various stages since the seventh century. Their cultural and linguistic disparity was manifest not only in rural regions but also in the major cities, which absorbed a great many inhabitants of both groups.[36]

Side by side with the Arabic language, often spoken in the modified Moroccan dialect, one heard the Berber idiom extensively used at home and on the street. Many native Jews, too, spoke a Berber dialect, while others had begun to develop a Judeo-Arabic dialect of their own. The Iberian newcomers, on the other hand, conversed in their own Castilian or Portuguese language which, in a somewhat different way than in the Balkan Ladino, remained a specific characteristic of the Sephardic settlers for generations thereafter. Remarkably, according to Louis S. Chenier who, in the mid-eighteenth century, served for many years as the French consul in Morocco, the local Jews spoke Arabic, "but many Rabbins have preserved the habit of translating the Bible into Spanish, without understanding it." Differences in religious rituals, and, to a lesser extent, in the cultural level continued to disturb the Moroccan Jewish communities for a long time.[37]

From the mid-sixteenth century on, however, Morocco in general and, even more so, Moroccan Jewry were drawn into the orbit of the Ottoman Empire in both its rise and decline. The history of the Jews from the mid-sixteenth century even in independent Morocco thus largely reflected the evolution of Ottoman Jewry. These close interrelations were manifest during the outwardly glorious reign of Aḥmad al-Manṣur (1578–1603) even after the Moroccan victory over King Sebastian in 1578. The notion that

Morocco was a great independent power supported by a powerful army and a stable gold currency made contemporaries, particularly in Europe, overlook the serious internal weaknesses of this regime, which survived largely by a successful balancing act between the great antagonists, the Spanish and Ottoman Empires. But these internal weaknesses came clearly to the fore in the early seventeenth century, when Morocco was, unofficially, broken up into a number of feuding principalities. At the same time Moroccan Jewry, as exemplified especially by the Pallache family, began playing an increasing role in international commerce and politics even beyond the Mediterranean area. An analysis of these far-reaching transformations must be relegated to the next volume.

GRANADA

The history of professing Jews in Muslim Spain ceased to all intents and purposes with the fall of Granada and their formal expulsion in 1492. Whatever relationships there existed between Granada and Morocco had been greatly weakened by Abu-Yusuf Ya'qub's four unsuccessful campaigns (1276–85) resulting in his final withdrawal from his Spanish ventures. Thereafter the Marinids were not only on the defensive against the Iberian kingdoms in Morocco but—except for Abu'l Ḥasan 'Ali's abortive efforts in the 1330s, which ended in his defeat at the Rio Salado in 1340 and left only Gibraltar in Muslim (not Marinid) hands until 1462—they no longer dared to interfere in Spanish affairs directly. Yet, at the very height of the Christian *reconquista* and its rhetoric about the crusade to rid the peninsula of Muslim "infidels," a great many Muslims were allowed to remain in their villages. In fact, the desperate need for manpower to cultivate the soil in the depopulated areas, such as the "kingdom" of Valencia, forced James the Conqueror (1213–76) to resettle thousands of Saracen refugees on labor-deficient lands. The coincidence of the Mongolian invasion in the East, climaxed by Hulagu's conquest of Baghdad in 1268, and the defeat of the last Almohades in the West, especially the fall of Marrakesh in 1269, set in motion a wave of Islamic migrations which, in part, brought new settlers into the Iberian Peninsula.[38]

Jews, whose loyalty to the new Christian rulers of Spain could be more readily taken for granted, now found new opportunities for enlarging the scope of their economic, cultural, and even political activities. Among the signal services rendered, as we recall, by an array of Jewish counselors to the Spanish rulers were their diplomatic activities in the kingdom of Granada, which remained as the only Muslim state on the Iberian Peninsula. Sporadically its Naṣrid or Banu al-Aḥmar dynasty had to recognize Castilian overlordship. But time and again, with the support of Aragon, it refused to pay its tribute. In their internecine conflicts the two major Christian realms on the Iberian Peninsula effectively used their Jewish diplomatic advisers during the thirteenth and early fourteenth centuries to maintain contacts with the Muslim rulers in Spain and North Africa. The brothers Abraham and Samuel Abengalell, in particular, often served as Aragonese envoys to Granada and Morocco. At one critical point in the 1290s, the so-called Samuel policy succeeded in establishing a modicum of peace between Granada and its Christian neighbors. This policy continued through most of the fourteenth century. Even the unfriendly King Henry II made use of his Jewish court physician, Joseph Ibn Waqqar, for a diplomatic mission to Granada. On this occasion, Ibn Waqqar was able to supply a local Muslim historian with material for the history of Granada.[39]

We also have records of some eminent Jewish physicians residing in Granada. One of them (who also dabbled in astrology), Abraham (Ibrahim) ibn Zarza, served as court physician of Muḥammad V (1354–59, 1362–91). By attracting a number of Muslim as well as Jewish pupils, Abraham aroused the envy of a Muslim colleague, Muḥammad b. Ali al-Laḥmi ash-Shaguri, who thereupon wrote a sharply anti-Jewish tract, *Qam' al-Yahud* (The Crushing of the Jews So That They May Not Exceed Their Limits). When a revolt forced the ruler to flee to Morocco in 1359, Ibn Zarza also left Granada and for a while served as court physician to Pedro I of Castile. In 1363, after Muḥammad V's resumption of his reign, Abraham returned to Granada as Pedro's envoy. Yet, despite Muḥammad's mild regime, it appears, Jews were obliged to wear distinguishing marks, although the regularity of their observance and even the varying shapes of the badges required by law are subject to debate. Similarly, the concentration of many Jews in their quarter (in 1492 replaced by a hospital, a church, and other Christian buildings) did not prevent some other Jews from inhabiting dwellings in different sections of the city. Such relative tolerance was made possible by the Naṣrid dynasty's general abstention from intensive pursuit of Muslim religious policies; the Naṣrids occasionally even showed outright hostility to their Moroccan neighbors. This attitude persisted also during the early years of Ferdinand and Isabella, when their dreams of Spanish unification were gradually beginning to unfold.[40]

During the preceding two and a half centuries of Granada's independence, Jews enjoyed a fair degree of toleration; they also could develop their Jewish culture along traditional lines. Although they had considerably declined in numbers after the pogrom of 1066 and the even greater shock of Almohade rule, the local Jews showed a remarkable recuperative power under the mild Naṣrid regime. It was toward the end of Almohade domination that Ya'qub al-Manṣur, partly with their aid, drove the Almohades from Granada back to Africa (1232). Individual Jews could now again reach high positions in society and government. For example, Yaḥya Ibn Assayag, who served as court physician to Abu'l Hayyaj Yussuf (1372–92), was able through his intervention to bring about the downfall and execution of the royal favorite, Khaled. If in the end he, too, fell victim to a court intrigue, this was a price frequently paid for political intrigues by royal advisers in many Muslim countries. On the whole, Jewish life in Granada was satisfactory enough for Solomon Ibn Verga to reminisce nostalgically, early in the sixteenth century, about conditions prevailing in the southeastern Spanish kingdom before 1066, eloquently exclaiming: "He who had not seen the Jews' glory in Granada, their good fortune and their magnificence, never saw genuine glory. They waxed truly great by their wisdom and piety." [41]

With the progress of Spain's unification under the Catholic monarchs, however, the days of Granada's independence were numbered. Even before the royal couple's accession to power, Castile began chipping away at the borders of the surviving Muslim principality, then divided into the four provinces of Almeria, Jaén, Málaga, and Granada proper. But major clashes were frequently interrupted by formal armistices. Even in 1478–84 the armed encounters still proceeded only in a desultory way. Yet the Jews, and even the Muslims, of Castile were made to contribute large sums to the financing of the war. In 1482 and 1485 the Jewish contribution amounted to 18,000 gold castellanos (of 485 maravedis each). In 1484 the communities had to raise 12,000 castellanos, plus 4,000 more for *logros* (interest). From 1486 on, the annual tribute was reduced to 10,000 castellanos. But when Málaga fell in 1487, Castilian Jewry was forced to spend 10,000,000 maravedis (about 20,000 castellanos) for ransoming 450 Jewish captives taken by the Spaniards in that city. These expenditures were often increased through administrative chicaneries in their collection. Finally, in 1488–92 the decisive battles were fought and on January 2, 1492 the last ruler of Granada, Boabdil (Muḥammad XI, 1482–83, 1487–92) signed a treaty of surrender and left for Morocco.[42]

Many other Muslims and Jews also started leaving the country immediately. But when, on March 31, 1492, the Catholic monarchs issued in Granada the decree of expulsion of all Jews from Spain, the local Jews, still numbering some 6,000 in a total population of 50,000 to 60,000 persons, were given the choice of conversion to Christianity or departure from the country. Most seem to have chosen exile, while those remaining behind joined the large group of *conversos* living in Spain ever since the mass conversions of 1391–1415. This new group baptism under pressure, understandably, gave rise to the usual suspicions of the neophytes' heterodoxy. Characteristically, the archbishop of Granada, Juan de Talavera, himself of *converso* descent was, as we recall, rather moderate in his outlook on dissenters. Perhaps for this reason, he was forced by the Inquisition to do penance and march barefooted and bareheaded through the streets of Granada. However, in 1507 Cardinal Francisco Ximénez de Cisneros became the Grand Inquisitor. He immediately ordered the burning of all Arabic books dealing with theology or law, while works devoted to science and medicine were donated to the university library of Alcalá de Henares, founded by him. The cardinal-inquisitor not only sharply prosecuted secret Jews and Muslims at home, but in 1507 he embarked on a large-scale military expedition to North Africa, which combined Christian missionary with Spanish imperialistic aims. After initial advances, he was forced to retreat, causing Moroccan Jewry to heave a sigh of relief.[43]

The later destinies of the Moriscos and the Jewish *conversos* were largely determined by the actions of the Spanish Inquisition—in the Morisco case, also by the harsh suppression of their uprisings in 1500–1502, 1571, and others. Regrettably, we hear little about the secret Jews of Granada, although even in 1541–43 the yield of confiscated property to the Granada Inquisition amounted to the substantial sum of 19,128,421 maravedis. By that time, the survivors living in North Africa and the Middle East were able to play an active role in Jewish as well as general affairs. From past experiences, however, they must have expected little sympathy from their former Morisco compatriots who had settled in Muslim lands. They doubtless knew that, even before the final surrender of Granada to the Spanish Christians, the preliminary agreement of November 25, 1491 between Boabdil and the Catholic monarchs included a clause (presumably inserted on the demand of the Muslim population of Granada) reading: "It has been agreed that no Jew shall be appointed tax collector or receiver, nor shall he hold any commission or judicial position over them [the Muslims]." These safeguards resembled similar provisions insisted upon, as we recall, by the surrendering Muslims of Tudela, Saragossa, and Tortosa in the early years of the Christian *reconquista* (1115–48). The Moriscos' anti-Jewish feelings were also dramatically illustrated by those who later settled in Rabat's twin city, Salé. In 1631, they offered to surrender their quarter to the Spanish troops besieging the city and soon thereafter to return to Spain as professing Christians. In recompense they asked the king to order that, on their arrival in Spain, they should get back their children who had been taken away from them before their departure. They also added a promise that

> having served your Majesty before their departure [from the home country], they will despoil the *judería* which is very wealthy. They will wait for the time of the arrival of the caravans and the Jews of Flanders with their merchant ships so that they may hand all of their spoils over to your Majesty. Additional possessions belonging to Dutch and French merchants will also be found in the quarter at the time of the surrender which should be of great value [to the conqueror].

This project, which probably met with derision at the court of Philip IV, was one more instance of a minority ready to fight another minority rather than their common enemy: in this case, the oppressive Spanish regime.[44]

CONFUSING STATUS

Basically, the Jewish legal status in North Africa and Muslim Spain continued to be shaped by the Muslim traditions as formulated in the classical age for the entire world of Islam. However, this region's numerous local and chronological variations were even greater than those affecting the position of the Jews in other medieval Muslim lands. The prevailing political instability throughout North Africa and the constantly shrinking area under Muslim domination in Spain make any broad generalization quite hazardous.

Moreover, the available source material is extremely fragmentary and at times contradictory. Generally, very few archival data relating to the medieval period have been preserved in the respective countries. Whatever documentary collections exist have been largely assembled by scholars and bibliophiles as private undertakings. Only for the last two centuries can one count on local public archives to supply an increasing amount of relevant documentary information. The medieval Jewish communities, even after emerging from the catastrophic destruction during the invasion of the Hilal and Sulaym tribes and the Almohade domination, must have been in disarray from the very beginning of their resettlement era. Nor were the North African countries blessed by a dry climate like that of Egypt, which would have made possible the preservation of ancient papyri, and by a Genizah like that of Cairo.

We owe some evidence to the privately assembled collection of the scholarly Ibn Danan family, although many of its notations were based on generally less reliable personal recollections and family traditions. The Arabic historical literature, on the other hand, our major source of information for the general history of these countries, furnishes us only meager data on Jews. As Évariste Lévi-Provençal has pointed out, the historians of the reigning dynasties narrated mainly events pertaining to the sultans and other personalities active in central governments but had little to say even about the provincial and local administrations. Apart from court intrigues and palace conflicts, they evinced interest mainly in wars and foreign relations. They paid some attention to revenues from taxation but largely neglected other domestic policies. Moreover, as is usual owing to faulty memories, negligence, or diverse biases, reports by contemporaries and near-contemporaries often differ greatly from one another; these disparities have forced modern historians to choose sides or to attempt varying harmonizations, leading to much confusion. The rich biographical literature, to be sure, about a variety of eminent personalities including theologians, poets, and scientists, offers some correctives to this one-sided type of historical presentation. But its concentrated attention on theological-juridical teachings, personal piety, scientific achievements, and the families of the individuals concerned, contributes little to our knowledge of the daily life of the Muslim masses. Rural districts are almost completely ignored. Jews are mentioned, as a rule, only when they played a role as court physicians, entertained personal relations with an important Muslim personality, or took part in some specific diplomatic or commercial negotiations. Occasionally space is also given, in that source material, to such dramatic events as anti-Jewish riots or literary polemics. But major aspects of legal practice, demography, and occupations, not to speak of Jewish religious and cultural life, are almost totally ignored.[45]

Jewish sources are particularly scarce for the period antedating the 1390s. After the arrival of several prominent Spanish rabbis, including R. Isaac b. Sheshet Perfet, R. Simon b. Ṣemaḥ Duran and his descendants, their wide correspondence yields many details illuminating not only the life of the exiles from the Iberian Peninsula but also that of the existing older groups of Moroccan, Algerian, and Tunisian Jews. However, the picture presented by this type of material is necessarily one-sided and fragmentary. Consisting, as it does, of inquiries largely relating to questions of law arising from individual incidents, the descriptions of events tend to stress specific halakhic aspects rather than to furnish exact names of persons, localities, and the dates on which these events took place. It is mainly from occasional broader descriptions or generalizations inserted into both the inquiries and the replies that modern historians have gained some new insights into North African Jewish life, internally and externally. In the case of Perfet's responsa, Abraham H. Hershman made a valiant effort to identify the Aragonese versus the Algerian provenance of the individual replies, and thus to date them broadly as written before 1392, or sometime between 1392 and 1402. Naturally, however, some identifications have proved unattainable, while some others must remain dubious. Moreover, even while living in Algeria, Perfet sent replies to inquirers in other countries, including Italy; of course, these replies contribute relatively little to our knowledge of conditions among the North African Jews. Of considerable value, therefore, are the data furnished, however briefly, by the sixteenth-century Jewish historians Abraham b. Solomon of Torrutiel (Adrutiel), Abraham b. Samuel Zacuto, Solomon Ibn Verga, Joseph b. Joshua ha-Kohen, Elijah b. Elqana Capsali, and their late-seventeenth-century successor Joseph b. Isaac Sambari. Further assistance is furnished by European visitors, whose travelogues occasionally refer to the conditions under which Jews lived in the North African countries. Among the most informative travelers were Leo Africanus and Luis de Marmol Carvajal in the sixteenth century, and Lancelot Addison who, in 1675, devoted an entire volume to a review of *The Present State of the Jews* (*More Particularly Relating to Those in Barbary*). Yet, the picture emerging from the totality of these sources still leaves much to be desired.[46]

The fundamental law regarding the position of *dhimmis* in western, as well as eastern, Islamic lands was the Covenant of 'Umar. Nor could rulers or jurists be completely oblivious of such sayings, attributed to the Messenger himself, as "Allah does not permit us followers to break into the Jews' homes without authority, to mistreat their women, or consume their food, so long as they fulfill their obligations." To be sure, voices were occasionally heard trying to defend the abrogation of that Covenant by various arguments. We recall Al-Mu'min's contention that, after the passage of 500 years since the *Hejira,* the failure of the Jewish Messiah to appear and of Christ to reappear caused the

Covenant to lose its validity. We hear less about this argument in later centuries, since the continued operation of the Covenant in intervening periods made its repudiation doubly difficult. Yet, no lesser jurist than Ibn Taimiya asserted that, when the "unbelievers" failed to live up to their obligations including the payment of the capitation tax, the Islamic governments were free to disregard the Covenant. Along similar lines the aforementioned late-fifteenth-century Muslim apologist Muḥammad al-Majili of Tuat argued that the violation of a single stipulation in the Covenant by any "infidel" invalidated all of its protective provisions and rendered the shedding of his blood and appropriation of his possessions perfectly legal. Although Al-Majili admitted that the lengthy earlier debates over this question had cast doubt on his doctrine, he insisted that the lack of continuity in governmental protection and the obstinate perseverance of the Jews in their illegal conduct rendered the Covenant, in their case, quite obsolete. Such manifestations of illegality applied, in his opinion, particularly to the Jews of Tlemcen, Tuat, Tigurarin, and Dra'. Nonetheless, neither he nor Ibn Taimiya really expected that the Muslim governments would repudiate the Covenant. They proceeded, therefore, to discuss its various discriminatory provisions and demanded that these be strictly enforced against the "unbelievers." [47]

Clearly, the general acceptance of the Covenant of 'Umar in legal theory did not necessarily guarantee the Jews' peaceful coexistence with the Muslim majority. Not only did agitators like Al-Majili often poison the atmosphere for all intergroup relations, but biased local chiefs sometimes denied the very right of Jews to live in their territories. For example, the ruler of Timbuktu (now in the republic of Mali), a prosperous center of trade in the western Sudan until its destruction in 1591 by a Turkish detachment, was characterized by Leo Africanus as "a declared enemy of Jews. He does not wish that any of them live in his city. If he hears that one of the Barbary merchants associates or does business with Jews, he confiscates his property." Moreover, many another temperamental ruler did not hesitate to violate the law if it suited his plans or even whims. Although few were as outspoken as was the Sa'adian sultan Aḥmad al-Manṣur, who was quoted by Al-

Wufrani (Al-Ifrani) as saying: "The Maghrib people are mad and their madness can be dealt with only by keeping them in chains"—paradoxically, he happened to treat his *dhimmi* subjects rather well—the religious minorities were often, under a variety of other rulers, the chosen targets for fiscal exploitation and other arbitrary acts of government.[48]

A major source of contention in Western, as in Eastern, Islam was the employment of Jews in high governmental positions, formal or informal. We recall, for example, Harun's tragic end in 1465, as well as the wise restraint of the physician Mushi b. Samuil, who did not mix in politics although he did later accept the post of chief of physicians of Tlemcen. An incident which allegedly occurred in Tunisia under the relatively tolerant regime of the Zirid dynasty illustrates the fairly widespread rejection by Muslim jurists of even lowly Jewish messengers from the royal court. At one time, we are told, the long-reigning Sharaf-ad-Dawla al-Mu'izz b. Badis (1016–62) ordered his Jewish courtier-physician Ibrahim ibn 'Ata to obtain a juridical opinion from the jurist Abu Imran al-Fasi. The doctor was received with the unexpected scolding: "Don't you know that my home is like a mosque? How did you dare to enter it?" Abu Imran refused to entrust the Jew with his written opinion, because no infidel was supposed to carry a paper containing the name of Allah. When the Jew reported the incident to the sultan, Al-Mu'izz exclaimed: "I merely wished to show you the power of Islam and the general veneration in which we hold Muslim scholars." Nevertheless, quite a few Jews accepted various governmental assignments, including such an unusual task as that of poisoning a rebel leader, allegedly performed by a Jew sent by the king of Fez to Ait Attab (Eit Hitab) in order to pacify the district of Tedle. More frequently, Jews were entrusted with formal diplomatic missions, especially to the courts in Aragon and Castile, and, at times, also to North African rulers. When the position of the Jews in Spain deteriorated in the course of the fourteenth century and became disastrous during the period of 1391 to 1415, the place of Jewish diplomats was frequently taken by merchants in the continually developing western Mediterranean commerce.[49]

Jews also played an active part in the Portuguese military expansion, on the one hand, and in the defense of Moroccan cities against the invaders, on the other hand. A noteworthy illustration was offered by Isaac Zamiro of Safi, who first held the command over a section of the wall during the Portuguese siege but, sometime after the city's occupation by the enemy, served as the Portuguese representative to the sultan in Marrakesh in seeking his recognition of the surrender. Not surprisingly, here, as in many other localities, Jews served as scapegoats blamed for the city's downfall. Leo Africanus must have heard from local Muslims that "the Jews, having shortly before concluded an agreement with the king of Portugal to deliver the city to him under the condition that he would not cause them any harm, had opened the city's gates [to the Portuguese] with general approval." This was clearly the reverse of the widespread Christian accusation that the Jews had been mainly responsible for the speedy Saracen conquest of Spain in 711–12. Both assertions were obvious exaggerations circulated by persons and groups trying to shift the blame from themselves onto an ever mistrusted minority. In fact, we have little evidence about large-scale physical participation of Jews in actual warfare. To be sure, an oft-cited legend claimed that 12,000 Jews had fallen in the renowned battle of Zalaca. According to Leo Africanus (cited from John Pory's quaint English translation of 1600), in the Demsera area deep in the Atlas Mountains, "great numbers of Iewes . . . live as stipendarie soldiers under diuers princes and are continually in armes." But as a rule, Jews were entrusted, or forced, to perform corvée labor in the defense of North African cities by building bridges, supplying weapons, billeting Muslim soldiers (a requirement which most Jews in Europe succeeded in evading because they feared the soldiers' brutality), and also by furnishing them clothing, food, and other necessary supplies.[50]

It must not be assumed, however, that relations between ordinary Jews and Muslims were always hostile. One of Al-Majili's major objections was (using an Arabic phrase comparable to "birds of a feather") to the close association of his coreligionists with Jews, whom he called the sworn enemies of their faith. The following story, reported half a millennium earlier by Abu l'Arab (d. 944 C.E.) in his biographical work, well reflects both the occasional intimate social contacts between Jews and Muslims in North Africa and the recurrent interventions of learned Muslim extremists to stop them. It might also have happened almost anywhere in North Africa in the post-Almohade age, although probably less frequently than in the generally more liberal tenth century:

We were at food in Jazira when a Jew came in. We invited him to join us, and he sat eating until Isma'il b. Rabāḥ came up, and we sent the Jew to an upstairs room. When Isma'il came in we invited him to partake of our food. He stretched out his hand to eat, then withdrew it, saying: "Your food is vile, or something vile has partaken of it!" "Yes," he was told, "a wandering Jew whom we invited, and who ate with us!" "Are you not ashamed," said he, "to eat with one who does not believe [*sic*] in God?"

The fifteenth-century Belgian Anselm Adorne, traveling on a Genoese ship from Tunis to Alexandria, noted with amazement the very friendly relations between the Muslim, Jewish, and Christian passengers, and their peaceful celebration of their respective weekly days of rest on Fridays, Saturdays, and Sundays.[51]

Needless to say, there were also many hostile incidents, including local massacres of Jews, which added many a blood-stained page to the annals of medieval Judeo-Muslim relations. After Harun's assassination in 1465, the aroused Moroccan populace staged a bloodbath among the Jews of Fez and, to a lesser extent, in several provincial cities. According to certain reports, only five men and six women survived the Fez massacre—surely an exaggeration. Yet this pogrom put to flight a great many survivors, and Jewish communal activities ceased until after the return of some Jewish settlers in 1472. Generally, however, even the Waṭṭasids, who were the immediate beneficiaries of the sanguinary removal of the Marinid dynasty, felt obliged to protect their Jewish subjects against assaults. In some cases even local Jews joined their Muslim compatriots in complaining about the expected arrival of a mass of exiles, whose presence would cause an inflation in prices and a general shortage of foodstuffs. In a famous instance in Algiers, the local qadhi, Ibn Meḥrez, is said to have rejected the proposal to stem the influx by telling the complaining Muslims, "I thought that you were believers. I see, however, that you are men of little faith. Is it beyond the power of God to provide sustenance for all His creatures?" In general, the rulers were more cognizant of their countries' need to include a commercially active Jewish population, and hence were more consistently tolerant, than the majority of their Muslim subjects who were easily swayed by extremist agitators. In response to momentary exigencies, especially, the people readily demanded the total exclusion of Jews or, at least, a sharp curtailment of their rights.[52]

Jewish feelings of insecurity contributed strongly to the segregation of many Jewish communities in special quarters, called *mellaḥs* in Morocco and *haras* in Tunisia. In Fez, for example, Jews were moved out of their older quarters to the newly founded section of Fez-Jedid, where Sultan Abu-Yusuf Ya'qub had erected the chief government buildings, mainly in order that he might more readily protect them in emergencies. According to Nicolas Clénard's (Cleynaerts') eyewitness account, in 1541 the "New City" of Fez was located at a distance of half a league from the Old City. "There is the Sultan's palace. Quite close to it is the Jewish quarter [Judaea], surrounded by its own wall. It pays tribute at the sultan's discretion. It contains, I believe, eight or nine synagogues, for 4,000 Jews reside in it, many of whom are remarkably well educated." Similarly in 1557, after Muḥammad ash-Shaykh al-Mahdi transfererd his capital to Marrakesh, he assigned a quarter, long to be called by the Spanish name *judería,* for the Jews who had theretofore lived in various districts. As it turned out, the new sections around the Jewish quarters in both Fez and Marrakesh became the most fashionable residential areas. For example, the French and English ambassadors to Morocco stated that their homes were close to the Jewish quarter. After his arrival in Marrakesh on September 14, 1585, Queen Elizabeth's envoy Henry Roberts wrote: "I was lodged by the Emperor's appointment in a faire house in the Judaria or Jurie which is the place where the Jewes have their abode in the fairest place and quietest lodging in all the 'Citie.'" Even Philip II's representative, Francisco da Costa, possibly a secret Jew, lived and died there and, following the wish expressed in his testament, was buried in the Jewish residence where he had lived rather than in the church cemetery. In other cities the Jewish streets were placed in an area which also embraced one or another Italian *funduq* (*fondaco*). These buildings, combining the functions of central marketplaces and hostelries for merchants and consuls of the major Italian republics, may have been located in Jewish quarters, which often included numerous immigrants, because the government preferred to have all the aliens concentrated in the same area. These arrangements may also have been preferred by the Italians themselves to facilitate their business transactions and exchanges of information with the Jews, many of whom served as their interpreters, agents, or business associates.[53]

Incidentally, living in the Jewish quarter did not necessarily make foreign envoys, merchants, or scholars friends of either the Jews or the country at large. During his three-year sojourn in the *judería* of Marrakesh, Henry Roberts got into several squabbles with his Jewish neighbors and in 1603, fifteen years after his return to England, he submitted to King James I a project for an English attack on Morocco with the aim of conquering and Christianizing the country. But he evidently was an intemperate person, and his autobiographical record is filled with complaints about his alleged mistreatment and underpayment by the English Barbary Company.[54]

In short, like many early medieval European ghettos, the North African Jewish quarters were not the result of enforced segregation but rather had either grown naturally from haphazard residences of new settlers or else were selected by the authorities for the security and convenience, internal as well as external, of their inhabitants. It was only in the nineteenth and twentieth centuries that their extreme overcrowding and the ensuing unsanitary conditions added to the contumely in which the Jews were often held by their Muslim neighbors. To unwary European visitors the continued segregation of Jews, in what by that time had become rather undesirable locations, must have appeared as the effect of conscious social degradation. This is not to gainsay that, under whatever guise, contempt for all *dhimmi*s had from time immemorial been fostered by the concerted efforts of Muslim theologians and jurists; it greatly nurtured the inbred feeling of superiority by the Muslim masses. This attitude was succinctly stated in the 1520s by two envoys to the Sharif of Marrakesh, during a purported conversation with Jewish tribesmen in the Sahara region. When asked whether there were Jews in the envoys' home country, they allegedly replied: "Yes, we have many, in order to make them pay a capitation tax, and in order to slap, curse, and insult them." Of course, this view sharply contrasted with the Jews' own traditional belief in the superiority of their religious heritage.[55]

Some of the ever proud, if much-suffering, Spanish-Portuguese exiles more deeply resented the Muslims' disdainful treatment and occasional physical assaults than did the native Jews who had grown up in the Moorish environment. An echo of this resentment is heard, for example, in R. Abraham Saba's commentary on the Book of Esther. Although he had endured grave trials and tribulations in both Spain and Portugal before he found relative peace during his ten-year sojourn in Fez, Saba graphically described the difference between living under a Christian and a Muslim domination. In his imaginary dialogue between "Two Men of Two Diasporas" he showed how "each tells about his experiences in his home country. . . . Each believes that his suffering was greater than that of the other, until he is almost yearning to live in the other exile." The Iberian refugee claimed that the worst part of the Christian oppression was that "they inflict all wrongs upon Israel in an intellectual way, but they do not kill or physically assail us as do the Ishmaelites. . . . They [the Muslims] slap us in the face and pull out the hair of our beards and skulls. . . . They blacken a man's face with wordless beatings." Another exile, R. Joseph b. Abraham Ḥayyun, contrasted the more sophisticated intolerance and miscarriage of justice of the Christian regimes with the crude pretentiousness of the Muslim nations who "give themselves the appearance of saintliness, while in fact they fornicate, rob, and steal." [56]

Saba's annoyance at the Muslims' contemptuous attitude reflected, in part, the greater sensitivity of many Spanish exiles who had long been accustomed to regarding their community as the salt of the earth. Saba himself contended that "the Jews were banished from Castile for they had lived there like kings." Don Isaac Abravanel voiced the prevailing opinion among his fellow exiles when he commented on the biblical phrase, "For the portion of the Lord is His people" (Deut. 32:9), as referring to the "Jerusalem exile which is in Spain." Yet, this pride in their native land did not prevent these refugees from following the traditional Jewish penchant for self-accusation and blaming their sufferings on their own shortcomings.[57]

This sense of Sephardic superiority also made itself felt in the intracommunal Jewish relations. These debates were in practice much more significant than the similar ones between the Muslim Spaniards of European ancestry and their Arab-Berber conquerors. Led by writers like Ibn Garcia in his *Risala* (Missive), the Shu'ubiyya movement liked to point out the great contributions to civilization made by the ancient European nations at a time when the Arabs were "herders of dirty camels." Nor were the Jews the sole offenders of Arab pride when they emphasized the biblical tradition about the Arabs' purported ancestor, Ishmael, being the *ben ha-amah,* or son of a slave girl, Hagar. Some Hebrew-writing Jews even dared to allude to Mohammed as "the madman," although any "blasphemy" aimed at the Messenger was considered a capital crime in most Muslim lands. But while the dominant Arab majority was prone to denigrate all such aspersions, members of the older Jewish communities in Africa and Asia were deeply impressed by the newcomers from the Iberian Peninsula, whose superiority in Jewish and general learning, manners, and frequently also financial success, appeared undeniable. Occasionally they could fall back on local patriotism and glorify their native-born coreligionists over arrivals from other lands. Such was the case in Fez, where being born to the *Ahl Fas* or *Al-Fasiyyun,* whether Jew or Gentile, was considered a special mark of distinction. Yet in time the weight of numbers helped the Iberian arrivals to overwhelm the native communities and to impress upon them many of their own cultural patterns, although this happened less frequently in North Africa than in the Middle East.[58]

Even the Sephardim had to learn early how to take in stride the studied humiliation of all "unbelievers" by the Muslim authorities. Such denigration was frequently connected with the ceremony accompanying the payment of the capitation tax (here called *jaliya* as well as *jizya*). On the assumption that this tax was intended as a ransom for the lives of the unbelieving people, graciously granted them by the Muslim governments, the authorities frequently attempted to demonstrate tangibly to these taxpayers how much gratitude they owed the rulers for sparing them. On occasion these ceremonies were conducted in public. Louis S. Chenier was later to state succinctly: "The lowest among the Moors imagines he has the right to illtreat a Jew, nor does the latter defend himself." We also recall the humiliating tax-gathering performance recorded in thirteenth-century Baghdad, with no exemption granted even to outstanding Jewish leaders. While we do not hear of similar proceedings in North Africa, we learn at least about demands to institute them by such Jew-baiters as Al-Majili. In his aforementioned anti-Jewish tract the Tuat polemist demanded that at the *jizya* payments

> [Jews] should be assembled in a public place such as the bazaar. They should present themselves there standing upright in the vilest and lowest location. Attendants of the law should stand above them assuming a menacing attitude such as would demonstrate, in their eyes and in the eyes of others, our intention to humiliate them by making it appear that they would be deprived of their property. They should take account of the fact that it is by our grace that we accept their *jizya* and let them go. Then they should be dragged one after another [before the functionary charged] with the collection. While paying, the *dhimmi* is to receive a slap and be pushed back in such a fashion that he should consider himself happy for being graciously allowed to escape the spear. Thus have proceeded the Lord's friends of the earlier and later generations toward their miserable enemies, for power belongs to God, his Messenger, and the believers.

Like many of his other proposals, Al-Majili's extremist recommendation seems to have found no practical application.[59]

It was this attempt to demonstrate *dhimmi* inferiority which also underlay the numerous laws concerning distinguishing marks. From its inception the Covenant of 'Umar provided that members of each "unbelieving" denomination be outwardly distinguished by the color of their attire. Subsequently specific decrees throughout the Muslim world ordained various methods of implementation. Sometimes a badge of a particular color worn on a visible garment sufficed. In other cases different headgear was also required. Curiously, the incoming Spanish and Portuguese Jews were for generations thereafter called men of the "bireta" in contrast to the local men of the "turban," because each group considered its particular head cover, originally imposed by outsiders, as a sign of superior dignity. At times, of course, one or another ruler could introduce highly detestable forms. We recall the Faṭimid Caliph Al-Ḥakim's decree forcing Jews and Christians to wear ludicrous symbols of their degradation. In the Almohade empire, too, Sultan Abu-Yusuf Ya'qub al-Manṣur in 1199 C.E. forced the Jews (though officially converted to Islam) to wear a *shikla* with sleeves long enough to reach the ground. In this connection the chronicler Muḥammad al-Kairuani reports a saying among the people of Tenes, Algeria: "Oh Jew, man of the *shikla,* your father has given you a kick for he has found you to be a pearl in the mire, may your father perish and the father of your grandfather be cursed." Yet, despite that hue and cry, it appears that the laws concerning badges were less effectively enforced in the North African and other Muslim lands, where they originated, than among late medieval Christian peoples who were their imitators.[60]

Most enduringly troublesome was the loss of much of North African Jewry's wide-ranging communal autonomy, which had existed in the days of the Great Caliphate and its Faṭimid successors. In theory, to be sure, the personal rather than territorial principle of Islamic law in religious, family, and personal matters was recognized in almost all medieval Muslim lands. Accordingly, each ethnoreligious group could adhere to its religious rites and requirements, and regulate its internal relations referring to marriage, divorce, and inheritance, in conformity with its own tradition. The differences of opinion regarding specific laws were, as a rule, to be adjudicated by the leaders of each such group; in the Jewish case, by rabbinic courts. In practice, however, after their great population losses during the Almohade flood, few Jewish communities had a sufficiently large and affluent membership to maintain the expensive religious and social institutions built up by their ancestors. Nor were there enough learned Jews to man adequately the special Jewish tribunals. Hence, the Jews often acquiesced (without any governmental pressure) in repairing to Muslim courts and being judged by Muslim law. On the contrary, the sultans were often willing to grant foreign, particularly Italian, merchants the right of judicial self-government administered by their own consuls. This prerogative, held by the Venetian consulate in Tunis from 1274 onward, was soon obtained by representatives of other European states. Similarly, after the arrival of the Spanish rabbis in Algeria in the 1390s, Jews had no difficulty in securing governmental approval, in practice if not through specific decrees, for submission to the jurisdiction of their own judges. On its part, the community was often held responsible for actual or alleged misdeeds of its members. According to a contemporary report reproduced by Solomon Ibn Danan, in 1595 a Fez Jew named Sa'id b. Awad was walking in the sultan's gardens—which evidently were open to the public, including Jews—when he became involved in an altercation with a Muslim. As a result of the ensuing fight, the Jew was executed for an alleged blasphemy, and the community at large was fined 2,000 ounces of silver.[61]

Judicial self-determination became particularly important for the Jews in adjudicating cases of "informers," a perennial plague of minorities which became most troublesome in critical periods. The Spanish refugees of 1391 must have become exceptionally aware of the dangers of informing, which they held partially responsible for the tensions which had led to the widespread anti-Jewish massacres in both Castile and Aragon. Some five years before that upheaval, R. Isaac b. Sheshet Perfet himself had repeatedly insisted that an informer should

> legally pay the extreme penalty because of the potential ultimate effects of his actions. Even if he had not yet denounced anybody, but merely threatened to do so, we put him to death, as we do a pursuer [of a man with the intent to kill], in order to save the person threatened by that delator. And not only shall the court condemn him to death, but any person who slays him first, as in the case of the pursuer, will perform a meritorious deed.

In 1390, as we recall, Queen Violante had appointed the distinguished rabbi Ḥisdai Crescas to serve as *judex malsinorum* (this loanword from the Hebrew word for informer had long become a part of the Spanish language) in charge of prosecutions of Jewish informers throughout Aragon. Not surprisingly, therefore, soon after their settlement in Algiers, R. Isaac and his associates influenced the community to adopt a sharp ordinance against delators. Couched in traditional biblical phrases severely condemning evildoers, this Hebrew ordinance concluded with a series of curses written in the local Judeo-Arabic dialect. Evidently its authors intended this section to be read from time to time in the synagogues as a warning to would-be offenders. Unlike some of the Aragonese kings, who out of self-interest considered informing within the Jewish community a cancerous growth—Pedro III in 1279 forced two leading rabbis to condemn an informer to death—the North African rulers seem to have wished to benefit from any information which could lead to the confiscation of the property of alleged culprits. However, in the long run they, too, apparently agreed that Jewish courts be entitled to condemn dangerous informers to death; they merely stipulated that the actual execution should be carried out exclusively by state officials, for the payment of a very high fee of 500 to 1,000 dinars by the community concerned.[62]

SOCIOECONOMIC DICHOTOMIES

Our knowledge of Jewish demography in the late medieval Maghrib is even more limited than of the Jewish political and legal status. After the days of Benjamin of Tudela, the existing late medieval Jewish and non-Jewish sources rarely refer to the size of the Jewish communities. Since the calamitous regime of the Almohades caused many Jewish settlements to start afresh, the figures preserved by the famous traveler of Tudela are of little use for estimating their population in the thirteenth to the fifteenth centuries. We owe most of our limited information, therefore, to Muslim and Christian travelers in the sixteenth and seventeenth centuries, especially Leo Africanus and Luis de Marmol Carvajal. To be sure, the figures quoted by them are far from reliable. We recall the conflicting data supplied by such long-term residents of Fez as Clénard and Marmol with respect to its Jewish population in the 1540s. Such outside observers may be somewhat more dependable in regard to smaller communities that embraced less than 100 Jewish families. There most inhabitants belonging to a single group knew one another and could give a fair estimate of their totals to casual visitors. Some other demographic aspects could also be studied a bit more closely by a resident of eight years duration, like Marmol. In general, however, we are told more about the urban Jews than about those living in villages, particularly in the Maghrib's southern districts close to the Sahara Desert. There quite a few Jews still lived in tents, if not in caves. Some "troglodyte Jews" were found in Tripolitania even in the twentieth century; they were viewed with amazement by the British combatants, Jewish and non-Jewish, fighting the Germans over the Libyan sand dunes during the Second World War. We also recall the family Perez which, from tent settlements, developed two Jewish townships. Another Jewish family inhabiting a tent village established a *duhar,* a locality, where "every head of the landowning family assembles around his tent his children, his relatives or allies, and his farmers, with whom he forms a *duhar,* of which he is the representative; he thus becomes head or sheikh of a tribe bearing his name." However, neither these Jewish tent dwellers nor even their cave-dwelling coreligionists were primitive people of the type usually associated with aborigine tribes in various parts of the world. Some of them had learned Hebrew and preserved considerable familiarity with the Jewish religious tradition. On one of his visits to a Jewish *duhar* of some twenty tents, Nahum Slouschz was amazed to find that its rabbi, Abraham, had come from a troglodyte community and that thus "a cave dweller [was] teaching tent dwellers." [63]

Of course, conditions in areas under Portuguese or Spanish occupation greatly differed from those prevailing in the Muslim-dominated cities, villages, and hamlets. Understandably, our best information stems from the occupied territories. Together with the Portuguese, quite a few professing Jews arrived from the Iberian Peninsula, and they were followed in 1497–1547 by "New Christians" as yet little disturbed by the Inquisition. After the evacuation of these cities by the Portuguese under the pressure of the Barbary corsairs and Turks, the newcomers could publicly profess Judaism without fear of prosecution. We may thus understand why, according to the distinguished contemporary Portuguese historian Damião de Góis, on the Atlantic coast the population of the occupied district of Safi, consisting of 4,500 families, embraced 400 Jewish houses. Among the inhabitants De Góis mentions specifically a Jewish physician and a Portuguese-speaking rabbi, Abraham. Azammur seems to have included even more Jewish residents.

At the same time a number of Old and New Christians genuinely professed Christianity. A community of *Chuetas* from Majorca lived in the fortress of Sueta into the nineteenth century.[64]

In the interior of Morocco the outstanding Jewish community, next to that of Fez, was in Marrakesh. While Diego de Torres mentioned over 200 Jewish families as living there in two Jewish quarters, Marmol raised that figure for 1551 to more than 3,000 houses, that is, to some 15,000–20,000 persons. This high figure is indirectly confirmed by the eighteenth-century French diplomat Louis Chenier who claimed that the Jewish population, which had once amounted to "more than 30,000 families" (an obvious exaggeration), had interveningly shrunk to one-twelfth of that number, or to about 2,500 families. This is another example of divergent, probably equally unreliable, estimates. Remarkably, even in the deep south some observers reported the presence of scores or even hundreds of Jewish families in certain localities. Regrettably, these scattered rural Jewries, which in the aggregate may have outnumbered their urban coreligionists, are passed over in total or partial silence by most natives and outsiders, Leo Africanus being a notable exception. This deficiency is doubly evident in Algeria, Tunisia, and Tripolitania-Libya, where the Jewish population was definitely much smaller. Hence, the total size of North African Jewry before 1650 is subject to mere conjecture.[65]

The few glimpses of the general or Jewish populations in North Africa are further vitiated by their dating from different periods. We are even worse off with respect to such other basic demographic data as birth and death rates, family sizes, and relative longevity. Nor do we learn to what extent the Jews, along with other inhabitants, were victims of the fairly frequent pestilences, famines, and fires. For example, quite apart from the Black Death, which also ravaged various parts of the Maghrib, we are told by Fray João Alvares (a former Portuguese captive in Morocco) that in 1441–42 a plague lasting 18 months destroyed 400–500 lives daily in Fez alone. According to Luis de Marmol, among the 15,000 Spanish soldiers stationed in Bougie in 1509, about 100 men died daily from a communicable disease; it certainly did not spare the town's civilian population. A Jewish record copied by Saadiah b. Samuel Ibn Danan informs us that in the year 5318, after Passover [April 11, 1558] the epidemic began to rage among the Jews. Many inhabitants of Fez fled in all directions. The pest continued to rage in Fez until the 29 of Ab [August 14, 1558]. The Jews returned after Saturday the Ninth of Ab [July 24]. During that epidemic 1,640 Jews perished in Fez, while 5,660 Jews, all learned in the law, died in Marrakesh. Subsequently Marrakesh Jews arriving in Fez reported that exactly 7,500 persons [of their community] had passed away.

The ravages of the plague, which four decades later engulfed Morocco for nine years (1598–1607), so impressed the English envoy George Wilkins that he reported home that 7,700 Jews had died in Marrakesh alone in 1604. Another deadly epidemic, the so-called French disease (syphilis), which around 1500 spread like wildfire in Europe, North Africa, and the Middle East, was actually attributed to Jews. Because its sudden appearance among the Muslim peoples coincided with the arrival of many Spanish exiles after 1492, rumors circulated that the Jews brought the malady from Spain, "for some sad individuals among the Moors had relations with Jewish women. So little by little in the course of ten years, there was not a family which was immune to it." Leo Africanus, who repeated that canard, also glibly asserted that it sufficed for persons stricken by that disease to reach the more salubrious regions of Nubia or Black Africa in order to be immediately healed. Remarkably, we hear very little from Jewish sources about the spread of that virulent disease among Jews, whose fairly general abstention from sexual relations with non-Jews may have minimized their contamination.[66]

Nor can we estimate, even remotely, how many persons died in the Maghrib as a result of the frequent famines. One extended disturbance of this kind, which was connected with the plague, lasted from late 1603 to 1606 and involved 3,000 Jewish victims of starvation, while more than 2,000 others apostasized to Islam, probably because they had lost faith in the God of Israel. Other famines, whether caused by drought (often lasting several months at a time), human negligence, or difficulties in transporation, were doubtless also responsible for a considerable increase in Jewish mortality. In ordinary times, on the other hand, the Jewish population in North Africa may have had substantial natural growth, if we may take a cue from late nineteenth-century conditions—admittedly a somewhat risky assumption. We learn that in 1891–93 Algerian Jewry, although at that time subject to incipient Westernization with the concomitant phenomena of lower birth and death rates, still had a natality rate of over 57 per 1,000 Jewish inhabitants and a mortality rate of 38 per 1,000. It thus was gaining at the rate of about 2 percent annually from natural causes. Most remarkably, as late as the interwar period of 1919–38 the Jews' birth rate exceeded that of the Muslims, while their death rate was smaller.[67]

Under these circumstances, it is impossible to offer even an informed "guestimate" of the totals of the Jewish population in any late medieval North African country. The same holds true for independent Morocco during the sixteenth-century "population explosion" in the Western and Ottoman areas. Certainly, the figure suggested by Olfert Dapper in 1686, that 160,000 Jewish families (or a total Jewish population of well over 800,000 persons) lived in the kingdom of Fez, is a clear exaggeration. As late as the beginning of this century, Western scholars differed in their estimates of the total number of inhabitants of that vast, but sparsely populated, land; these ranged anywhere between 5,000,000 and 10,000,000. In fact, at that time not even the precise boundaries of Morocco were fully known. In their pertinent article in the 11th edition of the *Encyclopaedia Britannica* (1911), Budgett Meakin and Kate A. Meakin wrote:

> Morocco is still the portion of Northern Africa about which European information is most defective, and all maps are still to a considerable extent composed of unscientific material eked out by probabilities and conjecture.

While our geographical knowledge has greatly increased over the last decades, the demographic history of Morocco's earlier periods still is in the early stages of investigation. As to the Jewish population, we must be satisfied with the data (even if often divergent) about major communities supplied to us by travelers and other contemporaries. But we must never lose sight of the fact that, between them, these communities embraced only a minority of a Jewry which was widely scattered over scores, if not hundreds, of towns, villages, and hamlets.[68]

We are a little better informed about the economic activities of the North African Jews, especially after the arrival of the Iberian refugees. True, the flourishing Mahdiya, Kairuwan, Sijilmassa, and other communities of the Genizah period had been effectively destroyed by the Almohades. Under the politically unstable conditions that followed, the renascent Jewish communities had to struggle for sheer survival. After his arrival in Algeria in 1392, R. Isaac b. Sheshet pointed out to an inquirer who expressed surprise about the small size of marriage settlements provided as a rule by local Jewish husbands:

> You are thinking of Majorca, where the rich possessed large fortunes, had houses stored with gold and silver and pearls and caves full of gold *denarii;* those who were denied such great wealth were classed with the poor, though they had precious stones and a good trade which yielded them a comfortable living. Think, however, of the Jews of this country, who have not the wherewithal to satisfy the very necessities of life—their hunger and their thirst—who sleep upon the bare ground, using their wearing apparel for their covering, whose clothes are full of patches and who are compelled to walk barefoot.

This contrast is overdrawn, but there is no question that many Algerian Jews lived in dire poverty, as did the majority of their non-Jewish compatriots. The newcomers of both the 1390s and the 1490s had a very hard time at first in earning a living, as is attested by the numerous complaints voiced by Yehudah Ḥayyat and other contemporaries. But many exiles brought with them considerable expertise in commerce, industry, or the medical profession. Even those who were unable to salvage much of their former Iberian possessions often succeeded within a relatively short time in raising their own and their coreligionists' economic level through activities which, as a rule, also accrued to the benefit of their North African Muslim hosts.[69]

North Africa's trade with late medieval Europe was largely limited to the Iberian and Italian cities, however, whereas the countries north of the Alps and Pyrenees, with a slight or no Islamic heritage of their own, engaged in relatively little business with the western Maghrib. There are very few records of North African Jews trading, for example, with Marseilles before its expulsion of Jews (about 1500). Even maritime travel from Marseilles to the Middle East (although it took twenty-five or more days to reach Alexandria, it was but "a humdrum experience" according to

S. D. Goitein) was hampered by an old prohibition against transporting more than four Jewish passengers on any Marseilles ship. Only during the dynamic sixteenth century did French trade with North Africa assume significant proportions. It has been shown that in 1553 France exported no less than 900,000 pounds of paper and hardware and 600,000 pounds of linen to Morocco alone. But at that time there were too few Jews in France significantly to participate in these exchanges. On the other hand, some North African Jews, particularly those residing in the Ottoman provinces, began more actively to share in that expanding branch of international trade. Before long they (and many Armenians), seeking protection for themselves and their merchandise under the treaties between France and the Ottoman Empire, used Marseilles Christian merchants to lend their names to the otherwise forbidden shipments. The frequency of that camouflage caused the Marseilles officials to complain to the Intendant of Provence regarding "the considerable transactions" made in this way by two Tunisian Jews, Jacob and Raphael Lumbroso, under the name of the Marseilles merchant François Lament (January 22, 1693). These disguises had evidently been practised for a long time and had continued in defiance of the strict governmental prohibition of 1687, which placed them under the sanction of confiscation of the ships transporting such merchandise plus a fine of 3,000 livres.[70]

On the whole, the economic life of most Maghribian Jews, except for those living in the Spanish or Portuguese-occupied cities or in the Berber south, resembled that of their coreligionists in the Mameluke Empire. The information transmitted by the extant sources is very sketchy, and we shall point out here only a few highlights of the Maghribian conditions. In international trade North Africa was a major supplier of grain, fruits, hides, and other agricultural products, while it imported from Europe mainly manufactured articles. Regrettably, our sources do not allow for an estimate of the occupational distribution of the late medieval Jews in any North African country or in what remained of Muslim Spain. Even the aforementioned three lists preserved in the Genizah are moderately relevant only for Egypt or Syria of an indeterminate earlier period.[71]

Jewish participation in international commerce was most concentrated in the export and import business with the Iberian Peninsula and the Balearic Islands. The difference between the cost of grain in the interior of Morocco and that prevailing in Catalonia and Tunisia was sufficiently great to secure for the Moroccan exporters a sizable profit, despite the high expenses of transportation and customs duties. It has been shown that in the period of 1280 to 1330, a container of 100 kilograms (220 pounds) of grain was sold in Catalonia for the average equivalent of 1.41 dinars, and in Tunisia for 1.06 dinars, but was obtainable on the Atlantic coast of Morocco (from which it could easily be shipped to either market) for as little as 0.3 dinars.[72]

Jewish farmers are mentioned in our sources particularly in connection with problems of Jewish ritual concern. From an eleventh-century responsum by Hai Gaon we even learn of sales in Kairuwan of containers of cheese bearing the Hebrew inscription *berakhah* (blessing), a practice confirmed by the discovery of a boxwood seal reading *berakhah* and dating from the Faṭimid era. The chances are that, since dairy products were a staple foodstuff for Jews and non-Jews in the Arabic-speaking lands, this practice continued during, or was resumed after, the Almohade period. The cost of cheese also compared favorably with that of other foods; in the fourteenth and fifteenth centuries it seems to have averaged one-half to one-third of the cost of meat, and one-third to one-eleventh of the cost of sugar. Numerous Jews also cultivated vineyards and sold wine both locally and for export. We learn from Leo Africanus that the Jewish community of Taza, located on the main route from Fez to Tlemcen, embraced fully 500 Jewish families, many of whom were engaged in viticulture; he describes their wine as being "absolutely perfect. It is said that theirs are the best wines in the entire area." Although the Jewish wine business with the Muslim majority was hampered by the Islamic prohibition of its consumption and the Jews' own restraints regarding the "wine of libation," there were various means of evasion as well as outright lawbreaking on the part of both denominations. We need but mention, for example, the Marinid Sultan Abu-Ya'qub Yusuf's wine parties with his Jewish councillor, Khalifa Ibn Waqqaṣa. We also recall Emperor Frederick II's decision to entrust to some Jewish immigrants from North Africa the cultivation of a palm grove and the production of henna and indigo in the Sicilian capital of Palermo, undoubtedly because they had acquired these skills in their home country.[73]

In Morocco and, perhaps to a lesser extent, in other North African countries, many Jews derived their livelihood from various crafts, although our information about this aspect of Jewish life there between 1200 and 1650 is extremely limited. It appears that when the Muslim craftsmen began organizing associations of their own, as they did in the sixteenth and seventeenth centuries, they were not primarily motivated by the wish to combat Jewish competition. They may even have admitted Jews to membership. Yet the concentration of Jewish artisans in their traditional areas of clothing, meat processing, and gold- and silversmithing was stimulated by such religious factors as the Jews' avoidance of mixing wool and linen in garments, consuming only kosher food, and manufacturing more or less costly ritual objects for synagogues and Jewish households. Chenier's observation in the eighteenth century that in Morocco "tailors, who are usually Jews, work for the Emperor gratis," doubtless held true for earlier periods as well. However, in handling gold, silver, and other metals, Jews had the advantage over their Muslim competitors because the Islamic doctrine of usury (*riba*), going farther than the corresponding Jewish anti-usury laws, forbade Muslims to charge customers more for gold and silver objects than the worth of the metal contained in them. Theoretically, at least, costs of workmanship, transportation, customs duties, and other additions to the metallic value of such merchandise were regarded as a usurious gain. These considerations helped Jews to continue playing a preeminent role in the gold and jewelry trade.[74]

According to David Cazès, the Jewish artisans of Tunis included tanners, cobblers, tailors, manufacturers of red bonnets, and especially jewelers and goldsmiths. In fact, even in the nineteenth century some of these trades still bore Spanish-sounding names and undoubtedly had been brought into North Africa by Spanish immigrants, particularly Jewish exiles. Some material about Jewish occupations may also be gleaned from the documents preserved by the Spanish Inquisition. From the records of one such trial Haim Beinart has described the life story of Juan Robles, son of a New Christian father and an Old Christian mother, who left Spain for Fez, became a Jew, and even intended to emigrate to Jerusalem. In Morocco Robles continued to work as a glass blower. He seems to have been fairly successful, since he was able to support his Christian mother who had remained behind in Spain. Despite her own continued profession of Christianity, the Holy Office did not hesitate to confiscate at least one shipment of 15 ducats and 8 reals which he had sent her.[75]

Jewish commercial activities are far more frequently reflected in our sources, partly because of the greater availability of mercantile documents, especially from European countries which traded with North Africa. In some branches Jews seem to have played a prominent role. Apart from adhering to their old traditions of working and trading in precious metals, Jews also had the edge as merchants in gold and gold dust. In fact, the gold route from the Sudan to the western Maghrib was sometimes called the "Jewish route," indicating an intensive activity which was facilitated by the prevailing practice that the rulers appropriated both gold bullion and gold coins, but left the gold dust to the workers and merchants, including Jews. This advantage may also have enhanced the Jewish role in minting and money exchange. However, banking was no more a major branch of Jewish trade in Morocco than it was in Egypt or Syria; it definitely was less peculiarly Jewish than in contemporary Europe. At the other extreme, we have more records of Jewish peddling in Morocco than in the Middle East. Probably the vast expanse of the North African territories, with many areas dotted with small Jewish settlements, encouraged peddling from village to village, as well as in cities. From contemporary responsa we learn about Jewish peddlers leaving their homes on Sunday morning and returning on Friday afternoon. There also were Jews active in professions, particularly medicine. Many performed a variety of religious, educational, and literary functions for the Jewish communities. But apparently these activities were, on the whole, pursued quite smoothly and gave rise to relatively few litigations; they rarely raised legal issues considered worthy of recording by contemporary rabbis or chroniclers. Hence, our sources do not evince particular interest in them unless the story concerned, for instance, a prominent physician who became involved in some court intrigue and for this reason had to be mentioned by his employer's biographer or political historian.[76]

Remarkably, despite their important role in the manufacture of and commerce in gold and silver objects, we hear very little about Jews in moneylending and allied occupations. If debts to Jews are mentioned in the sources, they often concern those arising from ordinary business transactions. For instance, after the death of the English consul in Algiers, A. Stanyford, the British government had to pay off the large sum of almost £1,000 which he owed to Jews and Moors. The negotiations, conducted over the years 1754–57, clearly indicated that these debts stemmed from purchases of merchandise on credit. But minting, exchange of coins, and moneylending generally belong to the gray areas in North Africa's economic evolution, concerning which the relative silence of the extant sources does not necessarily imply absence.[77]

The fiscal system of the North African countries broadly resembled that of other Muslim lands, although there apparently was much less stability in Morocco than under the early Mameluke regime. Basically, Jews paid their capitation tax according to the provisions of the Covenant of 'Umar. Jews also paid the land tax on whatever rural or urban real estate they owned, but in this respect they were seemingly treated more or less on a par with the rest of the population. The same apparently held true in regard to customs duties, which were generally imposed on all exported and imported goods at a rate of 10 percent of the value of the merchandise. Only rarely do we hear of a distinction being drawn between Jews and other *dhimmis*, who paid that amount, and Muslims, who were charged less—at times as little as 3 percent. As mentioned before, some governments also exacted from Jews corvée labor in wartime and also for building bridges for peacetime use and the like. But here, too, the situation is far from clear. More frequently, we hear about special protection money exacted by the authorities from Jews in the Maghrib as in the rest of the Muslim world, whether this happened in a systematic legal fashion or in extralegal extortions. Nor was the peculiar Jewish tax which later, under the name of *Leibzoll* (corporeal tax), was to play a significant role in the struggle for Jewish emancipation in Germany, completely overlooked. Leo Africanus describes a "bad castle," Ummi al-Hadaj (Umelheffen), twenty-five miles from Sijilmassa, the chiefs of which exacted a quarter ducat for every camel and every Jew passing through its territory. Leo also reminisced about a journey in the company of fourteen Jews. When the passengers declared that they consisted of two Muslims and thirteen Jews, the chiefs made the two Muslims recite the Arabic prayers to prove their Muslim faith. Apparently one of the Jewish passengers was able and willing to deliver such a recitation. Jews were also obliged frequently to give presents to their rulers, high and low.[78]

At times communities at large were forced to contribute money to the royal treasuries, in lieu of individual contributors or in addition to them. During the turmoil created by the Turkish raids into Morocco in 1554, the Turkish commander collected from the Fez Jewish community a tribute of 20,000 dinars during his occupation, which lasted only 39 days. The returning sultan Muḥammad ash-Shaykh imposed another contribution of the same amount on the community, which had in the interim paid 12,000 dinars to a third contender. On another occasion, Ash-Shaykh is said to have imposed upon the Muslim inhabitants of Tetuan a war tax of 100,000 ounces, on the "Andalusians" one of 150,000 ounces, and on the Jews one of but 10,000 ounces; this disparity was undoubtedly due mainly to the small size of the local Jewish community and its impoverishment by the war. In fact, the unnamed author of the excerpt, recorded by Saul b. David Serero, complained that after exacting that "modest" Jewish share in Tetuan, "they left us naked down to the [covers of the] scrolls of Law." In general, rightly observes Edouard Michaux-Bellaire, a student of Morocco's fiscal organization, the taxation imposed on each ethnic and tribal group "was not in proportion to its wealth but in proportion to the greater or lesser dependence in which it found itself in relation to the Makhzen [central administration] and to the means of enforcement the Makhzen was able to employ against it." Even outsiders were struck by the intolerable fiscal burden often resting on Jewish shoulders. Nicolas Clénard doubtless was not alone in noting that Jewish taxpayers in Morocco

> pay here a very heavy tax monthly, so that I often deplore their lot. Each time the king needs money, they have to pay. Because they are humiliated, weighed down by adversity, they react through their keen

wits. They make provisions in advance for such payments to the king in a fashion which neither a Christian nor a Moor can circumvent, namely through Jewish tricks—which I readily forgive them. For how could these unfortunates pay so high a tax except through agile manipulations which they prefer to violent death in prison.

Yet, the entire ramified fiscal and economic structure of the Maghrib's medieval Jewish communities has been sadly neglected by modern scholars. Careful studies into the existing documentation, however meager, and some attempts at tentative generalizations, definitely are a major scholarly desideratum.[79]

STAGNATION AND RESURGENCE

A general review of the Muslim countries bordering the Mediterranean during the Late Middle Ages give the impression of spreading stagnation. After the great upsurge of the first centuries of Islam, centered in the Middle East, Kairuwan, and Spain, came a period of inner dissolution and growing external pressures. Although the challenge of the Christian Crusades initiated a temporary revival under the Ayyubid monarchs in the East and the Almohade unitarianism in the West, this passed after the reigns of Saladin and Abu-Yusuf Ya'qub al-Manṣur. What followed was a more or less continuous turmoil under changing dynasties in both East and West. Sultans followed one another frequently, for the most part after brief periods of reign. A sultanate did not always imply actual rule, since real authority was often held by viziers and provincial governors. Moreover, as Louis Massignon observed, because of the persistent tribal divisions few Moroccan sultans of the post-Almohade age exercised effective and constant control over more than one-fifth of the population. Chronologically, too, periods of relative stability and peace alternated with frequent uprisings, whether of a mass character or under the shape of palace revolts. The resulting instability led to the weakening of the countries' economic structure, inflationary price rises, and a spreading political fatigue. Among the first impressions received by R. Zechariah b. Joshua Ibn Saruq upon his arrival in Algiers in 1493 was that "the nature of the Ishmaelite country consists of endless quarrels and disputes." [80]

By the end of the Middle Ages, Muslim Spain was entirely recaptured by the Christian powers, which also began encroaching on the coast of the Maghrib along the Mediterranean and Atlantic shores. Only toward the end of the fifteenth century did the rising star of the Osmanlis help to keep the western Muslim possessions under the rule of the Crescent. After the Turkish conquest of Constantinople in 1453, Islam resumed its role as a world power; in the sixteenth century it appeared again as a prime contender for world supremacy in the struggle with the equally expanding power of the Austrian and Spanish Habsburgs.

From the Jewish point of view, the last three centuries of the Middle Ages marked a low point in the history of the Jewish people in the southern parts of the Mediterranean basin. Under the vast Almohade Empire Judaism (along with Christianity) was for the first time formally outlawed by a Muslim regime. Whatever Jewish communities survived from Libya to Spain consisted largely of secret Jews practicing their religious rites in the privacy of their homes, while outwardly paying lip service to the regnant faith. In the eastern Mediterranean the flourishing communities of the Faṭimid Empire obtained a certain respite under the Ayyubid dynasty, but they suffered a severe decline during the Mongolian invasions. In the Maghrib and Granada, too, the former great intellectual and economic efflorescence gave way to a quiet, restrained, almost subdued sort of existence.

Only after the arrival of refugees from the Iberian persecutions in 1391 and 1492–97 did the Jewish communities of the Maghrib reveal signs of a new vibrant life. This restoration, however slow at first, helped them to overcome the enormous difficulties set in their paths by the frequently hostile Muslim majorities and the mostly arbitrary governmental authorities. To be sure, the revival of the Islamic protection of the "people of the book" made their continued toleration by the respective regimes a basic fact of life. But the definitions of toleration varied from time to time and from area to area. Under some regimes Jews were able to reach pinnacles of commercial and political success, particularly as advisers to the rulers or as court physicians, while their majority suffered from constant humiliations by their haughty neighbors. Contrasting the conditions in the Late Middle Ages with those of the classical period of Islam, A. S. Tritton rightly observed, "The position of the dhimmis did change for the worse. They were more liable to suffer from the violence of the crowd, and the popular fanaticism was accompanied by increasing strictness among the educated. The spiritual isolation of Islam was accomplished." Although themselves internally often divided, the Jewish communities—especially in the Maghrib where the Berber Jews long differed from the Jews of Arabic-speaking lands and the newcomers from Christian Europe—also faced an incipient though still weak growth of local nationalism among the Islamic peoples, which underscored the Jews' existence as an "alien" group in the population.[81]

Under these circumstances many Jews withdrew into an inner shell, cultivated their religion along accustomed ways, and made occasional contributions to Jewish learning along well-trodden paths. The rise of the great Jewish communities in the Ottoman Empire in the sixteenth century injected a new, vitalizing force into Jewish life throughout the Muslim world by developing major new centers of learning in Palestine, Egypt, Syria, and the Balkans, followed also by an independent creativity among the revived communities of the Maghrib. The Jews under Islam were now able to resume their position in world Jewry as a counterpart to the upsurging Jewish communities in Poland-Lithuania and soon thereafter also in Western Europe.

NOTES

ABBREVIATIONS

AHR	American Historical Review
Annales ESC	Annales Économies, Sociétés, Civilisations
AOH	Acta Orientalia of the Hungarian Academy
Baer Jub. Vol.	Sefer Yobel le-Yitzhak Baer (Yitzhak Baer Jubilee Volume). Jerusalem, 1960.
Baron Jub. Vol.	Essays on Jewish Life and Thought in Honor of Salo Wittmayer Baron. Ed. by Joseph L. Blau *et al.* New York, 1959.
	Salo Wittmayer Baron, Jubilee Volume: On the Occasion of His Eightieth Birthday. Ed. by Saul Lieberman, 3 vols. New York, 1974 [1975].
BSOAS	Bulletin of the School of Oriental and African Studies (University of London)
BZ	Byzantinische Zeitschrift
CSCO	Corpus scriptorum christianorum orientalium
CSSH	Comparative Studies in Society and History
EI	Encyclopaedia of Islam
Essays . . . Israel Brodie	Essays Presented to Chief Rabbi Israel Brodie. Ed. by H. J. Zimmels *et al.*, 2 vols. London, 1967 [1968].
Festschrift . . . A. Harkavy	Festschrift . . . A. Harkavy. Ed. by David Günzburg and Isaac Markon. St. Petersburg, 1908.
GRBS	Greek, Roman and Byzantine Studies
GS	Gesammelte Schriften
HJ	Historia Judaica
HUCA	Hebrew Union College Annual
HZ	Historische Zeitschrift
JA	Journal Asiatique
JAOS	Journal of the American Oriental Society
JC	The Jewish Community: Its History and Structure to the American Revolution, by Salo W. Baron. Philadelphia, 1942; reprint ed., Westport, Conn., 1972.
JE	The Jewish Encyclopedia. 12 vols., New York, 1901–1906.

JESHO	Journal of the Economic and Social History of the Orient
JGOE	Jahrbücher für Geschichte Osteuropas (new series unless otherwise stated)
JJS	Journal of Jewish Studies
JQR	Jewish Quarterly Review (new series unless otherwise stated)
JRAS	Journal of the Royal Asiatic Society
JSS	Jewish Social Studies
Mélanges Cénival-Lopes	Mélanges d'Études Luso-Marocaines dédiés . . . à David Lopes et Pierre de Cénival. Lisbon, 1945
MGH	Monumenta Germaniae Historica
MGWJ	Monatsschrift für Geschichte und Wissenschaft des Judentums
M.T.	Moses ben Maimon, *Mishneh Torah* (Code)
OLZ	Orientalistische Literaturzeitung
PAAJR	Proceedings of the American Academy for Jewish Research
PG	J. P. Migne's Patrologiae cursus completus, series Graeca
PL	J. P. Migne's Patrologiae cursus completus, series Latina
REB	Revue des études byzantines
REI	Revue des études islamiques
REJ	Revue des études juives
RESEE	Revue des études sud-est européens
Resp.	Responsa (*Teshubot* or *She'elot u-teshubot*)
RHC	Recueil des historiens des croisades
RHPR	Revue d'histoire et de philosophie religieuse
ROC	Revue de l'Orient chrétien
ROL	Revue de l'Orient Latin
RSO	Rivista degli studi orientali
Starr Mem. Vol.	The Joshua Starr Memorial Volume: Studies in History and Philology. Ed. by Abraham G. Duker *et al.* New York, 1953.
VSW	Vierteljahrsschrift für Sozial- und Wirtschaftsgeschichte
WZKM	Wiener Zeitschrift für die Kunde des Morgenlandes
Zakhor le-Abraham	Mélanges Abraham Elmaleh. Ed. by H. Z. Hirschberg. Jerusalem, 1972.
ZDMG	Zeitschrift der Deutschen Morgenländischen Gesellschaft
ZRG	Zeitschrift der Savigny-Stiftung für Rechtsgeschichte

NOTES

CHAPTER LXXI: BYZANTINE WORLD IN DECLINE

1. See the *Fragmentum* attributed to Marino Sanudo Torsello, reed. from an Oxford MS by R. L. Wolff in his "Hopf's So-Called 'Fragmentum' of Marino Sanudo Torsello," in the *Joshua Starr Memorial Volume: Studies in History and Philology* [ed. by A. Duker *et al.*, with a Foreword by S. W. Baron], pp. 149–59, esp. pp. 150 f., with further data in Wolff's "Mortgage and Redemption of an Emperor's Son: Castile and the Latin Empire of Constantinople," *Speculum,* XXIV, 45–84; and such general works as G. Ostrogorsky, *History of the Byzantine State,* English trans. by J. Hussey; D. Obolensky, *The Byzantine Commonwealth: Eastern Europe, 500–1453;* the chapters included in the second edition of the *Cambridge Medieval History,* Vol. IV, Parts 1–2, ed. by J. M. Hussey *et al.;* and a similar Russian 3-volume collection entitled *Istoriia Vizantii* (A History of Byzantium), ed. by S. D. Skatskin *et al.,* These last two works, collaborative efforts of some of the leading Western and Soviet specialists, respectively, with their diverse strengths and weaknesses, are reviewed by J. Meyendorff *et al.* in "The Cambridge and Soviet Histories of the Byzantine Empire," *Slavic Review,* XXX, 619–48.

Of considerable interest also is Peter Wirth's thoughtful survey of the work done in Byzantine studies during the quarter century after World War II, in his "Forschungsbericht: Byzantinische Geschichtswissenschaft in den Jahren 1945–1967," *HZ,* Sonderheft 3, pp. 575–640; also in *Byzantinische Forschungen,* III, 262–336. However, Wirth has little to say about the ethnic and religious minorities, including the Jews, living in the various provinces of the Empire, or about the Slavic states and Italian colonies which emerged from the disintegrating imperial structure but maintained constant interrelations with the Constantinopolitan center until its fall to the Turks in 1453 and beyond. See also the extensive literature listed in all these works and *supra,* Vols. III, Chap. XIX, *passim;* IV, pp. 107 f., 294 nn. 23–24, where the destinies of the Jews in the Byzantine Empire until 1204 are briefly analyzed.

I wish to note here with special gratification that the history of Byzantine Jewry, after the minor pioneering effort by Samuel Krauss before World War I, has been primarily investigated by two of my former pupils, the late Joshua Starr and Zvi Ankori. See Krauss's *Studien zur byzantinisch-jüdischen Geschichte;* Starr's *The Jews in the Byzantine Empire, 641–1204;* his *Romania: the Jewries of the Levant after the Fourth Crusade;* and Ankori's *Karaites in Byzantium.* Numerous pertinent articles by these authors are quoted in the following notes. Only during the last decade and a half have further monographic studies by David Jacoby and others, likewise cited in these notes, considerably enriched our knowledge of this little cultivated, yet important, phase of medieval Jewish history in its sociopolitical aspects.

2. To be sure, M. Hellmann and V. Glötzner, among others, have recently argued against this long-accepted nexus between the conquest of Constantinople by the Turks

in 1453 and the Muscovite claims under Ivan III. They pointed out, in particular, that Ivan's alleged designation of *samoderzhets* (the equivalent of the Byzantine *autocrator*) does not occur in any contemporary document. See Hellmann's "Moskau und Byzanz," *JGOE,* XVII, 321–44, esp. pp. 330 ff.; and V. Glötzner's "Das Moskauer Cartum und die byzantinishe Kaiseridee," *Saeculum,* XXI, 393–418. Yet the historical trend in this direction was inescapable, even if Ivan himself, or any of his contemporaries, dimly perceived the far-ranging implications of the great contemporary events. See also *infra,* Chap. LXXII, nn. 91 ff.; and on the designation "tsar," see G. Moravcsik's comparative study "Zur Geschichte des Herrschertitels 'Caesar-Tsar' " (1963), reprinted in his *Studia Byzantina,* pp. 267–74.

3. The figure of 60,000 Latins in Constantinople after 1175 is derived, from an epistle of Patriarch Eustathios of Thessalonica (see *infra,* n. 17), by G. I. Bratianu in his *Recherches sur le commerce génois dans la Mer Noire au XIIIe siècle,* p. 70. The general conditions in the decaying Byzantine Empire before 1204 are well analyzed in C. M. Brand's detailed study of *Byzantium Confronts the West: 1180–1204.* At the same time the old Western dream of taking over Byzantium now appeared to be a realistic possibility. See S. Kindlimann, *Die Eroberung von Konstantinopel als politische Forderung des Westens im Hochmittelalter. Studien zur Entwicklung der Idee eines lateinischen Kaiserreiches in Byzanz.* Among the countless monographic studies relating to twelfth-century Byzantium we need but mention here J. Herrin, "The Collapse of the Byzantine Empire in the Twelfth Century: a Study of a Medieval Economy," *University of Birmingham Historical Journal,* XII, 188–203; L. Halphen, "Le Rôle des 'Latins' dans l'histoire intérieure de Constantinople à la fin du XIIe siècle," *Mélanges Charles Diehl,* I, 141–45, both showing the extent to which the presence of a large minority stemming from the Western countries, for the most part endowed with extensive commercial and political privileges, was detrimental to the defenses of the country at the crucial moment of the Crusaders' invasion.

Incidentally, the public law of the Empire had long fully recognized the right of conquerors to loot possessions of the conquered population and their subsequent orderly division according to established patterns. See A. Dain, "Le Partage du butin de guerre d'après les traités juridiques et militaires," *Actes* of the Sixième Congrès International d'Études Byzantines, held in Paris, July 27–August 2, 1948, I, 347–52; with the additional comments thereon by H. F. Schmid, referring particularly to the repercussions of the pertinent Byzantine laws in the southern Slavic codes in "Le Partage du butin dans le soi-disant ancien code slave. La 'Loi pour juger le gens' (*Zakon soudnyj ljudem*)," *ibid.,* pp. 352*–54*.

4. Benjamin b. Jonah of Tudela, *Sefer Massa'ot* (Itinerary), critically ed. and trans. into English by M. N. Adler (reprinted from *JQR,* [o.s.] XVI–XVIII), pp. 16 f. (Hebrew), 14 (English); with a good summary thereof and additional comments in J. Starr's *Jews in the Byzantine Empire,* pp. 228 ff. No. 182, 238 No. 186; Petaḥiah b. Jacob of Ratisbon, *Sibbub* (Travelogue), ed. with a German trans. entitled *Die Rundreise des R. Petachjah aus Regensburg,* by L. Grünhut, I, 36 (Hebrew), 49 (German); in A. Benisch's English trans. entitled *The Travels of Rabbi Petahyah,* pp. 66 f.; Elisha bar Shinaya, *K. Al-Būrhān 'alā saḥiḥ al-'iman* (A Demonstration of the Truth of Faith), Arabic text reproduced from a Vatican MS by J. Starr and excerpted in English, in *The Jews in the Byzantine Empire,* pp. 190 No. 131 and

246 App. B; also in L. Horst's German trans., *Des Metropoliten Elias von Nisibis Buch vom Beweis der Wahrheit des Glaubens,* pp. 42, 103; *supra,* Vol. III, pp. 180, 195 f., 315 f. n. 7, 322 f. n. 29.

All population estimates of the Jewish inhabitants of the twelfth-century Byzantine Empire have relied heavily on Benjamin's figures, despite their frequent ambiguity and hearsay character. Among the outstanding scholars dealing with this problem was M. A. Andréadès, a leading Byzantine economic historian. See esp. his "Sur Benjamin de Tudèle," *BZ,* XXX, 457–67; idem, "The Jews in the Byzantine Empire," *Economic History,* III, 1–23; and, more generally, idem, "La Population de l'Empire Byzantin," *Bulletin de l'Institut Archéologique Bulgare,* IX, 117–26. Summing up the figures relating to the Byzantine areas visited by Benjamin and adding to them a few thousand more for places not recorded in Benjamin's *Itinerary,* Andréadès estimated the Jewish population at 15,000 out of a total of some 15,000,000 inhabitants in the entire Empire. This computation was based on the assumption that Benjamin referred to individuals, rather than families. J. Starr went even further and reduced the Jewish demographic strength to but 12,000 (pp. 34 ff.). These scholars overlooked, however, the likelihood that at least many of the figures mentioned by Benjamin related to families, taxpayers, or males attending synagogues. Considering these other possibilities, I have suggested a more likely figure of close to 100,000 Jews, or a little more than 0.5 percent of the imperial population. See *supra,* Vol. III, pp. 195 f., 322 f. n. 29.

Subsequently, Zvi Ankori carefully reviewed the entire record and pointed out, in particular, the large omissions in Benjamin's *Itinerary.* He referred especially to Asia Minor, the vast territories of which, reconquered by the emperors Nicephorus II Phokas (963–69) and John I Tzimiskes (969–76), included many Jewish communities. Also accepting the suggestion that some cities visited by Benjamin had more than one Jewish quarter, not fully reflected in the figures given by him, and that these figures usually related to families, Ankori came to the conclusion that the Jewish population probably ranged in the vicinity of 85,000. See his *Karaites in Byzantium,* pp. 159 f.

More recently, however, P. P. Argenti, basing his views exclusively on the brief statement by Benjamin relating to Chios' 400 Jews and comparing this figure with the 15 Jewish families whose taxes had been donated by Constantine IX to a local monastery in 1049 (see *infra,* n. 9), took issue with Ankori's and my calculations and reverted to the far smaller number suggested by Andréadès. See his *Religious Minorities of Chios: Jews and Roman Catholics,* pp. 93 ff. In his critique of my methodological suggestions, however, he not only overlooked the references I gave to the impressions made on other contemporaries by the very large number of Jewish communities in the Empire (as reflected by Petaḥiah, Yehudah b. David, and Elisha bar Shinaya, mentioned in the text), but also my remarks on the general methods employed by Benjamin, *supra,* Vols. III, pp. 163 f., 283 f. n. 48; VI, pp. 222 ff., 435 f. nn. 88–90. Nor must we completely overlook the presence of sizable and influential Jewish communities in Asia Minor during the Graeco-Roman period, which, it may be taken for granted, did not completely disappear under the Byzantine and Muslim regimes. See my tentative estimates, *supra,* Vol. I, pp. 170, 370 ff. n. 7; and, on their likely contributions to the spread of Christianity, Vol. II, pp. 83 ff., etc. See also such other relevant studies as A. Galanté, *Histoire des Juifs d'Anatolie,* with the *Appendices* thereto (though mainly useful for the period under Ottoman rule, this work includes some information on the earlier periods as well); P. Charanis's "A

Note on the Population and Cities of the Byzantine Empire in the Thirteenth Century" in the *Starr Mem. Vol.*, pp. 135–48; his other population studies collected in his recent volume entitled *Studies on the Demography of the Byzantine Empire;* and such local investigations as Andréadès's "Sur la population de Constantinople sous les empereurs byzantins," *Metron,* I, 68–120; and D. Jacoby's more recent "La Population de Constantinople à l'époque byzantine: un problème de démographie urbaine," *Byzantion,* XXXI, 81–109, esp. pp. 104, 107 f. Tables I and III.

In another remarkable study, "Les Quartiers juifs de Constantinople à l'époque byzantine," *Byzantion,* XXXVII, 167–227, Jacoby raises another serious objection to estimating the population of the Jewish quarter in Constantinople in Benjamin's day as high as 10,000–12,500. On the basis of his expert topographical knowledge of the Byzantine capital, he believes that the quarter covered only an area of 20–25 hectares and that the resulting population estimate of 400–500 persons per hectare is impossible (*absolument exclue;* p. 217). See also R. Janin's comprehensive study, *Constantinople byzantine, Développement urbain et répertoire topographique,* esp. pp. 47 and 274. Jacoby overlooks the great population density of Middle Eastern cities. Even if we disregard the exceptional case of ancient Tyre where, upon his conquest, Alexander the Great is said to have found a population of 70,000 persons living on 90 hectares, we must remember that such underdeveloped cities as Jerusalem, Jaffa, and Baghdad in the 1880s, long before the population explosion of the twentieth century, averaged one inhabitant per 30–35 square meters. In other words, they had more than 300 inhabitants per hectare. What is true of an entire city, with its numerous public buildings, squares, and streets, holds doubly true for special quarters. Compared with the ornate and vast mosques and churches, most medieval synagogues occupied little more space than ordinary houses. Moreover, special quarters, whether growing organically or "assigned" to a particular minority by governmental authorities, usually started with a relatively small population. When in the course of decades their inhabitants doubled or trebled in number, they often found that, because adjacent neighborhoods were occupied by other ethnic, religious, or occupational groups, they could not enlarge the area of their habitation in order to take adequate care of their increased numbers. Famous instances of such overcrowded Jewish quarters are the ghettos of Frankfort and Rome. When the Jews of Frankfort were relocated to a new quarter in 1463, they numbered only some 200 souls. Three centuries later basically the same area had to accommodate a population of 3,000. The Roman Jewish quarter had its origin in a papal decree of 1555. At that time this artificially created ghetto embraced a population of about 3,000 Jews. By the early eighteenth century their number had increased to 10,000–12,000, with little addition of living space. When Benjamin arrived in Constantinople in the 1160s the Jewish quarter in the Golden Horn area seems to have reached its maximum occupancy before it was destroyed by the Crusaders in 1203–1204. Hence, a population of 500–600 or even more per hectare is wholly within the realm of possibility, and even likelihood. See the data cited in my *Ancient and Medieval Jewish History: Essays,* ed. by L. A. Feldman, pp. 68 ff., 396 ff.; and *supra,* Vols. IX, pp. 35 f., 256 n. 38; XIII, pp. 273 f., 452 f. n. 78; and XIV, pp. 35, 318 nn. 31–32; and the literature listed there. See also *infra,* n. 17. Under these circumstances a population of 12,000 or even 15,000 Jews inhabiting, in the 1160s, a quarter covering some 25 hectares would not be greatly disproportionate within a population of some 400,000 to 500,000 persons living on the city's surface of about 13 square kilometers, or 1,300 hectares. In other words, the Jewish quarter extending over 2 percent of the city's area, which included many gardens and at times open fields, could well have accommodated some 3 percent of the city's population. See A. M. Schneider, "Die Bevölkerung Konstantinopels im XV. Jahrhundert," *Nachrichten* of the Akademie der Wissenschaften in Göttingen, Phil.-hist. Klasse, 1949, pp. 233–44.

It may readily be admitted, however, that all these debates have a certain aura of unreality about them. Where general medieval demography leaves very much to be desired and is even more dubious in regard to the Jewish population under both Islam and Western Christendom (see esp. *supra,* Vol. XII, pp. 4 ff., 243 ff., etc.; and my essay on "Population," in the recent English *Encyclopaedia Judaica,* XIII, 866–903), we have at least sporadic tax lists from both these areas which gives us some guidance on the number of Jewish inhabitants. No such tax lists concerning Jews in the Byzantine Empire have been preserved, if they ever existed at all. We shall presently see that the entire problem of special Jewish taxation in Byzantium still is under debate. Nor do we have any data whatever concerning such basic demographic facts as the Jewish birth and mortality rates, especially whether Jews shared in their neighbors' penchant for birth control, on which see E. Patlagean's "Sur la limitation de la fécondité dans la haute époque byzantine," *Annales ESC,* XXIV, 1353–69, a penchant which may have lost some of its appeal in the Late Middle Ages even among the non-Jewish population. But, as elsewhere, demographic aspects of life are too important to be ignored and scholars have to grapple with whatever small bits of evidence may be available in order to reach at least some plausible "guesstimates." See also the latest general review of the pertinent figures by A. Sharf in his *Byzantine Jewry from Justinian to the Fourth Crusade,* esp. pp. 3 f., 136 ff., 145 f. This volume, despite the severe strictures in D. Jacoby's review in *BZ,* LXVI, 403–406, still offers the most comprehensive survey of these six crucial centuries.

5. See M. Angold's recent monograph, *A Byzantine Government in Exile: Government and Society under the Lascarids of Nicaea, 1204–1261,* esp. pp. 29, 32, and 105; and the comprehensive works by G. Ostrogorsky and D. Obolensky (*supra,* n. 1); and A. A. Vasiliev, *History of the Byzantine Empire 324–1453,* esp. Vol. II. Of considerable interest also are such biographies of thirteenth-century rulers as A. Heisenberg, "Kaiser Johannes Batatzes der Barmherzige, eine mittelalterliche Legende," *BZ,* XIV, 160–233 (briefly alluding to the emperor's religious intolerance toward infidels and suggesting that the crucial word in the source may originally have read *Israelitai,* rather than *Ismaelitai;* p. 188); and C. Chapman, *Michel Paléologue, restaurateur de l'empire byzantin (1261–1282).* Studies of certain segments of the old Empire, such as those relating to Trebizond, likewise contribute a good deal to our knowledge of general Byzantine history of the period. See W. Miller, *Trebizond, the Last Greek Empire of the Byzantine Era, 1204–1461,* 2d ed.; and F. I. Uspenskii, *Ocherki iz istorii Trapezentskoi imperii* (Essays on the History of the Empire of Trebizond). Most of these studies also list their primary as well as secondary sources, some of which are mentioned *supra,* Vol. III and in subsequent volumes; see the *Index to Volumes I–VIII* under the pertinent entries. Very useful also are the current bibliographies regularly appearing in *BZ.*

Not surprisingly, Russian scholars have taken a particular interest in Byzantine history, which sheds much light on the antecedents of the history and culture of their own people, although in the first years of the Soviet regime there was little governmental encouragement for studies which willy-nilly would have treated aspects of life intimately connected with the Byzantine religion. See such general bibliographical surveys as Z. V. Udaltsova, *Sovetskoe vizantinovedenie za 50 let* (Soviet Byzantine Scholarship of the Last Fifty Years); I. Sorlin, "Les Recherches soviétiques sur l'histoire byzantine de 1945 à 1962," *Travaux et memoires* of the Centre de Recherches d'Histoire et Civilisations Byzantines, II 489–568; idem, "Les Recherches soviétiques sur l'histoire byzantine, II: 1963–1968," *ibid.*, IV, 487–517; and A. P. Každan, "La Byzantinologie soviétique en 1968–1969," and "1970," *Byzantion,* XLI, 520–44; XLIII, 525–45.

6. The obscure events which had led to John III's intolerant decree and the reversal of his policies by Michael VIII are briefly alluded to in Vatatzes' *Vita,* ed. by Agathangelos, p. 40, and summarized in F. Dölger and P. Wirth's ed. of *Regesten der Kaiserurkunden des oströmischen Reiches von 565–1453,* III, 24 No. 1817 (*ca.* 1254); and in the *Iggeret* (A Polemical Letter) by Jacob b. Elijah de Lattes of Valencia [or Venice] to his relative, the well-known convert and anti-Jewish controversialist Pablo Christiani, ed. by J. Kobak in *Jeschurun,* VI, Hebrew section, pp. 1–34, esp. pp. 24 ff., with the comments thereon by L. Lewin, "Eine Notiz zur Geschichte der Juden im byzantinischen Reiche," *MGWJ,* XIX, 117–22; and by J. Mann in "Une Source de l'histoire juive au XIIIe siècle: la lettre polémique de Jacob b. Élie à Pablo Christiani," *REJ,* LXXXII, 363–77. See also *supra,* Vol V, p. 294 n. 4. The effectiveness of Vatatzes' intolerant decree seems to have been greatly reduced by his general arbitrariness. A story has it that, when he once asked the advice of Nicaea's clergy, he was told: "But what is the use of asking us, Sire, what we think, when you always do whatever you think good?" See A. Gardner, *The Lascarids of Nicaea: the Story of an Empire in Exile,* p. 194. On Nicaea and the other Asian communities, see J. Starr, *The Jews in the Byzantine Empire,* pp. 119 ff. No. 54; idem, *Romania,* pp. 20 ff.; and other data assembled by Z. Ankori in his *Karaites in Byzantium,* pp. 104 ff., 113 ff., 120 f., 134 ff.

7. The original patriotic upsurge which enabled Theodore I Lascaris and John III to expand their Nicaean possessions, and which led Karl Marx to designate Nicaea as the "center of Greek patriotism," is partially qualified by J. Irmscher in his "Nikäa als 'Zentrum des griechischen Patriotismus,' " *RESEE,* VIII, 33–47. But he must admit that, despite the patriotic appeal to Greek-Orthodox universalism, it was the revival of the Byzantine tradition which made Nicaea the focus of the national resurgence. It also was the persistence of the people's belief in Byzantium's destiny to play the role of the "second Rome," and Rome's universal monarchy, which helped the Nicaean regime surmount the despair over the temporary fall of Constantinople into the hands of the Latin "heretics." See E. von Ivanka's *Rhomäerreich und Gottesvolk; das Glaubens-, Staats- und Volksbewusstsein der Byzantiner und seine Auswirkung auf die ostkirchlich-osteuropäische Geisteshaltung.* On the other hand, after the recapture of Constantinople and other European territories which included a religiously and ethnically far more heterogeneous population, the Palaeologi could more readily afford to follow their personal bent toward religious tolerance with respect to the Jews as well.

8. Andronicus II's chrysobull of February 1319 is reproduced in F. Miklosich and J. Müller, eds., *Acta et diplomata graeca medii aevi sacra et profana,* V, 77 ff., and

carefully analyzed in its Jewish aspects by N. A. Bees in his "Übersicht über die Geschichte des Judentums von Janina (Epirus)," *Byzantinisch-neugriechische Jahrbücher,* II, 159–77. See also the more comprehensive reviews of extant data by P. Charanis in his "The Jews in the Byzantine Empire under the First Palaeologi," *Speculum,* XXII, 75–77; and by J. Starr in his *Romania,* esp. pp. 15 ff., 85 ff. The greater toleration of religious diversity under the Palaeologi surely also reflected lessons derived from the Greek experiences in the Nicaean Empire and its constant exchanges with the neighboring Muslim principalities. While still adhering to the old division of the world into Hellenes and barbarians, some thoughtful Greeks began to evince a new appreciation of foreign cultures, including that of Islam. See K. Lechner's Munich dissertation, *Hellenen und Barbaren im Weltbild der Byzantiner. Die alten Bezeichnungen als Ausdruck eines neuen Kulturbewusstseins,* esp. pp. 115 ff.; and S. Vryonis, Jr.'s "Byzantine Attitudes toward Islam in the Late Middle Ages," *GRBS,* XII, 263–86. Combined with Byzantium's growing economic and military dependence on the Italian republics, this new appreciation of strangers doubtless also tended to moderate the official attitude toward Jews. On the general impact of foreign relations, always a potent factor in influencing domestic policies as well, see, for instance, A. E. Laiou, *Constantinople and the Latins: the Foreign Policy of Andronicus II, 1282–1328;* and U. V. Bosch, *Kaiser Andronikos III. Palaiologos. Versuch einer Darstellung der byzantinischen Geschichte in den Jahren von 1321 bis 1341.*

Benjamin of Tudela's lack of interest in visiting either Iannina or Castoria is especially noteworthy, since both these cities were to play a significant role in Jewish affairs in later centuries. See M. Molho (in collaboration with Abraham Meborah), *Histoire des Israélites de Castoria.* In contrast, Benjamin referred to either Arta or Leukas as the first community he had observed after leaving Italian Otranto and Corfu. See his *Massa'ot,* ed. by M. N. Adler, pp. 11 (Hebrew), 10 (English) with A. M. Andréadès's and J. Starr's comments thereon in their respective studies, "Sur Benjamin de Tudèle," *BZ,* XXX, 457 ff.; *The Jews in the Byzantine Empire,* p. 233 item k.

9. See the Greek texts of the 1049 chrysobull and its renewals, reproduced with an English trans. by P. P. Argenti in *The Religious Minorities of Chios,* pp. 64 f.; and previously somewhat differently translated by J. Starr in *The Jews in the Byzantine Empire,* pp. 197 f. No. 143 (with notes thereon). The conclusion drawn from this document by Argenti (who follows in the footsteps of Franz Dölger and, to a lesser extent, of M. A. Andréadès), that there existed a universal tax imposed specifically upon Jews throughout the Empire and that it owed its origin to the ancient *fiscus judaicus* is debatable. See esp. Dölger's "Die Frage der Judensteuer in Byzanz," but slightly revised in his *Paraspora. 30 Aufsätze zur Geschichte, Kultur und Sprache des byzantinischen Reiches,* pp. 358–77. It appears that the *fiscus judaicus* had been discontinued in practice in the middle of the third century (possibly as a result of raging inflation which made the collection of a *didrachmon* financially unrewarding) and formally abolished in the fourth century by Julian the Apostate. See *supra,* Vol. II, pp. 185 f., 399 n. 17. True, not long thereafter (in 429) followed the abolition of the Jewish patriarchate, whereupon the Empire appropriated the Jewish *aurum coronarium* previously collected for the patriarchs' benefit. But we have very little evidence about its actual collection; in any case this tax seems not to have endured for any length of time. Certainly, the system of gathering it from all

Jewish males aged twenty "and upward," as originally stated in the Bible, bears little resemblance to the special tax allegedly imposed upon the later Byzantine Jews.

In fact, the decree of 1049 here cited concerning the *kephaleiton,* which was to be paid by the fifteen Chios families to the local monastery of Nea Moné, clearly conveys the impression that it was an extraordinary impost. Despite its designation, it resembled a hearth rather than a poll tax, in return for which the Jews were freed from all other fiscal obligations. There probably existed some other local taxes of this kind in particular localities during the period after 1204. But our meager documentation allows for even less firm conclusions regarding the nature, size, and frequency of these imposts than may be derived from the earlier documentary allusions quoted by Dölger in support of his theory. See *supra,* Vol. III, pp. 191 ff., 320 f. n. 23.

10. See G. M. Thomas and R. Predelli, eds., *Diplomatarium veneto-levantinum sive acta et diplomata res venetas graecas atque Levantis illustrantia,* I, 142; G. L. F. Tafel and G. M. Thomas, eds., *Urkunden zur älteren Handels- und Staatsgeschichte der Republik Venedig,* I (XII), 179 ff. No. lxx; H. F. Brown, "The Venetians and the Venetian Quarter in Constantinople at the Close of the Twelfth Century," *Journal of Hellenic Studies,* XL, 68–88, esp. pp. 82 ff.; and *infra,* nn. 14–15. On the equivocal meaning of "The Terms 'Serf' and 'Villein' in the Latin East" even when applied to the peasant subjects of feudal landlords, see G. Dmitriev's pertinent Russian article in the *Sbornik* of the Soviet Byzantine Institute, XIII, 127–41.

11. See F. Miklosich and J. Müller, *Acta et diplomata,* V, 105 f. No. xi; G. M. Thomas and R. Predelli, *Diplomatarium,* I, 153; and other sources quoted by J. Starr in his *Romania,* pp. 112 f., 116 nn. 6–7. None of these sources, however, with their general lack of juridical precision, have any connotation of a tax.

12. See the discussion of the complicated problems connected with the development of "Jewish serfdom" in the medieval Western lands and the extensive modern literature thereon, *supra,* Vol. XI, Chap. XLVII; and my studies on the " 'Plenitude of Apostolic Powers' and Medieval 'Jewish Serfdom' "; and "Medieval Nationalism and Jewish Serfdom," reprinted in my *Ancient and Medieval Jewish History: Essays,* pp. 284–307 and 308–322. On the legal aspects of the Jewish status in Poland-Lithuania, with its large Greek-Orthodox population, see *supra,* Vol. XVI, pp. 141 f., 385 n. 7. That none of these controversies found an echo in the Byzantine world was owing not only to the absence of the sharp conflict there between the Papacy and Empire, but also to the general Byzantine aloofness from, and general ignorance of, the major phases of the Western evolution. See D. M. Nicol, "The Byzantine View of Western Europe," *GRBS,* VIII, 315–39.

13. Andronicus II's privilege confirming the possessions of the Iannina Church, reproduced in F. Miklosich and J. Müller, eds., *Acta et diplomata,* V, 84 ff., esp. p. 86; C. Bernheimer, ed., "Document relatif aux Juifs de Négropont," *REJ,* LXV, 224–30; and the variant readings of that document, with some additional observations, and further source references by J. Starr in his *Romania,* pp. 48 ff., 59 f. nn. 39 and 44. On the Clarentza episode, see D. Zakythinos, *Le Despotat Grec de Morée,* p. 209 n. 3, corrected from the Paris MS by Starr, pp. 73, 76 n. 2.

14. See the texts of the four codes of law, in J. Zépos and P. Zépos, eds., *Jus Graecoromanum;* in the partial English trans. by E. H. Freshfield entitled *A Manual of Later Roman Law;* and the *Basilicorum libri LX,* ed. by G. E. Heimbach and C. G. E. Heimbach; or in the new ed., together with its Scholia, by H. J. Scheltema *et al.,* Ser. A. Vols. I–VI; Ser. B Vols. I–VII. The dates of these compilations, their special meaning for the Jewish subjects of Byzantium, and their impact on later legislation, also in the Eastern-Slavic countries are discussed *supra,* Vol. III, pp. 185 ff., 316 ff. nn. 8 ff. There is no evidence that they, and particularly the *Basilika,* ever were formally abrogated. On the contrary, to the end of the Late Middle Ages this code, compiled under the auspices of Leo VI (886–912), and other enactments of the early Byzantine emperors were being recopied and translated with partial modifications in Bulgaria, Serbia, and even in remote Muscovy. Nor were the older compilations of the fifth and sixth centuries (the Theodosian Code and Justinian's *Corpus*) completely neglected. To the vast literature on their treatment of the Jewish question, listed in our earlier volumes, add the more recent studies by S. Grayzel, "The Jews and Roman Law," *JQR,* LIX, 93–117; and K. L. Noethlichs's Cologne dissertation, *Die Gesetzgeberischen Massnahmen der christlichen Kaiser des vierten Jahrhunderts gegen Häretiker, Heiden und Juden.*

15. See V. Grumel, ed., *Les Régestes des actes du patriarcat de Constantinople,* I, Part 3, pp. 100 ff. No. 1034, esp. p. 101 qu. 7; Joannes Anagnostes, *De extremo Thessalonicensi excidio narratio,* ed. with a Latin trans. by I. Becker in *Corpus scriptorum historiae byzantinae,* XXXVI, section 4, Bonn, 1838 ed., pp. 481–534, esp. p. 489; O. Tafrali, *Théssalonique au quatorzième siècle,* pp. 17 f., 39 f. It appears, however, that such secondary anathemas of persons guilty of associating with men or women enjoying conviviality with Jews and other "infidels" were no more effective than the primary bans hurled at the original lawbreakers. In general, the Church's proneness to excommunicate "sinners" for a variety of minor transgressions was in the long run as self-defeating here as it was in the medieval West. See *JC,* II, 228 ff.; III, 177 ff. nn. 18 ff. On the situation in Thessalonica, see also J. Nehama, *Histoire des Israélites de Salonique,* esp. I, 89 ff., 100 ff.

16. See N. G. Svaronos, "Le Serment de fidelité à l'empereur byzantin et sa signification constitutionelle," *REB,* IX, 106–142, esp. pp. 109 ff., 116 ff.; F. Miklosich and J. Müller, eds., *Acta et diplomata,* I, 174 ff.; F. Dölger, "Zur Frage des jüdischen Anteils an der Bevölkerung Thessalonikes im XIV. Jahrhundert," *Starr Mem. Vol.,* pp. 129–33; J. Nehama, *Histoire des Israélites de Salonique,* I, 89 ff., 104 ff., 111 f. On the specific oaths of abjuration of any earlier beliefs by a new convert from Judaism to Christianity, recorded in a Byzantine document of 1027, and on the possible connection with the oath *more judaico,* taken as part of court proceedings also in the West, see *supra,* Vol. III, pp. 194 f., 322 n. 28. However, if these oaths were ever more elaborate, it was because the legislators did not consider the Jews trustworthy enough and wished to reinforce the oath's reliability by the curses on the potential perjurer. But the elimination of some christological passages from an oath of fidelity to a monarch was, if granted at all, considered a favor to Jews.

17. See Archbishop Demetrios Chomatianos' reply to Metropolitan Constantine Cabasilas, reproduced in J. B. Pitra in his ed. of *Analecta sacra et classica specilegio*

Solesmensi parata, VI, 661 ff. No. xxii (on the authorship of that epistle, see D. Jacoby's remark in *Byzantion,* XXXVII, 181 n. 5; *infra,* n. 19), here cited from the English trans. by P. Charanis in "The Jews in the Byzantine Empire under the First Palaeologi," *Speculum,* XXII, 75–77 (reprinted in his *Studies on the Demography of the Byzantine Empire,* Chap. ix); Eustathios' *Epistolae,* No. 32, reed. in J. P. Migne, *PG,* CXXXVI, 1215–1334, esp. cols. 1298 f., here quoted in J. Starr's English trans. in *The Jews in the Byzantine Empire,* p. 237 No. 184. Regrettably, we do not know what, if any, instructions Eustathios may have received from Constantinople. See V. Grumel, ed., *Les Régestes des actes du patriarcat de Constantinople;* and *infra,* n. 23. In any case, it appears that despite the city's turbulent history and subjection to different masters during the first decades of the fourteenth century, Jews continued to live in its various quarters. This is at least the impression given by O. Tafrali's studies, *Topographie de Thessalonique* and *Thessalonique au quatorzième siècle,* pp. 40, 86. See also J. Starr's *Romania,* pp. 30 and 34 f. n. 18a; and, more generally, A. E. Vacalopoulos, *A History of Thessaloniki,* trans. from the Greek by T. F. Carney. The ancient and early medieval antecedents of the Thessalonican Jewish community are discussed in our earlier volumes. See the *Index to Volumes I–VIII,* 133 ff. *s.v.* Salonica and Thessalonica. To the literature listed there add S. D. Goitein's recent study, "The Jewish Communities of Saloniki and Thebes in Old Documents from the Genizah" (Hebrew), *Sefunot,* XI (= Book on Greece, I), 9–33, with an English summary. On the slow development of the compulsory ghetto, even in the West, see *supra,* Vols. XI, pp. 87 ff., 324 ff. nn. 15–24; XIV, pp. 114 ff., 322 ff. nn. 45 ff., etc.

18. A suggestion that the Pera Jewish quarter rose from an occupational rather than ethnoreligious distinction, made by me in 1942 (see my *JC,* I, 365; III, 94 n. 19), has been accepted by both J. Starr and Z. Ankori. See Starr's *Romania,* p. 33 n. 1; and Ankori's *Karaites in Byzantium,* p. 161. See also, more generally, G. Zoras, *Le Corporazioni bizantine;* and L. Cracco Ruggini, *Le Associazioni professionali nel mondo romano-bizantino, Artigianato e tecnica nella società dell'alto medioevo occidentale; studio sull'En archikón biblion,* I.

19. See Nicolò [Niccolò] Barbaro, *Diary of the Siege of Constantinople 1453,* trans. by J. R. Jones, p. 66; Muḥammad ibn Muḥammad Al-Jazari's account published by M. Izeddin in "Un Texte arabe inédit sur Constantinople byzantine," *JA,* CCXLVI, 453–57; Abu 'Abd-Allah Muḥammad Ibn Baṭṭuṭa, *Voyage,* ed. and trans. into French by C. Defrémery and B. R. Sanguinetti, II, 428 f., or in his *Travels, A.D. 1325–1354,* trans. into English with Revisions and Notes by H. A. R. Gibb, esp. II, 304 ff.; Stephan of Novgorod's journey of *ca.* 1350 reproduced in B. de Khitrovo (Sofiia Petrovna), ed., and trans., *Itinéraries russes en Orient,* I, 1, p. 121; and other sources cited by D. Jacoby in "Les Quartiers juifs de Constantinople," *Byzantion,* XXXVII, 167–227. More specific was the monk Maxim Planudes, compiler of a well-known collection of Greek epigrams, whose letters give us the best lead for the existence of a Jewish quarter in the district of Vlanga in the years 1295–96. See M. Treu, ed., *Maximi monachi Planudis epistulae,* pp. 50 ff. No. xxxi, 260 ff. No. c. See also the additional data to be analyzed in the next volume in connection with the broader aspects of the Ottoman conquest of Constantinople.

20. See *supra,* Vols. I, 198 f., 331 f. n. 10; III, 251 n. 60; XI, 95 f., 327 f. n. 23, etc. Some obscure recollections of these events seem to have been orally transmitted in

certain Jewish circles in Constantinople. While not much stock can be placed in legends such as those which Solomon Ibn Verga "heard from old people," they ought not to be dismissed out of hand. According to this chronicler-apologist, at one time a royal decree ordered an enforced conversion in some "Greek cities," mainly Constantinople. Since the Jews resisted fiercely, the ruler, on the advice of his councilors, decided to remove all of them forcibly from their dwellings and to keep them in an open field for three days without supplying them with any food or water. Only some small children, unable to withstand the hardships, ran away to Christian homes, but the large majority persisted in preferring starvation to apostasy and, finally, was allowed to return to the city. Yet, "to appease the population the king issued other evil ordinances and commanded them not to live within the city of Constantinople but in a neighboring town called Pera. He also ordained that a segment of them should have no other occupation but that of tanning, and that they should establish shops for that craft near the sea." See Ibn Verga's *Shebeṭ Yehudah* (Judah's Rod), xxviii, ed. by M. Wiener, pp. 47 f.; in Wiener's German trans., pp. 94 f.; ed. by A. Shochet, p. 72. The author not only fails to supply any date or other identifications of these events, but himself expresses doubts about the specific facts reported, claiming that he had heard from other persons that such an ordinance had been issued at another time and under different circumstances.

21. See J. Zépos and P. Zépos, eds., *Jus Graecoromanum,* I, 426 f.; and *supra,* Vol. V, pp. 57 f., 317 n. 70. On the high position of a *strategos* in twelfth-century Byzantium and the various stages in the evolution of that office, see R. J. Guilland, *Recherches sur les institutions byzantines,* I, 380 ff.

22. See A. M. Schneider, "Brände in Konstantinopel," *BZ,* XLI, 382–403, esp. pp. 387 ff., enumerating the major recorded fires in chronological order. The list is probably incomplete, but it is noteworthy that none of the devastating fires of that period seem to have started in a Jewish quarter, as against those which were to destroy much of the city in 1510 and 1606, then under the Turkish regime. Here, of course, the overcrowding caused by the tremendous immigration, particularly of Spanish and Portuguese Jewish exiles, was a major contributory factor. However, in sharp contrast to contemporary Prague and some Polish cities, Jews were not blamed as the arsonists responsible for the fires which happened to have originated in their quarter. See *supra,* Vol. XVI, pp. 193 f., 406 n. 33.

23. Patriarch Athanasius I's letters to Andronicus II, long known particularly by their inclusion in J. P. Migne's ed. of *PG,* CXLII, 473–523, esp. cols. 509 ff., are now available in their fully annotated French trans. on the basis of a Vatican MS in V. Laurent, comp., *Les Régestes des actes du patriarcat de Constantinople,* I, Part 4 (a continuation of V. Grumel's publication, mentioned *supra,* n. 15); and in a critical ed. and English trans. by A. M. Talbot in *The Correspondence of Athanasius I, Patriarch of Constantinople (1289–1293; 1303–1309): Letters to the Emperor Andronicus II, Members of the Imperial Family and Officials.* Athanasius' juxtaposition of Jews and Armenians underscores some of the existing similarities between these two ethnoreligious minorities in the Empire. One may, indeed, learn a good deal about both groups from their respective legal and socioeconomic developments. See P. Charanis, *The Armenians in the Byzantine Empire;* see also J. Starr, *Romania,* pp. 27, 34 f. n. 13 and Addendum. However, in his analysis of Athanasius' unpub-

lished letters R. Guilland does not refer to this particular anti-Jewish accusation, although he points out the patriarch's zeal for his Church and enmity toward all schismatics. See his "La Correspondance inédite d'Athanase, patriarche de Constantinople (1289–1293, 1304–1310)," *Mélanges Charles Diehl,* I, 121–40; P. Charanis, "The Jews of the Byzantine Empire under the First Palaeologi," *Speculum,* XXII, 75–77 (or in his *Studies on the Demography,* Chap. IX). On the Greek Ecumenical Patriarchate which, together with Michael VIII, moved back from Nicaea to Constantinople, see also V. T. Istavridis's succinct survey of "The Ecumenical Patriarchate," *The Greek Orthodox Theological Review,* XIV, 198–225, esp. p. 200.

24. See *Basilika,* ed. by G. E. Heimbach, I, 1, 47, summarized by Starr in *The Jews in the Byzantine Empire,* pp. 144 f. No. 83; *supra,* Vol. II pp. 189, 401 n. 24. The paucity of Byzantine records concerning synagogues is entirely understandable, since the majority of the late medieval Jewish congregations were very small and required no special buildings for their divine services. Most Jews, both Rabbanite and Karaite, doubtless gathered in small chapels or even in sections of private dwellings, set aside for worship. Generally, the Byzantine Jews maintained a very low profile. In his work *De oboedientia Ecclesiae Romanae debita* (written in 1358–59, and published by T. Kneppeli in his "Deux nouveaux ouvrages de Fr. Philippe Incontri de Pera, O.P.," in the *Archivum fratrum Praedicatorum,* XXIII, 163–99, esp. p. 176), the Dominican Philip de Bindo Incontri contended that on his missionary journeys through the Empire he had encountered many clandestine Catholics because "they were afraid of the populace." Similarly, the Jews, though perhaps less widely hated by the Orthodox masses who vividly remembered the Crusaders' atrocities during their conquest of Constantinople in 1204, had equally good reasons not to flaunt their ethnoreligious disparity. This factor may help explain the paucity of "Jewish" names occurring in the contemporary Byzantine sources, except for those borrowed from the Bible, like Isaac, Jacob, or Simeon, which were frequently borne also by Greek-Orthodox churchmen and lay persons.

25. See esp. S. Bernstein, ed., "New Liturgical Poems and Poets of the Byzantine Period" (Hebrew), *Horeb,* V, 43–122; and Y. L. (L. J.) Weinberger, ed., "New Poems of the Byzantine Period" I–II (Hebrew), *HUCA,* XXXIX, 1–62; XLIII, 270–308. These poems culled from the then widely used *Maḥzor Romania* and *Maḥzor Corfu* (the latter extant only in several MSS) reveal but slight differences from doctrinal and customary presuppositions accepted in the Western communities. By way of contrast, cf. B. Schultze, "Das Nicaenoconstantinopolitanum und das Filioque," *Orientalia christiana periodica,* XXXV, 334–46; and W. Ullmann, "Das *Filioque* als Problem oekumenischer Theologie," *Kerygma und Dogma,* XVI, 58–76. However, we must not minimize the continued impact of Justinian's and his successors' outlawry of the *deuterosis* (the Second, or Oral Law) on Byzantine Jewry's prayers, music, and entire educational system—a factor which but tangentially affected the Western Jews. See *supra,* Vol. VII, pp. 89 ff., 125 ff., 259 ff. nn. 36 ff., 281 ff. nn. 86 ff. See also the additional data presented by L. J. Weinberger in his "On the Provenance of Benjamin b. Samuel Qūštani," *JQR,* LXVIII, 46–60; and the pertinent evolution in the Orthodox Church, analyzed by M. Alexion in *The Ritual in Greek Tradition.*

26. *Codex Theodosianus,* ed. by P. Krüger, II, 1, 10; Justinian's *Corpus iuris civilis,* I, 9, 8.15, ed. by T. Mommsen and P. Krüger, II, 61 f.; Thalelaios, *Synopsis*

Basilicorum, Letter I, iv, 3, in J. Zépos and P. Zépos, eds., *Jus Graecoromanum,* V, 318, cited by F. Dölger in "Zur Frage des jüdischen Anteils an der Bevölkerung Thessalonikes im XIV. Jahrhundert," *Starr Mem. Vol.,* pp. 129–33, esp. pp. 132 f. (reprinted in his *Paraspora,* pp. 378–83, esp. p. 382); my comments thereon *supra,* Vols. II, pp. 268 f., 419 n. 43; III, 11 ff., 232 f. nn. 9–11; and my debate with G. Kisch in his "Zur Frage der Aufhebung jüdisch-religiöser Jurisdiktion durch Justinian," *ZRG,* Romanistische Abteilung, LXXVII, 395–401; my "Berichtigung" thereto, *ibid.,* LXXIX, 547–48; and his "Entgegnung," *ibid.,* pp. 548–49.

27. The astounding similarity between the Byzantine-Jewish betrothal ceremony and that solemnizing marriage is discussed by Isaiah b. Mali of Trani (the Elder) in his *Resp.* No. 40, cited from a Cambridge MS by H. Gross in his "Jesaja b. Mali da Trani," *Zeitschrift für hebräische Bibliographie,* XIII, 46–58, 87–92, 118–23, esp. pp. 53 f.; and, more fully, by S. Assaf in his "On the Family Life of the Jews in Byzantium" (Hebrew), *Sefer ha-Yobel* (Jubilee Volume) in honor of Samuel Krauss, pp. 169–77, reprinted in Assaf's *Be-Ohole Ya'aqob* (In the Tents of Jacob. Chapters from Jewish Cultural Life in the Middle Ages), pp. 99–106; and J. Starr, *Romania,* pp. 17 ff. In this connection, we may also note that the prevailing marriage regulations and practices among the Byzantine non-Jews included much of the people's pagan heritage from the pre-Christian age. See H. Hunger, "Christliches und Nichtchristliches im byzantinischen Eherecht," *Österreichisches Archiv für Kirchenrecht,* XVIII, 305–315.

On the linguistic borrowings from Greek, see D. Sperber, "Contribution to Byzantine Lexicography from Jewish Sources," *Byzantion,* XLVI, 58–81 (offering 16 examples out of a great many he had assembled; 110 of them in Hillel b. Eliakim's Commentary on the Sifra, ed. by S. Koloditzky, alone); and J. Starr, "A Fragment of a Greek Mishnaic Glossary," *PAAJR,* VI, 353–67. Some of the ancient antecedents are discussed *supra,* Vols. II, pp. 147, 387 n. 26; IV, pp. 240 f. n. 17; VI, p. 441 n. 3; and in the literature listed there.

28. See P. Lemerle, "Le Juge général des Grecques et la réforme judiciaire d'Andronic III," *Mémorial Louis Petit. Mélanges d'histoire et d'archéologie byzantines,* pp. 292–316, esp. p. 301; P. Charanis, "Internal Strife in Byzantium during the Fourteenth Century," *Byzantion,* XV, 208–230; K. P. Matschke, *Fortschritt und Reaktion in Byzanz im 14. Jahrhundert. Konstantinopel in der Bürgerkriegsperiode von 1341 1354;* H. Hunger, ed., "Anonymes Pamphlet gegen eine byzantinische 'Mafia,'" *RESEE,* VII, 95–107. See also, more generally, U. V. Bosch's *Kaiser Andronikos III. Palaiologos.*

29. See Benjamin of Tudela's *Massa'ot,* pp. 12 (Hebrew), 10 (English); Yehudah b. Solomon al-Ḥarizi, *Sefer Taḥkemoni* (Maqamae), ed. by P. de Lagarde, pp. 92, 184; Giovanni Badoer, *Il Libro dei conti (Constantinopoli, 1436–1440),* ed. by U. Dorini and T. Bertelé; *supra,* n. 17; Vols. II, pp. 180, 398 n. 12; IV, pp. 184 f., 319 f. n. 20; VII, 184 ff., 307 f. nn. 66–67. See also, more generally, R. S. Lopez, "Silk Industry in the Byzantine Empire," *Speculum,* XX, 9–42, pointing out that in Byzantium the manufacture of silk and the wearing of silk garments, the quality of which depended on the class status of the wearer as regulated by law, were a matter of both finance and prestige (pp. 20 ff.). Of considerable interest also are the studies relating to the peculiar structure of the Byzantine cities. See C. P. Kyrris, "The Political

Organization of the Byzantine Urban Classes between 1204 and 1341," *Liber memorialis* in Honor of Antonio Era, pp. 19–32; and E. Kirsten, *Die Byzantinische Stadt,* a continuation of his study of the ancient period, entitled, *Die griechische Polis als historisch-geographisches Problem des Mittelmeerraumes.*

30. See D. A. Zakythinos, *Crise monétaire et crise économique à Byzance du XIIIe à XVe siècle;* D. M. Metcalf, *Coinage in the Balkans, 820–1355.* The Empire's financial situation became doubly precarious when, beginning in 1379, it assumed the obligation of paying an annual tribute to Turkey equivalent to 15,000 Venetian gold ducats, an amount the Treasury could ill afford. See the details in O. Iliescu's "Le Montant du tribut payé par Byzance à l'Empire Ottoman en 1379 et 1424," *RESEE,* IX, 427–32. To be sure, such payments to a neighboring ruler in order to stave off the ill effects of piracy or raids did not involve any real political dependence. No less an authority than George Ostrogorsky conveys the wrong impression, therefore, when in his "Byzance, état tributaire de l'empire turc," *Zbornik Radova Vizantiiskogo Instituta,* V, 49–58, he depicts the Empire as being practically a vassal state of the sultan between the battle of Maritsa in 1371 and the fall of Constantinople in 1453. This was no more the case here than it was with the powerful Venetian Republic when it first agreed in 1400 to pay a regular *haraj* to a Turkish captain in Albania, and in 1406 offered to pay the sultan 2,000 ducats annually to secure noninterference with its shipping in the Adriatic Sea and elsewhere. Such payments to buy off unwelcome attackers were also made by Genoa and other states. See M. Spremić, "I Tributi veneziani nel Levante nel secolo XV," *Studi Veneziani,* XIII, 221–51. On the general ups and downs in the imperial policies of the period, see esp. J. W. Barker, *Manuel II Palaeologus (1391–1425): a Study in Late Byzantine Statesmanship,* esp. pp. 123 ff., 433 App. i. In all that turmoil the Jews seem essentially to have been mere passive bystanders and victims. See also my forthcoming comments on the Ottoman aspects of these relationships in the next volume.

31. On the relatively few earlier records of Jewish life in the eastern Balkans, but not in Adrianople as such, see J. B. Frey in his *Corpus Inscriptionum Judaicarum,* I, 683 ff.; and other sources listed by J. Juster in *Les Juifs dans l'Empire romain,* I, 187 f.; and by J. Starr in *The Jews in the Byzantine Empire,* p. 235. Even in his *Romania,* where, combining great industry with much ingenuity, Starr assembled most of the available data concerning the Jews of the Byzantine area in the Late Middle Ages, he was unable to furnish information about the Adrianople community. Nor did Simon Marcus, who wrote a special study, "A Contribution to the History of the Jews in Adrianople" (Hebrew), *Sinai,* XIV, Vol. XXVIII, nos. 171–76, pp. 7–23, 318–44, shed any light on the pre-Turkish period. Most astonishing is the controversy over the date of the transition from Byzantine to Ottoman sovereignty. While Turkish scholars have favored the early years 1359–62, the Byzantine writers assumed the later date of 1369 for this momentous event. In his 1937 lecture at the University of Cracow, Franz Babinger asserted that there was "general agreement" that that conquest had taken place in the spring of 1361, but in 1961 Irene Beldiceanu-Steinherr again pointed out, with some hesitation, the questionable value of the reports thereon by the medieval Turkish chroniclers. Finally Elizabeth A. Zachariadou, writing in 1970, has claimed that there were, in fact, several different stages in that conquest. Referring to the dates 1361, 1362, 1367, and 1371 variously suggested by scholars, she came to the conclusion that it was after 1366, and most

probably in 1369, that the Turkish regime was fully anchored in the new capital. See Babinger, "Quelques problèmes d'études islamiques dans le sud-est européen" (lecture delivered at the Jagiellon University, Cracow, 1937), reprinted in his *Aufsätze und Abhandlungen zur Geschichte Südosteuropas und der Levante,* pp. 76–87, esp. p. 77; I. Beldiceanu-Steinherr, "La Conquête d'Adrianople par les Turcs: la pénétration turque en Thrace et la valeur des chroniques ottomanes," *Travaux et Mémoires* of the Centre de Recherches d'Histoire et Civilisation Byzantines, I, 439–61; and E. A. Zachariadou, "The Conquest of Adrianople by the Turks," *Studi Veneziani,* XII, 211–17. Zachariadou's final date remains questionable, however, because of her excessive reliance on a tedious Greek poem extolling John V Palaeologus.

Even less definitive assertions can be made about the immediate effects of the Turkish occupation upon the local Jewish community. Although the conquerors seem to have ruthlessly slaughtered or evacuated most of the inhabitants, it appears that from the outset there were quite a few Jewish survivors. Together with the returning refugees, they seem quickly to have rebuilt their community, including their old synagogue.

32. Johannes Cantacuzenus (Emperor John VI, 1347–54), *Historiae,* ed. by L. Schopen *et al.,* III, 85; G. Ostrogorsky, *History of the Byzantine State,* pp. 376 f.; and on the various meanings given to the term "Romania," see R. L. Wolff's "Romania: the Latin Empire of Constantinople," *Speculum,* XXIII, 1–34. In general, Cantacuzenus' assertions have to be treated with considerable caution, particularly since his works have come down to us in a somewhat disorderly fashion. See R. J. Loenertz, "Ordre et désordre dans les mémoires de Jean Cantacuzène," *REB,* XXII, 222–37, esp. pp. 228 ff. His statement about Morea, especially, is to be understood against his background in contemporary Byzantine society as described by G. Weiss in his *Johannes Kantakuzenus—Aristokrat, Staatsmann, Kaiser, Mönch—in der Gesellschaftsentwicklung von Byzanz im 14. Jahrhundert.* The fullest story of the Morea is offered by D. Zakythinos, *Le Despotat grec de Morée;* J. Longnon, *L'Empire Latin de Constantinople et la principauté de Morée;* and A. Bon, *La Morée franque. Recherches historiques, topographiques et archéologiques sur la principauté d'Achaïe (1205–1430),* with a volume of plates. See also Longnon's earlier study of "Problèmes de l'histoire de la principauté de Morée," *Journal des Savants,* 1946, pp. 77–93, 147–61; and D. Jacoby's "The Encounter of Two Societies: Western Conquerors and Byzantines in the Peloponnesus after the Fourth Crusade," *AHR,* LXXVIII, 873-906.

33. Benjamin of Tudela, *Massa'ot,* ed. by M. N. Adler, pp. 12 (Hebrew), 10 (English); Abraham b. Samuel Abulafia, *Iggeret* (Epistle or Missive), ed. by A. Jellinek in his *Ginze ḥokhmat ha-qabbalah* (Auswahl kabbalistischer Mystik), pp. 13 ff., German section, pp. 16 ff.; the excerpt from Abulafia's *Sefer ha-'Edut* (Book of Testimony; a kabbalistic treatise), reproduced by H. Graetz in his Note, "Abraham Abulafia, der Pseudomessias," *MGWJ,* XXXVI, 557–58; A. Berger, "The Messianic Self-Consciousness of Abraham Abulafia: a Tentative Evaluation," *Baron Jub. Vol.,* 1959, pp. 55–61.

34. E. Gerland, *Neue Quellen zur Geschichte des lateinischen Erzbistums Patras,* pp. 90 n. 4, 113 f., 191 ff. Doc. 9, 201 ff. Doc. 14 (cosigned by a Jewish witness), 211 ff. Doc. 17, 218 ff. Doc. 19 (a Jewish owner of a garden in the vicinity of Patras), 234 ff.

Doc. 22; other data succinctly summarized by J. Starr in his *Romania,* pp. 73 ff.; and his "Jewish Life in Crete," *PAAJR,* XII, 104 (see *infra,* Chap. LXXII, n. 2). See also the brief sketch in A. Bon, *La Morée franque,* pp. 449 ff. In connection with the 1533 incident we must bear in mind, however, that, because of the fundamental changes introduced by the Turkish regime, we must be very cautious in hypothesizing about the fate of Jewish communities in the late Byzantine period.

35. See Bayezid's letter to the Doge of April 7, 1504 and other documents in A. Bombaci's "Il 'Liber Graecus,' un cartolario veneziano comprendente inèditi documenti ottomani in greco (1481–1504)" in *Westöstliche Abhandlungen, Rudolf Tschudi . . . überreicht,* ed. by F. Meier, pp. 288–303, esp. pp. 294 ff.; the comments thereon by H. Hunger in his "Piraterie in der Aegaeis anno 1504. Brief Bajazeds II. an Leonardo Loredan," *Byzantion,* XL, 361–76; and J. Starr, *Romania,* pp. 70, 72 n. 21, 75. See also, more generally, D. Zakythinos, *Corsairs et pirates dans les mers grecques;* and P. Charanis, "Piracy in the Aegean during the Reign of Michael VIII Palaeologus," *Annuaire* of the Université Libre of Brussels, X (*Mélanges Henri Grégoire,* II), 127–36. On the general slave trade, which continued to flourish in many parts of the Empire, see H. Köpstein's succinct observations in her "Zum byzantinischen Sklavenhandel," *Wissenschaftliche Zeitschrift der Karl Marx Universität Leipzig,* Gesellschafts- und sprachwiss. Reihe, XV, 487–93; and her general review, "Die Byzantinische Sklaverei in der Historiographie der letzten 125 Jahre," *Klio,* XLIII–XLV, 560–75.

36. Benjamin of Tudela, *Massa'ot,* ed. by M. N. Adler, pp. 12 (Hebrew), 10 (English); *supra,* Vol. IV, pp. 168 f., 293 ff. n. 20; J. Longnon, *L'Empire Latin de Constantinople,* in the numerous pages listed in the Index, p. 363 *s.v.* Thèbes. Since the contemporary Christian chroniclers generally evinced but moderate interest in the Jews, and Jewish leadership had greatly declined and become quite inarticulate, we are reduced to guessing what happened to the Jews of Thebes and of most other provincial communities after 1204. On the local silk industry, see also R. S. Lopez's pertinent essay, cited *supra,* n. 29.

37. See the sources cited *supra,* n. 6; Benjamin, *Massa'ot,* pp. 12 (Hebrew), 10 (English); A. H. Freimann, "Palestine Emissaries and Pilgrims: Fifteenth Century Documents from Candia" (Hebrew), *Zion,* I, 185–207, esp. p. 188 n. 11. Ancient Jewry's connections with Sparta and other Greek cities are discussed *supra,* Vols. I, pp. 185, 377 n. 23; III, pp. 184, 318 n. 14. On that city's and Mistra's Jewish communities, see N. A. Bees, "Jews in the Lacedaemonian Area and in Mistra" (Greek), *Noumas,* III, esp. p. 166 n. 10. The frequent changes in the names of localities, even of some well known in ancient times, often have led to much confusion among modern students. That is why O. Markl's *Ortsnamen Griechenland's in "fränkischer" Zeit* has served as a useful tool for historical research as well. See also, Z. Avneri, "The Jews of Mistra" (Hebrew), *Sefunot,* XI, 12–35 (mainly about the Turkish period); and more generally, A. Struck, *Mistra. Eine mittelalterliche Ruinenstadt,* esp. pp. 13 and 38; and I. P. Medvedev's recent work, *Mistra: Ocherki istorii i kultury* (Mistra: Sketches of the History and Culture of a Late Byzantine City).

38. See Georgios Gemistos Plethon, *Peri ton en Peloponeso pragmaton logos* (Denkschrift über die Angelegenheiten des Peloponnes), ed. and trans. into German

with notes by A. Ellissen in his *Denkschriften,* part of his *Analekten der mittel- und neugriechischen Literatur,* IV, 2; and the interesting observations by A. F. Vacalopoulos in his *Origins of the Greek Nation: the Byzantine Period, 1204–1461,* trans. from the Greek by I. Moles, esp. pp. 121, 126 ff.; and Moles's "Nationalism and Byzantine Greece," *GRBS,* X, 95–107, esp. pp. 105 f.

Perhaps one may secure some new insights into the Judeo-Greek exchanges, practical as well as intellectual, from a careful study of medieval Greek belles lettres and folklore. This resource has largely been neglected even in the general modern historiography. An interesting attempt in this direction was made by P. E. Pieler through an analysis of five Greek novels for the light they shed on Byzantine society, especially the courts, officials, legal relationships, and so forth. See his "Recht, Gesellschaft und Staat im byzantinischen Roman der Paläologenzeit," *Jahrbuch der österreichischen Byzantinistik,* XX, 189–221. With reference to Jews we learn about the romantic appreciation of Jewish ladies in certain Cretan folk songs which differed greatly from the official line of promoting segregation between Jews and Greeks. See some examples cited by S. Xanthoudidis in "The Jews in Crete under Venetian Rule" (Greek), *Kretiké Stoà,* II, 209–224, esp. pp. 223 f.; and the German trans. of one such song in L. Ross's *Reisen auf den griechischen Inseln des Ägäischen Meeres,* ed. by E. Wiedermann and H. Hauff in their *Reisen und Länderbeschreibungen der älteren und neueren Zeit, eine Sammlung,* III, 49, 175 ff., cited by J. Starr in his "Jewish Life in Crete under the Rule of Venice," *PAAJR,* XII, 74 n. 43.

39. See *The Chronicle of Morea: a History in Political Verse* (To Chronikon tou Moreos), ed. with an Intro. and Critical Notes by J. Schmitt, vv. 2093–95, cited by D. Jacoby in "The Encounter of Two Societies," *AHR,* LXXVIII, 890; Jacoby, *La Féodalité en Grèce medievale. Les "Assises de Romanie," sources, application et diffusion;* A. Bon, *La Morée franque,* and D. A. Zakythinos, *Le Despotat grec de Morée.* Regrettably, the texts of the various decrees issued by the Angevin kings, Charles I, Charles II, and their successors Philip II of Tarent (1317, 1324), Robert of Anjou (1338), Maria of Bourbon (1365), Philip III (1370), Joanna I (d. 1382), and Charles III (1382), were unavailable to Umberto Cassuto when he wrote his succinct but very informative article on "Korfu" for the *Encyclopaedia Judaica* (German), X, cols. 325–30. J. Starr's assumption that the Angevin rule in Durazzo (Albania) necessarily reflected Charles II's intolerant decree suppressing Judaism in Sicily in 1288 appears unjustified. See his *Romania,* pp. 81 ff.; and, on the sudden outbreak of the Sicilian and Neapolitan intolerance at home, his "The Mass Conversion of the Jews in Southern Italy (1290–1293)," *Speculum,* XXI, 203–211; and *supra,* Vols. X, pp. 226 ff., 400 f. nn. 7–8; XI, pp. 253 ff., 410 f. nn. 77–78. On Philip II's anti-Jewish decree of 1182 and its abrogation sixteen years later, see *supra,* Vol. IV, pp. 61 ff., 268 ff. nn. 80–81.

40. See *supra,* n. 13; J. Longnon, *L'Empire Latin de Constantinople,* pp. 295 ff.; and A. Lowe, *The Catalan Vengeance,* p. 1. The complicated international developments in connection with the Catalans' eastern adventure are well summarized in A. E. Laiou's *Constantinople and the Latins,* pp. 134 ff.; K. M. Setton's *Catalan Domination of Athens, 1311–1388;* and D. Jacoby's "Catalans, Turcs et Vénitiens en Romanie (1305–1332), un nouveau témoignage de Marino Sanudo Torcello," *Studi medievali,* 3d ser. XV, 127–36. Remarkably, A. Rubio y Lluch, who in his other works frequently made available important documents of Jewish interest, does not

refer to Jews in his study of *La Població de la Grecia catalana en XIVèn segle;* see esp. p. 19. It should also be noted that, despite their great interest in developing political and economic relations with the Middle East, the Aragonese rulers at home tried to discourage journeys of Jews to the eastern Mediterranean countries. In 1342 the royal treasurer of Barcelona entered in his ledger the receipt of fines from Jews who had gone there without authorization. For example, one Jacme Cap de Bon of Barcelona was punished for having traveled to Cyprus and Syria. At the same time Pedro IV of Aragon ordered an investigation of losses sustained by a German Jew who, on his way back from Jerusalem, had been attacked by pirates near Cyprus, robbed of his merchandise worth some 500 gold florins, and forced to pay 50 additional florins as a ransom for his person (about 1343). The outcome of this investigation is unknown. See Y. F. Baer, *Die Juden im christlichen Spanien,* I, 295 No. 212, 303 No. 216. The further developments of Spanish trade with the eastern Mediterranean countries under Venetian and especially under Ottoman rule will be discussed more fully in the forthcoming chapters.

41. See *supra,* Vols. I, pp. 236 f., 397 f. n. 22; III, pp. 16 f., 235 n. 16; Benjamin of Tudela, *Massa'ot,* ed. by M. N. Adler, pp. 17 (Hebrew), 14 (English); A. Galanté, *Histoire des Juifs de Rhodes, Chio, Cos, etc.* (mentioning that even the small village of Malona, on that island, still had a street called *Evraiké* [Jewry] as late as 1935; he assumes that the name may have come down from the late medieval period; p. 6); and other sources cited by J. Starr in his *Romania,* pp. 85 ff.

42. N. Iorga, *Notes et extraits pour servir à l'histoire des croisades au XVe siècle,* reprinted from *ROL,* II, 98; L. Conrady, ed., *Vier Rheinische Palästina Pilgerschriften des XIV., XV. und XVI. Jahrhunderts,* p. 108; Meshullam b. Menaḥem (Bonaventura di Manuello) da Volterra, *Massa' be-Ereṣ-Yisrael bi-shenat RMA* (A Journey to Palestine in the Year 1481), ed. from a Unique MS with an Intro. and Notes by A. Yaari, pp. 43 f.; A. Galanté, *Histoire des Juifs de Rhodes,* pp. 7 ff.; idem, *Appendice,* thereto. On the date of the Hospitallers' occupation of Rhodes (August 15, 1308, rather than 1309, as frequently stated), see V. Grumel, *La Chronologie* in *Traité d'études byzantines,* ed. by P. Lemerle, I, 401 f.

Some doubts have been expressed about the veracity of Meshullam da Volterra's narrative, especially concerning the report of his audience with the Grand Master. However, fourteenth- and fifteenth-century rulers were generally rather easily accessible to foreign visitors. Not only did Ibn Baṭṭuṭa visit the emperor in Constantinople in 1332, at which time a Jew (originally from Damascus) served as an interpreter but, for instance, the Spanish visitor Pero Tafur, a more ordinary traveler through the Middle East in 1435–39 apparently had no difficulty in securing audiences with John IV, Greek emperor of Trebizond, and Murad II, Turkish sultan in Adrianople. To be sure, the accuracy of many of Tafur's detailed assertions has been impugned by Alfred Morel-Fatio and others. But we have no reason to doubt his visits to these courts. See Ibn Baṭṭuṭa's *Travels,* cited *supra,* n. 19; Pero Tafur's *Andanças e viajes por diversas partes del mundo avidos (1435–1439),* ed. by M. Jimenez de la Espada, esp. I, 158 ff.; in the English trans., ed. with an Intro. by M. Letts, *Travels and Adventures, 1435–1439,* esp. pp. 126 f., 131 f.; and with the comments thereon by A. Morel-Fatio in his review of Jimenez de la Espada's ed. of Tafur's work in the *Revue critique d'histoire et de la littérature,* IX, 135–41; and by A. A. Vasiliev in his "Pero Tafur: a Spanish Traveller of the Fifteenth Century and His Visit to Constantinople, Trebizond and Italy," *Byzantion,* VII, 75–122, esp. pp. 97 ff. Moreover, as far as Meshullam was concerned, while visiting Rhodes in 1481, after the warlike events of the preceding year in which the Jews distinguished themselves as codefenders of the city against the Turks, he must have found the ruling circles of the Order favorably disposed toward his coreligionists. D'Aubusson's subsequent change of mind may have been owing to some untoward events during the intervening years, including the ruinous plague in 1498–1500. It is possible that, because of the good impression the island had made on Meshullam, his brother Nathan settled there. See also, more generally, E. Billiotti and Abbé Cottret, *Histoire de l'île de Rhodes,* pp. 330, 563; and the literature listed *infra,* n. 43.

43. Obadiah Yare b. Abraham di Bertinoro, *Iggarot* (Epistles), reed. on the basis of M. Artom's critical ed. in his unpublished dissertation at the University of Rome in A. Yaari's collection of *Iggerot Ereṣ Yisrael* (Letters from Palestine, Written by Jews Living in the Country to Their Brethren in the Dispersion from the Babylonian Exile to the Return to Zion in Our Days), pp. 98–143, 542–43, esp. p. 111. The arguments about the unsatisfactory nature of the earlier editions and translations of Bertinoro's epistles voiced by M. D. [U.] Cassuto in his "R. Obadiah Bertinoro's Epistles" (Hebrew) in *Ve-zot li-Yehudah* (Dissertationes hebraicae . . . Ludwig Blau), pp. 296–302, are still largely valid today; see Yaari's comments, pp. 542 f. See also J. Delaville le Roulx, *Les Hospitaliers à Rhodes jusqu'à la mort de Philibert de Naillac (1310–1421),* esp. p. 356 n. 1; the Lower Rhenish report reproduced by L. Conrady in his ed. of *Vier Rheinische Palästina Pilgerschriften des XIV., XV. und XVI. Jahrhunderts,* pp. 49 ff., 108; Pietro Casola, *Pilgrimage to Jerusalem in the Year 1494,* English trans., by M. Newett, p. 208; and other sources cited in J. Starr's *Romania,* pp. 92 f. Regrettably, all research in the history of late medieval Rhodes is hampered by the inadequacy of the records even if kept in the Hospitallers' Chancery after its establishment in 1314. See A. Luttrell, "Notes on the Chancery of the Hospitallers of Rhodes, 1314–1342," *Byzantion,* XL, 408–420.

44. See V. A. Vertot's *Histoire des chevaliers hospitaliers de St. Jean de Jérusalem,* 5th ed., III, 146; Elijah b. Elqana Capsali, *Seder Eliyahu Zuta. History of the Ottomans and of Venice and That of the Jews in Turkey, Spain, and Venice,* ed. from Hebrew MSS and annotated by A. Shmuelevitz, S. Simonsohn, and M. Benayahu, I, 116 ff. Capsali is far more informative about the subsequent period of the Ottoman conquest of the island (*ibid.,* Vol. II), to which reference will be made in the next volume. See also N. Iorga, "Rhodes sous les Hospitaliers," *Revue historique du sud-est européen,* VIII, 32–51, 98–113, 169–87; C. Marinescu, "L'Île de Rhodes au XVe s. et l'Ordre de Saint-Jean de Jérusalem d'après des documents inédits," *Miscellanea Giovanni Mercati,* V, 382–401. Marinescu describes, in particular, the Hospitallers' military and financial difficulties in the face of the Turkish demand, after the fall of Constantinople, that their island pay tribute to the Porte. These difficulties, aggravated by a plague raging in Rhodes in 1456, were but temporarily relieved by the Western subsidies and the intervention of a papal fleet; pp. 383, 391 ff., 399.

45. See *supra,* Vols. I, pp. 374 f. n. 13; II, pp. 94 ff., 102, 370 f. nn. 7–10; III, pp. 19 f., 236 f. n. 20; Benjamin of Tudela, *Massa'ot,* pp. 17 f. (Hebrew), 14 f. (English). On the Cypriot Mishawites and their strained relations with both Rabbanites and Karaites, see Z. Ankori, *Karaites in Byzantium,* pp. 385 ff.

46. See A. A. Beugnot, ed., *Assises de Jérusalem,* I, 98 Chap. lx; II, 171 f. Chap. ccxli; and the Abrégé therefrom *ibid.*, II, 254 f. Chap. xxiv; Francesco Amadi, *Chronique,* ed. by R. de Mas Latrie in *Collection des documents inédits sur l'histoire de France,* VII, Part 1, pp. 214 f., 326 f., 405 f. (probably quoting from the older chronicle, *Gestes des Cyprois*); other sources cited by J. Starr in *Romania,* pp. 95 ff.; and the brief summary by B. (C.) Roth in "The Jews in Cyprus" (Hebrew), *Sefunot,* VIII (= *Itzhak Ben-Zvi Memorial Volume*), 283–98, esp. pp. 288 f. See also, more generally, L. de Mas-Latrie, *Histoire de l'île de Chypre sous le règne des princes de la maison de Lusignan;* the new data offered by J. Richard in his *Chypre sous les Lusignans. Documents chypriotes des Archives de Vatican* (*XIVe et XVe siècles*); G. Hill's comprehensive *A History of Cyprus,* Vols. I–IV; and on the island's role in international commerce, B. Mitrović's older study of *Cipro nella storia medioevale del commercio levantino.* The impact of the Order of the Hospitallers on Cypriot affairs particularly in 1290–1310 is described by J. Riley-Smith in *The Knights of St. John in Jerusalem and Cyprus c. 1050–1310,* esp. pp. 198 ff. (offers no further data on Raymond de Pins' mission).

Because of the great changes which took place under the Venetian administration (1485–1571, about which more in the next chapter) and the subsequent three centuries of Ottoman rule, few conclusions can be drawn from these later developments for the period of the Lusignan regime. This is particularly true in the case of Jews, who seem practically to have disappeared from the island until their repopulation by the governmentally sponsored and partly enforced immigration under the Turks. That is why the references to Jews in T. Papadopoullos's *Social and Historical Data on Population (1570–1881)* do not substantially help to clarify the conditions of the Jewish community in the Late Middle Ages.

47. See R. Fishman-Duker, "The Second-Temple Period in Byzantine Chronicles," *Byzantion,* XLVII (= *Homage à Ivan Dujčev*), 126–56; Demetrius Cydonius, *Correspondance,* ed. by R. J. Loenertz, esp. II, 117 ff. No. 226 (addressed to Atamano in 1380–81), 241 f. No. 314 (to an unknown person, mentioning Jewish unleavened bread; line 24), 388 ff. No. 432, esp. line 90) with Loenertz's earlier observations in his ed. of *Les Recueils de lettres de Démétrius Cidonès;* E. Voordecker's Ghent dissertation, *Johannes VI. Kantakuzenos, Ketzer en Monnik* (typescript, cited by Fishman-Duker, p. 154 n. 98); idem, "Les Juifs de l'empire byzantin au XIVe siècle," *Actes* of the XIV International Congress of Byzantine Studies held in Bucharest, September 6–12, 1971, II, 285–90, citing among other things a MS of Theophanes III of Nicaea's polemical tract, written sometime between 1370 and 1390—one of eight aimed at Jews, of which only small fragments have been published in later works. See K. Krumbacher, *Geschichte der byzantinischen Litteratur vor Justinian bis zum Ende des oströmischen Reiches (527–1453),* I, 105. See also, more generally, E. G. Beck, *Kirche und theologische Literatur im Byzantinischen Reich.*

48. See G. Mercati, *Se la versione dell'ebraico del Codice Veneto Greco VII sia di Simone Atamano arcivescovo de Tebe, ricerca storica con notizie e documenti sulla vita dell'Atamano,* esp. pp. 12 f., 19, 30 ff., 41 f., with comments thereon by K. M. Setton in his *Catalan Domination of Athens, 1311–1388,* p. 232; Jacques Le Saige, *Voyage . . . à Rome, Notre Dame de Lorette, Venise, Jérusalem, et autres saints lieux,* new ed. by H. R. Duthilloeul, p. 52.

CHAPTER LXXII: ITALO-SLAVIC PENETRATION

1. See G. L. F. Tafel and G. M. Thomas, *Urkunden zur älteren Handels- und Staatsgeschichte der Republik Venedig mit besonderer Beziehung auf Byzanz und die Levante,* I (XII), 43 ff.; F. Dölger, *Regesten zu den Kaiserurkunden des oströmischen Reiches,* II, 27 f. No. 1081; C. G. Fernand, "The Amount of Constantinopolitan Booty in 1204," *Studi Veneziani,* XIII, 95–104 (although expressing some doubts about the reliability of the data supplied by our main informant, Geoffrey de Villehardouin); A. Kretschmayr, *Geschichte von Venedig,* I, 161 ff. See also W. Heinemeyers' careful analysis of "Die Verträge zwischen dem oströmischen Reiche und den italienischen Städten Genua, Pisa und Venedig vom 10. bis 12. Jahrhundert," *Archiv für Diplomatik,* III, 79–161; and D. Minnes, "À propos des privilèges vénitiennes à Constantinople sous les Paléologues," *Bulletin* of the Faculté des Lettres of the University of Strasbourg, XXVIII, 235–41. The importance, for domestic stability, of maintaining the Republic's commerce and food supply even in times of great scarcity was emphasized, for example, by Gasparo Contarini, the eminent diplomat and humanist, in his celebrated *De magistratibus et republica Venetorum libri quinque* (1543), Leiden, 1628 ed., p. 237 (this work was written in the 1520s and 1530s under the unforgettable impact of the Republic's war with the League of Cambrai). See F. Gilbert, "The Date of the Composition of Contarini's and Giannotti's Books on Venice," *Studies in the Renaissance,* XIV, 172–85, esp. pp. 174 ff. See also, more generally, G. Ostrogorsky's *History of the Byzantine State, passim.*

On the Venetian administration of its growing colonial empire see esp. the large collections of summaries from primary sources compiled by F. Thiriet, *Régestes des délibérations du Sénat de Venise concernant la Romanie;* and *Délibérations des Assemblées vénitiennes concernant la Romanie,* Vol. I; his analytical study, *La Romanie vénitienne au moyen âge. Le développement et l'exploitation du domaine colonial vénitien (XIVe–XVe siècles*); and the older but still very useful work by S. Romanin, *Storia documentata di Venezia.* See, for one example, the instruction given in 1389 to the departing podesta for Napoli di Romania, Vettor Morosini, concerning his duties to safeguard the various local cultures under his administration (*ibid.,* III, 358 n. 1). Other more recent authors of relevant monographs are briefly mentioned by Z. Ankori in his "Jews and the Jewish Community in the History of Mediaeval Crete," *Pepragména* (Proceedings) of the Second International Congress of Cretan Studies, III, 312–67, esp. p. 361. Some of these writers will be mentioned in the following notes.

The contrast between the rather favorable treatment by the Venetian authorities of Jews in the colonies and their generally rigid intolerance in the mother city, until after the war with the League of Cambrai, has often been noted. To the extensive literature on Venetian Jewry cited in our earlier volumes, one may add R. C. Muller's recent essay, "Charitable Institutions, the Jewish Community, and Venetian Society: a Discussion of the Recent Volume by Brian Pullan," *Studi Veneziani,* XIV, 37–82 (with reference to Pullan's *Rich and Poor in Renaissance Venice: the Social Institutions of a Catholic State to 1620*). Here (p. 63) Muller states that he expects to discuss more fully the status of the Jews in Venice and Mestre before Cambrai in a special monograph. Much new information is also in P. F. Grendler's "The Destruction of Hebrew Books in Venice, 1568," *PAAJR,* XLV, 29–45; and B. Ravid's *Economics and Toleration in Seventeenth Century Venice: the Background and Context of the* Discorso *of Simone Luzzatto,* esp. the four charters reproduced in the App., pp. 99 ff.

2. See I Macc. 15:23; *supra,* Vols. I, p. 63; V, pp. 168, 366 f. n. 29; and the numerous biblical references to *Kaftor* and *Kretim* easily located in any concordance. A succinct story of the Jews of Crete under Venetian domination was first told by S. Xanthoudidis in "The Jews in Crete under Venetian Rule" (Greek), *Kretikė Stoà,* II, 209–224; and, more fully, by J. Starr in his "Jewish Life in Crete under the Rule of Venice," *PAAJR,* XII, 59–114. It has been further elaborated in a series of investigations by Z. Ankori, who effectively used a combination of interdisciplinary tools employed in archaeological digs, detailed examination of epigraphic minutiae, and critical philological-historical analysis of the extant multilingual documents. The fruits of these dedicated labors are gradually unfolding. See for the time being his aforementioned essay (*supra,* n. 1); his "The Living and the Dead: the Story of Hebrew Inscriptions in Crete," *PAAJR,* XXXVIII-XXXIX, 1–100 (was to be continued); and his "From *Zudecha* to *Yahudi Mahallesi:* The Jewish Quarter of Candia in the Seventeenth Century (A Chapter in the History of Cretan Jewry under Muslim Rule)," *Baron Jub. Vol.,* 1975, pp. 63–129. These and many other data are to be included in Ankori's forthcoming documentary and analytical volumes, which are to appear under the titles of *Creta Judaica: Documents and Regesta* and *Cretan Jewry through the Ages,* and which promise to become models for future histories of important Near- and Middle-Eastern Jewish communities.

3. See C. N. Sathas, *Hellenikė anėkdota* (Greek Curiosities), I, 61 ff., 86 ff.; II, xxxii; H. Noiret, ed., *Documents inédits pour servir à l'histoire de la domination vénitienne en Crète tirés des archives de Venise de 1380 à 1845,* esp. p. 399; the contemporary rabbinic sources reproduced by S. Assaf in his "Jewish Executioners (a Contribution to the History of the Jews of Candia)" (Hebrew), *Tarbiz,* V, 224–26 (including a discussion as to whether such a forced executioner was to be treated as an immoral person disqualified from serving as a witness and from being redeemed from captivity at communal expense); *supra,* Chap. LXXI, n. 26.

4. See *supra,* Chap. LXXI, nn. 42–43; D. Jacoby, "Venice, the Inquisition and the Jewish Communities of Crete in the Early 14th Century," *Studi Veneziani,* XII, 127–44, partly derived from an unpublished letter from the doge to the duke of Crete dated August 22, 1314 and reproduced in the Appendix (pp. 143 f.). According to Jacoby, another Cretan Jew, Jeste Cazorea, "a wealthy man of great substance," likewise served as a *messetus* in the city of Canea in 1422 (p. 132 n. 29). This equivocal title, translated by C. de F. Du Cange (in his *Glossarium ad scriptores mediae et infimae latinitatis,* V, 364) as courtier, which equals a broker or an agent, evidently refers to someone in a semiofficial position. On Elias *fisicus,* see E. Santchi, "Médecine et justice en Crète vénitienne au XIVe siècle," *Thesaurismata, Bulletino* of the Istituto Ellenico di Studi Bizantini in Venice, VIII, 17–48, esp. p. 24; and *infra,* n. 15.

5. See D. Jacoby, "David Mavrogonato of Candia: a Fifteenth-Century Jewish Merchant, Intercessor and Spy" (Hebrew), *Tarbiz,* XXXIII, 388–407; also in French under the less dramatic title, "Un Agent juif au service de Venise: David Mavrogonato de Candie," in *Thesaurismata,* IX, 68–96, esp. p. 93 App. ii. Here Jacoby used to good advantage numerous documents published by M. I. Mamousakas in his *He en Krete synomosia tou Séphi Vlastou* (The Cretan Conspiracy of Sephos Vlastos 1452–54 and the New Conspiratorial Movement of 1460–62) with the addition of other archival sources from the inexhaustible treasure trove of the Archivio di Stato in Venice. Mavrogonato's intercessions for the Cretan Jews are mentioned *infra,* n. 30, while Jacopo of Gaëta's services to Meḥmed the Conqueror are to be treated more fully in the next volume. On the Turko-Venetian encounters of 1463–65, fought on both sides with little perseverance, see N. Iorga's *Geschichte des osmanischen Reiches,* II, 127 ff.

6. See H. Noiret, ed., *Documents inédits,* pp. 239 ff., 246, 298 f.; F. Thiriet, *La Romanie vénitienne,* pp. 299 f., 407 f.; Meir b. Isaac Katzenellenbogen, *Resp.,* Fürth, 1766 ed., fol. 85a–b No. 76; J. Starr, "Jewish Life in Crete," *PAAJR,* XII, 81 ff. On the changing fortunes of the large Cretan class of feudal vassals, see E. Gerland's "Histoire de la noblesse crétoise au moyen âge, I," *ROL,* X, 172–247; XI, 7–144. Although written in the early years of this century, this study has not yet been superseded.

7. Z. Ankori's theory about the peculiar "argo-urban" type of an important segment of Cretan Jewish economy was developed especially in his essays, "Jews and the Jewish Community," *Pepragména,* III, 355 ff.; and his "From *Zudecha,*" *Baron Jub. Vol.,* 1975, pp. 80 ff. See also, more generally, F. Thiriet, "Villes et campagnes en Crète vénitienne aux XIVe–XVe siècles," *Actes* of the IIe Congrès International du Sud-Est Européen, II, Athens, 1972, pp. 44–59 (stressing the great improvement in the lot of the Cretan peasant and the general increase of agricultural production, particularly in viticulture; see *infra,* n. 41); and R. Ziegler's earlier Vienna dissertation, *Wirtschaftsgeschichte, wirtschaftliche Struktur und Entwicklung der Insel Kreta* (typescript).

8. See E. S. Artom and [U.] M. D. Cassuto, eds., *Taqqanot Qandiah ve-zikhronoteha* (Statuta Judaeorum Candiae eorumque memorabilia), esp. pp. 74 ff. Nos. 71, 74–75; F. Thiriet, *La Romanie vénitienne,* p. 320; J. Starr, "Jewish Life in Crete," *PAAJR,* XII, 90. On the great importance of viticulture and wine exports in the entire Cretan economy until the present day, see H. Koepstein's "Zur Landwirtschaft Kretas Ende des 15. Jahrhunderts (nach Stephanos Sachlikis)," *Studi Veneziani,* XI, 43–56, esp. p. 49; and F. Thiriet, "Les Lettres commerciales des Bembo et le commerce vénitien dans l'Empire Ottoman à la fin du XVe siècle," *Studi in onore di Armando Sapori,* II, 911–33, esp. pp. 923 ff.

Although we do not hear in Crete of any Jewish artisan guilds, such as existed on the Greek mainland (see *supra,* Chap. LXXI, n. 18), the Cretan Jewish craftsmen seem to have had no difficulty in getting the assistants they required. In general, Cretan artisans were very liberal in training apprentices of different ethnic or class origins. They were only forbidden by law to employ them as boatmen because of fear that such pupils might flee from the country. We even hear of female apprentices. Nor is there any mention of slaves held by Cretan Jews either for domestic or industrial work, or as objects of trade, although, in general, Crete had an important slave market. Only in the Venetian, as well as Genoese, colonies and trading posts in the Black Sea area do some local Jews seem to have occasionally participated in the more extensive business in such human merchandise. See *infra,* n. 61; C. Verlinden, "La Crète débouché et plaque tournante de la traité des esclaves aux XIVe et XVe siècles," *Studi in onore di Amintore Fanfani,* III, 593–609; and E. Santschi, "Contrats de travail et d'apprentisage en Crète vénitienne au XIVe siècle d'après quelques notaires," *Schweizerische Zeitschrift für Geschichte,* XIX, 34–74.

9. See T. Reinach, "Mutuum date nihil inde sperantes," *Revue des études grecques,* VII, 52–58; *supra,* Vols. IV, pp. 198, 200 f., 338 n. 61, 339 f. n. 64; XII, pp. 193 ff., 307 ff.; J. Starr, "Jewish Life in Crete," *PAAJR,* XII, 84 f.; F. Thiriet, *La Romanie vénitienne,* pp. 300 f.; idem, *Régestes,* II, 110 No. 1469. The crucial passage in Luke 6:35 had greatly puzzled the Church Fathers, and has never been fully clarified by their successors. See G. W. H. Lampe, ed., *A Patristic Greek Lexicon,* pp. 181 f. Yet, perhaps to allay whatever compunctions a party to a "usurious" deal may have had, many notarial documents included in the borrower's testimony the standard phrase that the loan was granted *causa amoris* (because of the creditor's love) for him or her. See the passages quoted *infra,* nn. 12–13.

As to the influence of the Aristotelian doctrine that money has no children, it must be remembered that, while Aristotle's writings in the metaphysical field enjoyed increasing acceptance in the Byzantine world, which in fact communicated its enthusiasm for the peripatetic philosophy to the West, they had far less influence on economic theory and practice. See, for instance, L. von Mohler's comprehensive biography, *Kardinal Bessarion als Theologe, Humanist und Staatsmann;* P. Moraux, *D'Aristote à Bessarion. Trois exposés sur l'histoire et la transmission de l'aristotélisme grec,* esp. pp. 76 ff.; and, with special reference to Venice's cultural interchanges with Byzantium, the fine collection of essays ed. by A. Pertussi, *Venezia e l'Oriente fra tardo medioevo e rinascimento.* Apparently Byzantium was fully cognizant of its own different social needs, which had led to substantial compromises as early as the days of Justinian.

10. See *supra,* Vol. IV, pp. 198, 338 n. 61; *infra,* n. 17; H. Noiret, ed., *Documents inédits,* pp. 287, 372, etc.; F. Thiriet, *Régestes,* II, 81 No. 1326, 91 No. 1377, 104 No. 1441, 190 No. 1820; III, 18 No. 2263, 49 No. 2400, 173 No. 2880, etc.; idem, *La Romanie vénitienne,* pp. 300 f., 408 f. Not surprisingly, in 1326 the Venetian authorities strongly rejected a proposal that the obligation of Cretan Jewry to extend loans to the government be modified; Thiriet, *Régestes,* I, 50 No. 144. Such a financial reserve became doubly important when Venice began paying tribute to the Ottoman Turks in order to secure peace for its ships and traders. See M. Spremič, "I Tributi veneziani nel Levante nel secolo XV," *Studi Veneziani,* XIII, 221–51.

11. See F. Thiriet, *Régestes,* III, 70 No. 2488, 147 No. 2761; *Del Viaggio in Terra Santa fatto e descritto da Ser Marianno da Sienna nel secolo XV,* ed. by D. Moreni, p. 9; Felix Fabri, *Evagatorium in Terrae Sanctae, Arabiae et Aegypti peregrinationem,* ed. by C. D. Hassler, III, 278 ff., 285; other data cited by J. Starr in "Jewish Life in Crete," *PAAJR,* XII, 81 ff.; and by D. Hemmerding Iliadou in "La Crète sous la domination vénitienne et lors de la conquête turque (1322–1684). Renseigne-

ments nouveaux ou peu connus d'après les pèlerins et les voyageurs," *Studi Veneziani,* IX, 535–623, esp. pp. 553, 559, 578 f. (apparently she was unfamiliar with Starr's work). Of interest also is Fabri's explanation of the Jewish control of the pharmaceutical business. He claimed that Crete was a favored center of that trade because its soil produced much of the raw materials needed for the preparation of medicinal drugs. Other materials were imported from Egypt, Africa, and Arabia. Crete thus helped to supply "all of Europe" with pharmaceuticals, and "Jews handle all this trade."

12. See H. Noiret, *Documents inédits,* pp. 245 ff., 322 f., 359 f.; F. Thiriet, *Régestes,* I, 87 No. 321, 139 No. 1594, 146 ff. Nos. 1626–27; II, 249 No. 2091; III, 33 No. 2328, 151 No. 2804, 193 No. 2950, etc.; idem, *La Romanie vénitienne,* pp. 408 f. Sometimes an entire class secured relief from the government. For example, in 1344 at the request of the feudal vassals represented by their envoy in Venice, the Senate decided that they should not be forced to pay their debts except in seven equal annual installments in addition to interest of only 8 percent. Thiriet, *Régestes,* I, 56 No. 172. Since we are restricted to the documents in the archives of the Senate, we cannot tell to what extent these and other compromise resolutions were carried out in Crete. At the most we may say that no complaints from either side seem to have been subsequently discussed on the Senate floor. But their mere absence from the records evidently is far from conclusive. Similarly, the final outcome of the controversy of 1416–21 is not known. It stands to reason that the Jews did not give up their claims because of the debtors' refusal to adopt the compromise plan and undoubtedly pursued them further in the local courts.

As elsewhere, one may learn more about the prevailing actual practices from notarial records referring to specific transactions. For example, in an agreement dated July 18, 1352 of a Jew Mordechai Plumari and a Jewess Dolce, widow (*relicta*) of Lingiachi Plumari, with a Christian Nicolaus Filarto, we learn without much ado that interest of 18 percent was charged. See A. Lombardo, ed., *Zaccaria di Fredo notaio di Candia (1352–1355),* pp. 24 f. No. 15. However, quite apart from the incompleteness of these records—we are offered here a selection of documents from 5 out of 21 years (1352–73) of that notary's activities—we depend in each case on the specific identification of a party as Jewish (*iudeus* or *iudea*). Otherwise the names of Candiot residents can easily be misleading. For instance, one Jacobus Habramo mentioned in a later document (*ibid.,* p. 84 No. 124) was probably a Christian, since these and other biblical names were very common among the Cretan Greeks, as they were among their conationals on the Byzantine mainland. Even Michael son of Moses, mentioned in a document of April 20, 1357 (*ibid.,* pp. 68 ff. No. 94), may be presumed to have been a Jew only because he is recorded as the purchaser of *vinum iudaicum* at the price of 10 hyperpera. The same difficulty confronts us also with the other notarial documents mentioned *infra,* n. 13.

13. H. Noiret, *Documents inédits,* pp. 213 f., 359 f.; F. Thiriet, *La Romanie vénitienne,* pp. 408 f. Pure business transactions probably could still be mediated between seller and buyer by a competent Jewish go-between. Fuller information on this score might be derived from an examination of the business documents recorded by notaries. The records of some of them, like Leonardo Marcello, Benvenuto di Brixano, and the aforementioned Zaccaria di Fredo, have been studied and partially reproduced. See M. Chiaudano and A. Lombardo, eds., *Leonardo Mar-*

cello, notaio in Candia, 1278–81; R. Morozzo della Rocca, ed., *Benvenuto di Brixano, notaio in Candia, 1301–1302,* esp. pp. 59 No. 154 and 104 No. 282, where the Magister Elia *medicus fisicus,* the lender, was probably a Jew identical with the Elias mentioned *supra,* n. 4; and *infra,* n. 15. Much can also be learned from some extant business correspondence, such as that ed. by R. Morozzo della Rocca in *Lettere de mercanti a Pignol Zucchello* (*1336–1350*); and, more generally, idem and A. Lombardo, eds., *Documenti del commercio veneziano nei secoli XI–XIII.* To be sure, in the Venetian colonies, particularly, notaries often engaged in private business on the side, thus creating many conflicts of interest. See, for instance, Mario Poppi, "Ricerche sulla vita e cultura del notaio i cronista veneziano Lorenzo de Monacio [Monaco], cancelliere cretese (*ca.* 1351–1428)," *Studi Veneziani,* IX, 153–86, esp. pp. 179 ff. (among other activities during his stay in Crete in 1419–28, Lorenzo lent money at 20 percent interest, bought and sold slaves, and so forth). Moreover, even in Venice itself the notarial records are not quite comparable in size and depth to the famous Genoese or Amsterdam notarial archives. Nonetheless they possess considerable merit and are outstanding in their own right. But they have only recently begun to be satisfactorily examined. As far as Jews are concerned, they may indeed be a new resource to be explored for the light it might shed on Jewish economic history in the Venetian Republic and maritime empire.

14. Emmanuel Piloti, *Traité sur le passage en Terre Sainte* (*1420*), ed. by P. H. Dopp, esp. p. 94 No. 59; and the comments thereon by F. Thiriet in his "Quelques observations sur le trafic des galées vénitiennes d'après les chiffres des Incanti (XIVe–XVe siècles)," *Studi . . . Amintore Fanfani,* III, 495–522, esp. p. 519; M. Bazzale, *Il Mercato del sale nella Repubblica Veneta nella seconda metà del XVI secolo;* and, more generally, M. Mollay, *Le Rôle du sal dans l'histoire.* Probably as a result of bureaucratic mismanagement the importation of grain from Venice's maritime territories seems to have dwindled considerably just at a time when the size and affluence of the metropolitan population was near its peak. According to M. Aymard's careful explanation of the records, in 1587 the grain imports from the eastern Mediterranean amounted to only 0.22 percent of the total. See his *Venise, Raguse et le commerce du blé pendant le seconde moitié du XVIe siècle,* I, 16 Table 1, 112 f. Table 12, 148 Table 15; and F. Thiriet, "Les Lettres commerciales des Bembo et le commerce vénitien dans l'Empire Ottoman," *Studi . . . Armando Sapori,* II, 911–33, esp. pp. 923 ff., 928 ff., 932 f. Evidently, Cretan Jews had little incentive to play any significant role in this branch of their island's exports.

15. See C. N. Sathas, ed., *Documents inédits relatifs à l'histoire de la Grèce au moyen âge,* 1st ser., VI, 661 ff., 686 f.; H. Noiret, *Documents inédits,* p. 399; and other sources, cited by J. Starr in "Jewish Life in Crete," *PAAJR,* XII, 90 f.; R. J. H. Jenkins, "Social Life in the Byzantine Empire," *Cambridge Medieval History,* ed. by J. M. Hussey *et al.,* 2d ed., IV, Part 2, pp. 79–103, esp. p. 88 n. 1; K. Vogel, "Byzantine Sciences," *ibid.,* pp. 265–305, esp. p. 291; O. Temkin, "Byzantine Medicine: Tradition and Empiricism," *Dumbarton Oaks Papers,* XVI, 95–115; and E. Trapp, "Die Stellung der Ärzte in der Gesellschaft der Palaiologenzeit," *Byzantinoslavica,* XXXIII, 230–34. It may be noted that, despite their general aversion to employing Jews in any form of public service, the Venetian authorities increasingly availed themselves of the help of Jewish doctors for forensic services. See E. Santchi, "Médecine et justice en Crète vénitienne au XIVe siècle," *Thesaurismata,* VIII, 17–48, esp.

pp. 25 ff., mainly based on data preserved in the Archives of the Duke of Candia in the Venetian Archivio di Stato, especially from the years 1318–24 and 1366–97, listing 20 Jews among the recorded 29 Cretan state doctors of the latter period. The ratio was probably even greater among the practitioners not used by the state for forensic purposes. See *supra*, n. 4; and on the Jewish pharmacists, n. 11. The Jewish role in late medieval and early modern medical science and practice will be more fully discussed in a later volume.

Incidentally, Santchi's study also sheds a noteworthy light on another aspect of Cretan Jewry's social life. In an ethnic list of both victims and aggressors who appeared at court in those years, the Greeks, who formed the majority of the population, understandably had the largest number of victims, 231 males plus 47 females, as against 271 male plus 5 female aggressors. They were followed by "Latins," with 51 male and 3 female victims as against 37 male and 4 female aggressors; and the Venetians, with 41 male and 5 female victims and 42 male and 6 female aggressors. The Jews, the next largest group, had a sizable share of victims, 15 males and 4 females, but they did not include a single aggressor. In fact, they were the only significant ethnic group with no alleged aggressor. See Santchi, p. 37.

16. See *infra*, n. 31. Needless to say, the official census of 1627 leaves much to be desired, even more than most other censuses of that period. It was conducted at a time when the Venetian rule over the island was drawing to its close and when the socioeconomic, as well as demographic, strength of the population had already peaked. This was doubly true of Cretan Jewry.

17. See H. Noiret, *Documents inédits*, pp. 417 f.; F. Thiriet, *Régestes*, I, 81 No. 293, 175 No. 724, 209 No. 887; idem, *La Romanie vénitienne*, pp. 227 f., 409 n. 2; *supra*, nn. 10–11; and, most comprehensively, J. Starr, "Jewish Life in Crete," *PAAJR*, XII, 76 ff. On the 4 percent rate see *ibid.*, p. 84 n. 74a. Apparently, in writing his valuable recent studies, Thiriet was unaware of Starr's significant contribution.

As early as 1342 the Senate rejected various suggestions regarding alleviation of the fiscal burdens of the local population. It made a special point that Jews should not be relieved of their obligation to lend money to the Republic. See Thiriet, *Régestes*, I, 50 No. 144. At any rate, the often forced nature of public loans converted them into fiscal contributions and relieved the local Treasury from the obligation of accumulating cash reserves to meet recurrent emergencies.

18. See F. Thiriet, *Régestes*, III, 11 No. 2232, 242 f. No. 3161; P. Grierson, "La Moneta veneziana nell'economia mediterranea del Trecento e Quattrocento," *La Civiltà veneziana del Quattrocento*, pp. 75–97; and the passages quoted here in the last several notes. In arguing in 1395 for the increase of the Jewish annual fiscal contribution from 2,000 to 4,000 hyperpera, the Senate pointed out that the wealth of the Jewish community was constantly increasing by the large immigration of Jews attracted to the island, and also referred to the exemption of Jews from serving as guards during the night. It has been suggested that the large wave of Jewish immigration in the 1390s was occasioned by the Spanish massacres of 1391 and the expulsion of Jews from the city of Venice in 1394. See I. Lévi, "Les Juifs de Candie de 1380 à 1485," *REJ*, XXVI, 198–208, esp. p. 205 (this essay is largely based on H. Noiret's *Documents inédits*); Noiret, p. 71.

19. The attitude of the Venetian Treasury toward payments by the clergy was rather ambivalent. In 1402, for example, when a decision was made to arm two galleys for war against the Turks, it was proposed that the Republic pay for one galley while the expenses for the second should be divided into 24 "carats." Six of these were to be paid by the Republic, 9 by the Cretan nobility, 6 by the Jewish community, and 3 by the clergy. This proposal was modified, however, by exempting the clergy completely and retaining the 6 "carats" for the Republic, but imposing upon the burghers 1 "carat," and raising the nobles' contribution to 10, the Jewish to 7 "carats." On other occasions, however, the Church was made to contribute a fairly substantial share. See Thiriet, *Régestes,* II, 22 No. 1035, etc.

20. C. N. Sathas, *Documents inédits,* I, 283 ff. No. 198, esp. p. 294; H. Noiret, *Documents inédits,* p. 71; F. Thiriet, *Régestes,* I, 59 No. 182, 81 No. 293, 209 No. 887; idem, *La Romanie vénitienne,* pp. 299 f.; idem, "Quelques observations," *Studi . . . Amintore Fanfani,* III, 511 ff., 516 ff. Of course, like the other inhabitants, the Jews were sometimes drafted to help build fortifications, especially in the vicinity of their quarters. But these services were not to be equated with the forced labor of villeins, a comparison which Samargia, with the approval of the Venetian Senate, rightly repudiated. See *supra,* Chap. LXXI, nn. 9–10.

21. See F. Thiriet, *Régestes,* III, 218 f. No. 3046. On the contrasting behavior of the Jews of Negroponte, see *infra,* n. 37. The general Ottoman policy aiming at replenishing the manpower of depopulated areas with Jews and others will be discussed in the next volume.

22. See the graphic narrative by the local Jewish chronicler, Elijah Capsali, in N. Porges' ed. of "Élie Capsali et sa chronique de Venise," *REJ,* LXXVII, 20–40; LXXVIII, 15–34; LXXIX, 28–60, esp. LXXVII, 23 ff., LXXIX, 29 ff. No. ii (the result of the balloting at the Consiglio Maggiore in Venice was 220 to 130 for acquittal and 89 abstentions on July 15, 1452, and 261 to 120 for acquittal and 125 abstentions on July 13, 1454. In both cases the abstentions were considered as votes against condemnation); L. A. Schiavi, "Gli Ebrei in Venezia e nelle sue colonie," *Nuova Antologia,* CXXXI, 489 f.; E. S. Artom and M. D. Cassuto, eds., *Taqqanot Qandiah,* I, 87 No. 78; and other sources cited by Starr in "Jewish Life in Crete," *PAAJR,* XII, 66 f.

The relative paucity of host libels in Crete and the entire Byzantine world may have been owing to the peculiar outlook of the Eastern Churches. The diverse approaches to the doctrine of Transubstantiation, though quite different from that of the Protestant Reformation, may have accounted for the fewer suspicions of Jewish curiosity about the wafer. The Blood Accusation which originated, as we recall, in the Hellenistic world, was so long aimed first at Jews and then at Christians during the pagan regime in the Middle East, that there was less incentive to use that same weapon against Jews until it was imported by the Western conquerors and settlers. Similarly, the accusation of well poisoning by Jews as the cause of the Black Death, allegedly accepted by the Dubrovnik population, seems to be a Western import. See *infra,* n. 77. However, these problems would merit further documentation and careful consideration.

23. Oldrado da Ponte, *Consilia seu responsa et quaestiones aureae,* Venice, 1585, fols. 16b–17a No. xxvi; E. S. Artom and M. D. Cassuto, eds., *Taqqanot,* I, 146 ff. Nos. 112–14; *supra,* n. 4; Vols. XIII, pp. 149, 386 n. 92; XIV, pp. 132 f., 354 n. 62; J. Starr, "Jewish Life in Crete," *PAAJR,* XII, 64 f. Oldrado, whose *consilium* is quoted here in a variant from both Starr's and D. Jacoby's English translations (see *Studi Veneziani,* XII, 140 n. 67), in other connections proved to be much more tolerant toward Jews. See *supra,* Vol. XIII, pp. 101, 359 f. n. 44. On the Venetian Inquisition and its persecutions of Iberian Marranos, see esp. the several studies by C. Roth mentioned in Vols. XIII–XIV.

In general, the inquisitorial prosecutions had few repercussions in the Venetian island colonies. In 1547 the Venetian authorities severely censured Lorenzo da Bergamo, a vicar of the archbishop, for casting aspersion on the Greeks, "calling them in his public writings nefarious heretics, who had defamed the holy cross, renounced the faith, and paid homage to the devil." In 1569 Venice generally forbade the Inquisition to prosecute the Greek "heretics" in Candia. See V. Lamansky, *Secrets d'État de Venise, documents, extraits, notices et études servant à éclaircir les rapports de la Seigneurie avec les Grecs, les Slaves, et la Porte Ottomane à la fin du XVe au XVIe siècles,* II, 063 No. 4, 069 No. 13. By that time, Venice itself pursued a more liberal policy toward the Levantine Jews residing in the capital, a policy which presumably also affected Venice's colonial subjects who happened to settle there. Evidently, because of commercial considerations, the authorities could no longer be quite so exacting in the latter part of the sixteenth century, when both Venice's political power and its economic prosperity showed incipient signs of decline. The situation on the island in the early stages of the Ottoman occupation is well analyzed (with the aid of descriptions by Evliya Chelebi, himself a participant in the 1667 campaign) by P. Hidiroglu in *Das Religiöse Leben auf Kreta nach Ewlijā Čelebi.* However, the occasional historical references to Jews in that volume shed no light on their religious life during this period.

24. See E. Santchi, "Procès criminal en Crète vénitienne (1354–1389)," *Thesaurismata,* VI, 82–96; Ludovico Foscarini's letter of 1450, on which Syndicus Antonio Gradonico [Gradenigo] reported to the Venetian Senate, is partially reproduced from F. Corner's (Cornelio's) compilation, *Creta Sacra, sive de episcopis utriusque ritus graeci et latini in insula Cretae,* II, 382 ff., by H. Noiret in his *Documents inédits,* p. 425 n. 1. To be sure, as pointed out by Starr, the text did not clearly indicate Foscarini's belief in Jewish murder of human beings for ritual purposes. Yet its implications seemingly justified Corner's heading of that letter as relating to *Pugnandum contra nefandum Judaeorum genus, qui homines et agnos crucifigunt.* See the remarks thereon by I. Lévi in "Les Juifs de Candie," *REJ,* XXVI, 205 f.; and Starr in *PAAJR,* XII, 65 ff., 73 f. (includes a variant English trans. of the excerpt from Giacomo Foscarini's report cited in the text).

25. See *supra,* n. 15; and Vols. XIII, pp. 174 f., 401 nn. 17–18; XV, pp. 60, 405 n. 71; E. S. Artom and M. D. Cassuto, eds., *Taqqanot,* pp. 28 No. 38, 67 No. 65. On the location of the Church of St. Peter in relation to the Jewish quarter of Candia, see Z. Ankori, "Jews and the Jewish Community," *Pepragména,* III, 330. A bibliographical survey of Candiot Jewish scholarship was published a century ago by M. Steinschneider in his "Candia. Cenni di storia letteraria," *Mosé, Antologia Is-*

raelitica, II–V. Various aspects of the intellectual life of Mid-Eastern Jewries under the Latin regimes will be discussed in later volumes.

26. See *supra,* n. 6; Vol. XI, pp. 87 ff.; J. Jegerleiner, "Der Aufstand der kandiotischen Ritterschaft gegen das Mutterland Venedig, 1363–65," *BZ,* XII, 78–125; E. Gerland, *Das Archiv des Herzogs von Kandia im Königlichen Staatsarchiv zu Venedig,* p. 125 [131]; H. Noiret, ed., *Documents inédits,* pp. 239 ff.; F. Thiriet, ed., *Régestes,* I, 32 No. 44.

27. Lorenzo da Mula's observation on the Candiot Jewish quarter, cited by G. Gerola in his comprehensive *Monumenti Veneti nell'isola di Creta,* II, 380 n. 4, with Z. Ankori's analysis and critique of this work in "The Living and the Dead," *PAAJR,* XXXVIII–XXXIX, pp. 5 ff.; Ankori's own studies of the various synagogues and their location, *ibid.,* pp. 15 ff. (Rethimo), 18 ff. (Candia), 32 ff. (Canea-Khania); and his "Jews and the Jewish Community," *Pepragména,* V, esp. pp. 323 ff. In 1333 a Jew argued that, since the authorities had allowed a coreligionist to open a window by piercing the wall of his house *near* the quarter, he should also be permitted to open two windows in his wall. He even asserted that, in this way, the city might be better defended against enemies. We also remember the Rethimo burghers' complaint that Jews kept shops outside their quarter. See Thiriet, *Régestes,* I, 29 No. 32; *supra,* n. 13. It seems, therefore, that the main reason for the continued settlement of Jews within their established Candia quarter was the relative absence of population pressure, such as was generated elsewhere by the sudden arrival of numerous immigrants.

28. See E. S. Artom and M. D. Cassuto, *Taqqanot,* I, 118 ff. No. 99; A. Rubiò i Lluch, ed., *Diplomatario de l'Orient català (1301–1409). Collecció de documents per la história de l'expedició catalana a Orient i dels Ducats d'Atenes i Neopatria. Recollida y anotata,* pp. 115 f. No. xcvi, 121 f. No. c, 124 ff. No. ciii; J. Starr, "Jewish Life in Crete," *PAAJR,* XII, 67 ff.

29. The story of how Jews were saved from the mob in 1538 and their subsequent observance of an annual Purim-like festival are described by Elijah Capsali in an autobiographical memoir reproduced in Hebrew and French by A. Danon in "Quelques Pourim locaux," *REJ,* LIV, 113–37, esp. pp. 115 f., 125 ff. According to a letter received by Salomon A. Rosanes of Sofia in 1902 from the local rabbi of Candia, that festival was still being observed there at that time. See Rosanes, *Dibre yeme Yisrael be-Togarma* or *Qorot ha-Yehudim be-Turqiah ve-Arṣot ha-Qedem* (A History of the Jews in Turkey and the Mideast), II, 2d ed., p. 55 n. 15; and J. Starr, "Jewish Life in Crete," *PAAJR,* XII, 70 n. 29.

30. See C. N. Sathas, *Helenikà anékdota,* II, xxix ff.; J. Starr, "Jewish Life in Crete," *PAAJR,* XII, 67 f.; and *supra,* n. 5. It appears that the family Mavrogonato or Maurogonato, a member of which was to play a significant role in the Venetian revolution of 1848, kept a family record book which included transcripts of the various governmental privileges granted to the descendants of David Mavrogonato. Such a manuscript collection of "Privileggi degli Ebrei Mavrogonati in Candia," held in private possession, was still available in the 1860s to one of the outstanding pioneers in modern Byzantine research, Karl Hopf. See his *Geschichte Griechen-*

lands vom Beginn des Mittelalters bis auf unsere Zeit, photo-offset of the 1867–68 ed. in J. S. Ersch and J. G. Gruber's *Allgemeine Encyklopädie der Wissenschaft und Kunst,* Vols. LXXXV–LXXXVI, esp. II (LXXXVI), 176 n. 18.

31. Meshullam b. Menaḥem da Volterra, *Massa',* ed. by A. Yaari, pp. 81 f.; in the excerpt translated in E. N. Adler's *Jewish Travellers,* pp. 201 f.; Z. Ankori, "Jews and the Jewish Community," *Pepragména,* III, 354; Starr, "Jewish Life in Crete," *PAAJR,* XII, 60 f., esp. nn. 5–6; and the excerpt reproduced by V. Lamansky in his *Secrets d'état de Venise,* II, 630 ff., esp. p. 632. On Foscarini see also *supra,* n. 24. Understandably, the demographic data supplied by the census of 1627 do not reflect the great fluctuations in the Jewish and general population in the preceding and subsequent centuries. It is indeed possible that in 1481 the Candiot Jewish community, and perhaps also the total population of the city, greatly exceeded the numbers given in 1627, since at its height in the fifteenth century the Republic's prosperity had communicated itself to the various Venetian colonies, including Crete. Similarly, the subsequent decline in the Levantine trade generally, and the Venetian share therein, as well as the numerous warlike disturbances in the eastern Mediterranean owing to the rapid Ottoman expansion, may also have greatly narrowed the economic opportunities of the local population. Jews especially may have been induced to emigrate to the more promising centers under Ottoman rule including Constantinople, Salonica, Smyrna, and Alexandria. Yet it is difficult to assume without positive evidence that the demographic gyrations in the Venetian colonies vastly exceeded those in the metropolis, as briefly described *supra,* Vol. XII, pp. 18 f. and 252 f. n. 15.

32. The basic similarity of the Italian colonial expansion into the eastern Mediterranean and that of the subsequent Western European powers into the Afro-Asian and American lands is, like most historical parallels, incomplete. Even in the age of the Palaeologi, when Venice and Genoa had to be treated by the Byzantine emperors as sovereign powers, rather than as vassal states, the Italian conquerors still felt flattered by signs of recognition on the part of the august Byzantine dynasty, heir to the celebrated ancient Roman world power. In fact, many more Byzantine Greeks were still prone to view the Western "Franks" as "barbarians" than vice versa. See N. Iorga's pertinent observations in his chapter, "Y-a-t-il là un moyen âge byzantin?" in his *Études Byzantines,* I, 299–311, esp. pp. 306 f. Yet, this psychological factor but slightly modified the practical relationship between masters and subjects in the Italian colonies.

33. See C. N. Sathas, ed., *Documents inédits,* II, 81 ff. No. 303, esp. pp. 83 ff.; III, 279 ff. No. 932, 347 f., 462 f. No. 1047; H. Noiret, ed., *Documents inédits,* pp. 131 ff., 297 f.; L. A. Schiavi, "Gli Ebrei," *Nuova Antologia,* CXXXI, 315; F. Thiriet, *Régestes,* I, 79 No. 284; idem, *Déliberations des Assemblées vénitiennes,* I, 175 f. No. 395; and, more generally, J. Starr, *Romania,* pp. 37 ff. Starr also calls attention to the diplomatic intervention by Venice in Constantinople in 1321. On this occasion the Republic protested against an attack by Greek seamen on Italian merchant ships, which resulted in considerable damage to a number of Italian merchants, including some Negroponte citizens. Three merchants bearing Jewish names collected an indemnity in this fashion. See G. M. Thomas and R. Predelli, eds., *Diplomatarium,* I, 183 f.

This example of the Venetian umbrella over Jewish international trade in the eastern Mediterranean shows how important a role Venice played in defending the interests of its Jewish subjects in all its possessions. Remarkably, all this happened before the Jews were officially readmitted to Venice itself and without any formal abrogation of the Byzantine decree of 992, which had prohibited Venetian captains from transporting Jewish passengers or goods on Venetian bottoms. See *supra*, Vol. IV, pp. 24 f., 183, 244 nn. 25–26. Evidently, that decree had long before fallen into oblivion. We find no evidence that it ever was invoked by hostile competitors in the Late Middle Ages.

34. See C. N. Sathas, ed., *Documents inédits*, III, 344 ff. No. 932 end; C. Bernheimer, "Document," *REJ*, LXV, 224 ff.; F. Thiriet, *Régestes*, III, 18 No. 2263; *supra*, Chap. LXXI, n. 13. If the terms *servi sive villani* originated from some earlier claims of the Frankish feudal lords, one is reminded of the rather bizarre treaties concluded by various lords in France in the early thirteenth century concerning Jews departing from one feudal fief to another, who were to be forcibly returned to their original masters. See *supra*, Vols. IV, pp. 62 f., 269 f. n. 81; XI, pp. 4 ff., 11 f., 289 ff., esp. n. 10. But under the conditions prevailing in the Byzantine area such phrasing undoubtedly had even fewer implications of true serfdom than it did in France.

35. See C. N. Sathas, ed., *Documents inédits*, II, 81 ff. No. 303, esp. pp. 83 ff. (1402); III, 344 ff. No. 932, 462 ff. No. 1047, esp. pp. 404 f., the document referring to the decision of 1402. It was renewed on September 26, 1423 by a resolution not reproduced by Sathas, but by Noiret in his *Documents inédits*, pp. 297 f. See also Thiriet, *Régestes*, II, 210 No. 1905.

36. See C. N. Sathas, *Documents inédits*, III, 279 ff. No. 856; H. Vast, *Le Cardinal Bessarion (1403–1472)*, pp. 272 f., 457 ff.; L. Mohler, *Kardinal Bessarion als Theologe, Humanist und Staatsmann*, III, 529 f.; and *supra*, n. 9. In his Hebrew essay, "On the Status of Jews in the Venetian Colonies in the Middle Ages" *Zion*, XXVIII, 57–69, D. Jacoby has argued, with much ingenuity, that the official documents affirming the "citizen" status of the family of David of Negroponte (1368–1473) or of David b. Elijah Mavrogonato of Candia and his descendants were not intended to convey the idea that these families were to enjoy full-fledged Venetian citizenship. He also pointed out that in these decrees appear such qualifying phrases as *nostrum fidelem et Venetum*, or *cives et fideles nostri*, and that in some general enactments conferring citizenship on large groups in order to attract new settlers (for instance to Crete in 1353 and 1368 after the great population losses of the Black Death era), Jews were specifically excluded. See C. N. Sathas, *Documents inédits*, II, 60 No. 272, 61 f. No. 274; F. Thiriet, *Régestes*, II, 116 f. No. 455.

Jacoby might have observed, however, the ambiguity of the entire medieval terminology of *civis* or *civitas*. Especially in the case of Jews, their designation as *cives* in Worms or in Marseilles, in Rome or in Sicily, did not mean that they would necessarily enjoy full equality of rights with the Christians including, for instance, eligibility for public office or military command. See the numerous examples quoted by me *supra*, Vol. XI, pp. 14 ff., 292 nn. 13–17, etc. Certainly, not even a Venetian Christian of the lower classes enjoyed the same rights as the city's renowned "aristocracy" and particularly some of its leading families. On the other hand, when it pleased the rulers they could entrust important fiscal functions to a Jew even if he was not called a "citizen," as was the case of Sambati-Shabbetai, the *messetus*, which so puzzled our author. See *surpa*, n. 4. Although living under different regimes, the Jews of Negroponte maintained close relations with the Jewish community of Thebes. But we know very little about their communal and intellectual exchanges with their coreligionists on the other Aegean Islands. Not even a scholar like Shemaryah b. Elijah al-Iqriti, admiringly mentioned (about 1360) by a visitor, Yehudah (Leon) Mosconi, seems to appear in any of the known records of Negroponte. See *infra*, n. 37.

37. See F. Thiriet, *Régestes*, III, 70 f. Nos. 2488 and 2492, 175 No. 2887, 218 f. No. 3046, 222 f. No. 3065; S. Rosanes, *Dibre yeme Yisrael*, I, 2d ed., pp. 45, 120 f.; U. Heyd, "The Jewish Communities of Istanbul in the Seventeenth Century," *Oriens*, VI, 299–314, esp. p. 300 *s.v.* Aguboz; and other sources cited by D. Jacoby in his "On the Status of Jews," *Zion*, XXVII, 30 ff. See also H. Inalcik, "The Policy of Mehmed II toward the Greek Population of Istanbul and the Byzantine Buildings of the City," *Dumbarton Oaks Papers*, XXIII–XXIV, 229–49. The Jewish situation in Constantinople after 1453 will be discussed more fully in the next volume. Before the Turkish conquest, however, the Jews still living in Negroponte displayed their unswerving loyalty to the Venetian regime. They not only defended their segment of the city wall against Ottoman assailants, but at least one of them is said to have furnished the local authorities with some valuable information concerning Turkish funds sent to one Zeffar claiming to be Bayezid's son (1430). See N. Iorga, *Notes et extraits pour servir à l'histoire des Croisades au XVe siècle*, I, 520.

38. See Meshullam da Volterra's *Massa'*, ed. by A. Yaari, p. 81; E. N. Adler's English trans. in his *Jewish Travellers*, p. 200; Moses b. Mordecai Bassola (previously known as the anonymous traveler of the year 5282 = 1542!), *Massa'ot Ereṣ-Yisrael* (A Pilgrimage to Palestine), ed. from the original manuscript by I. Ben-Zevi, pp. 33 f.; and Elijah of Pesaro, *Massa'* (Itinerary), reproduced in A. Yaari's *Massa'ot Ereṣ-Yisrael* (Travels to Palestine), pp. 165–95, esp. pp. 168 f.

39. See Elijah of Pesaro's account, *ibid.*, pp. 186 ff. (includes an interesting account of moneylending practices on the island, some loans being negotiated only for a few days; pp. 189 f.); Johann Helffrich, *Kurtzer und wahrhafftiger Bericht von der Reyss aus Venedig nach Jerusalem* in *Reyssbuch des Heyligen Landts*, ed. by S. Feyrabend, fols. 375–99, esp. fol. 378a. All these and other sources are cited by J. Starr in his *Romania*, pp. 101 ff., 109 f. See also G. F. Hill's *History of Cyprus*.

40. V. Lamansky, *Secrets d'état de Venise*, II, 014 ff., esp. 031 No. 19; B. Lewis, *Notes and Documents from the Turkish Archives: a Contribution to the History of the Jews in the Ottoman Empire*, pp. 28 ff. and 44 f.; U. Heyd, ed., *Ottoman Documents on Palestine, 1552–1615*, pp. 167 f.; T. Papadopoullos, *Social and Historical Data on Population (1570–1881)*, pp. 29 f. On Don Joseph Nasi's relations to Cyprus see C. Roth, *The House of Nasi: the Duke of Naxos*, pp. 138 ff.; and, more fully, the forthcoming analysis in Vol. XVIII. See also, more generally, N. Banescu, *Le Declin de Famaguste. Fin du royaume de Chypre. Notes et documents;* and G. F. Hill, *History of Cyprus*. On the antecedents of the great war between Turkey and the Western alliance and the occupation of Cyprus by Turkish troops, see F. Braudel's renewed analysis in *La Méditerranée et le monde méditerranéen à*

l'époque de Philippe II, 2d ed. rev. and enlarged, esp. I, 370 ff.; and the fuller description of the contemporary developments in the Ottoman Empire in my next volume.

41. Pierre Belon, *Les Observations de plusieurs singularitez et choses observables trouvées en Grèce, Asie, Judée, Égypte, Arabie et autres pays étranges,* Paris, 1553 ed.; Pero Tafur, *Travels and Adventures, 1435–1439,* in M. Letts's English trans., pp. 49 f.; Mariano da Siena, *Del Viaggio in Terra Santa fatto e descritto . . . nel secolo XV,* ed. by D. Moreni, p. 9.

42. Meshullam da Volterra, *Massa',* pp. 82 f.; in E. N. Adler's trans. in his *Jewish Travellers,* p. 203; Johann von Hassenstein (Hašištensky), *Putovàni k Svatemu Hrobu* (Pilgrimages to the Holy Sepulchre), p. 38; Arnold von Harff, *The Pilgrimage . . . from Cologne through Italy, Syria, Egypt, etc.,* English trans. from the German by M. Letts, p. 81 (incidentally, the traveler's anti-Jewish bias is evident in his description of Trent [p. 9]); Georges Lengherand, *Voyage à Venise, Rome, Jérusalem, Mont Sinaï et le Kayre, 1485–1486,* ed. with an Intro., Notes and Glossary by Marquis de Godefroy Ménilglaise, p. 98; Pietro Casola, *Pilgrimage to Jerusalem in the Year 1494,* English trans. by M. N. Newett, pp. 152 f., 192; Felix Fabri, *Evagatorium in Terrae Sanctae, Arabiae, et Aegypti peregrinationem,* ed. by C. D. Hassler, III, 285; C. N. Sathas, *Documents inédits,* IV, 33 f., 64 f., 87 f., 107 f., 112, 127 f., 145, 154, 159 ff., 169, 176; most of them cited by J. Starr in *Romania,* pp. 63 ff. On the ability of the medieval Balkan lands, together with Egypt, to supply Venice with grain, see Nicola Kondov's educated estimates in "Über den wahrscheinlichen Weizenertrag der Balkanländer im Mittelalter," *Études Balkaniques,* 1974, no. 1, pp. 97–109; and *supra,* n. 14. See also V. Hrechová, "Le Commerce vénitien et les changements dans l'importance des centres de commerce en Grèce du 13e au 15e siècles," *Studi Veneziani,* IX, 3–34, esp. pp. 24 f.

43. David b. Joseph Ibn Yaḥya's circular letter summarized by I. Loeb in his "Josef Haccohen et les chroniqueurs juifs," *REJ,* XVI, 28–56, 211–35; XVII, 74–95, 242–71, with some corrections; *ibid.,* XVIII, 310, esp. XVI, 37 item 36, 46 f. See also J. [I.] Kracauer, "Rabbi Joselmann de Rosheim," *REJ,* XVI, 84–105, esp. p. 99 item 19; the derogatory description of Modon in an earlier *Voyage de la Saincte Cyte de Hierusalem,* cited by D. A. Zakythinos in "La Population de la Morée byzantine," *Hellénisme Contemporain,* 2d ser. III, 130; and S. R. Luce's broader "Modon—a Venetian Station in Mediaeval Greece," *Classical and Mediaeval Studies in Honor of Edward Kennard Rand,* ed. by L. W. Jones, pp. 195–208, esp. pp. 196 ff., 202, 204 f. The Jewish sister community of Coron seems to have been so completely overshadowed by that of Modon that it left few traces in the extant documentation. Apparently it generally shared the destinies of its nearby coreligionists under the same Venetian or Turkish administration.

44. Meshullam da Volterra, *Massa',* p. 84; Moses Bassola, *Massa'ot,* pp. 30 f.; E. N. Adler, *Jewish Travellers,* p. 204; F. Braudel, *La Méditerranée,* II, 116 f.; Andrea Marmora, *Della historia di Corfu,* VIII, 437 (on that author see E. Legrand, *Bibliographie héllenique du XVIIe siècle,* II, 281 ff.); J. A. Romanos, "Histoire de la communauté israélite de Corfou," *REJ,* XXIII, 63–75; D. Kaufmann, "Contributions à l'histoire des Juifs de Corfou," *ibid.,* XXXII, 226–35; XXXIII, 64–76, 219–32; XXXIV, 263–75; L. A. Schiavi, "Gli Ebrei in Venezia," *Nuova Antologia,* CXXXI,

485 ff.; and C. Roth's interesting summary in his *Venice* (Jewish Communities Series), pp. 310 ff. Immanuel Aboab's correspondence with Horatio del Monte was reproduced in Aboab's *Nomologia o Discursos legales,* Amsterdam, 1629, pp. 143–57; with the comments thereon by M. Kayserling in his biographical sketch, "Immanuel Aboab und seine Nomologia," *Jeschurun,* ed. by S. R. Hirsch, IV, 566–73; V, 643–47.

45. See "The Petition by the Jews of Corfu to the Doge of Venice in 1611" reproduced, from a copy extant in Vienna, in Italian with a Hebrew translation and analysis, in the pertinent Hebrew article by J. Schneider in *Zion,* XII, 82–87; and, more generally, W. Miller, *Essays on the Latin Orient* (a collection of studies originally written in 1897–1921), esp. pp. 200 ff., 209 ff. (also quoting the passage relating to religious liberty), 224, etc.; and the literature mentioned *infra,* n. 46. Of interest also is that Don Isaac Abravanel was able to find in Corfu the manuscript of the early part of his *Commentary* on Deuteronomy, which many years before he had left behind during his hurried departure from Lisbon. Evidently it was brought there by another Portuguese refugee. It now stimulated the author to bring it to completion. See his *Perush ha-Torah,* Venice, 1579, Intro.; B. Netanyahu, *Don Isaac Abravanel,* 2d ed., pp. 71 ff., 285 nn. 39–41.

46. F. Thiriet, *Régestes,* II, 78 No. 1308, 226 No. 1982; III, 77 Nos. 2231–32; A. Marmora, *Della historia di Corfu,* V, 255 f.; *supra,* n. 18. Understandably, most later writers discuss developments after 1650, for which we have much richer documentation than for the earlier period. For example, the first Jewish lawyer, Mordecai Cohen, known to have practiced law in Corfu is mentioned in the sources in 1654. He was followed by a number of others so that, in 1698, seven of the twenty candidates admitted to the bar were Jews. However, the chances are that this system was inherited from the Byzantine law which had provided that, even in their litigations with coreligionists, Jews should appear before general courts. There they understandably preferred to be represented by lawyers of their own faith, unless they felt that, in certain cases, a Christian attorney's special skill, prestige, or personal contacts with judges and others might prove more useful to them. Indeed, much more can be learned in retrospect from somewhat later documentation such as is offered, for example, in my three essays, "A Contribution to the History of Palestine Relief and the Ransom of Captives (From Corfu Records)" (Hebrew), *Sefer ha-Shanah li-Yehude Amerika* (American Hebrew Year Book), VI, 167–79 (also listing some of the general literature on Corfu; pp. 168 f. n. 5); "On the History of the Corfu Communities and Their Organization" (Hebrew), *Qobeṣ Madda'i, Studies in Memory of Moses Schorr,* ed. by L. Ginzberg and A. Weiss, pp. 25–41; and "Jewish Immigration and Communal Conflicts in Seventeenth-Century Corfu," *Starr Mem. Vol.,* pp. 169–82. Some additional data, likewise mainly for the period after 1650, are supplied by several documents ed. by D. Benvenisti and Ḥ. Mizrachi in their "Sources for the History of the Jewish Community of Corfu" (Hebrew), *Sefunot,* I, 303–314, with an English summary, p. [16]. In view of that growing accumulation of source materials over the years, the time has decidedly come for a competent scholar to undertake a comprehensive history of the Jews of Corfu from ancient times to the present.

47. See the few scattered data offered by Moses Bassola in his *Massa'ot,* p. 32; Elijah of Pesaro's *Massa'* in A. Yaari's ed. of *Massa'ot Ereṣ Yisrael,* pp. 183 f.; C. N.

Sathas, *Documents inédits,* VI, 264; Jacob b. Israel ha-Levi, *Resp.,* Venice, 1632 ed., fol. 174c No. 82; Johann Helffrich, *Reyssbuch,* ed. by S. Feyrabend, col. 376a; J. Starr, *Romania;* and C. Roth, *Venice,* in the Indices *s.v.* Zante. On R. Jacob b. Israel, who called himself quaintly *le-bet Levi* (of the House of Levi), see I. Broydé's brief biographical sketch in the *Jewish Encyclopedia,* VII, 33 *s.v.* Jacob ben Israel ha-Levi. See also W. Miller, *Essays on the Latin Orient,* esp. pp. 213 ff. The Venetian possessions on the Dalmatian shore and the adjoining islands, which largely belonged to the southern Slavic sphere, are discussed *infra,* nn. 76 ff.

48. See F. Dölger, *Regesten der Kaiserurkunden,* III, 53 f. No. 1960 (1268), 68 f. No. 2026 (1277); and other aspects discussed by D. J. Geanakoplos in his *Emperor Michael Palaeologus and the West, 1258–1282: a Study in Byzantine-Latin Relations,* esp. p. 300 n. 2; G. M. Thomas and R. Predelli, *Diplomatarium,* esp. I, 164; and particularly, in D. Jacoby's excellent analysis of "Venetian Diplomatic Protection for Jews in Constantinople in the Fourteenth and Fifteenth Centuries" (Hebrew), *Zion,* XXVII, 24–35 (with an English summary, pp. ii–iii), which is closely followed in our presentation here. Needless to say, the Byzantine authorities did not formally accept the Venetian postulates and from time to time protested against the violation of their sovereign rights over Byzantine subjects. On similar arrangements in Cyprus, where Genoa was the main driving force in securing extraterritorial rights (though of lesser scope than demanded, and often secured, by Venice) see, for instance, the decree of 1232, reproduced by L. de Mas-Latrie in his *Histoire de l'île de Chypre sous le règne des princes de la maison de Lusignan,* II, 51 ff.

The extraordinary position of the Venetian bailo in Constantinople, which he inherited in part, though with somewhat diminished authority, from the Venetian podesta during Venice's overpowering influence on the Latin Empire in Constantinople before 1261, is analyzed by R. L. Wolff in his "A New Document from the Period of the Latin Empire of Contantinople; the Oath of the Venetian Podestà," *Annuaire* of the Institut de Philologie of the Université Libre in Brussels, XII (= *Mélanges Henri Grégoire,* IV), 539–73, esp, pp. 566 ff. See also J. Chrysostomides, "Venetian Commercial Privileges under the Palaeologi," *Studi Veneziani,* XII, 267–356, esp. p. 291 (describing Venetian private property in Constantinople) and 331 ff. (reproducing twenty documents ranging from 1342 to 1420).

49. See *supra,* Vols. IV, pp. 24 f., 183, 244 nn. 25–26; X, pp. 292 f., 430 f. n. 86; U. Heyd, "The Jewish Communities of Istanbul," *Oriens,* VI, 299 ff. (on the location of the later Jewish quarters); H. Noiret, ed., *Documents inédits,* pp. 182 f. (1404); F. Thiriet, *La Romanie vénitienne,* p. 300 n. 2; J. Starr, *Romania,* pp. 28 ff. On the rapidly improving Veneto-Byzantine relations in that period, notwithstanding the mutual recriminations in their diplomatic correspondence—recriminations which, for the most part, seem to have remained unresolved—see A. E. Laiou's lucid analysis in his *Constantinople and the Latins,* pp. 267 ff. Admittedly we have no direct evidence of converted Jews, of either sex, being counted among the Venetian (or Genoese) *gasmuli.* But in view of the frequency of mixed marriages in the Byzantine world it would be surprising if none had joined that privileged class. See D. M. Nicol, "Mixed Marriages in Byzantium in the Thirteenth Century," *Studies in Church History,* I, 160–72. Our general knowledge of Jewish converts in Byzantium and its successor states is extremely hazy even with respect to the recurrent outlawries of the Jewish faith, which were doubtless followed by formal mass conversions.

Because of the absence of an effective and sustained Inquisition, we possess no data to enable us to reconstruct the number and image of Jewish converts to Christianity in either the Greek or the Latin environment in the eastern Mediterranean.

50. The situation of the "white Venetian" Jews, especially in Constantinople, was first described by D. Jacoby in his aforementioned Hebrew essay, *Zion,* XXVII, 24–35; and was then supplemented by him in "Les Juifs vénitiens de Constantinople et leur communauté du XIIIe au milieu du XVe siècle," *REJ,* CXXXI, 397–410. Utilizing to good advantage especially the documents recently reproduced by C. A. Maltezou in her *Ho Thesmós tou en Konstantinoupólei Venétou bailou* (The Institution of the Venetian Bailo in Constantinople, 1268–1453), Jacoby was also able to discuss some interesting facets of the communal organization and the domestic life of the small but influential Jewry residing in the Venetian quarter of the Byzantine capital. On the size of a Venetian barrel of wine, see U. Tocci, "Un Problema di metrologia navale; la botte veneziana," *Studi Veneziani,* IX, 213–17. That the exceptional treatment of specially privileged foreign protégés—an adumbration of the future "capitulations"—was not limited to the Byzantine world in decline may be seen from the example of the two Jewish brothers-in-law from Leghorn who, in 1669, were given permission to trade freely in Marseilles (they did it effectively with both North Africa and the Middle East) in defiance of the existing law. See *supra,* Vol. XV, pp. 85 f., 417 n. 16. Needless to say, neither the French nor the Venetians were disinterested protectors. Apart from the general commercial advantages they derived from such protective arrangements, Venice, as we recall, also imposed upon its Jewish protégés a variety of special taxes in addition to the prescribed gifts to the bailo. Probably the highest revenue was produced by a 10 percent charge on all dowries given to a Jewish couple. See F. Thiriet, *La Romanie vénitienne,* p. 300 n. 2.

51. On the Byzantine protests, see esp. G. M. Thomas and R. Predelli, eds., *Diplomatarium,* I, 164; F. Thiriet, ed., *Régestes,* I, 91 f. No. 342; C. N. Sathas, *Documents inédits,* I, 139 No. 97; and other sources cited by D. Jacoby in his "Venetian Diplomatic Protection," *Zion,* XXVII, pp. 26, 29; and his "Venice, the Inquisition and the Jewish Communities of Crete," *Studi Veneziani,* XII, 127–44. The protectionist system naturally lent itself to abuses. Among the objections raised by the Byzantine diplomacy was the purportedly fraudulent claim by some "white Venetians" that they owned merchandise which, in fact, belonged to local Greeks or Turks, in order to secure its exemption from duties and other imposts. This complaint was voiced particularly by Manuel II in his letter to Venice of July 31, 1418, as summarized by N. Iorga in his *Notes et extraits pour servir à l'histoire des croisades du XVe siècle,* I, 281 f.

52. See F. Dölger, *Regesten der Kaiserurkunden,* II, 82 f. Nos. 1488, 1497–98; III, 48 ff. Nos. 1934, 1941, 1960; G. L. F. Tafel and G. M Thomas, *Urkunden zur älteren Handels- und Staatsgeschichte der Republik Venedig,* I, 151 ff.; G. Ostrogorsky, *History of the Byzantine State,* pp. 345, 403 f., 436 f., 469; E. Dalleggio d'Alessio's twin essays, "Galata et la souveraineté de Byzance," *REB,* XIX (= *Mélanges Raymond Janin),* 315–27; and "Listes des potestas de la colonie génoise de Péra (Galata), des prieures et sous-prieures de la Magnifica Communità," *ibid.,* XXI, 151–57 (covering the years 1264–1453 and 1539–1793, respectively). Much can still be learned from L. Sauli's old *Della colonia dei Genovesi in Galata;* and L. T. Belgrano's "Prima

serie di documenti riguardanti la colonia di Pera," *Atti* of the Società Ligure di Storia Patria, XIII, 97–336; and "Seconda serie," *ibid.*, pp. 931–1003; G. I. Bratianu, ed., *Actes des notaires génois de Péra et de Caffa de la fin du XIII*e *siècle* (covering the years 1281–90); N. Banescu, "Archives d'État de Gènes, officium provisionis Romaniae," *RESEE,* IV, 576–91; V, 225–63 (includes 45 documents of 1424–25). On the struggle between Genoa and Venice, see also the numerous documents published by F. Suditch in his *Genova e Venezia fra Tre e Quattrocento,* esp. pp. 143 ff.

Both republics also faced for a time strong competition from the Pisans who, as early as 1111, 1136, and 1170, had concluded favorable treaties with Emperors Alexius I, John II, and Manuel I. Although Genoa and Venice soon realized the danger of fighting one another and in 1299 concluded a treaty of "perpetual peace" (see Dölger, *Regesten,* II, 53 Nos. 1254–55, 60 No. 1312, 84 No. 1499; Tafel and Thomas, III, 391 ff.), their commercial rivalry was so intense that that treaty was quickly disregarded. Their recurrent hostilities made life extremely difficult for the native populations as well. See also, more generally, the highly informative work by W. Heyd, *Histoire du commerce du Levant au moyen-âge,* revised French trans. from the German by R. Raynaud, I, 264 ff.; G. I. Bratianu, *Recherches sur le commerce génois dans la Mer Noire au XIII*e *siècle;* R. Lopez, *Storia delle colonie genovesi nel Mediterraneo;* the lucid chronological survey of "Genoese Colonies in Greek Lands," in W. Miller's *Essays on the Latin Orient,* pp. 296 ff.; A. E. Laiou's analysis of the vicissitudes during the crucial reign of Andronicus II in *Constantinople and the Latins,* esp. pp. 260 ff.; and other writings, critically reviewed by V. Vitale in his "La Colonizzazione dei Genovesi nella storiografia più recente" in *Atti* of the III Congresso di Studi Coloniali.

53. Bartolomeo Senarega, *De rebus Genuensibus Commentaria ab anno MCDLXXXVIII usque ad annum MDXLIV,* ed. by E. Pandiani, in L. A. Muratori's ed. of *Rerum italicarum scriptores,* new ed. by G. Carducci *et al.*, XXIV, Part 8, pp. 24 f.; Joseph b. Joshua ha-Kohen, *'Emeq ha-bakha,* ed. by M. Letteris, pp. 100 f.; in W. Wiener's German trans., pp. 66 f., 199 f. nn. 233a–234, and other passages listed in his two indices, p. 222 *s.v.* Joseph ha-Cohen and p. 224 *s.v.* Genua; in H. S. May's recent English translation entitled *The Vale of Tears* (*Emek Habacha*), trans. plus critical commentary, esp. pp. 80 ff.; M. Stagliano, "Degli Ebrei in Genoa," *Giornale ligustico di archeologia, storia e belle arti,* III, 173–86, 394–415; G. Musso, "Per la storia degli Ebrei nella Repubblica di Genova tra il Quattro e il Cinquecento," *Miscellanea storica ligure,* III, 102–128, 203–225; idem, "Per la storia degli Ebrei nella seconda metà del Cinquecento," *Scritti in Memoria di Leone Carpi, Saggi sull'Ebraismo italiano,* ed. by D. Carpi *et al.*, pp. 101–111; and *supra,* Vols. IV, pp. 26, 331 f. n. 47; X, pp. 278, 424 f. n. 70; XIV, pp. 80, 336 n. 8.

54. See G. M. Thomas and R. Predelli, eds., *Diplomatarium,* pp. 103 ff. No. lix; N. Iorga, "Notices et extraits pour servir à l'histoire des croisades au XV*e* s.," *ROL,* IV, 71; Bertrandon de La Brocquière, *Voyage d'outre mer,* ed. by C. Schefer, p. 141; H. Noiret, *Documents inédits,* pp. 179 ff.; F. Thiriet, *Régestes,* I, 51 No. 152; II, 68 No. 1238; D. Gioffré, "Atti rogati in Chio nella seconda metà del XIV secolo," *Bulletin* of the Institut Historique Belge de Rome, XXXIV, 319–404, esp. pp. 348 f. No. 45, 389 f. No. 78 (referring to Sabata Petino and Elia Grammatico of Pera and their transactions with Jews of Chiòs in 1398; see *infra,* nn. 55–56); D. Jacoby, "Les Quartiers juifs de Constantinople," *Byzantion,* XXXVII, esp, pp. 215 f. Jacoby ex-

pected to find additional data in Genoa's famed notarial archives, which have not yet been utilized as effectively for the Genoese colonies as they have for the home community. See also *supra*, n. 49. Only in recent years have a series of partial studies based on the records of the Genoese notaries in such commercial Black Sea centers as Kilia, Kaffa, and Licostomo seen the light of day. See G. Pistarino, *Notai genovesi in Oltremare. Atti rogati a Chilia da Antonio di Ponzò,* followed by similar publications relating to Kaffa and other localities in 1973 and so forth, ed. by S. Raiteri *et al.* See also O. Iliescu's observations, "Nouvelles éditions d'actes notariés instrumentés au XIVe siècle dans les colonies génoises des bouches de Danube," *RESEE,* XV, 113–27. However, these monographs cover, as a rule, only the records of brief spans of time.

More significantly, in comparison with Venice, the Genoese colonies generally do not have that splendid resource of the quantitatively and qualitatively unsurpassed dispatches of the Constantinople bailos and other envoys to their home office. For several generations past these reports have served as an inexhaustible source of information and insights for scholars of many nations concerning various phases of modern European and mid-Eastern history. Yet, a more thorough investigation of the entire correspondence between the Genoese authorities at home and their representatives in the colonies and other lands, including the as yet unpublished materials, is likely to shed some new and important light on many aspects of Byzantine, colonial, and Ottoman history. The Genoese podestas in Pera-Galata alone had numerous occasions to report home on events and trends in their locality and the areas around it. On their names and periods of service, see E. Dalleggio d'Alessio, "Listes," *REB,* XXI, 151–57 (*supra,* n. 52).

55. Benjamin of Tudela's *Massa'ot,* ed. by M. N. Adler, pp. 14 (English), 17 (Hebrew); *supra,* Vol. III, pp. 191 f., 330 n. 23; W. Miller, *The Latins in the Levant: a History of Frankish Greece (1204–1566),* esp. pp. 283 ff., 298 ff.; idem, *Essays on the Latin Orient, passim* (see Index *s.v.* Chios); A. Galanté, *Histoire des Juifs de Rhodes, Chio, Cos, etc.,* pp. 145 ff.; and particularly D. Jacoby's pertinent study of "The Jews of Chios under Genoese Rule, 1346–1566" (Hebrew), *Zion,* XXVI, 180–97. The most comprehensive treatment of the Jews of Chios under Genoese and Ottoman domination is included in P. P. Argenti's *The Religious Minorities of Chios,* pp. 100 ff., 371 ff. with documentary excerpts, largely dating from the Turkish period. See also D. Jacoby's corrections in his review of that work in *BZ,* LXIX, 108–111.

Much can also be learned from Argenti's general works dealing with Chios. See especially his ed. of Hieronimo Giustiniani's *History of Chios;* his and S. P. Kuriakides' collection of source materials in their comp. of *He Chios parà toîs geográphois kaì periegetaîs* (Chios According to the Geographers and Travelers); and his analytical works *Chius Vincta, or The Occupation of Chios by the Turks (1566), Their Administration of the Island (1566–1912) in Contemporary Diplomatic Reports and Official Dispatches,* with a Preface by S. Gaselee; and *The Occupation of Chios by the Genoese, 1346–1566, and Their Administration of the Island,* with a Preface by S. Runciman. See also Argenti's *Bibliography of Chios from Classical Times to 1936,* with a Preface by T. C. Myers. All these works are replete with excerpts from archival and printed sources which bring much new light to the history of the Aegean islands in general. For instance, Vol. III of *The Occupation of Chios by the Genoese* consists entirely of excerpts from notarial deeds, at least two of which relate to Jews, pp. 743 ff. No. 263 (1456), 769 ff. No. 277 (1457).

56. Nicolas de Nicolay, *Les Quatre premiers livres des navigations et pérégrinations orientales,* Lyons, 1568, p. 52, or in the English trans. by T. Washington the Younger entitled *The Navigations, Peregrinations and Voyages Made into Turkey,* London, 1585, fol. 37b, referring to "a number of Jews which seuerally haue one streete to dwell in, and because they should be better knowen from others, they are constrayned to weare for a token a great cappe of yellowe colour" (this work is also available in an Italian translation, published in Venice in 1580); Hieronimo Giustiniani, *History of Chios,* ed. with an Intro. by P. P. Argenti, p. 65; and other sources quoted in Argenti's *The Occupation of Chios,* esp. p. 442 n. 2; and his *The Religious Minorities of Chios,* pp. 118 f. We greatly depend, however, on Italian-writing notaries for economic data on the Jews of Chios. See, in particular, the data offered by Argenti, as well as by D. Gioffré in his "Atti Rogati in Chio," *Bulletin* of the Institut Historique Belge de Rome, XXXIV, 393 No. 81, 396 f. No. 83 (also *supra,* n. 54); and by P. Villa in "Documenti sugli Ebrei a Chio nel 1394" in *Atti* of the Società Ligure di Storia Patria, n.s. V (LXXXIX), fasc. 1.

As to Argenti's query, however, about the presence of Jewish notaries in Chios, we may assume that there were some Jewish scribes on the island. They were needed for the copying of biblical, rabbinic, liturgical, and literary texts, as well as for the preparation of marital and business deeds. On the other hand, the public notarial profession as such, bearing a semiofficial character, was probably closed to Jews, although in some Western areas like Sicily, Jewish notaries were allowed to exercise their profession. See my *JC,* II, 110 ff.; III, 139 f. No definite answer to such problems can be given, so long as we possess almost no data about the Jewish communal and intellectual activities in Chios. Even a Jewish scholarly visitor like Yehudah (Leon) b. Moses Mosconi of Ochrida, who in his extensive travels had come to Chios about 1360, mentions the Jews of the island only in passing without referring to any rabbi by name, as he did, for instance, in Negroponte. See *supra,* n. 35; and the brief biographical sketches by A. Berliner in his "Super-Commentare zu Abraham ibn Esra, I: Jehuda b. Mosconi," *Magazin für die Wissenschaft des Judenthums,* III, 41–51; and M. Steinschneider, "Jehuda Mosconi, Nachtrag," *ibid.,* pp. 94–100, 140–53, 190–206.

57. See H. Giustiniani, *History of Chios,* ed. with an Intro. by P. P. Argenti, pp. 403 f. (also mentioning without special emphasis the continued practice in the Chios churches of the recitation on Good Friday of the old prayer for Jews and other "infidels" which long antedated the Great Schism between the Roman Catholic and the Eastern Churches; p. 405); see *supra,* Vols. II, pp. 169, 395 n. 52; V, pp. 351 f. n. 68. Pope Martin V's letter of 1423 was ed. from a Vatican MS by Argenti in *The Religious Minorities,* p. 373 App. I No. 1; the excerpt here quoted is given in a variant from Argenti's translation, *ibid.,* p. 123. Generally speaking, however, Martin V was more friendly to Jews than were other popes of the period. See F. Vernet, "Le Pape Martin V et les Juifs," *Revue des questions d'histoire moderne,* LI, 373–423. Nicolas de Nicolay's report (in his *Les Quatre premiers livres,* pp. 52, 150) probably refers to his visit to Chios in 1551 and his subsequent observations in the Ottoman Empire before the publication of his book. See Argenti, p. 124, esp. n. 3.

58. A. Galanté, *Histoire des Juifs de Rhodes, Chio, Cos, etc.,* pp. 146 f.; J. Starr, *Romania,* pp. 96 f.; P. P. Argenti, *The Religious Minorities,* pp. 140, 142 f. See also, more generally, Argenti's *Chius Vincta,* pp. lxxii ff., 56 ff. Docs. 24–30; idem, *The Occupation of Chios by the Genoese,* esp. I, 361 f. To be sure, in his list of Chios

rabbis (*The Religious Minorities*, p. 541 App. II) Argenti mentions three rabbis who resided on the island in the years 1360–98. However, we know practically nothing about these individuals and even their title, as given in non-Jewish documents (quoted by Argenti on pages listed in the Appendix), may be a reflection of the practice, widespread since the anti-Karaite reaction, of naming ordinary laymen with the prefix rabbi. See *supra,* Vol. V, pp. 283, 416 n. 85.

59. See the sources listed in the preceding note; and *supra,* Vol. III, pp. 12 f., 233 n. 11. The relative weakness of the Chian Inquisition may also have been the result of the absence of a serious Protestant threat among the dominant Italian minority on the island. Perhaps the most important sixteenth-century native of Chios who played a certain role in the "heretical" activities of the time, Jacob Palaeologus, evinced his radical propensities only after he left the island and spent some time in a Constantinople monastery (1553–54). He subsequently made an adventurous career in Italy, Austria, Poland and Transylvania, where he died in 1585 under inquisitorial indictment. See L. Szczucki, "Jacob of Chios Palaeologus (a Biographical Sketch)" (Polish), *Odrodzenie i Reformacja w Polsce,* XI, 63–91; XIII, 5–50; and other literature, including Palaeologus' *Catechesis christianae dies XII,* which shows his attitude to Jews and Judaism, quoted *supra,* Vol. XVI, pp. 70, 347 f. n. 76.

60. See P. P. Argenti's analysis of the Jewish economic activities in Chios in his *The Religious Minorities,* pp. 137 ff.; idem, *The Occupation of Chios,* III, 743 ff. No. 264, 769 ff. No. 277, 803 f. No. 315, etc.; idem and K. J. Rose, *The Folk-Lore of Chios,* II, 596 item 11, 944 item 19; and D. Jacoby, "The Jews of Chios," *Zion,* XXVI, 194 ff. Argenti's contention, however, that a Jewish shipwright named Moyse Lachano appears in a document of 1457 (which he reproduces in *The Religious Minorities,* pp. 373 ff. App. I No. 2) seems to be erroneous. The date given in the Appendix is 1456 and Lachana (!) is characterized as a *judeus cirugicus,* that is surgeon. But that some such maritime occupation could have occurred among Jews is not to be ruled out. The *escama* of 1537 adopted by the Rhodian community is reproduced in its characteristic mixture of Ladino and Hebrew by A. Galanté in his *Histoire des Juifs des Rhodes, Chio, Cos, etc.,* pp. 55 f. While this is couched in a purely religious terminology and probably prompted primarily by concern for the ritualistic purity of the wine to be consumed by Jews, it is not impossible that the Rhodian elders were also motivated by a desire to reduce the business competition from their coreligionists residing in Chios, Crete, and Naxos. On Z. Ankori's thesis concerning the "agro-urban" character of Cretan Jewry see *supra,* n. 7.

61. See O. Iliescu, "Nouvelles éditions," *RESEE,* XV, 119; the notarial and other records cited *supra,* nn. 12 and 54; Vol. XVI, pp. 49, 335 n. 53. The myth of the early medieval Jewish dominance in the slave trade has been controverted by E. Täubler in his "Zur Handelsbedeutung der Juden in Deutschland vor Beginn des Städtewesens," *Martin Philippson Festschrift,* pp. 370–92, esp. pp. 381 ff., 392. See also, more broadly, my discussion, *supra,* Vol. IV, pp. 187 ff., 332 ff. nn. 48 ff., esp. n. 59.

62. See *supra,* Chap. LXXI, nn. 4 and 9; N. D. Fustel de Coulanges's graphic sketch of the monastery's history in the "Mémoire sur l'île de Chios" in his *Questions historiques,* rev. and completed from his notes by C. Jullian, pp. 325–38, esp. p. 332. Despite their reluctance to allow ecclesiastical courts to interfere in the in-

ternal affairs of other than their own respective denominations and their rejection of inquisitorial prosecutions by any Holy Office on the island, the Genoese authorities generally tried to promote the interests of the Catholic Church, their most dependable ally in their colonial ventures. See *supra,* nn. 58–59; and G. Hofmann, *Vescovadi cattolici nella Grecia* (*Orientalia christiana,* XCII, CVII, CXII, CXV, CXXX), esp. Vol. I: *Chios.*

63. See Nicolas de Nicolay, *Les Quatre premiers livres,* p. 150, or *The Navigations,* fol. 131b; J. Starr, *Romania,* p. 98; D. Jacoby's strictures on Starr's thesis in his "The Jews in Chios" (Hebrew), *Zion,* XXVI, 191; P. P. Argenti, *The Religious Minorities,* pp. 143 ff., 160. The Turkish decree transmitted by Don Joseph to the Jew of Chios on his visit in 1567 is reproduced in a French trans. by A. Galanté in his *Histoire des Juifs des Rhodes, Chio, Cos, etc.,* pp. 13 ff., 53 ff.

Subsequently Jewish life in Chios remained unaffected by either the application of the original Turkish charter issued on May 29, 1453 in favor of the Genoese citizens principally in Constantinople, or by the short and inept, if temporarily destructive, Florentine invasion of Chios in 1599, which left a permanent imprint on the local folklore. Until recently mothers trying to frighten naughty children threatened them with "The Florentines are coming." See N. D. Fustel de Coulanges, *Questions historiques,* p. 357. By mere chance a Jewish refugee from a famine in Safed, Jacob b. Yehudah Ashkenazi, landed in Chios on May 1, 1599 and thus became an eye-witness to the Florentine attack. See his brief Hebrew description of that event, ed. with an English trans. and notes by J. Leveen in "An Eye-Witness Account of the Expedition of the Florentines against Chios in 1599" in *BSOAS,* XII, 542–54; and, more generally, P. P. Argenti's *The Expedition of the Florentines to Chios (1599). Described in Contemporary Diplomatic Reports and Military Dispatches.*

64. See I Macc. 15:23; Josephus, *Antiquities,* xiv, 7, 2.112; xvi, 2, 2.18–20; and the brief data assembled by A. Galanté in his *Histoire des Juifs des Rhodes, Chio, Cos, etc.,* pp. 161–78. Most of Galanté's notes are largely based on what he was able to ascertain on his numerous trips to these localities while serving as Turkish inspector of education for that district. See A. Elmaleh's biographical sketch *Ha-Professor Abraham Galante* (Le Professeur A. G.; sa vie et son œuvre littéraire, historique et scientifique), pp. 16 f., 26 ff. With respect to Mytilene, Galanté was also able to add bits of information in his monograph, *Don Salomon Aben Yaèche duc de Mételin,* pp. 20 f. However, we are poorly informed about the extent to which the title of duke influenced Alvaro Mendes in actually governing the island and we know still less about the impact, if any, of his regime upon his coreligionists there. Alvaro's scintillating career, mentioned *supra,* Vol. XV, pp. 83 f., 128 ff., 415 f. n. 13, 434 nn. 65–68, will be more fully discussed in the next volume.

65. L. de Mas-Latrie, *Histoire de l'ile de Chypre,* II, 359, etc.; G. F. Hill, *A History of Cyprus,* III; N. Banescu, *Le Déclin de Famagouste; supra,* nn. 38–39; and Vol. XIV, pp. 79 ff., 335 f. nn. 7–8.

66. See M. Balard, *Gênes et l'Outremer,* Vol. I: *Les Actes de Caffa du notaire di Sambuceto, 1289–1290,* esp. pp. 141 f. No. 371; G. Pistarino, *Notai genovesi in Oltremare. Atti rogati a Chilia da Antonio di Ponzo;* with additional data in O. Iliescu's "Nouvelles éditions d'actes notariés instrumentés au XIVe siècle dans les colonies

génoises des bouches de Danube—Actes de Kilia (1360–61) et de Licostomo (1373 et 1383–84)," *RESEE,* XV, 113–27. See also other notarial documents ed. by G. Balbi and S. Raiteri, *Notai genovesi in Oltremare. Atti rogati a Caffa e a Licostomo (sec. xiv)*; S. Raiteri, *Atti rogati a Licostomo da Domenico da Carignano (1373), Oberto Grasso da Voltri (1383–84).*

The English Naturalization Act of 1740 and its sequel in the "Jew Bill" of 1753 have been discussed extensively in the pertinent literature. Here it suffices to refer to the sources cited in my *Steeled by Adversity,* ed. by J. M. Baron, esp. pp. 93 ff., 595 nn. 27–32.

67. See the large collection of important documents assembled by S. Ljubič *et al.* in their *Monumenta spectantia historiam Slavorum meridionalium;* and such comprehensive general works as A. Philippson, *Das Byzantinische Reich als geographische Erscheinung;* F. Dölger, *Byzanz und die europäische Staatenwelt. Ausgewählte Vorträge und Aufsätze,* esp. pp. 70 ff. ("Rom und die Gedankenwelt der Byzantiner"), 140 ff. ("Bulgarisches Zartum und byzantinisches Kaisertum"); F. Dvornik, *The Slav in European History and Civilization;* N. Iorga, *Byzance après Byzance. Constinuation de l'histoire de la vie byzantine,* new impression with a Preface by M. Berza and a Postscript by V. Chudova; I. Dujčev, *Medioevo bizantino-slavo* (a comprehensive collection of 104 essays pertaining to political, socioeconomic, and literary history); idem, *Slavia orthodoxa: Collected Studies in the History of the Slavic Middle Ages,* with a Preface by I. Sevčenko; such briefer surveys as W. Miller, "The Byzantine Inheritance in South-Eastern Europe" in *Byzantium: an Introduction to East Roman Civilization,* ed. by N. H. Baynes and H. St. L. B. Moss, pp. 326–37; S. Runciman, "Byzantium and the Slavs," *ibid.,* pp. 338–68; and M. Dinić, "The Balkans, 1018–1499," *The Cambridge Medieval History,* IV, i, pp. 519–65. Many additional insights and up-to-date bibliographical materials are found in D. Obolensky's study, *The Byzantine Commonwealth: Eastern Europe, 500–1453;* the numerous monographs listed in the *Südosteuropa-Bibliographie,* Vols. I–IV; and the *Südosteuropa Dissertationen, 1918–1960. Eine Bibliographie deutscher, österreichischer und schweizerischer Hochschulschriften,* ed. by A. Scherer.

68. King Agrippa I's letter to Caligula, reproduced in Philo Judaeus, *Legatio ad Caium,* xxxvi.276 ff., cited here in the new English trans. by E. M. Smallwood in her *Philonis Alexandrini Legatio ad Gaium,* ed. with an Intro., Trans. and Commentary, pp. 122 ff., esp. p. 124, with the comments thereon, pp. 291 f.; Acts of the Apostles, 2:9–11; J. B. Frey, ed., *Corpus Inscriptionum Judaicarum,* I, 487 ff. Nos. 675 ff., esp. pp. 492 No. 681, 504 f. No. 694, 592 No. 102*; and other sources listed *supra,* Vols. I, pp. 167 ff., 218, 369 ff. nn. 3 f.; II, pp. 10, 210, 330 f. n. 8, 406 f. n. 42; III, pp. 208 f., 328 n. 39, 330 n. 46; to which is to be added A. (S.) Scheiber, ed., *Magyarországi zsidó feliratok* (Corpus inscriptionum Hungariae judaicarum, a temporibus saeculi III., quae exstant, usque ad annum 1686), with a German summary; and E. R. Goodenough, *Jewish Symbols in the Greco-Roman Period,* Vols. I–XIII. On the available general archaeological data on the ancient Roman provinces in the Balkans, see R. F. Hodinott, *Bulgaria in Antiquity: an Archaeological Introduction,* Part II.

69. Pope Nicholas I's reply to Boris I of 866 is reproduced in the pope's "Epistolae et decreta," *PL,* CXIX, 978 ff., No. xcvii, 1014 f. Art. civ. On Cyril and Methodius, the Glagolitic and Cyrillic alphabets, and related problems, see *supra,* Vol. III, pp. 209 f.,

330 f. nn. 45–47. To the bibliography listed there add H. Scheleskiner's "Konstantinisches Alphabet und glagolitisches und kyrillisches Schriftzeichensystem," *Wiener Slawistisches Jahrbuch,* XVIII, 96–99. See also, more generally, W. N. Zlatarsky *et al., Geschichte der Bulgaren,* esp. Vol. I, covering the period of 677–1396, with good historical maps showing at a glance the changing frontiers of medieval Bulgaria. On the title tsar, see G. Moravcsik, "Zur Geschichte des Herrschertitels Caesar-Tsar" (1963), reprinted in his *Studia byzantina,* pp. 267–74; and, more broadly, V. Beševliev's "Die Kaiseridee bei den Protobulgaren," *Byzantiná,* III, 83–92.

Evidently, the almost constant wars, the fluidity of frontiers, the incessant ethnocultural mixtures, and limited economic opportunities were all conducive to holding down both the size and the security of Jewish settlements in the entire Balkan area. They were even more detrimental to the creation of permanent Jewish institutions, the development of well-rooted Jewish cultural centers and traditions, and the preservation of valuable historical records. Nor were there enough modern Jewish scholars and organizations able and willing to devote concentrated energies to the recapture of all the surviving vestiges of the medieval and early modern Jewish civilization in the Balkan areas before their incorporation into the Ottoman Empire. It is therefore not surprising that, for instance, S. Israel's valuable survey of the "État actuel, problèmes et perspectives de historiographie judéo-balcaniques," *Études Balkaniques,* VII, no. 2, pp. 120–34, reveals, despite its relatively rich bibliography, esp. for Yugoslavia, so many gaps in our knowledge.

70. See Pope Gregory IX's letters of 1238 to John Assen II, Bela IV, and Baldwin II in his *Epistolae,* excerpted in his *Registres,* ed. by L. Auvray, II. See also the Hebrew letter addressed by a physician Elijah to the convert Pablo Christiani, reproduced in H. Kishales, *Qorot Yehude Bulgariah* (A History of the Jews of Bulgaria), I, 60 ff., 74 f.

71. See S. Mézan, *Les Juifs espagnoles en Bulgarie,* Vol. I: *Histoire, statistique, ethnographie* (the introductory chapter repeats many fanciful conjectures advanced by S. A. Rosanes and others); M. Molho and A. Meborah, *Histoire des Israélites de Castoria;* and, more generally, D. Angelov, "La Formation de la nationalité bulgare," *Études Balkaniques,* V, no. 4, pp. 14–37. Much new information on the history of the Jews in Bulgaria and other Balkan countries during the medieval and early modern periods can be found in numerous articles in the English-language *Annual,* published by the Social, Cultural and Educational Association of the Jews in the People's Republic of Bulgaria. See esp. the list of contributions by the late Eli Eshkenazy, listed in the "Index of the Articles and Materials Published in the *Annual* during the Period 1966–1972" in Vol. VII, pp. 307–310. Although most of his data are derived from long-familiar rabbinic writings and, regrettably, are devoid of much new archival documentation, these papers mark a significant step in the investigation of that much-neglected area. A good deal can also be learned from outside sources, such as those stemming from the Dubrovnik archives (see *infra,* nn. 103 ff.). For instance, in her "De l'activité des associations commerciales de Ragusa (Dubrovnik) dans les terres bulgares au XVe et XVIe siècles," *Bulgarian Historical Review,* II, 90–104, I. D. Spisarevska mentions a Jewish partnership of Juda Benjamin of Bursa (Brusa) and Esdra Navarro of Sofia which traded extensively in skins and clothes in Sofia and Dubrovnik. At its liquidation in 1542, Esdra owed Juda the substantial sum of 50,000 piastres (p. 100). See also the recent, more

comprehensive treatment in *Qorot Yehude Bulgariah* by H. Kishales, esp. pp. 66–92 covering the period of 1018–1389. This work is more informative for the later periods.

72. See the literature cited *supra*, n. 67; and Z. Pljakov, "Über das soziale Gepräge der bulgarischen Stadt im XV. bis zur Mitte des XVII. Jahrhunderts," *Byzantinobulgarica*, III, 231–44; E. Chrysos, "Zur Entstehung der Institution der autocephalen Erzbistümer," *BZ*, LXII, 263–86; and D. Angelov's somewhat overdrawn picture of "Die Feudalen Verhältnisse und der Klassenkampf in den balkanischen Staaten im Spätmittelalter (13.–15. Jahrhundert)," *Zeitschrift für Geschichte*, VI, 1283–1308. Bogomilism, founded by the tenth-century Bulgarian heresiarch Bogomil (a Slavonic version of Theophilus), spread all over the Balkans, became for a time the state religion of Bosnia, and, through returning Crusaders, influenced the "heretical" movements in France and Italy. See especially D. Obolensky, *The Bogomils: a Study in Balkan Neo-Manichaeism;* D. Dragojlović, "Bogomilisme et mouvements hérétiques dualistes du moyen âge," *Balcanica*, IV, 121–43; and T. S. Thomov, "Les Appellations des 'Bogomiles' et 'Bulgares' et leurs variants et équivalents en Orient et en Occident," *Études Balkaniques*, 1973, no. 1, pp. 77–99. The ideological and practical interrelations between the exponents of the Bogomil doctrines and Jews and Judaism, a field hitherto almost totally neglected by scholars, would merit monographic treatment. See also L. Kirkova and M. Petrova, "Bibliographie des publications les plus importantes sur l'histoire bulgare du moyen âge et sur l'histoire de Byzance parues en 1907–1970," *Byzantinobulgarica*, IV, 371–410.

73. See particularly Y. Eventov, *Toledot Yehude Yugoslavia* (A History of Yugoslav Jews), ed. by Z. Rotem, Vol. I: From Ancient Times to the End of the Nineteenth Century (with English and Serbian summaries); and the brief comments thereon by Z. Laker in his "New Books on the History of Yugoslavia's Jews," *JQR*, LXIII, 323–37. The great difficulties (even regarding terminology) of segregating the different ethnic strains which combined in making up the medieval mixture from which the present Yugoslav nation has emerged, have rightly been pointed up by B. Grafenauer in his analysis of *Die Ethnische Gliederung und geschichtliche Rolle der westlichen Südslaven im Mittelalter*, with interesting graphic illustrations; and S. Liser's comments thereon in "Die Konzeption von Prof. B. Grafenauer über die Ethnogenese der Balkanslaven," *Byzantinobulgarica*, IV, 345–54. See also J. C. Jireček, *Geschichte der Serben*, Vols. I–II, I (to 1537); idem, *Staat und Gesellschaft im mittelalterlichen Serbien. Studien zur Kulturgeschichte des 13.–15. Jahrhunderts* in *Denkschriften* of the Vienna Academy, LVI, Parts 2–3; LVIII, Part 2; LXIV, Part 2 (this concluding section was posthumously ed. from the author's MS by V. Jagič), esp. II (LVI, 3), 52; M. Maladinovitsch's stimulating Paris dissertation, *Le Caractère de l'État Serbe au moyen âge*, esp. pp. 94 ff. Without referring to Jews Maladinovitsch argues—not too convincingly—that next to the territorial principle, the personal principle had played no role in Serbian laws. Yet, despite the absence of any direct evidence, it appears likely that the few Jews living in medieval Serbia were treated differently than members of the majority or of the other ethnic minorities. Numerous more recent publications are analyzed in the bibliographical work edited by J. Tadić *et al.* and published by the Comité National Yougoslave des Sciences Historiques, for the benefit of the participants in the X International Congress of Historical Sciences in Rome, September 1955, *Dix années d'historiographie*

yougoslave 1945–1955; continued in Tadić's ed., for the Federation of Historical Societies of Yugoslavia, of the *Historiographie yougoslave, 1955–1965.*

74. See D. Obolensky, *The Byzantine Commonwealth,* esp. pp. 242 ff., 247 f., 250, 254 f., Stephen Dushan's *Zakonik* (Code), ed. by S. Navakovič; or in the new ed. by N. Radojčić; in M. Burr's English translation in his "The Code of Stephan Dušan Tsar and Autocrat of the Serbs and Greeks. Trans. from the Old Serbian, with Notes," *The Slavonic* [*and East European*] *Review,* XXVIII, 198–217, 516–39, esp. pp. 199 f. Arts. 6 and 9–10, 214 Art. 85; and the general comments on that code by A. Soloviev in his *Zakonodavstvo Stefana Dušana* (The Legislative Activities of Stephen Dushan, the Tsar of Serbs and Greeks), *passim.* The importance attached to Dushan's law code by modern Serbo-Croatian historians is well illustrated by the numerous publications, referring to text, substance, and influence of that code, by N. Radojčić and others, as analyzed by J. Tadić *et al.* in *Dix années d'historiographie,* pp. 202 ff. Nor was the code limited to the Serbo-Croatian area. That (together with some older Byzantine materials) it also penetrated Rumania has been shown, with the aid of a fifteenth-century MS found in Bistritsa, Walachia, by V. A. Georgesco in his "Présentation de quelques manuscrits juridiques de Valachie et de Moldavie (XVe–XIXe siècles). Contribution à l'étude de la réception du droit byzantin en Roumanie," *RESEE,* VI, 625–38; VII, 335–45; esp. VI, 626 ff.

75. See, for instance, G. Stökl's Breslau dissertation, *Der Südslawische Bibeldruck im 16. Jahrhundert und die Südostgrenze des Reiches;* E. Tardeanu's twin essays, "L'Apocalypse de Baruch en Slave," *Revue des études slaves,* XLVIII, 23–48; and "Les Testaments des douze patriarches," *Journal for the Study of Judaism,* I, 48–84; and G. Freidhof, "Zur ersten Übersetzung des 3. Buches der Makkabäer ins Ostslawische," *Slawistische Studien,* 1972, pp. 75–80. On the Belgrade Jews of 1688, see Moses b. Michael Kohen's autobiographical *'Eṭ sofer* (Pen of a Scribe: a Guide to Letter Writing), Fürth, 1691; with D. Ginsberg's brief analysis in his "Moses Kohen aus Beograd und sein Epistolarium," *Revue internationale des études balkaniques,* II, nos. 5–6, pp. 574–80; and the shorter allusions thereto in another refugee's report, ed. and interpreted by D. Kaufmann in his "Joseph ibn Danon de Belgrade," *REJ,* XXXVII, 284–98, esp. pp. 288 f., 292 f.

76. See J. B. Frey's *Corpus Inscriptionum,* I, 491 No. 680; B. Gabričević, "The Jewish Community in Ancient Salona" (Serbo-Croatian), *Jevrejski Almanach,* 1959–60, pp. 9–15; various other essays in that journal, Vols. I–VI; V. Lamansky, *Secrets d'État de Venise,* I, 502 ff. (citing a fragment from Nicolò Contarini's historical work); and, more generally, R. Paci, *La "Scala" di Spalato e il commercio veneziano nei Balcani fra Cinque e Seicento.* Because of the highly diverse conditions in Albania, Dalmatia, Croatia, and Slovenia, the literature on the Jewish inhabitants of these areas is extremely scattered. Among the best monographs are those by G. Novak, *Židovi u Splitu* (Jews in Split-Spalato); D. Kečkemet, *Zidovi v povijesti Splita* (Jews in the History of Split); and I. Šlang, *Jevreji u Beogradu* (Jews in Belgrade). The insecurity of travel on the Adriatic Sea is well illustrated by the incident described in I. Dujčev's ed. of *Avvisi di Ragusa,* pp. 159 ff., relating to a ship captured at sea with forty families from Candia including some Jews; S. Mitrani-Samarian in his note, "Deux Juifs captivés par les uscoques," *REJ,* LIV, 280–81 (reproducing a brief document from the *Monumenta Hungariae Historica*). See also

Monumenta historiam Uscocorum illustrantia; J. Tadić, "Venezia e la costa orientale dell'Adriatico fino al secolo XV," *Civiltà Veneziana, Studi,* XXVII, 687–704; and, more generally, the older but still very informative studies by J. K. Jireček, *Die Romanen in den Städten Dalmatiens während des Mittelalters;* idem, *Staat und Gesellschaft im mittelalterlichen Serbien.*

77. See *supra,* n. 22. From the large literature on Dubrovnik-Ragusa we need mention here only the comprehensive recent study by F. W. Carter, *Dubrovnik (Ragusa): a Classic City-State;* such earlier monographs as J. Tadić's *Pomorska tragovina Dubrovnika svšetskom sredniego vijeka* (Dubrovnik's Maritime Trade during the Middle Ages); idem, "Les Archives économiques de Raguse," *Annales ESC,* XVI, 1158–75, esp. pp. 1168 ff.; idem, *Ragusa e il suo porto nel Cinquecento. Per una storia tra le due sponde Adriatiche;* and B. Krekić, *Dubrovnik in the 14th and 15th Centuries: a City between East and West.*

78. See the standard work on the Jews of Dubrovnik by J. Tadić, *Jevreji u Dubrovniku do polovine XVII stoljeća* (The Jews in Dubrovnik to the Middle of the Seventeenth Century), with a documentary appendix, pp. 413–16, and a fairly detailed French summary, pp. 437–58, esp. pp. 52, 59 ff. (with reference to Isaac and Yehudah Abravanel).

79. The statement by Jacob Salomonis is reproduced by M. J. Dinić in his *Iz Dubrovačkog archiva* (From the Dubrovnik Archive), III, 169 f. No. 336. On the two contracts of 1402 and 1431, see B. Krekić, *Dubrovnik (Raguse) et le Levant au moyen âge,* esp. pp. 223, No. 361, 246 No. 503, 294 No. 790. The involvement of a Jew of Trani with two Catalan Christians in 1422–31 is the less surprising as the kingdom of Naples was at that time under Aragonese domination and mercantile relationships between Dubrovnik and the Aragonese possessions were quite intensive, particularly under the reign of the enterprising and pro-Jewish King Ferrante (1458–84). See M. Spremić, *Dubrovnik i Aragontsi, 1442–1495* (Dubrovnik e gli Aragonesi, 1442–1495; with an Italian summary); and P. Sposato, "Attività commerciali degli Aragonesi nella seconda metà del Quattrocento," *Studi in onore di Riccardo Filangieri,* II, 213–31, esp. pp. 215 f. (on Ferrante), 225 f. App. i (Ferdinand the Catholic's letter of October 3, 1484, relating to Anello Perosso's company, which had a contract with Sidi Ahametto Albehyes of Cairo involving the large investment of 100,000 gold ducats by each party). Even earlier, however, King Frederick III of Sicily successfully intervened in 1309 in favor of the heirs of a Syracuse Jew, Leon Turtuvideo in the district of Jadar (Western Serbia), where seemingly he had owned some land. See *Monumenta spectantia historiam Slavorum meridionalium,* ed. by S. Ljubič, K. Horvat, *et al.,* I, 235 f. No. cclxii. On the reign of the enterprising King Ferrante, when Jewish businessmen were favorably treated on both sides of the Adriatic, see *supra,* Vol. X, pp. 241 ff., 245, 406 ff. nn. 26 and 31.

80. N. H. Biegman, *The Turco-Ragusan Relationship According to the Firmāns of Murād III (1575–1595) Extant in the State Archives of Dubrovnik,* esp. pp. 40, 108, 110 (citing the *Lettere di Levante);* J. Tadić, *Jevreji u Dubrovniku,* esp. pp. 361 ff. See also, more generally, I. Mitić, "Le Service consulaire de la République Ragusaine" (Serbo-Croatian), *Pomorski Zbornik,* II, 1733–45; and N. Steengaard, "Consuls and Nations in the Levant from 1570 to 1650," *Scandinavian Eco-*

nomic History Review, XV, 13–55. On the extensive slave trade within the Byzantine area including that under Venetian control see, for instance, the following reprints of C. Verlinden's essays: "Le Recrutement des esclaves à Venise aux XIVe et XVe siècles," *Studia historica Gandensia,* No. 108, 83–202; idem, "La Législation vénitienne du bas moyen âge en matière d'esclavage," *ibid.,* No. 40, pp. 129–72; idem, "L'Esclavage sur la côte dalmate au bas moyen âge," *ibid.,* No. 41, pp. 57–140; and H. Köpstein, "Zum byzantinischen Sklavenhandel," *Wissenschaftliche Zeitschrift der Karl Marx Universität Leipzig,* XV, 487–93. We must bear in mind, however, that the occasional restrictive policies of the Salonican Jewish community did not always enjoy the unanimous support of its members. In 1675 and later, the Jewish merchants themselves petitioned the rabbis to annul the earlier impeditive Jewish ordinance which, they claimed, only helped to enrich their non-Jewish competitors. Nonetheless the ordinance remained in force for a total of some 250 years. See I. S. Emmanuel, *Histoire de l'industrie des tissus des Israélites de Salonique,* pp. 60 f. The underlying economic factors will be more fully discussed in connection with the general economic developments in Ottoman Jewry in the next volume.

It has also been observed that, under the difficult and perilous Balkan system of communications, many conquering soldiers found that captives yielded them much larger sums when ransomed or sold as slaves than they could obtain from the disposal of looted goods which they were able to carry away. See P. F. Sugar, "The 'Professional Prisoner' on the Western Borders of the Empire in the Sixteenth and Seventeenth Centuries," *Études Balkaniques,* VII, no. 2, pp. 82–91. Jews probably appeared as preferred objects for seizure because of the readiness of their foreign coreligionists to redeem them at high prices. Such cases were recorded even in the period of relative security and affluence of the Byzantine Empire; see *supra,* Vol. IV, pp. 109 ff., 177 f., 295 f. nn. 25–28, 326 n. 34.

81. J. Tadić, *Jevreji u Dubrovniku,* pp. 77, 92 ff., 415, 421 f., 425 (reproducing excerpts from the protocols concerning the decrees of May–June 1498, December 7, 1514, May 4, 1515, and June 16, 1571); *supra,* n. 76; Vol. XIV, pp. 78 f., 325 n. 6.

82. H. Bjelovučić, *The Ragusan Republic: Victim of Napoleon and Its Own Conservatism,* p. 60; G. Fedalto, *La Chiesa latina in Oriente,* Vol. I. The Ragusan pride in independence found expression even more frequently in secular matters. In its oft-quoted sentence of 1551 a Dubrovnik tribunal repudiated a judgment of the Venetian Consulato del Mare as "not valid, for this city governs itself according to its own laws, and not by those of others." Cited by A. Marinović in "Étude sur la législation maritime de la République de Dubrovnik," *Études Balkaniques,* VII, no. 3, p. 82.

83. J. Tadić, *Jevreji u Dubrovniku,* pp. 243 ff., 429 f., 450 f.; B. Krekić, *Dubrovnik in the 14th and 15th Centuries,* pp. 91 ff.; H. Bjelovučić, *The Ragusan Republic,* pp. 47, 60 ff. Another contract of a *cirurgieno* who, though salaried, was promised an additional fee, is reproduced by M. J. Dinić in his ed. of *Odluke veča Dubrovačke republike* (Decisions of the Councils of the Republic of Dubrovnik), I, 37, dated May 8, 1380 (perhaps more correctly 1330, like the other documents).

84. J. Tadić, *Jevreji u Dubrovniku,* pp. 275 ff., 298 ff., 315 ff.; T. Popović, *Turke i Dubrovnik v XVI veku* (Turkey and Dubrovnik in the Sixteenth Century), esp.

pp. 245, 250, 277 (on Don Joseph Nasi); and my essay on "Solomon ibn Ya'ish and Sultan Suleiman the Magnificent," *Joshua Finkel Festschrift,* pp. 29–36. On the agreements between doctors and patients in Dubrovnik, see also the earlier samples reproduced by G. Cremošnik in "A Few Medical Contracts from Dubrovnik," *Zbornik iz Dubrovački prašlosti* (Collection from the Past of Dubrovnik = *Mélanges Milan Rešetar*), pp. 43–45 (citing excerpts from four contracts, dated 1305–1313). See also the data presented by L. Šik in his *Jüdische Ärzte in Jugoslawien,* German trans. from a Croatian article in *Liječnički Vijesnik,* which mainly deals with the later period. It appears that some Jewish doctors from Venice's Adriatic colonies were able to practice medicine on the Italian mainland, if not in the mother city itself. As early as 1400 a Jewish physician, native to Durazzo, was abducted by a Tatar slave and a valet of two Christian doctors. We may suspect that this crime was committed in order to discourage an unwelcome competitor. Not unexpectedly the authorities were all too easily persuaded that this was merely an innocuous "prank" and took no action against the culprits. Regrettably, the full story of this miscarriage of justice does not emerge from the brief summary presented by C. Verlinden in "La Législation vénitienne du bas moyen âge en matière d'esclavage (XIIIe–XVe siècles)," *Ricerche storiche ed economiche in memoria di Carrado Barbagello,* pp. 147–72, esp. p. 165; reprinted in his *Studia historica Gandensia,* No. 40. See also, more generally, N. Korin, "Contributions to the History of Medicine on the Eastern Shore of the Adriatic Sea" (Serbo-Croatian), *Pomorski Zbornik,* X, 747–71.

85. H. Bjelovučić, *The Ragusan Republic,* p. 47; J. Tadić, *Jevreji u Dubrovniku,* pp. 108 ff., 119 ff., 225 ff., 233 f. Jewish ownership or co-ownership of vessels was facilitated by Dubrovnik's relatively liberal laws of navigation, especially its remarkable Statute of 1272, which served as the basic Ragusan maritime law code for generations. Jews apparently were able to serve also as mariners, although we do not possess documentary evidence to this effect (perhaps by mere chance). For unlike Venice, which specifically excluded minors under eighteen years of age, soldiers, foreigners, and slaves, the Dubrovnik statute kept that occupation open to everybody. See the *Liber statutorum civitatis Ragusii,* ed. with an Intro., commentaries and index by V. Bogisič and C. Jireček, and the analysis thereof by A. Marinovič, "Étude sur la législation maritime," *Études Balhaniques,* VII, no. 3, esp. pp. 68 ff., 80. On the noble family Juda (Zuda), see, for instance, *Monumenta spectantia historiam Slavorum meridionalium,* ed. by S. Ljubič *et al.,* I, 31 ff. No. xi (1221–23), 37 f. No. liii (1226); II, 70 ff. (1203–1204); and other data cited by J. C. Jireček in *Die Romanen,* in the passages listed *s.v.* Juda in the Index, III, 34.

86. J. Tadić, *Jevreji u Dubrovniku,* pp. 119 ff., 367 ff.; F. W. Carter, *Dubrovnik (Ragusa),* pp. 15 f. Isaac Yeshurun's trial and sentence was also the subject of a typical Hebrew folktale entitled *Ma'aseh Yeshurun* (The Story of Yeshurun), first published in Venice, 1657, together with the biblical commentary and homilies entitled *Shemen ha-ṭob* (The Good Oil), by the Dubrovnik savant-businessman, Solomon Oheb (mentioned in the local documents of 1577 and 1586, under the name Oëf; see Tadić, pp. 326 ff.), and a tract by Solomon's grandson, Aron Koen. It is noteworthy that, in its document of December 18, 1622, the government not only used the phrase "ghetto" but also enumerated all its Jewish heads of family by name. They were compelled to sign a pledge on behalf of the three elders who had been imprisoned in connection with the blood libel against Isaac Yeshurun. On the use

of the term *Judeca,* resembling the Venetian *Giudecca,* see J. C. Jireček, *Staat und Gesellschaft,* II (LVI, 3), 52. On the other hand, in a document dated April 18, 1625, the Ragusan council spoke of the *synagoga hebraeorum* as being obliged to pay 250 gold ducats a year for the lease of the seven houses assigned to the Jews for their habitation. Here, of course, the synagogue stands as a synonym for community. See Tadić, pp. 428 f. The peculiar Jewish forms of life of that interesting, if very small, community and its relatively high intellectual standing (including some of its rabbinic leaders like Oheb-Oëf and Aron Koen) will be discussed in our treatment of various phases of Jewish communal and intellectual life in later volumes.

87. See *supra,* Vols. III, pp. 210 f., 331 n. 48; XIV, 183 f., 374 n. 39; G. Schwarz, "Geschichte der Zagreber Juden," *Annalen des K. Kroatisch-slawonisch-dalmatischen Landesarchivs,* III–V, XVI; L. Šik, *Die Juden in den kroatischen Ländern;* L. Glesinger's and other articles in *Jevrejski Almanach,* 1954, 1955–56, 1965–67, etc. Additional publications are reviewed in S. Israel's aforementioned essay and Y. Eventov's volume, cited *supra,* nn. 69 and 73. On the general background, see S. Guldescu's twin volumes, *History of Medieval Croatia* and *The Croatian-Slavonic Kingdom, 1526–1792.*

88. See, for example, D. Dvorchenko-Markova's study, "The Origin of the Vlachs," in the *Romanian History Symposium* held at the Hardin-Simonsohn University, November 21–22, 1975, pp. 13–22. The long and heatedly debated problem of the historic continuity of the Rumanian civilization from Roman Dacia, through the Barbarian Migrations, into the late medieval and early modern Danubian Principalities and Transylvania also has important implications for the region's Jewish settlements. This discussion, especially between Rumanian and Hungarian historians, became very intense in the nationalistically overheated atmosphere of the 1920s and 1930s. Suffice it to mention here G. I. Bratianu's study, *Le Problème de la continuité daco-romaine.* In this booklet, written during World War II, the author not only responded sharply to various anti-Rumanian theories advanced by Hungarians, but also rejected the relatively friendly reservations by F. Lot. More recent Rumanian writers, however, controverted Bratianu's repeated emphasis on the "enigma" or "miracle" of the emergence of the Rumanian nation and looked for more rational and "scientific," that is, largely Marxist, explanations. Nonetheless, they, too, have insistently argued for the basic continuity of Rumanian history and marshaled some additional archaeological, linguistic, and toponomastic data in its favor.

Generally speaking, the assumption that after the 163-year-long Roman domination the area north of the lower Danube was completely emptied of its population and replaced by another has little to recommend it, although one may readily admit that from time to time new immigrants, voluntary or involuntary (such as prisoners of war or purchased slaves), added to the existing ethnic mixture. See the succinct summaries offered by C. Daicoviciu *et al.* in *Die Entstehung des rumänischen Volkes und der rumänischen Sprache.* See also D. Tudor's more recent analysis of *Unitate et continuitate in istoria poporului romăni* (Unity and Continuity of the Rumanian People); the related survey of *Rumanian Archaeology in the 20th Century* by E. Condurachi; *The Romance Character of Rumanian* by A. Graur; and, from another angle, D. Ghermani, *Die Kommunistische Umdeutung der rumänische Geschichte unter besonderer Berücksichtigung des Mittelalters.*

Among the newcomers the percentage of Jews may have been higher than that of some other ethnic groups, but their mingling with the existing remnants of ancient Jewry doubtless was greatly facilitated by their common faith and traditions. However, in view of the nearly total absence of reliable sources, the observation made some forty years ago by R. W. Seton-Watson with respect to general Rumanian history is doubly relevant to Jewish history in the country: "The methods inevitably adopted by the historian in his enquiry into Roumanian origins differ widely from those applicable to the early period in any other European country, even Russia or the Balkans. We are dealing with perhaps the most obscure corner of all Western history." See his *A History of the Roumanians from Roman Times to the Completion of Unity,* pp. 15 f.

89. Benjamin of Tudela, *Massa'ot,* pp. 11 (English), 13 (Hebrew). The use of the term Walachians here, as referring to a mountaineer people without clear tribal characteristics, is the less astonishing because for centuries afterward the Slavs applied the name of "Vlach" indiscriminately to the Rumanians and the Latin settlers in Dalmatia. See J. C. Jireček, *Die Romanen,* p. 34. On the title *logofet,* see R. Guilland's "Les Logothètes. Études sur l'histoire administrative de l'empire byzantin," *REB,* XXIX, 5–115. Among the numerous biographies of individual rulers, see, for example, N. Stoicescu, *Vlad Ţepeş* (Vlad l'Empereur), with the comments thereon by M. Berza in his "Vlad Ţepeş, ses règnes et sa légende. En marge de deux livres récentes," *RESEE,* XV, 325–54 (also referring to a study by Stefan Andreescu); M. T. McNally, *Dracula: a Biography of Vlad the Emperor (1431–1476)*; and the eight Rumanian articles published in the special issue of the *Revista de Istorie* (XXIX, no. 11) on the 500th anniversary of Vlad Ţepeş' death (1976), which includes a bibliography of some 200 studies devoted to various aspects of his controversial personality and reign.

It is noteworthy that, although Rumania played such an important role in Jewish life during the nineteenth and twentieth centuries, relatively little research has been done on the earlier history of the Jews in its core provinces of Walachia and Moldavia. Fortunately, research in this field is being facilitated by the ever increasing availability of critical editions of sources, the publication of new archival materials, and bibliographical aids. See, for example, the edition of the *Cronicile medievale ale Romanîei* (Rumanian Chronicles of the Middle Ages), ed. by I. Crăciun, A. Ilies *et al.,* of which Vols. I–VIII have appeared since 1963; and I. Crăciun *et al.,* comps., *Bibliografia istorică a Romanîei* (Historical Bibliography of Rumania), Vol. I: 1944–1969, both works sponsored by the Rumanian Academy. There has also been a growth of interest in Rumanian studies in Western Europe and the United States. See, for instance, E. D. Tappe, ed., *Documents Concerning Rumanian History (1427–1601): Collected from British Archives,* with an Intro. by C. Marinescu; and S. Fischer-Galati, "New Approaches to the Study of Southeast European History in the United States of America," *RESEE,* VIII, 133–34.

With respect to Jewish history, however, the progress in recent years has been very slow. True, because of the raging controversies on the Jewish question in the country, even non-Jewish scholars took some (more or less biased) interest in the Jewish past. The leading Rumanian historian, Nicholas Iorga, published in 1914 an essay "Histoire des Juifs de Roumanie," *Bulletin de la Section Historique* of the Rumanian Academy, II, 33–81, in which he strongly argued against the presence of the Jews in Rumania before the seventeenth century. But this denial, clearly disproved by subsequent research, was obviously colored by his partisan nationalistic views which later led to his premiership of the realm and ultimately, in 1940, to his assassination by Rumanian fanatics. On the Jewish side the best efforts were put forth by Meir Halevi and his journal, *Sinaï. Annuar de Studi Judaice* during the late 1920s and 1930s, but they were unfortunately cut short by the outbreak of the Second World War. See, for instance, his "The Jewish Community of Jassy before the End of the Seventeenth Century" (Rumanian), *ibid.*, II. We can also learn something about the early developments from the more extensive literature dealing with the Jewish settlements in areas inhabited by Rumanians which, before the First World War, had formed part of Austria-Hungary or Russia, especially Transylvania, Bukovina, and Bessarabia. See also, in general, N. Iorga, *Histoire des Roumains et de la Romanité orientale;* R. W. Seton-Watson, *History of the Roumanians;* and the recent collective work by M. Constantinescu *et al., Histoire de la Roumanie des origines à nos jours.*

90. See Balthasar Walther's Latin chronicle which, largely based upon the account by the Walachian court marshal as authorized by Michael himself, is reproduced in A. Papiu-Harianu's ed. of *Tésaur de Monimente istorice pentru România* (Treasury of Historical Monuments for Rumania), I, 12 f. The pertinent passage is cited here from I. Lupas's trans. in his *Zur Geschichte der Rumänen. Aufsätze und Vorträge,* pp. 272 f. Though he was devious and bloodthirsty, Michael's military and political exploits were extolled not only by his Rumanian compatriots in songs and ballads, but also by numerous Western contemporaries who cherished the deeds of "the great and redoubtable lion of the Orient" against the dreaded "Turkish menace." See A. Desei, "Les Relations entre Michel le Brave et l'Empire Ottoman," *Revue Roumaine d'Histoire,* XIV, 457–82; and, more generally, R. W. Seton-Watson's *History of the Roumanians,* pp. 61 ff.; and M. Constantinescu *et al.*, eds., *Histoire de la Roumanie,* pp. 169 ff. In their generally laudatory description of Michael's regime, the author (S. Pascu) and the editors, despite their Marxist orientation, largely gloss over their national hero's sell-out of the Rumanian peasantry.

91. See M. Markreich, "Notes on the Transformation of Place Names by European Jews," *JSS,* XXIII, 265–84, esp. pp. 276 f. From the very large literature on Byzantine-Muscovite relations we need but refer again to Johannes Irmscher, "Das Nikäische Kaisertum und Rusland," *Byzantion,* XL, 377–84; the various studies by D. Obolensky, "Byzantium, Kiev and Moscow: a Study in Ecclesiastical Relations," *Dumbarton Oaks Papers,* XI, 21–78; his "The Relations between Byzantium and Russia (Eleventh to Fifteenth Century)," paper delivered at the XIII International Congress of Historical Sciences, Moscow, 16–23 August, 1970 (also reprint); and esp. his *The Byzantine Commonwealth: Eastern Europe, 500–1453,* pp. 164 ff., 237 ff., and *passim.* A fine review of "The Byzantine Inheritance in Russia" is offered by Baron Meyendorff and Norman H. Baynes in Baynes and H. St. L. B. Moss's ed. of *Byzantium: an Introduction to East Roman Civilization,* pp. 369–91; the two quotes in our text come from the English translation in that chapter, pp. 384 f.

Of course, along with the dominant Byzantine heritage, the Russian people had also absorbed many cultural strains from the tribes and nations it had encountered in its long evolution from prehistoric times. One of the last medieval factors to place its permanent imprint upon the political and cultural, as well as biological, make-up of the medieval Muscovite state and society was the Tatar Golden Horde; the ultimate political theory of Russian tsardom betrayed many ingredients taken over from the Tatar realities and world outlook. See M. Cherniavsky, "Khan or Basileus: an Aspect of Russian Mediaeval Political Theory," *Journal of the History of Ideas,* XX, 459–76. Many scholars, moreover, both Russian and Western, have long recognized that even in the Middle Ages there was a trend among the Russian leaders to reduce Muscovite spiritual dependence on Byzantium. See, for instance, E. Hösch's succinct observations on this subject in his "Byzanz und die Byzanzidee in der russischen Geschichte," *Saeculum,* XX, 6–17. See also, from other angles, M. Hellmann, "Moskau und Byzanz," *JGOE,* n.s. XVII, 321–44; *supra,* n. 67; and Vols. IX, pp. 139 ff., 309 ff. nn. 5–14; XI, pp. 4 ff., 289 nn. 2–6.

92. See *supra,* Vol. III, pp. 214 ff., 335 ff. nn. 53–55; the literature listed there; and Benjamin's *Massa'ot,* ed. by M. N. Adler, pp. 80 f. (English), 72 f. (Hebrew). On Benjamin's travelogue, the aims of his journey, and his general reliability, see *supra,* Vol. VI, pp. 222 ff., 435 f. nn. 88–90. The more recent Soviet investigations of the manifold problems relating to the medieval Russian chronicles are analyzed by H. J. Grabmüller in "Die Russischen Chroniken des 11.–18. Jahrhunderts im Spiegel der Sowjetforschung (1917–1975)," *JGOE,* n.s. XXIV, 394–416; XXV, 66–90. The Jewish aspects of the period under Mongol domination are almost totally unknown. In general, Soviet, as well as tsarist, historians have been prone to describe the two and one-half centuries of the Golden Horde's regime as having contributed almost nothing to the national character and culture of the Russian people. Some of them like to quote their great national poet, Alexander Sergeevich Pushkin, who had repudiated any comparison of the Mongol heritage of Russia with that of the Moorish legacy in Western Europe: "They [the Mongols] conquered Russia, but they did not present it with either algebra or Aristotle." See, for instance, A. M. Sakharov's arguments based on archaeological evidence of the wholesale destruction in his "Les Mongols et la civilisation russe," *Studies in Russian History,* Special issue of the *Journal of World History,* 1958, pp. 77–97. See, however, *infra,* Chap. LXXIII, nn. 27 and 31.

93. See J. B. Frey, *Corpus Inscriptionum Judaicarum,* I, 495 ff. Nos. 683–91, 576 No. 79*; Johannes Schiltberger, *Reisen . . . in Europa, Asien und Afrika von 1396 bis 1427,* ed. from a Heidelberg MS by K. F. Neumann, p. 106 or *The Bondage and Travels . . . in Europe, Asia and Africa, 1396–1427,* English trans. by J. B. Telfer, with notes by P. Brunn, pp. 49, 176 n. 7; the text of "The Decree Concerning the Genoese Colonies on the Black Sea Issued in Genoa in 1449," ed. with a Russian intro. and commentary by V. Yurgevich in *Zapiski* of the Odessa Historical Society, V; A. P. Vigna, ed., *Codice diplomatico delle colonie Tauro-Liguri durante la signoria dell'Ufficio di San Giorgio (1453–1475).* Vols. I–III; and, particularly I. Kaia, "Letters of Privilege Granted by the Khans to Crimean Jews" (Russian), *Evreiskaya Starina,* VII, 102–103 (reproducing the Charters of 1003 and 1156 A.H. = 1597 and 1742 C.E. in Russian trans.); and, more generally, the older comprehensive work by M. G. Canale, *Della Crimea e dei suoi dominatori dalle sue origini fino al trattato di Parigi;* and R. Lopez's aforementioned *Storia delle colonie genovesi nel Mediterraneo.* See also *supra,* Vols. III, pp. 197 ff., 201 ff., 323 n. 60; V, pp. 237, 247, 407 f.

On the commercial importance of these Crimean cities in the Black Sea trade, see also C. Verlinden's concise review in the lecture he delivered at the XIII International Congress of Historical Sciences in Moscow, 1970 and published under the title, *Le Commerce en Mer Noire des débuts de l'époque byzantine au lendemain de la conquête de l'Égypte par les Ottomans (1517)*; K. P. Matschke, "Zum Charakter des byzantinischen Schwarzmeerhandels im 13. bis 15. Jahrhundert," *Wissenschaftliche Zeitschrift der Karl-Marx-Universität Leipzig,* Ges. und sprachwiss. Reihe XIX, 447–58 (pointing out that the demands voiced, for instance, by Georgios Gemistos Plethon, that Byzantine public officials be forbidden to take part in wholesale and retail trade, had more than mere theoretical importance; they naturally reinforced the role of Jewish and other civilian merchants, p. 458); M. Nystazopoulou-Pélekidis, "Venise et la Mer Noire du XIe au XVe siècle," *Thesaurismata,* VI, 15–51; and, particularly, M. Malowist's detailed study, *Kaffa, kolonia genueńska na Krymie* (Kaffa: a Genoese Colony in the Crimea, and the Eastern Question in 1453–1475); and G. I. Bratianu's comprehensive posthumous work, *La Mer Noire des origines à la conquête ottomane* (includes V. Lorent's eulogy of Bratianu, as well as bibliography of his writings). Of considerable value still is J. von Hammer-Purgstall's old *Geschichte der Chane der Krim unter osmanischer Herrschaft. Aus türkischen Quellen.*

94. Ivan III's letters to Guizolfi, dated March 14, 1484; October 18, 1487; and March 18, 1488; and Guizolfi's reply of June 8, 1487, are reproduced in *Sbornik Imperatorskago Ruskago Istoricheskago Obshchevstva,* XLI, 40 ff., 71 f., and are cited here from the English trans. by H. Rosenthal in his "Guizolfi (Giexulfis), Zacharias De," *Jewish Encyclopedia,* Vol. VI, pp. 107 f. See also J. Brutzkus, "Zechariah, the Prince of Taman" (Russian), *Evreiskaya Starina,* X, 132–43 (claiming, with F. K. Brun, that Guizolfi was addressed by Ivan as "the Jew" by mistake); G. Vernadsky, "The Heresy of the Judaizers and the Policy of Ivan III of Moscow," *Speculum,* VIII, 436–54, esp. pp. 448 ff. (suggesting that Zechariah may indeed have been a Judaizer); B. D. Weinryb, "The Beginnings of East-European Jewry in Legend and Historiography," *Studies and Essays in Honor of Abraham A. Neuman,* pp. 445–502, esp. pp. 488 ff.; and *infra,* n. 95. See also my brief remarks in *The Russian Jew under Tsars and Soviets,* 2d ed. rev., pp. 6 ff., 344; and, more generally, A. Bennigsen and C. Lemercier-Quelquejay, "Le Khanat de Crimée au début du XVIe siècle de la tradition mongole à la souzeraineté ottomane d'après un document inédit des Archives Ottomanes," *Cahiers du monde russe,* XIII, 321–37.

These friendly relations with the Crimean Jews did not necessarily influence Ivan III's ambiguous policy with relation to the Jews in Muscovy. One incident often adduced as an illustration of his Judeophobia proves very little, since the individual concerned was coresponsible for the unfortunate outcome. The story has it that Messer Leon (perhaps identical with the eminent Jewish physician and Hebraic scholar who, because of a raging controversy within the Jewish community, was expelled from his native Mantua), came to Moscow about 1490 and served there as court physician. On one occasion his ministrations to the tsarevich during a critical illness proved unsatisfactory and the young prince died. Thereupon the physician was beheaded, because he had allegedly suggested in advance that, if he did not heal the prince, his life be forfeited. See V. Colorni, "Note per la biografia di alcuni dotti Ebrei vissuti a Mantova nel secolo XV," *Annuario di studi ebraici,* I, 172 ff., 175 n. 5. This story, if authentic, reveals more the cruelty of the contemporary Moscow rulers than their intolerance toward Jews. One might actually argue, on the contrary, that the employment of a Jewish physician at court was a sign of moderate religious toleration.

95. Like many other secret groups, the *Judaizanti* are known to us almost exclusively from reports by opponents; in their case especially through the polemical attacks in Joseph Sanin's (Volotsky's) *Prosvietitel* (The Enlightener, or the Detection of the Judaizing Heresy), Kazan, 1855 ed., esp. pp. 43 ff. We know very little, in particular, about the crucial years between 1471, when Zechariah arrived in Novgorod, and 1488 when the real struggle against his preachment began. It is, therefore, no surprise to find modern scholarship deeply divided about the nature of this movement, its background and founder, and its impact upon subsequent sectarian trends. In the defense of Orthodoxy Joseph Sanin used such old Western classics as Nicholas de Lyra's aforementioned anti-Jewish tracts. Yet, even in the nineteenth century scholars were not unanimous about the Jewish antecedents of that heritage. The historian Dmitri Ivanovich Ilovaiskii, for example, tried to prove that the *Judaizanti* had nothing to do with Judaism, that Zechariah himself was not a Jew, and that the sect arose under the stimulus of Western proto-Reformation tendencies. Variants of this theory, and of other aspects of that heresy supported by a much greater array of archival documents and scholarly reasonings, have been advanced in modern Soviet literature—of course, with the addition of arguments from the socioeconomic life in fifteenth-century Novgorod and Moscow.

Among the proponents of this interpretation in recent years has been S. Y. (or J.) Lur'e (Luria) whose work (together with N. A. Kazakova), *Antifeodalniie ereticheskiie dvizheniia na Rusi XV i nachala XVI v.* (Antifeudal Heretical Movements in Russia in the Fifteenth and the Beginning of the Sixteenth Centuries) has aroused a considerable amount of discussion and controversy in both the Soviet Union and other countries. See also his *Ideologicheskaia borba v russkoi publitsistike kontsa XV–nachala XVI veka* (Ideological Struggles in the Russian Publicist Literature of the End of the Fifteenth and the Beginning of the Sixteenth Centuries); the summary of his views in "L'Hérésie dite des judaïsants et ses sources historiques," *Revue des études slaves,* XLV, 49–67—all denying the Jewish origin of that heresy and even presenting Zechariah as a figment of Gennadius' imagination. Connected with this controversy was another over the background and implications of Fedor Kuritsin's *Laodikiiskoe poslanie* (Laodicaean Missive), evidently inspired by the chancellor's conscientious scruples as well as political objectives. See esp. J. V. A. Fine, "Fedor Kuritsyn's 'Laodikijskoe poslanie' and the Heresy of the Judaizers," *Speculum,* XLI, 500–504; J. Maier, "Zum jüdischen Hintergrund des sogenannten 'Laodicenischen Sendschreibens,'" *JGOE,* XVII, 1–12; and other essays in this periodical.

The most convincing arguments in favor of the Jewish origin of the Judaizing sect have been presented by S. Ettinger in his "Jewish Influence on the Religious Ferment in Eastern Europe at the End of the Fifteenth Century" (Hebrew), in *Yitzhak F. Baer Jubilee Volume,* ed. by S. W. Baron *et al.,* pp. 228–47. He pointed out, in particular, the availability of Russian translations not only of the Bible, which show some influences of the Jewish interpretation, but also of Jewish liturgical pieces, though not in the form in which they were incorporated in the normative Ashkenazic prayerbook. He also referred to related manifestations across the border in Lithuania which inevitably influenced the religious turmoil in contemporary Muscovy. According to Gennadius' admittedly biased contention, in 1490 the Lithuanian Jews greeted with joy the progress of judaization of the Muscovite population. See also the additional data and publications cited in E. Hösch's detailed review of "Sowjetische Forschungen zur Häresiengeschichte Altrusslands.

Methodologische Bemerkungen," *JGOE,* XVIII, 279–312; and J. Juszczyk, "On Studies about Judaizantism" (Polish), *Kwartalnik Historyczny,* LXXVI, 141–51. Both authors lean toward accepting the Jewish origin of the sect. Yet, because of the great differences which prevailed among the adherents of that and related heresies and because of the host of contradictions and other obscurities enveloping the entire early history of Russian sectarianism, many of the uncertainties which plagued George Vernadsky (in his essay on the Judaizers cited *supra,* n. 94) and other scholars over generations have not yet been resolved. See also *supra,* Vols. IX, pp. 288 ff. n. 4, esp. item 3; and XVI, pp. 71 f., 349 f. n. 78.

96. See the sources cited in J. Hessen, *Istoriia evreiskago naroda v Rossii* (A History of the Jewish People in Russia), I, 39; S. M. Dubnow, *History of the Jews in Russia and Poland,* in the English trans. by I. Friedlander, esp. I, 242 ff. (from whose rendition some passages cited in the text are taken); and, particularly, S. Ettinger, "The Muscovite State and Its Attitude toward the Jews" (Hebrew), *Zion,* XVIII, 136–68, with an English summary, p. iii. The allusion to "poisonous herbs" which Jews allegedly imported into Muscovy may refer to medicines, since Jews were widely engaged in both the medical treatment of patients and the dispensation to them of medical drugs. However, some scholars have interpreted this allusion as referring to tobacco, then a rather recent transplant into the European markets. Understandably, from the outset its use aroused antagonism in conservative circles. On the tragic events in Polotsk, see *supra,* Vol. XVI, pp. 175 and 398 n. 11.

97. See S. A. Bershadskii *et al.,* ed., *Regesti i nadpisi,* I, 338; *supra,* n. 96; Vol. XVI, pp. 170 f., 176 f., 396 ff. nn. 5, 12 ff., and the literature cited there. On the Romanov dynasty and its founder, see E. M. Almedingen's general survey, *The Romanovs: Three Centuries of an Ill-Fated Dynasty.*

98. See *supra,* Vol. XVI, pp. 178 ff., 400 ff. nn. 15–18; and Basil Posniakov's *Khozhdenie po sviatym mestam* (Journey to Holy Places), reproduced in a French trans. in S. P. de Khitrovo, comp., *Itinéraires russes en Orient,* Vol. I, 283–334, esp. pp. 290 f.

99. See Paolo Giovio, *Libellus de legatione Basilij magni principis Moschouiae ad Clementem VII. pontificem maximum in qua situs regionis antiquis incognitus, religio gentis mores et causae legationis fidelissime referendum,* Basle, 1527; idem, *Historiarum sui temporis tomus primus* [secundus], Venice, 1553–69.

CHAPTER LXXIII: LATE MEDIEVAL ISLAM

1. The age of Saladin, his spectacular victories, and the fall of the Latin Kingdom of Jerusalem have attracted much attention from both contemporaries and modern historians. See esp. such recent monographs as A. S. Ehrenkreutz, *Saladin;* H. A. R. Gibb, *The Life of Saladin: From the Works of 'Imad ad-Dīn and Bahā' ad-Dīn;* J. Hartmann, *Die Persönlichkeit des Sultans Saladin im Urteil der abendländischen Quellen:* F. Gabrieli, *Arab Historians of the Crusades: Selected and Translated from the Arab Sources,* English trans. from the Italian by E. J. Costello; and A. Luders, *Die Kreuzzüge im Urteil syrischer und armenischer Quellen.*

Among the numerous detailed studies, we may mention the reconstruction of the topography of the decisive battle of Ḥaṭṭin, which led to the conquest of Jerusalem by Saladin in 1187, by J. Prawer in "La Bataille de Ḥaṭṭîn," *Israel Exploration Journal,* XIV, 160–79; and J. Kraemer's *Der Sturz des Königreichs Jerusalem (583/1187) in der Darstellung des 'Imād ad-Dīn al-Kātib al-Isfahani (Nach dem 1. Buch des "Fatḥ al-qudsī fil' fatḥ al-qudsī")."* This work by 'Imād ad-Din al-Isfahāni, a primary source for the Ayyubid period, is now available in H. Massé's French trans., entitled *Conquête de la Syrie et de la Palestine par Saladin.* The impact of the Muslim conquests upon Christian opinion in Europe was well expressed by a contemporary chronicler who spoke of the "incomparable pain and ineffable sadness which afflicted all of Christianity." See the *Continuatio Acquicinctina* (for the years 1149–1237) of Sigebert of Gembloux's *Chronica,* ed. by L. C. Bethmann in G. H. Pertz *et al.,* eds., *MGH* Scriptores, VI, 268 ff.

We know less about the impression these events made upon the Jews of Europe. But it stands to reason that many of them rejoiced over the setback suffered by the Crusaders, whose atrocities in the first three Crusades had remained a living memory in the Jewish communities in many lands. The Jews may also have received direct reports about Saladin's personal humanity and sense of justice and believed some more or less exaggerated news about the sultan's favors toward his Jewish subjects. See E. Ashtor-Strauss, "Saladin and the Jews," *HUCA,* XXVII, 305–326; and *supra,* Vol. IV, pp. 115 f., 298 f. n. 35.

2. These world-shaking events have been described in a vast array of primary sources and modern investigations. Suffice it to mention here such standard histories of the Crusades as those by R. Grousset, *Histoire des croisades et du Royaume franc de Jerusalem;* S. Runciman, *A History of the Crusades* (also in paperback in Harper's Torchbooks); and K. M. Setton *et al.,* eds., *A History of the Crusades,* 2d ed. See also H. E. Mayer's "Literaturbericht über die Geschichte der Kreuzzüge. Veröffentlichungen 1958–1967," *HZ,* Sonderheft 3, pp. 641–731. However, the traditional enumeration of the First through the Fifth Crusades represents only a part of a long historic process which extended over the entire first half of the second millennium. These aspects have been repeatedly emphasized by A. S. Atiya in "The Crusades: Old Ideas and New Conceptions," *Journal of World History,* II, 469–75; his *The Crusade in the Later Middle Ages;* and several other works. See *infra,* nn. 18–19. On the impact of these greatly exacerbated religious conflicts upon such

Jewish leaders as Yehudah Halevi, see *supra,* esp. Vol. IV, Chapter XXI; and H. Liebeschütz, "The Crusading Movement in its Bearing on the Christian Attitude towards Jewry," *JJS,* X, 97–111. This factor made itself immediately felt in the Middle East as well. The holy wars on both sides of the conflict and their implications for the entire Mediterranean world are discussed, for instance, in A. Noth's Bonn dissertation, *Heiliger Krieg und heiliger Kampf im Islam und Christentum. Beiträge zur Vorgeschichte und Geschichte der Kreuzzüge;* and A. R. Naqvi, "Laws of War in Islam," *Islamic Studies* (Islamabad), XIII, no. 1, pp. 25–43.

3. The anonymous Syriac chronicle, ed. by J. B. Chabot *et al.* in the *Corpus scriptorum christianorum orientalium,* 3d ser., XV; and in the English trans. by A. S. Tritton in "The First and Second Crusades from an Anonymous Syriac Chronicle. With Notes by H. A. R. Gibb," *JRAS,* 1933, pp. 69–101, 273–305, esp. pp. 291 ff.; Benjamin of Tudela, *Massa'ot* (Itinerary), ed. and trans. into English by M. N. Adler, pp. 32 f. (Hebrew), 32 (English); Yehudah ben Solomon al-Ḥarizi, *Taḥkemoni* (Maqamae), xxviii, xlvi, ed by P. de Lagarde, pp. 120 f., 167 f.; S. Krauss, "L'Émigration de 300 rabbins en Palestine en l'an 1211," *REJ,* LXXXII, 333–52. The figure of 5,000 Jews in Aleppo, reported by Benjamin, is doubtless exaggerated even if it refers to persons rather than to families, as is often done in his other computations. We shall presently see that the total Jewish population of Syria (including Palestine) at that time hardly exceeded 40,000 persons. See *supra,* Vol. III, pp. 113 f., 283 f. n. 48; and *infra,* nn. 44 ff.

Aleppo happened to be one of the oldest communities in northern Syria, and its Jewry living under Muslim domination inherited a rich tradition going back to the Graeco-Roman period. True, the date corresponding to 342 C.E. that the local community read into an inscription found in its synagogue, rather than the more correct one of 833 C.E., may have been invented for the benefit of the Muslim administration to support the Jewish contention that the synagogue antedated the Muslim regime. In this way the community might have hoped to evade the Muslim prohibition against the erection of new synagogues without special permission from the authorities. See M. Sobernheim and E. Mittwoch, "Hebräische Inschriften in der Synagoge von Aleppo," *Festschrift . . . Jacob Guttmann,* pp. 273–85, esp. p. 279 and my remarks thereon in *JC,* I, 164 f.; III, 35 f. n. 6; A. Dothan's rejection of that hypothesis without offering an alternative date in his "On the History of the Ancient Synagogue in Aleppo" (Hebrew), *Sefunot,* I, 25–64, esp. pp. 27 f.; and J. Sauvaget, *Alep. Essai sur le développement d'une grande ville syrienne, des origines au milieu du XIXe siècle,* pp. 60 ff. Apart from major warlike disturbances, the internecine strife between the Sunni and Shi'ite Muslims caused much suffering to all inhabitants, including Jews. See H. M. Khayat, "The Shi'ite Rebellions in Aleppo in the VIth Century A.H./XIIth Century A.D.," *RSO,* XLVI, 167–95, esp. pp. 183 ff., 191 f. (on the outbreaks of 1157 and 1173). Similarly dubious is Saladin's purported invitation to Jews to settle in Jerusalem, reported by Al-Ḥarizi. Its historicity is denied by S. D. Goitein in his "Letters from Eretz-Israel Dating to the Crusader Period" (Hebrew), *Yerushalayim* (Review), II–V, 54–70, esp. p. 56; and by E. Ashtor-Strauss in his "Saladin and the Jews," *HUCA,* XXVII, 324 ff.; but it is defended by J. Prawer in his authoritative *Toledot Mamlekhet ha-Ṣalbanim be-Ereṣ-Yisrael* (A History of the Latin Kingdom of Jerusalem), esp. II, 79 n. 16; or *Histoire du Royaume Latin de Jérusalem,* trans. from the Hebrew by G. Nahon, revised and completed by the author, II, 85 n. 16. See also, more generally, B. Z. Kedar's Hebrew analysis of "The

Jewish Community of Jerusalem in the Thirteenth Century," *Tarbiz,* XLI, 82–94, with an English summary, pp. vi–vii.

4. See S. Y. Labib's *Handelsgeschichte Ägyptens im Spätmittelalter (1171–1517),* p. 59; F. P. Bargebuhr's Munich dissertation, *Über das Beamtentum unter Saladin;* E. Ashtor-Strauss, remarks in *HUCA,* XXVII, 306 f., and the sources listed there. We recall that even Maimonides may not have been allowed to use a horse on his daily trips from Fusṭaṭ to the sultan's court in Cairo and therefore employed the equivocal term "animal" in his description. A Jewish or Christian court physician riding on horseback ran the risk of being attacked by overzealous Muslims. This happened to the Jewish surgeon and oculist Muwaffaq ibn Shawa, at whom a visiting Syrian Ṣufi courtier threw a stone, permanently blinding him in one eye. See *supra,* Vol. III, pp. 298 f. n. 23; Ibn abi 'Uṣaibi'a. *K. 'Uyūn al-Anbā'* (Choicest News on the Classes of Physicians, or a History of Arab Physicians), ed. by A. Müller, II, 116; and M. Meyerhof, "Jewish Physicians under the Reign of the Fatimid Caliphs in Egypt," *Medical Leaves,* II, 131–39, esp. p. 138.

5. See *supra,* Vol. VIII, pp. 248 ff., 398 ff. nn. 38 ff. The extent of Maimonides' personal contacts with Saladin is still uncertain. His failure to dedicate any of his medical treatises to the sultan, as he did to several other members of the Ayyubid family, is inconclusive. As far as we can tell from the dedications of individual tracts, these were all written on specific requests rather than on the physician's own initiative. See the extensive literature listed *supra,* Vol. VIII, and in M. Meyerhof's careful review of "The Medical Work of Maimonides," *Essays on Maimonides,* ed. by me, pp. 265–99.

6. See the passages cited by M. Perlmann in his edition of *Asnawi's Tract against Christian Officials, passim;* H. A. R. Gibb, "The Achievement of Saladin," reprinted in his ed. of *Studies in the Civilization of Islam,* pp. 99 f.; and E. Sivan in *L'Islam et la croisade. Idéologie et propagande dans les réactions musulmanes aux croisades,* esp. p. 97.

7. H. Corbin, *Suhrawardi d'Alep (1191), fondateur de la doctrine illuminative ishrâqî;* L. Massignon, *La Passion d'al-Hosayn ibn Mansour al-Hallaj, martyr mystique de l'Islam exécuté à Bagdad le 26 Mars 922. Étude d'histoire religieuse;* A. J. Arberry, *A Sufi Martyr: the Apologia of 'Ain al-Quḍat al-Hamadhani,* trans. with Intro. and Notes, esp. pp. 14 f.; S. Y. Labib, *Handelsgeschichte,* pp. 59 f.; A. S. Ehrenkreutz, "The Standard of Fineness of Gold Circulating in Egypt at the Time of the Crusades," *JAOS,* LXXIV, 162–66, esp. pp. 163, 166 n. 26 (largely based upon the important manual by Manṣur ibn Bara' written between 1218 and 1238, as well as upon the author's personal examination of some specimens of Saladin's coins extant in Damascus). See also Ehrenkreutz's "Extracts from the Technical Manual on the Ayyūbid Mint in Cairo," *BSOAS,* XV, 423–47, and, more broadly, his "Monetary Aspects of Medieval Near Eastern Economic History" in M. A. Cook, ed. *Studies in the Economic History of the Middle East from the Rise of Islam to the Present Day,* pp. 37–50. In contrast to Saladin's legalized coin debasement, his predecessors, the Faṭimids, usually issued far purer gold coinage. See, for example, G. C. Miles, *Fatimid Coins in the Collections of the University Museum, Philadelphia and the American Numismatic Society.*

The *Karimi* merchants have been the subject of several scholarly investigations in recent years. Yet many important aspects of their activities have not yet been elucidated; these include their relations with Jewish merchants and even their possible Jewish antecedents. See esp. W. J. Fischel, "Über die Gruppe der Karimi-Kaufleute. Ein Beitrag zur Geschichte des Orienthandels unter den Mamluken," *Studia Arabica,* I (*Analecta Orientalia,* XIV), 67-82, showing, among other matters, the government's overriding power. For example, when in 1288 Sultan Qala'un ordered these merchants to advance 700,000 dirhems to six notables from Damascus so that they might pay a fine in Cairo, the Karimis complied, although they may have doubted that this substantial loan would ever be repaid, as indeed it was not (pp. 74 f.); E. Ashtor, "The Karimi Merchants," *JRAS,* 1956, pp. 45–56 (emphasizing that they did not form a patrician group, no family lasting more than three generations; also includes some references to their relations with Jews; pp. 50, 55); S. D. Goitein, "New Light on the Beginnings of the Karimi Merchants," *JESHO,* I, 175–84, revised in his "The Beginnings of the Karim Merchants and the Character of Their Organization," in his collection of essays entitled *Studies in Islamic History and Institutions,* pp. 351–60. Here Goitein cites five passages in Genizah documents showing the presence of these merchants in Egypt and Aden in the first half of the twelfth century, contrary to the older assumption that they began to flourish under the Ayyubid dynasty. We shall also see that, despite their great successes and ever-growing economic power, they were not able completely to displace the Jews in the India trade in Egypt and other Mediterranean countries.

8. Al-Qadhi al-Fadhil's decree, published from a Berlin MS and trans. into German by H. A. Hein in his *Beiträge zur ayubidischen Diplomatik,* pp. 183 ff. (undated but evidently enacted some time between Aleppo's conquest in 1183 and Al-Fadhil's death in 1193); Abraham b. Hillel, *Scroll,* ed. by A. Neubauer in "Egyptian Fragments: *Megillot,* Scrolls Analogous to That of Purim, with an Appendix on the First *Negidim,*" *JQR,* [o.s.] VIII, 541–61, esp. p. 549; and his additional "Note" thereon, *ibid.,* IX, 721. See also *supra,* Vol. VI, pp. 215, 431 f. n. 78; and B. Lewis, "Maimonides, Lionheart, and Saladin" (Hebrew), *Eretz Israel,* VII (= *Leo A. Mayer Mem. Vol.*), 70*–75*, reprinted under the title, "The Sultan, the King, and the Jewish Doctor" in his *Islam in History: Ideas, Men and Events in the Middle East,* pp. 166–76, 323.

The apparent conflict between these laudatory statements and the reference to the "Days of the Armenian Kingdom When the King Was a Lover of Money" in the introductory poem to the scroll (if Neubauer's identification of this king, p. 545, with Saladin because of his Kurdish ancestry is accepted) is not necessarily serious. Saladin's perennial shortage of funds was aggravated by his generosity in giving them away. Certainly, his unconditional freeing of Richard Lion-Heart from imprisonment sharply contrasted with the greed of the Austrian lord who later detained the English king on his way home and released him only after receiving a very high ransom. This and other magnanimous acts made Saladin a legendary figure even to his European enemies. See J. Hartmann's *Die Persönlichkeit des Sultans Saladin im Urteil der abendländischen Quellen.* The excessive praise of the Syro-Egyptian sultan later included his alleged religious toleration of non-Muslims. Ultimately, in his famous dramatic poem, *Nathan the Wise,* Gotthold Ephraim Lessing chose Saladin as the exponent of the parable of the Three Rings, symbolizing the equality of Judaism, Christianity, and Islam.

9. See J. Mann, *The Jews in Egypt and in Palestine under the Fatimid Caliphs: A Contribution to Their Political and Communal History Based Chiefly on Genizah Materials Hitherto Unpublished,* and a *Second Supplement* thereto, with a Preface and Readers' Guide by S. D. Goitein, reprinted from the Oxford 1920–22 ed., esp. I, 255 f. (following R. J. H. Gottheil's summary of Qalqashandi's description in his "An Eleventh-Century Document Concerning a Cairo Synagogue," *JQR,* [o.s.] XIX, 467–539, esp. pp. 500 f., 527 ff. App. iii); Mann, *Texts and Studies,* I, 394 ff.; and, more generally, D. Neustadt (Ayalon), "Some Problems Concerning the 'Negidut' in Egypt during the Middle Ages" (Hebrew), *Zion,* IV, 126–49; and Y. L. Fishman (Maimon), *Ha-Negidut be-Yisrael* (The Institution of Nagid among the Jews), reprinted from *Ha-Tor,* VII, nos. 6–8, 11–17; and other older literature listed *supra,* Vol. V, pp. 308 f. n. 45; and *JC,* I, 177 ff.; III, 43 ff. nn. 29–30. The operations of this important office will be more fully analyzed in connection with the general aspects of Jewish self-government under medieval Islam in a later chapter.

It may also be noted that, apart from the sultans, some of their leading advisers often proved very helpful to the Jewish chiefs. Just as Moses Maimonides was extremely friendly with Saladin's vizier Al-Qadhi al-Fadhil—who is recorded to have visited the sage of Fusṭaṭ and, on one occasion, saved him from serious complications arising from a denunciation by a hostile medical student—Maimonides' son frequently enjoyed the cooperation of Ibn Shukr (Ṣafiaddin 'Abdallah ibn 'Ali adh-Dhamiri), the sultan's otherwise very ruthless adviser, in 1200–1212 and 1219–25. See A. M. Helbig, *Al-Qāḍī al-Fāḍil, der Wezir Saladins, eine Biographie* (Diss. Heidelberg); and other literature listed by H. L. Gottschalk in *Al-Malik al-Kāmil von Egypten und seine Zeit. Eine Studie zur Geschichte Vorderasiens und Egyptens in der ersten Hälfte des 7./13. Jahrhunderts,* p. 23 n. 1 (on Ibn Shukr).

10. See S. D. Goitein, "New Documents from the Cairo Geniza," *Homenaje a Millás-Vallicrosa,* I, 707–720 (with an Appendix of three documents in Arabic and Hebrew); idem, *A Mediterranean Society: the Jewish Communities of the Arab World as Portrayed in the Documents of the Cairo Geniza,* II, 406 f. Goitein also points out that Abraham Maimonides' general tolerance of liturgical diversity was illustrated by his responsum to a legal inquiry; see Abraham's *Teshubot* (Responsa), collected from MSS and ed. with an Intro. and Notes by A. H. Freimann. The Arabic Text revised and annotated by S. D. Goitein, pp. 62 ff. No. 62. In a somewhat similar situation, Moses Maimonides, too, against his better judgment regarding the merits of the case, had advised a provincial cantor to retain the insertion of certain liturgical passages into the established text rather than give rise to communal dissension. See Moses Maimonides' *Teshubot* (Resp.), ed. by J. Blau, II, 329 f. No. 181.

11. H. L. Gottschalk, *Al-Malik al-Kāmil,* pp. 82 f.; Al-Ḥarizi, *Taḥkemoni* (*supra,* n. 3); Abraham Maimonides, *Resp.,* ed. by A. H. Freimann and S. D. Goitein, p. 15; B. Z. Kedar, "The Jewish Community of Jerusalem," (Hebrew), *Tarbiz,* XLI, 84. On the emergency created by the Third Crusade and the attack on Damietta, see *infra,* n. 18. The changing fiscal policies of the various Muslim regimes will be discussed more fully in later contexts. For the time being we refer to such monographs as C. Cahen, "Le Régime des impôts dans le Fayyūm ayyūbide," *Arabica,* III, 8–30, based on a report by 'Utman b. Ibrahim al-Nabulusi, a fiscal official, which showed that in 1241–43 the administration collected the capitation tax only from

1,142 *dhimmis* including 293 non-residents, paying on the average slightly over 2 dinars per taxpayer (*ibid.*, pp. 21 f.); H. L. Gottschalk, *Al-Malik al-Kāmil,* pp. 15 f.; and, more generally, H. M. Rabie (Rabi'), *The Financial System of Egypt, A.H. 564–741/A.D. 1169–1341,* esp. pp. 73 ff., 123 ff.

12. See S. D. Goitein, "Jerusalem in the Arab Period, 638–1099" (Hebrew), *Yerushalayim* (Review), [I] 1953, pp. 82–103, esp. pp. 99 f.; idem, "New Sources on the Fate of the Jews during the Crusaders' Conquest of Jerusalem" (Hebrew), *Zion,* XVII, 129–44, with an English summary, pp. viii–ix, and in its revised English trans. entitled, "Contemporary Letters on the Capture of Jerusalem by the Crusaders," *JJS,* III, 162–77, esp. p. 176 (from which the trans. of the Egyptian Jewish pilgrim's statements here and *infra,* n. 14 are taken); the qadhi's lamentation reproduced by the leading Arab chronicler of the period, 'Imād ad-Din al-Isfahāni, in his *K. Al-Fatḥ al-qudsī,* and in the French trans. by H. Massé, *Conquête de la Syrie et de la Palestine par Saladin;* cited by E. Sivan in his "Réfugiés syro-palestiniens au temps des croisades," *REI,* XXXV, 135–47, esp. p. 141.

The figure of 70,000 victims, though repeated by several chroniclers, is exaggerated. In 1047, before the various invasions, Jerusalem's population was estimated at 20,000 inhabitants, a figure stemming from the general predilection of Arab writers for round numbers rather than from any close statistical approximation. In the quarter century following the Seljuk occupation of the city in 1070, the total population must have diminished considerably. It could not have increased sufficiently to reach the number allegedly killed by the Crusaders even though, on their approach, many Jewish and non-Jewish provincials fled to the metropolis and its assumed greater security.

13. Urban II's Clermont address partially reproduced in four complementary versions and trans. into English by A. C. Krey in *The First Crusade: The Accounts of Eye-Witnesses and Participants,* pp. 24 ff., 28 ff.; Matthew of Edessa, *Chronique,* trans. from the Armenian by E. Dulaurier, *Bibliothèque historique arménienne ou choix des principaux historiens arméniens,* esp. pp. 233 f.; H. Hagenmayer, ed., *Die Kreuzzugsbriefe aus den Jahren 1088–1100,* p. 164 No. 16; and other sources cited by J. Prawer in *The Crusaders' Kingdom: European Colonialism in the Middle Ages,* pp. 214 ff. On the Maronites and their relations with the Roman Church, see K. B. Salibi, "The Maronites of the Lebanon under Frankish and Mamluk Rule, 1099–1516," *Arabica,* IV, 288–303, esp. pp. 290 f. After a while, the Crusaders allowed the Eastern Orders to return to their old monasteries, perhaps because not enough Catholic monks accompanied the expeditions to fill the empty spaces. In time, the new rulers established two new militant orders of Templars and Hospitallers (1109–1110), which had to be evacuated after the Muslim reoccupation of Jerusalem and other West-Asian areas. We recall the important effects upon the Jews in the Mediterranean islands, such as Rhodes, Cyprus, and Malta, which these Orders controlled after their departure from the Holy Land. See *supra,* Chap. LXXII, nn. 38 ff.; and Vol. XIV, p. 323 n. 47.

14. See J. Prawer's detailed analysis, "The Jews in the Latin Kingdom of Jerusalem" (Hebrew), *Zion,* XI, 38–82; and in the broader context of his standard work, *Toledot Mamlekhet ha-Ṣalbanim,* esp. I, 420 ff.; or in the revised French trans., *Histoire du Royaume Latin de Jérusalem,* esp. I, 522 ff., 528 ff.; S. D. Goitein, "Con-

temporary Letters," *JJS,* III, 176; Baudri (Baldricus) of Bourgueil, *Historia Jerosolomitana,* iv.14, in *RHC,* Historiens occidentaux, IV, 103 n. 7; *supra* Vol. IV, pp. 110, 294 ff. nn. 23 and 27. A pathetic description of the Jewish sufferings during the First Crusade was presented also by the contemporary rabbi of Aleppo, Baruch b. Isaac, although his flowery language makes it difficult to pinpoint the underlying facts. See the Hebrew text ed. by S. A. Wertheimer in the *Ginze Yerushalayim* (From Jerusalem Collections), II, 169 f.; and on R. Baruch, J. Mann's data in his App. to "The Messianic Movements during the First Crusade" (Hebrew), *Hatekufah,* XXIII, 243–61; XXIV, 335–58, esp. pp. 352 ff. (reprinted in his *The Collected Articles,* photo-offset ed., I, 218 ff.). See also the partial French trans. of R. Baruch's letter in J. Prawer's *Histoire,* pp. 530 f.; and B. Z. Dinaburg (Dinur), "A Study of the History of the Jews in Palestine during the First Crusade" (Hebrew), *Ṣiyyon,* II, 38–66, discussing also that Crusade's aftereffects on the Jewish settlement in twelfth-century Palestine.

15. See L. Massignon, "L'Umma et ses synonymes. Notions de 'communauté sociale' en Islam" (1946), reproduced in his *Opera minora,* collected, classified, and ed. with a bibliography by A. Moubarac, I, 97–103; M. Ahmed, "Umma: the Idea of a Universal Community," *Islamic Studies,* XIV, 27–54; E. Sivan, "Réfugiés Syro-Palestiniens," *REI,* XXXV, 135 ff.; and, more broadly, idem, *L'Islam et la croisade. Idéologie et propagande dans les réactions musulmanes aux croisades.* R. Baruch b. Isaac has recently become more widely known in connection with the letter of recommendation he issued in behalf of Obadiah (Johannes), the Norman proselyte. See *supra,* Vols. III, pp. 141, 169, 190, 320 n. 21; IV, 294 n. 24. On the intriguing personality of this proselyte, see also the additional recent publications by A. Scheiber, "Obadiah Scroll," *AOH,* IV, 271–96 (reproducing the texts which had previously come to light), and "Ein aus arabischer Gefangenschaft befreiter christlicher Proselyt in Jerusalem," *HUCA,* XXXIX, 163–75, esp. p. 168 n. 4 (listing the older literature on the subject), 169 ff. (publishing an additional fragment in the original Hebrew); and N. Golb, "A Study of a Proselyte to Judaism Who Fled to Egypt at the Beginning of the Eleventh Century" (Hebrew), *Sefunot,* VIII, 85–104, esp. App. pp. 102 ff.

16. A. A. Beugnot, ed., *Livre des Assises de la Cour des Bourgeois,* ccxli, in *Les Assises des Jérusalem, Lois* II, 171 ff.; Benjamin of Tudela, *Massa'ot,* ed. by M. N. Adler, pp. 20 ff. (Hebrew), 18 ff. (English); and other sources cited by J. Prawer in his aforementioned essay in *Zion,* XI, esp. pp. 55 ff.; and *The Crusaders' Kingdom,* pp. 233 ff. The conflict in the number of Tyre's Jewish inhabitants as quoted by Benjamin and the mere nine families, or approximately fifty persons, mentioned but a few years earlier by the Venetian agent, Marsilius Georgius (in R. Röhricht's *Regesta Regni Hierosolymitani (MXCVII–MCCXCI),* I, 290 No. 1114), is persuasively explained by Prawer by the likelihood that Marsilius had in mind only the Jews residing in Tyre's Venetian quarter. (Incidentally, efforts to ascertain the number of Jews in any locality of the Latin Kingdom on the basis of names are hampered, as in Europe, by the records of certain indubitable Christians bearing such names as Petrus Judaeus or Johannes de Judea. See Röhricht, *ibid.,* pp. 77 f. No. 302, 89 No. 340, 95 No. 362; *Additamentum,* p. 97 No. 1413c.) On the legal conditions in the Crusader kingdom, see also Prawer's succinct observations in his *Estates, Communities and the Constitution of the Latin Kingdom* (*Proceedings* of the Israel Academy of Sciences and Humanities, Vol. II, no. 6). See also J. S. C. Riley-

Smith, *The Feudal Nobility and the Kingdom of Jerusalem, 1174–1277*, esp. pp. 83 f., 88 ff. This author overstates, however, the discriminatory treatment of Jews by the Latin rulers; it was, if anything, less extensive than in the European countries from which the Franks had come.

17. See, for instance, the treaty concluded in 1173 between the Republic of Pisa and Egypt in M. Amari's *I Diplomi arabi nel R. Archivio Fiorentino*, pp. 257 ff. No. vii, 262 ff. Nos. viii–xii (under Saladin), etc.; and, more generally, K. H. Almendinger, *Die Beziehungen zwischen der Kommune Pisa und Ägypten im hohen Mittelalter. Eine rechts- und wirtschaftshistorische Untersuchung* (Beiheft, *VSW*, 54), esp. p. 60. Of considerable interest also are the older but still very useful studies by E. H. Byrne, "Genoese Trade with Syria in the Twelfth Century," *AHR*, XXV, 191–219, esp. pp. 209, 216 ("one interesting transformation in the trade between 1154 and 1205 is the gradual displacement of gold and silver by cloth as the most important article of export"), and *Genoese Shipping in the Twelfth and Thirteenth Centuries;* C. Brizzolari's brief notes, particularly on the early Genoese quarters in the Middle East, in his *Gli Ebrei nella storia di Genova*, pp. 27 ff.; and G. Wiet, *Les Marchands d'épices sous les sultans mamlouks*, which also includes data on the pre-Mameluke period. See also *supra*, Vols. IV, pp. 26, 186, 245 n. 28, 331 f. n. 47; X, pp. 272 f., 278, 421 f. n. 65, 424 n. 70.

The newly established relationships between the Italian and the Middle-Eastern Christians may have enhanced, rather than reduced, the opportunities for Jewish businessmen and agents. See the documentary collection by G. (J.) Müller, *Documenti sulle relazioni delle città toscane coll'Oriente cristiano e coi Turchi fino all'anno MDXXXI;* and such recent analyses as B. Spuler's "Les Chrétiens orientaux et leur relations avec les Vénitiens et les Italiens en général pendant la domination latine dans le Levant," in A. Pertusi, ed., *Venezia e il Levante fino al secolo XV*, I, 679–86. On the impact of these new developments on the European gold reserves, see the stimulating essay by F. Braudel, "Monnais et civilisations. De l'or du Soudan à l'argent d'Amérique, un drame méditerranéen," *Annales ESC*, I, 9–22. Though in the main leading up to the epochal transformations during the sixteenth century, Braudel's remarks have a bearing also on the late medieval period.

18. See S. Runciman's comprehensive *History of the Crusades*, esp. III, 270 ff.; A. S. Atiya's reiterated insistence during the last four decades that the Crusades were a long-lasting, more or less continuous process which covered practically the entire Late Middle Ages, in his *The Crusade in the Later Middle Ages*, and in his aforementioned essay in the *Journal of World History*, II, 469–75; and the Syriac chronicler's observation in A. S. Tritton's trans., "The First and Second Crusades from an Anonymous Syriac Chronicle, with Notes by H. A. R. Gibb," *JRAS*, 1933, pp. 69–101, 273–305, esp. pp. 296 f. See also such recent analyses as G. Valentini, "La Crociata da Eugenio IV a Callisto III (dai documenti d'archivi di Venezia)," *Archivum historiae pontificiae*, XII, 91–123; and J. A. Brundage, "Recent Crusade Historiography: Some Observations and Suggestions," *Catholic Historical Review*, XLIX, 493–507.

19. J. I. Smith, "The Meaning of 'Islam' in Hadīth Literature," *Islamic Culture*, XLVIII, 139–48, esp. p. 140; A. S. Atiya, *Crusade, Commerce and Culture*, esp. pp. 130 ff.; and other literature on the *jihad* listed *supra*, n. 2. After frequent changes in the Muslim attitude concerning the sanctity of Jerusalem, the loss of the city to

the Crusaders strongly reinforced its veneration as Islam's third holiest city. Even then, some influential voices were heard trying to lower its dignity as compared with Mecca and Medina. From among the large literature on the subject see particularly J. W. (H. Z.) Hirschberg's twin essays, "The Place of Jerusalem in the Muslim World" (Hebrew), *Yerushalayim* (Quarterly), II, 55–60, and "The Sources of Moslem Traditions Concerning Jerusalem," *Rocznik Orientalistyczny,* XVII, 314–50; S. D. Goitein, "The Sanctity of Jerusalem in Early Islam" (1945–46), reprinted in his *Studies in Islamic History and Institutions,* pp. 135–48; E. Sivan, "Le Caractère sacré de Jérusalem dans l'Islam aux XIIe–XIIIe siècles," *Studia Islamica,* XXVII, 149–82; and C. D. Matthews, *Palestine, Mohammedan Holy Land.* Among those opposing the exaltation of Jerusalem was the leading fourteenth-century theologian, Taqi ad-Din Ibn Taimiya. See idem, "A Muslim Iconoclast (Ibn Tamiyyeh) on the 'Merits' of Jerusalem and Palestine," *JAOS,* LVI, 1–21; and, more generally, H. Laoust, *Essai sur les doctrines sociales et politiques de Taki-D-Din Ahmad b. Taimīya, canoniste ḥanbalite, 661–728/1262–1328.* Ibn Taimiya's bias may well have been connected with his general denigration of Jews and Judaism, about which see *infra,* nn. 61, 64 ff. On the changing attitudes toward Jerusalem, see also M. J. Kister, " 'You Shall Not Set Out Only For Three Mosques': a Study of an Early Tradition," *Le Muséon,* LXXXII, 173–96, showing how efforts to reduce the number to two mosques by eliminating Jerusalem from the triad alternated with endeavors to enlarge the number by adding Damascus or other cities.

20. Innocent III's Letters xvi, Nos. 28 and 37 of 1216 in Migne's *PL,* CCXV, 817–22, 831 f.; R. Röhricht, *Regesta Regni Hierosolymitani,* I, 232 No. 864; S. Runciman, *History of the Crusades,* III, 145 f.; H. L. Gottschalk, *Al-Malik al-Kāmil,* pp. 50, 88 ff., 152 ff., and the sources cited there; L. Massignon, "La Légende 'De Tribus Impostoribus' et des origines islamiques" (1920), reproduced in his *Opera minora,* I, 82–85.

Needless to say, Frederick II staunchly denied the rumor of his authorship of the incriminating tract. See J. L. A. Huillard-Bréholles, ed., *Historia diplomatica Friderici Secundi,* V, 339. Massignon has indeed shown that this theme had been attributed to the Qarmatian leader Abu Tahir (d. 932) and been reproduced by the famous eleventh-century Seljuk vizier Nizam al-Mulk in his *Siyasat namah* (*Siasset Nameh,* Book of Government), xlvii, ed. and trans. into French by C. Schefer, pp. 197 (Arabic), 288 (French). The accusation had been disseminated in the Middle East some 150 years before it began to be circulated in Europe. The Arabic text read briefly: "In this world three men have corrupted the people: a shepherd, a medicine man, and a camelier. And the camelier was the worst juggler, the worst conjurer of the three." See *supra,* Vol. V, pp. 103 f., 336 f. n. 29.

21. See my "Yehudah Halevi: an Answer to a Historic Challenge," *JSS,* III, 243–72, reprinted in *Ancient and Medieval Jewish History: Essays,* ed. by L. A. Feldman, pp. 128–48, 433–43; *supra,* Vol. V, pp. 159 ff., 197 ff., 334 ff., 349 ff., esp. p. 198; J. Mann, "The Messianic Movements during the First Crusades" (Hebrew), *Hatekufah,* XXIII–XXIV, reproduced in his *The Collected Articles,* I, 182–224. On the provisions relating to residence in Palestine, see esp. Bab. Talmud, Ketubot 110b; R. Ḥayyim b. Ḥananel ha-Kohen's statements quoted in *Tosafot, ibid., s.v. Hu;* Maimonides, *Commentary* on the Mishnah, Ketubot, XIII, 11 end; E. E. Urbach, *Ba'ale ha-Tosafot* (The Tosafists, Their History, Works, and Methods), pp. 107 ff.;

H. Z. Zimmels, "Erez Israel in den Responsen-Literature des Mittelalters," *MGWJ*, LXXIV, 44–64, esp. p. 52; *Sifre on Deuteronomy*, No. 80, ed. by H. S. Horowitz, reed. with variants and notes by L. Finkelstein, p. 146 (although the lengthy discussion here may have been a later interpolation [see *ibid.*, n. 4], it nevertheless reflected the prevailing tannaitic concept and was, as such, accepted by Naḥmanides and others), together with the literature listed in these studies.

Since the publication of Zimmels's noteworthy essay, much ado has been made about R. Ḥayyim's legal decisions. In fact, this distinguished Tosafist did not wish to give vent to any anti-Palestinian feelings. On the contrary, on other occasions, he himself stressed the difference between the essentially temporary nature of the exilic Diaspora and the far superior permanent ancestral home. But being confronted with the practical question of a husband trying to force his wife to join him in emigrating to the Holy Land, he had to take a realistic stand. According to the same talmudic provision, the wife, too, had the right to force her husband to settle in Palestine. But in practice these and other strongly pro-Palestinian utterances of the ancient and medieval rabbis were rarely enforced. For similar reasons another Talmudic provision that a Jew must not emigrate from Palestine for economic reasons, unless there were famine conditions exemplified by a measure of wheat being sold, if at all, at the inflated price of one *sela'*, went into total disuse.

22. Shem Ṭob Sonzolo's data, summarized by Joseph Ibn Verga in his Supplement to his father's work, Solomon Ibn Verga, *Shebeṭ Yehudah* (Judah's Rod, A Chronicle), ed. and trans. into German with additions by M. Wiener, I, 113 (Hebrew), II, 232 (German); rev. ed. with notes by A. Shohet and an intro. by Y. Baer, pp. 147, 222; S. Krauss, "L'Émigration des 300 rabbins en Palestine en l'an 1211," *REJ*, LXXXII, 333–52; *supra*, Vol. IX, pp. 94, 238 n. 9, 284 f. n. 5; Naḥmanides (Moses b. Naḥman), *Perush* (Commentary) on the Pentateuch, esp. on Lev. 18:25, 26:32; and other data quoted by P. Grajewsky in his *Ha-Ramban vi-Yerushalayim* (Naḥmanides and Jerusalem); J. Prawer in his *Crusaders' Kingdom*, pp. 249 ff. It may be noted that another illustrious scholar of that period, R. Meir bar Baruch of Rothenburg (ca. 1215–93), not only took the decisive step of trying to leave the Holy Roman Empire for Palestine, but also generally claimed—along lines similar to those of Naḥmanides—that Gentiles usually did not flourish while in control of Palestine, whereas Jews did. See his *Resp.*, ed. by M. Bloch, No. 15; the German trans. by Zimmels, pp. 52 f.; in the English trans. by I. A. Agus in his *Rabbi Meir of Rothenburg, His Life and His Works*, II, 680 f. No. 787.

We recall that similar changes in attitude toward the religio-historical role of Jerusalem had taken place in Islam in response to changing historical conditions. See *supra*, n. 19. The Christian world, too, varied in its evaluation of the Holy City's position within the framework of its faith. See S. Möhl's noteworthy summary, "Jerusalem in mittelalterlicher Sicht," *Die Welt als Geschichte*, XXII, 11–26. This is not surprising, as all three religions shared one interlocking vision of a transcendental mystical-spiritual Jerusalem (*Yerushalayim shel ma'alah*, or heavenly Jerusalem) with that of a real earthly city, with all the usual shortcomings of a relatively small town located in an unstable political and economic environment.

23. See the general description by A. Hartmann, "Türken in Bagdad zur Zeit der späten Abbasiden, am Beispiel der Herrschaft von An-Nasir li-Din Allahs (1180–1225)," *Der Islam*, LI, 282–97. At one point the Assassins allegedly were ready to

adopt Christianity, a conversion which might have seriously affected the over-all power structure in the Middle East before the Mongolian invasion. See J. Hauziński's Polish analysis of "The Alleged Attempts to Convert the Syrian Assassins to Christianity in the Light of William of Tyre's Report," *Przegląd historyczny,* LXIV, 243–53, with Russian and French summaries.

24. See esp. J. Mann, "The Exilarchic Office in Babylonia and Its Ramifications at the End of the Geonic Period" (Hebrew), *Livre d'hommage (Sefer Zikkaron) à . . . Samuel Poznanski,* pp. 18–32, esp, p. 27; the "Letters of R. Samuel b. 'Ali and His Contemporaries" (Hebrew), ed. by S. Assaf in *Tarbiz,* I, Part 1, pp. 102–130; Part 2, pp. 43–84; Part 3, pp. 15–80 (also reprint); and *supra,* Vols. II, pp. 95 ff.; V, pp. 5 ff., 24, 43 ff., 293 f. n. 2, 302 n. 25, 311 n. 51. On the situation in Baghdad in the late twelfth and early thirteenth centuries, see the material analyzed by W. J. Fischel in his "Arabische Quellen zur Geschichte der babylonischen Judenheit im 13. Jahrhundert," *MGWJ,* LXXIX, 302–322; and, apparently without the knowledge of this essay, by A. Ben Jacob in his Hebrew study, "New Sourses with Regard to the History of the Jews in Babylonia in the Twelfth and Thirteenth Centuries," *Zion,* XV, 56–69; and, more fully, in his *Yehude Babel* (A History of the Jews in Iraq. From the End of the Gaonic Period [1038 C.E.] to the Present Time). A lengthy decree of appointment of Gaon Daniel b. Eleazar b. Ḥibbat Allah (Netanel), dated 1209, was reproduced by the Arab chronicler, 'Ali b. Anjab ibn as-Sa'i in his *K. al-Jāmi' al-Mukhtaṣar* (an annalistic history), ed. by M. Jawad and A. al-Karmeli. It is cited in I. Goldziher's German trans. in S. Poznanski's *Babylonische Geonim im nachgaonäischen Zeitalter,* pp. 37 ff.; in Ben Jacob's fuller Hebrew version in *Zion,* XV, 66 f.; and in a condensed English rendition in W. J. Fischel's *Jews in the Economic and Political Life of Medieval Islam,* pp. 128 f. Another decree of 1250, installing R. Eli b. Zechariah of Arbil (or Irbil) as gaon was issued by the chief justice rather than by the caliph himself; it is briefly summarized by 'Abd ar-Razzaq b. Aḥmad ibn al-Fuwati in his *K. Al-Hawadiṭ al-Jamia'h* (The Comprehensive Events and Useful Experience of the Seventh Century [A.H.]), ed. by M. Jawad, p. 248; and in the German rendition by Fischel in *MGWJ,* LXXIX, 315 f. On these two authors, see F. Rosenthal, "Ibn al-Fuwati, Kamal," *EI,* III, 769–70 (denying, however, with Jawad, Ibn al-Fuwati's authorship of that work), pp. 925 f.; and, more generally, D. S. Sassoon, *The History of the Jews in Baghdad,* esp. pp. 99 ff.; and H. J. R. Ghanima's Arabic *Ta'rikh Yahud al-Iraq* (A History of the Jews in Iraq), esp. pp. 139 ff.

25. See Fischel in *MGWJ,* LXXIX, 308 ff.; Ben Jacob in *Zion,* XV, 56 ff.; S. M. Stern, "A New Description by Judah Al-Ḥarizi of His Journey to Iraq" (Hebrew), *Sefunot,* VIII, 145–56, with English summary p. [17], esp. pp. 150 f. (Arabic and Hebrew); Benjamin of Tudela, *Massa'ot,* ed. by M. N. Adler, pp. 35 f. (Hebrew), 35 (English); Petaḥiah of Ratisbon, *Sibbub* (Rundreise), ed. and trans. into German by L. Grünhut, pp. 8 ff. (Hebrew), 9 ff. (German); in A. Benisch's English trans., *Travels.* See also *supra,* Vol. III, pp. 100, 276 f. n. 32.

26. See Ben Jacob's analysis of the Arabic text of Abu 'Abdallah Muḥammad ibn Yaḥya abu Fadhlan's letter of 1228 in *Zion,* XV, 62 ff. On the denigrating ceremony connected with the payment of the Jewish poll tax see the passage quoted *supra,* Vol. III, pp. 167 f., 311 n. 53. Despite their one-sidedness, these few glimpses of the life of Baghdad Jewry in the first half of the thirteenth century compare favorably

with the extreme paucity of information available to us about Jews in the other Babylonian cities of that period. For example, in narrating "The History of the Jews in Basra," probably the second largest community in the area, D. S. Sassoon has little more to contribute than a discussion of the purported tomb of Ezra the Scribe and practically glosses over the entire history of that community from the eleventh to the end of the seventeenth century. See his pertinent essay in *JQR,* XVII, 407–469, esp. pp. 412 f.

27. See Paul Pelliot (in collaboration with H. Borchesius, H. Massé, and E. Tisserant), "Les Mongols et la Papauté. Documents nouveaux, édités, traduits et commentés," *Revue de l'Orient chrétien,* XXIII, 3–30; XXIV, 225–335; XXVIII, 3–84, esp. XXIII, 13 ff., here given in a variant from the English translation in B. Spuler's *History of the Mongols: Based on Eastern and Western Accounts of the Thirteenth and Fourteenth Centuries,* trans. by H. and S. Drummond, pp. 69 f. (also reproducing a contemporary Latin translation of Göyük's letter to Innocent IV); Gregory Abu'l-Faraj Barhebraeus, *Chronicum ecclesiaticum,* ed. by J. B. Abeloos and T. J. Lamy; idem, *Chronography,* ed. and trans. by E. A. Budge, esp. fols. 575 (Syriac), 490 (English), cited by W. J. Fischel in his *Jews in . . . Medieval Islam,* p. 91. According to the leading near-contemporary chronicler of the early Mongol conquests, 'Ala ad-Din 'Ata Malik Juvaini, before the conquest of Bukhara Jenghiz Khan's messenger was ordered to advise the local rulers "to stand out of the way of a dreadful deluge." Ultimately, since the local garrison still held out in the citadel, Jenghiz Khan gave orders "for all the quarters of the town to be set on fire; and since the houses were built entirely of wood, within several days the greater part of the town had been consumed, with the exception of the Friday mosque and some of the palaces, which were built with baked bricks." See Juvaini's *Ta'rīkh-i Jahān gushā* (History of the World Conquerer), ed. by Mīrzā Muḥammad ibn 'Abd al-Wahhāb-e Qazwīnī; in the new ed. and English trans. from the Persian by J. A. Boyle, entitled *The History of the World Conqueror,* esp. I, 75 ff. (Persian), 97 ff. (English). The events leading up to the fall of Bukhara (including its important Jewish community) were typical of the general approach of Jenghiz Khan and many of his successors to cities and countries under attack.

28. The overwhelming catastrophe which befell Western Asia and Eastern Europe in the mid-thirteenth century has often been described by contemporary chroniclers and modern historians. Of considerable value still are the older voluminous works by C. M. d'Ohsson, *Histoire des Mongols depuis Tschinguiz Khan jusqu'à Timour Bey ou Tamerlan;* and H. H. Howorth, *History of the Mongols from the 9th to the 19th Century;* as well as such more recent analyses as R. Grousset's study, mentioned *infra,* n. 31. On the situation in Syria, see esp. also such monographs as G. Levi Della Vida, "L'Invasione dei Tatari in Siria nel 1260 nei ricordi di un testimonio occulare," *Orientalia,* IV, 353–76; and W. M. Brinner, "Some Ayyubid and Mamluk Documents from Non-Archival Sources," *Israel Oriental Studies,* II (= *S. M. Stern Mem. Vol.*), 117–43, esp. pp. 119 ff., 127 ff. Damascus did not wholly escape the Mongol wrath, however. It suffered much destruction in a renewed Mongol attack some forty years later. See J. Somogyi's annotated English trans. of the pertinent passage of "Adh-Dhahabī's Record of the Destruction of Damascus by the Mongols in 699–700/1299–1301," in *Ignace Goldziher Mem. Vol.,* ed. by S. Löwinger *et al.,* I, 353–86, esp. pp. 360 ff.

29. See W. J. Fischel, *Jews in . . . Mediaeval Islam,* p. 117; A. Ben Jacob, "New Sources" (Hebrew), *Zion,* XV, 63 f.; and, more generally, E. Ashtor (Strauss), "The Mongol Storm and the Jews: a Contribution to the History of Oriental Jewry from the Arabic Sources" (Hebrew), *Zion,* IV, 51–70, with an English summary, p. iii. Because of the extreme paucity of reliable documentation, Ashtor's pioneering effort has necessarily remained quite incomplete. Nor has the additional information which has come forth through the ongoing general study of the Mongolian invasions during the last three decades shed much new light on the position of the Jews during that "deluvial" transformation. Remarkably, though at first but fellow-sufferers, Jews were often accused by their Muslim neighbors of having supported the invaders. There was no more truth in this assertion—which had some validity in the case of Christians, some of whom viewed the Mongols as liberators from Muslim oppression—than the corresponding rumors in Europe that the Jews had been furnishing weapons to the invading Tatars in 1241. See *supra,* Vols. IX, pp. 218, 343 n. 26; X, pp. 22, 310 n. 24.

30. See H. H. Howorth, *History of the Mongols,* III, 105 f.; Raymond Lull's "Petitio Raymundi (pro conversione infidelium) ad Coelestinum V et ad Cardinales directa" in his *Opera,* ed. by I. Sulzinger, II: Liber de quinque sapientibus, pp. 174 f.; *supra,* Vol. IX, pp. 289 f. n. 4; F. Y. Baer, "Eine jüdische Messiasprophetie auf das Jahr 1186," *MGWJ,* LXX, 113–22, 155–65, esp. pp. 161 ff.; Meshullam b. Solomon Dapiera's poem in J. N. Epstein, "On the Messianic Movement in Sicily" (Hebrew), *Tarbiz,* XI, 218–19; J. Mann, "A Messianic Excitement in Sicily and Other Parts of Southern Europe" in his *Texts and Studies,* I, 34 ff., 41; and other sources discussed by E. Strauss in his *Toledot ha-Yehudim be-Miṣraim,* I, 50 ff. On the monotheistic faiths professed by Jenghiz Khan and his sons see K. Lech's *Das Mongolische Weltreich, Al-'Umari's Darstellung der mongolischen Reiche in seinem Werk* Masālik al-alṣār fī mamālik al-amṣār, with a paraphrase and commentary, pp. 95, 193 n. 39, referring also to B. Spuler's publications on the Mongols and particularly the Golden Horde.

31. See the excerpts from more or less contemporary sources cited by B. Spuler in his *History of the Mongols,* pp. 61, 72 f., 80, 92 f., etc.; and his *Die Mongolen in Iran: Politik, Verwaltung und Kultur der Ilchanenzeit 1220–1350,* esp. pp. 245 ff. On the Mongolian legislation and its impact on Western Asia, see also D. Ayalon, "The Great Yāsa of Chingiz Khan: a Reexamination," *Studia Islamica,* XXXVI, 113–58. Remarkably, despite their inclusion for a time in the same Mongolian Empire, the knowledge of its western, Islamic provinces among the Chinese people was still quite rudimentary. See, for example, F. Hirth's older, but still useful, study of *China and the Roman Orient: Researches into Their Ancient and Medieval Relations as Represented in Old Chinese Records.* Of course, their information about Jews and Judaism was even more limited. This aspect will be more fully discussed *infra,* Vol. XVIII.

32. On the general evaluation of the impact of the Mongol conquests upon the conquered peoples, see the suggestive arguments presented by C. Lemercier-Quelquejay in *La Paix Mongole: joug tatar ou paix mongole?;* and by W. Kotwicz in "Les Mongols, promoteurs de l'idée de paix universelle au début du XIIIe siècle," *Rocznik Orientalistyczny,* XVI, 428–34; and A. M. Sakharov's study mentioned *supra,* Chap.

LXXII, n. 92. See also R. Grousset's suggestive *L'Empire des steppes. Attila, Genghis-Khan, Tamerlan;* or in the English trans. by N. Wolford entitled, *The Empire of the Steppes: a History of Central Asia* (comparing the Mongolian expansion in Asia to the "Barbarian invasions" of early medieval Europe); and H. Lamb, *Genghis Khan, Emperor of All Men.*

33. W. Popper, *Egypt and Syria under the Circassian Sultans 1382–1468 A.D.: Systematic Notes to Ibn Taghri Birdi's Chronicles of Egypt,* I, 87 ff.; E. Strauss (Ashtor), *Toledot ha-Yehudim be-Miṣraim,* I, 3 (mentions the two Jewish Mamelukes); S. D. Goitein, "The Rise of the Middle Eastern Bourgeoisie in Early Islamic Times," *Journal of World History,* III, 583–604, reprinted in his *Studies in Islamic History,* pp. 217–41, esp. p. 235; 'Abd ar-Raḥman Ibn Khaldun, *K. Al-'Ibar* (Book of Examples: a World History), Bulaq, 1867–68 ed., V, 371; excerpt trans. into Hebrew with brief observations by D. Ayalon in his "Ibn Khaldun's View of the Mameluks," *Eretz-Israel,* VII (= *Leo A. Mayer Mem. Vol.*), Hebrew section, pp. 142–43; other sources cited by Ayalon in "The European-Asiatic Steppe: a Major Reservoir of Power for the Islamic World," *Proceedings* of the XXV International Congress of Orientalists, II, 46–52; idem, "The Circassians in the Mamluk Kingdom," *JAOS,* LXIX, 135–47 (arguing, among other matters, that a major reason for the Mameluke weakness in resisting the Ottoman onslaught after a century of relative peace following Timur, was the preceding dwindling of the supply of Kipchak slaves owing to the downfall of the Golden Horde); and by B. Lewis in "The Coming of the Steppe Peoples: II, Egypt and Syria," *Cambridge History of Islam,* ed. by P. M. Holt *et al.,* I, 175–230. See also W. J. Fischel, *Ibn Khaldun in Egypt: His Public Functions and His Historical Research, 1382–1406.*

The peculiar kind of Mameluke slavery is analyzed by D. Ayalon in *L'Esclavage du Mamelouk;* and with respect to black slaves in particular, G. Rotter, *Die Stellung des Negers in der islamisch-arabischen Gesellschaft bis zum 16. Jahrhundert.* The curious antecedents of Sultan Lachin or Lajin have never been satisfactorily ascertained. After he had served for two years as the supreme ruler, he and his chief advisers were assassinated. See P. M. Holt, "The Sultanate of Al-Manṣūr Lāchīn (696–8/1296–9)," *BSOAS,* XXXVI, 521–32.

34. See the sources cited by E. Strauss (Ashtor) in his *Toledot ha-Yehudim,* I, 62 ff.; and, more generally, S. F. Sadeque's comprehensive biography of *Baybars I of Egypt, passim.* Regrettably, the evidence presented by the Muslim historians of the period is often both inadequately transmitted and contradictory. See C. Cahen, "Les Chroniques arabes concernant la Syrie, l'Égypte et la Mesopotamie de la conquête arabe à la conquête ottomane dans les bibliothèques d'Istanbul," *REI,* IV, 333–62; U. Haarmann, *Quellenstudien zur frühen Mamelukenzeit* (analyzing, with some translations, the fourteenth-century chronicles by Al-Jazari and Ibn al-Dawadari); E. Ashtor, "Études sur quelques chroniques mamloukes," *Israel Oriental Studies,* I, 272–97; and, particularly, D. P. Little's detailed analysis in *An Introduction to Mamlūk Historiography: an Analysis of Arabic Annalistic and Biographical Sources for the Reign of al-Malik an-Nāsir Muḥammad ibn Qalā'un.* Little's observation that "a substantial number—half at least—of the major historians of the period have yet to be edited and published" (p. 97) holds true for the days of Baybars as well. A critical edition of Mameluke historiography, along lines similar to the *Monumenta Germaniae Historica* is a major desideratum for Mid-Eastern research.

See C. Cahen's observations in his "Editing Arabic Chronicles: a Few Suggestions," *Islamic Studies,* I, 1–25.

35. See W. Muir, *The Mameluke or Slave Dynasty of Egypt, 1260–1517 A.D.,* esp. pp. 225 ff., App. ii, 229 n. 1. We must not overlook, however, the frequent riots in the Middle-Eastern cities, where the highly mixed and volatile population often reacted temperamentally to the regime's oppressive measures. Because of the religious fanaticism fanned by Muslim leaders, especially in the period of the holy wars against the Crusaders, the Muslim populace also frequently resorted to attacks on "unbelieving" neighbors. Sharp religious controversies also occurred within Islam itself, as attested by the major Shi'ite rebellions of 1157 and 1173, on which see H. M. Khayat, "The Shi'ite Rebellions in Aleppo," *RSO,* XLVI, 167–95, esp. pp. 183 ff., 191 f. They were followed by similar clashes in the subsequent three centuries. See also, more generally, A. N. Poliak, "Les Révoltes populaires en Égypte à l'époque des Mameloukes et leur causes économiques," *REI,* VIII, 251–73, esp. pp. 270 f.; and C. Cahen, "Mouvements populaires et autonomisme urbain dans l'Asie musulmane du moyen âge," *Arabica,* V, 225–62; VI, 25–56, 233–65.

36. See A. N. Poliak, "L'Arabisation de l'Orient sémitique," *REI,* XII, 35–63; A. S. Tritton, "The Tribes of Syria in the Fourteenth and Fifteenth Centuries," *BSOAS,* XII, 567–73, esp. p. 567. It appears that a great many Mamelukes, including quite a few sultans, preferred to communicate with one another in their Turkic dialects, and that their knowledge of Arabic was quite deficient. At the same time the majority of native Jews and Christians, including many Copts, conversed and wrote letters and contracts in Arabic. Yet, at that time the linguistic differences were far overshadowed by the denominational criteria, and hence the equation of Sunni Muslim with Arab was widely accepted in Egypt and Syria.

37. Of the vast literature relating to the interplay of forces affecting East–West relations during that period see, for instance, S. Vryonis, Jr., "Byzantine Attitudes toward Islam during the Late Middle Ages," *GRBS,* XII, 263–86; M. Canard, *Byzance et les musulmans du Proche Orient,* with a Preface by C. Cahen; A. Pertusi, ed., *Venezia e l'Oriente fra tardo medioevo e rinascimento;* U. Benigni, "Documenti e note sulla politica orientale dei Papi," *Bessarione,* V, 238–58, 489–510 (offering excerpts and summaries of documents dating from 1534 to 1623 and 1696); V. Salavert y Roca, "La Expansión catalano-aragonese por el Mediterráneo en el siglo XIV," *Anuario de estudios medievales,* VII, 17–37 (also listing the earlier literature on this subject; p. 17 n. 1); and, more generally, K. M. Setton, *Europe and the Levant in the Middle Ages and the Renaissance;* D. Baker, ed., *Relations between East and West in the Middle Ages,* with an Intro. by D. M. Nicol. At times even generally less hostile nations, such as Aragon, resorted to total prohibitions for their citizens to visit the Middle-Eastern countries. We shall see how some Aragonese Jews were punished by the authorities upon their return. See *infra,* n. 50.

38. The confusing array of rulers under both the Baḥri and Burji sultanates has often puzzled modern historians, since, at times, rival factions recognized different sultans. Good surveys and chronologies are offered by S. Lane-Poole in *The Mohammadan Dynasties: Chronological and Genealogical Tables with Historical Introductions;* C. E. Bosworth in *The Islamic Dynasties: a Chronological and Genealogical*

Handbook; and the older, not yet superseded, work by E. von Zambaur, *Manuel de généalogie et de chronologie pour l'histoire de l'Islam.*

39. See the characteristic quotations from the *Ḥadith* in J. P. Charney's "Action et politique en Islam" in his ed. of *L'Ambivalence dans la culture arabe,* pp. 407–418, esp. pp. 412 f., to which might be added Al-Ghazzali's similar advice in his handbook for royal guidance: "One day of justice is equal to seventy years of prayer," cited by H. Kh. Sherwani in his *Studies in Muslim Political Thought and Administration,* 2d ed. rev., p. 166; and, more generally, É. Tyan, *Histoire de l'organisation judiciaire dans les pays de l'Islam,* stressing the positive and negative sides of the medieval Muslim judiciary. That *dhimmis*, and particularly Jews, could nevertheless not expect equal justice from the Muslim judges was intimated in Sultan Zangi's oft-quoted boast, "Even if the plaintiff were a Jew, and the accused his own son, he would do justice to the plaintiff." The observation of the well-informed eighteenth-century French consul, L. S. Chenier, that in mixed litigations the Muslim "judges are always in favor of the Mahomedan" party, largely held true for the medieval period as well. See his *The Present State of the Empire of Morocco,* English trans. from the French, p. 158.

The excesses of the Syro-Egyptian regimes before the Mongolian invasion were rightly stressed by the historian 'Ala ad-Din Juvaini (1226–83) as one of the reasons why the Mongolian invaders found receptive listeners among the masses of peasantry. Juvaini stated: "The practice of tyranny and oppression having exceeded all bounds and the peasants in particular being crushed and ground underfoot by the collection of casual levies to such an extent that the produce of their crops did not amount to the half of the contribution [required] from them, he [the Mongolian emperor, Mengus] gave orders [that all officials] behave with self-control." See Juvaini's *The History of the World Conqueror,* trans. (from the Persian text, ed. by Mirza Muhammad Qazwini) by J. A. Boyle, II, 599. As we shall see, the urban population, and particularly Jews and Christians, did not fare any better.

The balance of power between sultan and emirs often varied; at times it resulted in the demotion or banishment, even imprisonment, of governors guilty of undue harshness or other abuses of power. See D. Ayalon, "Discharges from Service, Banishments and Imprisonments in Mamluk Society," *Israel Oriental Studies,* II (= *S. M. Stern Mem. Vol.*), 25–50, emphasizing that Jerusalem was the most frequently chosen locale to which the guilty governors were dispatched. Apart from the Holy City's pleasant climate and emotional appeal, it was favored because it had neither fortifications nor a substantial garrison, which increased the difficulty for any rebellious emir to start an uprising against the sultan (pp. 34 f.). See also P. M. Holt, "The Position and Power of the Mamluk Sultans," *BSOAS,* XXXVI, 237–49.

40. See K. S. Salim, "Listes chronologiques des grands cadis de l'Égypte sous les Mamelouks, établies, annotées et documentées," *REI,* XXV, 81–125; A. Schimmel's analytical study of *Kalif und Kadi im spätmittelalterlichen Ägypten;* C. Cahen, "Mouvements populaires," *Arabica,* V, 230, 233; VI, 25 f., 29 ff.; F. Taeschner, "Die Islamischen Futuwwabünde. Das Problem, ihre Entstehung und die Grundlinien ihrer Geschichte," *ZDMG,* LXXXVII, 6–50 (emphasizes the looseness of the *futuwwas*' organization, their long history, the more honorary conferral of membership in them to dignitaries, including sultans even during the groups' periods of weakness, like that under the Mamelukes, and the strong opposition to them by Ibn Taimiya and others); idem, "Futuwwa, eine gemeinschaftbildende Idee im mit-

telalterlichen Orient und ihre verschiedenen Erscheinungsformen," *Schweizerisches Archiv für Volkskunde,* LII, 122–58; idem, "Futuwwa," *EI,* 2d ed., II, 967. On the impact of these loosely organized societies on Jews and particularly Jewish artisans, see *infra,* nn. 94–95. Their communal aspects will be discussed in a later volume.

41. See B. Lewis, "The Islamic Guilds," *Economic History Review,* VIII, 22–37, showing some anti-guild reactions, voiced by Ibn Taimiya and others, and pointing out four basic differences between the Islamic and West-European guilds, including the eastern interconfessionalism. By the thirteenth century the overwhelming majority of Mid-Eastern Jewry lived in cities, large and small. Hence Jewish life was greatly influenced by the structure and life-style of the urban environment. Of the large literature, partially written in response to the great interest in urban problems evinced by modern scholars, we need but mention the following studies: N. A. Ziadeh, *Urban Life in Syria under the Early Mamluks* (pointing out the great changes in the Middle East's urban population by listing the cities mentioned by Muqaddasi in the tenth century which, in the course of the following half a millennium, had been destroyed or turned into villages, while others persisted or even grew larger; pp. 52 f.); I. M. Lapidus, *Muslim Cities in the Later Middle Ages;* idem, "The Evolution of Muslim Urban Society," *CSSH,* XV, 21–50, esp. pp. 24 ff., 37 ff.; E. Wirth, "Strukturwandlungen und Entwicklungstendenzen der orientalischen Stadt. Versuch eines Überblicks," *Erdkunde,* XXII, 101–128; and the succinct observations by G. E. von Grunebaum in "Die Islamische Stadt," *Saeculum,* VI, 138–53. Of considerable interest also are the various points of view advanced at two recent symposia: I. M. Lapidus, ed., *Middle Eastern Cities: a Symposium on Ancient, Islamic and Contemporary Middle-Eastern Urbanism;* and A. H. Hourani and S. M. Stern, eds., *The Islamic City: a Colloquium.*

42. See *supra,* Vols. III, pp. 99 ff.; VI, pp. 222 ff., 435 f. nn. 88–90; A. N. Poliak, "The Demographic Evolution of the Middle East," *Palestine and Middle East,* X; S. D. Goitein, "The Social Services of the Jewish Community, as Reflected in the Cairo Geniza Records," *JSS,* XXVI, 3–22, 67–86; idem, *A Mediterranean Society,* II, 138 ff., 438 ff. App. B, 469 f. Tables 1–3, 471 ff. App. C. While such lists of contributors to, and recipients of, charities do not necessarily cover the entire membership of the Jewish community and, because of the voluntary character of the donations and the selectivity in distribution, may not quite equal the records of compulsory taxes, the fact that we have here fifty authentic documents of different years allows for conclusions which are in some ways even more satisfactory. Certainly, the trends in growth or decline of a Jewish community can more easily be deduced from such figures even if the absolute numbers may not be reliably estimated.

43. See W. Popper, *Egypt and Syria under the Circassian Sultans, 1382–1468,* I, 82, 88 f.; the memorandum written by Yacoub Artin Pasha in reply to queries by William Muir and published in Appendix 2 of Muir's *The Mameluke . . . Dynasty,* pp. 224 ff.; Bertrandon de La Brocquière, *The Travels to Palestine and His Return from Jerusalem Overland to France 1432–33,* English trans. by T. Johnes, pp. 154, 160.

44. G. Wiet, "La Grande peste noire en Syrie et en Égypte," *Études d'orientalisme dédiées . . . à Lévi Provençal,* I, 367–83; M. W. Dols, *The Black Death in the Middle East* (includes a brief survey of later epidemics); D. Ayalon, "The Plague and Its

Effects on the Mamluk Army," *JRAS,* 1946, pp. 67–73; the Aleppo scribe's report in Muḥammad ibn Ṣaṣra's *A Chronicle of Damascus,* ed. and trans. by W. M. Brinner (see *infra,* nn. 59 and 63), I, 182 f. (II, fol. 140b); E. Strauss (Ashtor), *Toledot,* I, 6 f., 55; II, 417 ff., 429 ff., etc.; idem, *Histoire des prix et des salaries dans l'Orient médiéval,* pp. 272 f., 387 f.; idem, "The Number of Jews in Medieval Egypt," *JJS,* XVIII, 9–42; XIX, 1–22, and the sources listed there. The Mamelukes were not exclusively responsible for these unfortunate conditions. Just as the plague of 1202–1203 occurred before their seizure of power, so were the large-scale massacres of civilians by hostile armies a frequent accompaniment of all wars. See, for instance, the graphic description of the devastation of Mosul and its neighboring Imramiyya (a place of pilgrimage for both Muslims and Jews), by the Mongols in 1236, in the letter published by S. D. Goitein in his "Glimpses from the Cairo Geniza on Naval Warfare in the Mediterranean and on the Old Mongol Invasion," *Studi orientalistici* in honor of Giorgio Levi della Vida, I, 393–408. On the enlarged district of Aleppo, see M. Gaudefroy-Demombyne, *La Syrie à l'époque des Mameloukes d'après les auteurs arabes,* pp. 85 ff.

Typical of some Westerners in the Mameluke camp are the two German Mamelukes encountered by the German pilgrim Arnold von Harff. One of them, we are told, had been sold seven times, and on his world-wide peregrinations had come across ten Christian and three Jewish sects. See Harff's *The Pilgrimage from Cologne, through Italy, Syria, Egypt, Arabia, Ethiopia, Nubia, Palestine, Turkey, France and Spain, Which He Accomplished in the Years 1496 to 1499,* trans. from the German and ed. with Notes and an Intro. by M. Letts, pp. 128 f.

45. See Meshullam da Volterra, *Massa' be-Ereṣ Yisrael* (A Journey to Palestine), ed. by A. Yaari, p. 53. On the identity of Taghri Birdi, a Jewish convert to Islam, see the numerous references to him by the contemporary historian, Muḥammad b. Aḥmad Ibn Iyas in *Die Chronik,* ed. by P. Kahle, M. Mustafa, and M. Sobernheim, 2d ed., revised and provided with Indices by M. Mustafa, Parts III–V; and *infra,* n. 49.

46. See Ashtor's and Goitein's studies cited *supra,* nn. 42 and 44; and W. J. Fischel's "*Ascensus Barcoch:* a Latin Biography of the Mamluk Sultan Barqūq in Egypt (died in 1399) Written by B. de Mignanelli in 1416, Rendered into English with an Intro. and a Commentary," *Arabica,* VI, 57–74, 152–72, esp. p. 67. It is not surprising that the two Jewish travelers Meshullam da Volterra and Obadiah di Bertinoro who visited the Middle East in 1481 and 1488, respectively, differed somewhat in their estimates. See Da Volterra's *Massa',* ed. by A. Yaari, pp. 53, 57; and Bertinoro's *Letters* (*Epistles*) in various editions but readily available in Yaari's compilation of *Iggerot Ereṣ Yisrael,* pp. 119 ff., estimating the total of Cairo Jewry at 700 families, *including* 150 Karaite and 50 Samaritan households (that is 300 fewer Rabbanite families than in Da Volterra's report), or a total of more than 3,500 persons. Neither this discrepancy in reports only seven years apart nor the even greater divergence between the two travelers concerning Jerusalem's Jewish population is generally attributed by scholars to their personal unreliability. See, for instance, I. Ben Zvi, *Ereṣ Yisrael ve-yishubah bimei ha-shilṭon ha-'ottomani* (Eretz-Israel under Ottoman Rule: Four Centuries of History), pp. 140 f. Indeed, their respective informants may themselves have been uncertain about the number of their fellow Jews; at times two informants in the same community may have furnished somewhat conflicting

data to two successive visitors. Basically, however, it appears that Ashtor's revised estimate is too low. At the same time his careful review of the situation in the individual Egyptian Jewish communities is very valuable; it may in part be supplemented by W. Niemeyer's data in his Hamburg dissertation, *Ägypten zur Zeit der Mamluken kulturlandeskundliche Skizze.*

47. See Da Volterra's *Massa'*, pp. 71 f.; Felix Fabri's *Evagatorium in Terrae Sanctae . . . peregrinationem* (Jerusalem Journey), trans. into English by H. F. M. Prescott, in the Palestine Pilgrim's Translation Series, VII, 226; Bernard von Breydenbach, *Die Reise ins Heilige Land, ein Reisebericht aus dem Jahre 1483,* modernized German trans. with a Postscript by E. Geck, p. 26; Bertinoro in Yaari's *Iggerot,* pp. 122, 127. See also M. Ish-Shalom's comments in *Massa'ei Noṣrim* (Christian Travels in the Holy Land), pp. 22, 254, 259.

48. E. Ashtor, "Un Mouvement migratoire au haut moyen âge: migrations de l'Irak vers les pays méditeranéens," *Annales ESC,* XXVII, 185–214; S. D. Goitein, *A Mediterranean Society,* I, 53, 67 f. The Western immigration continued to the end of the Middle Ages and beyond. The Iberian Peninsula, the German-speaking countries, and Italy furnished not only contingents of temporary visitors but also some permanent settlers. See J. Braslavsky, "On the Immigration of German Jews to Palestine in the Fifteenth Century (from Non-Hebrew Sources)" (Hebrew), *Zion,* II, 56–69; with the comments thereon by M. Shulvass and L. Lewis, *ibid.,* III, 86–87 and 88. We also recall A. H. Freimann's essay on "Palestine Emissaries and Pilgrims: Fifteenth Century Documents from Candia" (Hebrew), *ibid.,* I, 185–207, cited *supra,* Chap. LXXII, n. 37. Quite apart from pilgrimages to holy places, many scholars, both Muslim and Jewish, were moved by intellectual curiosity to traverse the countries of the Mediterranean world. See the examples from the earlier period assembled by S. D. Goitein, *A Mediterranean Society,* I, 51 ff.

49. See S. D. Goitein, *ibid.,* II, 67 f., 382 ff.; and A. N. Poliak, "Nafis ben David and Sa'd ad Dawla" (Hebrew), *Zion,* III, 84–85, with an English summary, p. vi, describing one such fourteenth-century convert from Karaism. After conversion, Nafis could freely enter Arabia. Another convert, the dragoman Taghri Birdi who befriended Da Volterra (*supra,* n. 45), was a Spanish immigrant. Of course, Nehemiah Brüll's interpretation of the pertinent passages in Da Volterra's travelogue (in "Der Ägyptische Vezir Tagri Berdi," *Jahrbücher für jüdische Geschichte und Literatur,* VIII, 41–42), that Taghri Birdi was none other than the distinguished historian, is untenable, since this Taghri Birdi had died in 1469, twelve years before Meshullam's arrival in Egypt. Apparently the dragoman, like many other converts, had enough nostalgia to try to be helpful to some new Jewish arrivals.

50. F. I. Baer, *Juden im christlichen Spanien,* I, 295 No. 212; E. Strauss, *Toledot,* II, 59; Meshullam da Volterra, *Massa',* pp. 39 ff. On the whole, the toleration of Jews and Christians in the Muslim world was based upon the treaties concluded by Mohammed and the first caliphs with the surrendering masses of non-Muslims. See the review of these compacts, reproduced in a French trans. by A. Fattal in *Le Statut légal de non-Musulmans en pays d'Islam,* pp. 18–69. Fattal also reproduces in French a "model convention" prepared for future occasions by Abu 'Abdallah Muḥammad b. Idris ash-Shafi'i, founder of the school of jurisprudence bear-

ing his name (pp. 72 ff.). See also *supra,* Vol. IV, pp. 24, 244 n. 25. In all, both riots and expulsions did not assume countrywide dimensions but were local and sporadic. Certainly, Egyptian and Syrian Jewry was never the subject of a comprehensive decree of expulsion or forced conversion, such as was enacted against its coreligionists in Spain and North Africa by the Almohade regime.

51. See R. J. H. Gottheil, "Dhimmis and Moslems in Egypt," in *Old Testament and Semitic Studies in Memory of William Rainey Harper,* II, 353–414; and on the documents preserved by the Jewish community in Cairo, see his "An Eleventh-Century Document Concerning a Cairo Synagogue," *JQR,* [o.s.] XIX, 467–539; "A Document of the Fifteenth Century Concerning Two Synagogues of the Jews in Old Cairo," *ibid.,* n.s. XVIII, 131–52; "A Decree in Favour of the Karaites of Cairo dated 1024," *Festschrift . . . A. Harkavy,* pp. 115–25. Additional material from the same source was made available by D. S. Richards in his "Arabic Documents from the Karaite Community in Cairo," *JESHO,* XV, 105–164. Some documents also found their way into the Genizah and other Jewish repositories and were published by Jacob Mann, S. D. Goitein, and others.

Understandably, similar materials affecting other denominations or originally dispatched to foreign powers have likewise been preserved, particularly if they were of direct interest to the recipients. See, for example, H. Ernst's annotated ed. and German trans. of *Die Mamlukischen Sultansurkunden des Sinai-Klosters;* and the aforementioned work by M. Amari, ed. and trans., *I Diplomi arabi nel R. Archivio Fiorentino.* Among more recent publications are S. M. Stern and H. Hourani, eds., *Documents from Islamic Chanceries;* Stern's *Fatimid Decrees: Original Documents from the Fatimid Chancery;* G. Wiet, "Décrets mamlouks d'Égypte," *Eretz-Israel,* VII (= *L. A. Mayer Mem. Vol.*), pp. 128*–143*; J. Sauvaget, "Décrets mamlouks de Syrie," *Bulletin d'études orientales* of the Institut Français de Damas, II, 1–52; III, 1–29; XII, 5–60; and H. R. Roemer's "Arabische Herrscherurkunden aus Ägypten," *OLZ,* LXI, 325–47; and *infra,* n. 82.

These documents recovered from collections of originals, however, form but a small minority of enactments and other proclamations cited by historians, including those whose works still exist only in manuscripts scattered through many libraries in Muslim and Christian countries. Of no less interest are, of course, private documents of individual citizens or associations. While we do not have any Muslim collection comparable in size to the Cairo Genizah, which had preserved about 10,000 items of some length from the private sector (in addition to many more pieces of a literary nature), stray documents have been preserved in many localities. They still await fuller discovery, publication, and careful analysis, such as was offered by R. Vesely in "Die Hauptprobleme der Diplomatik arabischer Privaturkunden aus dem spätmittelalterlichen Ägypten," *Archiv Orientální,* XL, 312–43, including a bibliography. On the size of the Genizah collections, see S. D. Goitein, *A Mediterranean Society,* I, 13. Nor must we overlook the specific difficulties of editing Arabic documents, governmental or private. Because many scribes liked to adorn their handwriting with various quirks and flourishes—the pride and joy of numerous calligraphers, an art highly praised by contemporaries—the very reading of manuscripts is often quite arduous. It is made doubly difficult by the absence of vowels and the flowery style beloved by many writers. See, for instance, C. Cahen's pertinent warnings in his "Editing Arabic Chronicles: a Few Suggestions," *Islamic Studies,* I, no. 3, pp. 1–25.

"The need of early cataloguing of all Arabic manuscripts" has also long been felt. It was expressed in a pertinent resolution adopted on January 8, 1971 by the Twenty-Eighth International Congress of Orientalists in Canberra, which also urged that some international initiative to this effect be taken as soon as possible; cited by R. Sellheim in his interesting paper on "The Cataloguing of Arabic Manuscripts as a Literary Problem," *Oriens,* XXIII–XXIV, 306–311, esp. pp. 310 f. Such an effort might, hopefully, extend also to the numerous collections preserved in mosques and major private libraries. In the meantime, however, we ought to be grateful for A. J. W. Huisman's meritorious compilation, *Les Manuscrits arabes dans le monde: une bibliographie des catalogues.* Perhaps the time has come for the Arab oil-producing countries to employ a small fraction of their newly accumulated wealth to sponsor large-scale research projects to make these vast treasures of the Arab past accessible in critical editions to scholars throughout the world.

52. See *supra,* Vol. VI, pp. 26, 78, 332 n. 27, 363 n. 85; Ibn al-'Arabi's dictum and the adage concerning the blessing of divergence, cited by J. Berque in "L'Ambiguité dans le fiqh" in J. P. Charney, ed., *L'Ambivalence dans la culture arabe* (a collection of essays written between 1958 and 1967), pp. 232–52, esp. pp. 235 f. On the other hand, the sharply divergent views concerning the total or partial rejection of any *bid'a* (innovation unsupported by tradition) greatly aggravated the jurists' tasks in making the necessary adjustments of law to life. See I. Goldziher's historical analysis of that concept in his *Muhammedanische Studien,* II, 22 ff., or in the English trans. by C. R. Barber and S. M. Stern, and ed. by Stern, *Muslim Studies,* II, 34 ff.; and numerous more recent studies such as S. Labib's "The Problem of Bid'a in the Light of an Arabic Manuscript of the 14th Century," *JESHO,* VII, 191–96 (referring to the Berlin MS of Idris at-Turkmani's *K. al-Luma fi l'Hawadith w'al Bida',* opposing all *bida*'s).

53. See S. Boustany and D. Cohen, "Essai de traduction des Ad'dād," in J. P. Charney's collection, *L'Ambivalence,* pp. 452–61; C. Chemata, *Essai d'une théorie générale de l'obligation en droit musulman,* I, 171; As-Suyuti's claim cited by R. Brunschvig in "Variations sur le thème du doute dans le *fiqh,*" *Studi Orientalistici* in honor of Giorgio Levi della Vida, I, 61–82. See also, more generally, the other illuminating essays in Charney's *L'Ambivalence,* including the article by D. Cohen, "Ad'dad et ambiguité linguistique en arabe," pp. 25–50; and Charney's own "Action et politique en Islam," pp. 407–418. Although largely documented from Moroccan sources, these analyses have broad validity for the Muslim world at large. On the question of the divine attitude toward evil deeds, see D. Gimaret, "Un Problème de théologie musulmane: Dieu veut-il les actes mauvaises? Thèse et arguments," *Studia Islamica,* XL, 5–73; XLI, 63–92; and G. Scholem, "Fulfillment of a Commandment through a Sinful Act" (Hebrew), *Knesset,* II, 347–92.

One of the major difficulties in analyzing the regnant political views of medieval Muslim thinkers and statesmen—notwithstanding the plethora of incidental observations on political facts of life included in many distinguished philosophical and historical works—is the paucity of specialized writings devoted to Muslim public law and political theory. The most important single work by 'Ali b. Muḥammad al-Mawardi, *Al-Aḥkam al-sulta'aniyat* (Treatise on Muslim Law), trans. into French by É. Fagnan under the title *Les Statuts gouvernementaux ou règles du droit publique et administratif,* was not followed, as might have been expected, by a legion of other medieval tracts and commentaries composed by authors facing diverse challenges under the different conditions evolving in various parts of the Muslim world. See also Q. Khan, *Al-Mawardi's Theory of State,* and, more broadly, the noteworthy survey by E. I. J. Rosenthal in his *Political Thought in Medieval Islam: an Introductory Outline.*

54. A. Fattal, *Le Statut légal,* pp. 116 ff.; E. Strauss, *Toledot,* I, 78 ff., 84 ff., etc.; E. Fritsch, *Islam und Christentum im Mittelalter: Beiträge zur Geschichte der muslimischen Polemik gegen das Christentum in arabischer Sprache,* esp. pp. 146 ff.; E. Strauss, "Scheich Ḥidr. Ein Beitrag zur Geschichte der Juden in Damaskus," *WZKM,* XLIV, 227–30. On the increasingly sharp anti-Jewish and anti-Christian polemics in the Mameluke Empire, see *infra,* nn. 66 ff.

55. 'Abd ar-Raḥman b. Muḥammad Ibn Khaldun, *K. al-Muqaddima* (Prolegomènes Historiques), ed. by M. E. Quatremère, Chap. ii, 25 and 27, the quotations being variants from F. Rosenthal's English trans., *The Muqaddimah: an Introduction to History,* I, 302 and 306; S. D. Goitein, *Jews and Arabs,* p. 104; Bab. Talmud, Yoma, 22b; Maimonides, *M.T.* De'ot, vi.i. Ibn Khaldun's and some other historians' critical comments are readily available in a French trans. presented by J. Sauvaget in his *Historiens arabes. Pages choisis, traduits, et presentées,* esp. pp. 137 ff. See also S. D. Goitein's comparative study, "Attitudes towards Government in Islam and Judaism," in a rev. English trans. in his *Studies in Islamic History and Institutions,* pp. 197–213; and my "Some Medieval Jewish Attitudes to the Muslim State," in *Ancient and Medieval Jewish History: Essays,* ed. by L. A. Feldman, pp. 72–94. On the other hand, the Christians, and particularly the Copts, seem to have objected to government service less vigorously not only in practice, but also in theory. See O. Meinardus, "The Attitude of the Orthodox Copts towards the Islamic State," *Ostkirchliche Studien,* XIII, 153–70 (mainly discussing the period of 600–1200 C.E.).

56. Niẓam al-Mulk, *Siyasat namah* (The Book of Government, or, Rules for Kings), trans. from the Persian by H. Darke; S. D. Goitein, "The Origin of the Vizierate and Its True Character," reprinted from *Islamic Culture,* XVI, 255–62, 380–92; and *JAOS,* LXXXI, 425–26, in his *Studies in Islamic History,* pp. 168–96, esp. pp. 190 f.; and *supra,* Vol. III, 150 ff., 159, 302 ff. nn. 34 and 44. See also A. Schimmel, *Kalif und Kadi im mittelalterlichen Ägypten.*

57. Gazi ibn al-Wasiti, *K. ar-Rad 'ali ahl adh-dhimma* (A Polemical Work against the Protected Subjects and Their Followers), published from a Columbia University manuscript with an English translation by R. J. H. Gottheil in "An Answer to the Dhimmis," *JAOS,* XLI, 383–457 (pointing out that, though relatively moderate, the author did not refrain from using the then customary abusive language; for example, any mention of a Jew or Christian bore the prefix "cursed"); E. Strauss, *Toledot,* I, 4, 104 ff., 204 f.; II, 65 ff., 73 f., and so forth. It appears that many local populations had become so inured to the preponderance of *dhimmis* in high places that they rarely staged revolts against the system. See A. N. Poliak in "Les Révoltes populaires en Égypte," *REI,* VIII, 251–73, esp. pp. 270 f. Foreign Muslim visitors, on the other hand, were more keenly aware of this seemingly privileged position of "infidels." It appears that a visit to Cairo by a Moroccan vizier in 1292 gave rise to a chain reaction which ultimately resulted in the sharply discriminatory decree of 1301. Soon after his arrival in the Egyptian metropolis, the vizier observed with

chagrin that a high Christian official riding on horseback was surrounded by a crowd of Muslim petitioners whose requests he treated with contempt. Understandably, such a spectacle deeply irked the visitor from a country which had behind it a century of Almohade religious intolerance. See Strauss, I, 85 ff. See also *supra,* n. 6.

58. Aḥmad b. 'Ali Maqrizi, *K. aṣ-Ṣuluk li-ma'rifat duwal al-muluk* (Histoire des Sultans Mamlouks), ed. by N. A. Ziadeh, French trans. with historical and geographic notes by E. Blochet entitled "Histoire d'Égypte de Makrizi," *ROL,* VI, 435–89; VIII, 165–212, 501–553; IX, 6–163, 466–530; X, 248–341; XI, 192–260; and M. E. Quatremère, *Histoire des sultans mamlouks de l'Égypte;* M. Perlmann, "Notes on Anti-Christian Propaganda in the Mamluk Empire," *BSOAS,* X, 843–61, mainly summarizing, from a British Museum MS, the arguments by Jamal ad-Din al-Asnawi (1305–1370) followed by his ed. of "Asnawi's Tract against Christian Officials," *Ignace Goldziher Mem. Vol.,* I, 172–208; and other sources quoted by A. Darrag in *L'Égypte sous le règne de Barsbay, 825–841/1422–1438,* pp. 140 ff.

59. See Benjamin of Tudela, *Massa'ot,* pp. 31 (Hebrew), 31 (English); Muḥammad b. Aḥmad al-Sarakhsi, *K. al-Mabsut* (comprehensive Ḥanafite work on Muslim law), X, 77 ff., briefly summarized by A. Fattal in *Le Statut légal,* pp. 266 f.; W. M. Brinner, ed. and trans. of *A Chronicle of Damascus* by Muḥammad ibn Ṣaṣra, I, 115 (in the Arabic MS, fols. 82b–83a). On the price paid by Barquq for Mintash, see Bertrando de Mignanelli's aforementioned (n. 46) Latin biography of Barquq, *Ascensus Barcoch,* trans. by W. J. Fischel in *Arabica,* VI, 153. Not surprisingly, a year later these very Jewish defenders were accused—on the basis of a single Jew's torture-exacted confession, later recanted—of setting fire to a local mosque. They were fined 100,000 dirhems and banished from the city. But this decree was speedily revoked. See Ibn Ṣaṣra's *Chronicle,* I, 167 ff. (126b ff.). See also, more generally, D. Ayalon, *L'Esclavage du Mamelouk,* describing the operation of that system from the slave's purchase from a dealer, through his training in the military school, to his emancipation and career in the army. See also the contemporary account in *L'Égypte au commencement du quinzième siècle d'après le traité d'Emmanuel Piloti de Crète (incipit 1420),* ed. by P. H. Dopp, pp. 14 ff.

60. See S. D. Goitein, "The Medical Profession in the Light of the Cairo Geniza Documents," *HUCA,* XXXIV, 177–94 (with a brief postscript on "the Pharmacists"); idem, *A Mediterranean Society,* II, 240 ff., esp. pp. 241, 250. Goitein also quotes a Muslim visitor to Egypt in the 1240s who had observed that most prominent Christians and Jews were either government officials or physicians. A reference work for the market police, written in that period, claimed that there were many towns which, for their medical treatment, depended exclusively on *dhimmi* doctors (*ibid.,* p. 242). We also recall Maimonides' famous description of his extremely busy medical practice in 1199 and Ibn Fadhlan's comment in 1230 regarding the large incomes of Jewish doctors and their luxurious life-style. See *supra,* Vol. VIII, pp. 232, 237, 388 ff. nn. 14 and 20. We shall see that only a small minority of Syro-Egyptian Jewry enjoyed such a high standard of living. But to casual observers and persons suffering from want or envy, it was easy to generalize and attribute the behavior of a few to all "protected subjects."

61. See Maimonides, *M.T.* Akum x.2; L. Nemoy, "A Scurrilous Anecdote Concerning Maimonides," *JQR,* LXII, 158–92; E. Strauss, *Toledot,* I, 106 ff., 112, 173 ff., 202 f.,

and so forth, showing also that the enmity of Muslim physicians toward Jews and Christians at times led them to refuse to give aspiring Jewish students of medicine any instruction, which, in the absence of regular medical schools, was the only method of securing adequate professional training in medicine. Both Muslim and non-Muslim physicians, however, often found themselves in the embarrassing position of having to prescribe medical treatment which in their opinion was most efficacious for curing a disease but which in some way ran counter to the accepted notions of the dominant faith. We recall Maimonides' Introduction to his *Discourse on Sexual Intercourse,* in which he apologized for mentioning wine and music as appropriate stimulants. He stated that he was not advising his princely patient to break Muslim law, but rather indicating what, from the medical point of view, might be a useful remedy. See *supra,* Vol. VIII, pp. 251, 402 n. 40. Some extreme Muslim pietists went so far as completely refusing the aid of secular medicine in curing their ailments. See H. Laoust, *Essai sur les doctrines sociales,* p. 492. One wonders how many Muslim thinkers insisted on such a refusal of medical ministrations by "infidel" doctors when their lives were at stake—a situation for which Jewish law made special allowance for breaking all except three specified basic commandments of the Torah.

62. See S. D. Goitein, *Jews and Arabs,* pp. 66, 74; E. J. Worman, "Notes on the Jews in Fusṭaṭ from Cambridge Geniza Documents," *JQR,* [o.s.] XVIII, 1–39, esp. p. 10 (referring to deeds dated in 1245, 1280, 1282, 1458–59, 1483, and 1496); and J. L. Abu-Lughod, *Cairo: 1000 Years of the City Victorious,* esp. pp. 58, 60, 200 ff. To understand the intricacies of the pertinent Muslim legislation one must bear in mind the strong ties between religion and society under Islam. While occasionally governmental policies deviated from the more extreme postulates of theologians (who at the same time were leading jurists), there was no real separation of church and state even to the extent prevailing in medieval western Europe. Certainly, there was no room in the Muslim world for a protracted conflict resembling the struggle between the Papacy and the Empire. See also the pertinent observations in G. E. von Grunebaum's lectures on *Theology and Law in Islam;* and J. Schacht's *An Introduction to Islamic Law.* Perhaps for that very reason the Muslim theologians had to modify their teachings concerning the toleration of "protected subjects" in order to conform with both their religious traditions and the needs of the state. See J. Gauss, "Toleranz und Intoleranz zwischen Christen und Muslimen in der Zeit vor den Kreuzzügen," *Saeculum,* XIX, 362–89 (which, of course, did not prevent extensive mutual criticism, pp. 378 ff.); and R. Paret, "Toleranz und Intoleranz im Islam," *ibid.,* XXI, 344–65.

63. See S. D. Goitein, *A Mediterranean Society,* I, 19; II, 346; P. Casanova, *Essai de reconstruction topographique de la ville d'al-Fusṭaṭ ou Miṣr;* Ibn Ṣaṣra, *Chronicle of Damascus,* ed. by W. M. Brinner, I, 171 f. (in the Arabic MS, fol. 130ab); and, on Egypt's provincial communities, N. Golb, "The Topography of the Jews in Medieval Egypt: Inductive Studies Based Primarily upon Documents from the Cairo Genizah," *Journal of Near Eastern Studies,* XXIV, 251–70 (mentioning also the Hebrew names for the Nile River, pp. 264 ff.). Continuity in settlement was also promoted by the Muslim predilection for safeguarding the rights of heirs as fully as possible. At least according to the Ḥanafite school of jurisprudence, even the right of a testator to establish a charitable or educational trust (*waqf*) was to be restricted if it seriously deprived the heirs of the inheritance due them. See J. Kresmárik, "Das Wakfrecht

vom Standpunkte des Šari'atrechtes nach der ḥanefitischen Schule. Ein Beitrag zum Studium des islamischen Rechtes," *ZDMG*, XLV, 511–76, esp. pp. 554 ff., 557 f., 573 ff. To be sure, as far as the religious minorities were concerned, inheritance laws were governed by the precepts of the religious community to which the testator belonged. Yet the tendency in general society to preserve family fortunes also affected, to some extent, the outlook of the minorities.

64. See Ibn Taimiya, *Iḥtiyarat,* reproduced in a French trans. by H. Laoust in *Essai sur les doctrines sociales,* p. 276 n. 1. Ibn Taimiya's statement about the governmental repression of internal Jewish heresies may have represented the thinker's personal preference, rather than a general rule of law. There is no evidence that Ibn Taimiya himself ever practiced what he taught, while he was serving as an influential government official. This statement reminds one of a parallel contention of his near-contemporary, the Christian Spanish inquisitor Nicholas Eymeric, that the pope had the right to interfere in Jewish religious affairs. But Eymeric, too, admitted that in practice the pope may consider any such intervention inadvisable. See *supra,* Vol. XIII, pp. 4, 17, 303 n. 1, 311 f. n. 17. However, Ibn Taimiya often spoke and acted as a maverick, antagonizing the established authorities. He also gave the impression of being an unbalanced person, according to such an acute observer as the world traveler Ibn Baṭṭuṭa. See D. T. Little's recent query: "Did Ibn Taimiyya Have a Screw Loose?" *Studia Islamica,* XLI, 93–111. Little believes that no definite answer can be given until all of Ibn Taimiya's writings—many of them are still extant in MSS only—are published, critically analyzed, and chronologically arranged.

65. See the description of one such joint interconfessional reception extended in 1390 to Sultan Barquq on his return to Cairo, presented by E. Strauss in *Toledot,* II, 8.

66. See Aḥmad ibn Idris al-Qarafi, *K. Al-Ajwiba al-faḥira 'an al-ad'ila al-fajira* (Precious Answers to Abominable Questions), pp. 119, 157; Ibn Taimiya, *K. Al-Jawab aṣ-ṣaḥiḥ liman baddala din al-Masiḥ* (A Correct Answer to Those Who Falsify Christ's Religion), II, 102 ff.; III, 123 f.; M. Belin's French trans. of Muḥammad ibn 'Ali ibn an-Naqqash's "Fetoua relatif à la condition des Zimmis . . . jusqu'au milieu du VIIIe siècle de l'Hegire," *JA*, 4th ser. XVIII, 417–516; XIX, 97–140 (includes a partial Arabic text and excerpts from other documents). See also S. M. Stern, "The Oxford Manuscript of Ibn Taimiyya's Anti-Christian Polemics," *BSOAS,* XXII, 124–28 (trying to unravel some of the complications in the literary tradition about this work). Among the anti-*dhimmi* polemists of the period, Ibn Taimiya was indubitably the most thoughtful. Despite his general independence, which more than once landed him in prison, he exerted an enduring influence on both contemporaries and successors. See the complementary studies by H. Laoust: "La Biographie d'Ibn Taimīya d'après Ibn Katir," *Bulletin d'études orientales,* IX, 115–62; *Essai sur les doctrines sociales et politiques;* and his edition and French translation of Ibn Taimiya's *Siyasa Shariya,* or *Le Traité de droit public;* Q. Khan, *The Political Thought of Ibn Taymiyah,* I. Most satisfying to some Muslim readers must have been an anti-Christian polemic by 'Abdallah al-Taryuman who, in many ways, resembled the ninth-century convert 'Ali b. Rabban al-Ṭabari. See M. de Epalza, *La Tuḥfa, autobiografía y polémica islamica contra el Cristianesimo de 'Abdallah al-Taryūman (fray Anselm Turmeda).*

Needless to say, Christians and Jews answered in kind. Clearly, in Christian countries they enjoyed greater freedom in their attacks on Islam than in Muslim areas where any "blasphemy," genuine or fabricated, against the Messenger was subject to capital punishment. See, for example, the excerpts from Byzantine writings translated into French by A. T. Khoury, *Les Théologiens byzantins et l'Islam. Textes et auteurs, VIII–XIIIe s.*, 2d ed.; and his analysis of the *Polémique byzantine contre l'Islam (VIII–XIII s.)*. See also, more broadly, M. Steinschneider's partially outdated and yet most comprehensive bibliographical work, *Polemische und apologetische Literatur in arabischer Sprache zwischen Muslimen, Christen und Juden.*

67. See M. J. Kister, "*Ḥadithū 'an banī isra'īla wa-lā ḥaraja':* a Study of an Early Tradition," *Israel Oriental Studies,* II (= *S. M. Stern Mem. Vol.*), 215–39. It appears, however, that such borrowings from postbiblical Jewish literature and folklore diminished in the later Middle Ages, as Muslim self-assertion grew, and the number of Muslim scholars interested in comparative religious practices and teachings for other than polemical purposes greatly declined. Perhaps it also was more difficult for them to find well-informed Jewish scholars who were willing to engage in friendly theoretical discussions with them in that period of Crusades and Counter Crusades. Certainly, there was no longer room for such dispassionate "godless" assemblies as met regularly in tenth-century Baghdad, which so shocked the Spanish visitor, Ibn Sa'id. See *supra,* Vol. V, p. 85.

68. Al-Qarafi, *K. Al-Ajwiba al-fahira,* pp. 4, 67, 124 ff., cited by E. Fritsch in *Islam und Christentum,* pp. 140 ff. Al-Qarafi's observations betrayed some familiarity with Scriptural rather than contemporary Judaism. Otherwise, since the Jews of his time were overwhelmingly monogamous (the vast documentation in the Genizah refers only to monogamous Jewish families, according to its outstanding student, S. D. Goitein, in *A Mediterranean Society,* I, 73), Al-Qarafi would undoubtedly have included the Jews, too, in his peroration against single wives. Only after the Sephardic influx of the fifteenth and sixteenth centuries did some polygamous marriages begin to play a minor role among Mid-Eastern Jews. It is also barely possible that the great indebtedness of Muslim law to Judaism in regard to marriage and family life deterred the Muslim polemists from attacking the Jewish religion on this score. See S. Bialoblocki, *Materialien zum islamischen und jüdischen Eherecht, mit einer Einleitung über jüdische Einflüsse auf den Ḥadith.* On the relatively few Jewish plural marriages in North Africa and the Ottoman Empire, see *infra,* Chap. LXXIV; and Vol. XVIII.

69. Sa'id ibn Manṣur Ibn Kammuna's statement is quoted *supra,* Vol. V, p. 102. See, more fully, M. Perlmann's introduction to Ibn Kammuna's *K. Tanqîḥ al-abḥāṭ lil-milal aṭ-ṭalāṭ,* ed. by him with an Intro. and Notes; and trans. into English under the title *Ibn Kammuna's Examination of the Three Faiths: a Thirteenth-Century Essay in the Comparative Study of Religion* (pointing out, among other matters, that "the Islamic religion cannot exist, unless it teaches the abrogation of the religion of Moses"; p. 76); and L. Hirschfeld's earlier Heidelberg dissertation, *Sa'ad B. Mansur Ibn Kammūna und seine polemische Schrift* Tankiḥ al-abhat li'l-milal aṭ-ṭalaṭ. The severe penalties imposed by the Muslim authorities for offenses against the Muslim faith are analyzed by A. Turki in his "Situation de 'tributaire' qui insulte l'Islam au regard de la doctrine et de la jurisprudence musulmanes," *Studia Islamica,* XXX, 39–72 (emphasizing that only few condemnations for that transgres-

sion are recorded in the sources). On the other hand, some exceptional cases are also recorded of Muslim scientists of the thirteenth and fourteenth centuries who surrounded themselves with scholars of differing outlooks on life, Muslim, Jewish, and Christian. See *supra,* Vol. V, pp. 83 ff.; and E. Strauss, "L'Inquisition dans l'état mamlouk," *RSO,* XXV, 11–26, esp. p. 12.

70. See E. Strauss, *ibid., passim,* and *Toledot,* I, 73, 96 f., 279 ff., etc.; J. Mann, "Moses b. Samuel, a Jewish Katib in Damascus and His Pilgrimage to Medinah and Mekkah," reproduced from *JRAS,* 1919, pp. 155–84, in *The Collected Articles,* I, 83–112; and the description of a conversion ceremony by a Cologne traveler in "Ein niederrheinischer Bericht über den Orient," ed. by R. Röhricht and H. Meissner in *Deutsche Philologie,* XIX, 22 f. The Almohades, as well as the Shi'ite persecutors of the crypto-Jews in Meshed, imposed upon the converts a distinguishing garment and tried to inhibit even commercial relations between them and the Old Muslims. See S. D. Goitein, *Jews and Arabs,* pp. 80 f. Although the Mameluke regimes generally refrained from following this intolerant example, they often used other, more subtle, ways of discriminating against recent converts. They found a favorable audience among the masses, as reflected in the adage which S. D. Goitein heard in Aden as recently as 1949: "Do not trust a Jew, even forty years after his conversion to Islam." See *A Mediterranean Society,* II, 275; L. Brunot and E. Malka, *Textes judéo-arabes de Fés,* p. 393.

71. See H. Hirschfeld, "A Karaite Conversion Story," *Jews' College Jubilee Volume,* pp. 81–100, esp. p. 89; *supra,* Vol. V, pp. 9 f., 222, 295 n. 6, 395 n. 16; Joseph b. Isaac Sambari, *Liqquṭim mi-Dibre Yosef* (Selections from Joseph's Narrative: a Chronicle), ed. by A. Neubauer in his *Mediaeval Jewish Chronicles,* I, 115–62; the excerpt also reproduced by B. Dinur in his *Yisrael ba-Golah* (Israel in the Diaspora), 2d ed., II, Part 1, pp. 337–39; E. Strauss, *Toledot,* I, 96 f.; and, more generally, S. D. Goitein's analysis in the section devoted to "Converts and Proselytes" in *A Mediterranean Society,* II, 299 ff. Here one also finds some material on the reverse action, namely, conversions to Judaism by either a Muslim or a Christian. These formally constituted a major crime in the entire world of Islam but were more severely prosecuted in the case of proselytes from Islam, just as conversion of a Christian to either Islam or Judaism was treated with great harshness in the Christian world. It is not surprising, therefore, that in the Middle East we find more European than native proselytes. See N. Golb, "Notes on the Conversion of European Christians to Judaism in the Eleventh Century," *JJS,* XVI, 69–74. The most prominent of these new arrivals was the Norman convert Obadiah, about whom see *supra,* n. 15; and Vol. III, p. 320 n. 21. In most cases, these proselytes arrived penniless and depended on the charity of the Jewish community. It appears that on occasion such support was inadequate, if we are to believe the complaints of an interested dependent. See A. Scheiber, "A Proselyte Letter to the Congregation of Fustat," *Essays . . . Israel Brodie,* pp. 377–80; and Goitein, II, 306, 596 nn. 37–38.

72. See H. Laoust, *Essai sur les doctrines sociales,* pp. 462 ff.; *supra,* Vol. III, pp. 10, 143 f., 158, 300 n. 27, 307 n. 43, 331 n. 7, and so forth.

73. Aḥmad b. 'Ali al-Qalqashandi, *K. Ṣubḥ al-a'sha fi ṣina't al-insha* (On the History, Geography and Government of Egypt), XIII, 378 f.; in the excerpt trans. into

Hebrew by L. A. Mayer in his "The Status of the Jews under the Mamelukes" (Hebrew), *J. L. Magnes Anniversary Book,* pp. 161–67; and into English by B. Lewis in his ed. and trans. of *Islam: From Prophet Muhammad to the Capture of Constantinople,* II, 234 f. See also *supra,* Vol. III, pp. 129 f. and the literature listed there, p. 289 n. 10. In addition many eminent jurists wrote *fatwas* (responsa) such as that composed by Muḥammad ibn 'Ali ibn an-Naqqash in 1357–58, trans. into French by M. Belin in his "Fetoua relatif à la condition des Zimmis," *JA,* 4th ser. XVIII–XIX; and that more recently ed., trans. into English, and annotated by A. S. Atiya in "An Unpublished XIVth-Century *Fatwa* on the Status of Foreigners in Mamluke Egypt and Syria," in *Studien zur Geschichte und Kultur des Nahen und Fernen Ostens: Festschrift Paul Kahle,* pp. 55–68. In this responsum, written in 1353, Taki ad-din al-Subḥi drew a sharp line between the safe-conduct extended to foreign traders and the general compact safeguarding the rights of the local "people of the book." The safe-conduct, without which the foreigner was to be rightless, "it being lawful to slay him," was revocable, though the sultan alone was entitled to do so "on what seems to be the good of the Muslims." In such cases the ruler could impose on the alien any kind of penalty, including enslavement or execution. The rights of the *dhimmis,* on the other hand, however restricted, had to be preserved in accordance with the provisions of the Covenant of 'Umar.

See also, more broadly, W. Heffening, *Das Islamische Fremdenrecht bis zu den islamisch-fränkischen Staatsverträgen. Eine rechtshistorische Studie zum Fiqh;* and the texts analyzed a century ago by M. Steinschneider in his *Polemische und apologetische Literatur,* pp. 165 ff. App. I. On Ibn Taimiya's extremist views, see the passages quoted and analyzed by H. Laoust in his *Essai sur les doctrines sociales,* esp. pp. 266 ff. and 276. The distinction between the treatment of male and female bathers becomes comprehensible in the light of the importance attached to baths in the Muslim civilization, on which see H. Grotzfeld's dissertation, *Das Bad im arabisch-islamischen Mittelalter. Eine kulturgeschichtliche Studie.*

How tenuous even the general protection extended to the "people of the book" often was may be noted from the status of the Parsees. Originally included by Mohammed and his early successors in the category of *Ahl al-kitab* (people of the book) who were to be tolerated under Muslim rule, the Zoroastrians greatly dwindled in numbers and political and economic power. Thereupon they lost much of their privileged position. According to Ibn Taimiya, they occupied an intermediate rank between the underprivileged *mushrik* and the protected "people of the book." See his *fatwa,* cited by Laoust, p. 265 n. 1.

74. S. D. Goitein, "The Rise of the Middle Eastern Bourgeoisie in Early Islamic Times," reprinted from the *Journal of World History,* III, 583–604, in his *Studies in Islamic History and Institutions,* pp. 217–41, esp. p. 226; *supra,* Vol. III, pp. 135, 296 n. 16; the document reproduced with an English trans. and an informative introduction by R. J. H. Gottheil in his "Dhimmis and Moslems in Egypt" in *Old Testament and Semitic Studies in Memory of William Rainey Harper,* ed. by R. F. Harper *et al.,* II, 353–414; and the additional materials assembled by Ibn 'Ubayya, the qadhi in Jerusalem, an active protagonist of the destruction of the Naḥmanides Synagogue in Jerusalem in 1474, cited in part and fully analyzed by S. D. Goitein in his "Ibn 'Ubayya's Book Concerning the Destruction of the Synagogue of Jerusalem in 1474" (Hebrew), *Zion,* XIII–XIV, 18–32; Laoust, *Essai sur les*

doctrines sociales, p. 26 n. 4. See also the dozen photographs of impressive extant buildings or tombs from the Mameluke era in W. Muir's *The Mameluke, passim.*

75. The unnamed Damascus poet of 1321 is quoted by Ibn Ṣaṣra in his *Chronicle of Damascus,* ed. and trans. by W. M. Brinner, I, 170 f. (fol. 129ab). On the Cairo incident, see R. J. H. Gottheil in his "Dhimmis and Moslems," *Harper Mem. Vol.,* II, 379. Evidently, however, the twenty-eight synagogues which Benjamin of Tudela found in Baghdad were never leveled by the caliphs, although most of them were doubtless eliminated during the Mongol onslaught. Similarly Cairo's four synagogues of the early fifteenth century, which elicited Al-Maqrizi's comment that they all had been "built under Muslim rule," escaped official suppression as Jewish houses of worship. See *supra,* Vol. III, pp. 134 f., 296 n. 16. On the twelve Christian churches which existed in Cairo in Maqrizi's time, see his descriptions, often translated and analyzed, esp. in L. Leroy's "Les Églises des chrétiens. Traduction de l'arabe d'al-Maqrizi," *ROC,* XII, 190–208, 269–79.

76. See the literature cited *supra,* n. 73; and R. J. H. Gottheil's essays pertaining to the Cairo synagogue in *JQR,* [o.s.] XIX, 467–539; n.s. XVIII, 131–52, cited *supra,* n. 51. See also S. D. Goitein, "The Synagogue Building and Its Furnishings According to the Records of the Cairo Genizah" (Hebrew), *Eretz-Israel,* VII, 81–97; and, more generally, J. Pinkerfeld, *Bate ha-knesiot be-Ereṣ Yisrael* (Synagogues in Palestine from the Geonic Period to the Ḥasidic Immigration). As we recall, the Muslim administration and, still more strongly, some zealous jurist-theologians carefully watched over their coreligionists, as well as over the *dhimmis,* so that they should not enter one another's sanctuaries except in emergencies. In a quandary owing to a muezzin's illness in the Syrian city of Homs (Hims or Hums), they actually hired a professing Jew who had a good voice to fill his place. Not to do violence to his own conscience, the substitute recited the traditional call as follows: "God is most great, the Muslims say that Mohammed is the Messenger of God." See A. S. Tritton's notes from a MS of Muhammad b. Hilāi b. al Ṣābi's *Kitab al-Hafawat* in his "Sketches of Life under the Caliphs," *The Muslim World,* LIV, 104–111, 170–79; LXII, 137–47, esp. LXII, 137.

77. R. J. H. Gottheil in his "Dhimmis and Moslems," *Harper Mem. Vol.,* II, 368 ff., 382 ff. (English), 406 ff. (Arabic). In his notes Gottheil gives numerous variants from related texts, some of which had previously been translated into European languages (p. 383 n. 134). He also refers to a passage in the Hebrew summary of Joseph Sambari's chronicle extant in a Paris MS, which, however, has been omitted in A. Neubauer's ed. (see *supra,* n. 71). The pledge to admit Muslims to churches (and synagogues) doubtless aimed chiefly at needy travelers or investigating officials, because otherwise Muslim pietists usually tried to discourage their coreligionists from entering *dhimmi* houses of worship. Some versions obligated the "protected subjects" to vacate their seats for the benefit of any lower-ranking Muslims as well.

78. See Maimonides, *M.T.* Akum xi.1, 3 with supporting biblical quotations. The literature on the provisions included under the umbrella of the Covenant of 'Umar and their innumerable variations is enormous. Almost all contemporary and modern historians have constantly mentioned them in various contexts. For the time being

we need but refer to the main writings listed *supra,* Vol. III, pp. 139 ff., 298 ff. nn. 22 ff. Of special interest are the examples cited in L. A. Mayer's "Jewish Clothing in the Mameluke Period" (Hebrew), in *Sefer Zikkaron* (Studies in Memory of Asher Gulak and Samuel Klein), pp. 115–18; I. Lichtenstadter's "The Distinctive Dress of Non-Muslims in Islamic Countries," *HJ,* V, 35–52; and, more generally, in L. A. Mayer's, "The Status of the Jews under the Mamelukes" (Hebrew), *Magnes Anniversary Book,* pp. 161–67, succinctly analyzing the rights of, and the restrictions placed on, the "protected people" under the Covenant. On occasion the authorities interpreted the royal edicts as narrowly as possible, however. When in 1321 An-Naṣir ibn Qala'un issued his punitive decree against the Christians and renewed the requirement of distinguishing hats for them, he failed to mention Jews. Thereupon some Christians in Cairo, we are told, borrowed yellow hats from their Jewish neighbors and thus escaped possible retribution. See Al-Maqrizi's *K. Al-Khiṭaṭ,* II, 516; E. M. Quatremère, *Mémoires géographiques et historiques sur l'Égypte et sur quelques contrées voisines,* II, 246 f.; and G. Wiet, *L'Égypte arabe,* pp. 487 ff.

The great emphasis in the Covenant and most subsequent legislation on the shape and colors of the clothing by which the "infidels" were to be distinguished from the conforming majority derived partly from the belief (reflected in a tradition attributed to Mohammed himself) that "when Allah gives riches to a man, he wants it to be seen on him." This sentiment was expressed in various forms in the medieval Arabic literature. See S. D. Goitein in "The Rise of . . . Bourgeoisie," *Journal of World History,* III, 589; or in his *Studies in Islamic History,* p. 224.

79. See R. J. H. Gottheil, "Dhimmis and Moslems," *Harper Mem. Vol.,* II, 380; A. S. Tritton's "Sketches of Life under the Caliphs," *The Muslim World,* LXII, 137; A. Fattal, *Le Statut légal,* pp. 120, 151 f.

80. See Ibn abi Zimra's *Resp.* III, No. 637; IV, No. 22; cited by I. M. Goldman in *The Life and Times of Rabbi David ibn abi Zimra: a Social, Economic, and Cultural Study of Jewish Life in the Ottoman Empire in the 15th and 16th Centuries as Reflected in the Responsa of RDBZ,* pp. 155 f.; H. J. Zimmel's earlier German study, *Rabbi Dawid ibn abi Zimra. Ein Beitrag zur Kulturgeschichte der Juden in der Türkei im 16. Jahrhundert,* Vol. I. On the geonic objections to Jewish taverns, see *supra,* Vol. IV, pp. 164 f. In any case, the alcoholic prohibition as an obstacle to Judeo-Muslim symbiosis and the general aspects of the Jewish wine trade in the Muslim world as well as the problem of the extent to which specific Jewish oaths (see the next note) were administered deserve fuller monographic treatment—admittedly, not an easy task in view of the relative paucity of reliable source materials in either field.

81. See L. A. Mayer's Hebrew translation in "The Status," *Magnes Anniversary Book,* p. 167. Another lengthy formula of the oath *more judaico* had previously been published by I. Goldziher in "Le Serment des Juifs (Mélanges judéo-arabes, xiii)," *REJ,* XLV, 1–8, reprinted in his *Gesammelte Schriften,* IV, 333–40. From the tenor of these oaths one may perhaps assume that their authors had first adopted Christianity before they embraced Islam. Apart from thus masking their Jewish antecedents before their new Muslim neighbors, their initial conversion to another minority faith would give the appearance of having been motivated by conviction,

rather than careerism. On the old interrelations between the oath *more judaico* in judicial proceedings and the oath of abjuration of their former faiths by new converts to Christianity, see *supra,* Vols. III, pp. 194 f., 322 n. 28; XI, pp. 106 ff., 334 ff. nn. 40–43. Of interest also is the long formula of abjuration trans. into French from an anonymous Christian polemical tract by A. T. Khoury in *Les Théologiens byzantins et l'Islam,* pp. 181 ff. The persistence of an oath *more judaico* even in civil proceedings is understandable because of the long-lasting distrust of documents as decisive means of evidence. On the gradually changing Muslim and Jewish attitudes toward proof by documents rather than the testimony of witnesses, see É. Tyan, *Le Notariat et la preuve par écrit dans la pratique du droit musulman;* J. A. Wakin, ed., *The Function of Documents in Islamic Law: the Chapter on Sales from Ṭaḥawi's* Kitab al-Shurūṭ al-Kabir, with an Intro. and Notes; S. D. Goitein, *A Mediterranean Society,* II, 357, 601 nn. 23 ff.; and *supra,* n. 51.

82. See Obadiah di Bertinoro's "Epistles," reproduced in A. Yaari's compilation of *Iggerot Ereṣ Yisrael* (Letters from Palestine), pp. 98 ff., esp. pp. 128, 158 f. On Ibn Taimiya's boast that he had ransomed *dhimmi* prisoners, see H. Laoust, *Essai sur les doctrines sociales,* pp. 268 f. See also, more generally, E. Strauss's (Ashtor's), "The Social Isolation of Ahl adh-dhimma," *Pa'l (Gershon) Hirschler Memorial Book,* pp. 73–94.

83. See A. Grohmann, *Einführung und Chrestomathie zur arabischen Papyruskunde,* I, 56; A. Udovitch, "Introductory Remarks" to M. A. Cook, ed., *Studies in Economic History,* pp. 3–10, esp. p. 4; and particularly the informative essay by B. Lewis, "Sources for the Economic History of the Middle East," *ibid.,* pp. 78–92, esp. p. 84. See also C. Cahen's succinct comments on these and other pertinent essays in his review of this volume, in *JESHO,* XIV, 74–78; *supra,* n. 51; to which add: W. M. Brinner, "Some Ayyubid and Mamluk Documents from Non-Archival Sources," *Israel Oriental Studies,* II (= *S. M. Stern Mem. Vol.*), 117–43 (esp. reconstructing the exchanges of letters during the first Mongolian invasion of 1258–60, pp. 119 ff., 127 ff.; and during Timur's invasion, pp. 121 ff.); H. H. Roemer, "Über Urkunden zur Geschichte Ägyptens und Persiens in islamischer Zeit," *ZDMG,* CVII, 519–38; idem, "Vorschläge zur Sammlung von Urkunden zur islamischen Geschichte Persiens," *ibid.,* CIV, 362–70. Roemer's suggestions are, needless to say, equally valid for the documentation available from the Mameluke Empire.

The situation is somewhat different with respect to the epigraphic materials. The two major collections by M. van Berchem *et al.,* eds., *Matériaux pour un Corpus inscriptionum arabicarum,* Vols. I–X; and by E. Combe, J. Sauvaget, G. Wiet, *et al.,* eds., *Répertoire chronologique d'épigraphie arabe,* Vols. I–XVI, though still incomplete (Vol. XVI reaches only the year 762 A.H. = 1361 C.E.), have assembled a vast amount of important sources along these lines. However, some deficiencies in these works have also long been recognized. They readily came to the fore when an effort was made to prepare a new complete collection for a single area like Palestine. See the comments by M. Sharon on the planned "Au Nouveau Corpus des inscriptions arabes de Palestine," *REI,* XLII, 185–91. Incidentally, Sharon mentions that one of the leaders in this specialty, Leo A. Mayer, left behind some 20,000 cards with valuable notations of Arabic source materials for the history of Palestine, many of which have not yet been satisfactorily utilized.

84. See H. Sauvaire's pioneering studies, still of great value today, in his "Matériaux pour servir à l'histoire de la numismatique et de la métrologie musulmanes, traduits ou recueillis et mis en ordre," *JA*, CXV (7th ser., XIV), 455–533; CXVI (XV), 228–77, 421–78; CXIX (XVIII), 499–516; CXX (XIX), 281–327; Part II, CXXIV (8th ser., III), 368–445; CXXV (IV), 207–321; CXXVI (V), 498–506; with a "Complement" thereto, *ibid.*, CXXXI, 200–259 (the first instalments were reprinted in a volume under the same title in 1882); P. Balog, "History of the Dirhem in Egypt from the Fatimid Conquest until the Collapse of the Mamluke Empire," *Revue Numismatique*, 6th ser. III, 109–146; idem, *The Coinage of the Mamluk Sultans of Egypt and Syria;* various essays by A. S. Ehrenkreutz, esp. "Studies in the Monetary History of the Near East in the Middle Ages," I: "The Standard of Fineness of Some Types of Dinars," *JESHO*, II, pp. 128–61; II: "The Standard of Fineness of Western and Eastern Dinars before the Crusades," *ibid.*, VI, 243–77; and his "Monetary Aspects of Medieval Near Eastern Economic History," in M. A. Cook, ed., *Studies in Economic History*, pp. 37–50; S. D. Goitein, *A Mediterranean Society*, I, esp. pp. 359 f. App. B, 370 ff. App. D, 390 ff. (dealing with the extremely complicated problem of the exchange rate of gold and silver money); and E. Ashtor, *Histoire des prix et des salaires*, esp. pp. 277 ff., 383 ff. (with detailed tables and charts); idem, *Les Métaux précieux et la balance des payments du Proche Orient à la basse époque.*

85. The vast pertinent literature is listed in L. A. Mayer's *Bibliography of Moslem Numismatics, India Excepted*, 2d ed. enlarged; with T. Lewicki's review of that work and with his pupil A. Kmietowicz's "Supplements to L. Mayer's 'Bibliography of Muslim Numismatics'" in *Folia Orientalia*, I, 356–60, and II, 259–75, respectively (adding 53 and 201 items). See also Lewicki's "Nouveaux travaux russes concernant les trésors des monnais musulmanes trouvés en Europe Orientale et en Asie Centrale (1959–1963)," *JESHO*, VIII, 81–90; and *infra*, n. 110.

The diminishing role played by Jews in the Mameluke versus Faṭimid minting is illustrated by A. N. Poliak in "The Jews and the Egyptian Mint in the Period of the Mamelukes and the Beginning of the Turkish Regime" (Hebrew), *Zion*, I, 24–36; with the comments thereon by S. Assaf in his "The Jews and the Egyptian Mint" (Hebrew), *ibid.*, pp. 256–57. On the impact of the declining supply of gold available to the Mameluke mints in the fifteenth century, see also F. Braudel's aforementioned article "Monnais et civilisations. De l'or du Sudan," *Annales ESC*, I, 9–22; the older essay by A. Rangé van Gennep, "Le Ducat vénitien en Égypte, son influence sur le monnayage de l'or dans ce pays au commencement du XVe siècle," *Revue Numismatique*, 4th ser., I, 373–81, 494–508; and C. M. Cipolla's stimulating observations on *Money, Prices and Civilization in the Mediterranean World, Fifth to Seventeenth Centuries.* Cipolla's contention, however, that the lower classes in Italy very rarely came in contact with gold coins (pp. 34 f.) is contrasted by S. D. Goitein with the evidence from the Genizah which shows that Middle-Eastern Jews, even among the poor, wrote marriage contracts and other deeds referring to payments in gold dinars. See his "The Exchange Rate of Gold and Silver Money in Fatimid and Ayyubid Times: a Preliminary Study of the Relevant Geniza Materials," *JESHO*, VIII, 1–46; XII, 112.

86. See A. N. Poliak, "Some Notes on the Feudal System of the Mamluks," *JRAS*, 1937, pp. 97–107, esp. pp. 103 (with an interesting table of revenues and expenses), 104; idem, *Feudalism in Egypt, Syria, Palestine, and the Lebanon, 1250–1900;*

C. H. Becker, "Zur Kulturgeschichte Nordsyriens im Zeitalter der Mamluken," *Der Islam,* I, 93–100, esp. pp. 95 f. (reprinted in his *Islamstudien, Vom Werden und Wesen der islamischen Welt;* W. Heyd, *Histoire du commerce du Levant au moyen-âge,* French trans. by F. Raynaud from the author's revised German manuscript, esp. II, 23 ff. showing how in reaction to the fall of Acco, the Crusaders' last bastion in the Middle East, the Papacy had initiated the European boycott movement against supplying the Mameluke Empire not only with war materials but also with anything helpful to the Mameluke civilian economy. Among the first measures taken was the equipping of a naval force of twenty ships which, together with the Cypriot fleet, were to attack indiscriminately all shipping to Middle-Eastern ports. After a short time, however, the business interests of the Western nations prevailed over this religiously inspired hostility and business returned to normal. However, piracy remained a permanent obstacle to all commercial exchanges. In addition to the literature listed *supra,* Chap. LXXII, nn. 32, etc. see the data from the Genizah analyzed by S. D. Goitein in *A Mediterranean Society,* I, 327 ff.

87. See E. Ashtor, *Histoire des prix et des salaires,* pp. 267 ff., 282 ff., 383 ff., 392 ff.; S. D. Goitein, *A Mediterranean Society,* I, 116 ff., 425 ff., esp. p. 118, citing from an unpublished Jerusalem letter in the Genizah; and *supra,* Vols. III, pp. 168 f., 311 f. nn. 55–56; and IV, pp. 152 ff., 312 f. nn. 2–3; Arnold Harff, *Pilgrimage,* p. 211. On the early impact of the Muslim legislation on landownership and land cultivation see W. Schmucker, *Untersuchungen zu einigen wichtigen bodenrechtlichen Konsequenzen der islamischen Eroberungsbewegung.* The repeated redistribution of land (especially in 1298 and 1315 in Egypt, in 1313 in Syria) is discussed by E. Strauss in *Toledot,* I, 5, showing that the sultans appropriated anywhere from 4 to 10 *qirats* (each constituting one twenty-fourth) of the total land under cultivation. The legal difficulties created by the government's handling of the *iqta'* system, whereby the sultan conferred on an emir or other dignitary a leasehold on a larger or smaller area of land, are analyzed by C. Cahen in his "L'Évolution de l'*iqtā'* du IXe au XIIIe siècle," *Annales ESC,* VIII, 24–52; and by H. Rabie in "The Size and Value of the Iqṭā' in Egypt 564–741 A.H./1169–1341 A.D.," in M. A. Cook, ed., *Studies in Economic History,* pp. 129–38.

88. See A. Fattal, *Le Statut légal,* pp. 141, 359 f.; Moses Maimonides, *M.T.* Naḥlot, I, 3. On the general Maimonidean reinterpretation of the ramified talmudic teachings regarding private property, particularly in land, and the laws of inheritance thereof, see "The Economic Views of Maimonides" in my ed. of *Essays on Maimonides,* pp. 145 ff., reprinted in my *Ancient and Medieval Jewish History: Essays,* pp. 159 ff., 453 ff. nn. 41 ff. On the Nile floods and their varying impact on Egyptian agriculture, see M. Verner, "Periodical Water Volume Fluctuations of the Nile," *Archiv Orientální,* XL, 105–123, referring to the apparent variations between abundance and shortage in seven-year cycles, so familiar from the biblical story of Joseph.

89. See Moses Maimonides, *Resp.,* in the Hebrew trans. ed. by A. H. Freimann, pp. 135 No. 139, 186 ff. No. 196, etc.; and in J. Blau's Arabic ed., II, 610 f. No. 339, 648 No. 371, etc.; R. David Ibn abi Zimra, *Resp.,* I, Nos. 67 and 296; II, No. 408; IV, Nos. 30 and 38; cited together with other sources by D. Neustadt (Ayalon) in his "Economic Life of the Jews in Egypt during the Middle Ages" (Hebrew), *Zion,* II, 216–55, esp. pp. 239 f. See also M. Goldman, *The Life . . . ibn abi Zimra,*

pp. 145, 231 nn. 1–7. On the frequent earlier instances of Jewish houseownership acquired through purchase, inheritance, foreclosures of mortgages, and the like, see S. D. Goitein, *A Mediterranean Society,* I, *passim* (consult the index to that volume, p. 537 *s.v.* houses); idem, "Documents from Damascus and Tyre Concerning Buildings Belonging to Jews" (Hebrew), *Eretz-Israel,* VIII (=*E. L. Sukenik Mem. Vol.*), pp. 288–97. We also find records of Jewish owners being compensated for some ruined property. See, for instance, the 1209 (?) document of conveyance of such property published by D. S. Richards in his "Arabic Documents from the Karaite Community in Cairo," *JESHO,* XV, Nos. 1–2, pp. 105–164, esp. pp. 107 f., 152 ff. App. A. Of considerable interest also is the detailed analysis of the price fluctuations for the various grains, fruits, and vegetables in E. Ashtor's *Histoire des prix et des salaires,* pp. 282 ff., 392 ff., showing how greatly the prices were influenced by climatic, even seasonal, changes, as well as by man-made disturbances such as wars and revolts and the frequently violent fluctuations in the general socioeconomic conditions in Egypt and Syria.

90. See M. Canard, "Le Riz dans le Proche Orient aux premiers siècles de l'Islam," *Arabica,* VI, 113–31; *supra,* Vol. II, pp. 246 f. The various articles of the Jewish diet, which consisted of vegetables much more than did that of the Mamelukes, who lived principally on meat and dairy products, are discussed by S. D. Goitein in *A Mediterranean Society,* I, in various contexts. See esp. the numerous references, pp. 116 ff.

91. See W. Davy, trans., *Institutes, Political and Military Written Originally in the Mogul Language by the Great Timoor, Improperly Called Tamerlane,* trans. from the Persian rendition by Abu Tanbib al-Husseini with notes, p. 134; E. N. Adler, "Aleppo," in *Gedenkbuch . . . David Kaufmann,* pp. 128–37, esp. pp. 136 f.; and other sources cited by E. Strauss in *Toledot,* II, 14 ff., 154. See also the literature listed *supra,* nn. 27 ff.

92. See M. Sobernheim, "Das Zuckermonopol unter Sultan Barsbai," *Zeitschrift für Assyriologie,* XXVII, 75–84, esp. pp. 76 f.; the excerpt from Maqrizi, cited *ibid.,* pp. 81 ff.; and J. Mazuel, *Le Sucre en Égypte. Étude de géographie historique et économique.* The general deterioration of business conditions in the Syro-Egyptian area under the Burji dynasty is well illustrated by the erratic prices of sugar. Until the middle of the fourteenth century its costs of production and distribution had remained fairly stable, and sugar could sell at the moderate price of a little over 6 dinars per *qinṭar* (a quintal, approximately 100 pounds). Maqrizi himself recalled how, in his youth, a *qinṭar* fetched 6.4 dinars. By 1384, however, the Italian pilgrim G. Gucci found that refined sugar was valued at about 30 dinars per *qinṭar.* By 1405, according to Maqrizi, the price of a *qinṭar* had gone up to 46.4 dinars. This price was basically maintained at least until the establishment of the royal monopoly in 1423 and the official price fixing of the *qinṭar* at 16.66 dinars, which may have led to the rise of a black market.

In Syria, too, the price of a *qinṭar* of the even more expensive "Damascene" sugar went from 1,250 dirhems in 1379 to 4,000–4,300 dirhems or 90 ducats in 1411, and fluctuated between 100 and 130 ducats in the following two years. See E. Ashtor, *Histoire des prix et des salaires,* pp. 269 f., 316 ff., and the noteworthy Table, p. 405, all revealing tremendous variations in prices. See also *infra,* n. 100. On "The Main Industries of the Mediterranean Area as Reflected in the Records of the Cairo

Geniza" see S. D. Goitein's article under this title in *JESHO,* IV, 168–97; or in a somewhat revised form, idem, *A Mediterranean Society,* I, 99 ff.

93. The relationship between the cost of slaves and that of houses naturally fluctuated greatly from time to time and differed according to the skills or physical qualities of the slaves and the size, location, and price of materials used for the construction of houses. Just as some palatial buildings commanded a price of 10,000 dinars or more, individual slaves had to be acquired at ever-higher prices if they possessed special skills in much demand. For instance, a Mameluke whose physique and courage made him eligible for military training usually cost 100 dinars or more. Beautiful female slaves, as well as gifted dancers and musicians, were acquired at multiples of that figure. Some sources record purchases of slaves for over 1,000 dinars each. As to houses, there is a curious paucity of documentary evidence not only for the costs of building a house but also for prices paid for houses when sold. Yet we do know that the ordinary small house, even if built of brick, which was customary in Cairo (lumber was always in short supply in Egypt), could often be acquired for as little as 30 dinars. See the few data offered for both houses and slaves by Ashtor in his *Histoire des prix et des salaires,* pp. 356 ff., 361 ff., 437 f. On labor and slaves in Jewish households and on Jewish slave trade in Europe and the Middle East, see S. D. Goitein, "Slaves and Slave Girls in the Cairo Geniza Records," *Arabica,* IX, 1–20; idem, *A Mediterranean Society,* I, 130–47; *supra,* Vol. IV, pp. 189 ff., 253 ff. nn. 52 ff.; and *infra,* nn. 100–101.

94. See E. Strauss, *Toledot,* I, 176 ff. Regrettably, the documents reviewed by the same author relating to the Burji period are even less precise. At the most they merely confirm the general impression that the Jews continued to engage in various crafts, but that they suffered even more than their predecessors from the economic shortcomings of the Mameluke administration. See *ibid.,* II, 150 ff.

95. See S. D. Goitein's brief analysis of "Artisans en Méditerranée orientale au haut moyen-âge," *Annales ESC,* XIX, 847–68; and his *A Mediterranean Society,* I, 80 ff., 92 ff., 410 ff., 413 ff. Of considerable interest is the rich documentation summarized in his App. C on "Industrial Partnerships," *ibid.,* pp. 362 ff. This documentation clearly reveals how Jewish workers could avoid service as employees of either Jewish or Gentile entrepreneurs by simply forming a partnership with someone who had capital or special skills, with contractually varying shares in profits and losses. See Goitein, *ibid.,* I, 169 ff. On early Muslim professional corporations, see, for instance, L. Massignon's seminal paper, "Le Corps de métiers et la cité Islamique" (1920) reprinted from the *Revue Internationale de Sociologie* in his *Opera minora,* I, 369–84; N. Elisséeff, "Corporations de Damas sous Nūr al-din. Matériaux pour une topographie économique de Damas au XIIe siècle," *Arabica,* III, 61–79, listing 69 corporations with their possessions and system of penalties; and G. Baer in his "Guilds in Middle Eastern History," in M. A. Cook, ed., *Studies in Economic History,* pp. 11–30. Baer cogently demonstrates that not until the development of the Ottoman guilds in the seventeenth and eighteenth centuries could the Mid-Eastern corporations be compared in any way with the Western guilds.

96. It may also be noted that, notwithstanding the frequent repetition of the governmental requirement that *dhimmis* wear distinguishing clothing and/or badges, we hear of no specialized craft devoted to the manufacture of such articles

of clothing among the 450 specialties counted by Goitein in the Genizah documents or in A. Morabia's related "Recherches sur quelques noms de couleur en Arabe classique," *Studia Islamica,* XXI, 61–99. Very likely, despite the constant reiteration of the regulations pertaining to Jewish and Christian distinguishing marks and the rhetoric often combined with the demands by zealous Muslims for their rigid application, their enforcement was too sporadic and variable in different places to create a steady market for such articles and thus give rise to a special class of artisans to supply them.

97. R. B. Serjeant, "Material for a History of Islamic Textiles up to the Mongol Conquest," *Ars Islamica,* IX, 54–92; X, 71–104; XI–XII, 98–145; XIII–XIV, 75–117; XV–XVI, 29–85; L. A. Mayer, *Islamic Metalworkers and Their Works;* E. Ashtor, *Histoire des prix et des salaires,* pp. 269 f., 340 ff., etc., and the sources cited there.

98. See *supra,* Chap. LXXI, nn. 10–11; Vol. IV, esp. pp. 166, 318 f. n. 17: S. D. Goitein, *A Mediterranean Society,* I, 111 f.; and the literature listed *supra,* nn. 95 and 97. See also, more generally, R. Brunschvig, "Métiers vils en Islam?" *Studia Islamica,* XVI, 41–60, pointing out that, next to the odiferous tanners, weavers and cuppers were held in low esteem—a circumstance which may have prevented any such artisans from marrying into another class of craftsmen. Though most concerned with conditions in Morocco, this essay sheds considerable light on general economic, as well as psychological, implications of the various lowly crafts throughout the world of Islam.

99. See S. D. Goitein, *A Mediterranean Society,* I, 92 ff., 169 ff. (on partnerships which included both commercial and manufacturing arrangements); Moses Maimonides, *Iggerot* (Epistles) ed. by D. H. Baneth, I, 68; A. L. Udovitch, *Partnership and Profit in Medieval Islam;* and his more specific analysis of "Labor Partnership in Early Islamic Law," *JESHO,* X, 62–80, showing that, while the Ḥanafite school was fairly flexible in adjusting the law to the newly developing occupational contingencies, other jurists were far more traditionalist.

100. E. Strauss, *Toledot,* II, 271 ff.; idem, "Le Coût de la vie dans l'Égypte médiévale," *JESHO,* III, 56–67, 240; idem, "Le Coût de la vie dans la Syrie médiévale," *Arabica,* VIII, 59–73; idem, "Essai sur les prix et les salaires dans l'empire califien," *Rivista storica italiana,* XXXVI, 19–69; and particularly idem, *Histoire des prix et des salaires,* pp. 372 ff., 464 ff.

101. R. David Ibn abi Zimra, *Resp.,* I, No. 67; III, No. 481. The fact that Jewish women had to seek employment in non-Jewish establishments at a considerable distance from their homes was another sign of the economic decline of the Jewish communities. In earlier periods, well-to-do Jewish households undoubtedly employed quite a few coreligionists as domestic servants, since Muslim law forbade them to use the services of Muslim slaves. Pagan slaves, however, seem to have been but little used by Jews even for domestic work. See also *supra,* n. 93.

102. See Aḥmad b. 'Ali al-Qalqashandi, *K. Ṣubḥ al-a'sha fi ṣina'at al-insha* (On the History, Government, and Geography of Egypt), esp. VIII, 77 f.; XIII, 340, cited by S. Y. Labib in his *Handelsgeschichte,* pp. 84 f.; *supra,* nn. 93 and 100; Vol. IV,

pp. 187 f., 193 f., 335 ff. nn. 57, 59, and the sources listed there. The earlier Jewish slave employment and slave trade are discussed by S. Assaf, "Slavery and the Slave Trade among the Jews during the Middle Ages (from Hebrew Sources)" (Hebrew), *Zion,* IV, 91–125; V, 271–80, reproduced in his collection of essays *Be-Ohole Ya'aqob* (In the Tents of Jacob: Chapters from Jewish Cultural Life in the Middle Ages), pp. 223–56; and supplemented by his "From the Genizah Records" (Hebrew), *Sinai,* XIII, reprinted in his other collection, *Meqorot u-meḥqarim* (Texts and Studies), pp. 166–70; S. D. Goitein in his aforementioned essay in *Arabica,* IX, 1–20; and in *A Mediterranean Society,* I, 140, 147. The prevailing attitude to the Jewish public and its leaders, as represented by their outstanding spokesman Maimonides, is analyzed in "The Economic Views of Maimonides," in my ed. of *Essays on Maimonides,* pp. 127–264, esp. pp. 229 ff. (or in the revised reprint thereof in my *Ancient and Medieval History: Essays,* ed. by L. A. Feldman, pp. 149–235, 443–501, esp. pp. 212 ff. and the notes thereto). On the difficulties arising for both slaveholders and slave traders from the Jewish legal requirement of circumcising Gentile slaves within a year, see also B. Z. Wacholder, "The Halakah and the Proselyting of Slaves during the Geonic Period," *HJ,* XVIII, 89–106.

At any rate, the conclusion reached *supra,* Vol. IV, concerning the conditions before 1200 was doubly true in the Late Middle Ages. No one has thus far produced evidence against the view that "neither slave trade nor slaveholding seem ever to have been an important factor in Jewish economic life. . . . As a commercial branch, in particular, it doubtless was always insignificant and dwindled to very minor proportions after the Christianization of the Slavic peoples in the tenth century" (IV, 196). As early as 1939, David Neustadt (Ayalon), after reviewing the then available Genizah fragments, stated: "In one commercial branch the Egyptian Jews played absolutely no part, namely in the slave trade. From the beginning of the Faṭimid regime to the days of R. David Ibn abi Zimra [tenth through the fifteenth centuries] I found in the sources not a single case of a Jewish slave trader despite the fact that in the tenth century and long thereafter Egypt had served as the chief market for Nubian slaves." This observation, reinforced by much richer Genizah and other materials, has been confirmed by S. D. Goitein. See Neustadt's aforementioned Hebrew essay on the "Economic Life of the Jews in Egypt," *Zion,* II, 225 f.; S. D. Goitein, *A Mediterranean Society,* I, 140. Incidentally, the small, and rather undistinguished, Italian Jewish poem on the subject of the slave trade does not even prove that this line of business was important for tenth-century Italian Jewry. See Z. Malachi, "A Hebrew Poem from Italy on the Slave Trade," *Israel Oriental Studies,* II (= *S. M. Stern Mem. Vol.*), 288–89. On the exceptional situation in the Black Sea area, see *infra,* n. 103.

103. F. Altheim and R. Stiehl, eds., *Christentum am Roten Meer;* A. Kammerer, *La Mer Rouge, l'Abyssinie et l'Arabie depuis l'antiquité,* with an Intro by G. Hanotaux; idem, *La Mer Rouge, l'Abyssinie at l'Arabie aux XVIe et XVIIe siècles et la cartographie de Portulans du monde oriental; étude d'histoire et de géographie historique;* O. Löfgren, *Arabische Quellen zur Kenntnis der Stadt Aden im Mittelatler; Abū Maḥrama, Adengeschichte nebst einschlägigen Abschnitten aus den Werken von Ibn al-Muǧāwir, Al-Ǧanadi und Al-Ahdal;* and S. Y. Labib, *Handelsgeschichte,* pp. 56 f., 71; *supra,* Vol. III, pp. 114 ff.; and on the fairs in Mecca (which antedated Islam) and elsewhere in the Muslim world, see R. Brunschvig, "Coup d'oeil sur l'histoire des foires à travers l'Islam," *Recueil de la Société Jean Bodin,* V: La Foire,

pp. 43–75 (pointing out that, although Meccan fairs dated from pre-Islamic times, late medieval Islam paid little attention to them in both legal theory and actual practice).

Jewish journeys to, and trade with, India have been known from Genizah records for quite some time. But our information was largely limited to the Faṭimid period. See J. Braslavsky, "Jewish Trade Between the Mediterranean and India in the Twelfth Century" (Hebrew), *Zion,* VII, 135–39 (reproduces a Judeo-Arabic letter written in 1149 by a Cairo spice dealer, Abraham b. Peraḥiah, who had traveled to India); E. Strauss (Ashtor), "A Journey to India (A Letter from Aden to Egypt of 1153 C.E.)" (Hebrew), *ibid.,* IV, 217–31; and the report by Musada b. Sadaqa published by S. M. Stern in his "Three Petitions of the Fātimid Period," *Oriens,* XV, 172–209, esp. pp. 179 ff.

New vistas on Egyptian Jewry's business and other relations with India were opened by S. D. Goitein in his essays, "From the Mediterranean to India: Documents on the Trade to India, South Arabia and East Africa from the Eleventh and Twelfth Centuries," *Speculum,* XXIX, 181–97; and "Letters and Documents of the India Trade in Medieval Times," *Islamic Culture,* XXVII, 188–205, both combined and revised in his *Studies in Islamic History,* pp. 329–50. Further data were supplied by him in "A Document from the African Port of Aidhab in the Period of the Head of the Academy Joshua ben Dosa (From the Archives of the Institute for the Study of the Jewish Communities in the Middle East)" (Hebrew), *Tarbiz,* XXI, 185–91. How self-assured the leaders of the Jewish community of Aydhab were may be seen from the episode related in the *Tarbiz* document concerning the difficulties encountered by Ṣafi, Joshua's slave and business agent [*ghulam*], who was brought before the governor of Aydhab by one Ibn Jamahir who accused Ṣafi of slander. Ṣafi was supposed to have spread the rumor, in the presence of some Muslim merchants, that the plaintiff had killed a slave girl who was bearing his child. In view of the high standing of Ṣafi's master, the governor wanted to review the accusation with the local Jewish merchants. Characteristically, the Jewish representatives disregarded the governor's invitation, apparently because they did not wish to get involved in that quarrel. As a result, however, the unfortunate Ṣafi was flogged and jailed. See also Goitein, *A Mediterranean Society,* I, 133. Trade with India was greatly facilitated by the availability of much Arab shipping in that direction. See G. R. Tibbetts, *Arab Navigation in the Indian Ocean. Before the Coming of the Portuguese. Being a Translation of* Kitāb al-Fawā'id fi usūl al-baḥr wa'l-qawā'id *of Aḥmad b. Majid al-Najdi;* R. S. Lopez, "European Merchants in the Medieval Indies: the Evidence of Commercial Documents," *Journal of Economic History,* III, 164–68; with corrections by P. Kunitsch in his review of that work in *Der Islam,* LI, 344–53; and the literature cited in the next note.

104. See W. Heyd, *Histoire du commerce du Levant au moyen-âge,* II, 23 ff.; S. Y. Labib, *Handelsgeschichte,* pp. 74 ff.; idem, "Capitalism in Medieval Islam," *Journal of Economic History,* XXIX, 79–96, esp. pp. 84 ff.; M. Rodinson's suggestive, though rather doctrinaire, analysis of the broader aspects of *Islam and Capitalism,* trans. from the French by B. Pearce; *supra,* Vol. IV, pp. 186, 331 n. 47; E. Strauss, *Toledot,* I, 190 ff., 280 ff. The ease with which 'Abd al-Aziz made his five trips to China demonstrated that Marco Polo's famous journey was not at all exceptional. Much has been done in recent years to uncover new sources and open new vistas on the exchanges between China and the Mediterranean world. See, for example, C. E. Dubler, "El Extremo Oriente visto por los Musulmanes anteriores a la invasión de

los Mongoles en el siglo XIII. La Deformación del saber geográfico y etnológico en los cuentos orientales," *Homenaje á . . . Millás Vallicrosa,* I, 465–519; J. Kuwabara, "On Pou Shou-Kêng. . . . A Man of the Western Regions . . . toward the End of the Sung Dynasty . . . with a General Sketch of Trade of the Arabs in China during the T'ang and Sung Eras," *Mémoires* of the Research Department of the Toyo Bunko (The Oriental Library), II, 1–79; VII, 1–104; and the papers presented at the two Oxford colloquia of 1967 and 1970 and edited by D. S. Richards under the title, *Islam and the Trade of Asia: a Colloquium* [held at Oxford, June 1967] (including the articles by B. Spuler and C. Issawi). Of interest also are the reciprocal views of the Chinese on their trade with lands along the Indian Ocean. See, for instance, W. Mayer, "Chinese Explorations of the Indian Ocean during the XVth Century," *China Review,* III. On the early settlements of the Jews in India and China, see *supra,* Vols. III, pp. 115, 285 f. n. 51; IV, 329 n. 40. Their subsequent evolution will be treated here in a later volume.

105. See *supra,* Chap LXXII, nn. 91 ff.; Vol. III, 114 ff., 213 ff., 284 nn. 49–51, 333 ff. nn. 51–52 and the literature listed there, to which add J. Heers, *L'Occident aux XIVe et XVe siècles; aspects économiques et sociaux,* pp. 142 ff.; K. P. Matschke, "Zum Charakter des byzantinischen Schwarzmeerhandels im 13. bis 15. Jahrhundert," *Wissenschaftliche Zeitschrift* of the University of Leipzig, Gesellschafts- und sprachwissenschaftliche Reihe, XIX, 447–58; A. N. Poliak, "Le Caractère colonial de l'état mamelouk dans ses rapports avec la Horde d'Or," *REI,* IX, 231–48; B. Spuler, *Die Goldene Horde; die Mongolen in Russland, 1228–1502,* 2d enlarged ed.; A. S. Atiya, *Crusade, Commerce and Culture,* p. 138; R. David Ibn abi Zimra, *Resp.*, published from manuscript by A. Marx in his "Contribution à l'histoire des Juifs de Cochin," *REJ,* LXXXIX, 293–304, esp. p. 299; English trans. reproduced in Marx's *Studies in Jewish History and Booklore,* pp. 174–77 (without the documentary Appendix).

The much-debated problem of the Radhanites (see the quotation, *supra,* Vol. IV, pp. 180 f.) still is unresolved, despite the numerous recent contributions to the discussion. See esp. L. I. Rabinowitz, *Jewish Merchant Adventures: a Study of the Radanites;* C. Cahen, "Y-a-t'il eu des Rādhānites?" *REJ,* CXXIII, 499–505; idem, "Quelques questions sur les Radanites," *Der Islam,* XLVIII, 333–34 (lists five unanswered questions); F. Kmietowicz, "The Term Ar-Rādāniya in the Work of Ibn Ḫurdadhbeh," *Folia Orientalia,* XI, 163–73 (explaining the term as relating to diplomatic couriers, among whom Jews were all represented): J. Jacobi, "Die Rāḏāniya," *Der Islam,* XLVII, 252–62; M. Gil, "The Rādhānite Merchants and the Land of Rādhān," *JESHO,* XVII, 298–328; J. Jacobi, "Antwort auf einige Fragen über die Rāḏāniya," *Der Islam,* LII, 226–38. Evidently not until the discovery of some new source material will the riddle posed by Postmaster Ibn Khurdadhbah in 846 be fully disentangled, paving the way for a certain consensus among scholars.

We must bear in mind, however, that the alternate route via the Caspian Sea to the Persian Gulf, taken by some Jewish and other Western merchants, was not devoid of peril. Even after reaching Ormuz which, as we recall, had a growing Jewish settlement, especially after its conquest by the Portuguese (see *supra,* Vol. XV, pp. 356 ff., 543 ff. nn. 108 ff.), the travelers were exposed to piratical raids both by the corsairs of the neighboring island Kish and by freebooters throughout the Indian Ocean.

106. See S. Y. Labib, *Handelsgeschichte,* pp. 337 ff., 481 ff. To the long-lasting debate on the causes of the economic decline of the Mameluke Empire in the four-

teenth and fifteenth centuries, A. L. Udovitch added a rather sophisticated interpretation through his part in the comparative study of late medieval conditions in England, Italy, and Egypt, presented under the title, "England to Egypt, 1350–1500: Long-term Trends and Long-distance Trade," by R. Lopez, H. Miskimin, and him at the London Conference of 1967 in M. A. Cook, ed., *Studies in Economic History*, pp. 93–128, esp. pp. 115–28. Udovitch pointed out, in particular, the importance of the demographic downgrade and the disproportionate rise of the wages of urban workers as major contributory causes to that decline. The Jewish share in the commercial exchanges was also deeply affected by the shift in political and military power from the Eastern to the Western states, which made Jewish participation much more difficult.

107. See A. O. Citarella, "A Puzzling Question Concerning the Relations between the Jewish Communities of Christian Europe and Those Represented in the Geniza Documents," *JAOS*, XCI, 390–97; and, more broadly, G. Salles's studies of "L'Institution des consulats," *Revue d'histoire diplomatique*, IX, 536–73; X, 253–73, and continued in "Les Origines des premiers consulats de la nation française à l'étrangers. Son origine, son développement au moyen âge chez les different peuples," *ibid.*, XI, 161–91, 409–26, 565–614; and the Middle-Eastern examples supplied in 1438 by Emmanuel Piloti, in P. H. Dopp's *L'Égypte . . . d'après . . . Piloti*, pp. 76 ff. No. 70, 83 f. No. 75. To the literature listed *supra*, nn. 86 and 103, add the documentary publications by G. L. Tafel and G. M. Thomas, *Urkunden zur älteren Handels- und Staatsgeschichte der Republic Venedig mit besonderer Beziehung auf Byzanz und die Levante;* H. Lammens's twin essays, "Relations officielles entre la Cour Romaine et les sultans mamlouks d'Égypte," *ROC*, VIII, 101–110; and "Correspondances diplomatiques entre les sultans mamlouks d'Égypte et les puissances chrétiennes," *ibid.*, IX, 151–87, 359–92; G. Müller, comp., *Documenti sulle relazioni delle città toscane coll'Oriente cristiano e coi Turchi fino all'anno MDXXXI raccolti e annotati;* A. S. Atiya, *Egypt and Aragon. Embassies and Diplomatic Correspondence between 1300 and 1330 A.D.;* and R. Nicolas's Berne dissertation, *Geschichte der Vorrechte und des Einflusses Frankreichs in Syrien und der Levante vom Beginn des Mittelalters bis zum Friedensvertrag von Paris 1802*.

Christian merchants from the West often encountered on their Eastern travels many more coreligionists than did the Jews. Despite their mutual suspicions of infidelity or heresy arising from denominational differences, the Eastern Christian townsmen were, as a rule, quite hospitable toward European visitors. See B. Spuler, "Les Chrétiens orientaux et leur relations avec les Vénitiens et les Italiens en général pendant la domination latine dans le Levant," in A. Pertusi, ed., *Venezia e il Levante fino al secolo XV*, I, 679–86. These relationships probably became even more friendly after the fall of the Latin Kingdom of Jerusalem greatly reduced the ecclesiastical conflicts.

108. See 'Amr b. Baḥr al-Jaḥiẓ, *K. at-Tabaṣṣur bi't-tijāra* (On Praise of Merchants and Condemnations of Officials), ed. by Ḥasan Ḥusni 'Abd al-Wahhab, partially available also in a German translation in O. Rescher, *Excerpte und Übersetzungen aus den Schriften des ibn Ǧahiz;* Muḥammad ibn al-Ḥasan ash-Shaybani, *K. al-Kasb* (On Earning), still available only in a selective summary, largely for purposes of refutation, by his pupil Ibn Sama'a under the title *Al-Iktisāb fi'l-rizq al-mustaṭāb* (On Lawful Livelihood), both analyzed together with other sources in S. D. Goitein's

aforementioned essay, "The Rise of the Middle-Eastern Bourgeoisie in Early Islamic Times" in his *Studies*, pp. 217–41. See also H. Ritter, "Ein Arabisches Handbuch der Handelswissenschaft," *Der Islam*, XVII, 1–91 (with reference to Ja'far b. 'Ali ad-Dimashqi's works), with comments thereon by C. Cahen, "À propos et autour d' 'Ein arabisches Handbuch der Handelswissenschaft'," *Oriens*, XV, 160–71; and the excerpts from, as well as analysis of the twelfth-century financial treatise by Qadhi Al-Makhzumi by C. Cahen, cited *infra*, nn. 119–20.

109. See Bab. Talmud B. B. 110a; *supra*, Vol. II, 256, 416 n. 3. The problems of Jewish work ethic versus dependence on charity will be discussed in a later volume. For the time being see my *JC*, I, 131 f.; III, 25; and Chap. XVI *passim*. On the two Jewish businessmen mentioned in the text, see J. Starr, "Contributions to the Life of Nahrai ben Nissim of Fusṭaṭ" (Hebrew), *Zion*, I, 436–53; and N. A. Stillman, "The Eleventh-Century Merchant House of Ibn 'Awkal (a Geniza Study)," *JESHO*, XVI, no. 1, pp. 15–88. The careers of the leading Jewish merchants may profitably be compared with that of one of their Muslim counterparts described, on the basis of Ibn Hawqal's report, by S. M. Stern, in "Rāmisht of Sīrāf; a Merchant Millionaire of the Twelfth Century," *JRAS*, 1967, pp. 10–14 (he supposedly owned a silver tray weighing over 1,000 kilograms; other Sirafians included a man whose fortune was said to have exceeded 3,000,000 dinars). The conduct of ramified business by a sedentary merchant was facilitated by the existing fairly dependable communications. See J. Sauvaget, *La Poste aux chevaux dans l'empire des Mamelouks;* S. D. Goitein, "The Commercial Mail Service in Medieval Islam," *JAOS*, LXXXIV, 118–23; idem, *A Mediterranean Society*, I, 281 ff., mentioning, in particular, the use of government and private couriers and postal agents and occasionally even carrier pigeons (pp. 290 f.). The great speed with which the river boats traveled on the Nile and Tigris (they covered as much as 115 miles a day) was also very helpful. However, the sort of telegraph service through a relay of luminous signs, mentioned by Marrakushi (ed. by Fagnan, p. 299), seems to have been limited to government agencies. See A. Mazahéri, *La Vie quotidienne des musulmans au moyen âge, Xe au XIIIe siècle*, pp. 293 ff.

Of course, all such services were often interrupted by both elementary and human forces. Quite apart from naval piracy, all travelers were constantly endangered by attacks of highwaymen, especially in the more deserted areas. The difficulties experienced by Meshullam da Volterra, particularly in crossing over from Egypt to Palestine and Syria, are vividly described in his travelogue (*Massa'*, pp. 60 ff.). His experience may not have been entirely typical, however, since a near-contemporary, R. David Ibn abi Zimra, assured a questioner that a journey from Egypt to Palestine "is not at all dangerous even for a pregnant woman or a child." See his *Resp.*, III, No. 408. In addition, there were frequent raids of Bedouins and other tribesmen on the more advanced areas of both countries, which naturally also affected passing strangers. On the situation in Northern Syria, for example, see A. S. Tritton, "The Tribes of Syria in the Fourteenth and Fifteenth Centuries," *BSOAS*, XII, 567–73. Examples of itinerant scholars in search of learning are quoted by S. D. Goitein in *A Mediterranean Society*, I, 51 ff.; and *supra*, Vol. V, pp. 53 f., 315 n. 65.

110. J. Thenaud, *Le Voyage d'outremer* (*Égypte, Mont Sinaÿ, Palestine*), ed. with notes by C. Schefer, p. 51; E. Strauss, *Toledot*, II, 158 f.; E. Wirth, "Zum Problem des Bazaars (sūq, çarṣi). Versuch einer Begriffsbestimmung und Theorie des tradi-

tionellen Wirtschaftszentrums der orientalisch-islamischen Stadt," *Der Islam,* LI, 203–260; LII, 6–46; H. K. N. Al-Ganabi, *Der Suq (Bazar) von Bagdad. Eine wirtschafts- und sozialgeschichtliche Untersuchung;* S. D. Goitein, *A Mediterranean Society,* I, 209 ff.; idem, "Bankers' Accounts from the Eleventh Century A.D.," *JESHO,* IX, 28–68; and A. L. Udovitch's demonstration of how important credit was in both providing capital for commercial purchases and facilitating payments in remote localities. See his "Credit as a Means of Investment in Medieval Islamic Trade," *JAOS,* LXXXVII, 260–64. Among the objects of trade in which the Jews undoubtedly had more than a proportionate share was jewelry. See, for instance, the excursus in O. Mugler's Munich dissertation *Edelsteinhandel im Mittelalter und im 16. Jahrhundert mit Excursen über den Levante- und asiatischen Handel überhaupt.*

Far more important for the East-West exchanges was the spice trade, especially of pepper. According to F. C. Lane's computations, the Venetians, Egypt's major customers, were annually importing from Alexandria 1,150,000 pounds of pepper and about the same amount of other spices, drugs, and aromatics. See his "The Mediterranean Spice Trade: Further Evidence for Its Revival in the Sixteenth Century," *AHR,* XLV, 581–90, esp. p. 587 n. 28; and "Venetian Shipping during the Commercial Revolution," *ibid.,* XXXVIII, 219–39, esp. p. 228. On the basis of these data, A. Udovitch calculated that the Egyptian revenue from this source totaled about 500,000 dinars. See his remarks in M. A. Cook, ed., *Studies in Economic History,* p. 128. We must bear in mind, however, that even this very large sum was a small fraction of the value of the total trade in the Venetian harbor. In his report to the Signoria, Thomas Mocenigo da Campofregoso, who served as doge in 1413–20, had estimated that the merchandise exported from the Venetian warehouses during the year 1420 was valued at 10,000,000 ducats and yielded a profit of 4,000,000 ducats. See Marino Sanudo, the Younger, *Le Vite dei Dogi di Venezia,* in L. A. Muratori, ed., *Rerum italicarum scriptores,* XXIV/2 (under the date of 1420); and A. S. Atiya, *Crusade, Commerce and Culture,* p. 180. See also, more generally, C. H. Becker's "Zur Kulturgeschichte Nordsyriens," *Der Islam,* I, 93–100; and *supra,* n. 85.

111. See S. D. Goitein, *A Mediterranean Society,* I, 158 f., 186 ff., 347 ff.; II, 26; *supra,* Vols. IV, pp. 212 f., 347 f. nn. 81–82; V. pp. 50 f., 314 n. 61. In general, international Jewish trade was greatly facilitated by the talmudic regulations concerning the employment of Jewish agents. See I. H. Levinthal's detailed examination of "The Jewish Law of Agency," *JQR,* XIII, 117–91; and, more fully, N. Rakover's *Ha-Sheliḥut ve-ha-harsha'ah ba-mishpaṭ ha-'ibri* (The Jewish Law of Agency in Legal Proceedings). On the Muslim aspects, see R. Grasshoff's older but still noteworthy Königsberg dissertation, *Die Suftaja und Ḥawāla der Araben. Ein Beitrag zur Geschichte des Wechsels.* Of considerable interest also is the presence of numerous Jewish women in brokerage as in most other lines of business. See S. D. Goitein's graphic description of the activities of "A Jewish Business Woman of the Eleventh Century," *JQR,* Jubilee Volume, pp. 225–42; and, more generally, his *A Mediterranean Society,* I, 127 ff.

112. See *supra,* nn. 84 f.; Vol. IV, pp. 68 f., 344 nn. 76–77; A. N. Poliak, "The Jews and the Egyptian Mint in the Period of the Mamelukes and Beginning of the Turkish Regime" (Hebrew), *Zion,* I, 24–36; Maqrizi, *K. al-Suluk,* I, 602 f.; Maimonides, *M.T.* She'elah u-piqqadon, VIII; my "Economic Views of Maimonides" in *Essays on*

Maimonides, pp. 205 f., or in *Ancient and Medieval Jewish History: Essays,* pp. 196, 480 nn. 136–37; S. Y. Labib, *Handelsgeschichte,* pp. 72, 273, and the sources listed there. Deposits could be made not only at mosques and banking firms, but in major cities also in special *Funduqs* for Money Trade, such as existed in Cairo. These business centers, similar to the Venetian *Fondachi,* were frequently established by business associations, native as well as foreign, in order to facilitate various kinds of mercantile transactions. As in Venice, some of them functioned as combinations of markets and hostelries for merchants arriving from foreign emporia. Among the Italian banks, we must remember, some Mid-Eastern branches or affiliates not only enjoyed the political backing of their home states, but at times were protected by their own armed forces. The famous Banco di San Giorgio of Genoa, on occasion, even took over the military and administrative functions from the Republic in some of its endangered colonies in the Black Sea and the Aegean. See W. Heyd, *Histoire du commerce du Levant,* II, 322, 383 ff., 423. No such authority was enjoyed by the Jewish *funduq,* which rather served in the main as a charitable hospice for strangers, similar to the European *heqdesh.* One such institution was recorded as located between the synagogues of the Babylonians and Palestinians in Cairo, probably in order to serve both congregations. It was hardly suitable for serving as a safe repository. See S. D. Goitein, *A Mediterranean Society,* II, 113 ff., 154. See also A. P. Usher, *The Early History of Deposit Banking in Mediterranean Europe,* I.

113. Maimonides, *Commentary* on the Mishnah of Baba Meṣiah IV, 6; *M.T.* Mekhirah xii.8–12; my "Economic Views on Maimonides" in my *Essays on Maimonides,* p. 195, or in *Ancient and Medieval Jewish History: Essays,* pp. 189 f., 474 f. n. 124. As in the case of deposits, there existed in Cairo a special central exchange market (*Suq aṣ-ṣarrafin*). However, this did not prevent an entire class of money-changers from plying their trade on small tables (hence the owner's designation reminiscent of the Greek term *trapezites,* and the corresponding Hebrew designation, *shulḥani*) in major thoroughfares throughout the capital. See the sources listed by S. Y. Labib in his *Handelsgeschichte,* p. 277 n. 73. Not surprisingly, some pietists voiced conscientious objections even to the use and exchange of coins, particularly those which were marked by crosses, feminine pictures, and the like. They were particularly concerned about persons who took such coins into their mouths, who might give the appearance that they were kissing idols. R. David Ibn abi Zimra, questioned about this practice, replied that "the Gentiles of our time are no idolators, but merely adhere to their ancestral customs, thus wrote R. [Jacob] Tam. Secondly, they do not engrave such figures for worship, but merely for identification." For these and other reasons he found the use of such coins totally unobjectionable. See his reply published by Z. J. (H. J.) Zimmels in "Eight Manuscript Responsa by R. David ibn abi Zimra" (Hebrew), *Sefer ha-Yobel* (Jubilee Volume) in honor of Samuel Krauss, pp. 178–87, esp. pp. 182 ff.

114. See E. Sachau, ed., *Syrische Rechtsbücher,* ed. with a German trans., II, 157; S. D. Goitein, *A Mediterranean Society,* I, 250 ff., esp. pp. 254 f.; and, more generally, E. Cohn's Heidelberg dissertation, *Der Wucher (Ribā) im Qor'ān, Chadīth und Fiqh. Ein Beitrag zur Entstehungsgeschichte des mohammedanischen Rechtes;* S. Y. Labib's more recent "Geld und Kredit. Studien zur Wirtschaftsgeschichte Ägyptens im Mittelalter," *JESHO,* II, 225–46, esp. p. 232 (showing that in the fif-

teenth century Italian ducats and florins were exchanged in Alexandria for twice as many silver dirhems as in Cairo); J. Schacht, "Riba," *EI,* III, 1148–50; his *Origins of Mohammedan Jurisprudence,* pp. 251, 287; *supra,* Vol. IV, pp. 199 ff., 338 ff. See also A. L. Udovitch's aforementioned "Credit as a Means of Investment," *JAOS,* LXXXVI, 260–64; idem, "Reflections on the Institutions of Credit and Banking in the Medieval Islamic Near East," *Studia Islamica,* XLI, 5–21. It appears that the fear of openly charging interest to a coreligionist deterred the moneylenders and their agents from imposing upon a defaulting debtor a charge over the original balance as a penalty for the delay. This is confirmed, for example, by the Genizah document published by R. J. H. Gottheil and W. H. Worrell in their edition of *Fragments from the Cairo Genizah in the Freer Collection,* pp. 24 f. No. iv. On the various methods of evading the prohibition of usury (*ḥilal*), see, for instance, Maḥmud ibn al-Ḥasan al-Qazwini's tract *K. al-Ḥilal f'il fiqh* (Book of Legal Tricks), ed. by J. Schacht, esp. pp. 9 f., 33. See also *infra,* n. 115.

115. Arnold von Harff, *The Pilgrimage,* pp. 185 f.; Sebald Rieter's hearsay story in *Das Reisebuch der Familie Rieter,* ed. by R. Röhricht and H. Meissner, esp. p. 147; the report of the anonymous traveler of 1495, a pupil of Bertinoro, in his letter reproduced in A. Yaari's *Iggerot,* pp. 144–60, esp. pp. 150 f.; Moses b. Mordecai Bassola, *Massa'ot Ereṣ Yisrael* (A Pilgrimage to Palestine), ed. by I. Ben-Zvi, pp. 65 ff. (both referring to Jewish moneylending in Damascus); E. Strauss, *Toledot,* II, 171, on the basis of Muḥammad b. Aḥmad Ibn Iyas' *K. Bada'i' az-Zuhar fi waqa'i' ad-duhar* (Die Chronik), ed. by P. Kahle, M. Mustafa, and M. Sobernheim (2d ed. rev. with an Intro. and Indices by Mustafa), IV, 53, 235; in G. Wiet's French trans., *Histoire des Mamlouks circassiens, passim.* Governmental rapacity ultimately affected even the formerly very influential Karimi merchants, who now tried to evade lending money to the authorities. In their increasing reluctance to serve as royal bankers and their ultimate flight to escape the rulers' insatiable appetites, see the examples cited by A. Darrag in *L'Égypte sous le règne de Barsbay,* p. 200; and by S. Y. Labib in his *Handelsgeschichte,* pp. 283 f., and *supra,* n. 7. According to Labib, no accounts by Arab bankers of that period have been preserved. Despite the various attempts at camouflaging interest, such bankers' ledgers might well prove useful for the detection of hidden interest charges. We are not much more fortunate with respect to business records of Jewish firms, especially for the late medieval period. Even S. D. Goitein's study of "Bankers' Accounts from the Eleventh Century A.D." *JESHO,* IX, 28–68 (partially identified by him as written in Nahrai b. Nissim's hand), may not be quite so instructive about the practices under Mameluke rule as it has been for those under the Faṭimid regime. In any case, the sparse references to Jewish usury even in the hostile Arabic polemical literature and the paucity of data on actual interest charges in the contemporary rabbinic responsa confirm the general impression that, during the Late Middle Ages, banking in general and moneylending in particular played a relatively minor role in the Syro-Egyptian Jewish economy.

116. See *supra,* Vol. XII, pp. 68 ff., 276 ff.; *JC,* II–III, Chap. XI; E. Strauss, *Toledot,* II, 137 ff.; S. D. Goitein, *A Mediterranean Society,* II, 68 ff., 211 ff., 219 ff., 228 ff., etc.

117. See the Arabic poem cited from Zayāt, *Ḥizana,* 1937, p. 492, by A. Fattal in *Le Statut légal,* p. 157; *supra,* nn. 53–54; Vol. VIII, Chap. XXXVI. Among the ac-

cusers of the Jews we need but mention 'Abd ar-Raḥman b. 'Umar al-Jaubari, whose *K. al-Muqhtar* (Book of Chosen Subjects in the Detection of Secrets [and Tearing Down Veils]), Chap. V, is analyzed by M. Steinschneider in his *Polemische und Apologetische Literatur,* pp. 188 ff.; and other data supplied by E. Strauss in his *Toledot,* II, 173 ff. (includes a list of 23 physicians specifically recorded in the sources between 1380 and 1514); and M. Perlmann in his "Notes on the Position of Jewish Physicians in Medieval Muslim Countries," *Israel Oriental Studies,* II (1972 = *S. M. Stern Mem. Vol.*), 315–19; and numerous other publications listed by R. Y. Ebied, *Bibliography of Mediaeval Arab and Jewish Medicine and Allied Sciences,* with a Foreword by A. M. Honeyman. Jewish contributions to pharmacology both in theory and practice have been discussed *supra,* Vol. VIII, pp. 256 f., 403 f. n. 45. To the literature listed there add M. Levey's posthumous study, *Early Arabic Pharmacology: an Introduction Based on Ancient and Medieval Sources.* It may be noted that in 1259–60 a Jewish pharmacist Abu'l-Muna al-Cohen al-'Aṭṭar compiled for private use an extensive handbook of medical drugs, based in part on his own observations. Nor must we overlook the impact of hashish and other addictive drugs on the medieval Islamic civilization. See S. Hamarneh, "Pharmacy in Medieval Islam and the History of Drug Addiction," *Medical History,* XVI, 226–37.

Much of the trade in drugs, both wholesale and retail, often combined with that of cosmetics and other related goods, was concentrated in a special bazaar located in the Cairo "Square of Perfumers." But many traders handled their sales in various other shops throughout the city. According to S. D. Goitein, perhaps fully one-third of the extant Genizah letters bearing a specific address were directed to that Square. See M. Meyerhoff, "Der Basar der Drogen und Wohlgerüche in Kairo," *Archiv für Wirtschaftsforschung im Orient,* IV, no. 3, p. 37; *supra,* n. 110; Vol. IV, pp. 179, 327 n. 36; S. D. Goitein, *A Mediterranean Society,* II, 264 f. and the numerous other passages listed in his Index to Vols. I and II *s.v.* "Druggists and Physicians."

Remarkably, many medical ministrations, including the dispensing of drugs, were performed by Jewish women. Most of them undoubtedly had no formal medical education but acquired certain expertise from their practice at home. On the great variety of drugs used in medieval Egypt, see also the inquiries addressed to R. David Ibn abi Zimra by questioners disturbed over the ritual aspects of certain drugs which might not be permissible under Jewish law. Such queries included the use of contraceptive devices. See the references in I. M. Goldman's *The Life . . . ibn abi Zimra,* pp. 140 f., 229 nn. 64–81.

118. See Maqrizi's *K. . . . Al-Khitat,* I, 104 f.; and the numerous other sources, cited esp. by H. Rabie in *The Financial System of Egypt A.H. 564–741/A.D. 1169–1341,* with the comments thereon by D. Ayalon in his review of that volume in *Der Islam,* LI, no. 2, 317–19. Other comprehensive studies include F. Løkkegard, *Islamic Taxation in the Classic Period; with Special Reference to Circumstances in Iraq;* A. Fattal, *Le Statut légal,* pp. 264–343; A. Ben Shemesh, *Taxation in Islam,* Vols. I and III, presenting annotated trans. of Yahya b. Adam's and Abū Yūsūf's standard treatises, each entitled *Kitab al-Kharaj.* These new translations reflect, of course, mainly the state of affairs up to their original authors' lifetime. For those periods see *supra,* Vol. III, pp. 161 ff., 308 ff. and the literature cited there. See also Z. Ahmad's more recent analysis of "The Concept of Jizya in Early Islam," *Islamic Studies,* XIV, 293–305; W. Hinz's study of "Das Rechnungswesen orientalischer

Reichsfinanzämter," *Der Islam,* XXIX, 1–29; and particularly C. Cahen's succinct review of the "Djizya" in the *EI,* new ed. by T. H. Kramers *et al.,* II, 559–62. Regrettably, however, even Rabie's work stops before the period of the Burji Mamelukes when the fiscal disarray, occasioned by the great economic crisis and governmental mismanagement, reached its climax. There is only a partial contribution to the fifteenth-century taxation system in B. Michel's "L'Organisation financière de l'Égypte sous les sultans mameloukes d'après Qalqachandi," *Bulletin d'Institut d'Égypte,* VII, 127–47, although many data presented by this medieval Muslim historian also refer to earlier conditions and do not necessarily mirror the situation of his own time.

On the Jewish aspects of Muslim taxation we must rely principally on the incidental references in the Genizah. This material has been extensively reviewed by S. D. Goitien in his *A Mediterranean Society,* esp. I, 266 ff., and II, 345 ff., where he also analyzes various other aspects of "government control" over the Jewish community. For the Mameluke period, however, we must still rely almost exclusively on the chapters relating to taxation in E. Strauss's *Toledot,* II, 259 ff., 293 ff., 310 ff. Here the author also made a valiant effort to correlate the data relating to taxes with those concerning costs of living—a subject to which he was later to devote special studies in his three aforementioned essays on "Le Coût de la vie" (see n. 100) and particularly in his comprehensive *Histoire des prix et des salaires.*

119. S. D. Goitein, "Evidence on the Muslim Poll Tax from Non-Muslim Sources: a Geniza Study," *JESHO,* VI, 278–95; idem, *A Mediterranean Society,* II, 380 ff.; H. Rabie, *The Financial System of Egypt,* pp. 100 ff. In his careful review of material that had been presented in 641–43 A.H. (1244–46 C.E.) by 'Utman b. Ibrahim al-Nabulusi and published by B. Moritz in the collection of the *Egyptian* (*Khedival*) *Library,* Cairo, XI, C. Cahen concluded that the average revenue from the 1,142 *dhimmis,* including 293 nonresidents, amounted to a little more than 2 dinars per taxpayer. See his "Le Régime des impôts dans le Fayyūm ayyūbide," *Arabica,* III, 8–30, esp. pp. 21 f. It may also be noted that the transfer of the poll tax collections from the central government to the governors of the *iqta'* lands, which greatly benefited a large number of Coptic peasants, was of minor advantage to the Jewish taxpayers who were concentrated in the larger cities. Those taxpayers who came under the *iqta'* influence may have found that, unlike the Copts who could claim to have paid the poll tax in another village, they merely suffered from the greater arbitrariness of the lesser landlords. See H. Rabie, "The Size and Value of the Iqta' in Egypt 564–741 A.H./1169–1341 A.D.," in M. A. Cook, ed., *Studies in Economic History,* pp. 129–38, esp, pp. 137 f.

120. A. Cowley, "Bodleian Genizah Fragments, I–VI," *JQR,* [o.s.] XVIII, 399–405; XIX, 104–108, 250–56 (with S. Poznanski's comments thereon, *ibid.,* pp. 399–401), esp. pp. 107 f. No. iii; J. Mann, *Texts and Studies,* I, 427, 431 ff. No. ii; Muḥammad b. Aḥmad Ibn Iyas, *K. Bada'i' az-Zuhar* (Die Chronik), ed. by P. Kahle *et al.,* 2d ed.; in the French trans. by G. Wiet, *Histoire des Mamlouks circassiens,* II, 367 f; E. Strauss, *Toledot,* I, 63 f.; II, 171. On the extent to which the "threat of high tax" had often become the incentive for wealthy Jews to convert to Islam, see the pertinent remark by the thirteenth-century thinker, Sa'id ibn Manṣur Ibn Kammuna, cited *supra,* n. 69; and Vol. V, p. 102. See also C. Cahen's "Contribution à l'étude des impôts dans l'Égypte médiévale," *JESHO,* V, 244–78, based in part on

the *K. al-Minhadj* by Qadhi Al-Sa'id Thiqat al-Makhzumi, analyzed in his "Un Traité financier inédit d'époque fatimide-ayyubide," *ibid.*, pp. 139–59.

121. See H. Rabie, *The Financial System of Egypt,* pp. 89 ff.; C. Cahen, "Douanes et commerce dans les ports méditerranéens de l'Égypte médiévale d'après le Minhādj d'al-Makhzūmī," *JESHO,* VII, 217–81; M. Awad, *Al-Ma'assir: Land and Sea Toll Barriers in the Byzantine and Mameluke Empires,* stressing the similarities, as well as the differences, between the two imperial systems. In this respect Western Europe was no better off. Because of the great feudal fragmentation of most countries, customs duties and tolls were often collected at short distances from one station to another. In addition, individual cities often imposed excise taxes on goods brought into their areas. However, there seems to have been a little more stability in most European areas than under the ever-changing regulations and practices of the Mameluke Empire.

122. See O. Löfgren's *Arabische Texte . . . Aden,* I, 76; A. Darrag, *L'Égypte sous le règne de Barsbay,* p. 199; and *supra,* n. 118.

123. See Ya'qūb b. Ibrāhīm Abu Yūsuf, *K. al-Kharaj* (Treatises on Taxation), pp. 125 f., in the French trans. by E. Fagnan, *Le Livre de l'impôt foncier,* and the English translation by Aharon Ben Shemesh in his *Taxation in Islam,* Vol. III, with the comments thereon, with special reference to the noteworthy theories by Al-Muqaffa', in S. D. Goitein's "A Turning Point in the History of the Muslim State (À propos of the Kitāb al-Ṣaḥāba of Ibn Muqaffa')," reprinted from *Islamic Culture,* XXIII, 120–35 in his *Studies in Islamic History and Institutions,* pp. 149–67, esp. p. 159; Goitein, *A Mediterranean Society,* II, 358 ff., and *passim;* H. Rabie, *The Financial System of Egypt,* pp. 136 f. The Mameluke regime seems to have become so diffident even of its ability to run mints efficiently that at times it entrusted them to agents. See A. S. Ehrenkreuz, "Contributions to the Knowledge of the Fiscal Administration of Egypt in the Middle Ages," *BSOAS,* XVI, 502–514; and some of his other essays, cited *supra,* nn. 7 and 84 f.

124. To be sure, the state tried to prevent abuses by tax farmers through making them adhere strictly to the existing regulations. However, in 1336–37 the inhabitants of Fusṭaṭ complained to the sultan that the *dhamin* had extended his collections to taxes on cucumbers, pomegranates, and sugar cane, even on fruits offered for sale in a single shop. Thereupon An-Naṣir ordered the tax farmer to be arrested and reduced the total collection by 10,000 dirhems. See Maqrizi, *K. aṣ-Ṣulūq,* II, 420; Rabie, *The Financial System of Egypt,* p. 137. Cases of miscalculating Jewish tax farmers were mentioned by David Ibn abi Zimra in his *Resp.,* I Nos. 136, 417. In some of these instances, entrepreneurs unable to fulfill their three-year contracts were tortured and, occasionally, lost their lives. See other instances cited by I. M. Goldman in *The Life . . . ibn abi Zimra,* pp. 152 f. On the respective attitudes to tax farming among the Muslims and the "protected subjects," see Z. Hacque's brief observations on "Métayage and Tax Farming in the Medieval Muslim Society," *Islamic Studies,* XIV, 219–37; and *supra,* Vol. II, p. 185.

125. A. S. Tritton, *The Caliphs and Their Non-Muslim Subjects: a Critical Study of the Covenant of 'Umar.* Admittedly, David Ayalon is quite correct in stressing

the great service the Mamelukes rendered to Islam through their military prowess and that without their aid the great expansion of Islam into the far corners of Asia and Africa might have been almost impossible. See his brilliant recent essay, "Aspects of the Mamlūk Phenomenon," *Der Islam,* LIII, 196–225; LIV, 1–32 (also stressing the continuity from the Ayyubid to the Mameluke Empires). He seems to underestimate, however, the long-range effects of the dead hand of an absolutist regime whose totalitarian controls were circumscribed only by their inability to master the unavoidable internal dissensions and their complete unfamiliarity with the autonomous operation of the economic and cultural factors.

CHAPTER LXXIV: NORTH AFRICA AND MUSLIM SPAIN

1. See N. Barbour, "The Significance of the Word *Maurus* with Its Derivative *Moro, Moor* and the Other Terms Used by Medieval Writers in Latin to Describe the Inhabitants of Muslim Spain," *Actas* of the IV Congresso de Estudos Arabes e Islamicos, held at Coimbra and Lisbon on September 1–8, 1968, pp. 253–66. The persistence of the Berber element in North Africa and its powerful impact on the history of all countries west of Egypt have long been recognized by modern scholars. See also *infra,* n. 37.

2. See A. Huici Miranda, *Historia política del imperio almohade;* R. Le Tourneau, *The Almohad Movement in North Africa in the XIIth and XIIIth Centuries;* and other literature listed *supra,* Vol. III, pp. 124 ff., 289 ff. nn. 5 ff. Regrettably, one of our major sources of information, the near-contemporary Muslim chronicler 'Abd al-Wahid Ibn Idhari al-Marrakushi in his *K. al-Bayan al-Maghrib,* ed. from a Leiden manuscript by R. P. A. Dozy, 2d ed. rev., and trans. into French with notes by E. Fagnan, as *Histoire de l'Afrique et de l'Espagne* (also trans. into Spanish by A. Huici Miranda, in the *Colección de crónicas árabes de la Reconquista,* II–III), is a none-too-reliable witness of events and still less acceptable in his interpretations. However, if it is used with the necessary caution, much can still be learned from his chronicle and its reinterpretation in the light of more recently accumulated evidence. All along, the Almohades employed to good military advantage the doctrine of the *jihad* which, in reaction to the Christian Crusades, was preached with growing intensity throughout the world of Islam. See, for example, its effect upon Spain according to D. Urvoy, "Sur l'évolution de la notion de *ğihād* dans l'Espagne musulmane," *Mélanges de la Casa Velázquez,* IX, 335–71. On the meteoric rise and the equally intriguing rapid disappearance of the Almohade regime, see also R. Le Tourneau, "Sur la disparition de la doctrine almohade," *Studia Islamica,* XXXII, 193–201.

3. There is, of course, an enormous literature on the history of western Islam and of its individual components from Muslim Spain to Libya. The best comprehensive handbooks are those by E. Mercier, *Histoire de l'Afrique septentrionale (Berbérie) depuis des temps les plus reculés jusqu'à la conquête française (1830)*; and, more up to date, by C. A. Julien, *History of North Africa: Tunisia, Algeria, Morocco from the Arab Conquest to 1830,* 2d ed. rev. by R. Le Tourneau, trans. into English by J. Petrie, and ed. by C. C. Stewart; C. Sanchez Albornoz, *La España musulmana según los autores islamitas y cristianos medievales.* A more general survey in English is offered by A. G. Chejne in his *Muslim Spain, Its History and Culture.* Regrettably, Évariste Lévi-Provençal's premature death limited his standard work, *Histoire de l'Espagne musulmane,* rev. ed., to three volumes. On the relationships between western and eastern Islam in the medieval period, see esp. M. Canard, "Les Relations entre les Mérinides et les Mamelouks au XIVe siècle," *Annales de l'Institut d'études orientales,* V, 41–81; G. S. Colin, "Contribution à l'étude des relations diplomatiques

entre les musulmans d'Occident et l'Égypte au XVe siècle," *Mémoires* of the Institut Français d'Archéologie Orientale au Caire, LXVIII (=*Mélanges Maspéro,* III), 197–206; and, more generally, G. Marçais in his *La Berbérie musulmane et l'Orient au moyen âge*. Some of the literature on the individual countries is quoted in the later notes.

On the Jews in the entire Maghrib see the comprehensive work by H. Z. (J. W.) Hirschberg, *Toledot ha-Yehudim be-Afriqah ha-ṣefonit* (A History of the Jews in North Africa from Antiquity to Our Time); or in the revised English trans. by M. Eichelberg in consultation with the author, *A History of the Jews in North Africa,* Vol. I (the only one thus far published); and, with its major emphasis on the modern period, A. N. Chouraqui, *Between East and West: a History of the Jews of North Africa,* trans. by M. M. Bernet, as well as other literature, both primary and secondary, listed by R. Attal in his *Yahadut Ṣefon Afriqah* (Les Juifs de l'Afrique du Nord. Bibliographie). We must look forward, moreover, to the fruits of a major basic research project undertaken by Bar-Ilan University, in Ramat Gan, Israel, to assemble the data concerning North African Jewish history that are scattered in the large rabbinic literature. See the preliminary publications by H. Z. Hirschberg, "Research on the History and Culture of the Jewries in the Muslim East" (Hebrew), *Bar-Ilan Annual,* VII–VIII, 420–36, with an English summary, pp. lxv–lxxvii; M. Slae, "References to Marranos in the Responsa of Rabbi Isaac ben Sheshet: Information Retrieved by Computer" (Hebrew), *ibid.,* pp. 397–419, with an English summary, pp. xlvii–lxiv.

4. See *supra,* Vol. III, pp. 124 f., 290 nn. 5–6; I. Goldziher's seminal paper, "Materialien zur Kenntnis der Almohadenbewegung in Nordafrika," *ZDMG,* XLI, 30–140, reprinted in his *GS,* II, 191–301, esp. pp. 268 ff.; Saadiah's *Sefer ha-Galui* (Book of Disclosure) in A. E. Harkavy's *Zikhron la-Rishonim,* cited *supra,* Vol. V, pp. 21, 300 f. n. 21; and, more fully, in my "Saadia's Communal Activities," *Saadia Anniversary Volume* of the American Academy for Jewish Research (Texts and Studies, II), pp. 9–74, reprinted in my *Ancient and Medieval Jewish History,* ed. by L. A. Feldman, pp. 95–127, 403–433, esp, pp. 119 f., 425 n. 110. The similarity between Saadiah and Ibn Tumart extends to their references, explicit or implied, to spurious genealogies. See also E. Lévi-Provençal, ed., *Documents inédits d'histoire almohade.*

5. See Shlomo Cohen's epistle, first published by J. M. Toledano in his "Documents from Manuscripts" (Hebrew), *HUCA,* IV, 449–67, with J. Mann's corrections, pp. 466 f.; and in a revised form by H. Z. Hirschberg in "The Almohade Persecutions and the India Trade (A Letter from the Year 1148)" (Hebrew) in *Baer Jub. Vol.,* pp. 134–53, esp. pp. 142 (Arabic), 147 f. (Hebrew), also mentioning the high figures of 100,000 dead at the conquest of Fez and 120,000 dead at Marrakesh.

6. See S. Munk, "Notice sur Ioseph ben Iehouda, ou Aboulhadjadj Youssouf ben Yaḥya al-Sabti al-Maghrebi disciple de Maïmonide," *JA,* 3d ser. XIV, 5–70, esp. pp. 40 f., 57 f.; and on the Visigothic example, *supra,* Vol. III, pp. 36 ff., 245 ff. nn. 44–56. Almohade intolerance toward Jews, Christians, and Muslim sectarians has long been accepted by both medieval writers and modern scholars. Contemporary poets like Abraham Ibn Ezra in his renowned poem, *Ahah yarad 'al Sefarad* (Oh, Evil Descended on Spain from Heaven), graphically described the ensuing destruction of many Jewish communities in Spain and North Africa. This poem has been

reproduced in his *Diwan,* ed. by J. Egers, pp. 69 f. No. 169. See also the comments thereon relating to North Africa by D. Cazès in his "Antiquités judaïques en Tripolitaine," *REJ,* XX, 78–87, esp. pp. 84 ff. Ibn Ezra knew some of the destroyed communities from his previous visit there. See Y. L. Fleischer, "R. Abraham Ibn Ezra in Africa" (Hebrew), *Mizraḥ u-ma'arab* (East and West), III, 81–91. Understandably, in his enumeration of the settlements ruined by the new rulers, he omitted a number of cities, especially in Tunisia. He was called to account for this oversight by another contemporary poet whose elegy was published by H. (J.) Schirmann in his ed. of "Lamentations about the Persecutions in Palestine, Africa, Spain, Germany, and France" (Hebrew), *Qobeṣ al-Yad,* n.s. III (XIII), 23–74, esp. pp. 31 ff. Similar views were held by the Jewish chroniclers from Abraham Ibn Daud onward (he died a martyr in 1180 in Christian Toledo), who depicted in very somber colors the great sufferings of the Jews in all countries ruled by Ibn Tumart's disciples.

The Maimonidean family, which had lived dangerously under the Almohade regime until it reached Egypt, and Maimonides' pupil, Joseph Ibn 'Aqnin, who succeeded in ultimately escaping to Aleppo, have also left some records of that persecution. These and other sources served as the basis for the reconstruction of the events by S. Munk, followed by almost all succeeding writers.

7. See D. Corcos-Abulafia, "The Attitude of the Almohadic Rulers towards the Jews" (Hebrew), *Zion,* XXXII, 137–60 (the passage quoted here is from his English summary, p. ii). This article and several others referred to in the following notes have been reproduced in Corcos's collection of essays in their original languages, entitled *Studies in the History of the Jews in Morocco,* with an Intro. by E. Ashtor. See also *supra,* Vol. III, pp. 124 ff., 290 ff. nn. 6 ff. (The suggested replacement of Fez by Marrakesh, on p. 124, as the Almohade capital is herewith gratefully accepted.) This is not the place to discuss Corcos's arguments—some of them quite valid—in detail. Suffice it to say that there may, indeed, have been an intensified persecution of "infidels" in 1165, as evidenced by the execution of Ibn Shushan in Fez. But the general attitude of the Almohade rulers from Al-Mu'min on was undoubtedly dictated by the fundamental doctrine of the founder, Ibn Tumart, whose integral monotheism made him persecute even Muslim mystics and the Marabuts (dervishes), who claimed descent from Mohammed, merely because they accepted some anthropomorphic features of the Deity. He equated such beliefs with an outright denial of God's uniqueness. Anthropomorphism also was his major objection to the Hebrew Bible with its corporeal descriptions of God and His actions. Ibn Tumart doubly condemned the Christian Trinitarian dogma, which he equated with unabashed polytheism. He insisted that outlawry of such "infidelity" was consonant with the traditional toleration of Christians and Jews which, he taught, had been intended only for a temporary waiting period to see whether the Jewish Messiah would arrive and Christ would reappear. How impressive Ibn Tumart's extreme interpretation of monotheism appeared even to his enemies may be seen from its impact on Maimonides and the Christian thinker Mark of Toledo. See *supra,* Vol. III, pp. 290 ff. n. 7 end.

The prevalence of many traditional ways of life, despite the Almohade revolution, is well illustrated by E. Lévi-Provençal's description of *Seville musulmane au début du XIIe siècle: le traité d'Ibn 'Abdun sur la vie et les corps des métiers* (see also *infra,* n. 55). What was true of Seville was even more true of the outlying Berber districts which had, long before Ibn Tumart, successfully resisted any serious interference with their living habits. Ignaz Goldziher may have cogently argued that Ibn Tumart's teachings and the upheaval generated by them in North Africa's and Spain's public life stemmed to a great extent from the old Berber quest for independence from the innovations of the Arab conquerors; see his aforementioned "Materialien" in *ZDMG,* XLI, 35 ff. or his *GS,* II, 196 ff. But the same individualistic, or rather tribal, self-assertive streak must now have operated to strengthen the local forces of continuity. In such a highly fragmented society as that of the Almohade empire, the preservation of ancestral beliefs and mores by secret Jews or Christians, though not devoid of danger, doubtless was quite feasible.

8. E. Tisserand and G. Wiet, eds., "Une Lettre de l'Almohade Murtadhe au Pape Innocent IV," *Hespéris,* VI, 27–53 (reproducing the letter in facsimile, Arabic transcription, and a French translation with extensive comments); A. Huici Miranda, *Historia política del imperio almohade,* I, 330 n. 3; F. Javier Simonet, *Historia de los Mozárabes de España,* esp. pp. 759 ff., 770; P. de Cénival, "L'Église chrétienne de Marrakech au XIIIe siècle," *Hespéris,* VII, 69–83. Al-Murtadha's letter to the pope, along with those addressed by Innocent III to Muḥammad an-Naṣir on March 8, 1199, by Gregory IX to 'Abd al-Wahid ar-Rashid on May 27, 1233, and by Innocent IV to 'Ali as-Sa'id on October 31, 1246, had in part been analyzed previously by L. de Mas-Latrie in his *Relations et commerce de l'Afrique septentrionale ou Magreb et les nations chrétiennes au moyen âge,* pp. 227 ff., 229 ff.

9. See J. Filliozat and P. Huard, "Les Épidémies au temps de Saint Louis," *JA,* CCLVIII, 35–42, esp. pp. 39 f.; and M. Mollat, "Le 'Passage' de Saint Louis à Tunis. Sa place dans l'histoire des croisades," *Revue d'histoire économique et sociale,* L, 289–303, contending that Louis IX may have been stimulated to his missionary assault by noticing the arrival in Paris, in 1269, of envoys from Sultan Muḥammad I al-Mustanṣir (1249–77) to settle debts of a high Tunisian dignitary to a Parisian merchant. These envoys had attended the solemn baptism of a Jewish convert at the church of St. Denis. See also *supra,* Vol. X, pp. 59 ff., 328 f. nn. 7–9. On Sidi Maḥrez, his role at the defense of Tunis in 1159 and the relatively favorable treatment of the local Jews by the otherwise implacable Al-Mu'min, see D. Cazès, *Essai sur l'histoire des Israélites de Tunisie depuis les temps les plus reculés jusqu'à l'établissement du Protectorat de la France en Tunisie,* pp. 77 ff. See also M. Eisenbeth, "Les Juifs en Algérie et en Tunisie à l'époque turque (1516–1830)," *Revue Africaine,* XCVI, 114–87, 345–84 (also reprint) which, though dealing with the Ottoman period, sheds much light on the preceding century as well.

10. Moses Maimonides' allegedly unflattering remarks concerning the Jews of Jerba are known only from a single letter purportedly addressed to his young son. It was published in 1757 by J. K. Neymann in his ed. of *Iggerot ha-Rambam* (Maimonides' Epistles), see esp. p. 3. Although there are good reasons to doubt its authenticity, the views expressed in it might indeed have been shared by Maimonides, who was generally an intellectual aristocrat looking down upon illiterate persons. See also the French trans. of that passage in D. Cazès' *Essai,* pp. 80 ff.; *supra,* Vol. VI, pp. 119 f., 387 f. n. 137; and N. Slouschz's observations during his visits to the island of Jerba early in the twentieth century, summarized in his *Travels in North Africa,* esp. pp. 250 ff. The lack of learning even on the part of lay judges in the central Maghrib continued into the fifteenth century and was unfavorably commented on

by the newly arrived Aragonese rabbis. R. Isaac b. Sheshet Perfet stated succinctly: "In this country [central Maghrib] the Jews apply Muslim law in most cases." See his *Resp.*, Constantinople, 1546 ed., No. 94. See also Simon b. Ṣemaḥ Duran, *Tashbeṣ,* II, 4b No. 5, repeated by his grandsons Ṣemaḥ and Simon, in *Yakhin u-Boaz* (Resp.), Leghorn, 1782 ed., I, 41a No. 192.

We must bear in mind, however, that even regular Jewish judges, fully equipped with the knowledge of the law, often tried to promote equitable settlements between the parties, especially in civil litigations, rather than to adhere to the letter of the law. The Tunisian Jewish elders may also have been stimulated by the example of their Muslim neighbors, among whom lay jurisdiction was quite widespread. Even in the sixteenth century Leo (Jean Léon) Africanus maintained that, in a metropolis like Marrakesh, he entertained "cordial relations" with a rich Muslim judge who was a student of North African history and had acquired much practical experience as a notary and royal favorite during forty years of service at Court while being but "slightly versed in juridical science." See Leo's *Description de l'Afrique,* new ed. by A. Époulard with notes by the editor *et al.,* p. 105 (or in the English trans. by John Pory, entitled *A History and Description of Africa,* ed. by R. Brown; see also *infra,* n. 62); and, more generally, Cazès, *Essai,* pp. 94 ff.; R. Brunschvig, "Justice religieuse et justice laïque dans la Tunisie des Deys et des Beys jusqu'au milieu du XIX siècle," *Studia Islamica,* XXIII, 27–70. Although concerned mainly with the Ottoman period, the data adduced by Brunschvig doubtless reflected local practices going back to the early Middle Ages.

11. See *supra,* n. 5. The long-accepted notion that Jewish life, together with the entire flourishing civilization of the east-central Maghrib, had suffered severely in the eleventh century from the sharp blows inflicted by the tribes of Banu Hilal and Banu Sulaym, is fully justified despite our growing realization that incipient symptoms of deep internal weakness were noticeable even before these attacks. J. Poncet has tried to minimize the total effects of the raids in "Le Mythe de la 'catastrophe hilalienne,'" *Annales ESC,* XXII, 1099–1120. But his arguments have been effectively refuted by H. R. Idris in his "De la réalité de la catastrophe hilalienne," *ibid.,* XXIII, 390–96. See also Poncet's rejoinder, *ibid.,* pp. 660–62; and the new data discussed by J. Berque in his "De nouveau sur les Beni Hilal?" *Studia Islamica,* XXXVI, 99–111.

12. See esp. *supra, Index to Volumes I–VIII,* under the pertinent entries. Here we may mention the following studies: M. Simon, "Le Judaïsme berbère dans l'Afrique ancienne," *RHPR,* XXVI, 3–31, 105–145; P. Monceaux, "Les Colonies juives dans l'Afrique romaine," *REJ,* XLIV, 1–28, reprinted in *Cahiers de Tunisie,* XVIII, 159–84; S. D. Goitein, "La Tunisie du XIe siècle," *Lévi-Provençal Mem. Vol.,* II, 559–79, or in the slightly revised English trans. entitled "Medieval Tunisia: the Hub of the Mediterranean," in his *Studies in Islamic History,* pp. 308–328, pointing out that even before 1045, central North Africa's economy and culture were on the downgrade (pp. 567 ff.). See also the two early-eleventh-century Genizah letters in the French trans. by N. A. Stillman in "Un Témoignage contemporain de l'histoire de la Tunisie ziride," *Hespéris-Tamuda,* XIII, 37–59; and on the cultural aspects, H. Z. Hirschberg, "The Role of North Africa in the Geonic Period" (Hebrew), *Horeb,* XIII, 71–121; XIV–XV, 75–126. Most direct, understandably, was the heritage of the Zirid period, which lasted for almost two centuries (972–1147) before the ad-

vent of the Almohades. See esp. H. R. Idris, *La Berbérie orientale sous les Zirides Xe–XIIe siècles,* which includes data on Jews, II, 671–74, 764–69, 802–808, and so forth.

13. See N. Slouschz, *Travels in North Africa,* p. 344 and *passim.* On some of the literature previously quoted, see *supra,* Vols. III, pp. 90 ff., 271 nn. 23–25; and XV, pp. 350 ff., 539 ff. nn. 100–107. More recently, H. Z. (J. W.) Hirschberg has been particularly impressed by the detailed anthropological investigations by L. C. Briggs *et al.* of a Jewish group living in the oasis of Mzab, southern Algeria. See Briggs's "Aperçu préliminaire sur l'anthropologie des Juifs de Mzab," *Bulletin* of the Société d'Histoire Naturelle de l'Afrique du Nord, XLVI, 135–54; his and (Mme) N. L. Guede's "Aperçu anthropologique et démographique sur les Juives du Mzab," *Bulletin* of the Société d'Anthropologie de Paris, 11th ser. IV, 506–530; some earlier studies mentioned by B. Cohen in his "Notes on the Jews of Mzab," *JQR,* XXIII, 398; P. Flamand, *Un Mellah en pays berbère: Demnate;* R. Basset, *Étude sur les Zenatia du Mzab, de Ouargla et de l'ouest de R'ir.* See also, more generally, C. Monteil's "Problèmes du Soudan occidental: Juifs et judaïsés," *Hespéris,* XXXVIII, 265–98; Briggs's *Tribes of the Sahara;* his and Guede's *No More for Ever: a Saharan Jewish Town. With Appendices on Physical Anthropology, Demography and Social Structure;* and some of the older writings, listed by C. Funck-Brentano in his "Bibliographie du Sahara occidental," *Hespéris,* XI, 203–296. Monteil emphasizes that in Mzab some families, both humble ones and those of the nobility, traced their ancestry to Jews, though many such claims were clearly spurious (pp. 292 ff.). On the basis of these and other researches, Hirschberg raised anew "The Problem of the Judaized Berbers" in a pertinent article in the *Journal of African History,* IV, 313–39; and in his *Toledot,* II, 9 ff. See also *infra,* n. 29.

Of considerable interest also is the fate of the once flourishing city-oasis, Sijilmassa, which had played a significant role in the pre-Almohade international trade with both East and West. Undermined by Berber raids, this great emporium was completely ruined by the Almohade rulers. See, for instance, J. M. Lessard, "Sijilmassa: La Ville et ses relations commerciales au XIe siècle d'après El-Bekri," *Hespéris-Tamuda,* V, 5–35 (mentioning that in 951 the oasis was able to deliver to the Faṭimid Treasury the huge amount of 400,000 dinars, or about half the Treasury's revenue from the Mahdiya region); H. Terrasse, "Notes sur les ruines de Sijilmasa," *Revue Africaine,* 1936; S. D. Goitein's *A Mediterranean Society,* I, Index, p. 547 *s.v.* Sijilmasa; and *supra,* Vol. IV, pp. 170, 320 f. n. 22.

14. Abi-Dinar al-Kairuani, *K. Al-Mu'nis fi Akhbar Ifriqiyya wa-Tunis,* in the French trans. by E. Pelissier and J. P. A. Remusat, entitled *Histoire de l'Afrique,* pp. 324 ff.; M. T. Ferrer i Mallol, "Documenti catalani sulla spedizione franco-genovese in Berberia (1390)," *Miscellanea di studi storici,* I, 211–61; and, more generally, the older but very useful works by L. de Mas-Latrie, ed., *Traités de paix et de commerce et documents divers concernant les relations des chrétiens avec les Arabes de l'Afrique septentrionale au moyen âge,* with a Supplement; idem, *Relations et commerce de l'Afrique septentrionale;* A. Sayous, *Le Commerce des Européens à Tunis depuis le XIIe siècle jusqu'à la fin du XVIe siècle.* These works have been used to good advantage by Jewish historians, especially H. Z. Hirschberg. How much could still be accomplished by thoroughgoing archival research in Europe was demonstrated by C. E. Dufourcq in his *L'Espagne catalane et le Maghrib aux*

XIIIe et XIVe siècles. De la bataille de Las Navas de Tolosa (1212) à l'avènement du sultan Mérinide Abou-l-Hasan (1331). This work includes a multitude of references to North African Jews. See the Index, p. 637 *s.v.* Juifs (les). See also M. Kraiem's comprehensive study, *La Tunisie précoloniale.*

Nor must we overlook the hitherto completely unexplored impact on the local Jews of Christian missionary efforts in North Africa, propagated particularly by such distinguished Spanish ecclesiastics as Raymond de Peñaforte and Raymond Lull. Begun with his *Petitio . . . pro conversione infidelium* in 1294, Lull's missionary career ended two decades later in a martyr's death in Bougie (1316). See J. M. Coll, "San Raimondo de Peñaforte y las missiones del Norte Africano de la Edad Media," *Missionalia Hispanica,* V, 117–457; A. S. Atiya, *The Crusade in the Later Middle Ages,* esp. pp. 74 ff.; and *supra,* Vol. IX, pp. 83 ff., 101, 279 nn. 34–35, 288 ff. n. 4 item 2, and so forth.

One wishes that scholars in other countries would similarly utilize their rich medieval archival collections to cast some light on life in North Africa during the Middle Ages, since there is little hope for the recovery of major documentary collections in the North African countries themselves. This paucity of archival information is especially pronounced in the case of Jewish communal repositories similar to the Cairo Genizah. Some samples, however, have been made available by Saadiah Ibn Danan, Abraham Gavison, Jacob Ben-Naïm, and Georges Vajda in their publications which were, or will be, mentioned in our notes. See also D. Cazès, *Note bibliographique sur la littérature juive-tunisienne,* and, more generally, R. Brunschvig, *La Berbérie orientale sous les Ḥafṣides des origines à la fin du XVe siècle,* esp. I, 404 f.

15. See M. Alarcón y Santón and R. García de Linares, eds., *Los Documentos árabes diplomáticos del Archivo de la Corona de Aragón,* pp. 311–14 No. 140bis (reproducing the Arabic text of the 1360 treaty between Aragon and Tunisia), 314–20 (Spanish trans.); I. de las Cagigas, "Un Traité de paix entre le roi Pierre IV d'Aragon et le sultan de Tunisie 'Abd Isḥak II (1360)," *Hespéris,* XIX, 65–77 (offering the Latin counterpart). The treaty uses the comprehensive term *aliquis* about the protection of ships and refers more specifically to *nullus Saracenus nec nullus Judeus* relating to the protection of captives. On consular protection, see A. Sacerdoti, "Il Consolato veneziano del regno Hafsida di Tunisi (1274–1518)," *Studi Veneziani,* XI, 531–35 (examining with the aid of some archival data the consulate's general administrative, judicial, and diplomatic functions); C. E. Dufourcq, "Les Consulats catalans de Tunis et de Bougie au temps de Jacques le Conquérant," *Anuario de Estudios medievales,* III, 469–79.

16. See Anselm Adorne's travelogue, ed. in its Latin original with a French trans. by R. Brunschvig in his *Deux récits de voyage inédits en Afrique du Nord au XVe siècle 'Abdālbasiṭ b. Ḫalīl et Adorne* (Diss. Paris), Part II, pp. 158, 29b (Latin), 192 (French); R. Isaac b. Sheshet Perfet, *Resp.,* Nos. 41–42, 70, 98–99, and *passim;* R. Simon b. Ṣemaḥ Duran, *Sefer Tashbeṣ* (Resp.), II, Nos. 93, 279, and *passim;* Ṣemaḥ and Simon Duran, *Yakhin u-Boaz, passim; supra,* Vol. XI, pp. 232 ff., 399 ff. nn. 52 ff. Good summaries of the historical material in the first two of these collections of responsa are offered by A. M. Hershman, *Rabbi Isaac ben Sheshet Perfet and His Times* (esp. pp. 177 f., 183); and I. Epstein, *The Responsa of Rabbi Simon b. Ẓemaḥ Duran as a Source of the History of the Jews in North Africa.* We must

bear in mind, however, that not all the responsa of these rabbis reflect conditions existing in Algeria. Those written by the aged Isaac b. Sheshet after his arrival there are but a small part of his printed responsa. See *infra,* n. 46. On the other hand, Duran, at least toward the end of his life, wrote a responsum on his own initiative on a complicated problem of levirate marriage created by the presence of a large class of *conversos* in Spain. The rabbi hoped thereby not only to prevent a miscarriage of justice in a pending case, but also to establish an effective precedent for the guidance of later rabbis and students. See his *Tashbeṣ,* III, No. 285; and M. Weinstein, "Fez and Its Connections with Algiers in the Fifteenth Century: a Responsum of R. Joseph Sasportas Addressed to the Community of Fez" (Hebrew), *Zakhor le-Abraham,* pp. 13–24 (includes the ed. from a MS, in private possession, of a responsum by R. Joseph Sasportas addressed to the community of Fez, pp. 20 ff.), esp. p. 14.

While almost all historians dealing with the history of North African Jewry have made extensive use of Simon Duran's responsa, the numerous other works of this prolific writer have been insufficiently utilized for historical purposes. Even his *Qeshet u-Magen* (Bow and Shield), an apologetic tract (part of a comprehensive commentary on Abot, written in Africa in 1423 and published in an anonymous collection *Milḥemet ḥobah* [Obligatory War], Constantinople, 1710) in which R. Simon rather frankly criticized both Christianity and Islam, has been examined for the author's philosophical and theological arguments rather than for the light it sheds on the community in which he lived. See the literature listed *supra,* Vol. IX, pp. 295 f. n. 7 item 14; and the succinct list of Duran's publications by S. A. Horodezky in his "Duran, Simeon ben Zemach," *Encyclopaedia Judaica* (German), VI, 130–34. See also, more generally, F. Braudel, *Les Espagnols et l'Afrique du Nord de 1492 à 1577* (reprinted from *Revue Africaine,* 1928); idem, "Les Espagnols en Algérie, 1492–1792," in J. Alazard *et al., Histoire et historiens de l'Algérie,* with an Intro. by S. Gsell, pp. 231–66; and numerous other data included in Braudel's comprehensive work, *La Méditerranée et le monde méditerranéen à l'époque de Philippe II,* 2d ed. rev. and enlarged, also in its English translation; and *infra,* Vol. XVIII, *passim.* Although dealing with the period of Ottoman domination, these studies are also useful for comprehending the conditions existing in the preceding centuries.

17. See, for the time being, S. Lane-Poole in collaboration with J. D. Jerrold-Kelley, *The Barbary Corsairs;* G. Fisher, *Barbary Legend;* the more popular but informed and attractively written sketch by P. Achard, *La Vie extraordinaire des frères Barberousse corsaires et rois d'Alger;* and such monographs as R. Coindreau, *Les Corsaires de Salé.* See also C. A. Julien, *History of North Africa,* esp. pp. 290 f., 302 ff.; and the extensive French literature analyzed by G. Turbet-Delof in his twin Sorbonne theses, *L'Afrique barbaresque dans la littérature française (1532–1715),* and the *Bibliographie critique* thereto.

18. See the list of Jewish communities in the respective areas as compiled in H. Z. Hirschberg's *A History,* I, 140 ff., and various other passages, esp. pp. 130 ff., 349 ff. nn. 54 ff. (or with somewhat fuller documentation in his *Toledot,* I, 95 ff., 103 ff.); S. D. Goitein, *A Mediterranean Society,* esp. II, 188, 256, and 395 f.; D. Cazès, "Antiquités judaïques en Tripolitaine," *REJ,* XX, 78–87, reproducing two tombstone inscriptions dating from 963 and 1159 C.E. On the Aragonese connections, see C. E. Dufourcq, *L'Espagne catalane et le Maghrib,* esp. pp. 314 n. 5, 506 n. 6; and

N. Slouschz, *Travels in North Africa,* pp. 11 ff. On Jason of Cyrene, see *supra,* Vol. I, pp. 198, 207, 217, 232, 390 n. 53. Remarkably, a Hebrew Bible which appeared in Tripoli in 1312 had chapter divisions which corresponded to neither the Masorah nor the Septuagint (Cazès, pp. 80 ff.). Though brought from Spain, it may have followed some older tradition of Tripolitanian-Libyan Jewry. To the literature listed *supra,* Vols. I–II, add J. Gray, "The Jewish Inscriptions in Greek and Hebrew at Tocra, Cyrene and Barca," *Cyrenaican Expedition of the University of Manchester,* ed. by A. Rowe, esp. pp. 56 f.

19. See Joseph b. Joshua ha-Kohen, *'Emeq ha-bakha,* ed. by M. Letteris, p. 110; in M. Wiener's German trans., p. 74; in H. S. May's English trans., *The Vale of Tears,* p. 74; Ḥ. Y. D. Azulai (ḤIDA), *Shem ha-Gedolim, Va'ad le-Ḥakhamim* (Names of the Great, Assembly of Scholars; a bio-bibliographical dictionary), ed. by Y. E. Ben-Yakob (Ben-Jacob), Part I (Biographies), p. 179 No. 166. According to Azulai, Simeon b. Labi also composed a large commentary on the *Zohar,* Books of Genesis and Exodus, which was extant in his day (late eighteenth century) in both Tunis and Tripoli. The section on Genesis had been published under the title *Ketem Paz* (Most Fine Gold). This high-sounding title was chosen because the numerical value of its Hebrew letters equaled that of the Hebrew letters in *Simeon Labi z. l.* (S. L. of blessed memory), and because the word Paz was an acronym of *Perush Zohar* (Commentary on the Zohar). See also, more generally, the Hebrew essays included in the collected volume *Yahadut Lub* (Libyan Jewry: Articles and Notes on the Life of the Jews in Libya). Although mainly concerned with modern developments, some of these studies shed light on the otherwise obscure evolution of Jewish life in Libya during the late medieval centuries. In general, Tripolitania vacillated in its allegiance between Egypt and Tunisia. See E. Rossi, *Storia di Tripoli e della Tripolitania dalla conquista araba al 1911,* ed. by M. Nallino; and the bibliographical studies by R. (A.) Attal, "A Bibliography of Publications Concerning North African Jewry" (Hebrew), *Sefunot,* V (=*Isaiah Sonne Mem. Vol.*), 467–508, with an English summary, p. [18]; idem, "A Bibliography of Publications Concerning Libyan Jewry" (Hebrew), *ibid.,* IX (=*Itzhak Ben-Zvi Mem. Vol.*), 383–98, with an English summary p. [21]; and, more generally, R. W. Hill, *A Bibliography of Libya;* H. Schlütter, *Index libycus. Bibliography of Libya 1957–1969,* with Supplementary Material for 1915–1956.

20. H. Z. Hirschberg, *Toledot,* I, 274 ff.; idem, *A History,* I, 363 ff.; Jacob b. Elijah de Lattes of Valencia (or Venice), *Iggeret* (Epistle), ed. by J. Kobak, *Jeschurun,* VI, Hebrew part, pp. 1–34; with the comments thereon by J. Mann in "Une Source de l'histoire juive au XIIIe siècle: La lettre polémique de Jacob b. Élie à Pablo Christiani," *REJ,* LXXXII, 363–77, reproduced in *The Collected Articles,* I, 230–44; and idem, "On the Time and Place of R. Jacob b. Elijah, the Author of a Polemical Letter against Fra Pablo" (Hebrew), *Alim,* I, 75–77. Whether the author lived in Valencia, in the midst of a still surviving large Muslim community, or in Venice (as argued by J. Mann), with its vast commercial and political contacts with the Muslim lands, he must have heard a good deal about the conditions in North Africa. See G. Sacerdoti's study mentioned *supra,* n. 15; and some of the extensive literature listed in R. L. Playfair's old compilations, *A Bibliography of Algeria;* and *Supplement to the Bibliography of Algeria from the Earliest Times to 1895.* More up-to-date compilations include the annual *Bibliographie de l'Algérie,* of which Vols. I–XIII appeared

in 1965–76. Of considerable interest also is the collection of essays published on the occasion of the 1930 centenary celebration of the French occupation of Algeria, ed. by J. Alazard *et al.*, *Histoire et historiens d'Algérie.*

21. See 'Abdalbasiṭ's comments reproduced by R. Brunschvig in his *Deux récits,* Part 1, pp. 43 ff., fol. 91b (Arabic), 105 ff. (French). One need not imagine that internally the life of the Jewish exiles in Algeria was free of conflict. Even the two greatest leaders, Isaac Perfet and Simon Duran, sometimes differed sharply on problems of Jewish law. On one occasion Duran even attacked a decision by his elder colleague as "sheer nonsense," although he later regretted this lack of consideration for a venerable sage. See A. M. Hershman, *Rabbi Isaac ben Sheshet Perfet,* pp. 222 f., 248 ff., Additional Notes, No. vii. The spread of the new arrivals into various communities outside Algiers is evident from the origins of the inquiries to the two rabbis. For example, Ephraim Alnaqua, son of Israel Alnaqua (the author of a celebrated ethical work, *Menorat ha-Ma'or* [Candlestick], and one of the 1391 martyrs of Toledo) settled in Honein and later in Tlemcen, where he died in 1442. Living close to the court in the royal capital, Ephraim early secured from the ruler the permission to attract Jews to Tlemcen and to erect a synagogue in the city. See *ibid.,* pp. 161 ff.; A. Mayer, *Étude sur la communauté de Tlemcen,* pp. 6 ff.; and R. I. Lawless's succinct observations on "Tlemcen, Capital City of the 'Abd al-Wahids: a Study of the Functions of a Medieval Islamic City," *Islamic Quarterly,* XVIII, 14–20, emphasizing that, although it was a large city with a population ranging from 80,000 to 125,000 inhabitants, it was mainly a military and administrative rather than commercial center. See also his and G. H. Blake's more comprehensive work, *Tlemcen: Continuity and Change in an Algerian Islamic Town,* ed. by J. C. Dewdney; and, more generally, H. Kurio, *Geschichte und Geschichtsschreiber der 'Abd al-Wadiden (Algerien im 13.–15. Jahrhundert). Mit einer Teiledition des* Nazm al-Durr *des Mohammed b. 'Abd al-Galil at-Tanas.*

22. See I. Block, "Les Israélites d'Oran," *REJ,* XIII, 85–104; the Arabic chronicle cited here in the English trans. by W. Marçais in his "Algeria," *JE,* I, 381–85, esp. p. 381; P. Ruff, *La Domination espagnole d'Oran sous le gouvernement du Comte d'Alcandate 1534–1558. Avec un appendice contenant six documents inédits,* pointing out that, because of the strongly centralized Spanish administration, the local governors had little chance to follow their personal inclinations. See also the additional sources quoted by H. Z. (J. W.) Hirschberg in *A History,* I, 441 ff. and *passim.*

23. See G. Vajda, "Un Traité Maghrébin 'Adversus Judaeos': *'Ahkām al-ḏimma'* du Šayḫ Muḥammad b. 'Abd al-Karīm al-Magīlī," *Lévi-Provençal Mem. Vol.,* II, 805–813, esp. p. 810. Al-Majili's tract was but a link in a long chain of Arabic polemical and apologetic writings, similar to the contemporary Syro-Egyptian literature of that type discussed *supra,* Chap. LXXIII, nn. 66 ff. and in our earlier volumes. Yet its survival in only a couple of manuscripts seems to indicate that it never achieved a wide circulation. It certainly left few traces in the subsequent Arabic literature and had little impact upon the local legislation in Tlemcen, Tuat, or the Sudan. The parts dealing with specific proposals affecting the sociopolitical standing of the Jews are discussed *infra,* nn. 29, 47, 58, 59. On Al-Majili's life and works, see also the biographical data summarized by Aḥmed Baba as-Sudani (d. 1623) and reviewed by I. Goldziher in his "Mélanges judéo-arabes, XXXIII. Sur les Juifs du

Maghrib," *REJ*, LX, 34–36, reprinted in his *GS*, V, 205–207; as well as the additional details supplied by Leo Africanus (see *infra*, n. 47); and by F. de la Chapelle in his "Esquisse d'une histoire du Sahara occidental," *Hespéris*, XI, 35–95, esp. p. 82 n. 2. On Tuat, see also R. Basset, "Notes de lexicographie berbérienne, 4th ser.: Vocabulaire du Touat et de Gourara; Argot de Mzab; Dialecte des Touaregs Aouelimmidens," *JA*, 8th ser. X, 365–464, esp. pp. 381 ff.; and H. Z. Hirschberg, *Toledot*, II, 18 ff.

24. H. Terrasse, *Histoire du Maroc des origines à l'établissement du Protectorat français*, II, 39, 46, 54 f.; 'Abd ar-Raḥman Ibn Khaldun, *The Muqaddimah: an Introduction to History*, trans. by F. Rosenthal, I, 278 ff., 343 ff., with the translator's observations thereon, *ibid.*, pp. lxxxii f.; in the annotated French trans. by W. M. de Slane entitled *Les Prolegomènes d'Ibn Khaldoun*, II, 347, with reference to Exod. 20:5; W. J. Fischel, "Ibn Khaldūn on the Bible, Judaism and the Jews," *Ignace Goldziher Mem. Vol.*, ed. by S. Loewinger *et al.*, II, 147–71, esp. pp. 160 ff.; A. Baumstark, "Der Bibelkanon bei Ibn Khaldūn," *Oriens Christianus*, IV, 393–98, showing that the historian was quite familiar with the Jewish and Christian Scriptures. See also, more generally, I. Goldziher, "Über Bibelcitate in muhammedanischen Schriften," *Zeitschrift für alttestamentliche Wissenschaft*, XIII, 315–21; and idem, "Ueber muhammedanische Polemik gegan Ahl al-Kitāb," *ZDMG*, XXXII, 341–87 (reprinted in his *GS*, I, 1–47), counting Ibn Khaldun among the relatively few Muslim authors who quoted biblical passages accurately, although he may not have gone as far as the Shafi'ite Al-Nadawi, who called any person denigrating the Scriptures of the "people of the book" a heretic (*kafir*) on a par with one daring to disparage the Qur'an. *Ibid.*, pp. 359 ff., 361 n. 4, 366 f. (*GS*, I, 19 ff., 21 n. 4, 26 f.). Yet, some of Ibn Khaldun's quotations did not conform with the masoretic text but were indebted to readings appearing in the Vulgate (according to Baumstark) or even in the Ethiopic versions (as postulated by August Dillmann and Ignaz Goldziher). Nonetheless, he seems to have had a fair knowledge of contemporary Jewish life as well. While still in Fez, he became acquainted with the influential Jewish family of the Banu Waqqaṣa at the court of Abu-Ya'qub Yusuf. However, it stands to reason that, like most of his contemporaries, Ibn Khaldun was an eclectic using citations taken from a variety of second-hand sources. In any case, a monograph on Ibn Khaldun's scattered discussions of ancient and medieval Jews and Judaism would still be of value. See, for example, a comparable study by I. Saade, "Cómo enjuicia Ibn Jaldūn el cristianismo," *Salmanticensis*, XVI, 275–97.

The vast historical literature on Morocco included, apart from the numerous Arabic chronicles and histories reviewed in F. Rosenthal's *A History of Muslim Historiography*, also some early Western studies; for example, the three-volume work by L. S. Chenier, *Recherches historiques sur les Maures et histoire de l'Empire de Maroc*, Paris, 1767, the latter part of which was trans. into English (1788) and published under the title, *The Present State of the Empire of Morocco* (see esp. pp. 156 ff.). Among the recent monographs are R. Thoden's *Abū'l Ḥasan 'Alī. Marinidenpolitik zwischen Nordafrika und Spanien in den Jahren 710–752 H./1310–1351;* and the more comprehensive summaries by M. P. Castellanos and F. S. Eijan, *Historia de Marruecos;* and J. Brignon *et al.*, *Histoire du Maroc*. It should also be noted that, in regard to the complicated chronology of the reigns of the Marinid and other North African rulers, I have generally followed the dates supplied by C. E. Bosworth in *The Islamic Dynasties*. Fuller data can be found in the sources and studies listed in the early bibliographical works by R. L. Playfair and R. Brown, *A Bibliography of Morocco to the End of 1891* in Supplementary Papers of the Royal Geographic Society, III (also published separately); and such compilations as P. de Cénival *et al.*, in the annual *Bibliographie marocaine,* in 1923–35, 1948–51; and J. Richer and O. Little, "Bibliographie marocaine," for the years 1940–43, 1944–47, 1948–51, 1952–53, published in *Hespéris,* XXXIV, 103–234; XXXVIII, 31–203; XLII, 294–708; and *Hespéris-Tamuda,* III, 159–591, respectively (totaling some 16,000 entries). See also *supra,* n. 3.

25. Muḥammad Ibn abi Zar, *K. Rawdh al-Qirtas* (A History of the Kings of Maghrib and Annals of the City of Fez), ed. with a Latin trans. by C. J. Thornberg as *Annales regum Mauritaniae a condito Idissarum imperio ad annum fugae 726,* and trans. into French by A. R. Beaumier, *Histoire des souverains du Maghreb (Espagne et Maroc) et annales de la ville de Fès,* esp. p. 55; H. Z. Hirschberg, *A History,* I, 370.

26. A. Bel, *La Religion musulmane en Berbérie. Esquisse d'histoire et de sociologie religieuse,* I, 311 ff. (on the spread of Ṣufism up to the sixteenth century), 361 ff. (its impact on juridico-religious studies), 376 ff. (the religious reaction to the Christian conquests); Don Joseph b. Shushan, *Commentary* on Abot, quoted (together with other pertinent passages) from a British Museum MS by H. H. Ben-Sasson in his stimulating essay on "The Generation of the Spanish Exiles on Its Fate" (Hebrew), *Zion,* XXVI, 23–64, with an English summary, pp. i–iii, esp. pp. 29 f. Information on the influential Jews in Moroccan history is widely scattered. They are frequently mentioned in connection with some broader treatment of Jewish history in the country as a whole, in individual communities such as Fez or Marrakesh, or in connection with specific events. Together with other aspects of Jewish life, they are often treated in the comprehensive reviews written by Jews of Morocco or of Moroccan origin, as well as by Western, especially French, scholars. Among the earlier writings we may mention N. Slouschz, "Études sur l'histoire des Juifs et du judaïsme au Maroc," *Archives marocaines,* VI, 1–167, esp. pp. 140 ff.; M. L. Ortega, *Los Hebreos en Marruecos: Estudio histórico, político y social,* 4th ed.; A. I. Laredo, *Bereberes y Hebreos en Marruecos; sus origines, segùn las leyendas, tradiciones y fuentes hebraicas antiguas.* Quite significant also are the Hebrew works by Saadiah Ibn Danan, *Seder ha-Dorot* in Z. H. Edelman's ed. of *Ḥemdah genuzah;* and J. M. Toledano, *Toledot Yisrael be-Maroqo* (A History of the Jews in Morocco); D. Corcos-Abulafia, "The Jews of Morocco under the Marinides," *JQR,* LIV, 271–87; LV, 55–81, 137–50; and such additional source materials as were edited in a French trans. by G. Vajda in *Un Recueil des textes historiques judéo-marocains.* Above all, we must refer constantly to H. Z. Hirschberg's comprehensive *Toledot* and its partial English trans., *A History,* I. The Hebrew Vol. II includes some extensive excerpts from Moroccan Hebrew manuscripts, including those underlying Vajda's French translations. Since in their legal and social status Jews were officially placed on a par with Christians—whose relatively small number, though it was constantly reinforced by new arrivals from European countries, grew but slowly because most of the newcomers returned home—it is of some use to compare the status of these two minorities. See, for instance, P. Mesnage, "Le Christianisme en Afrique," *Revue Africaine,* 1913, pp. 361–700.

27. H. Terrasse, *Histoire du Maroc,* II, 39; C. E. Dufourcq, *L'Espagne catalane et le Maghrib,* pp. 200 ff., 395; 'Abdalbasiṭ b. Ḥalil in R. Brunschvig's *Deux récits,* pp. 17 (Arabic text), 69 ff. (French trans.), esp. pp. 47 ff. (fol. 97b, Arabic), 113 ff. (French). Harun's enemies also claimed that, during his absence from Fez, his brother had diverted to Jews the alms collected for the Muslim poor according to the high religious principle of *sadaqa* (alms). This obvious loanword from the Hebrew *ṣedaqah* was given a different etymology by some Arab linguists—perhaps bent on drawing a sharper line of demarcation between Judaism and Islam—as meaning "to tell the truth." See E. Fagnan, "Le Signe distinctif des Juifs au Maghreb," *REJ,* XXVIII, 294–98, esp. p. 298 n. 1. On the frequency of wine drinking among the Muslims from the caliphs down, see A. von Kremer, *Culturgeschichte des Orients unter den Chalifen,* II, 62–86. The famed Harun ar-Rashid, for example, is said to have been induced by a song of one of his court musicians to quaff ten cups of wine in quick succession (pp. 64 f.).

28. Joseph b. Joshua ha-Kohen, *Dibre ha-Yamim le-Malkhe Ṣarefat u-Malkhe Bet Ottoman ha-Toger* (A History of the Frankish and Ottoman Kings; a World History), Amsterdam, 1733, esp. fol. 134b; the Ibn Danan family chronicle, likewise entitled *Dibre ha-Yamim,* and in Arabic *Al-Tawariḥ.* This collection consists of notes on contemporary events, interspersed with many legendary and anecdotal details, written in the sixteenth through the middle of the nineteenth centuries by successive members of that rabbinical family, in a flowery style. These notes were first compiled and edited, together with numerous additions of his own, by R. Samuel b. Saul Ibn Danan (1668–1730). They were subsequently amplified by additional notes, finally compiled from 1879 onward in a codex by another descendant of that family. It circulated in manuscript form among the cognoscenti of the community, but it has never been fully published. Only recently did Meir Benayahu undertake to prepare a critical ed. of the entire text (see Hirschberg's *Toledot,* II, 353 n. 3). However, thus far the work does not seem to have appeared in print. The more significant excerpts from this chronicle were reordered in a more systematic fashion and ed. in a French trans. by G. Vajda in *Un Recueil des textes historiques judéo-marocains.* However, the original notes had previously been utilized by numerous other Hebrew chroniclers of the history of Jews of Fez, such as Abner Sarfaty in his *Yaḥas Feṣ* (Distinction of Fez; see Y. D. Sémaḥ, "Une Chronique juive de Fès, le 'Yahas Fès' de Ribbi Abner Hassarfaty," *Hespéris,* XIX, 79–94); and Joseph Ben Naïm in his *Malkhe Rabbanan* (Kings–Rabbis), published in Jerusalem, 1931. See also N. Slouschz, "Les Juifs de Debdou," *Revue du Monde Musulman,* XXII, 221–69, esp. pp. 230, 245 f., 257; and his *Travels in North Africa,* esp. pp. 388 ff. Here Slouschz calls Debdu "a Jewish city," for he found that it embraced 1,400 Jews (other travelers estimated 1,500) among its 2,000 inhabitants.

Much information about Jews may also be derived from the general Arabic historical sources, and modern studies in part based on them, relating to the three successive Moroccan dynasties of the Marinids, Waṭṭasids, and Sa'adians (or the Sharif dynasty). See, for example, Muḥammad ibn al-Ahmar, *Histoire des Beni Merīn, Rois de Fās, intitulée Rowdat en-Nisrim,* ed. and trans. by C. Bouáli and G. Marçais; Muḥammad b. 'Abdallah al-Wufrani (Eloufrani), *Nozhet-Elhādi* (*Histoire de la dynastie saadienne au Maroc, 1511–1670*), ed. and trans. into French by O. V. Houdas; Muḥammad Ibn abi Zar, *K. Rawdh al-Qirtas* (*supra,* n. 25). See also

A. Cour, *La Dynastie marocaine des Beni Waṭṭas, 1426–1554* (Diss. Algiers; includes data on the Waṭṭasid viziers before 1456, pp. 46 ff.); idem, *L'Établissement des dynasties des Chérifs au Maroc (1509–1830)*. On the Jews under the early Sa'adian dynasty see M. Arribas Palau's brief summary in "Las Comunidades israelitas bajo los primeros Sa'díes," *Homenaje a Millás Vallicrosa,* I, 45–65, esp. p. 47. Aspects of Jewish life under the later Sa'adian dynasty, whose rule was intimately connected with the first century of Ottoman suzerainty over the rest of North Africa, will be further analyzed in the context of Jewish history in the Ottoman Empire.

29. See D. Corcos-Abulafia, "Moroccan Jewry in the First Half of the 16th Century" (Hebrew), *Sefunot,* X, 69 ff.; William Lemprière, *A Tour from Gibraltar to Tangier, Sallee, Mogadore, Santa Cruz, Tarudant and thence over Mount Atlas to Morocco,* London, 1791, p. 173. On the Berber Jews in the Atlas Mountains and elsewhere in North Africa, see *supra,* n. 13; and the following studies: G. S. Colin, "Les Juifs nomades retrouvés dans le Sahara marocain au XVIe siècle," *Mélanges Cénival-Lopes,* pp. 53–66, esp. pp. 59 ff.; M. Bugeja, "Les Juifs de Kabylie," *Bulletin* of the Société des Conférences Juives d'Alger, no. 3, pp. 101 ff.; E. W. Ikin *et al.,* "The Blood Groups and Haemoglobin of the Jews of the Tafilalet Oases of Morocco," *Man,* VII, 595–600; E. Margalis *et al.,* "Blood Groups in Jews from Morocco and Tunisia," *Annals of Human Genetics,* XXII, 65–68; and, more generally, A. E. Mourant, "The Blood Groups of the Jews," *JJS,* I, 155–76; J. Bourilly, *Éléments d'ethnographie marocaine;* and F. de La Chapelle, "Esquisse," *Hespéris,* XI, 82, also referring to Al-Majili's anti-Jewish propaganda in Sijilmassa and Tuat. See *supra,* n. 23.

30. See M. Bataillon, "Le Rêve de la conquête de Fès et le sentiment impérial portugais au XVe siècle," *Mélanges Cénival-Lopes,* pp. 31–39 (reprinted in his *Études sur le Portugal au temps du humanisme,* pp. 101–107), analyzing in particular Diogo de Gouvea's propagation of that enterprise. On the spelling of the name Gouvea, the likely New Christian antecedents of that prominent French family, and the general idea of the Portuguese expansion into Morocco, see *supra,* n. 17; Vol. XIII, pp. 52 f., 118 f., 330 f. n. 56, 376 n. 61. As early as the 1540s and 1550s, the then newly founded Jesuit Order, with its large complement of New Christian leaders, extended its missionary activities to Morocco and the rest of Africa. See D. M. dos Santos, "A Entrada dos Jesuítas em Marrocos no seculo XVI," *Mélanges Cénival-Lopes,* pp. 225–95.

Much documentation concerning the Portuguese expansion into Moroccan territories and its effects upon Jews is derived from Portuguese archival documents and their modern analyses. See, for example, P. A. de Azevedo, ed., *Documentos de chancelarias reais anteriores a 1531 relativos a Marrocos;* R. Ricard, *Les Portugais au Maroc de 1495 à 1521;* idem, "Le Problème de l'occupation restrainte dans l'Afrique du Nord (XVe–XVIIe siècles)," *Annales d'histoire économique et sociale,* VIII, 426–37; and, within the framework of Portuguese history, D. Lopes's standard work, *Historia de Portugal,* ed. by D. Peres.

31. See E. Rossi, *Storia di Tripoli,* pp. 112 f.; I. D. Abbou, *Musulmans andalous et judéo-espagnols,* p. 401 n. 1; the two special prayerbooks written for these festive occasions by Abraham b. Solomon Ṣarfati, *Shebi Elohim* (God's Bondage), Leghorn, 1545, listed by R. L. Playfair in his *Supplement to the Bibliography of Algeria from the Earliest Times to 1895,* p. 6 No. 4776; the *Siddur Ahabat ha-Qadmonim* (Love of the Ancients), in the excerpt cited and trans. into French by A. I. Laredo

in "Les Purims de Tanger," *Hespéris,* XXXV, 193–203, esp. pp. 195 f.; and *supra,* Vol. XV, pp. 235 f., 487 f. n. 86.

Not surprisingly, these local Jewish festivals were viewed with a jaundiced eye by interested outsiders. While in his section of the Hebrew chronicle of the Ibn Danan family Samuel b. Saadiah Ibn Danan matter-of-factly reported the Fez Jewish celebration of the anniversary of King Sebastian's defeat, an unnamed Portuguese observer, probably originally a captive from Sebastian's army, described the Jewish ceremony in exaggerated colors and with considerable venom. In his Portuguese *Copia do imperio e reino dos Xerifes,* written in 1596, he cited this festivity as an illustration of Fez Jewry's "haughtiness and enmity toward the Christians." See Ibn Danan's Hebrew excerpt, reproduced by H. Z. Hirschberg in his *Toledot,* II, 212 f., 353 nn. 1 ff.; G. Vajda in *Un Recueil des textes historiques judéo-marocains,* pp. 15 ff. No. V; and H. de Castries, ed. and trans., *Une Description du Maroc sous le règne de Moulay Ahmad al-Mansour (1596) d'après un manuscrit portugais de la Bibliothèque Nationale,* pp. 50 (Portuguese), 118 f. (French). The aspersion here cast upon the chastity of the Fez Jewish women was clearly refuted by another Portuguese survivor, Ieronymo de Mendoça (or Mendonça), who had spent several years as a captive sold to a Jewish family in Fez. His warm praise of the local Jews, men and women, was briefly cited earlier from his *Iornada de Africa,* published in 1607. In fact, Mendoça's sense of fairness on this point is underscored by his simultaneous sympathetic description of the missionary efforts among the local Jews by a Dominican friar, Vincente de Fonseca (who later, from 1587 on, served as archbishop of Goa, India, the center of the Portuguese Inquisition in Asia), and his mention of a Jewish girl made pregnant by a Gentile *qaid.* See *supra,* Vol. XV, pp. 461 n. 26, 547 f. n. 116 with the literature cited there, to which add R. Ricard, "Le Maroc à la fin du XVIe siècle d'après la *Jornada de Africa* de Jeronimo de Mendoça," *Hespéris,* XLIV, 179–204. Ricard prefers spelling the author's name as Mendoça, rather than the widely accepted Mendonça, because it appears thus on the title page of the first edition. See also E. Glaser, "Le Chroniqueur portugais Jeronimo de Mendonça et son esprit de tolerance," *Bulletin hispanique,* LVI, 38–48.

32. G. Rambert *et al.,* eds., *Histoire du commerce de Marseille,* III, 24 ff.; *supra,* Vol. X, pp. 216 f., 396 f. nn. 59–60; M. Kayserling, *Geschichte der Juden in Portugal,* pp. 143 ff. On the animosity frequently exhibited by the local population even toward Muslim refugees, see H. Pieri, "L'Accueil par les Tunisiens aux Morisques expulsés d'Espagne: un témoignage morisque," *IBLA,* XXXI, 63–70; and K. Brown, "An Urban View of Moroccan History: Salé, 1000–1800," *Hespéris-Tamuda,* XII, 5–106, esp. p. 47. See also, more generally, J. D. Latham's careful examination of what happened to the Morisco exiles in Tunisia after their expulsion from Spain in the early seventeenth century, in his "Towards a Study of Andalusian Emigration and Its Place in Tunisian History," *Cahiers de Tunisie,* IV, 203–252, esp. pp. 216 ff.; and other studies reviewed by M. de Epalza in his "Recherches récentes sur les émigrations des 'Moriscos' en Tunisie," *ibid.,* XVIII, nos. 69–70, esp. pp. 139–47. Apparently not even Morisco fugitives from the Spanish Inquisition (on which, see *infra,* n. 44) received a more favorable treatment.

33. A. Marx, "The Expulsion of the Jews from Spain: Two New Accounts," *JQR,* [o.s.] XX, 240–71; [n.s.] II, 257–58, reprinted in his *Studies in Jewish History and Booklore,* pp. 77–106; Yehudah b. Jacob Ḥayyat, *Sefer Minḥat Yehudah* (Yehudah's

Gift), a Commentary on Perez b. Isaac's kabbalistic work *Ma'arekhet ha-Elohut* (God's Order), published together with this work in Ferrara, 1558, Intro. p. [5]; H. Z. Hirschberg, *A History,* I, 405 f.

34. E. García Ontiveros y Herrera, *La Politica norte africana de Carlos I;* and M. Fernández Alvarez, *Felipe II. Isabel de Inglaterra y Marruecos* (both in Publications of the Instituto de Estudios Africanos); *infra,* n. 35; Nicolas Clénard (Cleynaerts), letter of December 4, 1540 to Jean Petit (Joannes Parvus) in his *Correspondance,* ed. with a French trans. and comments by A. Roersch, I, 169 f. No. 53 (Latin), III, 114 f. No. xxxii (French), with the editor's comments thereon, II, 130 f.; and R. Le Tourneau, in his "Notes sur les lettres latines de Nicolas Clénard relatant son séjour dans le royaume de Fès 1540–1541," *Hespéris,* XIX, 45–53; and *infra,* n. 53. See also idem, "Un Humaniste de Fès au XVIe siècle," *Revue de la Méditerranée,* XIII, 131–46, 298–310. On the Jesuits in the Spanish possessions and elsewhere in Morocco, see D. M. dos Santos's aforementioned "A Entrada dos Jesuítas," *Mélanges Cénival-Lopes,* pp. 225–95.

On the other hand, we are much less well informed about the internal Jewish migrations within the world of Islam during the Late Middle Ages, in contrast with the ample documentation available in the Genizah for the tenth to the twelfth centuries. See S. D. Goitein's succinct remarks in his *Jews and Arabs,* pp. 112 ff. While these Jewish migratory movements doubtless greatly diminished (along with the Jewish demographic decline) after the Almohade regime, they again assumed a mass character in the sixteenth century during the expansion of the Ottoman Empire, to be discussed more fully in Vol. XVIII.

35. See D. Corcos-Abulafia, "Moroccan Jewry" (Hebrew), *Sefunot,* X, 96, 104 ff. (on Rosales), 106 ff. (on Ruti), and *passim;* H. de Castries *et al.,* eds., *Les Sources inédites de l'histoire du Maroc de 1530 à 1845. Collection des lettres, documents et mémoires.* 1st ser., *Archives et Bibliothèques d'Espagne,* esp. III, Nos. 21, 26, and 29; Yehudah b. Joseph Peres, *Peraḥ Lebanon* (The Flower of Lebanon; homilies on the Pentateuch), Intro.; N. Slouschz, *Travels in North Africa,* pp. 483 ff., 486 (includes the reading of an epitaph dated 1615); H. Z. Hirschberg, *A History,* I, 409 ff. See also *supra,* nn. 29 and 33.

36. See Nicolas Clénard's (Cleynaerts') letters of April 9 and 12, 1541 in his *Correspondance,* ed. by A. Roersch, I, 174 No. 54, 186 No. 55 (Latin), III, 121, 137 f. (French) with the editor's comments thereon, II, 138 (citing another excerpt from Clénard); Luis de Marmol Carvajal, *Descripción general de Affrica,* II, 70; D. Corcos-Abulafia, "Moroccan Jewry" (Hebrew), *Sefunot,* X, 93 ff., 99 ff.; and *infra,* n. 53. On Marmol, see the study by T. García Figueros, "Españoles en Africa en el siglo XVI. Luis de Marmol Carvajal," *Archivos del Instituto de Estudios Africanos,* X, no. 2.

Because of its great importance to Moroccan and Jewish history, the city of Fez and its Jewry have been the subject of many studies. Among recent publications we may mention the following: M. Weinstein, "Fez and Its Connections with Algiers" (Hebrew), *Zakhor le-Abraham,* pp. 13–24; H. Beinart, "Fez, a Center of Return to Judaism in the XVI Century" (Hebrew), *Sefunot,* VIII (= *Itzhak Ben-Zvi Mem. Vol.*), pp. 319–34, with an English summary, pp. 27–28 (referring in particular to an inquisitorial investigation in 1530–35 of Juan Robles, son of a New Christian father and an Old Christian mother; see *infra,* n. 75); J. S. Gerber's *Jewish Society in Fez: Studies in Communal and Economic History* (typescript; Diss. Columbia University); and, more generally, R. Le Tourneau, *Fès avant le Protectorat. Étude économique et sociale d'une ville de l'Occident musulman;* and in the English trans. by A. Clement, *Fez in the Age of the Marinids.*

Needless to say, quite apart from the metropolis Jews were to be found in most cities and towns as well as in many villages and hamlets throughout Morocco and neighboring Algeria. Much can be learned, therefore, from such general and Jewish monographs relating to particular localities as: L. J. Goulven, *Les Mellahs de Rabat-Salé,* with a Preface by G. Hardy; K. Brown, "An Urban View of Moroccan History. Salé, 1000–1800," *Hespéris-Tamuda,* XII, 5–106 (considers Salé a "microcosm" of Moroccan history and emphasizes the blossoming of its culture especially after the establishment of its academy [*madrasa*] in 1340, pp. 7, 31 f.); J. Caillé's comprehensive study, *La Ville de Rabat jusqu'au Protectorat français. Histoire et archéologie;* J. Chaumeil, "Le Mellah de Tahala au pays des Ammeln," *Hespéris,* XL, 227–40 (referring to a Jewish tribe still called Udaym [Jews] and including seven photographs of the Jewish quarter); A. de la Porte des Vaux, "Notes sur le peuplement juif du Souss," *Bulletin économique et social du Maroc,* XV, 448–59, 625–32 (although largely oriented toward twentieth-century conditions, this essay shows how persistently these relatively backward southern communities clung to their old settlements and ways of life); V. Monteil, "Les Juifs d'Ifran (Anti-Atlas marocain). Situation actuelle—cimetières—ancêtres—tombe de Youssef ben Maimoun," *Hespéris,* XXXV, 151–62; R. Ricard, "Ibero-Africana, VI," *ibid.,* XXXVI, 233–35, esp. p. 233, referring to a converted Jewish doctor, João de Mazagan, who served at the Court of John II of Portugal (1481–95). See also the list of thirteen *mellahs* existing in the early 1500s, compiled by L. Massignon in his *Le Maroc dans les premières années du 16e siècle,* pp. 158 f.; and the study of developments in the second most important Moroccan city, Marrakesh, which often served as the rival capital of the whole country or of one of its major segments, by A. Mandleur, "Croissance et urbanisation du Marrakech," *Revue de Géographie du Maroc,* XXII, 31–60; R. Le Tourneau's comprehensive study of *Les Villes musulmanes de l'Afrique du Nord;* and I. M. Lapidus's general review of *Muslim Cities in the Later Middle Ages.*

37. See, for instance, L. Brunot and É. Malka, eds., *Textes judéo-arabes de Fès; textes, transcriptions, traduction annotée;* followed by their *Glossaire judéo-arabe de Fès;* M. Cohen, *Le Parler arabe des Juifs d'Alger,* esp. 386 ff. listing Hebrew loan words; idem, *Le Parler arabe des Juifs de Tunis;* C. Pellat, "Nemrod et Abraham dans le parler arabe des Juifs de Debdou," *Hespéris,* XXXIX, 121–45, offering the text and French trans. of that patriarchal legend with interesting textual and linguistic notes; and, more generally, J. Blau, *The Emergence and Linguistic Background of Judaeo-Arabic: a Study of the Origin of Middle Arabic;* and such monographs as A. L. Motzkin, "Some Aspects of Judaeo-Arabic in the Thirteenth Century," *Journal of Semitic Studies,* XV, 56–62; and, more generally, G. S. Colin, *La Vie marocaine. Textes éthnographiques en arabe dialectale sur les usages et les coûtumes des citadins et des ruraux du Maroc.*

Samples of the Judeo-Spanish dialect spoken in Morocco are offered by, among many others, A. de Larrea Palacín in his ed., *Cancionero judio del Norte de Marruecos. Romances de Tetuan;* idem, ed., *Cuentos populares de los Judios del Norte de Marruecos,* claiming that the Tetuan stories here reproduced show that the local

Jews had preserved the Spanish traditions and language in greater purity than did the rest of the Sephardic colonies (I, iii ff.); J. Martínez Ruiz in his "Poesia sefardi tradicional (Alcazarquivir)," *Archivum* (Oviedo), XIII, 79–215; Z. Nahón, comp., *Romances judéo-españoles de Tanger,* critical ed. with notes by S. G. Armistead and J. H. Silverman in collaboration with O. A. Librowicz, musical transcription by I. J. Katz. See also D. Corcos-Abulafia, "Les Juifs au Maroc et leurs mellahs," *Zakhor le-Abraham,* pp. xxvi ff.; and, more generally, H. Zafrani, *Les Juifs de Maroc. Études et recherches sur la vie intellectuelle juive au Maroc, de la fin du XVe au début du XXe siècle,* Vol. I: *Pensée juridique et environment social, économique et religieux.* On the use of Spanish translations of the Bible, see L. S. Chenier, *The Present State of the Empire of Morocco,* English trans., I, 157.

While Judeo-Arabic linguistic studies have been satisfactorily cultivated, those of the Jewish Berber dialects and of the North African adaptations of the spoken Spanish or Portuguese brought with them by the Iberian exiles have yet to be subjected to much additional scholarly investigation. See L. Galand's brief summary of "The Actual State of Research in the Berber Language" (Polish), *Przegląd Orientalistyczny,* LX, 331–36; and W. Cline's succinct observations on "Berber Dialects and Berber Scripts," *Southwestern Journal of Anthropology,* IX, 268–76. Among the ancient loanwords in the Berber language Cline also found some Punic, that is related to Hebraic borrowings. A fuller review of the state of our knowledge in these areas must await a later chapter dealing with the various Jewish dialects developed by the medieval and early modern Jewries.

38. See R. J. Burns, "Immigrants from Islam: The Crusaders' Use of Muslims as Settlers in Thirteenth-Century Spain," *AHR,* LXXX, 21–42. Socioeconomic realities thus overcame the scruples generated on both sides by the Christian Crusades and the Muslim *jihad.* See *supra,* n. 2. Incidentally, the same factors also accounted in part for the favorable treatment of Jews and the rise of a class of Jewish grandees in thirteenth-century Spain, particularly Aragon, in the face of the religious fanaticism generated by the *Reconquista.* See *supra,* Vol. X, Chap. XLIV, *passim;* and on the services rendered by Jewish financiers and diplomats in mediating between Spain and the North African countries, C. E. Dufourcq, *L'Espagne catalane et le Maghrib;* P. Prieto y Llovera, *Política aragonesa en Africa hasta le muerte de Fernando el Católico;* and other literature listed *supra,* nn. 15, 18, and so forth.

39. See M. M. Antuna, ed. and trans., "Una Versión arabe compendiada de la Estoria de España de Alonso el Sabio," *Al-Andalus,* I, 105–154, esp. pp. 115 f. (Arabic), 129 (Spanish); Y. Baer, *A History of the Jews in Christian Spain,* I, 367 f., 450 n. 53; and, more generally, the older study by M. Lafuente y Alcántara, *Historia de Granada, comprendendo la de sus cuarto provincias Almería, Jaén, Granada y Málaga, deste remotos tiempos hasta nuestros días,* new ed. with an Intro. and Biographical Sketch of the Author by J. Zorilla; the more recent surveys by R. Arié, *L'Espagne musulmane au temps des Naṣrides (1232–1492),* esp. pp. 331, 431 n. 3; and D. Gonzalez Maeso, *Garnata al-Yahūd* (*Granada en la historia del judaismo español*).

40. Muḥammad 'Abdallah b. 'Ali al-Laḥmi ash-Shaguri's tract, *Qam' al-Yahud* (The Crushing of the Jews So That They May Not Exceed Their Limits); H. P. J. Renaud, "Un Médecin du Royaume de Grenade, Muhammad as-Saguri," *Hespéris,*

XXXIII, 31–64, esp. pp. 32 f. and n. 15. Some interesting new general data have also been made available in W. Hoenerbach's ed. of *Spanisch-Islamische Urkunden aus der Zeit der Naṣriden und Moriscos;* and his more recent German translation of *Islamische Geschichte Spaniens. Übersetzung des A'mal Al-a'lam und ergänzenden Texte.* See also the pertinent chapters in C. Sanchez Albornoz's *La España musulmana.*

41. See C. E. Dufourcq, *L'Espagne catalane et le Maghrib,* p. 139 n. 7; Solomon Ibn Verga, *Shebeṭ Yehudah* (Rod of Judah: a Chronicle), ed. by M. Wiener, p. 3; in Wiener's German trans., p. 6; in A. Shohet's ed., p. 22. The memories of the tragedy of 1066 were still much alive in the Jewish community of Granada in later centuries. On that severe bloodletting, see H. (J.) Schirman, "Yehosef ha-Nagid: The Tragedy of a Jewish Statesman" (Hebrew), *Moznaim,* VIII, 48–58 (dealing with Joseph b. Samuel Ibn Nagrela); F. P. Bargebuhr, *The Alhambra: a Cycle of Studies on the Eleventh Century in Moorish Spain;* and *supra,* Vol. III, pp. 157 f., 307 n. 42.

Not surprisingly, the contacts between the Jews of Granada and of Majorca were particularly intensive. See the numerous archival data cited in A. Pons, "Los Judíos del reino de Mallorca durante los siglos XIII y XIV," *Hispania* (Madrid) XVI, 163–255, 503–594; XX, 3–54, 163–216, 368–540 (also reprint); the interesting samples of business, marriage, and other contracts published by L. Seco de Lucena (Parades) in his *Documentos arábigo-granadinos,* ed. with a Spanish trans., intro., notes, glossaries, and indexes; and, more generally, G. Rosseló Bordoy, *L'Islam a les illes Baléares,* trans. by G. Frontera. Going beyond the purely commercial relationships, Moroccan Jews, like their Muslim compatriots, doubtless also benefited from cultural exchanges with their Majorcan coreligionists. See D. Urvoy's survey of "La Vie intellectuelle et spirituelle dans les Baléares musulmanes," *Al-Andalus,* XXXVII, 87–132, and, more generally, I. S. Allouche, *La Vie intellectuelle et sociale à Grenade au XIVe siècle.* Ironically, in mentioning that in 1320 Abu'l Walil b. Abi-Sa'id b. Faraj introduced the Jewish badge into Granada, A. Fattal attributes this to the example set by his Christian neighbors. See his *Le Statut legal de non-musulmans en pays d'Islam,* p. 106. Clearly, however, the spread of the Jewish badge in the Christian countries during the preceding century had been but an imitation of long-accepted practices in the Islamic world. See also H. Z. (J. W.) Hirschberg, "The Almohade Persecutions and the India Trade (A Letter from the Year 1148)" (Hebrew), *Baer Jub. Vol.,* pp. 134–53, with an English summary, pp. xii–xiii; and *supra,* n. 4.

Since among the twenty-nine Naṣrid rulers of Granada between 1232 and 1492, quite a few were pleasure-loving individuals preferring to leave the affairs of state in the hands of trusted advisers, it is often useful to consult J. M. Casciano, "El Visirato en el reino nazari di Granada," *Anuario de Historia del Derecho Español,* XVIII, 233–58, which includes a biographical list of the viziers who served Granada (pp. 250 ff.). Needless to say, there was no Jewish successor to Samuel ha-Nagid in that post in the Late Middle Ages.

42. See esp. the studies by M. A. Ladero Quesada, *Castilla y la conquista del reino de Granada* (Diss. Valladolid), esp. pp. 221 ff.; and *Los Mudejares de Castilla en tiempos de Isabel I,* offering a valuable collection of documentary materials, some of which (for instance, Nos. 35, 48 and 59), reflect the regime's conflicting attitudes toward permitting the subjects to emigrate to Africa. See also *supra,* Vol. X,

pp. 205 f., 391 f. n. 46. On the ransom of the Málaga captives, which yielded to the crown the substantial sum of 56,000,000 maravedis, see M. A. Ladero Quesada, "La Esclavidud por guerra a fines del siglo XV: el caso de Málaga," *Hispania* (Madrid), XXVII, 63–88, esp. pp. 67 ff. No. 105.

The events leading up to the conquest of Granada and their effect upon the subsequent destinies of the non-Christian population in Spain have long intrigued Spanish and other European scholars. Among the more recent writings see J. Torres Fontes, "Las Relaciones castellano-granadinas desde 1475 a 1478," *Hispania* (Madrid), XXII, 186–229; idem, "Las Treguas con Granada de 1462 y 1463," *ibid.*, XXIII, 163–99; F. Henriques de Jorquera, *Anales de Granada: Descripción del reino y ciudad de Granada. Crónica de la reconquista (1482–1492). Sucesos de los años 1588 a 1646,* ed. from the original MS by A. Marin Oeste; and biographies of the main protagonists, the conqueror and the conquered, by J. P. de Florian, *Gonzalvo de Cordou, ou, Grande Reconquiste;* and F. Fernández Martínez, *Boabdīl* (popular). See also *supra,* Vol. XI, pp. 238 ff., 403 ff. nn. 59 ff.

43. The estimate of 50,000–60,000 persons in the city of Granada is offered by L. Torres Balbás in his "Esquema demográfico de la ciudad de Granada," *Al-Andalus,* XXI, 131–46, esp. p. 142. The population figures, first mentioned by the interested German traveler, Hieronymus (Jeronimo) Munzer, are questioned by R. Arié. See Munzer's *Itinerarium sive peregrinatio per Hispaniam, Franciam et Alemaniam,* ed. by L. Pfandl in *Revue hispanique,* XLVIII, 1–179, or in his *Viaje por España y Portugal en los años 1494 y 1495,* trans. from the Latin with an Intro. and Notes by J. Puyal (also in *Boletín* of the R. Academia de la Historia, LXXXIV, 32–119, esp. pp. 95 f.); and R. Arié's *L'Espagne musulmane,* p. 332. The fact, however, that in 1492, shortly before Granada's fall, only 110 Jewish households paid the hearth tax was doubtless owing, in part, to the departure of a great many Jews before the final siege of the city. Very likely many more had already left during the preceding decade. See also *supra,* Vols. X, p. 391 n. 46; XI, pp. 404 f. n. 61.

In contrast, the smaller communities in the principality seem to have embraced but few Jews. For example, Vélez was supposed to have had at that time only 50 Jews and a few Christians among a Muslim population of 2,500–3,000. See C. de la Veronne, "Recherches sur la population musulmane de la région de Málaga à la fin du XVe siècle d'après le 'Repartimiento,'" *Bulletin hispanique,* LXIV, 216–19, mentioning that, outside the capital, only Vélez and Caén had populations of more than 2,000 each. On the Granada Inquisition and Talavera's family and outlook, see *supra,* Vol. XIII, pp. 69 f., 75 f., 338 f. n. 7, 342 f. n. 13.

44. See M. A. Ladero Quesada, *Los Mudejares de Castilla en tiempos de Isabel I,* pp. 172 ff. No. 50, 176; K. Garrad, "La Inquisición y los Moriscos granadinos, 1526–1580," *Miscelanea de estudios árabes y hebráicos,* V, 73–104; B. Vincent, "L'Expulsion des Morisques du Royaume de Grenade et leur répartition en Castille (1570–1571)," *Mélanges de la Casa Velázquez,* VI, 211–46 (with good maps); G. S. Colin, "Projet de traité entre les morisques de la Casba de Rabat et le roi d'Espagne en 1631," *Hespéris,* XLII, 17–25, esp. p. 19 Art. xii; P. Dressendörfer, *Islam unter der Inquisition. Die Morisco Prozesse in Toledo (1575–1610),* esp. pp. 62 ff. (stressing the dissimilarities, but rather minimizing the similarities, with the position of the Jews), 64 f. n. 172 (listing some of the Morisco polemical writings); and the extensive literature cited *supra,* Vol. XV, pp. 184 ff., 462 ff. nn. 28–30. See also M. Asín Palacio's ed.

of "Un Tratado morisco polémico contra los Judíos," *Mélanges Hartwig Derenbourg. Recueil des travaux d'érudition*, pp. 343–66.

45. See E. Lévi-Provençal, *Les Historiens de Chorfa; essai sur la littérature historique et biographique au Maroc du XVIe au XXe siècle*, pp. 42 ff.; F. Rosenthal, *A History of Muslim Historiography*. The existing confusion and conflicts in the primary sources induced, for instance, a recent historian of Muslim Spain to follow the lead of the chronicler Abu al-Khatib al-Iḥaṭa as his guide in preference to all others. See M. K. Mas'ud, "Political Developments in Fourteenth-Century Muslim Spain," *Islamic Studies* (Islamabad), XV, 3–17. It is not surprising that Maimonides, generally rather antagonistic to disciplines other than law, philosophy, and science, repudiated the study "of books found among the Arabs describing historical events, the government of kings and Arab genealogy, or books of songs and similar works which neither possess wisdom nor yield profit for the body, but are merely a waste of time." See his *Commentary* on Mishnah Sanhedrin, X, 1; and my remarks thereon in the "Historical Outlook of Maimonides," *PAAJR*, VI, 5–113, esp. p. 7, reprinted in my *History and Jewish Historians*, pp. 111, 349 n. 4. Yet even the sage of Fusṭaṭ was interested at least in the history of biblical, talmudic, and posttalmudic traditions and incidentally referred to events and phenomena pertaining to Jewish history. See the data analyzed in my essay.

Even more serious is the paucity of documentary materials relating to the Middle Ages and early modern times in the local public archives. See R. Le Tourneau, "Les Archives musulmanes en Afrique du Nord," *Archivum, Revue Internationale des Archives*, IV, 175–78. To be sure, Germaine Ayache has made a valiant effort to analyze the strengths and weaknesses of the existing public and private archives and documentary collections in Morocco. See "La Question des archives historiques marocaines," *Hespéris-Tamuda*, II, 311–26; and "L'Utilisation et l'apport des archives historiques marocaines," *ibid.*, VII, 69–85. But apart from the listing of seven valuable private collections (II, 315 f.), we find here mainly references to public depositories of relatively recent vintage. See also J. Sauvaget's observations in his *Introduction à l'histoire de l'Orient musulman*, pp. 19 ff.; they are as valid today as they were three decades ago. We depend, therefore, mainly on the Arabic manuscript collections assembled in North African and foreign libraries, which at times include historically relevant documents. See, for example, J. Schacht, "On Some Manuscripts in the Libraries of Morocco," *Hespéris-Tamuda*, IX, 5–55 (analyzing 55 MSS); M. El-Fasi, "Les Bibliothèques du Maroc et quelques uns de leur manuscrits les plus rares," *ibid.*, II, 135–44; A. Cour, *Catalogue des manuscrits arabes conservés dans les principales bibliothèques algériennes;* and *supra*, Chap. LXXIII, nn. 34 and 51.

The situation is not better on the Jewish side. Only in modern times have a few Jewish communal minute books and other records escaped the ravages of Jewish neglect and non-Jewish vandalism. For example, the *pinqas* (minute book) of the Fez community of 1879–1925 has been fairly well preserved in manuscript. It is now located at the Ben-Zvi Institute in Jerusalem (No. 2651). This *pinqas* includes passages of older vintage; for example, a paragraph describing rather objectively the causes which had led to the downfall of the royal courtier Harun in 1465. See *supra*, nn. 27 and 28. If these causes are described here in a story-telling way and thus overlook the really fundamental reasons for the overthrow of 'Abd al-Ḥaqq and his Jewish adviser, this is owing to the general preference of Jewish and Muslim authors of the time to overemphasize the anecdotal aspects of history. This paragraph in the *pinqas,* copied from a document of 1689, has long been available, however, in a partially better rendition in Joseph Ben-Naïm's bio-bibliographical dictionary of Moroccan rabbis, entitled *Malkhe Rabbanan* (Kings-Rabbis), fol. 96 cd. Ben Naïm's text is cited from an old manuscript written by Moses Gavison of the family of Abraham b. Jacob Gavison, author of the *'Omer ha-Shikhah* (Forgotten Sheaf; an historical study). See H. Z. Hirschberg, *A History,* p. 400 n. 2.

Not surprisingly, we learn more about North African Jews from foreign than from domestic sources. We have seen how much information has been forthcoming from the Aragonese archives of the thirteenth and fourteenth centuries, so effectively utilized by C. E. Dufourcq. For the sixteenth century and after, our most important source of information still is the monumental collection of *Les Sources inédites de l'histoire du Maroc,* ed. by H. de Castries *et al.* in the several series of excerpts culled from Dutch, English, French, Spanish, and Portuguese archives.

46. See Lancelot Addison, *The Present State of the Jews (More Particularly Relating to Those in Barbary)*; A. M. Hershman, *Isaac ben Sheshet Perfet,* pp. 217–36. This study shows that the large majority of Perfet's responsa were undoubtedly written in Aragon, where the rabbi had spent the first seventy-two years of his life, while his stay in Algeria was limited to his last decade. Regrettably, the published editions of these responsa are not arranged in any chronological order and a great many replies are altogether undatable. For example, the last 67 numbers (452–518) include only six for which Hershman was able to ascertain dates. They all happen to antedate Perfet's departure from Aragon. The exiles of 1492, on the other hand, included a number of historians who, together with their successors of the sixteenth and seventeenth centuries, were able to record events which were not too distant in time and often were attested by eyewitnesses who reported them to the authors. See especially Abraham b. Solomon of Torrutiel's (Adrutiel's) chronicle, written as a continuation of the *Sefer ha-Qabbalah* by Abraham ibn Daud, and hence sometimes called *Tashlum Sefer ha-Qabbalah.* Excerpts from that tract were published from a Bodleian MS by A. Neubauer in his edition of *Mediaeval Jewish Chronicles,* I, 101–114, see esp. pp. 112 f. They were reedited with critical notes by A. E. Harkavy in the Appendix to S. P. Rabbinowitz's Hebrew trans. of H. Graetz's *Geschichte der Juden (Dibre yeme Yisrael),* Vol. IV (these supplements are also entitled *Ḥadashim gam Yeshanim* [New and Old], Part 2). They are further available in a Spanish trans. by Francisco Cantera Burgos entitled *El Libro de la Cábala.* Other well-known works by such contemporaries or near-contemporaries as Abraham Zacuto, Solomon Ibn Verga, Joseph ha-Kohen, and Elijah Capsali—all frequently quoted in our earlier volumes—likewise furnish extremely valuable information on events relating to North African Jews.

47. I. Goldziher, *Muhammedanische Studien,* II, 59; G. Vajda, "Un Traité maghrébin," *Lévi-Provençal Mem. Vol.,* II, 812; *supra,* n. 23; and *infra,* n. 59. On Al-Majili's later anti-Jewish propaganda in Tlemcen, Tigurarin, Gurara, and Tuat, see Leo Africanus, *Description de l'Afrique,* pp. 436 f. and nn. 96–97. The failure of the later jurists to refer to the 500-year limit of the Covenant of 'Umar is quite noteworthy. One of the reasons undoubtedly was that even before Al-Mu'min, this theory had little backing among prominent exponents of the Muslim tradition. It may even have vanished from the consciousness of most anti-*dhimmi* writers during

the following centuries. It certainly had no impact on the legislation in any Muslim country after the Almohade era.

48. See Leo Africanus, *Description de l'Afrique,* p. 468; Muḥammad b. 'Abdallah al-Wufrani (Al-Ifrani), *Nozhet Elhādi* (Histoire de la dynastie saadienne au Maroc 1511–1670), ed. and trans. into French by O. V. Houdas, II, 259 (French). On the generally successful reign of Aḥmad Al-Manṣur and his moderate policies toward his Jewish subjects, see H. Terrasse, *Histoire du Maroc,* pp. 191 ff.; and H. Z. Hirschberg, *Toledot,* II, 213 ff.

49. H. R. Idris, *La Berbérie orientale sous les Zirides,* I, 178 ff.; R. Brunschvig, *Deux récits,* pp. 44 f. [91b] (Arabic), 107 (French); C. E. Dufourcq, *L'Espagne catalane et le Maghrib,* pp. 139 ff., and *passim.* We also recall the Jewish physician from Tlemcen whom the sultan had sent to Toledo in 1512 as his envoy. Ferdinand the Catholic himself not only received this professing Jew, despite the general prohibition after 1492 for any Jew to visit Spain under the sanction of capital punishment, but also personally used his medical ministrations. Obviously, the Catholic monarch did not wish to intervene during the inquisitorial prosecution in 1515 of the visitor's New Christian host, Juan Serrano, for listening to the doctor's pro-Jewish arguments and accepting some Hebrew books from him. See *supra,* Vols. XIII, pp. 43, 325 f. n. 45; XV, 221 ff., 480 ff. nn. 69–71. Some Jewish court physicians and other dignitaries took great interest in the position of their coreligionists and doubtless often participated in communal deliberations. But only a few were qualified to assume a spiritually leading position, probably because of the lack of Jewish learning which characterized most North African Jewish communities before 1391. One of the few exceptions was Saul Astruc ha-Kohen who, before the distinguished Spanish rabbis' arrival, had not only been a busy physician ministering to both Jews and Muslims, high and low, and a philanthropist, but also had officiated as a *dayyan* (judge) of the Jewish community. Being quite wealthy, he served without salary. Soon after 1391, however, he recognized the newcomers' superior rabbinic learning and resigned his post. See I. Epstein, *The Responsa of . . . Duran,* pp. 18 ff.

50. H. de Castries *et al., Les Sources inédites,* Portuguese ser., I, 271, 273; other sources cited by H. Z. Hirschberg in *A History,* I, 435 n. 3; Leo Africanus, *The History and Description of Africa,* English trans., by J. Pory, ed. by R. Brown, II, 246, 339 f. n. 37 (or in A. Epoulard's French trans., pp. 85 f.). Leo, whose Andalusian name had been Al-Ḥasan b. Muḥammad al-Wazzan al-Zayati, made four extended journeys to North Africa. The fruits of his rich experiences are recorded in this work, which has long served as a primary source of information concerning the life of the sixteenth-century North African population, including the Jews. On some complicated aspects of his life and work, see R. Mauny, "Notes sur les 'Grands Voyages' de Léon l'Africain," *Hespéris,* XLI, 379–94, with a map of these voyages (p. 381).

51. G. Vajda, "Un Traité maghrébin," *Lévi-Provençal Mem. Vol.,* II, 808 f.; Abu l'Arab, quoted here from the English citation in J. F. P. Hopkins's *Medieval Muslim Government in Barbary until the Sixth Century of the Hijira,* p. 60; Anselm Adorne in R. Brunschvig, *Deux récits,* pp. 175 [44a] (Latin), 220 (French). Such conviviality of Jews and Muslims, was, of course, greatly impeded by the various ritualistic

taboos on both sides. On the pertinent Muslim customs, see A. Mazahéri, *La Vie quotidienne des musulmans au moyen âge*, pp. 84 ff. But, as we recall, even drinking wine together was not altogether rare. How much more closely could amicable relationships be cultivated by members of the two faiths in other areas of social life which were subject to fewer formal restrictions!

52. 'Abdalbasiṭ b. Ḥalil in R. Brunschvig, *Deux récits*, pp. 47 f. [fol. 97b] (Arabic), 111 f. (French); R. Isaac b. Sheshet Perfet, *Resp.*, No. 61, cited by A. H. Hershman, p. 47; D. Corcos, "Moroccan Jewry" (Hebrew), *Sefunot*, X, 99 n. 243. It was a great misfortune for the Jews that most of the North African rulers were quite insecure in the exercise of their power and often submitted to vociferous spokesmen of popular prejudices. In general, the Jews' position was relatively more stable under strong monarchs like the first two Marinids.

53. Nicolas Clénard (Cleynaerts), *Correspondance*, I, 174, 186 (Latin), III, 121, 137 (French); *supra*, n. 34; H. Terrasse, *Histoire du Maroc*, II, 30 f., 170 f.; Henry Roberts' statement of 1585 in *The Ambassage of Master Henry Roberts*, reproduced by R. Hakluyt in *The Principal Navigations, Voyages, Traffiques and Discoveries of the English Nation Made by Sea or Overland . . . Within the Compass of these 1600 Years*, 1905–1906 ed., VI, 426 f.; H. de Castries *et al.*, eds., *Les Sources inédites*, English ser., I, 1, p. 511; Jean Mocquet's report, in his *Voyage au Maroc, 1601–1607*, reproduced in *Les Sources inédites*, French ser., Part 2, II, 399 f.; D. Corcos, "Moroccan Jewry" (Hebrew), *Sefunot*, X, 91; idem, "Les Juifs au Maroc et leurs mellahs," *Zakhor le-Abraham*, pp. xiv–lxxviii, with a Hebrew summary, pp. 238–40, esp. pp. xxiii ff., xxix ff., and the sources listed there; D. Cazès, *Essai*, pp. 75 f. (the Jewish *funduq* accommodated some forty Jewish families); P. Sebag and R. Attal, *La Hara de Tunis*; E. Fagnan, *Extraits inédits relatifs au Maghreb*. See also S. D. Goitein's observations in *A Mediterranean Society*, I, 71; and *supra*, n. 36.

54. See *The Ambassage of Master Henry Roberts*; and, more generally, R. Lebel, "Le Maroc dans les relations des voyageurs anglais aux XVIe, XVIIe, et XVIIIe siècles," *Hespéris*, IX, 269–94.

55. The haughty observation of the two Arab envoys was reported by Yahudah ben Zamirro in an undated Arabic letter to his family, trans. from a Lisbon MS by G. S. Colin in his "Les Juifs nomades retrouvés," *Mélanges Cénival-Lopes*, esp. pp. 62 ff. Even in pre-Almohade Muslim Spain, where Muslim-Jewish relations had generally been less strained than in North Africa, voices were frequently heard demanding both segregation and humiliation of Jews and Christians. See the series of postulates presented after 1100 C.E. by Muḥammad Ibn 'Abdun of Seville in his administrative manual, cited *supra*, Vol. III, p. 302 n. 31, to which add G. Vajda's trans. of several excerpts in his "À propos de la situation des Juifs et des chrétiens à Seville au début du XIIe siècle," *REJ*, XCIX, 127–29, with reference to E. Lévi-Provençal's "Un Document sur la vie urbaine et les corps des métiers à Seville au début du XIIe siècle. Le Traité d'Ibn 'Abdūn," *JA*, CCXXIV, 177–299, esp. pp. 238 ff., 248 f. Vajda's trans. includes paragraphs 157, 164, 169, and 206. See also Lévi-Provençal's subsequent trans. in *Seville musulmane au début du XIIe siècle;* and *supra*, n. 7.

56. See R. Abraham Saba, *Sefer Eshkol ha-Kofer* (The Cluster of Henna; a Commentary on the Book of Esther) on Esther 3:8, Drohobycz ed., 1904, p. 66; R. Joseph b. Abraham Ḥayyun, *Perush* (Commentary) on Psalms 63:1, Salonica ed., 1522, fol. 63b, both cited by H. H. Ben-Sasson in his "Exile and Redemption through the Eyes of the Spanish Exiles" (Hebrew), *Baer Jub. Vol.*, pp. 216–27, with an English summary, p. xvi, esp. pp. 219 f.

57. See Isaac Abravanel's *Ma'yene ha-Yeshuah* (Springs of Salvation: a Commentary on Daniel), Intro.; and other passages quoted by H. H. Ben-Sasson in "The Generation of the Spanish Exiles" (Hebrew), *Zion,* XXVI, 23 ff.; *supra,* Vol. XI, pp. 240 f., 405 n. 62.

58. See Ibn García's *Missive* in *The Shu'ubiyya in Al-Andalus. The Risala of I. G., Five Refutations,* trans. into English, with an Intro. and Commentary by J. T. Monroe; I. Goldziher, "Die Šu'ubijja unter den Mohammedanern in Spanien," *ZDMG,* LIII, 601–620, reprinted in his *GS,* IV, 204–223; and his *Muhammedanische Studien,* I, 143 ff., 158, 208 ff., 268 f.; or in C. R. Barber and S. M. Stern's English trans., *Muslim Studies,* I, 137 ff. On the local pride of the native-born inhabitants of Fez, see R. Le Tourneau's succinct summary in his "Al-Fasiyyun or Ahl Fas," *EI,* 2d ed., I, 855–56. The possible impact of these debates on Yehudah Halevi is analyzed in my "Yehudah Halevi: an Answer to a Historical Challenge," *JSS,* III, 243–72; reprinted in my *Ancient and Medieval Jewish History: Essays,* pp. 128 ff., 144 f., 433 ff., 442 n. 49.

59. See *supra,* Vol. III, pp. 167, 311 n. 58; *infra,* n. 78; L. S. Chenier, *The Present State of the Empire of Morocco,* pp. 156 f.; Al-Majili's anti-Jewish tract in G. Vajda, "Un Traité maghrébin," *Lévi-Provençal Mem. Vol.,* II, 811 (in Vajda's translation, with some hesitation about one passage in n. 24 and with the quotation of the original Arabic text in n. 25). It appears that none of the Muslim controversialist's suggestions were ever applied in practice. Certainly, an officer like Ieronimo de Mendoça who spent some years in Morocco, for the most part as a servant in a Jewish home, might have mentioned something concerning this debasing ritual if he had known of it. See his *Iornada de Africa,* mentioned *supra,* n. 31. Nor would such keen observers as Clénard, Marmol, or Leo Africanus have failed to allude to such an interesting ceremony, if they had seen or merely heard about it.

60. See A. Huici Miranda, *Historia política del imperio almohade,* I, 380 ff.; Muḥammad Abi-Dinar al-Kairuani, *K. al-Mu'nis fi akhbar Ifriqiyya wa-Tunis,* p. 128 l. 4 (written in 1681); trans. into French by E. Pelissier and J. P. Rémusat, as *Histoire de l'Afrique;* E. Fagnan, "Le Signe distinctif des Juifs au Maghreb," *REJ,* XXVIII, 294–98, esp. p. 296; A. M. Hershman, *Rabbi Isaac ben Sheshet Perfet,* pp. 41, 46, 246 f. No. 5; A. Fattal, *Le Statut légal,* pp. 96 ff.; and the more general literature on badges in Muslim lands, cited *supra,* Chap. LXXIII, n. 78; and Vols. III, 139 ff., 298 n. 22; XI, 96 ff.; 328 ff. nn. 25 ff. According to R. Isaac b. Sheshet Perfet, Saul Astruc ha-Kohen induced the authorities to relieve the Jewish women from wearing special boots, apparently provided with a tinkling device, rather than regular shoes. The jingling sound (the Hebrew word *te'akhasna* is rather equivocal) was supposed to make their presence noticeable audibly as well as visually. The rea-

son for the women's distress apparently was the fear of mugging rather than of sexual molestation. This is at least the tenor of the passage stating that Astruc had "nullified the ordinance that the [Jewish] women should walk with bangles tinkling [*te'akhasna*] on their feet [a clear allusion to Isa. 3:16: 'making a tinkling with their feet'; perhaps for this reason the rabbi employed the ungrammatical masculine form for 'their feet']. If that ordinance would have spread, the mobsters would have recognized us [them] and robbed their jewels and clothing." See Perfet's *Resp.*, No. 60.

61. See H. Borrmans, "Statut personnel et droit familial en pays musulmans," *Proche Orient Chrétien,* XXIII, 133–37; A. M. Hershman, *Rabbi Isaac ben Sheshet Perfet,* pp. 125 ff.; I. Epstein, *The Responsa of Rabbi Simon b. Ẓemaḥ Duran,* pp. 60 ff.; G. Vajda, ed. and trans., *Un Recueil des textes historiques judéo-marocains,* pp. xix f. No. viii; *supra,* n. 26. On the jurisdiction of the foreign consuls, see the aforementioned studies by A. Sacerdoti and C. E. Dufourcq (*supra,* n. 15). The system of "capitulations," later developed more fully in the Ottoman Empire, was greatly to affect also the position of Jewish foreigners residing in Turkey and even of some Turkish Jewish subjects (*rayas*) who were able to secure special consular protection. See *infra,* n. 70; and Vol. XVIII. Certain parallel arrangements had already been made by the Venetian and other Italian republics with the Byzantine Empire, as mentioned *supra,* Chap. LXXIII, n. 19.

62. R. Isaac b. Sheshet Perfet, *Resp.,* Nos. 234–39; *supra,* Vol. XI, pp. 61, 312 f. n. 70; *JC,* I, 235 f.; II, 220 f.; III, 55 n. 22. The Algerian ban on informers was apparently enacted soon after 1391; it is reproduced in R. Solomon b. Simon Duran's *Resp.* No. 352 and in the English translation by I. Epstein in the *Responsa of . . . Duran,* pp. 66 ff.

63. See M. J. Daumas, *Mœurs et coûtumes de l'Algérie: Tell—Kabylie—Sahara,* pp. 9f. (on *duhar*); H. Basset, "Les Troglodytes de Taza," *Hespéris,* V, 427–42, with noteworthy illustrations; N. Slouschz, *Travels in North Africa,* pp. 304 f., and *passim.* The Taza region on the whole belonged to the economically and culturally more advanced areas. See *infra,* n. 73. The study of Muslim cities in the Middle Ages, which in recent years has made considerable progress with respect to the Mid-Eastern area, has somewhat lagged behind with respect to the Maghrib. There are, however, some interesting special studies, such as those mentioned *supra,* nn. 13, 36, and others. This survival of medieval types of settlement despite the impact of westernization under the rule of the colonial powers in the nineteenth and twentieth centuries is quite noteworthy. The blend of old and new forms has survived also in some larger cities. See, for example, L. C. Brown's study, *From Madina to Metropolis: Heritage and Change in the Near Eastern City.* See also, more generally, R. Le Tourneau, *Les Villes musulmanes de l'Afrique du Nord.* On the other hand, the conditions in the northern villages and the life of the African peasants in general have thus far been greatly neglected in modern historical literature.

64. See Damião de Góis, *Crónica do felicissimo rei D. Manuel,* new ed., II, 57 ff., Chap. xviii (on this distinguished Humanist author, see *supra,* Vol. XIII, pp. 327 f. n. 48); M. L. Ortega, *Los Hebreos en Marruecos: Estudio histórico, político y social,* 4th ed., p. 110. See also the literature listed *supra,* esp. n. 30.

65. Diego de Torres, *Relación del origén y sucesso de los Xerifes,* Seville, 1585, p. 225; or in the French trans. of 1636 by M. C. D. V. D. D. A. (Charles de Valois, duc d'Angoulème), entitled *Relation de l'origine et socces des chérifs, et de l'estat des royaumes de Marroc, Fez et Tarrodent, et autres provinces qu'ils vsurperent,* p. 399 (on the Jewish interpreter brought along by the king of Tlemcen on his visit to Charles V in Madrid, who tried to denigrate the beauty of the Christian services at the cathedral of Toledo and was duly reprimanded by his king); Luis de Marmol Carvajal, *Descripción general de Affrica,* II, 59; L. S. Chenier, *Recherches historiques,* III, 51; and in the partial English trans., *The Present State of the Empire of Morocco,* I, 187; and the numerous demographic data supplied by Leo Africanus in his *Description de l'Afrique,* pp. 55 f., 117, 121, 142, 232 f., 303, etc. On the conditions in Granada before its fall, see *supra,* n. 43.

The only contemporary scholar who has paid special attention to medieval and early modern demographic features in Morocco is David Corcos-Abulafia. He culled from the existing literature a number of references to Morocco's Jewish population. See esp. his "Morroccan Jewry" (Hebrew), *Sefunot,* X, 56, 71 ff., 76, 79 ff., 84 ff., 90 f., 95, and *passim.* However, the available data did not allow him to compile figures for various detailed aspects of North African Jewish life, such as were assembled a quarter of a century ago by A. de la Porte des Vaux in his "Notes sur le peuplement juif de Souss" in the *Bulletin économique et social du Maroc,* XV, 448–59, 625–32; or, on a broader scale, by M. Eisenbeth in "Les Juifs en Algérie et en Tunisie à l'époque turque," *Revue Africaine,* XCVI, 114–87, 345–84 (also reprint). Needless to say, our knowledge of the general North African population of that period is likewise extremely limited. Nor did the attempts by V. Magalhães Godinho and A. Dziubiński to come to grips with the demographic situation in Morocco during the sixteenth century yield acceptable approximations for more than a few localities. See, for instance, their totally divergent estimates of the population of Marrakesh (in about 1525), which ranged from over 100,000 down to 20,000, underscoring the difficulties of reaching any kind of consensus. See V. Magalhães Godinho's *História econômica e social da expansão portuguesa,* esp. I, 135; and A. Dziubiński's *Maroko w XVI wieku* (Morocco in the Sixteenth Century, 1510–1578), pp. 95 ff., 103 f. Nevertheless, further careful investigations of the existing source materials—admittedly none too rich or dependable—may yet lead to some more satisfactory, if still tentative, results.

66. See João Alvares, *Chrónica do Infante Santo D. Fernando,* ed. by Mendes dos Remedios, pp. 68 ff., Chaps. xxv–xxvi; L. de Marmol, *Description,* French trans., II, 417, 472 No. 1359; Leo Africanus, *Description de l'Afrique,* pp. 60 f.; G. Vajda, *Un Recueil des textes historiques judéo-marocains,* esp. pp. 11 ff. No. ii; D. Corcos, "Les Juifs au Maroc," *Zakhor le-Abraham,* pp. xxxi f.; and the other sources listed by H. P. J. Renaud in his "Recherches historiques sur les épidémies du Maroc. Les 'pestes' des XVe et XVIe siècles, principalement d'après des sources portugaises," *Mélanges Cénival-Lopes,* pp. 363–89. In this connection we may note such reckless generalizations as those propounded by an anonymous Portuguese chronicler of 1596. Reporting on the *judiaria* of Fez, he writes: "The Jewish women are beautiful, prudent [*avisadas*], well brought up, and greatly preoccupied with their personal appearance. They are greatly enamored of Christians and generously grant them everything." About the Muslim women he likewise asserts sweepingly: "They are very much in love with Christians." See H. de Castries, ed., *Une Description du Maroc*

. . . (*1596*), pp. 49 f., 51 f. (Portuguese), 118 f., 119 f. (French). See also *supra*, n. 31; and, more generally, L. Massignon, *Le Maroc*, pp. 79 ff.

67. See the brief remarks by R. Ricard in his "Ibero-africana, II: Le Fr. Toribio Motolinia et les famines africaines de 1521 et 1541," *Hespéris*, XXXIII, 157–59. On the demographic features of late nineteenth- and twentieth-centuries Algerian Jewry, see P. Leroy-Beaulieu in *L'Algérie et la Tunisie*, 2d ed rev. and enlarged, esp. p. 40; and N. Chouraqui, *Between East and West*, esp. App. V. We must bear in mind, however, that any comparison of demographic trends in the nineteenth with those of the previous centuries, especially if it relates to large cities, is subject to doubt. Suffice it to mention that eighteenth-century London required an annual immigration of some 6,000 persons from the countryside and abroad (or more than 1 percent of its total population) just to maintain its size.

68. See O. Dapper, *Description de l'Afrique*, Amsterdam, 1686, pp. 120, 131, 138, 150; B. Meakin and K. A. Meakin, "Morocco," *Encyclopaedia Britannica*, 11th ed., XVIII, 850–61, esp. pp. 850, 853. In his *Toledot*, II, 215 f., 353 n. 9, H. Z. Hirschberg points out that Dapper often used earlier sources, such as J. B. Gremay's *Africae illustratae libri X*, Tournay, 1623. But Hirschberg's effort in this connection to draw a median line between two or more conflicting estimates, and to assume that the median figure approximates the real situation, is too simplistic. Yet one need not despair of some future discoveries of new sources and a further refinement of demographic methods which would yield more satisfactory results in this important area as well.

69. R. Isaac b. Sheshet Perfet, *Resp.*, No. 153; the excerpt is trans. into English in A. M. Hershman, *Rabbi Isaac ben Sheshet Perfet*, p. 35; and see *supra*, n. 26.

70. See A. Cousin and D. Saurin, cited by A. N. Chouraqui in his *Between East and West*, p. 50. There are few references to Jewish traders in either the Marseilles or the Mid-Eastern sources of the Late Middle Ages. See esp. the comprehensive work by G. Rambert *et al.*, eds., *Histoire du commerce de Marseille*, Vols. II–IV, covering the period of 1291–1660, esp. II, 684 ff.; III, 24 ff.; IV, 22; S. D. Goitein, *A Mediterranean Society*, I, 40, 42, 301 (quoting an interesting document of *ca.* 1200 C.E.), 325; R. Pernoud, *Les Statuts municipals de Marseille*, p. 156. On the prohibition of 1687 and its evasions, see J. Weyl, "Les Juifs protégés français aux Echelles du Lévant sous les règnes de Louis XIV et Louis XV d'après des documents inédits tirés des archives de la Chambre du Commerce de Marseille," *REJ*, XII, 267–82; XIII, 277–94, esp. pp. 270 f. App. i. We must bear in mind, however, that the paucity of Marseilles records about local Jews trading with Maghribian coreligionists is not necessarily conclusive. We recall Armand O. Citarella's observation (*supra*, Chap. LXXIII, n. 107) that even the numerous Genizah records of the period before 1250 refer almost exclusively to exchanges between European Christians and Eastern Jews, rather than to Jews doing business with their coreligionists in the divided world of that period. See his "A Puzzling Question Concerning the Relations between the Jewish Communities of Christian Europe and Those Represented in the Geniza Documents," *JAOS*, XCI, 390–97. However, here, too, the *argumentum a silentio* is far from decisive. On the use of North African Jewish agents by a Marseilles capitalist, see *infra*, n. 76.

71. See R. J. H. Gottheil and W. H. Worrell, eds., *Fragments from the Cairo Genizah,* pp. 66 ff. No. xiii (List of Tax-Payers); J. Braslavsky, "A Genizah Poor List and a K'far Hananiah's Widow" (Hebrew), *Tarbiz,* XIII, 43–51 (from a British Museum MS); and E. Strauss (Ashtor), "Documents Pertaining to the Study of the Economic and Social History of the Jews in the Near East" (Hebrew), *Zion,* VII, 140–55; *supra,* Chap. LXXIII, n. 94. We do not even have evidence for the extent to which sons followed their fathers' occupations, as was often the case in Egypt. But there, too, many occupational shifts are reflected in the Genizah records. See S. D. Goitein, *A Mediterranean Society,* I, 79 f.

H. Z. Hirschberg's valiant effort (in *A History,* I, 267 ff. or *Toledot,* I, 200 ff.) to shed some light on the Jewish occupational distribution in North Africa west of Egypt was based mainly upon his study of names in the Gottheil-Worrell, Braslavsky, and Strauss lists which, at least in part, betray their bearers' Maghribian origin. However, this is not necessarily proof that the individuals concerned had been engaged in these occupations in their home countries, since both Cairo and Alexandria embraced substantial Maghribian communities, including persons whose parents or grandparents had immigrated into the land of the Nile. Some of them became oblivious of the warning repeatedly given to their predecessors by R. Isaac b. Sheshet, "not to try to change the usages of the native Jews if you wish to live at peace with them." By the early sixteenth century, the number of Jewish settlers from the Maghrib in Cairo had become so great and influential that their "Maghribian" congregation tried to claim supremacy over the older native Musta'rib Jews.

This fundamental conflict was settled before long (1527) by an agreement (*haskamah*), based on a decision of a committee of five arbiters from each party and sanctioned by a formal declaration at the court of R. David Ibn abi Zimra. Its first paragraph stated outright that "the Maghribian congregation has no preferential rights over the Musta'rib congregation with respect to being called to the reading of the Torah, nor in any other matter. Nor shall the Musta'rib congregation be discriminated against [by] them [the Maghribis] in any fashion or period of time whatsoever." See Hirschberg's essay, "The Agreement between the Musta'ribs and the Maghribis in Cairo 1527" in the *Baron Jub. Vol.,* 1975, II, 577–90, esp. pp. 580 ff. It is therefore quite likely that many Maghribian Jewish artisans had acquired their occupational training, or had entered new occupations, while residing in the Middle East. Moreover, the pertinent documents largely antedate the Almohade regime and hence are not particularly helpful in the reconstruction of the economic diversification of Maghribian Jewry in the Late Middle Ages. Furthermore, even with such dubious identifications the emergent classification is so incomplete that it does not add up to any statistical summary. See Hirschberg, *A History,* I, 267 ff.

72. See E. Ashtor, *Histoire des prix et des salaires,* pp. 465 f., 478 ff., partly based upon C. E. Dufourcq's "Prix et niveaux de vie dans les pays catalans et maghribiens à la fin du XIIIe et au début du XIVe siècle," *Le Moyen Âge,* LXXI, 475–520.

73. See R. Hai Gaon's responsum reproduced in *Teshubot ha-Geonim* (Geonic Responsa), ed. by A. E. Harkavy, No. 5; M. Narkiss in the *Bulletin of Israel Exploration Society,* XII, 72–74; H. Z. Hirschberg, *A History,* I, 462 f.; Leo Africanus, *Description de l'Afrique,* pp. 274, 303; and *supra,* n. 27; Vol. IV, pp. 160, 316 n. 11. We must also bear in mind the perils of caravan travel for Jews. Apparently many succeeded in hiding their Jewish identity. But when their faith was detected, they

sometimes suffered severely. In a dramatic fashion Leo Africanus describes his own vicissitudes when the caravan in which he journeyed was held up for three days by a sudden snowstorm. The Arabs in charge of that transport despaired of getting paid for their labors. But on recognizing a Jew among the passengers, they tried to force him to pay for the entire group from his fifty loads of dates. See Leo Africanus' *Description de l'Afrique,* p. 52.

74. L. S. Chenier, *The Present State of the Empire of Morocco,* II, 310; L. Massignon, *Enquête sur les corporations musulmanes d'artisans et des commerçants du Maroc.* On the ritual aspects of the production of, and trade in, dairy products and wine, see *supra,* Vols. IV, pp. 151 ff., 157 f., 312 f. nn. 2–3, 315 f. n. 10; and V, pp. 27 ff., 258 n. 24.

75. See D. Cazès, *Essai sur l'histoire des Israélites de Tunisie,* p. 106; H. Beinart, "Fez, a Center of Return to Judaism" (Hebrew), *Sefunot,* VIII, 319–34; *supra,* n. 36. See also the numerous references to North Africa's Jewish artisans in Leo Africanus' *Description de l'Afrique,* esp. pp. 74, 112, 114, 130, 234, etc.; and, more generally, such more detailed surveys as P. Ricard, "Les Métiers manuels à Fès," *Hespéris,* IV, 205–224 (particularly valuable for his explanation of many technical trade terms); R. Guyot, R. Le Tourneau, and L. Faye, "Les Corporations des tanneurs et l'industrie de la tannerie à Fès," *ibid.,* XXI, 167–240 (pointing out that, unlike in some other countries, even members of distinguished Moroccan families were engaged in the large-scale production of skins for both domestic and foreign use); and J. Lapanne-Joinville, "Les Métiers à tisser de Fès," *ibid.,* XXVII, 21–65 (also citing his pertinent earlier studies referring to Tlemcen, Tetuan, and Al-Kasr al-Kabir [Alcazarquivir] and emphasizing that technologically the Moroccan textile industry had undergone few changes since the Middle Ages). On the Jews in these occupations, see esp. the valuable review by H. Bentov of "Jewish Artisans in Fez in the Seventeenth and Eighteenth Centuries" (Hebrew), *Sefunot,* X, 413–82, with a French summary, pp. 23–27. Although based on a partially preserved Hebrew *pinqas* of Fez, dating from 1699 to 1715, it sheds considerable light on Jewish crafts in the earlier period as well.

76. See C. E. Dufourcq, *L'Espagne catalane et le Maghrib,* p. 142; P. H. Dopp, ed., *L'Égypte au commencement du quinzième siècle d'après le traité d'Emmanuel Piloti de Crète (incipit 1420),* pp. 57 ff.; E. W. Bowill, *The Golden Trade of the Moors,* esp. p. 112. A considerable amount of information about Jewish trade activities with European countries has been preserved in European archives, while the Cairo Genizah offers but little new documentation for the period after 1250. Nevertheless, Piloti is undoubtedly right when he attributes to the Maghrib a vital share in the trade with Egypt, Syria, and the rest of the Middle East. We must resort, therefore, to the general literature on the trade between the Mediterranean countries to get some glimpses of the Jewish part therein. See esp. J. Devisse, "Routes de commerce et échanges en Afrique Occidentale en relations avec la Méditerranée. Un essai sur le commerce africain du XIe au XVIe siècle," *Revue d'histoire économique et sociale,* L, 42–73, 357–97; L. de Mas-Latrie, *Relations et commerce de l'Afrique septentrionale ou Magreb et les nations chrétiennes au moyen âge;* R. Ricard, "Contributions à l'étude du commerce génois au Maroc durant la période portugaise 1415–1550," *Annales d'études orientales,* III, *passim;* E. A. Sayous, *Le Commerce des*

Européens à Tunis depuis le XIIe siècle jusqu'à la fin du XVIe siècle, esp. pp. 39 ff., recording no less than twenty contracts concluded in the years 1212–46 by a Marseilles capitalist, Mandurel, with North African importers of coinage minted in Marseilles through Jewish agents in Ceuta, Oran, Bougie, and Tlemcen.

It may be noted that, contrary to long-held assumptions, there is relatively little information about Jewish slave traders in North Africa. However, all assertions about it can be made only with considerable diffidence because of the paucity of the extant documentary material. There is more information available, however, about the general slave trade. In *The African Slave Trade and Its Suppression. A Classified and Annotated Bibliography of Books, Pamphlets and Periodical Articles,* P. C. Hogg listed fully 4,400 pertinent entries for the period from the fifteenth to the nineteenth centuries. It was this large supply of slaves, as well as of gold, which maintained the economy of the area on a relatively high plateau. In the long run, however, this relative stability turned out to be a retarding influence in economic progress. See M. Małowist, "The Social and Economic Stability of the Western Sudan in the Middle Ages," *Past and Present,* XXXIII, 3–14; idem, "Le Commerce d'or et des esclaves au Soudan occidental," *Africana Bulletin* (Warsaw), no. 4 (1966), 49–72 (reviewing the situation in the fourteenth to sixteenth centuries). According to a specialist like Charles Verlinden, the main supply of black slaves for France in the period of 1300–1490 came from Libyan Barqah. See his "Esclavage noir en France méridionale et courants de traité en Afrique," *Annales du Midi,* LXXVIII, 335–43.

77. See G. Fisher, *Barbary Legend,* pp. 299 ff.; J. M. Haddey, *Le Livre d'or des Israélites algériens, recueil des renseignements inédits et authentiques sur les principaux négociants juifs d'Alger pendant la période turque,* pp. 60 f. and *passim;* and other sources cited by H. Z. Hirschberg in his *Toledot,* II, 61 f., 334 ff. nn. 24 and 31. On the minting and circulation of coins, in which Morocco played an especially significant role, see for example, V. Prieto, *La Reforma numismatica de los Almohades;* and H. W. Hazard, *The Numismatic History of the Late Medieval North Africa.* The uncertainties prevailing in this entire area, however, are well illustrated by its fuzzy terminology. For example, the important governmental and social position of *jahbadh* (in Hebrew documents often equated with *gizbar;* both terms were of Persian origin) could mean a banker, a money changer, a government tax collector, or a tax farmer, or even a person simultaneously engaged in all these occupations. In the eleventh century this position was held in high esteem, but it declined to a secondary rank under the Mamelukes. Correspondingly, it became quite rare thereafter. See S. D. Goitein, *A Mediterranean Society,* I, 248 ff.; Hirschberg, *Toledot,* I, 199 f.; idem, *A History,* I, 266 f.; H. Rabie, *The Financial System of Egypt,* pp. 158 f. In the domestically more turbulent late medieval North Africa, with its small and struggling Jewish communities and the scarcity of dependable sources relating to their economic activities, the extent to which Maghribian Jews were involved in any phase of the money trade has, at least thus far, not been ascertained. The changes brought about in the sixteenth and seventeenth centuries will be discussed in the next volume.

78. Leo Africanus, *Description de l'Afrique,* pp. 431 f.; see also pp. 142 f., 147, 234, etc.; and *supra,* n. 59. Nor must we forget that originally the capitation tax had been conceived as a sort of ransom from the slavery to which a conquered population was supposed to be automatically reduced. This connotation of its being the permanent

remedy for bondage played into the hands of many Jew-baiters, as we have seen, who clamored for the revocation of the original Covenant. See also A. Abel's pertinent observations in "La Djizya. Tribut ou rançon?" *Studia Islamica,* XXXII, 5–19. We also have some additional information about Jewish taxes from rabbinic sources, particularly those written by the immigrant rabbis from Spain. See the data culled from their responsa in A. M. Hershman, *Rabbi Isaac ben Sheshet Perfet,* pp. 35 ff.; and I. Epstein, *The Responsa of Rabbi Simon ben Ẓemaḥ Duran,* pp. 52 ff. But these are more significant for the internal Jewish administration in collecting and delivering such taxes than for the actual amounts assessed by the governments and the degree to which the collections met the rulers' expectations.

79. G. Vajda, ed., *Un Recueil des textes historiques judéo-marocains,* pp. 11 f. No. ii, 21 ff. No. x; E. Michaux-Bellaire, "L'Organisation des finances au Maroc," *Archives Marocaines,* XI, 171–251, esp. p. 171; Nicolas Clénard's letter of April 12, 1541 to Arnold Streyters in his *Correspondance,* I, 186 (Latin), III, 137 f. (French), and the editor's comments, *ibid.,* II, 38. Regrettably, even the general fiscal structure of the Maghrib in the Late Middle Ages and early modern times has not yet been investigated to the same extent as that of the Mameluke Empire or of the classical period of Islam. Certainly, E. Michaux-Bellaire's study merely scratches the organizational surface. Hence we must rely on some general information stemming from the pre-Almohade period, which may or may not be fully applicable to the specific conditions of the late medieval North African lands. See the general publications listed *supra,* Vol. III, pp. 161 ff., 308 ff. nn. 47–56; and Chap. LXXIII, nn. 118 ff.

80. L. Massignon, *Le Maroc,* pp. 72 ff.; Zechariah b. Joshua Ibn Saruq, *Perush Megillat Aḥashverosh* (Commentary on the Book of Esther), Venice, 1565, Intro. fol. 3a, cited by H. H. Ben-Sasson in the *Baer Jub. Vol.,* pp. 219 f.

81. See E. Gellner and C. Micaud, eds., *Arabs and Berbers. From Tribe to Nation in North Africa* (a collection of articles); M. Hajji, "L'Idée de nation au Maroc et quelques-uns de ses aspects aux XVIe et XVIIe siècles," *Hespéris-Tamuda,* IX, 109–121; M. El-Menouni, "Apparition à l'époque mérinide et ouattavide des éléments constitutifs du sentiment national marocain," *ibid.,* pp. 219–27; R. Hartmann's more general observations on *Islam und Nationalismus* (*Abhandlungen* of the Deutsche Akademie der Wissenschaften, 1945–46, No. 5); A. S. Tritton, *The Caliphs and Their Non-Muslim Subjects: a Critical Study of the Covenant of Umar,* pp. 232 f.